Beginning
MFC
Programming

Ivor Horton

Wrox Press Ltd.®

Beginning MFC Programming

Published by Wrox Press Ltd. 30 Lincoln Road, Olton, Birmingham, B27 6PA , UK.
Printed in Canada
1 2 3 4 5 TRI 99 98 97

ISBN 1-861000-85-5

Trademark Acknowledgements

Wrox has endeavored to provide trademark information about all the companies and products mentioned in this book by the appropriate use of capitals. However, Wrox cannot guarantee the accuracy of this information.

Visual C++, Windows 95 and Windows NT are trademarks and ActiveX, ActiveX ControlPack, ActiveX ControlPad, ActiveX SDK, Developer Studio and Internet Explorer are registered trademarks of Microsoft Corporation.

Credits

Author
Ivor Horton

Editors
Julian Dobson
Jon Hill
Alex Stockton

Managing Editor
John Franklin

Technical Reviewers
from Beginning VC++ 5
Derek Paul
Mungo Henning
Lynn Mettler
Dave McGlade

Technical Reviewers
Previous Edition
Julian Templeman
Abe Klagsbrun
Bill Ibbetson
Justin Rudd
Lynn Mettler
Curt Krone
Hugh Gibson

Cover/Design/Layout
Andrew Guillaume
Graham Butler

Copy Edit/Index
Dominic Shakeshaft

Thanks to all those people, too numerous to mention, who have contributed feedback to the various versions of this book.

A Note from the Author

My objective is to minimize what, in my judgment, are the three main hurdles you will face when first learning MFC: getting to grips with the jargon that pervades every programming language and environment, understanding the *use* of the classes (as opposed to what they are), and appreciating how the classes can be applied in a practical context.

Jargon is an invaluable and virtually indispensable means of communication for the competent amateur as well as the expert professional, so it can't be avoided. My approach is to ensure that you understand what the jargon means and get comfortable with using it in context. In that way, you can use the documentation that comes along with Visual C++ more effectively, and can also feel competent to read and learn from the literature that surrounds most programming languages.

Comprehending the syntax and effects of the classes that make up MFC is obviously essential to learning this complex library, but I believe illustrating *how* the classes work together and *how* they are used is equally important. Rather than just use code fragments, I provide you with practical working examples that show the relationship of the MFC classes to specific problems. You can then use these as a basis for experimentation, to see at first hand the effects of changing the code in various ways.

The practical context goes beyond the mechanics of applying individual classes. To help you gain the competence and confidence to develop your own applications, I aim to provide you with an insight into how things work in combination and on a larger scale than a simple example with a few lines of code. That's why this book contains a working example that builds over several chapters. In that way it's possible to show something of the approach to managing code as well as how MFC classes can be applied together.

Finally, I know the prospect of learning about a class library as large as MFC can be quite daunting. For that reason it's important for you to realize three things that are true. First, there *is* a lot to it, but this means there will be a greater sense of satisfaction when you've succeeded. Second, it's great fun, so you really will enjoy it. Third, it's a lot easier than you think, so you positively *will* make it.

Ivor Horton

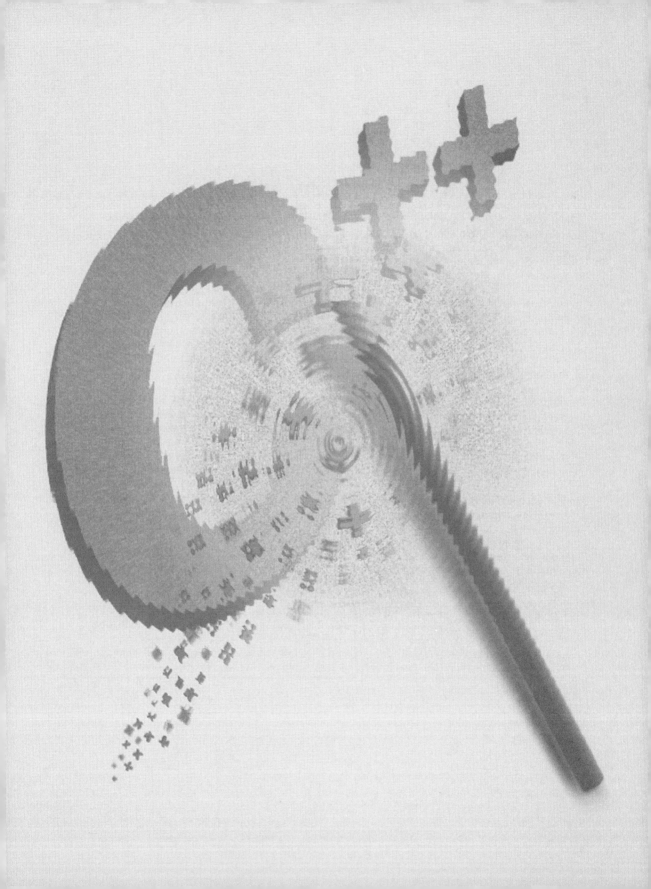

Beginning

MFC

Programming

Introduction   **1**

    Who Is This Book For?   1
      Who Isn't This Book For?   1
    What's Covered in This Book   2
    What You Need to Use This Book   2
    Conventions Used   3
    Tell Us What You Think   3
      Source Code and Keeping Up to Date
      Corrections and Clarifications   5

Chapter 1: Programming MFC with Visual C++   **7**

    Learning C++ and Windows Programming   8
      Introducing Windows Programming   8
    What is the Developer Studio?   10
      Components of the System   10
        The Editor   10
        The Compiler   10
        The Linker   10
        The Libraries   10
      Other Tools   11
        AppWizard   11
        ClassWizard   11
        The Wizard Bar   11
    Using the Visual C++ Development Environment   11
      Toolbar Options   12
      Dockable Toolbars   13
      Projects and Project Workspaces   14
        Defining a Project   14
        Debug and Release Versions of Your Program   15
      Creating a New Project   16
        Entering Your First Visual C++ Program   18
          Adding a Source File to a Project   21
          Building a Project   21
          Dealing with Errors   22
          Using Help with the Output Window   22
          Files Created by Building a Console Application   22
        Executing Your First Program   24
      Setting Options in Visual C++   24
        Setting Developer Studio Options   25
        Setting Project Options   26

Table Of Contents

Creating and Executing a Windows Program 27
Executing a Windows Program 30
Summary 32
Exercises 32

Chapter 2: A Taste of Old-Fashioned Windows 35

Windows Programming Basics 35
Elements of a Window 36
Comparing DOS and Windows Programs 37
Event-driven Programs 38
Windows Messages 38
The Windows API 38
Notation in Windows Programs 39
The Structure of a Windows Program 40
The WinMain() Function 41
Specifying a Program Window 42
Creating and Initializing a Program Window 44
Initializing the Client Area of the Window 46
Dealing with Windows Messages 46
Queued and Non-Queued Messages 46
The Message Loop 47
Multitasking 48
A Complete WinMain() Function 49
How It Works 51
Message Processing Functions 51
The WindowProc() Function 51
Decoding a Windows Message 52
Drawing the Window Client Area 53
Ending the Program 55
A Complete WindowProc() Function 55
How It Works 56
A Simple Windows Program 56
Old-Fashioned Windows 57
Debugging 58
Setting Breakpoints 59
Removing Breakpoints 60
Starting Debugging 60
Inspecting Variable Values 62
Viewing Variables in the Edit Window 63
Watching Variables' Values 64
Changing the Value of a Variable 66
Summary 67
Exercises 67

Chapter 3: Understanding Windows Programming 71

The Essentials of a Windows Program 71
The Windows API 73
Visual C++ and the Windows API 73
The Microsoft Foundation Classes 73
MFC Notation 74

How an MFC Program is Structured   74
  The Application Class   75
  The Window Class   76
  Completing the Program   77
  The Finished Product   77
The Document/View Concept   79
  What is a Document?   79
  Document Interfaces   79
  What is a View?   80
Linking a Document and its Views   80
  Document Templates   81
  Document Template Classes   81
Your Application and MFC   82

Windows Programming with Visual C++   83
What is the AppWizard?   83
Using AppWizard to Create an SDI Application   84
  Step 1   84
  Step 2   85
  Step 3   85
  Step 4   85
  Step 5   88
  Step 6   89
The Output from AppWizard   90
  Viewing Project Files   90
  Viewing Classes   91
  The Class Definitions   92
  Comments in AppWizard Generated Code   95
  Creating an Executable Module   96
    Precompiled Header Files   97
  Running the Program   98
  How the Program Works   98
    The Function InitInstance()   98
    The Function Run()   100
Using AppWizard to Create an MDI Application   101
  Running the Program   101
Using the ClassWizard   103

Summary   105
Exercises   105

Chapter 4: Working with Menus and Toolbars   **109**

Communicating with Windows   109
  Understanding Message Maps   110
    Message Handler Definitions   111
  Message Categories   113
  Handling Messages in Your Program   113
    How Command Messages are Processed   114
Extending the Sketcher Program   115
Elements of a Menu   115
  Creating and Editing Menu Resources   115
    Adding a Menu Item to the Menu Bar   117
    Adding Items to the Element Menu   117
      Defining Menu Item Properties   118
    Modifying Existing Menu Items   119

Completing the Menu   119
Using ClassWizard for Menu Messages   119
Choosing a Class to Handle Menu Messages   121
Creating Menu Message Functions   121
Coding Menu Message Functions   125
Adding Members to Store Color and Element Mode   125
Initializing the New Class Data Members   126
Modifying the Class Constructor   127
Running the Extended Example   128
Adding Message Handlers to Update the User Interface   129
Coding a Command Update Handler   130
Exercising the Update Handlers   132
Adding Toolbar Buttons   132
Editing Toolbar Button Properties   134
Exercising the Toolbar Buttons   135
Adding Tooltips   136
Summary   137
Exercises   138

Chapter 5: Drawing in a Window   141

Basics of Drawing in a Window   141
The Window Client Area   142
The Windows Graphical Device Interface   143
What is a Device Context?   143
Mapping Modes   143
The Drawing Mechanism in Visual C++   145
The View Class in Your Application   145
The OnDraw() Member Function   146
The CDC Class   146
Displaying Graphics   147
Drawing Lines   148
Drawing Circles   149
Drawing in Color   151
Creating a Pen   151
Using a Pen   153
Creating a Brush   154
Using a Brush   155
Drawing Graphics in Practice   156
Programming the Mouse   157
Messages from the Mouse   158
WM_LBUTTONDOWN   159
WM_MOUSEMOVE   159
WM_LBUTTONUP   159
Mouse Message Handlers   160
The ClassWizard Generated Code   161
Drawing Using the Mouse   162
Getting the Client Area Redrawn   164
Defining Classes for Elements   165
Storing a Temporary Element in the View   166
The CElement Class   167
The CLine Class   168
Implementing the CLine Class   169
The CLine Class Constructor   169

Drawing a Line   170
Creating Bounding Rectangles   170
Normalized Rectangles   173
Calculating the Enclosing Rectangle for a Line   173
The CRectangle Class   174
The CRectangle Class Constructor   174
Drawing a Rectangle   175
The CCircle Class   175
Implementing the CCircle Class   176
The CCircle Class Constructor   176
Drawing a Circle   177
The CCurve Class   177
Completing the Mouse Message Handlers   178
Setting the Drawing Mode   178
Coding the OnMouseMove() Handler   180
Creating an Element   182
Dealing with WM_LBUTTONUP Messages   184

Exercising Sketcher   **184**
Running the Example   185
Capturing Mouse Messages   186
Summary   **187**
Exercises   **188**

Chapter 6: Creating the Document and Improving the View   191

What are Collection Classes?   191
Types of Collection   192
The Type-Safe Collection Classes   192
Collections of Objects   193
The CArray Template Class   193
Helper Functions   195
The CList Template Class   195
Adding Elements to a List   195
Iterating through a List   197
Searching a List   198
Deleting Objects from a List   199
Helper Functions for a List   199
The CMap Template Class   200
Helper Functions Used by CMap   201
The Typed Pointer Collections   202
The CTypedPtrList Template Class   202
CTypePtrList Operations   203

Using the CList Template Class   **204**
Drawing a Curve   205
Defining the CCurve Class   206
Implementing the CCurve Class   208
Exercising the CCurve Class   209

Creating the Document   **211**
Using a CTypedPtrList Template   211
Implementing the Document Destructor   212
Drawing the Document   213
Adding an Element to the Document   215
Exercising the Document   215

Improving the View   **216**
Updating Multiple Views   216

Scrolling Views   218
    Logical Coordinates and Client Coordinates   220
    Dealing with Client Coordinates   221
  Using MM_LOENGLISH Mapping Mode   222

Deleting and Moving Shapes   224
Implementing a Context Menu   225
  Associating a Menu with a Class   226
  Displaying a Pop-Up at the Cursor   227
  Choosing a Context Menu   228
    Identifying a Selected Element   230
  Exercising the Pop-Ups   231
    Checking the Context Menu Items   232
Highlighting Elements   233
  Drawing Highlighted Elements   237
  Exercising the Highlights   237
Servicing the Menu Messages   237
  Deleting an Element   237
  Moving an Element   238
    Modifying the WM_MOUSEMOVE Handler   240
  Getting the Elements to Move Themselves   241
    Dropping the Element   243
  Exercising the Application   244

Dealing with Masked Elements   244
Summary   245
Exercises   246

Chapter 7: Working with Dialogs and Controls   249

Understanding Dialogs   249
Understanding Controls   250
Common Controls   251
Creating a Dialog Resource   252
Adding Controls to a Dialog Box   252
  Testing the Dialog   254
Programming for a Dialog   254
Adding a Dialog Class   254
Modal and Modeless Dialogs   255
Displaying a Dialog   256
  Code to Display the Dialog   257
Supporting the Dialog Controls   257
Initializing the Controls   258
Handling Radio Button Messages   259
Completing Dialog Operations   259
Adding Pen Widths to the Document   260
Adding Pen Widths to the Elements   260
Creating Elements in the View   261
Exercising the Dialog   262
Using a Spin Button Control   263
Adding the Scale Menu Item and Toolbar Button   263
Creating the Spin Button   264
  The Controls' Tab Sequence   265

Generating the Scale Dialog Class   265
Dialog Data Exchange and Validation   266
Initializing the Dialog   267
Displaying the Spin Button   268
Using the Scale Factor   268
Scaleable Mapping Modes   269
Setting the Document Size   270
Setting the Mapping Mode   270
Implementing Scrolling with Scaling   272
Setting Up the Scrollbars   273
Creating a Status Bar   274
Adding a Status Bar to a Frame   275
Defining the Status Bar Parts   276
Updating the Status Bar   277
Using a List Box   278
Removing the Scale Dialog   279
Creating a List Box Control   279
Creating the Dialog Class   280
Displaying the Dialog   281
Using an Edit Box Control   282
Creating an Edit Box Resource   282
Creating the Dialog Class   284
The CString Class   284
Adding the Text Menu Item   285
Defining a Text Element   286
Implementing the CText Class   287
The CText Constructor   287
Drawing a CText Object   288
Moving a CText Object   288
Creating a Text Element   288
Summary   291
Exercises   291

Chapter 8: Storing and Printing Documents   **293**
Understanding Serialization   293
Serializing a Document   294
Serialization in the Document Class Definition   294
Serialization in the Document Class Implementation   295
The Serialize() Function   296
The CArchive Class   296
Functionality of CObject-Based Classes   298
The Macros Adding Serialization to a Class   298
How Serialization Works   299
How to Implement Serialization for a Class   300
Applying Serialization   300
Recording Document Changes   301
Serializing the Document   302
Serializing the Element Classes   303
The Serialize() Functions for the Shape Classes   305
Exercising Serialization   307

Moving Text   308
Printing a Document   310
  The Printing Process   311
    The CPrintInfo Class   312
Implementing Multipage Printing   314
  Getting the Overall Document Size   315
  Storing Print Data   315
  Preparing to Print   316
    Cleaning Up After Printing   318
  Preparing the Device Context   318
  Printing the Document   319
  Getting a Printout of the Document   324
Summary   324
Exercises   325

Chapter 9: Writing Your Own DLLs   **327**

Understanding DLLs   327
  How DLLs Work   329
    Run-Time Dynamic Linking   330
  Contents of a DLL   332
    The DLL Interface   332
    The DllMain() Function   332
  Varieties of DLL   332
    MFC Extension DLL   332
    Regular DLL - Statically Linked to MFC 333
    Regular DLL - Dynamically Linked to MFC 333
Deciding What to Put in a DLL   333
Writing DLLs   334
  Writing and Using an Extension DLL   334
    Understanding DllMain()   336
    Adding Classes to the Extension DLL   337
    Exporting Classes from the Extension DLL 338
    Building a DLL   339
    Using the Extension DLL in Sketcher   339
    Files Required to Use a DLL   341
  Exporting Variables and Functions from a DLL   341
  Importing Symbols into a Program   342
  Implementing the Export of Symbols from a DLL   342
    Using Exported Symbols   344
Summary   345
Exercises   346

Chapter 10: Connecting to Data Sources   **349**

Database Basics   349
A Little SQL   352
  Retrieving Data Using SQL   352
    Choosing Records   353
  Joining Tables Using SQL   354
  Sorting Records   356

Database Support in MFC   356
DAO vs. ODBC   357
Classes Supporting DAO   358
Classes Supporting ODBC   359
Creating a Database Application   359
Registering an ODBC Database   360
Using AppWizard to Generate an ODBC Program   362
Snapshot vs. Dynaset Recordsets   364
Choosing Tables   364
Understanding the Program Structure   366
Understanding Recordsets   366
Recordset Creation   366
Querying the Database   367
Data Transfer between the Database
and the Recordset   368
Understanding the Record View   369
Creating the View Dialog   371
Linking the Controls to the Recordset   373
Exercising the Example   374
Sorting a Recordset   375
Modifying the Window Caption   376
Using a Second Recordset Object   376
Adding a Recordset Class   377
Adding a Record View Class   380
Creating the Dialog Resource   380
Creating the Record View Class   381
Linking the Dialog Controls to the Recordset   383
Customizing the Record View Class   383
Adding a Filter to the Recordset   383
Defining the Filter Parameter   384
Initializing the Record View   385
Accessing Multiple Tables   387
Switching Views   387
Enabling the Switching Operation   390
Handling View Activation   391
Viewing Orders for a Product   392
Viewing Customer Details   393
Adding the Customer Recordset   393
Creating the Customer Dialog Resource   394
Creating the Customer View Class   394
Adding a Filter   395
Implementing the Filter Parameter   397
Linking the Order Dialog to the Customer Dialog   398
Exercising the Database Viewer   400
Summary   400
Exercises   401

Chapter 11: Understanding OLE Documents   **403**

Object Linking and Embedding   403
Containers and Servers   404
Compound Documents   404
Activating an Embedded Object   405
How Does OLE Work?   406
The OLE Component Object Model   406

The Registry 407
MFC Classes Supporting OLE 408
OLE Object Classes 409
An Embedded Object in a Container 410
An Embedded Object in a Server 411
OLE Document Classes 411

Implementing an OLE Container 412

Initializing a Container Application 413
The CWrxContainerItem Class 415
Reacting to OLE Object Modification 417
Dealing with the Position of an Object in the Container 419
Managing Multiple Embedded Objects 420
Selecting an Object 421
Finding the Object Selected 422
Setting an Object as Selected 423
Setting the Tracker Style 424
Setting the Cursor 425
Activating an Embedded Object 426
Drawing Multiple Embedded Objects 426
Dealing with Object Insertion 427
Trying Out the OLE Container 429

Implementing an OLE Server 430

Generating a Server Application 431
Adding Sketcher Application Functionality 431
Document Data and Interface Functions 432
Adding the Menus 434
Adding the Toolbar Buttons 434
Adding the View Application Functionality 435
Drawing the Document 437
Running Sketcher as a Server 438
Server Resources 438
Updating Menu Resources 439
How Container and Server Menus are Merged 440
Updating Toolbar Resources 440
Adding Server Functionality 441
Implementing the Embedded Object 442
Scaleable Mapping Modes 442
Updating the View 443
Changing the Mapping Mode 443
Drawing the Embedded Object 444
Getting the Extent of an Embedded Object 445
Notifying Changes 446

Executing the Server 447
Summary 448
Exercises 448

Chapter 12: ActiveX Controls 451

ActiveX and OLE 451
What Are OLE Controls? 452
What About ActiveX Controls? 452
How OLE Controls Work 453
Properties 453
Ambient Properties 454
Control Properties 455

Extended Properties   455
Property Pages   456
Methods   456
Events   456
The Interface to an OLE Control   457
Implementing an ActiveX Control   457
Creating a Basic ActiveX Control   458
Structure of the Program   460
The Application Class   460
The Control Class   460
Implementation of the Control Class   462
The Property Page Class   463
Implementation of the Property Page Class   464
Defining a Traffic Signal Object   464
Implementing the NextState() Function   466
Implementing the Draw() Function   467
Adding a Constructor   471
Using a CTrafficSignal Object   471
Testing the Control   473
Using Stock and Ambient Properties   473
Adding Custom Properties to the Control   477
Using ClassWizard to Add Custom Properties   477
Initializing Custom Properties   479
Making the Signal Work   480
Starting and Stopping the Signal   481
Starting the Signal   481
Stopping the Signal   482
Handling WM_TIMER Messages   482
Implementing the Notify Function for the Control   483
Implementing the Property Get/Set Functions   483
Using the Property Page   484
Connecting Controls to Properties   485
Using the Control   487
Adding Events to a Control   487
The ODL File   489
Adding an Enumeration   491
Embedding an ActiveX Control in a Web Page   495
Summary   498
Exercises   498

Chapter 13: Using the Active Template Library   501

More About COM   501
COM and Interfaces   502
Dispatch Interfaces   503
COM Interfaces and Class Interfaces   504
Understanding the Active Template Library   505
Invisible Controls   505
Using the ATL COM AppWizard   506
Basic COM AppWizard Code   508
Adding a COM object to the Project   509
ATL Object Code   511

The COM Object Class   511
The Interface Definition   512
Extending the Interface   514
Implementing the Interface Functions   515
Building the Component   **516**
Using the Component   **518**
Visual Basic Access to the COM Component   518
Using the COM Component in C++   520
Creating the Interface   521
Using the COM Library   524
Component Objects   525
Obtaining the CLSID for a Component   525
Creating an Instance of a Component   527
Releasing the Component   528
Using Component Interface Functions   528
Using ATL to Create an ActiveX Control   **529**
The ATL Control Class   530
Defining the Signal   533
Implementing CTrafficSignal   535
Drawing the Signal   536
Adding the Signal to the Control   540
Drawing the Control   541
Starting and Stopping the Signal   542
Controlling the Signal   544
Exercising the Control   545
Adding Custom Properties   546
Adding Events   547
Adding a Connection Point   549
Running the Control   551
Summary   **552**
Exercises   **552**

Appendix A: Keywords in Visual C++   **555**

Appendix B: The ASCII Table   **557**

ASCII Characters 0 - 31   557
ASCII Characters 32 - 127   558

Appendix C: Solutions to Exercises   **561**

Chapter 1   561
Chapter 2   561
Chapter 3   563
Chapter 4   564
Chapter 5   565
Chapter 6   569
Chapter 7   574
Chapter 8   577

Chapter 9   579
Chapter 10   581
Chapter 11   585
Chapter 12   587
Chapter 13   592

Index   **599**

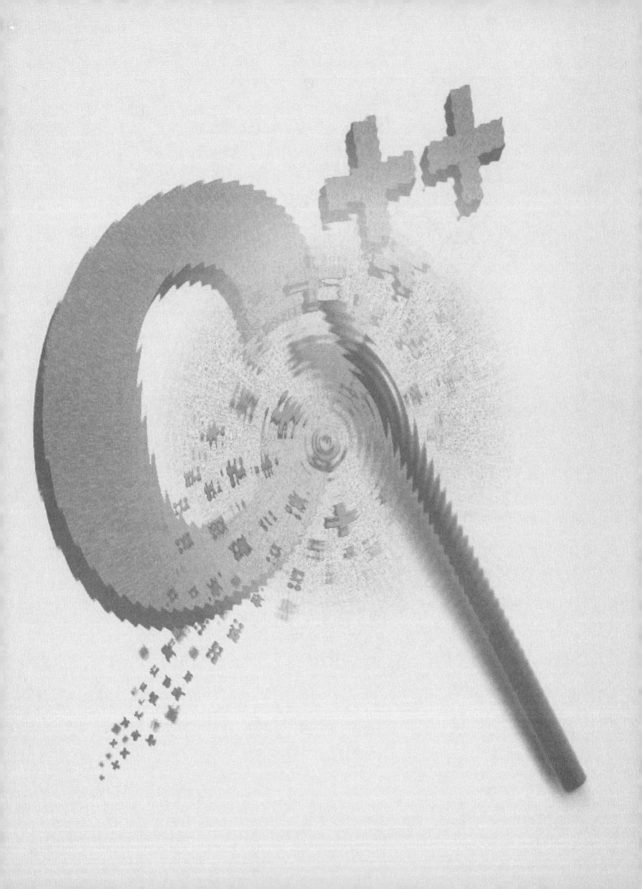

Beginning

MFC

Programming

Introduction

Welcome to *Beginning MFC Programming*. With this book you will quickly become a competent MFC Windows programmer.

Based on the proven success of *Beginning Visual C++ 5* and the feedback I have received on that title, I have created *Beginning MFC Programming* to better address your needs as a C++ programmer.

Who Is This Book For?

Beginning MFC Programming is designed to teach you how to use MFC to write useful programs as quickly and as easily as possible using Microsoft's Visual C++ compiler. This is the tutorial for you, if:

▶ You've done some programming before, and you understand C++. Now you want to move past writing simple text mode applications and start developing practical Windows programming skills using the most powerful tools available.

▶ You've developed simple Windows applications using C++ and the Windows SDK, but you've had enough of doing things the hard way. You know that it's time to get to grips with the industry standard Windows class library to increase your programming productivity.

▶ You've created C++ programs using other class libraries (perhaps even on non-Windows operating systems). This book will give you the solid MFC foundation you're looking for, but will move along fast enough to keep you excited.

In other words, if you know C++ and you're keen to learn MFC, this is the book for you.

Who Isn't This Book For?

This book isn't suitable if you're new to programming or don't already know C++. If that describes you then you should definitely check out *Beginning Visual C++ 5*, which features all the great coverage of MFC that's contained in this book plus an extensive C++ tutorial that provides the necessary grounding in the C++ language that you'll need to get the most out of MFC.

What's Covered in This Book

In this book, I will take you from your first contact with MFC right up to the cutting edge of Windows programming: developing ActiveX controls. The book starts with an introduction to Developer Studio, the integrated development environment provided with Visual C++, briefly covering the main components of the interface.

Soon you'll get to grips with the Microsoft Foundation Classes and Windows programming for real. We'll look at AppWizard and ClassWizard, two tools to speed up your application development. We'll cover building applications with menus, dialogs and scrollbars. Saving and reading data to and from disk will be discussed, along with how to print documents and write dynamic-link libraries. All these new topics are reinforced through the progressive development of a simple drawing application that grows in functionality as your knowledge increases.

Chapter 10 demonstrates how to connect to databases with Visual C++, showing you how easy it is to produce a dialog-based database interface using the classes provided by MFC for the purpose.

The last three chapters of the book form an introduction to one of the most important areas of development now and in the future: custom controls. We'll start by explaining the concept of object linking and embedding (OLE), and produce a version of our drawing application that allows you to edit your drawings *inside* other applications—Microsoft Word, for example. After that, we take the next step and use MFC to produce an ActiveX control, which as well as being embeddable inside other applications can also communicate with them. Finally, we use one of the new features of Visual C++ 5—the ATL Object Wizard—to create two more ActiveX controls without using MFC.

Every chapter is concluded with a summary and a set of exercises. These could form part of a structured course, or simply serve to consolidate the new things you've learned during the chapter.

What You Need to Use This Book

To use this book you need Visual C++ 5.0, the latest version of Microsoft's best-selling C++ compiler. This version is 32-bit only, so you'll need to install it on Windows 95, Windows NT 3.51 or NT 4, which means a 486 CPU or better and a minimum 16Mb of memory.

For Visual C++, you'll need quite a lot of hard disk space—a typical installation is 170 Mbytes. You can do a minimal installation, which takes up around 40 Mbytes, but this will mean longer compile times, as the CD-ROM will be utilized more often.

More importantly, however, to get the most out of this book you need a willingness to learn, a desire to succeed and the determination to master the most powerful tool there is to program Windows. You might believe that doing all this is going to be difficult, but I think you'll be surprised by how much you can achieve. I'll help you to start experimenting on your own and to become a successful programmer.

Conventions Used

We use a number of different styles of text and layout in the book to help differentiate between the different kinds of information. Here are examples of the styles we use and an explanation of what they mean:

> *These boxes hold important, not-to-be forgotten, mission critical details which are directly relevant to the surrounding text.*

 Extra details, For Your Information, come in boxes like this.

Background information, asides and references appear in text like this.

▶ **Important Words** are in a bold type font.

▶ Words that appear on the screen, such as menu options, are in a similar font to the one used on screen, for example, the File menu.

▶ Keys that you press on the keyboard, like *Ctrl* and *Enter*, are in italics.

▶ All filenames are in this style: **Videos.mdb**.

▶ Function names look like this: **sizeof()**.

▶ Code that is new, important, or relevant to the current discussion will be presented like this:

```
void main()
{
    cout << "Beginning MFC Programming";
}
```

▶ whereas code you've seen before, or which has little to do with the matter at hand, looks like this:

```
void main()
{
    cout << "Beginning MFC Programming";
}
```

Tell Us What You Think

We have tried to make this book as accurate and enjoyable for you as possible, but what really matters is what the book actually does for you. Please let us know your views, whether positive or negative, either by returning the reply card in the back of the book or by contacting us at Wrox Press using either of the following methods:

e-mail:	**feedback@wrox.com**
Internet:	**http://www.wrox.com/**
	http://www.wrox.co.uk/

Source Code and Keeping Up-to-date

We try to keep the prices of our books reasonable, so instead of providing disks, we make the source code for our books available on our web sites:

http://www.wrox.com/
http://www.wrox.co.uk/

We've done everything we can to ensure your download is as fast as possible. The code is also available via FTP:

ftp://ftp.wrox.com
ftp://ftp.wrox.co.uk

If you don't have access to the Internet, then we can provide a disk for a nominal fee to cover postage and packing.

Errata & Updates

We've made every effort to make sure there are no errors in the text or the code. However, to err is human and as such we recognize the need to keep you, the reader, informed of any mistakes as they're spotted and amended.

While you're visiting our web site, please make use of our *Errata* page that's dedicated to fixing any small errors in the book or, offering new ways around a problem and its solution. Errata sheets are available for all our books - please download them, or take part in the continuous improvement of our tutorials and upload a 'fix' or pointer.

For those without access to the net, if you've got a specific problem you can call us on **1-800 USE WROX**. Alternatively, send a letter to:

Wrox Press Inc.,
1512 North Fremont,
Suite 103,
Chicago
IL 60622
USA

Wrox Press Ltd,
30, Lincoln Road,
Olton,
Birmingham,
B27 6PA
UK

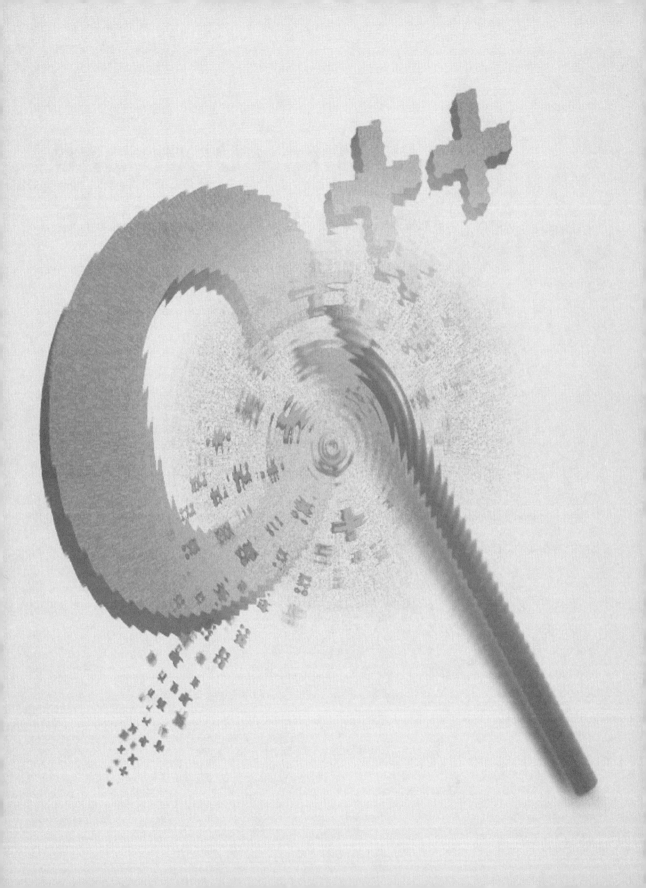

Programming MFC with Visual C++

The Microsoft Foundation Classes make Windows programming easy for you, the C++ programmer. This is because they expose the Windows programming interface in a way that's familiar to you: a well-defined hierarchy of interacting classes. All the key Windows functionality is implemented through member functions, while the classes themselves represent objects as diverse as dialog windows, linked lists and spin controls. In this book, I'll explain how Windows works in fairly broad terms, and I'll show you just how naturally MFC fits in with that scheme.

In this chapter, as a base for tackling MFC, we're going to take a rapid tour of the Developer Studio—the integrated development environment that comes with Microsoft Visual C++. Although there are other vendors whose compilers also support MFC—notably, Borland, Symantec and Watcom—the latest version invariably appears for Visual C++ first; therefore, using Visual C++ will tend to keep you ahead of the game. For that reason, the discussion and examples in this book center on using the Developer Studio. The things you'll learn about MFC will be true whatever environment you're working in, but if you're using one of the other compilers then your path with this book will be more difficult.

The Developer Studio is very straightforward, and generally intuitive in its operation, so you'll be able to pick up most of it as you go along. The best approach to getting familiar with it is to work through creating, compiling and executing a simple program. You'll get some insight into the philosophy and mechanics of the Developer Studio as you use it. We'll take you through this process and beyond, so that by the end of this chapter, you will have learned about:

- The principal components of Visual C++
- Projects and how you create them
- How to create and edit a program
- How to create a basic Windows program

So power up your PC, start Windows, load the mighty Visual C++ and we can begin our journey.

Learning C++ and Windows Programming

With this book, you'll learn how to write Windows programs. To give you a feel for where we are ultimately headed, we can take look at the characteristics of a typical Windows program.

Introducing Windows Programming

Our approach to Windows programming will be to use all the tools that Visual C++ provides. **AppWizard**, which can generate a basic Windows program automatically, will be the starting point for all the Windows examples in the book. We'll then be using **ClassWizard** to augment the code produced by AppWizard and create more useful programs. To get a flavor of how AppWizard works, later in this chapter we'll look at the mechanics of starting a Windows program.

A Windows program has quite a different structure to that of the typical DOS program, and it's rather more complicated. There are two reasons for this. Firstly, in a DOS program you can get input from the keyboard or write to the display directly, whereas a Windows program can only access the input and output facilities of the computer by way of Windows functions; no direct access to these hardware resources is permitted. Since several programs can be active at one time under Windows, Windows has to determine which application a given input is destined for and signal the program concerned accordingly. Windows has primary control of all communications with the user.

Secondly, the nature of the interface between a user and a Windows application is such that a range of different inputs is possible at any given time. A user may key some data, select any of a number of menu options, or click the mouse somewhere in the application window. A well-designed Windows application has to be prepared to deal with any type of input at any time, because there is no way of knowing in advance which type of input is going to occur.

These user actions are all regarded by Windows as **events**, and will typically result in a particular piece of your program code being executed. How program execution proceeds is therefore determined by the sequence of user actions. Programs that operate in this way are referred to as **event-driven programs**.

Therefore, a Windows program consists primarily of pieces of code that respond to events caused by the action of the user or by Windows itself. This sort of program structure can be represented as illustrated:

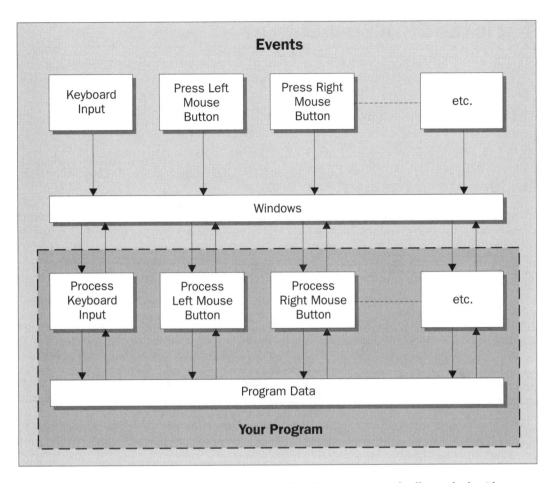

Each block in the illustration represents a piece of code written specifically to deal with a particular event. Although the program may appear to be somewhat fragmented, the primary factor welding the program into a whole is Windows itself. You can think of your Windows program as customizing Windows to provide a particular set of capabilities. Of course, the modules servicing various external events, such as selecting a menu or clicking the mouse, will all typically have access to a common set of application-specific data in a particular program. This application data will contain information that relates to what the program is about—blocks of text in an editor for example, or player scoring records in a program aimed at tracking how your baseball team is doing—as well as information about some of the events that have occurred during execution of the program. This shared collection of data allows various parts of the program, which look independent to communicate and operate in a coordinated and integrated fashion. We will, of course, go into this in much more detail later in the book.

Even an elementary Windows program involves quite a few lines of code, and with AppWizard-based Windows programs, 'quite a few' turns out to be rather a lot.

What is the Developer Studio?

The Developer Studio is a completely self-contained environment for creating, compiling, linking and testing Windows programs. It is the Integrated Development Environment (IDE) that comes with Visual C++ version 5.0.

The Developer Studio incorporates a range of fully integrated tools designed to make the whole process of writing Windows programs easy. We will see something of these in this and the following chapter.

Components of the System

The fundamental parts of Visual C++, provided as part of the Developer Studio, are the editor, the compiler, the linker and the libraries. These are the basic tools that are essential to writing and executing a C++ program. Their functions are as follows:

The Editor

The editor provides an interactive environment for creating and editing C++ source code. As well as the usual facilities, such as cut and paste, which you are certainly already familiar with, the editor also provides color cues to differentiate between various language elements. The editor automatically recognizes fundamental words in the C++ language and assigns a color to them according to what they are. This not only helps to make your code more readable, but also provides a clear indicator of when you make errors in keying such words.

The Compiler

The compiler converts your source code into machine language, and detects and reports errors in the compilation process. The compiler can detect a wide range of errors that are due to invalid or unrecognized program code, as well as structural errors, where, for example, part of a program can never be executed. The output from the compiler is known as **object code** and is stored in files called **object files**, which usually have names with the extension **.obj**.

The Linker

The linker combines the various modules generated by the compiler from source code files, adds required code modules from program libraries supplied as part of C++, and welds everything into an executable whole. The linker can also detect and report errors; for example, if part of your program is missing, or a non-existent library component is referenced.

The Libraries

A library supports and extends the C++ language by providing routines to carry out operations which are not part of the language. For example, libraries can contain routines such as calculating a square root, comparing two character strings or obtaining date and time information. There are two kinds of library provided by Visual C++.

The first kind contains routines that aren't platform-specific. There is a basic set of routines common to all C++ compilers which make up the **standard library**. There are also extensions to the standard set which will be supported in many other C++ compilers, but their universality isn't guaranteed.

The other kind of library is called the **Microsoft Foundation Class library**, or **MFC** for short, which is the cornerstone of Windows programming with Visual C++. MFC provides the basis for all the Windows programs you'll write. MFC is also referred to as an **application framework**, because it provides a set of structured components that provide a ready-made basis for almost any Windows program.

> *There is a further library provided with Visual C++, called the **Active Template Library** (**ATL**). This library allows the creation of programs based on COM and the ActiveX technologies. You'll be treated to a glimpse of ATL in Chapter 13. Microsoft sometimes refers to both MFC and ATL as a single entity called MFC & T.*

Other Tools

The Developer Studio also includes two important tools which work in a wholly integrated way to help you write Windows programs. These are the **AppWizard** and the **ClassWizard**. They aren't essential to the process of writing Windows programs, but provide such immense advantages in simplifying the development process, reducing the incidence of errors, and shortening the time to completing a program, that we will use them for all of our major examples. Read on for an idea of the services that these tools provide.

AppWizard

The AppWizard automatically generates a basic framework for your Windows program. In fact, the framework is itself a complete, executable Windows program, as we shall see later in this chapter. Of course, you need to add the specific functionality necessary to make the program do what you want, which is an essential part of developing a Windows program.

ClassWizard

Classes are the most important language feature of C++ and are fundamental to Windows programming with Visual C++. The ClassWizard provides an easy means of extending the classes generated by AppWizard as part of your basic Windows program and also helps you to add new classes based on classes in MFC to support the functionality you want to include in your program. Note that ClassWizard neither recognizes nor deals with classes that are not based on MFC classes.

The Wizard Bar

A further capability for managing, modifying, and extending your code is provided by the Wizard Bar, which is optionally displayed in the toolbar area of the Developer Studio window. It's particularly useful in the context of MFC-based Windows programs, so we'll see more of it then. For now let's just say that its particular forte is adding code to your programs to deal with the Windows events we discussed earlier.

Using the Visual C++ Development Environment

All our program development and execution will be performed from within the Developer Studio. When you start Visual C++, assuming no project was active when you shut it down last (we'll see what a project is, exactly, in a moment), you will see the window shown on the following page:

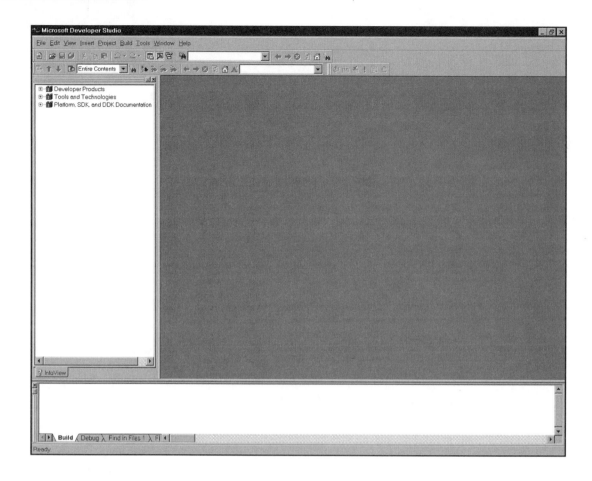

The window to the left is the **project workspace window**, the window to the right is the **editor window**, and the window at the bottom is the **output window**. The workspace window provides access to the on-line documentation and enables you to navigate through your program files, the editor window is where you enter and modify source code and other components of your application, and the output window displays messages that result from compiling and linking your program.

The toolbars below the main menu that you see above provide icons which act as an instant route to some of the functions available from the main menus. Just clicking on a toolbar icon will directly perform the function that it corresponds to. Developer Studio offers a whole range of dockable and customizable toolbars that you can use.

Toolbar Options

It may be that your Developer Studio window doesn't show the toolbars that appear above. If this is the case, just right click with the mouse in the toolbar area. You will see a pop-up with a list of toolbars, some of which have check marks alongside:

This is where you decide which toolbars are visible at any one time. You can make your set of toolbars the same as those shown by making sure the Output, Workspace, Standard, Build MiniBar and InfoViewer menu items are checked.

You needn't clutter up the application window with all the toolbars you think you might need at some time. Other toolbars will appear automatically when required, so you'll probably find the default toolbar selections are perfectly adequate most of the time. As you develop your applications, from time to time you might think it would be more convenient to have access to toolbars that aren't displayed. You can change the set of toolbars that are visible whenever it suits you by right clicking in the toolbar area and choosing from the pop-up.

Like many other Windows applications, the toolbars that make up the Developer Studio come complete with tooltips. Just let the mouse pointer linger over a button for a second or two and a little yellow label will provide you with the function and shortcut key combination of that button.

Dockable Toolbars

A **dockable** toolbar is one that you can drag around with the mouse to position it at a convenient place in the window. When it is placed in any of the four borders of the application, it is said to be *docked* and will look like the toolbars that you see at the top of the application window. The toolbar on the lower line of toolbar buttons which contains the up and down arrows, and the list box showing Entire Contents, is the InfoViewer toolbar. You can drag this away from the toolbar by placing the cursor on it and dragging it with the mouse while you hold down the left mouse button. It will then appear as a separate window that you can position anywhere.

If you drag any dockable toolbar away from its docked position, it will look like the InfoViewer toolbar that you see above, enclosed in a little window—but, of course, with a different caption. In this state, it is called a **floating toolbar**. All the toolbars that you see above are dockable and can be floating, so you can experiment with dragging any of them around. You can position them in docked positions where they will revert to their normal toolbar appearance. You can dock a dockable toolbar at any side of the main window.

13

You'll be familiar with many of the toolbar icons that Developer Studio uses from other Windows applications, but you may not appreciate exactly what these icons do in the context of Visual C++, so we'll describe them as we use them.

Since we'll use a new project for every program we develop, looking at what exactly a project is and understanding how the mechanism for defining a project works, a good place to start is to find out how we use the Developer Studio.

Projects and Project Workspaces

A **project** is simply a program of some kind—it might be a console program, a Windows program, or some other kind of program. A **project workspace** is a folder in which all the information relating to a project is stored. When you create a project, a project workspace is created automatically, and Developer Studio will maintain all of the source code and other files in the project workspace folder. This folder will also contain other folders to store the output from compiling and linking your project. When you have created a project along with its project workspace, you can add further projects to the same workspace. These are referred to as **subprojects** of the original project. Where a project has one or more subprojects, you can work on any of the files for the project or its subprojects.

Any kind of project can be a subproject of another, but you would usually only create a subproject in a project workspace where the subproject depends on the project in some way, sharing source code for example, or some operational interdependency. Generally, unless you have a good reason to do otherwise, each of your projects should have its own project workspace. This ensures you only access the files that belong to your project within Developer Studio, and there is no possibility of confusion with files for other projects which might have similar names. All the examples we will create will have their own workspace.

Defining a Project

The first step in writing a Visual C++ program is to create a project for it using the File | New... menu option from the main menu. As well as containing files that define and keep track of all the code that goes to make up your program, the project workspace also holds files that record the Developer Studio options you're using. The workspace folder will hold the project definition files and all your source code. A project definition includes:

- ▶ A project name.
- ▶ A list of all the source files.
- ▶ A definition of what sort of program is to be built from the source files, for example, a Windows **.exe** program, or a console application.
- ▶ The options set for the editor, the compiler, the linker and other components of Visual C++ that might be involved.
- ▶ The windows to be displayed in Developer Studio when the project is opened.

The basic definition of a project is actually stored on disk in a file with the extension **.dsp** (in previous versions of Visual C++ this was a **.mak** file). This contains information about how your program is to be created from the files in the project workspace and is produced when you create a project workspace. Your project workspace will also contain a file with the extension **.opt** which contains the settings for the project workspace. This will include information about the appearance of the project workspace so that this can be restored when you open a project you have worked on previously. Another file with the extension `.dsw` is used to store further information about the workspace, such as what projects it contains.

All of these files are created and maintained automatically by Visual C++ and the Developer Studio, so you shouldn't attempt to edit or amend them directly yourself. Any changes you want to make—for example, to the options in effect for a program—you should introduce using the menus for that purpose in Developer Studio.

Debug and Release Versions of Your Program

You can set a range of options for a project through the Project | Settings... menu. These options determine how your source code is to be processed during the compile and link stages; the set of options that produces a particular executable version of your program is called a **configuration**. When you create a new project workspace, Developer Studio will automatically create configurations for producing two versions of your application. One includes information which will help you to debug the program and is called the Debug Version. With the debug version of your program you can step through the code when things go wrong, checking on the data values in the program. The other, called the Release Version, has no debug information included and has the code optimization options for the compiler turned on to provide you with the most efficient executable module. These two configurations will be sufficient for our needs throughout the book, but when you need to add other configurations for an application, you can do so through the Build | Configurations... menu. Note that this menu won't appear if you haven't got a project loaded. This is obviously not a problem, but might be confusing if you're just browsing through the menus to see what's there.

You can choose which configuration of your program to work with by selecting the Build | Set Active Configuration... menu option:

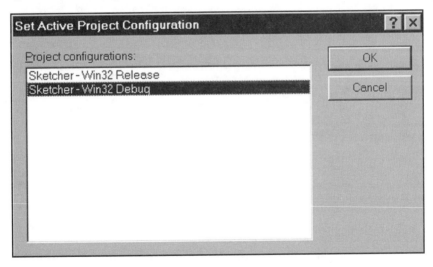

You just select the configuration you want to work with from the list, and click on the OK button. If you display the Build toolbar, this will provide a drop down list box on the toolbar from which you can select a configuration. While you're developing an application, you'll be working with the debug configuration. Once your application has been tested using the debug configuration and appears to be working correctly, you would typically rebuild the program as a release version—since this produces optimized code without the debug and trace capability, which will run faster and occupy less memory.

Creating a New Project

Let's take a look at creating a project for a console application. First select <u>N</u>ew... from the <u>F</u>ile menu to bring up the list of items shown below:

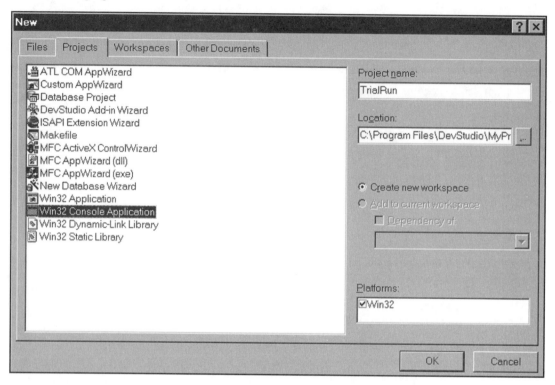

The default tab shown is the Projects tab, which displays the kinds of project that you can create. The selection that you make from the list determines what kind of program you are creating. For many of these options, a basic set of program source modules will be created automatically.

For the project we are creating, you should select Win 32 Console Application as the project's type. This won't generate any code, but will set the options for this kind of application. You can now enter a suitable name for your project by typing into the Project <u>N</u>ame: edit box—you could call this one TrialRun, for instance—or any other name that takes your fancy. Visual C++ supports long file names, so you have a lot of flexibility.

This dialog also allows you to enter the location for your project, as well as the platforms upon which you'd like it to run, where this is applicable. (We won't need to change the platform setting at all for the examples in this book.) If you simply enter a name for your project, the workspace folder will automatically be set to a folder with that name, with the path shown in the Lo<u>c</u>ation: edit box. The folder will be created for you if it doesn't already exist. If you want to specify a different path, just enter it in the <u>L</u>ocation: edit box. Alternatively, you can use the button to select another folder and path for your project's files.

When you click on the OK button, a new project workspace folder will be created in the folder that you have specified as the Location: entry. The folder will have the name that you supplied as the project name and will store all the files making up the project definition. If you use Explorer to look in the project folder, you will see there are just four files initially: the **.dsp**, **.opt**, and **.dsw** files that we mentioned earlier, plus the file **TrialRun.ncb**, which stores no compile browser information from your program which is used by several components of Developer Studio. So what's 'no compile browser' information? It's information that records where each entity in your program is defined, and where it's used. ClassView and the WizardBar use this information to help you manipulate and edit your source code.

The new workspace will automatically be opened in Developer Studio. You will see that two tabs have been added to the Project Workspace window, showing a ClassView and a FileView for your project. You can switch between these windows by clicking the tab for the window you want to see. All three tabs are shown below:

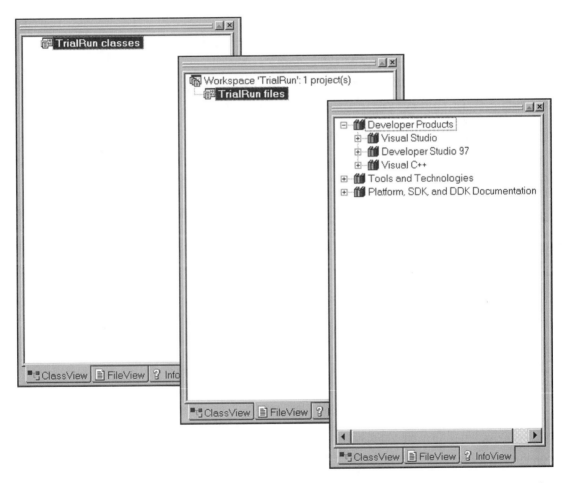

Although these views are looking rather empty at the moment, you'll see later that they provide a quick and convenient way of viewing and accessing various aspects of your project.

The **ClassView** displays the classes defined in your project and will also show the contents of each class. We don't have any classes in this application, so the view is empty. When we get into discussing classes, you will see that you can use ClassView to move around the code relating to the definition and implementation of all your application classes very quickly and easily.

The **FileView** shows the source program files that make up your project. You can display the contents of any of your project files by double clicking on a file name in FileView. This will open a window for the file and automatically invoke an editor to enable you to modify the file contents. At the moment we have no source program files, either.

The **InfoView** is a standard view that is the same for every project. It shows the contents for the Books Online reference material supplied with ClassWizard, or a subset of those contents if you've defined one. You can access this material by clicking on pages displayed on the InfoView tab, or by using the buttons on the InfoViewer toolbar to search the material.

On this toolbar you have buttons for searching the online documentation, for setting bookmarks to documentation you want to access frequently, and for stepping through the pages of the material. You can also define subsets of the documentation to divide it into more manageable chunks, which you can then select from the list box to the left.

Projects for Windows applications will also have a tab to display a **ResourceView** which will display the dialogs, icons, menus and toolbars that are used by the program.

Like most elements of the Developer Studio, the Project Workspace window provides context-sensitive pop-up menus when you right-click in the window. If you find that the Project Workspace window gets in your way when writing code, you can hide and show it most easily by using the Project Workspace button provided on the Standard toolbar.

Entering Your First Visual C++ Program

Since a project workspace isn't really a great deal of use without a program file, it's time we entered our first program. We'll keep away from the MFC and Windows programs so as not to muddy the water with new concepts. Select File then New... from the main menu. Developer Studio knows that we've already created a project, and this time offers the Files tab by default:

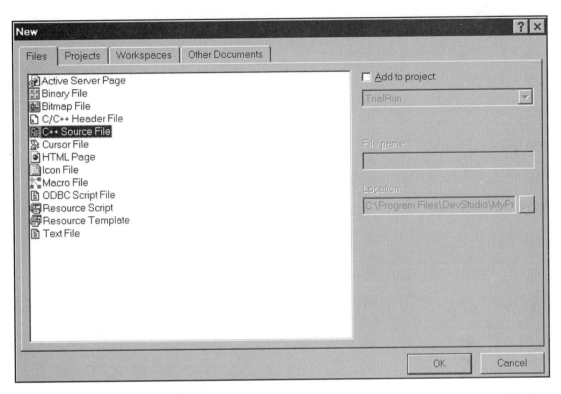

As the name suggests, this dialog lets you choose to create one from a range of different kinds of file. Select the type of file from the list as C++ Source File and click on OK. This will open a new editor window to display the file, which will have the default name **Cpp1**. You'll see that the file name is displayed in the Developer Studio title bar at the top. The asterisk following the name indicates that the contents of the file displayed in the window have been modified.

Because you chose to open the file as a C++ source file, the editor is already prepared to accept source code, so go right ahead and type in the program code exactly as shown in the window below. Don't worry about what it does. This is a very simple program which outputs some lines of text and is just meant to exercise the Developer Studio facilities.

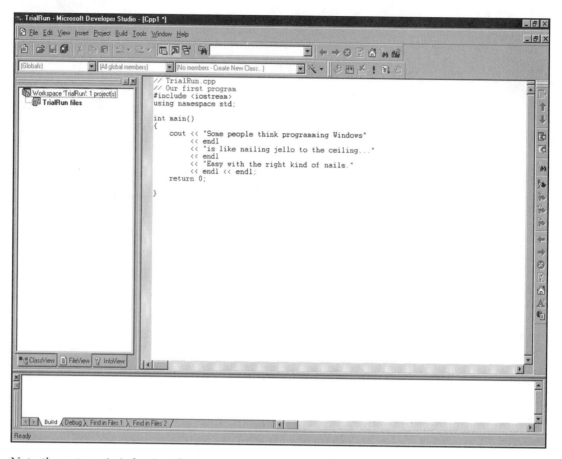

```
// TrialRun.cpp
// Our first program
#include <iostream>
using namespace std;

int main()
{
    cout << "Some people think programming Windows"
         << endl
         << "is like nailing jello to the ceiling..."
         << endl
         << "Easy with the right kind of nails."
         << endl << endl;
    return 0;

}
```

Note the automatic indenting that occurs as you type in the code. C++ uses indenting to make programs more readable, and the editor automatically indents each line of code that you enter, based on what was in the previous line. You can also see the syntax color highlighting in action as you type. Some elements of the program are shown in different colors as the editor automatically assigns colors to language elements depending on what they are.

Having entered the program, you need to save it with a suitable file name. C++ source programs are usually assigned a name with the extension **.cpp**, so, using the <u>S</u>ave option from the <u>F</u>ile menu (or the corresponding toolbar button), save this file as **TrialRun.cpp**. Files with the extension **.cpp** or **.cxx** are recognized as C++ source files, whereas files with the extension **.c** are assumed to be C source files. If you don't use one of these extensions, Developer Studio won't recognize the file as a source file. It's best to stick to the **.cpp** extension for C++ as this is most commonly used in the PC environment. You can save a file in any folder that you feel like, but, since we intend this file to be part of the TrialRun project that we just created, it's a good idea to store it in the same directory as the project files, which will be the default option.

Adding a Source File to a Project

Now that we have a program source file, we need to add it to our project (saving it in the project directory doesn't do that, it just stores it on disk). The easiest way to do this is to right-click in the text file window and select the Insert File into Project item from the pop-up. Alternatively, you could have chosen Add to Project from the Project menu on the main menu bar, selected Files... from the pop-up, and browsed for the file that you wished to add.

You could also have created the file as part of the project at the outset. By selecting Add to Project from the Project menu, and then choosing New... from the pop-up, the C++ file would automatically have been part of the project. In this case you are obliged to supply the name of the file in the New dialog, before Developer Studio creates the file. Once the file is part of the project, the file name appears on the FileView tab in the project workspace window.

Building a Project

The combined process of compiling the source files in a project to produce object code modules and then linking these to produce an executable file is referred to as **building** a project. The project file with the extension **.dsp** is used by Visual C++ in the build process to set the options for the compiler and linker to create the executable file. You can build a project in a number of ways:

▶ Click the [button] button on the Build toolbar.

▶ Choose the Build item from the menu that appears when you right-click the TrialRun files folder in the FileView.

▶ Choose the Build TrialRun.exe item from the Build menu on the main menu bar.

> *Note that open source files are automatically saved when a build is performed.*

When you build the executable the Output window, which provides you with status and error information about the process, will appear.

```
--------------------Configuration: TrialRun - Win32 Debug--------------------
Compiling...
TrialRun.cpp
Linking...
--------------------------------------------------------------------

TrialRun.exe - 0 error(s), 0 warning(s)
```
Build / Debug \ Find in Files 1 \ Find in Files 2 \ Results \ SQL Debugging /

Dealing with Errors

Of course, if you didn't type in the program correctly, you'll get errors reported. To show how this works, we could deliberately introduce an error into the program. If you already have errors of your own, you can use those to exercise this bit. Go back to the Text Editor window and delete the semicolon at the end of the second-to-last line and then rebuild the source file. The Output window should appear like this:

```
--------------------Configuration: TrialRun - Win32 Debug--------------------
Compiling...
TrialRun.cpp
C:\Program Files\DevStudio\MyProjects\TrialRun\TrialRun.cpp(14) : error C2143: syntax error : missing ';' before ')'
Error executing cl.exe.
--------------------------------------------------------------------

TrialRun.exe - 1 error(s), 0 warning(s)
```
Build / Debug \ Find in Files 1 \ Find in Files 2 \ Results \ SQL Debugging /

The error message here is very clear. It specifically states that a semicolon is missing and, if you double click on the error message you will be taken directly to the line in error. You can then correct the error and rebuild the executable.

Using Help with the Output Window

Sometimes, the cause of an error may not be quite so obvious, in which case some additional information can be very helpful. You can get more information about any error reported by placing the cursor in the output window, anywhere in the line containing the error code (in this case C2143). You can position the cursor just by clicking with the mouse anywhere in the line. If you now press the function key *F1*, you will automatically bring up a help page with more information on the particular error in question, often containing examples of the sort of incorrect code that can cause the problem.

The build operation works very efficiently because the project definition keeps track of the status of the files making up the project. During a normal build, Visual C++ only recompiles the files that have changed since the program was last compiled or built. This means that if your project has several source files and you've edited only one of the files since the project was last built, only that file is recompiled before linking to create a new **.exe** file.

You also have the option of rebuilding all files from the start if you want, regardless of when they were last compiled. You just need to use the Rebuild All menu option instead of Build TrialRun.exe (or whatever the name of the executable is).

Files Created by Building a Console Application

Once the example has been built without error, if you take a look in the project folder, you'll see a new subfolder called Debug. This folder contains the output of the build that you just performed on the project. You will see that this folder contains seven new files.

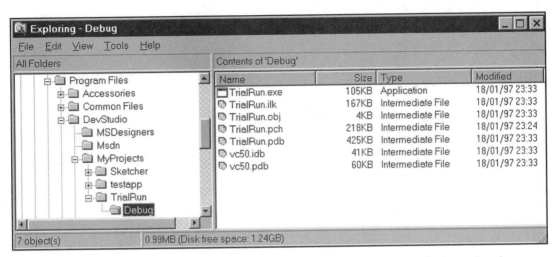

Other than the **.exe** file, which is your program in executable form, you don't need to know much about what's in these files. However, in case you're curious, let's do a quick run-through of what the more interesting ones are for:

File Extension	Description
.exe	This is the executable file for the program. You only get this file if both the compile and link steps are successful.
.obj	The compiler produces these object files containing machine code from your program source files. These are used by the linker, along with files from the libraries, to produce your **.exe** file.
.ilk	This file is used by the linker when you rebuild your project. It enables the linker to incrementally link the object files produced from the modified source code into the existing **.exe** file. This avoids the need to re-link everything each time you change your program.
.pch	This is a **pre-compiled header** file. With pre-compiled headers, large tracts of code which are not subject to modification (particularly code supplied by Visual C++) can be processed once and stored in the **.pch** file. Using the **.pch** file substantially reduces the time needed to build your program.
.pdb	This file contains debugging information that is used when you execute the program in debug mode. In this mode, you can dynamically inspect information that is generated during program execution.
.idb	Contains additional debug information.

If you have a **.exe** file for the TrialRun project, you can take it for a trial run, so let's see how to do that.

Executing Your First Program

We can, of course, execute the program in the normal way by double clicking the `.exe` file from Explorer, but we can also execute it without leaving the Visual C++ development environment. You can do this by selecting Execute TrialRun.exe from the Build menu, or by clicking on the toolbar button for this menu item.

```
TrialRun
Some people think programming Windows
is like nailing jello to the ceiling...
Easy with the right kind of nails.

Press any key to continue
```

 FYI The text Press any key to continue wouldn't normally appear in the console window - you could verify that by double-clicking the `.exe` file. Developer Studio is lending a helping hand by letting you peruse the output from your application at your leisure.

If we had changed any of the source files since the last build of the executable, or if we hadn't built the executable at all, we would be prompted to rebuild the project when we clicked the Go button.

You could also run your program from a DOS window under Windows 95. You just start a DOS session, change the current directory to the one that contains the `.exe` file for your program, then enter the program name to run it. You can leave the DOS session running while you are working with Visual C++ and just switch back to it when you want to run a console program.

Setting Options in Visual C++

There are two sets of options you can set. First, you can set options that apply to the tools the Developer Studio provides, which will apply in every project context. You can also set options that are specific to a project, which determine how the project code is to be processed when it is compiled and linked.

Setting Developer Studio Options

The Developer Studio options are set through a dialog that's displayed when you select Tools | Options... from the main menu.

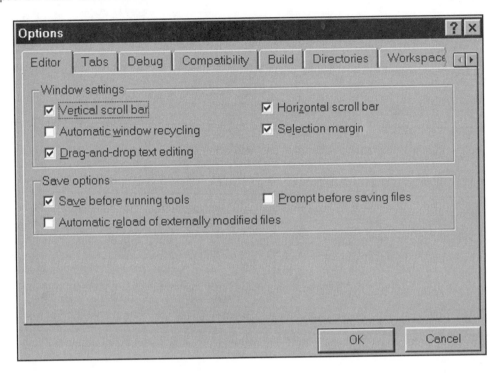

On each tab you'll see a range of options that you can select or deselect by clicking the check boxes. You can get an explanation of any of the options on a tab by clicking on the question mark at top right, and then clicking on the check box you're interested in. You only need concern yourself with a couple of these at this time, but it will be useful to explore the range of options available to you.

The Workspace tab allows you to set up which toolbars are dockable and which are not. It also has a range of other options relating to the way a workspace is handled. You may like to check the box for Reload last workspace at startup, then you will automatically pick up precisely where you left off when you closed Developer Studio last.

The Tools | Customize... menu option will display a dialog where you can change the contents of the toolbars in Developer Studio.

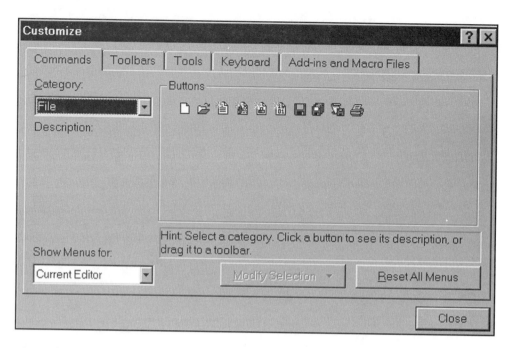

By selecting from the Category: list box on the Commands tab, you can view the toolbar buttons for any of the menus. You can see what any toolbar button on the Commands tab does by clicking it, and you can add any of the buttons shown to any toolbar by dragging it to where you want while holding down the left mouse button. You can also remove a button from an existing toolbar while this dialog is displayed simply by dragging the button that you want to remove off the toolbar.

If you're a keyboard fan, then through the Keyboard tab you can define your own shortcut key for any of the menu options on the main menu.

Setting Project Options

To set the options for a project, you select Project | Settings... from the main menu. This will display another dialog with a variety of tabs. Most of this you can ignore at this time, but one thing you'll find very useful for a project of any significant size is to create a browse information file. This will enable you to find out where in your source code any item is used, and where it is defined, just by right clicking it and selecting from the pop-up menu. You can get a browse information file generated by switching to the C/C++ tab.

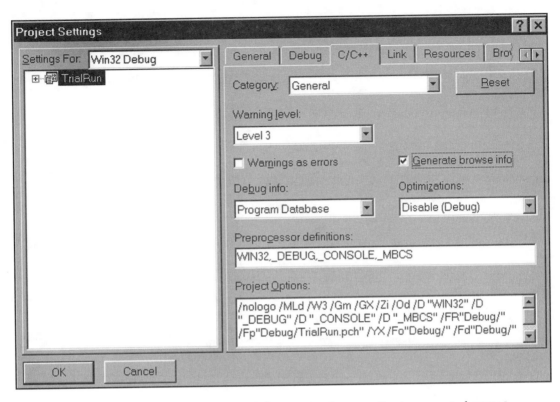

Just click on the Generate browse info check box to get the compiler to generate browse
information for each source file. Then switch to the Browse Info tab and click on the Build
browse info file check box. This will cause a composite of all the browse information to be
assembled into a file with the extension .bsc, which will be used when you're browsing your
source code.

Creating and Executing a Windows Program

Just to show how easy it's going to be, we'll now create a working Windows program, although
we'll defer discussion of the program that we generate until we've covered the necessary ground
for you to understand it in detail. You will see, though, that the process really is very
straightforward.

To start with, if an existing project is active—this will be indicated by the project name
appearing in the title bar of the Developer Studio main window—you can select Close
Workspace from the File menu. Alternatively, you can just go ahead and create a new project.

To create the Windows program we're going to use AppWizard, so select New... from the File
menu, and then select the Projects tab in the dialog. Select the project type as MFC AppWizard
(exe) and enter TrialWin as the project's name.

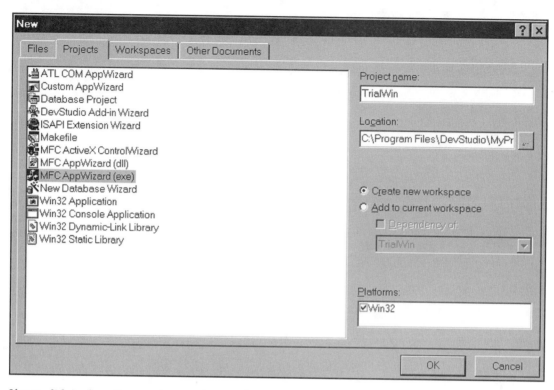

If you didn't close the previous project workspace, you'll need to check the Create new workspace radio button, otherwise the project will be created in the current workspace.

When you click on the OK button, the MFC AppWizard window will be displayed. The AppWizard consists of a number of dialog pages with options that let you choose which features you'd like to have included in your application, and we'll get to use most of these in examples later on.

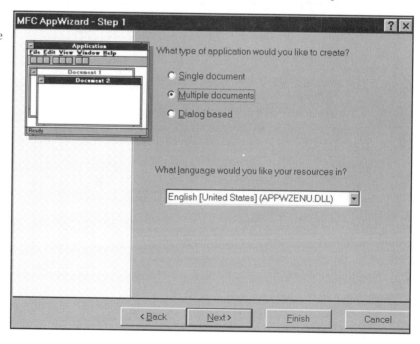

We'll ignore all these options and just accept the default settings, so click the Finish button. Another window will be displayed, as shown below:

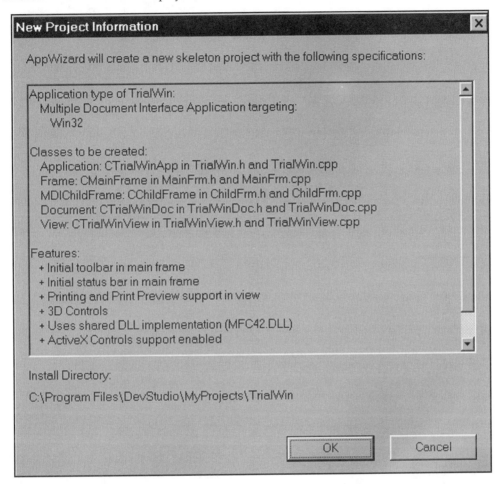

This is to advise you of what AppWizard is about to do, thus providing you with an opportunity to abort the whole thing if it doesn't seem to be what you want. It defines a list of the classes that it's going to create, and what the basic features of the program are going to be. We won't worry about what all these signify—we'll get to them eventually. It also indicates the folder that it will use to store the project and program files. Just click on the OK button and let AppWizard out of its cage. AppWizard will spend a few moments generating the necessary files and then eventually return to the main window. If you now expand the FileView in the project workspace window, you'll see the file list shown next:

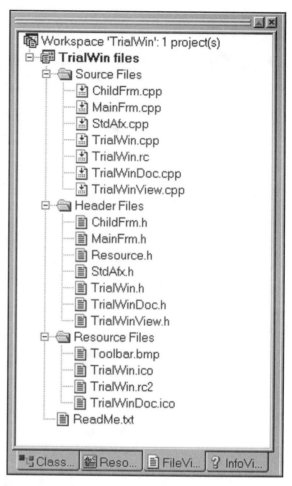

The list shows a large number of files that have been created. You need plenty of space on your hard drive when writing Windows programs! The files with the extension **.cpp** contain executable C++ source code, and the **.h** files contain C++ code consisting of definitions that are used by the executable code. The **.ico** files contain icons. FileView groups the files into the sub-folders you can see for ease of access. These aren't real folders, though, and they won't appear in the project folder on your disk.

If you now take a look at the **TrialWin** folder using Explorer, or whatever else you may have handy for looking at the files on your hard disk, you will see that we have generated a total of 23 files, four of which are in a sub-folder, **res**. The files in this sub-folder contain the resources used by the program—these are such things as the menus and icons used in the program. We get all this as a result of just entering the name we want to assign to the project. You can see why, with so many files and file names being created automatically, a separate directory for each project becomes more than just a good idea.

One of the files in the **TrialWin** subdirectory, **ReadMe.txt**, provides an explanation of the purpose of each of the files that AppWizard has generated. You can take a look at it if you wish, using Notepad, WordPad, or even the Visual C++ editor. To view it in the editor window just double click on it in FileView.

Executing a Windows Program

Before we can execute our program, we have to compile and link the program modules. You do this in exactly the same way that you did with the console application example. To save time, just select the Execute TrialWin.exe item from the Build menu or the toolbar button. Since you haven't built the executable yet, you'll be asked whether you want to do so. Click Yes.

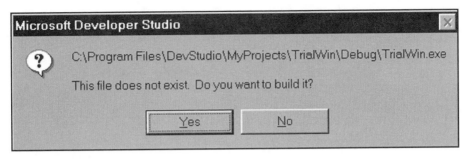

Compiling and linking the project will take a little time, even if you have a fast machine, since we already have quite a complex program. Once the project has been built, the Output window will indicate that there were no errors and the executable will start running. The window for the program we've generated is shown here:

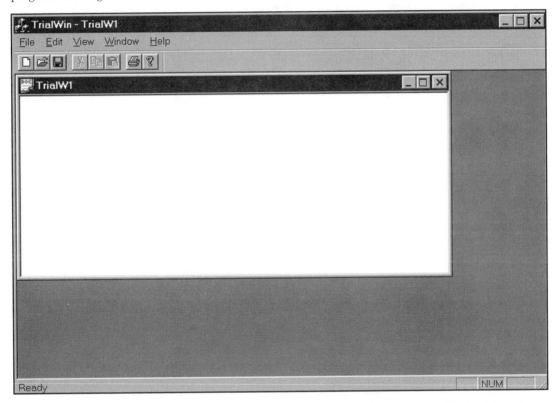

As you see, it's complete with menus and a toolbar. Although there is no specific functionality in the program—that's what we need to add to make it *our* program—all the menus work. You can try them out. You can even create further windows by selecting the New item from the File menu.

I think you'll agree that creating a Windows program with AppWizard hasn't really stressed too many brain cells. We'll need to get a few more ticking away when we come to developing the basic program we have here into a program that does something more interesting, but it won't be that hard. Certainly, for many people, writing a serious Windows program the old-fashioned way, without the aid of Visual C++, required at least a couple of months on a fish diet before making the attempt. That's why so many programmers used to eat sushi. That's all gone now with Visual C++. However, you never know what's around the corner in programming technology. If you like sushi, it's best to continue with it to be on the safe side.

Summary

In this chapter, we've run through the basic mechanics of using Developer Studio. We used the Studio to enter and execute a console application program and, with the help of AppWizard, we created a complete Windows program.

Every program should have a project defined for it. The project will store information as to the kind of program it is, what files need to be combined to construct the program and the options in effect for the program. All programs in this book will have a project defined.

Exercises

It's not easy to set exercises for this chapter, because we haven't got much new knowledge to exercise yet, so we'll use this opportunity to familiarize ourselves with the basics of the Developer Studio.

Ex1-1: List as many different ways as possible to build (i.e. compile and link) a project.

Ex1-2: List the three types of file used to store information about a project and describe the role of each.

Ex1-3: Describe the use of the following file types produced by the Visual C++ compiler: **.obj**, **.pch**, **.pdb**, **.exe**.

Ex1-4: Edit the **TrialRun** program to introduce various errors—miss out or put in the wrong curly braces, misspell names like **main** or **iostream.h**. Build the project, and use the help system to look at the error messages produced. Don't worry too much for now if you don't understand exactly what they mean; the idea is to get some practice in using the compiler and the help system.

Ex1-5: Read about the Development Environment and building projects in Books Online. A good place to start is under Visual C++\Developer Studio Environment User's Guide.

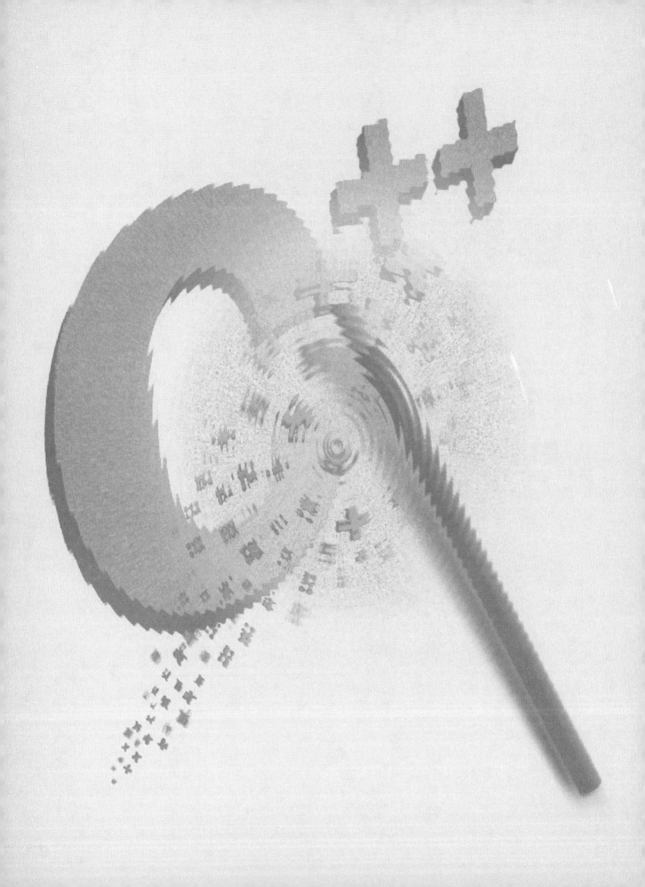

A Taste of Old-Fashioned Windows

In this chapter, we're going to take a look at the nuts and bolts of a Windows program to see how you can put one together without the assistance of the AppWizard and MFC.

In the next chapter, you'll be using MFC for your Windows application development, so that you can take advantage of its object-oriented approach and have the application framework set up for you by the AppWizard. In this chapter, you'll see how Windows operates behinds the scenes—knowledge that will be useful to you even when you are developing applications using MFC.

By the end of this chapter you will have learnt:

> What the basic structure of a window is

> What the Windows API is and how it is used

> What Windows messages are and how you deal with them

> What notation is commonly used in Windows programs

> What the basic structure of a Windows program is

We'll also take a look at what tools Developer Studio provides to help find those mistakes that as idealists you never make, but as realists crop up now and again in your code.

Windows Programming Basics

You have already created a Windows program in Chapter 1 with the aid of the AppWizard and without writing a single line of code. The user interface that was created was actually very sophisticated—we are going to create a much more elementary window for our example in this chapter—but we'll use the window generated by our example in Chapter 1 to illustrate the various elements that go to make up a window.

Elements of a Window

You will inevitably be familiar with most, if not all, of the principal elements of the user interface to a Windows program. However, we will go through them anyway, since we will be concerned with programming them as elements rather than just using them. The best way for us to understand what the elements of a window can be is to look at one. An annotated version of the window displayed by the example that we saw in Chapter 1 is shown below:

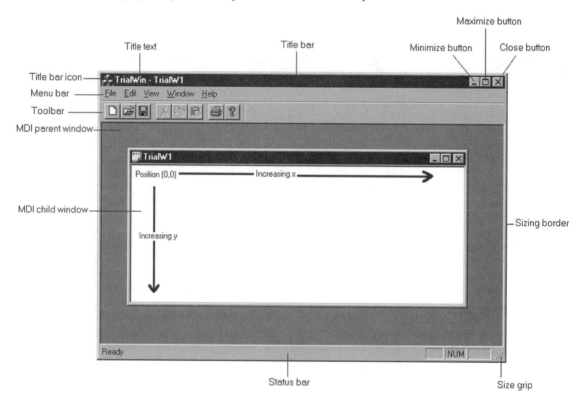

The example actually generated two windows. The larger window with the menu and the tool bars is the main, or **parent window**, and the smaller window is a **child window** of the parent. If you ran the example you will have seen that, while the child window can be closed by double-clicking the title bar icon without closing the parent window, closing the parent window automatically closes the child window as well. This is because the child window is owned by, and dependent upon, the parent window. In general, a parent window may have a number of child windows, as we shall see.

The most fundamental parts of a typical window are its **border**, the **title bar icon**, the **title bar** showing the name that you give to the window, and the **client area** (the area in the center of the window not used by the title bar or borders). We can get all of these for free in a Windows program. As you will see, all we have to do is provide some text for the title bar.

The border defines the boundary of a window and may be fixed or sizable. If the border is sizable, you can drag it to alter the size of the window. The window may also possess a size grip which you can use to alter the size of a window while maintaining its aspect ratio - that is, the ratio of the width to the height. When we define a window, if we need to, we can modify how the border behaves and appears. Most windows will also have the maximize, minimize and close buttons in the top right corner of the window. These allow the window to be increased to full screen size, reduced to an icon or closed.

When you click on the title bar icon with the left mouse button, it provides a standard menu for altering or closing the window called the 'system menu' or 'control menu'. The system menu also appears when you right-click on the title bar of a window. While it's optional, it is a good idea always to include the title bar icon in any main windows that your program generates. It can be a very convenient way of closing the program when things don't work as you anticipated.

The client area is the part of the window where you will usually want your program to write text or graphics. By default, the top left corner of the client area has the coordinates (0, 0), with x increasing from left to right, and y increasing from top to bottom.

The menu bar is optional, but is probably the most common way to control an application. The contents of a menu and the physical appearance of many objects that are displayed in a window, such as the icons on the toolbar that appear above, the cursor and many others, are defined by a **resource file**. We will see a lot more of resource files when we get to write some more sophisticated Windows programs.

The toolbar provides a set of icons that usually act as alternatives to the menu options that you use most often. Because they give a pictorial clue to the function provided, they can often make a program easier and faster to use.

Comparing DOS and Windows Programs

When you write a program for DOS, the operating system is essentially subservient. When you want some service to be provided, you call an operating system function. You can even bypass the operating system and provide your own function to communicate with your PC hardware if you want. You can address any of the hardware in your machine directly, and for some application areas where the ultimate performance is required—games programs, for example—this is how programs are regularly implemented.

With Windows, it's all quite different. Here your program is subservient and Windows is in control. You must not deal directly with the hardware and all communications with the outside must pass through Windows. When you use a Windows program you are interacting primarily with Windows, which then communicates with the application program on your behalf. Your Windows program is the tail, Windows is the dog, and your program wags only when Windows tells it to.

There are a number of reasons why this is so. First and foremost, since you are potentially always sharing the computer with other programs that may be executing at the same time, Windows has to have primary control in order to manage the sharing of machine resources. If one application was allowed to have primary control in a Windows environment, as well as inevitably making programming more complicated because of the need to provide for the possibility of other programs, information intended for other applications could be lost. A second reason for Windows being in control is that Windows embodies a standard user interface and needs to be in charge to enforce that standard. You can only display information on the screen using the tools that Windows provides, and then only when authorized.

Event-driven Programs

We have already seen, in Chapter 1, that a Windows program is event-driven. A significant part of the code required for a Windows application is dedicated to processing events caused by external actions of the user. Activities that are not directly associated with your application can nonetheless require that bits of your program code are executed. For example, if the user drags the window of another application that is active alongside yours, and this action uncovers part of the client area of the window devoted to your application, your application will need to redraw that part of the window.

Windows Messages

Events are occurrences such as the user clicking the mouse or pressing a key, or a timer reaching zero. Windows records every event in a message and places the message in a message queue for the program for which the message is intended. If your program is properly organized, then by sending a message Windows can tell it that something needs to be done, or that some information has become available, or that an event such as a mouse click has occurred. There are many different kinds of messages and they can occur very frequently—many times per second when the mouse is being dragged, for example.

A Windows program must contain a function specifically for handling these messages. The function is often called **WndProc()** or **WindowProc()**, although it doesn't have to be, since Windows accesses the function through a pointer to a function that you supply. The sending of a message to your program boils down to Windows calling this function that you provide, and passing any necessary data to your program by means of arguments to this function. Within your **WindowProc()** function it is up to you to work out what the message is from the data supplied and what to do about it.

Fortunately, you don't need to write code to process every message. You can filter out those that are of interest in your program, deal with those in whatever way you want, and pass the rest back to Windows. Passing a message back to Windows is done by calling a standard function provided by Windows called **DefWindowProc()**, which provides default message processing.

The Windows API

All of the communications between a Windows application and Windows itself use the Windows application programming interface, otherwise known as the **Windows API**. This consists of literally hundreds of functions that are provided as standard with Windows to be used by your applications. Structures are often used for passing some kinds of data between Windows and your program, which is why we needed to look at them first.

The Windows API covers all aspects of the dialog necessary between Windows and your application. Because there is such a large number of functions, using them in the raw can be very difficult - just understanding what they all are is a task in itself. This is where Visual C++ comes in. Visual C++ packages the Windows API in a manner which structures the functions in an object-oriented manner, and provides an easier way to use the interface with more default functionality. This takes the form of the Microsoft Foundation Classes, MFC.

Visual C++ also provides an application framework in the form of code generated by the AppWizard which includes all of the boilerplate code necessary for a Windows application, leaving you just to customize this for your particular purposes. The example in Chapter 1 illustrated how much functionality Visual C++ is capable of providing without any coding effort at all on our part. We will discuss this in much more detail when we get to write some examples using AppWizard.

Notation in Windows Programs

In many Windows programs, variable names have a prefix which indicates what kind of value the variable holds and how it is used. There are quite a few prefixes and they are often used in combination. For example, the prefix **lpfn** signifies a **l**ong **p**ointer to a **f**u**n**ction. A sample of the prefixes you might come across is:

Prefix	Meaning
b	a logical variable of type **BOOL**, which is equivalent to **int**
by	type **unsigned char**; a byte
c	type **char**
dw	type **DWORD**, which is **unsigned long**
fn	a function
h	a handle, which is used to identify something (usually an **int** value)
i	type **int**
l	type **long**
lp	**long** pointer
n	type **int**
p	a pointer
s	a string
sz	a zero terminated string
w	type **WORD**, which is **unsigned short**

This use of these prefixes is called **Hungarian notation**. It was introduced to minimize the possibility of misusing a variable by interpreting it differently from how it was defined or intended to be used. Such misinterpretation was easily done in the C language, a precursor of C++. With C++ and its stronger type checking, to avoid such problems you don't need to make such a special effort with your notation. The compiler will always flag an error for type inconsistencies in your program, and many of the kinds of bugs that plagued earlier C programs can't occur with C++.

On the other hand, Hungarian notation can still help to make programs easier to understand, particularly when you are dealing with a lot of variables of different types that are arguments to Windows API functions. Since a lot of Windows programs are still written in C, and of course since parameters for Windows API functions are still defined using Hungarian notation, the method is still widely used.

You can make up your own mind as to the extent to which you want to use Hungarian notation; it is by no means obligatory. You may choose not to use it at all, but in any event, if you have an idea of how it works, you will find it easier to understand what the arguments to the Windows API functions are. There is a small caveat, however. As Windows has developed, the types of some of the API function arguments have changed slightly, but the variable names that are used remain the same. As a consequence, the prefix may not be quite correct in specifying the variable type.

The Structure of a Windows Program

For a minimal Windows program, written using just the Windows API, we will write two functions. These will be a **WinMain()** function, where execution of the program begins and basic program initialization is carried out, and a **WindowProc()** function which will be called by Windows to process messages for the application. Usually, the **WindowProc()** part of a Windows program is the larger portion because this is where most of the application-specific code will be, responding to messages caused by user input of one kind or another.

While these two functions make up a complete program, they are not directly connected. **WinMain()** does not call **WindowProc()**, Windows does. In fact, Windows also calls **WinMain()**. This is illustrated in the diagram:

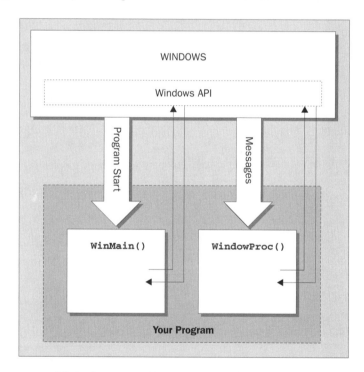

Links between Your Program and Windows

The function **WinMain()** communicates with Windows by calling some of the Windows API functions. The same applies to **WindowProc()**. The integrating factor in your Windows program is Windows itself, which links to both **WinMain()** and **WindowProc()**. We will take a look at what the pieces are that make up **WinMain()** and **WindowProc()**, and then assemble the parts into a working example of a simple Windows program.

The WinMain() Function

The **WinMain()** function is the equivalent of the **main()** function in a DOS (console) program. It's where execution starts and where the basic initialization for the rest of the program is carried out. To allow Windows to pass data to it, **WinMain()** has four parameters and a return value of type **int**. Its prototype is:

```
int WINAPI WinMain(HINSTANCE hInstance,
                   HINSTANCE hPrevInstance,
                   LPSTR lpCmdLine,
                   int nCmdShow
              );
```

Following the return type specifier, **int**, we have a specification for the function, **WINAPI**. This is a Windows-defined macro which causes the function name and the arguments to be handled in a special way, which happens to correspond to the way that a function is handled in the Pascal language (and the Fortran language) which is different from the way functions are normally handled in C++. The precise details are unimportant—this is simply the way Windows requires things to be, so we need to put the **WINAPI** specifier in front of the names of functions called by Windows.

You may wonder why there are types, such as **HINSTANCE** and others, defined by Windows. This is to provide for implementations of Windows in different machine environments. By defining its own, specific Windows types, Windows can control how these types are interpreted and how they can be adjusted to suit the needs of different computers. All the types used by Windows, as well as the prototypes of the Windows API functions, are contained in the header file **windows.h**, so we will need to include this header file when we put our basic Windows program together.

The four arguments passed by Windows to your **WinMain()** function contain important data. The first argument, **hInstance**, is of type **HINSTANCE** which is a handle to an instance, an instance here being a running program. A handle is a 32-bit integer value which identifies an object of some kind—in this case the instance of the application. The actual integer value of a handle is not important. The **hInstance** handle allows for the possibility of multiple copies of a Windows program being active simultaneously and individually identifiable. As we will see shortly, handles are also used to identify all sorts of other things. Of course, all handles in a particular context—application instance handles for example—need to be different from one another.

With DOS, only one program can be executed at one time; with Windows, on the other hand, there can be several. This raises the possibility of several copies of the same application being active at once, and this needs to be recognized. Hence the need for the **hInstance** handle to identify a particular copy. If you start more than one copy of the program, each one will have its own unique **hInstance** value.

The next argument, **hPrevInstance**, is a legacy from 16-bit days. Under Windows 3.*x* this parameter gave you the handle to the previous instance of the program, if there was one. If **hPrevInstance** was **NULL**, you knew that there was no previous instance of the program so this must be the only copy of the program executing (at the moment, anyway). This information was necessary in many cases because programs running under Windows 3.*x* share the same address space and multiple copies of a program executing simultaneously could cause complications. For this reason, programmers often limited their applications to only one running instance at a time, and having the **hPrevInstance** argument passed to **WinMain()** allowed them to provide for this very easily by testing it in an **if** statement.

Under 32-bit systems (Windows 95 and Windows NT) the **hPrevInstance** parameter is completely irrelevant since each application runs in its own address space, and one application has no direct knowledge of the existence of another that is executing concurrently. This parameter is always **NULL**, even if another instance of an application is running.

The next argument, **lpCmdLine**, is a pointer to a string containing the command line that started the program. For instance, if you started it using the Run... command from the Start button menu of Windows 95, the string will contain everything that appears in the Open box. Having this pointer allows you to pick up any parameter values that may appear in the command line. The type **LPSTR** is another Windows type, specifying a 32-bit pointer to a string.

The last argument, **nCmdShow**, indicates how the window is to look when it is created. It could be displayed normally or it might need to be minimized, for example if the shortcut for the program specifies that the program should be minimized when it starts. This argument can take one of a fixed set of values that are defined by symbolic constants such as **SW_SHOWNORMAL** and **SW_SHOWMINNOACTIVE**. There are a number of other constants like these which define the way a window is to be displayed and they all begin **SW_**. Other examples are **SW_HIDE** or **SW_SHOWMAXIMIZED**. You don't usually need to examine the value of **nCmdShow**. You typically pass it directly to the Windows API function responsible for displaying your application window.

If you want to know what all the other constants are that specify how a window will be displayed, you can find a complete list of possible values if you search on WinMain in the Visual C++ help facility and look at the WinMain topic.

The function **WinMain()** in our Windows program needs to do three things:

1 Tell Windows what kind of window the program requires.

2 Create and initialize the program window.

3 Retrieve Windows messages intended for the program.

Let's take a look at each of these in turn, and then create a complete **WinMain()** function.

Specifying a Program Window

The first step in creating a window is to define just what sort of window it is that we want to create. Windows defines a special **struct** called **WNDCLASS** to contain the data specifying a window. This data defines a window class, which determines the type of window. Do not confuse this with a C++ class. We need to create a variable from this **struct** and give values to each of its members (just like filling in a form). Once we've filled in the variables, we can pass it to Windows (via a function that we'll see later) in order to register the class. When that's been done, whenever we want to create a window of that class we can tell Windows to look up the class that we've already registered.

The definition of the **WNDCLASS** structure is as follows:

```
struct WNDCLASS
{
    UINT style;              // Window style
    WNDPROC lpfnWndProc;     // Pointer to message processing function
    int cbClsExtra;          // Extra byte after the window class
    int cbWndExtra;          // Extra bytes after the window instance
    HINSTANCE hInstance;     // The application instance handle
    HICON hIcon;             // The application icon
    HCURSOR hCursor;         // The window cursor
    HBRUSH hbrBackground;    // The brush defining the background color
    LPCSTR lpszMenuName;     // A pointer to the name of the menu resource
    LPCSTR lpszClassName;    // A pointer to the class name
};
```

The **style** member of the **struct** determines various aspects of the window's behavior, in particular, the conditions under which the window should be redrawn. You can select from a number of options for this member's value, each defined by a symbolic constant beginning **CS_**.

You'll find the possible constant values for **style** if you look at the section for **WNDCLASS** under **Platform, SDK, and DDK Documentation\Platform SDK\Reference\Structures\Win32 Structures** in InfoView.

Where two or more options are required, the constants can be combined to produce a composite value using the bitwise OR operator, |. For example, assuming that we have declared the variable **WindowClass**, we could write:

```
WindowClass.style = CS_HREDRAW | CS_VREDRAW;
```

The option **CS_HREDRAW** indicates to Windows that the window is to be redrawn if its horizontal width is altered, and **CS_VREDRAW** indicates that it is to be redrawn if the vertical height of the window is changed. In the statement above we have elected to have our window redrawn in either case. As a result, Windows will send a message to our program indicating that we should redraw the window whenever the width or height of the window is altered by the user. Each of the possible options for the window style is defined by a unique bit in a 32-bit word being set to 1. That's why the bitwise OR is used to combine them. These bits indicating a particular style are usually called **flags**. Flags are used very frequently, not only in Windows, because they are a very efficient way of representing and processing features that are either there or not, or parameters that are either **TRUE** or **FALSE**.

The member **lpfnWndProc** stores a pointer to the function in your program which will handle messages for the window that we will create. The prefix to the name signifies that this is a **long** pointer to a function. If you followed the herd and called the function to handle messages for the application **WindowProc()**, you would initialize this member with the statement:

```
WindowClass.lpfnWndProc = WindowProc;
```

The next two members, **cbClsExtra** and **cbWndExtra**, allow you to ask for some extra space internal to Windows for your own use. An example of this could be when you want to associate additional data with each instance of a window to assist in message handling for each window instance. Normally you won't need extra space allocated for you, in which case you must set the **cbClsExtra** and **cbWndExtra** members to zero.

The **hInstance** member holds the handle for the current application instance, so you should set this to the **hInstance** value passed to **WinMain()** by Windows.

The members **hIcon**, **hCursor** and **hbrBackground**, are handles which in turn define the icon which will represent the application when minimized, the cursor the window is to use and the background color of the client area of the window. (As we saw earlier, a handle is just a 32-bit integer used as an ID to represent something.) These are set using Windows API functions. For example:

```
WindowClass.hIcon = LoadIcon(0, IDI_APPLICATION);
WindowClass.hCursor = LoadCursor(0, IDC_ARROW);
WindowClass.hbrBackground = GetStockObject(GRAY_BRUSH);
```

All three members are set to standard Windows values by these function calls. The icon is a default provided by Windows and the cursor is the standard arrow cursor used by the majority of Windows applications. A brush is a Windows object which is used to fill an area, in this case the client area of the window. The background color is therefore set as gray so that a handle to the standard gray brush will be returned by the function **GetStockObject()**. This function can also be used to obtain other standard objects for a window, such as fonts for example.

The **lpszMenuName** member is set to the name of a resource defining the window menu, or to zero if there is no menu for the window. We will be looking into creating and using menu resources when we use the AppWizard.

The last member of the **struct** is **lpszClassName**. This member stores the name that you supply to identify this particular class of window. You would usually use the name of the application for this. You need to keep track of this name because you will need it again when a window is created. This member would therefore be typically set with the statements:

```
static char szAppName[] = "OFWin";        // Define window class name
WindowClass.lpszClassName = szAppName;  // Set class name
```

Creating and Initializing a Program Window

After all the members of your **WNDCLASS** structure have been set to the values required, the next step is to tell Windows about it. You do this using the Windows API function **RegisterClass()**. Assuming that our structure is **WindowClass**, the statement to do this would be:

```
RegisterClass(&WindowClass);
```

Easy, wasn't it? The address of the **struct** is passed to the function, and Windows will extract and squirrel away all the values that you have set in the structure members. This process is called **registering** the window class. The term *class* here is used in the sense of classification and is not the same as the idea of a **class** in C++, so don't confuse the two. Each instance of the application must make sure that it registers the window classes that it needs.

Once Windows knows the characteristics of the window that we want, and the function that is going to handle messages for it, we can go ahead and create it. You use the function **CreateWindow()** for this. The window class that we've already created determines the broad characteristics of a window, and further arguments to the function **CreateWindow()** add additional characteristics. Since in general, an application may have several windows, the function **CreateWindow()** returns a handle to the window created which you can store to enable you to refer to the particular window later. There are a lot of API calls that will require you to specify the window handle as a parameter if you want to use them. We will just look at a typical use of the **CreateWindow()** function at this point. This might be:

```
HWND hWnd;                                // Window handle
...
hWnd = CreateWindow(
       szAppName,                         // the window class name
       "A Basic Window the Hard Way",     // The window title
       WS_OVERLAPPEDWINDOW,               // Window style as overlapped
       CW_USEDEFAULT,           // Default  screen position of upper left
       CW_USEDEFAULT,           // corner of our window as x,y...
       CW_USEDEFAULT,           // Default window size
       CW_USEDEFAULT,           // ....
       0,                       // No parent window
       0,                       // No menu
       hInstance,               // Program Instance handle
       0                        // No window creation data
     );
```

The variable **hWnd** of type **HWND**, is a 32-bit integer handle to a window. We'll use this variable to record the value that identifies the window, returned from the function **CreateWindow()**. The first argument that we pass to the function is the class name. This is used by Windows to identify the **WNDCLASS struct** that we passed to it previously, in the **RegisterClass()** function call, so that the information from this **struct** can be used in the window creation process.

The second argument to **CreateWindow()** defines the text that is to appear on the title bar. The third argument specifies the style that the window will have once it is created. The option specified here, **WS_OVERLAPPEDWINDOW**, actually combines several options. It defines the window as having the **WS_OVERLAPPED**, **WS_CAPTION**, **WS_SYSMENU**, **WS_THICKFRAME**, **WS_MINIMIZEBOX**, and **WS_MAXIMIZEBOX** styles. This results in an overlapped window, which is a window intended to be the main application window, with a title bar and a thick frame which has a title bar icon, system menu and maximize and minimize buttons. A window specified as having a thick frame has borders that can be resized.

The following four arguments determine the position and size of the window on the screen. The first pair are the screen coordinates of the top left corner of the window, and the second pair define the width and height of the window. The value **CW_USEDEFAULT** indicates that we want Windows to assign the default position and size for the window. This tells Windows to arrange successive windows in cascading positions down the screen. This only applies to windows specified as **WS_OVERLAPPED**.

The next argument value is zero, indicating that the window being created is not a child window, which is a window that is dependent on a parent window. If we wanted it to be a child window, we would set this argument to the handle of the parent window. The next argument is also zero, indicating that no menu is required. We then specify the handle of the current instance of the program which was passed to the program by Windows, and the last argument is zero.

The window now exists but is not yet displayed on the screen. We need to call another Windows API function to get it displayed:

```
ShowWindow(hWnd, nCmdShow);    // Display the window
```

Only two arguments are required here. The first identifies the window and is the handle returned by the function **CreateWindow()**. The second is the value **nCmdShow** which was passed to **WinMain()**, and which indicates how the window is to appear on screen.

Initializing the Client Area of the Window

After calling the function **ShowWindow()**, the window will appear on screen but will still have no application content, so let's get our program to draw in the client area of the window. We could just put together some code to do this directly in the **WinMain()** function, but this would be most unsatisfactory: the contents of the client area cannot be considered to be permanent—we can't afford to output what we want and forget about it. Any action on the part of the user which modifies the window in some way, such as dragging a border or dragging the whole window, will typically require that the window *and* its client area are redrawn.

When the client area needs to be redrawn for any reason, Windows will send a particular message to our program and our **WindowProc()** function will need to respond by reconstructing the client area of the window. Therefore, the best way to get the client area drawn in the first instance is to get Windows to send the message requesting this to our program. Indeed, whenever we know in our program that the window should be redrawn, when we change something for example, we just need to tell Windows to send a message back to this effect.

We can do this by calling another Windows API function, **UpdateWindow()**. The statement to accomplish this is:

```
UpdateWindow(hWnd);            // Cause window client area to be drawn
```

This function only requires one argument: the window handle **hWnd**, which identifies our particular program window. (In general there can be several windows in an application.) The result of the call is that Windows will send a message to our program requesting that the client area be redrawn.

Dealing with Windows Messages

The last task that **WinMain()** needs to address is dealing with the messages that Windows may have queued for our application. This may seem a bit odd, since we said that we needed the function **WindowProc()** to deal with messages.

Queued and Non-Queued Messages

There are, in fact, two kinds of Windows messages. Firstly, there are **queued messages** which Windows places in a queue and which the **WinMain()** function needs to extract from the queue for processing. The code in **WinMain()** that does this is called the **message loop**. Queued message include those arising from user input from the keyboard, moving the mouse and clicking the mouse buttons. Messages from a timer and the Windows message to request that a window be repainted are also queued.

Secondly, there are **non-queued messages** which result in the **WindowProc()** function being called directly by Windows. A lot of the non-queued messages arise as a consequence of processing queued messages. What we are doing in the message loop in **WinMain()** is retrieving a message that Windows has queued for our application and then asking Windows to invoke our function **WindowProc()** to process it. Why can't Windows just call **WindowProc()** whenever necessary? Well it could, but it just doesn't work this way. The reasons are to do with how Windows manages multiple applications executing simultaneously.

The Message Loop

Retrieving messages from the message queue is done using a standard mechanism in Windows programming called the message loop. The code for this would be:

```
MSG msg;                                  // Windows message structure
while(GetMessage(&msg, 0, 0, 0) == TRUE)  // Get any messages
{
   TranslateMessage(&msg);                // Translate the message
   DispatchMessage(&msg);                 // Dispatch the message
}
```

This involves three steps in dealing with each message:

GetMessage()	retrieves a message from the queue.
TranslateMessage()	performs any conversion necessary on the message retrieved.
DispatchMessage()	causes Windows to call the **WindowProc()** function in our application, to deal with the message.

The operation of **GetMessage()** is important since it has a significant contribution to the way Windows works with multiple applications. Let's look into it in a little more detail.

The **GetMessage()** function will retrieve a message queued for our application window and will store information about the message in the variable **msg**, pointed to by the first argument. The variable **msg**, which is a **struct** of type **MSG**, contains a number of different members which we will not be accessing here. Still, for completeness, the definition of the structure is:

```
struct MSG
{
   HWND    hwnd;          // Handle for the relevant window
   UINT    message;       // The message ID
   WPARAM  wParam;        // Message parameter (32-bits)
   LPARAM  lParam;        // Message parameter (32-bits)
   DWORD   time;          // The time when the message was queued
   POINT   pt;            // The mouse position
};
```

The **wParam** member is an example of a slightly misleading Hungarian notation prefix that we mentioned was now possible. You might assume that it was of type **WORD** (which is **int**), which used to be true in earlier Windows versions, but now it is of type **WPARAM**, which is a 32-bit integer value.

The exact contents of the members **wParam** and **lParam** are dependent on what kind of message it is. The message ID in the member **message** is an integer value that can be one of a set of values that are predefined in the header file **windows.h** as symbolic constants. They all start with **WM_** and typical examples are **WM_PAINT** to redraw the screen or **WM_QUIT** to end the program. The function **GetMessage()** will always return **TRUE** unless the message is **WM_QUIT** to end the program, in which case the value returned is **FALSE**, or unless an error occurs in which case the return value is **-1**. Thus, the **while** loop here will continue until a quit message is generated to close the application or until an error condition arises. In either case, we would then need to end the program by passing the **wParam** value back to Windows in a **return** statement.

The second argument in the call to **GetMessage()** is the handle of the window for which we want to get messages. This parameter can be used to retrieve messages for one window separately from another but if this argument is 0, as it is here, **GetMessage()** will retrieve all messages for an application, so this is an easy way of retrieving all messages for an application regardless of how many windows it has (it may not have any!) When the user of your Windows program closes the application window, for example, the window is closed before the **WM_QUIT** message is generated. Consequently, if you only retrieve messages by specifying a window handle to the **GetMessage()** function, you will not retrieve the **WM_QUIT** message and your program will not be able to terminate properly.

The last two arguments to **GetMessage()** are integers that hold minimum and maximum values for the message IDs you want to retrieve from the queue. This allows messages to be retrieved selectively. A range is usually specified by symbolic constants. Using **WM_MOUSEFIRST** and **WM_MOUSELAST** as these two arguments would select just mouse messages, for example. If both arguments are zero, as we have them here, all messages are retrieved.

Multitasking

If there are no messages queued, the **GetMessage()** function will not come back to our program. Windows will allow execution to pass to another application and we will only get a value returned from calling **GetMessage()** when a message appears in the queue. This mechanism is fundamental in enabling multiple applications to run under Windows 3.*x*, and is referred to as **cooperative multitasking** because it depends on concurrent applications giving up their control of the processor from time to time. Once your program calls **GetMessage()**, unless there is a message for your program, another application will be executed and your program will only get another opportunity to do something if the other application calls **GetMessage()**.

With Windows 3.*x*, a program that does not call **GetMessage()** or includes code for a heavy computation that does not make provision for returning control to Windows from time to time, can retain use of the processor indefinitely. With Windows 95, the operating system can interrupt an application after a period of time and transfer control to another application. This is called **pre-emptive multitasking**. However, you still need to program the message loop in **WinMain()** using **GetMessage()** as before, and make provision for relinquishing control of the processor to Windows from time to time in a long running calculation (this is usually done using the **PeekMessage()** API function). If you don't do this, your application may be unable to respond to messages to repaint the application window when these arise. This can be for reasons that are quite independent of your application—when an overlapping window for another application is closed, for example.

The conceptual operation of the **GetMessage()** function is illustrated below:

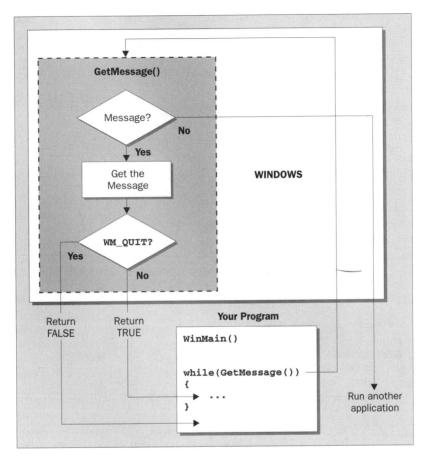

The Operation of GetMessage()

Within the **while** loop, the first function call to **TranslateMessage()** requests Windows to do some conversion work for keyboard related messages. Then the call to the function **DispatchMessage()** causes Windows to dispatch the message, or in other words, to call the **WindowProc()** function in our program to process the message. The return from **DispatchMessage()** will not occur until **WindowProc()** has finished processing the message. The **WM_QUIT** message indicates that the program should end, so this results in **FALSE** being returned to the application which stops the message loop.

A Complete WinMain() Function

We have looked at all the bits that need to go into the function **WinMain()**. So now let's assemble them into a complete function:

```
// Listing OFWIN_1
int WINAPI WinMain(HINSTANCE hInstance, HINSTANCE hPrevInstance,
                   LPSTR lpCmdLine, int nCmdShow)
{
    WNDCLASS WindowClass;        // Structure to hold our window's attributes
```

```
        static char szAppName[] = "OFWin";     // Define window class name
        HWND hWnd;                             // Window handle
        MSG msg;                               // Windows message structure

        // Redraw the window if the size changes
        WindowClass.style   = CS_HREDRAW | CS_VREDRAW;

        // Define our procedure for message handling
        WindowClass.lpfnWndProc = WindowProc;

        WindowClass.cbClsExtra = 0;     // No extra bytes after the window class
        WindowClass.cbWndExtra = 0;     // structure or the window instance

        WindowClass.hInstance = hInstance;   // Application instance handle

        // Set default application icon
        WindowClass.hIcon = LoadIcon(0, IDI_APPLICATION);

        // Set window cursor to be the standard arrow
        WindowClass.hCursor = LoadCursor(0, IDC_ARROW);

        // Set gray brush for background color
        WindowClass.hbrBackground = GetStockObject(GRAY_BRUSH);

        WindowClass.lpszMenuName = 0;  // No menu, so no menu resource name

        WindowClass.lpszClassName = szAppName;  // Set class name

        // Now register our window class
        RegisterClass(&WindowClass);

        //  Now we can create the window
        hWnd = CreateWindow(
             szAppName,                         // the window class name
             "A Basic Window the Hard Way",     // The window title
             WS_OVERLAPPEDWINDOW,               // Window style as overlapped
             CW_USEDEFAULT,          // Default screen position of upper left
             CW_USEDEFAULT,          // corner of our window as x,y...
             CW_USEDEFAULT,          // Default window size
             CW_USEDEFAULT,          // ....
             0,                      // No parent window
             0,                      // No menu
             hInstance,              // Program Instance handle
             0                       // No window creation data
          );

        ShowWindow(hWnd, nCmdShow);  // Display the window
        UpdateWindow(hWnd);          // Cause window client area to be drawn

        // The message loop
        while(GetMessage(&msg, 0, 0, 0) == TRUE)   // Get any messages
        {
           TranslateMessage(&msg);                 // Translate the message
           DispatchMessage(&msg);                  // Dispatch the message
        }

        return msg.wParam;          // End so return to Windows
}
```

How It Works

After declaring the variables we need in the function, all the members of the **WindowClass** structure are initialized and the window is registered.

The next step is to call the **CreateWindow()** function to create the data for the physical appearance of the window, based on the arguments passed and the data established in the **WindowClass** structure that was previously passed to Windows using the **RegisterClass()** function. The call to **ShowWindow()** causes the window to be displayed according to the mode specified by **nCmdShow**, and the **UpdateWindow()** function signals that a message to draw the window client area should be generated.

Finally, the message loop will continue to retrieve messages for the application until a **WM_QUIT** message is obtained, whereupon the **GetMessage()** function will return **FALSE** and the loop will end. The value of the **wParam** member of the **msg** structure is passed back to Windows in the **return** statement.

Message Processing Functions

The function **WinMain()** contained nothing that was application-specific beyond the general appearance of the application window. All of the code that will make the application behave in the way that we want is going to be included in the message processing part of the program. This is the function **WindowProc()** that we identified to Windows in the **WindowClass** structure. Windows will call this function each time a message for our main application window is dispatched.

Our example is going to be very simple, so we will be putting all the code to process messages in the one function, **WindowProc()**. More generally though, the **WindowProc()** function would be responsible for analyzing what a given message was and which window it was destined for, and then calling one of a whole range of functions, each of which would be geared to handling a particular message in the context of the particular window concerned. However, the overall sequence of operations, and the way in which the function **WindowProc()** analyses an incoming message, will be much the same in most application contexts.

The WindowProc() Function

The prototype of our **WindowProc()** function is:

```
long WINAPI WindowProc(HWND hWnd, UINT message, WPARAM wParam,
                       LPARAM lParam);
```

Since the function will be called by Windows, we need to qualify the function as **WINAPI**. The four arguments that are passed provide information about the particular message causing the function to be called. The meaning of each of these arguments is:

HWND hWnd	A handle to the window in which the event causing the message occurred.
UINT message	The message ID, which is a 32-bit value indicating the type of message.
WPARAM wParam	A 32-bit value containing additional information depending on what sort of message it is.
LPARAM lParam	A 32-bit value containing additional information depending on what sort of message it is.

The window that the incoming message relates to is identified by the first argument, **hWnd**, that is passed to the function. In our case, we only have one window, so we can ignore it.

Messages are identified by the value **message** that is passed to **WindowProc()**. You can test this value against predefined symbolic constants, each of which relates to a particular message. They all begin with **WM_**, and typical examples are **WM_PAINT**, which corresponds to a request to redraw part of the client area of a window, or **WM_LBUTTONDOWN** which indicates the left mouse button was pressed. You can find the whole set of these by searching for WM_ in the Visual C++ online help.

Decoding a Windows Message

The process of decoding the message that Windows is sending is usually done using a **switch** statement in the **WindowProc()** function, based on the value of **message**. Selecting the message types that you want to process is then just a question of putting a **case** statement for each case in the **switch**. The typical structure of such a **switch** statement, with arbitrary cases included, is as follows:

```
switch(message)
{
   case WM_PAINT:
      // Code to deal with drawing the client area
      break;

   case WM_LBUTTONDOWN:
      // Code to deal with the left mouse button being pressed
      break;

   case WM_LBUTTONUP:
      // Code to deal with the left mouse button being released
      break;

   case WM_DESTROY:
      // Code to deal with a window being destroyed
      break;

   default:
      // Code to handle any other messages
}
```

Every Windows program will have something like this somewhere, although it will be hidden from sight in the Windows programs that we will write later using MFC. Each case corresponds to a particular value for the message ID and provides suitable processing for that message. Any messages that a program does not want to deal with individually are handled by the default statement which should hand the messages back to Windows by calling **DefWindowProc()**. This is the Windows API function providing default message handling.

In a complex program, dealing specifically with a wide range of possible Windows messages, this **switch** statement can become very large and rather cumbersome. When we get to use AppWizard we won't have to worry about this because it is all taken care of for us and we will never see the **WindowProc()** function. All we will need to do is to supply the code to process the particular messages that we are interested in.

Drawing the Window Client Area

To signal that the client area of an application should be redrawn, Windows sends a **WM_PAINT** message to the program. So in our example, we will need to draw the text in the window in response to the **WM_PAINT** message.

We can't go drawing in the window willy nilly. Before we can write to our window, we need to tell Windows that we want to do so, and get Windows' authority to go ahead. We do this by calling the Windows API function **BeginPaint()**, which should only be called in response to a **WM_PAINT** message. It is used as follows:

```
HDC hDC;                        // A display context handle
PAINTSTRUCT PaintSt;            // Structure defining area to be redrawn

hDC = BeginPaint(hWnd, &PaintSt); // Prepare to draw in the window
```

The type **HDC** defines what is called a **display context**, or more generally a **device context**. A device context provides the link between the device-independent Windows API functions for outputting information to the screen or a printer, and the device drivers which support writing to the specific devices attached to your PC. You can also regard a device context as a token of authority which is handed to you on request by Windows and grants you permission to output some information. Without a device context you simply can't generate any output.

The **BeginPaint()** function provides us with a display context as a return value and requires two arguments to be supplied. The window to which we want to write is identified by the window handle, **hWnd**, which we pass as the first argument. The second argument is the address of a **PAINTSTRUCT** variable, **PaintSt**, in which Windows will place information about the area to be redrawn in response to the **WM_PAINT** message. We will ignore the details of this since we are not going to use it. We will just redraw the whole of the client area. We can obtain the coordinates of the client area in a **RECT** structure with the statements:

```
RECT aRect;                          // A working rectangle
GetClientRect(hWnd, &aRect);
```

*Rectangles are used a great deal in Windows programs. For this reason, there is a **RECT** structure predefined in the header file **windows.h**:*

```
struct RECT
{
    int left;                   // Top left point
    int top;                    // coordinate pair

    int right;                  // Bottom right point
    int bottom;                 // coordinate pair
};
```

*This **struct** is usually used to define rectangular areas on your display for a variety of purposes. Since **RECT** is used so extensively, **windows.h** also contains prototypes for a number of functions to manipulate and modify rectangles. For example, **windows.h** provides the function **InflateRect()** to increase the size of a rectangle and the function **EqualRect()** to compare two rectangles. MFC also defines a class called **CRect**, which is the equivalent of a **RECT** structure. We'll be using this in preference to the **RECT** structure later. The **CRect** class provides a very extensive range of functions for manipulating rectangles, and you'll be using a number of these when we're writing Windows programs* *using MFC. You can find the complete list of functions for manipulating* **RECT** *structures by looking up* Platform, SDK, and DDK Documentation\Platform SDK\Graphics and Multimedia Services\2-D Graphics\Rectangles *in InfoView.*

The **GetClientRect()** function supplies the coordinates of the upper-left and lower-right corners of the client area for the window specified by the first argument. These coordinates will be stored in the **RECT** structure **aRect**, which is passed through the second argument as a pointer. We can then use this definition of the client area for our window when we write the text to the window using the **DrawText()** function. Because our window has a gray background, we should alter the background of the text to be transparent, to allow the gray to show through, otherwise the text will appear against a white background. We can do this with the API function call:

```
SetBkMode(hDC, TRANSPARENT);                // Set text background mode
```

The first argument identifies the device context and the second sets the background mode. The default option is **OPAQUE**.

We can now write the text with the statement:

```
DrawText(hDC,                    // Device context handle
         "But, soft! What light through yonder window breaks?",
         -1,                     // Indicate null terminated string
         &aRect,                 // Rectangle in which text is to be drawn
         DT_SINGLELINE|          // Text format - single line
         DT_CENTER|              //             - centered in the line
         DT_VCENTER              //             - line centered in aRect
    );
```

The first argument is our certificate of authority, the display context **hDC**. The next argument is the text string that we want to output. We could equally well have defined this in a variable and passed the pointer to the text. The argument with the value -1 signifies our string is terminated with a null character. If it wasn't, we would put the count of the number of characters in the string here. The fourth argument is a pointer to a **RECT** structure defining a rectangle in which we want to write the text. In our case it is the whole client area defined in **aRect**. The last argument defines the format for the text in the rectangle. Here we have combined three specifications with a bitwise OR. Our string will be a single line, with the text centered on the line and the line centered vertically within the rectangle. This will place it nicely in the center of the window. There are also a number of other options which include the possibility to place text at the top or the bottom of the rectangle, and to left or right justify it.

Once we have output all the text we want, we must tell Windows that we have finished drawing the client area. For every **BeginPaint()** function call, there must be a corresponding **EndPaint()** function call. Thus, to end processing the **WM_PAINT** message, we need the statement:

```
EndPaint(hWnd, &PaintSt);  // Terminate window redraw operation
```

The **hWnd** argument identifies our program window, and the second argument is the address of the **PAINTSTRUCT** structure that was filled in by the **BeginPaint()** function.

Ending the Program

You might assume that closing the window will automatically close the application, but to get this behavior we actually have to add some code. The reason that our application won't close when the window is closed is that we may need to do some clearing up. It is also possible that the application may have more than one window. When the user closes the window by double-clicking the title bar icon or clicking the close button, this causes a **WM_DESTROY** message to be generated. Therefore, in order to close the application we need to process the **WM_DESTROY** message in our **WindowProc()** function. We do this by generating a **WM_QUIT** message with the following statement:

```
PostQuitMessage(0);
```

The argument here is an exit code. This Windows API function does exactly what its name suggests - it posts a **WM_QUIT** message in the message queue for our application. This will result in the **GetMessage()** function in **WinMain()** returning **FALSE** and ending the message loop, so ending the program.

A Complete WindowProc() Function

We have covered all the elements necessary to make up the complete **WindowProc()** function for our example. The code for the function is as follows:

```
// Listing OFWIN_2
long WINAPI WindowProc(HWND hWnd, UINT message, WPARAM wParam,
                       LPARAM lParam)
{
   HDC hDC;                           // Display context handle
   PAINTSTRUCT PaintSt;               // Structure defining area to be drawn
   RECT aRect;                        // A working rectangle

   switch(message)                    // Process selected messages
   {
      case WM_PAINT:                       // Message is to redraw the window
         hDC = BeginPaint(hWnd, &PaintSt); // Prepare to draw the window

         // Get upper left and lower right of client area
         GetClientRect(hWnd, &aRect);

         SetBkMode(hDC, TRANSPARENT);       // Set text background mode

         // Now draw the text in the window client area
         DrawText(
             hDC,                    // Device context handle
             "But, soft! What light through yonder window breaks?",
             -1,                     // Indicate null terminated string
             &aRect,                 // Rectangle in which text is to be drawn
             DT_SINGLELINE|          // Text format - single line
             DT_CENTER|              //               - centered in the line
             DT_VCENTER);            //               - line centered in aRect

         EndPaint(hWnd, &PaintSt); // Terminate window redraw operation
         return 0;

      case WM_DESTROY:                  // Window is being destroyed
         PostQuitMessage(0);
```

```
            return 0;

        default:              // Any other message - we don't want to know,
                              // so call default message processing
            return DefWindowProc(hWnd, message, wParam, lParam);
    }
}
```

How It Works

The function consists wholly of a **switch** statement. A particular **case** will be selected, based on the message ID passed to our function in the parameter **message**. Because our example is very simple, we only need to process two different messages: **WM_PAINT** and **WM_DESTROY**. We hand all other messages back to Windows by calling the **DefWindowProc()** function in the **default** case for the **switch**. The arguments to **DefWindowProc()** are those that were passed to our function, so we are just passing them back as they are. Note the **return** statement at the end of processing each message type. For the messages we handle, a zero value is returned.

A Simple Windows Program

Since we have written **WinMain()** and **WindowProc()** to handle messages, we have enough to create a complete source file for our Windows program. The complete source file will simply consist of an **#include** statement for the Windows header file, a prototype for the **WindowProc** function and the **WinMain** and **WindowProc** functions that we've already seen:

```
// OFWIN.CPP    Native windows program to display text in a window
#include <windows.h>

long WINAPI WindowProc(HWND hWnd, UINT message, WPARAM wParam, LPARAM lParam);

   // Insert code for WinMain() here (Listing OFWIN_1)

   // Insert code for WindowProc() here (Listing OFWIN_2)
```

Of course, you'll need to create a project for this program, so choose Win32 Application as the project type.

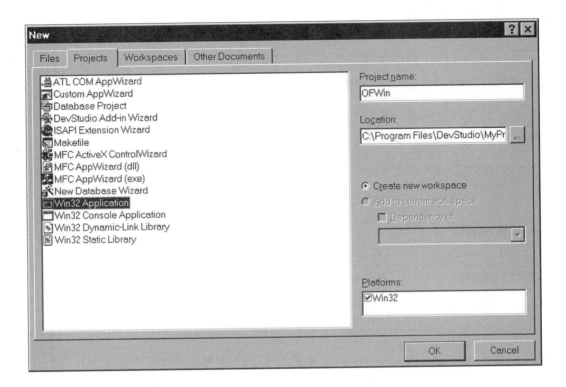

Old-Fashioned Windows

If you build and execute the example, it will produce the window shown below:

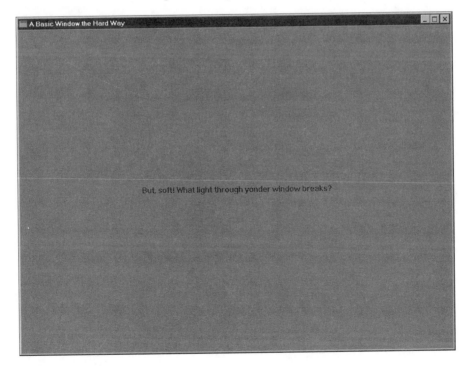

Note that the window has a number of properties provided by Windows that require no programming effort on our part to manage. The boundaries of the window can be dragged to resize it, and the whole window can be moved about on the screen. The maximize and minimize buttons also work. Of course, all of these actions do affect the program. Every time you modify the position or size of the window, a **WM_PAINT** message will be queued and our program will have to redraw the client area, but all the work of drawing and modifying the window itself is done by Windows.

The system menu and close button are also standard features of our window because of the options that we specified in the **WindowClass** structure. Again, Windows takes care of the management. The only additional effect on our program arising from this is the passing of a **WM_DESTROY** message if you close the window, as we have previously discussed.

Debugging

Now that you've seen the fundamentals of a Windows program, let's take another look at the features that Developer Studio provides to help you with your programming. Specifically, let's take a look at debugging. To debug code, you need something to work on. Take a quick look at the following code:

```
//EX2_01.CPP
// Exercising pointers
#include <iostream.h>

int main()
{
    long* pnumber = NULL;            // Pointer declaration & initialization
    long number1 = 55, number2 = 99;

    pnumber = &number1;              // Store address in pointer
    *pnumber += 11;                  // Increment number1 by 11
    cout << endl
         << "number1 = " << number1
         << "   &number1 = " << hex << pnumber;

    pnumber = &number2;              // Change pointer to address of number2
    number1 = *pnumber*10;           // 10 times number2

    cout << endl
         << "number1 = " << dec << number1
         << "   pnumber = " << hex << pnumber
         << "   *pnumber = " << dec << *pnumber;

    cout << endl;
    return 0;
}
```

This example is a good vehicle for an initial exploration of the basic debug capabilities of the Developer Studio. When you've written a program that doesn't work as it should, the debug facilities enable you to work through a program one step at a time to find out where and how it's going wrong. We'll arrange to execute our program one statement at a time and to monitor the contents of the variables that we are interested in. In this case, we want to look at **pnumber**, the contents of the location pointed to by **pnumber** (which is ***pnumber**), **number1**, and **number2**.

First we need to be sure that the build configuration for the example is set to Win32 Debug rather than Win32 Release (it will be unless you've changed it). The configuration is shown in the drop-down list on the *full* Build toolbar (only the MiniBar is shown by default). To display it, select Tools | Customize... and choose the Toolbars tab. Check the box against Build, and uncheck Build MiniBar. You can change the build configuration by extending the drop-down list and choosing the alternative. The toolbar is shown below:

The tooltips will tell you what each of the toolbar buttons are for. Just let the cursor linger over a toolbar button and the tooltip for that button will appear.

The 'debug' configuration in the project causes additional information to be included in your executable program so that the debugging facilities can be used. In this example, we won't use all the debugging facilities available to us, but we'll consider some of the more important features, starting with the buttons available on the Build toolbar. This will get you started on using debugging, so you should be able to experiment with using debugging on other examples as we go through the book.

Setting Breakpoints

Setting breakpoints enables you to define where in a program you want execution to pause so that you can look at variables within the program and change them if they don't have the values they should. We are going to execute our program one statement at a time, but with a large program this would be impractical. Usually, you will only want to look at a particular area of the program where you think there might be an error. Consequently, you would usually set breakpoints where you think the error is and run the program so that it halts at the first breakpoint.

To set a breakpoint, you simply place the cursor in the statement where you want execution to stop and click the Insert/Remove Breakpoint button, or press *F9*.

When debugging, you would normally set several breakpoints, each chosen to show when the variables that you think are causing a problem are changing. Execution will stop *before* the statement indicated by the breakpoint is executed. A breakpoint is indicated by a large circle at the start of a line of code, as you can see from this screen shot:

```
//EX2_01.CPP
// Exercising pointers
#include <iostream.h>

int main()
{
    long* pnumber = NULL;              // Pointer declaration & initialization
    long number1 = 55, number2 = 99;

    pnumber = &number1;                // Store address in pointer
    *pnumber += 11;                    // Increment number1 by 11
    cout << endl
         << "number1 = " << number1
         << "   &number1 = " << hex << pnumber;
```

You can set breakpoints by placing the cursor anywhere in a line of code, but the compiler can only break before a complete statement and not halfway through it. The breakpoint is set at the beginning of the line in which you have placed the cursor, so execution will stop before the line is executed. If you place a cursor in a line that doesn't contain any code (for example, the line above the one in the picture) and attempt to run the program, you'll see this dialog:

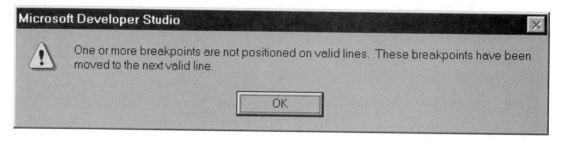

When you click OK, the Developer Studio will do exactly what it said it was going to do, and execution will begin as normal.

Removing Breakpoints

You can remove breakpoints by positioning the cursor on the same line as an existing breakpoint and clicking the Insert/Remove Breakpoint button or pressing *F9*. Alternatively, you can remove *all* the breakpoints in the active project by selecting the Remove All button on the Edit | Breakpoints... dialog, or by pressing *Ctrl-Shift-F9*. Note that this will remove breakpoints from all files in the project, even if they're not currently open in Developer Studio.

FYI There's a toolbar button to do this as well. If you want it available on your toolbar, right click in the toolbar area and select **Customize...** from the pop-up. In the **Debug** category there's a button that will remove all breakpoints which you can drag to wherever you want in the existing toolbars.

Starting Debugging

There are four ways of starting your application in debug mode, which you can see if you look at the options under Start Debug in the Build menu.

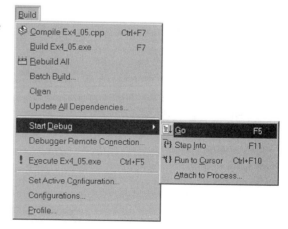

The Go option (also available from the button on the Build toolbar) simply executes a program to the first breakpoint, where execution will halt. After you've examined all you need to at a breakpoint, selecting Go again will continue execution up to the next breakpoint. In this way, you can move through a program from breakpoint to breakpoint, and at each halt in execution have a look at critical variables, changing their values if you need to.

Of course, just because you started debugging using Go doesn't mean that you have to continue using it; at each halt in execution you can choose any of the possible ways of moving through your code.

Run to Cursor does exactly what it says—it executes the program up to the statement where you left the cursor in the Text Editor window. In this way you can set the position where you want the program to stop as you go along.

The Attach to Process... option enables you to debug a program that is already running. This option will display a list of the processes that are running on your machine and you can select the process you want to debug. This is really for advanced users and you should avoid experimenting with this unless you are quite certain you know what you are doing. You can easily lock up your machine or cause other problems if you interfere with critical operating system processes.

Step Into executes your program one statement at a time. This would be something of a nuisance for us if we used it throughout the debugging process, since it would also execute all the code for stream output (from the header file we **#include**d) which we're not really interested in, since we didn't write it. To avoid having to step through all that code, we'll use the Step Over facility provided by the debugger. This will simply execute the statements in our function **main()** and jump over all the code used by the stream operations without stopping. First though, we'll start the program using Step Into, so click the menu item or press *F11* to begin.

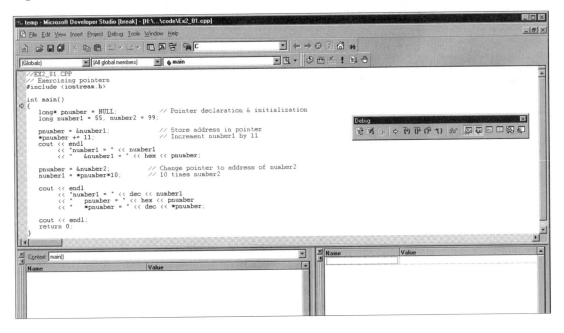

After a short pause (assuming that you've already built the project), Developer Studio will switch to debugging mode. The Project Workspace and Output windows will disappear to be replaced by the Variables window and the Watch window at the bottom of the screen; the Build menu will be replaced by the Debug menu and the Debug toolbar will appear. If you look at the Debug menu or the Debug toolbar, you'll see that it contains an option for Step Over as well as a number of other features, some of which we'll discuss shortly.

In the Text Editor window you'll see that the opening brace of our **main()** function is highlighted by an arrow to indicate that this is the current point in execution. At this point in the program, we can't choose any variables to look at because none exist at present. Until a declaration of a variable has been executed, you cannot look at its value or change it.

Inspecting Variable Values

Defining a variable that you want to inspect is referred to as **setting a watch** for the variable. Before we set any watches, we need to invoke Step Over three times to get the declarations for our variables executed. Use the Step Over menu item, the toolbar icon, or press *F10* three times so that the arrow now appears at the start of the line:

```
pnumber = &number1;              // Store address in pointer
```

If you look at the Variables window now, you should see the following (although the value for **&number1** may be different on your system as it represents a memory location). Note that the values for **&number1** and **pnumber** are not equal to each other since the line that the arrow is pointing at hasn't yet been executed. We initialized **pnumber** as a **null pointer** in the first line of the function, which is why the address it contains is zero. Remember this is not the same as a pointer which has not been initialized, which would contain a junk value.

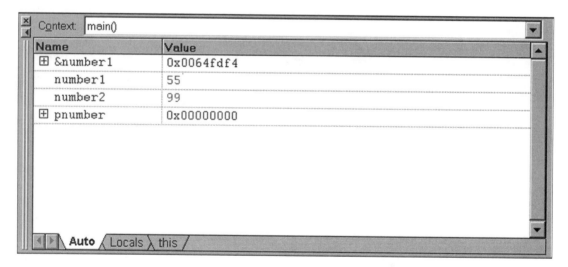

The Variables window has three tabs, each representing a different view of some of the variables in use in your program:

The Auto tab shows the variables in use in the current and previous statements (in other words, the statement pointed to by the arrow and the one before it).

The Locals tab shows the values of the variables local to the current function. In general, new variables will come into scope as you trace through a program and then go out of scope as you exit the block in which they are defined. In our case, this window will always show values for **number1**, **number2** and **pnumber** as we only have the function **main()**.

The this tab displays all the member variables of the current object when tracing through methods

You'll have noticed that **&number1** and **pnumber** both have plus signs next to their names in the Variables window. Plus signs will appear for any variable, such as an array or a pointer, for which there is additional information that can be displayed. In our case, we do have some pointer variables, so you can expand the view for each of these by clicking the plus signs. This will display the value stored at the address contained in the pointer.

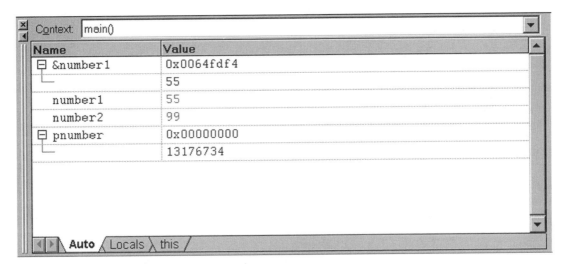

As you can see, the Variables window automatically provides us with all the information we need, displaying both the memory address and the data value stored at that address for pointers. You can view the variables that are local to the current function by selecting the Locals tab. There are also other ways that we can inspect variables using the debugging facilities of the Developer Studio.

Viewing Variables in the Edit Window

If we need to look at the value of a single variable, and that variable is visible in the Text Editor window, the easiest way to look at its value is to position the cursor over the variable for a second. A tooltip will pop up showing the current value of the variable. You can also look at more complicated expressions by highlighting them and resting the cursor over the highlighted area. Again a tooltip will pop up to display the value. Unfortunately, this method won't show the extended information that appears in the Variables window, such as the data stored at the address contained in a pointer, but there is another way to get at this information.

Watching Variables' Values

You can monitor a variable, and its extended information where it has any, by setting a **watch**. You can also monitor the value of an expression in this way. To set a watch for the pointer **pnumber**, first position the cursor in the Text Editor window in the middle of the pointer name, **pnumber**, then select QuickWatch... from the <u>D</u>ebug menu. You could also click on the Debug toolbar icon showing the spectacles to do this. You should see the window below:

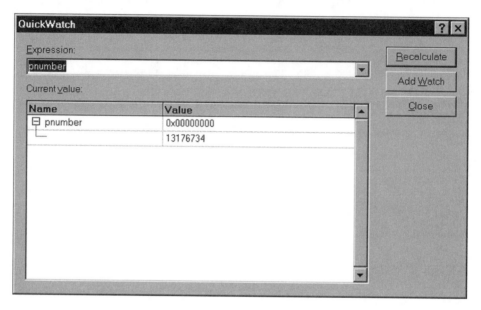

It should be clear to the debugger what you want to watch in this case, but in general if you have any problems setting a watch, highlight the whole name of the variable or expression in which you are interested.

In the QuickWatch window, as in the Variables window, the variable **pnumber** is automatically displayed in hexadecimal notation, because this is usually the most convenient form for an address. The QuickWatch facility shows us both the memory address and the value stored there, which is just what we want, but it only allows us to watch one expression at a time and, since the dialog is modal, we can't continue executing our code.

We can get around this by setting a permanent watch (or a SlowWatch if we extend Microsoft's terminology, which is what mine always seems to be!). Do this now by clicking the Add <u>W</u>atch button. This will add the watched expression into the Watch window. As execution proceeds, the Watch window will show all the variables we are watching, with their values and extended values.

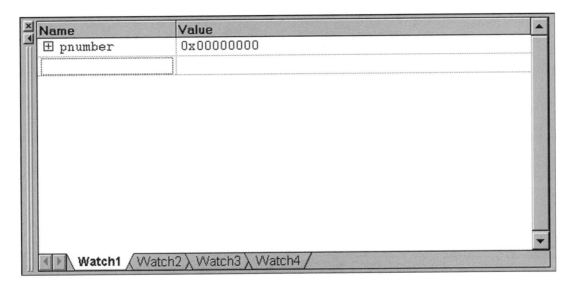

You can also add variables or expressions to the Watch window in two other ways: either type the name of the variable into the Name field of a line in the Watch window, or highlight and drag a variable or expression from the Text Editor window or the Variables window. We'll add some more expressions to the Watch window now.

First expand the view on **pnumber** in the Watch window by clicking the plus sign. Now, type ***pnumber** into the Name field of the last blank line. Since ***pnumber** is the value stored at the address given by **pnumber**, the last two lines should always have the same value throughout the execution of the program. With the help of the Watch window, you'll be able to confirm this for yourself.

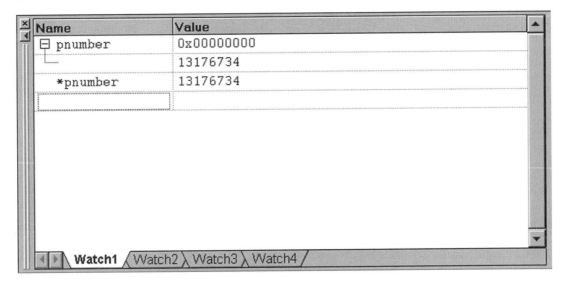

You could have achieved exactly the same result by highlighting the line under **pnumber** in the Variables window (the line that is shown when you click the plus sign) and dragging it into the Watch window. Now add the rest of the variables shown by dragging them from the Auto tab of the Variables window into the Watch window. Remember to start your drag by clicking in the Name field of the Variables window, otherwise you'll just drag the value. You can remove items from the Watch window by highlighting the line that they're on and pressing the *Delete* key.

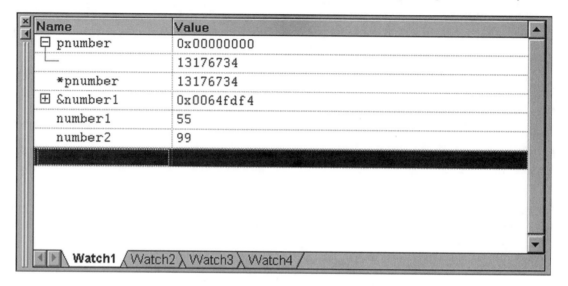

Name	Value
⊟ pnumber	0x00000000
	13176734
*pnumber	13176734
⊞ &number1	0x0064fdf4
number1	55
number2	99

> **Watch1** / Watch2 \ Watch3 \ Watch4 /

Now you're in a position to step through each line of code in the program using Step Over so that you don't have to step through all the stream output code. If you do accidentally step into some code that you don't recognize, you can always step out of it again by using the Step Out item from the Debug menu or the button on the Debug toolbar.

At each stage, you can see that everything operates as you would expect just by looking at the values of the variables in the Watch window. The program will end as soon as the last line of code has been executed, but if you wish, you can end debugging before that by choosing the Stop Debugging item from the Debug menu, clicking the Stop Debugging button on the Debug toolbar, or pressing *Shift-F5*. Make sure that you don't leave your programs hanging in the middle of the code.

There are various options you can experiment with for watching variables. For example, you can specify different formats for the value to be displayed. You can use any of the ways of stepping through a program in any combination, and in debugging a program for real this is exactly what you would do. Don't forget to try the Help menu if you get stuck.

Changing the Value of a Variable

Using Watch windows also allows you to change the values of the variables you are watching. You would use this in situations where a value displayed is clearly wrong, perhaps because there are bugs in your program, or maybe all the code is not there yet. If you set the 'right' value, your program will stagger on so that you can test out more of it and perhaps pick up a few more bugs.

To change the value of a variable in a Watch window, you should double-click the variable value shown, and type the new value. If the variable you want to change is an array element, you need to expand the array by clicking on the + box alongside the array name, then change the element value.

Naturally, you should be cautious about flinging new values into your program willy-nilly. Unless you are clear about the effect your changes are going to have, you may end up with a certain amount of erratic program behavior, which is unlikely to get you closer to a working program.

You'll probably find it useful to run a few more of the examples in debug mode as we progress through this book. It will enable you to get a good feel for how the programs work, as well as getting you familiar with the way that debugging operates under various conditions.

Summary

The example that we developed in this chapter was designed to introduce you to the basic mechanics of operating a program under Windows. As we said at the beginning of the chapter, we don't actually need to know about this when using the full capabilities of Visual C++ because all the details of creating and displaying a window, the message loop, and analyzing messages passed to an application are all submerged in the code that Visual C++ can provide automatically. However, you should find that the operation of programs generated by the AppWizard is much easier to understand if you have plowed through the material in this chapter, and this should make the AppWizard even easier to apply.

You may also be like me—never quite comfortable with taking things on trust, and not happy about using things without understanding how they really work. This has its downside of course. It can take a while to get comfortable with using something as mundane as a microwave oven, or even taking a plane. With the latter, understanding the theory still doesn't make sitting in a metal tube seven miles above the earth feel like a secure and natural thing to be doing!

You'll also need to be comfortable with running a program in debug mode. As soon as you start writing programs of your own which are more than a few lines of code, you will certainly find things will go wrong where the error is not obvious. You will then need to turn to debug mode for help.

Exercises

Ex2-1: Code up the **OFWin** program from this chapter, and make sure it runs correctly. Can you now modify it so that the program's main window is exactly in the center of your screen, and measures 300 by 200 pixels? (Hint: look up the **GetSystemMetrics()** API call in the help system to get the size of the screen.)

Ex2-2: Debug the following program, which takes a string and reverses it:

```
//EX2_02.CPP
// Debugging example for exercise 2-2
#include <iostream.h>
```

```
int len(char * strArray);

int main()
{
   char * strInput;

   cout << "Enter some text to process";

   cin >> strInput;

   // Processed entered text swapping around the text
   for(int i = 1; i != len(strInput); i++ )
   {
      strInput[i] ^= strInput[len(strInput) - i];
      strInput[len(strInput) - i] ^= strInput[i++];
   }

   cout << strInput << endl;

   return 0;
}


int len(char * strArray)
{
   int length = 0;

   do
   {
      if(strArray[length] = '\0')
         return length;
   }while(length++);

   return -1;
}
```

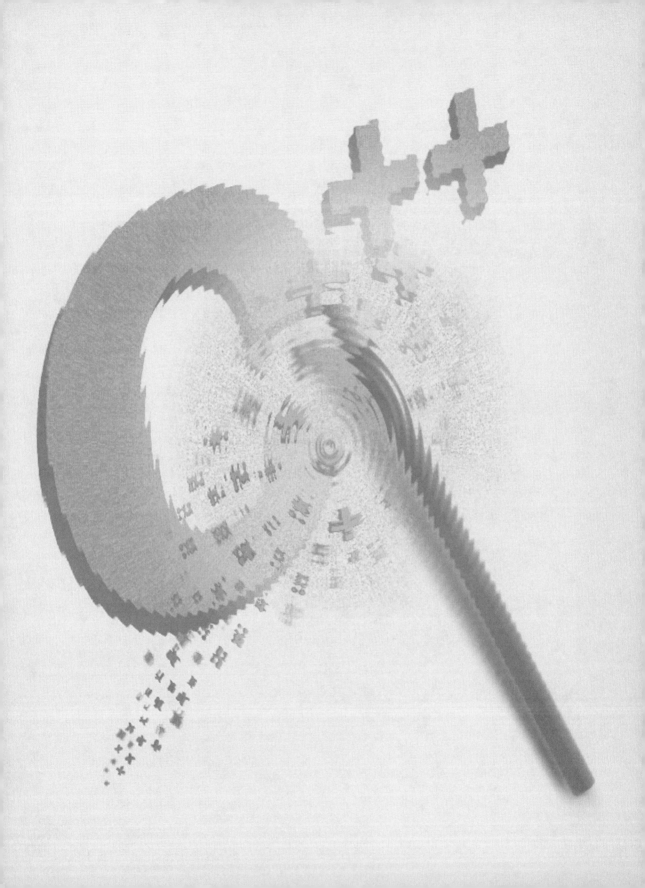

Understanding Windows Programming

This chapter is an overview of using Developer Studio for Windows programming. We'll look at how to use Visual C++ to generate a Windows program, and how that program is organized. By the end of this chapter, you will understand:

- What the Microsoft Foundation Classes are
- The basic elements of an MFC-based program
- Single Document Interface (SDI) applications and Multiple Document Interface (MDI) applications
- What the AppWizard is and how to use it to generate SDI and MDI programs
- What files are generated by the AppWizard and what their contents are
- How an AppWizard-generated program is structured
- The key classes in an AppWizard-generated program, and how they are interconnected
- What the principal source files in an AppWizard program contain
- The general approach to customizing an AppWizard-generated program

We'll expand the AppWizard programs that we generate in this chapter by adding features and code incrementally in subsequent chapters. By the end of the book, you should end up with a sizable, working Windows program that incorporates the basic user interface programming techniques.

The Essentials of a Windows Program

In the previous chapter, we saw an elementary Windows program which displayed a short quote from the Bard. It was unlikely to win any awards, being completely free of any useful functionality, but it did serve to illustrate the two essential components of a Windows program: providing initialization and setup, and servicing Windows messages. These are illustrated here:

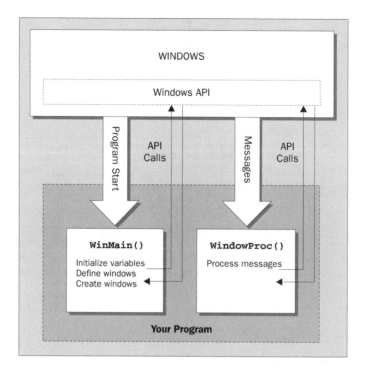

This structure is at the heart of *all* Windows programs. You can see the two essential pieces of a Windows program: the function **WinMain()**, which is called by Windows at the start of execution of the program, and a window procedure for each window class you've defined, often referred to as **WndProc()** or **WindowProc()**, which will be called by the operating system whenever a message is to be passed to your application's window.

The function **WinMain()** does any initialization that's necessary and sets up the window or windows that will be the primary interface to the user. It also contains the message loop for retrieving messages that have been queued for the application.

The function **WindowProc()** handles all the messages that aren't queued, which will include those initiated in the message loop in **WinMain()**. **WindowProc()**, therefore, ends up handling both kinds of messages. This is because the code in the message loop will sort out what kind of message it has retrieved from the queue, and then dispatch it for processing by **WindowProc()**. **WindowProc()** is where you code your application-specific response to each Windows message, which should handle all the communications with the user by processing the Windows messages generated by user actions, such as moving or clicking the mouse, or entering information at the keyboard.

The queued messages are largely those caused by user input from either the mouse or the keyboard The non-queued messages for which Windows calls your **WindowProc()** function directly, are either messages that your program created, typically as a result of obtaining a message from the queue and then dispatching it, or messages that are concerned with window management—such as handling menus and scrollbars, or resizing the window.

The Windows API

The example that you saw in the previous chapter used the **Windows Application Programming Interface**, abbreviated to the **Windows API**. The Windows API comes as part of every copy of Windows and consists of a large set of functions that provide all the services and communications with Windows that are necessary for producing an application that is to run in the Windows environment. The API actually contains over a thousand functions.

All the interactions between a program and the user are handled by Windows. Your program will receive information from the user second-hand, through Windows messages. Every Windows program uses the Windows API, regardless of how it is produced. All the programs we will write using Visual C++ will ultimately use the Windows API, so there's no getting away from it. Fortunately, we don't need to know very much about the Windows API in detail as MFC does such a terrific job of packaging it up in a much more organized and friendly form.

Visual C++ and the Windows API

Remember that the Windows API was not written with Visual C++ in mind, or even considering C++ in general, since it was written before C++ came into general use. Naturally, it needs to be usable in programs written in a variety of languages, most of which aren't object-oriented. The API functions don't handle or recognize class objects but, as we shall soon see, MFC encapsulates the API in a way that makes using it a piece of cake.

Visual C++ lets you develop a Windows program in two stages. First, you use Visual C++'s set of tools to generate code for a program automatically, then you modify and extend the code to suit your needs. As the basis for doing this, Visual C++ uses a hierarchy of classes called the **Microsoft Foundation Classes**, although they can also be used independently of the development tools in Visual C++.

The Microsoft Foundation Classes

The Microsoft Foundation Classes, usually abbreviated to **MFC**, are a set of predefined classes upon which Windows programming with Visual C++ is built. These classes represent an object-oriented approach to Windows programming that encapsulates the Windows API. The process of writing a Windows program involves creating and using MFC objects, or objects of classes derived from MFC. In the main, we'll derive our own classes from MFC, with considerable assistance from the specialized tools in Visual C++ to make this even easier. The objects created will incorporate member functions for communicating with Windows, for processing Windows messages, and for sending messages to each other.

These derived classes will, of course, inherit all of the members of their base classes. These inherited functions do practically all of the general grunt work necessary for a Windows application to work. All we need to do is to add data and function members to customize the classes to provide the application-specific functionality that we need in our program. In doing this, we'll be applying most of the techniques that we've been grappling with in the preceding chapters, particularly those involving class inheritance and virtual functions.

MFC Notation

All the classes in MFC have names beginning with **C**, such as **CDocument** or **CView**. If you use the same convention when defining your own classes or deriving them from those in the MFC library, your programs will be easier to follow. Data members of an MFC class are prefixed with **m_**. We'll also follow this convention in the examples, just as we've been doing throughout the book.

You'll find that MFC uses Hungarian notation for many variable names, particularly those that originate in the Windows API. As you will recall, this involves using a prefix of **p** for a pointer, **n** for an **int**, **l** for **long**, **h** for a handle, and so on. The name **m_lpCmdLine**, for example, would refer to a data member of a class (because of the **m_** prefix) that is of type 'pointer to **long**'. This practice of explicitly showing the type of a variable in its name was important in the C environment because of the lack of type checking; since you could determine the type from the name, you had a fair chance of not using or interpreting its value incorrectly. The downside is that the variable names can become quite cumbersome, making the code look more complicated than it really is. As C++ has strong type checking, which will pick up the sort of misuse that used to happen regularly in C, this kind of notation isn't essential, so we won't use it for our own variables in our examples in the book. However, we will retain the **p** prefix for pointers, and some of the other simple type denotations, since this helps to make the code more readable.

How an MFC Program is Structured

We know from Chapter 1 that we can produce a Windows program using the AppWizard without writing a single line of code. Of course, this uses the MFC library, but it's quite possible to write a Windows program which uses MFC without using AppWizard. If we first scratch the surface by constructing the minimum MFC-based program, we can get a clear idea of the fundamental elements involved.

The simplest program that we can produce using MFC is slightly less sophisticated than the example that we wrote in Chapter 2, using the raw Windows API. The example we'll produce here will have a window but no text displayed in it. This will be sufficient to show the fundamentals, so let's try it out.

An MFC Application Without AppWizard

First, create a new project workspace using the File | New... menu option, as you've done many times before. We won't use AppWizard here, so select the type of project as Win32 Application, as shown below:

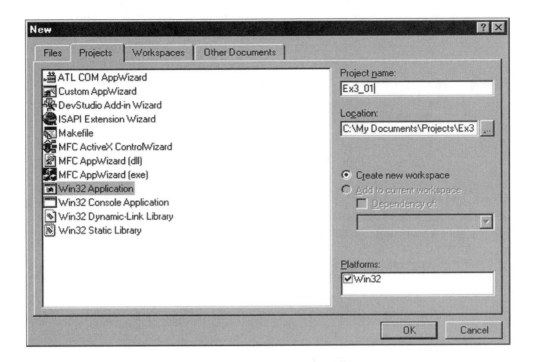

With this choice of project type, we must ensure that the linker knows that we intend to use MFC classes. If we don't do this, the wrong link options will be set and we will get some obscure linker errors. Use the Project | Settings... menu item to bring up the Project Settings dialog. Go to the General tab and make sure that the Microsoft Foundation Classes: option is showing Use MFC in a Shared DLL. Now you can create a new source file and insert it in to the project as **Ex3_01.cpp**. So that you can see all the code for the program in one place, we'll put the class definitions we need together with their implementations in this file. To achieve this, we won't use the Wizard Bar; we'll just add the code manually—there isn't very much of it.

To begin with, add a statement to include the header file **afxwin.h**, as this contains the definitions for many MFC classes. This will allow us to derive our own classes from MFC.

```
#include <afxwin.h>                    // For the class library
```

To produce the complete program, we'll only need to derive two classes from MFC: an **application class** and a **window class**. We won't even need to write a **WinMain()** function, as we did in the example in the previous chapter, because this is automatically provided by the MFC library behind the scenes. Let's look at how the two classes that we need are defined.

The Application Class

The class **CWinApp** is fundamental to any Windows program written using MFC. An object of this class includes everything necessary for starting, initializing, running and closing the application. The first thing that we need to do to produce our application is to derive our own application class from **CWinApp**. We will be defining a specialized version of the class to suit our application needs. The code for this is as follows:

```
class COurApp: public CWinApp
{
  public:
      virtual BOOL InitInstance();
};
```

As you might expect for a simple example, there isn't a great deal of specialization necessary in this case. We've only included one member in the definition of our class: the function **InitInstance()**. This function is defined as a virtual function in the base class, so it's not a new function in our derived class. We're redefining the base class function for our application class. All the other data and function members that we need in our class we'll inherit from **CWinApp** unchanged.

Our application class will be endowed with quite a number of data members that are defined in the base, many of which correspond to variables used as arguments in Windows API functions. For example, the member **m_pszAppName** stores a pointer to a string that defines the name of the application. The member **m_nCmdShow** specifies how the application window is to be shown when the application starts up. Don't panic: we don't need to go into the inherited data members now. We'll see how they are used as the need arises in developing our application-specific code.

In deriving our own application class from **CWinApp**, we must override the virtual function **InitInstance()**. Our version will be called by the version of **WinMain()** that's provided for us, and we'll include code in the function to create and display our application window. However, before we write **InitInstance()**, we need to look at a class in the MFC library which defines a window.

The Window Class

Our MFC application will need a window as the interface to the user, referred to as a **frame window**. We will derive a window class for our application from the MFC class **CFrameWnd**, which is designed specifically for this purpose. Since **CFrameWnd** provides everything for creating and managing a window for our application, all we need to add to our derived window class is a constructor. This will allow us to specify a title bar for our window to suit the application context:

```
class COurWnd: public CFrameWnd
{
  public:
      // Class constructor
      COurWnd()
      {
         Create(0, "Our Dumb MFC Application");
      }
};
```

The **Create()** function, which we call in our class constructor, is inherited from the base class and will create the window and attach it to the **COurWnd** object being created. Note that the **COurWnd** object is not the same thing as the window that will be displayed by Windows—the class object and the physical window are distinct entities.

The first argument value for the **Create()** function, 0, specifies that we want to use the base class default attributes for the window—you'll recall that we needed to define window attributes in our example in the previous chapter. The second argument specifies the window name which will be used in the window title bar. You won't be surprised to learn that there are other parameters to the function **Create()**, but they all have default values which will be quite satisfactory, so we can afford to ignore them here.

Completing the Program

Having defined a window class for our application, we can write the **InitInstance()** function in our **COurApp** class:

```
BOOL COurApp::InitInstance(void)
{
   // Construct a window object in the free store
   m_pMainWnd = new COurWnd;
   m_pMainWnd->ShowWindow(m_nCmdShow);       // ...and display it
   return TRUE;
}
```

This will override the virtual function defined in the base class **CWinApp**, and as we said previously, will be called by the **WinMain()** function that's automatically supplied by the MFC library. The function **InitInstance()** constructs a main window object for our application in the free store by using the operator **new**. We store the address returned in the variable **m_pMainWnd**, which is an inherited member of our class **COurApp**. The effect of this is that the window object will be owned by the application object. We don't even need to worry about freeing the memory for the object we've created—the supplied **WinMain()** function will take care of any clean-up necessary.

The only other item we need for a complete, albeit rather limited, program is to define an application object. An instance of our application class, **COurApp**, must exist before **WinMain()** is executed, so we should declare it at global scope with the statement:

```
COurApp AnApplication;     // Define an application object
```

The reason that this object needs to exist at global scope is that it is the application, and the application needs to exist before it can start executing. The **WinMain()** provided by MFC calls the **InitInstance()** function member of the application object to construct the window object and, thus, implicitly assumes the application object already exists.

The Finished Product

Now that you've seen all the code, you can add it to the project. In a Windows program, the classes are usually defined in **.h** files, and the member functions not appearing within the class definitions are defined in **.cpp** files. Our application is so short, though, that you may as well put it all in a single **.cpp** file. The merit of this is that you can view the whole lot together. The program code is structured as follows:

```
// EX3_01.CPP
// An elementary MFC program
#include <afxwin.h>                       // For the class library

// Application class definition
class COurApp:public CWinApp
{
   public:
      virtual BOOL InitInstance();
};
```

77

```
// Window class definition
class COurWnd:public CFrameWnd
{
   public:
      // Class constructor
      COurWnd()
      {
         Create(0, "Our Dumb MFC Application");
      }
};

// Function to create an instance of the main window
BOOL COurApp::InitInstance(void)
{
   // Construct a window object in the free store
   m_pMainWnd = new COurWnd;
   m_pMainWnd->ShowWindow(m_nCmdShow);        // ...and display it
   return TRUE;
}

// Application object definition at global scope
COurApp AnApplication;                        // Define an application object
```

That's all we need. It looks a bit odd because no **WinMain()** function appears but, as we noted above, the **WinMain()** function is supplied by the MFC library.

Now we're ready to roll, so build and run the application. Select the Build | Build Ex3_01.exe menu item, click on the appropriate toolbar button, or just press *F7* to build the project. You should end up with a clean compile and link, in which case you can select Build | Execute Ex3_01.exe or press *Ctrl-F5* to run it. Our minimum MFC program will appear as shown:

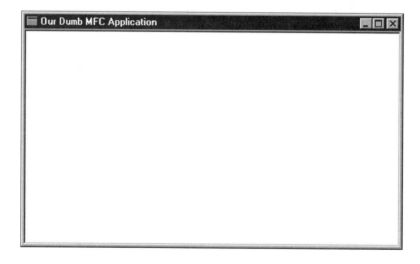

We can resize the window by dragging the border, we can move the whole thing around, and we can also minimize or maximize it in the usual ways. The only other function that the program supports is 'close', for which you can use the system menu, the close button at the top right of the window, or just key *Alt-F4*. It doesn't look like much but, considering that there are so few lines of code, it's quite impressive, particularly if you think of how much code you would need to do something like this in the old DOS world.

FYI

If you find that the linker throws some errors about the symbols __beginthreadex and __endthreadex, you need to change the **Microsoft Foundation Classes:** list box on the **General** tab of the **Project Settings** dialog to use MFC, either statically or with the DLL. The **Project Settings** dialog is accessed by selecting the **P**roject | **S**ettings...menu item, or by pressing *Alt-F7*.

The Document/View Concept

When you write applications using MFC, it implies acceptance of a specific structure for your program, with application data being stored and processed in a particular way. This may sound restrictive, but it really isn't for the most part, and the benefits in speed and ease of implementation you gain far outweigh any conceivable disadvantages. The structure of an MFC program incorporates two application-oriented entities—a document and a view—so let's look at what they are and how they're used.

What is a Document?

A **document** is the name given to the collection of data in your application with which the user interacts. Although the word 'document' seems to imply something of a textual nature, a document isn't limited to text. It could be the data for a game, a geometric model, a text file, a collection of data on the distribution of orange trees in California or, indeed, anything you want. The term 'document' is just a convenient label for the application data in your program, treated as a unit.

You won't be surprised to hear that a document in your program will be defined as an object of a document class. Your document class will be derived from the class **CDocument** in the MFC library, and you'll add your own data members to store items that your application requires, and member functions to support processing of that data.

Handling application data in this way enables standard mechanisms to be provided within MFC for managing a collection of application data as a unit and for storing and retrieving data contained in document objects to and from disk. These mechanisms will be inherited by your document class from the base class defined in the MFC library, so you will get a broad range of functionality built in to your application automatically, without having to write any code.

Document Interfaces

You have a choice as to whether your program deals with just one document at a time, or with several. The **Single Document Interface**, referred to as **SDI**, is supported by the MFC library for programs that only require one document to be open at a time. A program using this interface is referred to as an **SDI application**.

For programs needing several documents to be open at one time, you use the **Multiple Document Interface**, which is usually referred to as **MDI**. With the MDI, as well as being able to open multiple documents of one type, your program can also be organized to handle documents of different types simultaneously. Of course, you will need to supply the code to deal with processing whatever different kinds of documents you intend to support.

What is a View?

A **view** always relates to a particular document object. As we've seen, a document contains a set of application data in your program, and a view is an object which provides a mechanism for displaying some or all of the data stored in a document. It defines how the data is to be displayed in a window and how the user can interact with it. Similar to the way that you define a document, you'll define your own view class by deriving it from the MFC class **CView**. Note that a view object and the window in which it is displayed are distinct. The window in which a view appears is called a **frame window**. A view is actually displayed in its own window that exactly fills the client area of a frame window. The general relationship between a document, a view and a frame window is illustrated here:

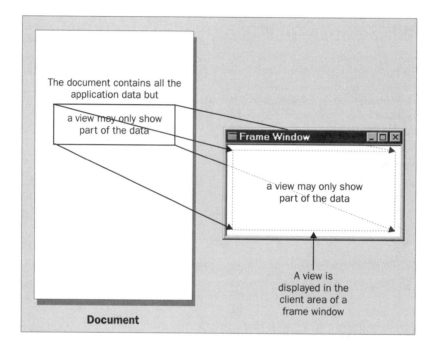

In this illustration, the view displays only part of the data contained in the document, although a view can display all of the data in a document if that's what's required.

A document object can have multiple view objects associated with it. Each view object can provide a different presentation or subset of the same document data. If you were dealing with text, for example, different views could be displaying independent blocks of text from the same document. For a program handling graphical data, you could display all of the document data at different scales in separate windows, or in different formats, such as a textual representation of the elements that form the image.

Linking a Document and its Views

MFC incorporates a mechanism for integrating a document with its views, and each frame window with a currently active view. A document object automatically maintains a list of pointers to its associated views, and a view object has a data member holding a pointer to the document that it relates to. Also, each frame window stores a pointer to the currently active view object. This is similar to the mechanism we used to link objects in our calculator program. The coordination between a document, a view and a frame window is established by another MFC class of objects called document templates.

Document Templates

A **document template** manages the document objects in your program, as well as the windows and views associated with each of them. There will be one document template for each different kind of document that you have in your program. If you have two or more documents of the same type, you only need one document template to manage them. To be more specific about the use of a document template, document objects and frame window objects are created by a document template object. A view is created by a frame window object. The document template object itself is created by the application object that is fundamental to any MFC application, as we saw in the last example. You can see a graphical representation of these interrelationships here:

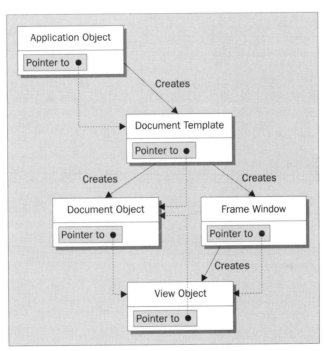

The diagram uses dashed arrows to show how pointers are used to relate objects. These pointers enable function members of one class object to access the **public** data or the function members in the interface of another object.

Document Template Classes

MFC has two classes for defining document templates. For SDI applications, the MFC library class **CSingleDocTemplate** is used. This is relatively straightforward, since an SDI application will have only one document and usually just one view. MDI applications are rather more complicated. They have multiple documents active at one time, so a different class, **CMultiDocTemplate**, is needed to define the document template. We'll see more of these classes as we progress into developing application code.

Your Application and MFC

MFC covers a lot of ground and involves a lot of classes. It provides classes that, taken together, are a complete framework for your applications, only requiring the customization necessary to make your programs do what you want them to do. It would be fruitless to try to go through a laundry list of all the classes that are provided; we can learn about them much more easily and naturally by exploring their capabilities as we use them.

However, it's worth taking a look at how the fundamental classes in an SDI application relate to MFC. This is illustrated in the diagram below:

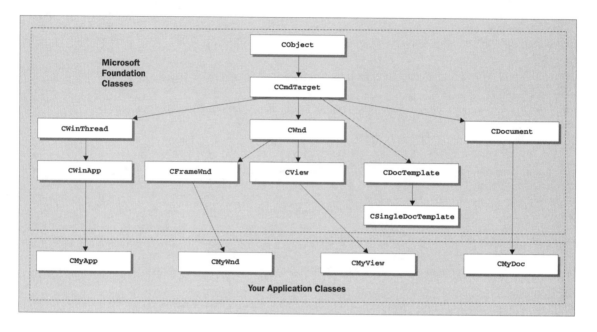

This shows the four basic classes that are going to appear in virtually all your Windows applications:

> The application class **CMyApp**

> The frame window class **CMyWnd**

> The view class **CMyView**, which will define how data contained in **CMyDoc** is to be displayed in the client area of a window created by a **CMyWnd** object

> The document class **CMyDoc** defining a document to contain the application data

The actual names for these classes will be specific to a particular application, but the derivation from MFC will be much the same, although there can be alternative base classes, particularly with the view class. As we'll see a bit later, MFC provides several variations of the view class that provide a lot of functionality pre-packaged for you, saving you lots of coding. The class defining a document template for your application will not typically need to be extended, so the standard MFC class **CSingleDocTemplate** will usually suffice in an SDI program. When you're creating an MDI program, your document template class will be **CMultiDocTemplate**, which is also derived from **CDocTemplate**.

The arrows in the diagram point from a base class to a derived class. The MFC library classes shown here form quite a complex inheritance structure, but in fact these are just a very small part of the complete MFC structure. You need not be concerned about the details of the complete MFC hierarchy in the main, but it is important to have a general appreciation of it if you want to understand what the inherited members of your classes are. You will not see any of the definitions of the base classes in your program, but the inherited members of a derived class in your program will be accumulated from the direct base class, as well as from each of the indirect base classes in the MFC hierarchy. To determine what members one of your program's classes has, you therefore need to know from which classes it inherits. Once you know that, you can look up its members using the Help facility.

Another thing you don't need to worry about is remembering which classes you need to have in your program and what base classes to use in their definition. As you'll see next, all of this is taken care of for you by Visual C++.

Windows Programming with Visual C++

You'll be using three tools in the development of your Windows programs:

1 **AppWizard** for creating the basic program code. You use this when you create a project.

2 **ClassWizard** for extending and customizing the classes in your programs. You access this through the Wizard Bar, or the context menu for a class from ClassView, or the View | ClassWizard menu item.

3 **Resource Editor** for creating or modifying such things as menus and toolbars.

There are, in fact, several resource editors; the one used in any particular situation is selected depending on the kind of resource that you're editing. We'll look at editing resources in the next chapter, but for now let's take a look at what AppWizard can do for us.

What is the AppWizard?

AppWizard is a programming tool that creates a complete skeleton Windows program using the MFC library. We'll be using AppWizard for the rest of the examples in the book. It's an extraordinarily powerful aid to Windows programming, since all you have to do to produce your application is to customize a ready-made program. AppWizard automatically defines all of the classes needed by your program that we have discussed. It even provides hooks and explanations for where you should add your application-specific code.

As we've already seen, you can invoke AppWizard when you create a new project workspace by selecting MFC AppWizard (exe) as the project type. Do this now and name the project **TextEditor**, as shown here:

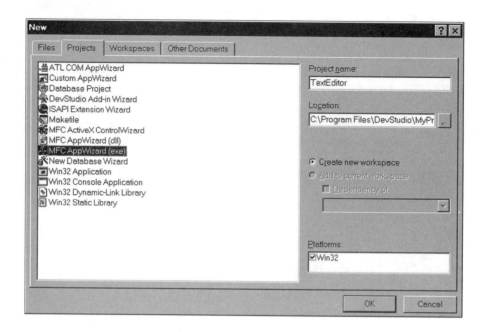

As you know, the name that you assign to the project, **TextEditor** in this case, will be used as the name of the folder which will contain all the project files, but it will also be used as a basis for creating names for classes generated in the application by AppWizard. When you click on OK, you'll find yourself at the first step in the AppWizard dialog to create the application. Initially, AppWizard allows you to choose an SDI, an MDI or a dialog-based application. Let's concentrate on the first two options. We'll generate both an SDI and an MDI application and see what the resulting programs look like.

Using AppWizard to Create an SDI Application

When you're in the AppWizard dialog, you can always go back to the previous step by clicking on the button labeled < Back. Try it out. If you felt like it, you could now rename the project and then click on OK again to return to Step 1 of the AppWizard dialog.

Step 1

The default option selected is MDI, and the appearance of an MDI application is shown so that you'll know what to expect. Select the SDI option and the representation for the application shown top left will change to a single window, as shown here:

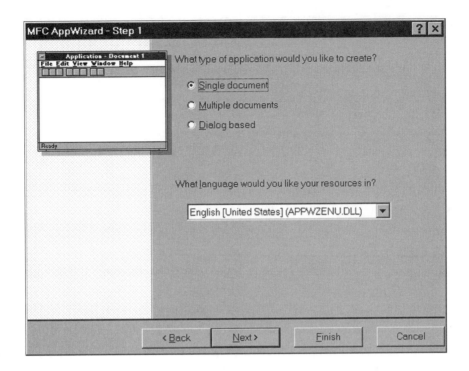

The drop-down list box shows the default language supported. Other languages will only appear in the list if your Visual C++ installation has been set up to support them.

Step 2

To move on to the next step in the dialog, you should click on **Next** >. Step 2 gives you choices about the database support in your application. We don't need any in this application, so click on **Next** > once again to move on.

Step 3

This step gives you a range of choices relating to OLE (Object Linking and Embedding), under the label of compound document support. OLE enables you to write programs that can import objects from other programs, or to import your program into another application. We'll see more about this in Chapter 11. There is also a default selection for the ActiveX Controls option. This means that AppWizard will include code that allows the possibility of using ActiveX controls in our application if we want. We won't be doing this in this case, but the option will do no harm. An ActiveX control is a reusable program component that you can apply in a program or in an Internet web page. We will see more about OLE and ActiveX controls towards the end of the book. For now, we'll accept the default set of choices and move to the next step.

Step 4

This step offers you a range of functions that can be included in your application by the AppWizard. The first group relate to menu and toolbar options. Let's take a brief look at them.

Feature	Meaning
Docking toolbar	The toolbar provides a standard range of buttons that are alternatives to using menu options. A docking toolbar can be dragged to the sides or the bottom of the application window, so you can put it wherever is most convenient. We'll see how to add buttons to the toolbar in Chapter 4.
Initial status bar	The status bar appears at the bottom of the application window. It comes with fully implemented standard functions including indicators for the *Num Lock*, *Caps Lock*, and *Scroll Lock* keys, as well as a message line to display prompts for menu options and toolbar selections.
Printing and print preview	This adds the standard Page Setup..., Print Preview, and Print... options to the File menu. The AppWizard will also provide code to support these functions.
Context-sensitive Help	Enabling this option results in a basic set of facilities to support context-sensitive help. You'll obviously need to add the specific contents of the help files if you want to use this feature.
3D controls	This option results in controls that appear in the application, such as buttons, being shaded to give them a 3D appearance.

All except Context-sensitive Help are default selections, and we'll keep the default set of options in our example. The second group of choices concern **WOSA**, which is **W**indows **O**pen **S**ervices **A**rchitecture. This is only relevant if your program is to implement communications with other computers. It provides two options for communications support in your program:

Feature	Meaning
MAPI (Messaging API)	This option will cause AppWizard to include support that allows you to send and receive messages.
Windows Sockets	This provides you with the ability to implement TCP/IP capability within your program. This is particularly applicable to applications that support the transfer of files over the Internet.

We will not be getting into either of these options, as they are beyond the scope of this book, so we'll leave them unchecked.

Towards the bottom of the dialog, you can vary the number of previously referenced file entries that will appear in the list at the end of the File menu. You can set this to any value from 0 to 16.

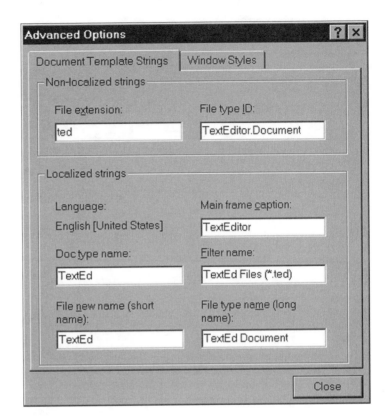

Clicking the Advanced... button brings up a range of options for your application, grouped under two tabs as shown here:

The tab shown allows you to choose the file extension which will identify files that are generated by your application and are to be associated with it. In this instance, we've associated **.ted** with our application. You'll notice that, when you fill in the file extension, the Filter name: box is automatically filled in for you—we'll be getting to what that does in a moment. From this tab, you can also modify the File Type ID: which is used to label the file type for your application in the system registry. The registry associates files with a given unique extension with a particular application.

AppWizard has already decided on a caption for the title bar in your application window but, like all the strings shown here, you can change it if you don't like it. For example, it might look better with a space between Text and Editor, or you might want to personalize it in some way.

The Doc type name: entry is a default name for a document. When you create a new document, MFC will use what is entered here as a basis for naming it. The Filter name: will be used to describe files associated with your application in the List Files of Type: box in the File | Open... and File | Save As... menu dialogs although, if you haven't specified a file extension for files produced by your application, this will do nothing. If you want to specify the filter name entry, you should put something descriptive to clearly identify the particular document type.

The option headed File new name (short name): is important if your application will support more than one type of document. This would mean that you had more than one document template implemented in your program. In that case, what you put here will be used to identify the document template in the File | New... menu dialog. Along with the option adjacent to it, it's also applicable if you're writing a program which is an OLE server. We'll see rather more about this towards the end of the book.

The Windows Styles tab is shown here:

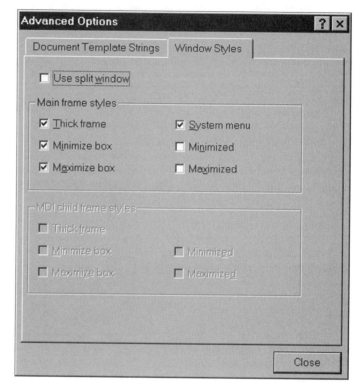

The bottom area is grayed out because the options here only apply to MDI applications. The Main frame styles area enables you to tailor your application window. Here, the Thick frame option is checked by default. It provides you with a window border that can be dragged to resize the window. The Minimize box, Maximize box, and System menu options, which are also checked by default, provide the three standard buttons that appear at the top of a window. The two unchecked options for Minimized and Maximized frame styles do not apply to Windows 95 programs, so you can ignore them.

We can now move to Step 5 by closing the Advanced Options dialog and clicking on Next >.

Step 5

This step offers two options for your consideration. The first is whether or not comments are to be included in the source code generated by AppWizard. In most instances, you will want to keep the default option of having them included, so that you can better understand the code generated for you.

The second option relates to how MFC library code is used in your program. The default choice of using the MFC library as a shared DLL (Dynamic Link Library) means that your program will link to MFC library routines at run time. This can reduce the size of the executable file that you'll generate, but requires the MFC DLL to be on the machine that's running it. The two programs together (**.exe** and **.dll**) may be bigger than if you had statically linked the MFC library. If you opt for static linking, the routines will be included in the executable module for your program when it is built. Generally, it's preferable to keep the default option of using MFC as a shared DLL. With this option, several programs running simultaneously using the dynamic link library can all share a single copy of the library in memory.

Step 6

The last step presents you with a list of the classes that AppWizard will be generating in your program code, as shown here:

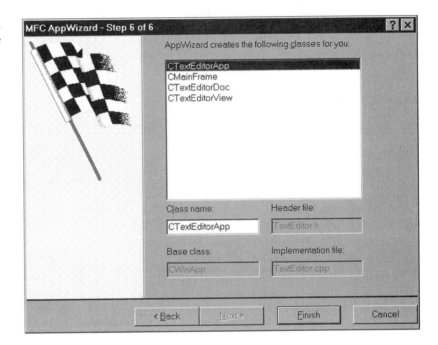

For the highlighted class in the list, the boxes below show the name given to the class, the name of the header file in which the definition will be stored, the base class used and the name of the file containing the implementation of member functions in the class. The class definition is always contained in a **.h** file, and the member function source code is always included in a **.cpp** file.

In the case of the class **CTextEditorApp** shown above, the only thing that you can alter is the class name and, since it's already a good choice, we'll leave it as it is. Try clicking on the other classes in the list. For **CMainFrame** and **CTextEditorDoc**, you can alter everything except the base class and, for the class **CTextEditorView**, you can change the base class as well. Click on the down arrow to display the list of other classes that you can have as a base class. There are a variety of view classes provided by the MFC with a range of capabilities, and the capability built into your view class will depend on which base class you select. Since we've called the application TextEditor, with the notion that it will be able to edit text, choose **CEditView** to get basic editing capability provided automatically.

If you click on Finish, you will see a summary of what AppWizard will include in your project. Just click on OK to have the program files containing a fully working base program generated by AppWizard, using the options you've chosen.

The Output from AppWizard

All the output from AppWizard is stored in the folder **TextEditor**. Developer Studio provides several ways for you to view the information in the project folder:

Tab	View	How project viewed
ClassView	ClassView	Viewed by class and function member name, plus the global entities in your program.
ResourceView	ResourceView	Viewed by resource type.
FileView	FileView	Viewed by file name.
InfoView	InfoView	Provides access to books online.

Each of these is selected using the appropriate tab at the bottom of the Project Workspace window in Developer Studio. The fourth tab provides access to all of the documentation available online with Visual C++.

Viewing Project Files

If you select FileView by clicking on the third tab, and expand the list by clicking on the + for TextEditor files, then on the ones for Source Files, Header Files and Resource Files, you'll see the complete list of files for the project, as shown here:

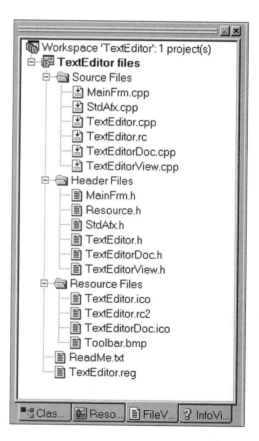

As you can see, there are a total of 18 files in the list. You can view any of the files simply by double-clicking on the filename. The contents of the file selected will be displayed in the right-hand window. Try it out with the **ReadMe.txt** file. You'll see that it contains a brief explanation of the contents of each of the files that make up the project. We won't repeat the descriptions of the files here, as they are very clearly summarized in **ReadMe.txt**.

Viewing Classes

As you may have started to see in the last chapter, ClassView is often much more convenient than FileView, since classes are the basis for the organization of the application. When you want to look at the code, it's typically the definition of a class or the implementation of a member function you'll want to look at, and from ClassView you can go directly to either. On occasions though, FileView will come in handy. If you want to check the **#include** directives in a **.cpp** file, using FileView you can open the file you're interested in directly.

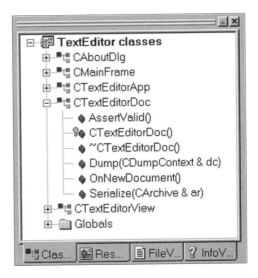

If you click the ClassView tab, you can expand the TextEditor classes item to show the classes defined for the application. Clicking on + for any of the classes will expand the class to show the members of that class. In the window shown below, the **CTextEditorDoc** class has been expanded:

The icons simply code the various kinds of things that you can display:

▶ Classes are dark blue

▶ Function members are purple

▶ Data members are light blue

▶ A key indicates that the member is **protected**

▶ A padlock will indicate that the member is **private**

You can see that we have the four classes we discussed earlier that are fundamental to an MFC application: **CTextEditorApp** for the application, **CMainFrame** for the application frame window, **CTextEditorDoc** for the document and **CTextEditorView** for the view. We also have a class **CAboutDlg**, which defines objects that support the dialog which appears when you select the menu item Help | About... in the application. If you expand Globals, you'll see that it only contains one definition: the application object **theApp**.

To view the code for a class definition, you just double-click the class name in the tree. To view the code for a member function, double-click the function name. Note that you can drag the edge of the Project Workspace window to the left or the right in order to view its contents or your code more easily. However, it's usually convenient to leave the left window fairly narrow since, if you leave the cursor over any line that is partially obscured, the complete contents of the line will be shown. You can hide or show the Project Workspace window by clicking the button at the right-hand end of the standard toolbar.

The Class Definitions

We won't examine the classes in complete detail here—we'll just get a feel for how they look and pick out a few important aspects. If you double-click the name of a class in the ClassView, the code defining the class will be displayed. Take a look at the application class, **CTextEditorApp** first. The definition for this class is shown below:

```
class CTextEditorApp: public CWinApp
{
public:
   CTextEditorApp();
// Overrides
   // ClassWizard generated virtual function overrides
   //{{AFX_VIRTUAL(CTextEditorApp)
   public:
   virtual BOOL InitInstance();
   //}}AFX_VIRTUAL

// Implementation

   //{{AFX_MSG(CTextEditorApp)
   afx_msg void OnAppAbout();
      // NOTE - the ClassWizard will add and remove member functions here.
      //    DO NOT EDIT what you see in these blocks of generated code!
   //}}AFX_MSG
   DECLARE_MESSAGE_MAP()
};
```

It may look complicated at first sight, but there isn't much to it. It's derived from **CWinApp** and includes a constructor, a virtual function **InitInstance()**, a function **OnAppAbout()**, and a macro **DECLARE_MESSAGE_MAP()**.

 FYI   A macro is not C++ code. It's a name defined by a **#define** pre-processor directive that will be replaced by some text that will normally be C++ code, but could also be constants or symbols of some kind.

The **DECLARE_MESSAGE_MAP()** macro is concerned with defining which Windows messages are handled by which function members of the class. The macro will appear in the definition of any class that may process Windows messages. Of course, our application class will inherit a lot of functions and data members from the base class, and we will be looking further into these as we expand our program examples.

The rest of the **CTextEditorApp** class definition is comments. However, they are very important comments. They include a note indicating where the ClassWizard will make changes to the code. Don't be tempted to delete or alter any of the comments, because some will be used as markers to enable the ClassWizard to find where changes to the class definition should be made. Modifying them may prevent ClassWizard from working properly with this project ever again!

If you take a look at the beginning of the **.h** file containing the class definition, you will notice that the directives preventing the file being included more than once look very much like the ones we've seen previously. Again, the long strings of letters and numbers will be different on your machine from the ones you see here.

The application frame window for our SDI program will be created by an object of the class **CMainFrame**, which is defined by the code shown here:

```
class CMainFrame: public CFrameWnd
{
protected: // create from serialization only
   CMainFrame();
   DECLARE_DYNCREATE(CMainFrame)

// Attributes
public:

// Operations
public:

// Overrides
   // ClassWizard generated virtual function overrides
   //{{AFX_VIRTUAL(CMainFrame)
   virtual BOOL PreCreateWindow(CREATESTRUCT& cs);
   //}}AFX_VIRTUAL

// Implementation
public:
   virtual ~CMainFrame();
#ifdef _DEBUG
   virtual void AssertValid() const;
   virtual void Dump(CDumpContext& dc) const;
#endif

protected:  // control bar embedded members
   CStatusBar   m_wndStatusBar;
   CToolBar     m_wndToolBar;

// Generated message map functions
protected:
   //{{AFX_MSG(CMainFrame)
   afx_msg int OnCreate(LPCREATESTRUCT lpCreateStruct);
      // NOTE - the ClassWizard will add and remove member functions here.
      //    DO NOT EDIT what you see in these blocks of generated code!
   //}}AFX_MSG
   DECLARE_MESSAGE_MAP()
};
```

This class is derived from **CFrameWnd**, which provides most of the functionality required for our application frame window. The derived class includes two protected data members, **m_wndStatusBar** and **m_wndToolBar**, which are instances of the MFC classes **CStatusBar** and **CToolBar** respectively. These objects will create and manage the status bar that will appear at the bottom of the application window, and the toolbar which will provide buttons to access standard menu functions.

93

The definition of the **CTextEditorDoc** class supplied by AppWizard is:

```
class CTextEditorDoc: public CDocument
{
protected: // create from serialization only
    CTextEditorDoc();
    DECLARE_DYNCREATE(CTextEditorDoc)

// Attributes
public:

// Operations
public:

// Overrides
    // ClassWizard generated virtual function overrides
    //{{AFX_VIRTUAL(CTextEditorDoc)
    public:
    virtual BOOL OnNewDocument();
    virtual void Serialize(CArchive& ar);
    //}}AFX_VIRTUAL

// Implementation
public:
    virtual ~CTextEditorDoc();
#ifdef _DEBUG
    virtual void AssertValid() const;
    virtual void Dump(CDumpContext& dc) const;
#endif

protected:

// Generated message map functions
protected:
    //{{AFX_MSG(CTextEditorDoc)
        // NOTE - the ClassWizard will add and remove member functions here.
        //    DO NOT EDIT.what you see in these blocks of generated code!
    //}}AFX_MSG
    DECLARE_MESSAGE_MAP()
};
```

As in the case of the previous classes, most of the meat comes from the base class and is therefore not apparent here. There are also a lot of comments, some of which are for you, and some are to help ClassWizard out.

The macro **DECLARE_DYNCREATE()** which appears after the constructor (and which was also used in the **CMainFrame** class) enables an object of the class to be created dynamically by synthesizing it from data read from a file. When you save an SDI document object, the frame window that contains the view is saved along with your data. This allows everything to be restored when you read it back. Reading and writing a document object to a file is supported by a process called **serialization**. We will be seeing in the examples we will develop how to write our own documents to file using serialization, and then reconstruct them from the file data.

The document class also includes the macro **DECLARE_MESSAGE_MAP()** in its definition to enable Windows messages to be handled by class member functions if necessary.

The view class in our SDI application is defined as:

```cpp
class CTextEditorView: public CEditView
{
protected: // create from serialization only
    CTextEditorView();
    DECLARE_DYNCREATE(CTextEditorView)

// Attributes
public:
    CTextEditorDoc* GetDocument();

// Operations
public:

// Overrides
    // ClassWizard generated virtual function overrides
    //{{AFX_VIRTUAL(CTextEditorView)
    public:
    virtual void OnDraw(CDC* pDC);  // overridden to draw this view
    virtual BOOL PreCreateWindow(CREATESTRUCT& cs);
    protected:
    virtual BOOL OnPreparePrinting(CPrintInfo* pInfo);
    virtual void OnBeginPrinting(CDC* pDC, CPrintInfo* pInfo);
    virtual void OnEndPrinting(CDC* pDC, CPrintInfo* pInfo);
    //}}AFX_VIRTUAL

// Implementation
public:
    virtual ~CTextEditorView();
#ifdef _DEBUG
    virtual void AssertValid() const;
    virtual void Dump(CDumpContext& dc) const;
#endif

protected:

// Generated message map functions
protected:
    //{{AFX_MSG(CTextEditorView)
        // NOTE - the ClassWizard will add and remove member functions here.
        //    DO NOT EDIT what you see in these blocks of generated code!
    //}}AFX_MSG
    DECLARE_MESSAGE_MAP()
};
```

As we specified in the AppWizard dialog, the view class is derived from the class **CEditView**, which already includes basic text handling facilities. The **GetDocument()** function returns a pointer to the document object corresponding to the view, and you will be using this to access data in the document object when you add your own extensions to the view class.

Comments in AppWizard Generated Code

You will probably have noticed a variety of comments in the class definitions created by AppWizard—things like **// Operations** and **// Implementation**. Before we get into adding our own code to that which AppWizard provides, let's look at what they mean. They can seem a little confusing when you're trying to work out where things fit as you start adding your own class members.

First of all, the comments are there as guidelines. They don't enforce anything on you as to where you should put your code. The only exceptions to this are the comments which quite clearly recommend against modifying code that was inserted by AppWizard. If you change or add code in such a section, you're on your own! The significance of the principal AppWizard comments within class definitions are as follows:

Comment	Meaning
// Implementation	This indicates that everything following it isn't guaranteed to be the same in the next release of Visual C++. Anything can be included in here—data members as well as function members. You can't rely on this code being the same when you move to another version of Visual C++. Of course, you can add your own code here if you want; the comment is just for information.
// Attributes	This indicates that the statements following it define properties of objects of the class—typically these will be data members of the class, but they can also be **Get()**/**Set()** types of functions that supply information about the class but don't change anything.
// Operations	The code following this comment will declare function members that act on the data members of the class, so they change the attributes of a class object in some way.
// Overrides	This defines a section of the class which declares function members that you can override in a derived class. Pure virtual functions will also appear in this section
// Constructors	Obviously, the section headed by this comment will house the class constructor declarations, but other functions that are used in the initialization of class members will also appear here

When you're modifying AppWizard-supplied classes, you can choose to add your own sections to accommodate your code. You're under no obligation to put it in the sections designated by the existing comments. We will endeavor to add code within the appropriately commented section in the remaining chapters, but it won't necessarily always fit.

Creating an Executable Module

To compile and link the program, click on Build | Build TextEditor.exe, press *F7*, or click on the build icon.

There are two implementations of the view class member function **GetDocument()** in the code generated by AppWizard. The one in the **.cpp** file for the **CEditView** class is used for the debug version of the program. You will normally use this during program development, since it provides validation of the pointer value stored for the document. (This is stored in the inherited data member **m_pDocument** in the view class.) The version that applies to the release version of your program you can find after the class definition in the **TextEditorView.h** file. This version is declared as **inline** and it does not validate the document pointer.

You will be using the **GetDocument()** function regularly as it provides a link to the document object. Using the pointer to the document, you can call any of the functions in the interface to the document class.

By default, you will have debug capability included in your program. As well as the special version of **GetDocument()**, there are lots of checks in the MFC code that are included in this case. If you want to change this, you can use the drop-down list box in the Build toolbar to choose the release configuration, which doesn't contain all the debug code.

When compiling your program with debug switched on, the compiler doesn't detect uninitialized variables, so it can be helpful to do the occasional release build even while you are still testing your program.

Precompiled Header Files

The first time you compile and link a program, it will take some time. The second and subsequent times it should be quite a bit faster because of a feature of Visual C++ called **precompiled headers**. During the initial compilation, the compiler saves the output from compiling header files in a special file with the extension **.pch**. On subsequent builds, this file is reused if the source in the headers has not changed, thus saving the compilation time for the headers.

You can determine whether or not precompiled headers are used and control how they are handled. Choose Project | Settings... and then select the C/C++ tab. From the Category: drop-down list box, select Precompiled Headers, and you'll see the dialog shown here.

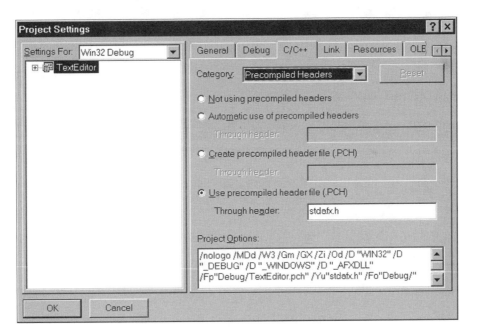

The option for automatic use of precompiled headers shown here is the easiest to apply. The **.pch** file will be generated if there isn't one, and used if there is. The option to create a **.pch** file does exactly that. The ability to specify the last header file to be included allows you to control what's included in the precompiled header. The option to use a precompiled header file presumes that one already exists. You can get more information on this through the button in the dialog.

Running the Program

To execute the program, press *Ctrl-F5*, or select the Execute option in the Build menu. Because we chose **CEditView** as the base class for our class **CTextEditorView**, the program is a fully functioning, simple text editor. You can enter text in the window as shown below.

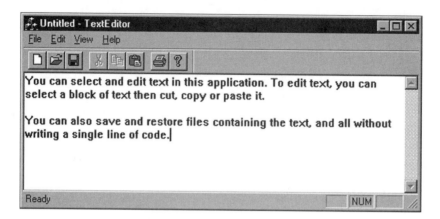

Note that the application has scroll bars for viewing text outside the visible area within the window, and of course you can resize the window by dragging the boundaries. When you save a document, it will automatically be given the extension **.ted**. All the options under the File menu are fully operational. As you move the cursor over the toolbar buttons or the menu options, prompts appear in the status bar describing the function that will be invoked, and if you let the cursor linger on a toolbar button, a tooltip will be displayed showing its purpose.

How the Program Works

As in the trivial MFC example we looked at earlier in this chapter, the application object is created at global scope in our SDI program. You can see this if you expand the Globals item in the ClassView, and then double-click on theApp. In the text editor window you'll see this statement:

```
CTextEditorApp theApp;
```

This declares the object **theApp** as an instance of our application class **CTextEditorApp**. The statement is in the file **TextEditor.cpp**, which also contains member function declarations for the application class, and the definition of the **CAboutDlg** class.

Once the object **theApp** has been created, the MFC-supplied **WinMain()** function is called. This in turn calls two member functions of the **theApp** object. First it calls **InitInstance()**, which provides for any initialization of the application that is necessary, and then **Run()**, which provides initial handling for Windows messages.

The Function InitInstance()

You can access the code for this function by double-clicking its entry in the ClassView after expanding the **CTextEditorApp** class in the Project Workspace window—or if you're in a hurry you can just look at the code immediately following the line defining the **theApp** object. The version created by AppWizard is as follows:

```
BOOL CTextEditorApp::InitInstance()
{
   AfxEnableControlContainer();

   // Standard initialization
   // If you are not using these features and wish to reduce the size
   // of your final executable, you should remove from the following
   // the specific initialization routines you do not need.

#ifdef _AFXDLL
   Enable3dControls();          // Call this when using MFC in a shared DLL
#else
   Enable3dControlsStatic();    // Call this when linking to MFC statically
#endif

   // Change the registry key under which our settings are stored.
   // You should modify this string to be something appropriate
   // such as the name of your company or organization.
   SetRegistryKey(_T("Local AppWizard-Generated Applications"));

   LoadStdProfileSettings();  // Load standard INI file options (including MRU)

   // Register the application's document templates.  Document templates
   //  serve as the connection between documents, frame windows and views.

   CSingleDocTemplate* pDocTemplate;
   pDocTemplate = new CSingleDocTemplate(
      IDR_MAINFRAME,
      RUNTIME_CLASS(CTextEditorDoc),
      RUNTIME_CLASS(CMainFrame),       // main SDI frame window
      RUNTIME_CLASS(CTextEditorView));
   AddDocTemplate(pDocTemplate);

   // Enable DDE Execute open
   EnableShellOpen();
   RegisterShellFileTypes(TRUE);

   // Parse command line for standard shell commands, DDE, file open
   CCommandLineInfo cmdInfo;
   ParseCommandLine(cmdInfo);

   // Dispatch commands specified on the command line
   if (!ProcessShellCommand(cmdInfo))
      return FALSE;

   // The one and only window has been initialized, so show and update it.
   m_pMainWnd->ShowWindow(SW_SHOW);
   m_pMainWnd->UpdateWindow();

   // Enable drag/drop open
   m_pMainWnd->DragAcceptFiles();

   return TRUE;
}
```

The string passed to the **SetRegistryKey()** function will be used to define a registry key under which program information will be stored. You can change this to whatever you want. If

I changed the argument to **"Horton"**, information about our program would be stored under the registry key

HKEY_CURRENT_USER\Software\Horton\TextEditor

All the application settings will be stored under this key, including the list of files most recently used by the program. The call to the function **LoadStdProfileSettings()** loads the application settings that were saved last time around. Of course, the first time you run the program, there aren't any.

A document template object is created dynamically within **InitInstance()** by the statement:

```
pDocTemplate = new CSingleDocTemplate(
    IDR_MAINFRAME,
    RUNTIME_CLASS(CTextEditorDoc),
    RUNTIME_CLASS(CMainFrame),          // main SDI frame window
    RUNTIME_CLASS(CTextEditorView));
```

The first parameter to the **CSingleDocTemplate** constructor is a symbol, **IDR_MAINFRAME**, which defines the menu and toolbar to be used with the document type. The following three parameters define the document, main frame window and view class objects that are to be bound together within the document template. Since we have an SDI application here, there will only ever be one of each in the program, managed through one document template object. **RUNTIME_CLASS()** is a macro that enables the type of a class object to be determined at runtime.

There's a lot of other stuff here for setting up the application instance that we need not worry about. You can add any initialization of your own that you need for the application to the **InitInstance()** function.

The Function Run()

The function **Run()** in the class **CTextEditorApp** is inherited from the application base class **CWinApp**. Because it is declared as **virtual**, you can replace the base class version of the function **Run()** with one of your own, but this is not usually necessary so you don't need to worry about it.

Run() acquires all the messages from Windows destined for the application and ensures that each message is passed to the function in the program designated to service it, if one exists. Therefore, this function continues executing as long as the application is running. It terminates when you close the application.

Thus, you can boil the operation of the application down to four steps:

1 Creating an application object, **theApp**.

2 Executing **WinMain()**, which is supplied by MFC.

3 **WinMain()** calling **InitInstance()**, which creates the document template, the main frame window, the document, and the view.

4 **WinMain()** calling **Run()**, which executes the main message loop to acquire and dispatch Windows messages.

Using AppWizard to Create an MDI Application

Now let's create an MDI application using AppWizard. Let's give it the project name **Sketcher**, as we will be expanding it into a sketching program during subsequent chapters. You should have no trouble with this procedure, as there are only three things that we need to do differently from the process that we have just gone through for the SDI application. On Step 1 you should leave the default option, MDI, rather than changing to the SDI option. Under the Advanced... button in Step 4, you should specify the file extension as **ske**, and on Step 6 you should leave the base class for the class **CSketcherView** as **CView**.

In Step 6, which is shown here, we get an extra class derived from MFC for our application:

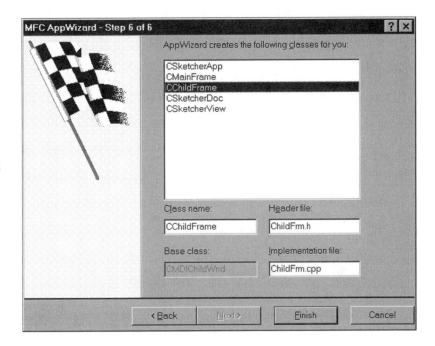

The extra class is **CChildFrame**, which is derived from the MFC class **CMDIChildWnd**. This class provides a frame window for a view of the document that will appear *inside* the application window created by a **CMainFrame** object. With an SDI application there is a single document with a single view, so the view is displayed in the client area of the main frame window. In an MDI application, we can have multiple documents open, and each document can have multiple views. To accomplish this, each view of a document in our program will have its own child frame window created by an object of the class **CChildFrame**. As we saw earlier, a view will be displayed in what is actually a separate window, but one which exactly fills the client area of a frame window.

Running the Program

You can build the program in exactly the same way as the previous example. Then, if you execute it, you will get the application window shown here:

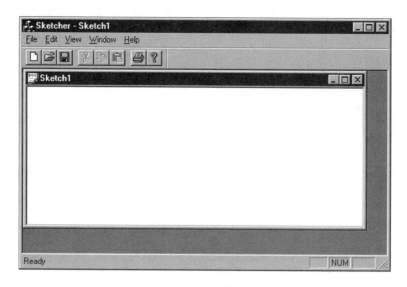

In addition to the main application window, we have a separate document window with the caption Sketch1. **Sketch1** is the default name for the initial document, and it will have the extension **.ske** if you save it. You can create additional views for the document by selecting the Window | New Window menu option. You can also create a new document by selecting File | New, so that there will be two active documents in the application. The situation with two documents active, each with two views open, is shown here:

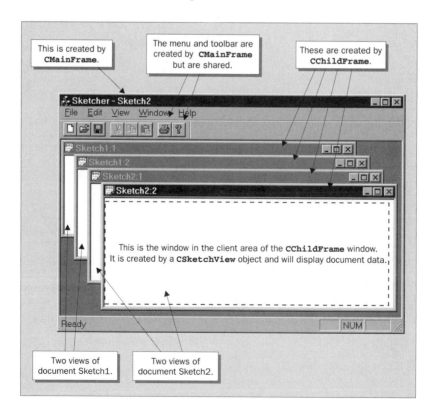

You can't yet actually create any data in the application, since we haven't added any code to do that, but all the code for creating documents and views has already been included by AppWizard.

Using the ClassWizard

We've mentioned the ClassWizard several times in this chapter. Since most of the rest of the book will be concerned with using the ClassWizard in various ways, let's make sure we have a good grasp of how we can use it. Once the AppWizard has generated the initial application code, you'll be using the ClassWizard to implement most of the additional code necessary to support your specific application needs, so a good platform for trying out how to use it in practical situations is the Sketcher program we just created.

You can invoke the ClassWizard by selecting the <u>V</u>iew | Class<u>W</u>izard... menu option, by pressing *Ctrl-W*, or easiest of all, by clicking on the toolbar button on the menu bar. If the toolbar button for the ClassWizard isn't displayed, you can add it by right-clicking on the menu bar and selecting Customize... from the pop-up.

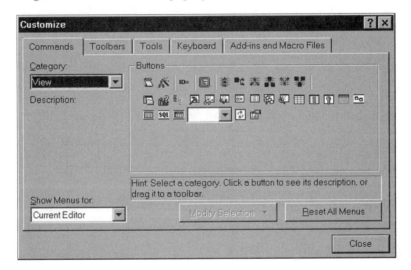

You can then drag the toolbar button from the Customize dialog to the menu bar. You can get at toolbar buttons for any of the menus by this means. When you have all the toolbar buttons you want, click on the Close button to end the dialog. If you now click on the ClassWizard button with the **Sketcher** application open, you'll get the ClassWizard dialog displayed for the current project. The dialog below shows the **Sketcher** project with the **CSketcherDoc** class selected in the right-hand drop-down list.

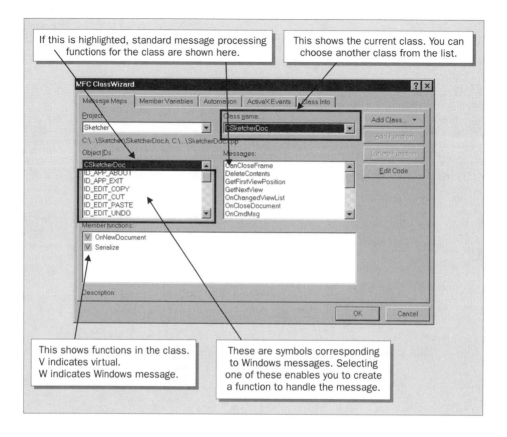

If this is highlighted, standard message processing functions for the class are shown here.

This shows the current class. You can choose another class from the list.

This shows functions in the class.
V indicates virtual.
W indicates Windows message.

These are symbols corresponding to Windows messages. Selecting one of these enables you to create a function to handle the message.

Here you can see the **Message Maps** tab, where you can add functions to the classes in your application to process specific Windows messages. The name of the current class is shown in the drop down list box at the top right. For the Object ID highlighted in the left list box, the messages applicable to it are shown in the **Messages:** list box on the right. You can also edit or delete any of the existing functions in a class. Highlighting one of the existing member functions will enable the grayed out button for **D**elete Function.

The **A**dd Class... button enables you to derive a new class in your application. This is the same dialog as you get by selecting the down arrow on the Wizard Bar and selecting **N**ew Class... from the pop-up menu. Because Sketcher uses MFC, the dialog gives you the option of deriving a class from the MFC, in addition to the possibility of creating a generic class. The other tabs in the ClassWizard dialog provide a wealth of other facilities for extending your program. We'll be going further into how we actually use the ClassWizard, starting in the very next chapter.

Although there is overlap between the functions accessible through the Wizard Bar, the class context menu, and selecting the ClassWizard toolbar button, you'll find yourself using all three, since they each have some unique abilities. If you just want to add a variable to a class for instance, the class context menu is the way to go. Of course, none of these options prevent you from modifying your source code directly. Indeed, you should be doing so from time to time, if only to make sure your code is adequately commented.

Summary

In this chapter we've been concerned mainly with the mechanics of using the AppWizard. We have looked at how a Windows program is structured, and we've taken a peek at MFC. We have also seen the basic components of MFC programs generated by the AppWizard. All our examples will be AppWizard-based, so it's a good idea to keep the general structure and broad class relationships in mind. You probably won't feel too comfortable with the detail at this point, but don't worry about that now. You'll find that it becomes much clearer once we have applied the ClassWizard and other Developer Studio tools a few times in the succeeding chapters. They'll be taking care of most of the detail automatically, and an appreciation of what fits where will become quite obvious after a bit of practice.

The key points that we have discussed in this chapter are:

▶ The AppWizard generates a complete, working, framework Windows application for you to customize to your requirements.

▶ The AppWizard can generate single document interface (SDI) applications which work with a single document and a single view, or multiple document interface (MDI) programs which can handle multiple documents and views simultaneously.

▶ The four essential classes in an SDI application that are derived from the foundation classes are:

> the application class
>
> the frame window class
>
> the document class
>
> the view class

▶ A program can have only one application object. This is defined automatically by the AppWizard at global scope.

▶ A document class object stores application-specific data and a view class object displays the contents of a document object.

▶ A document template class object is used to tie together a document, a view and a window. For an SDI application, a **CSingleDocTemplate** class does this, and for an MDI application, the **CMultiDocTemplate** class is used. These are both foundation classes and application-specific versions do not normally need to be derived.

Exercises

It isn't possible to give programming examples for this chapter, as it really just introduces the Windows programming side of the IDE. There aren't solutions to all the exercises, because the reader will either see the answer for themselves on the screen, or be able to check their answer back with the text.

Ex3-1: What is the relationship between a document and a view?

Ex3-2: What is the purpose of the document template in an MFC Windows program?

Ex3-3: Why do you need to be careful, and plan your program structure in advance, when using AppWizard?

Ex3-4: Code up the simple text editor program. Build both debug and release versions, and examine the types and sizes of the files produced in each case.

Ex3-5: Generate the text editor application several times, trying different window styles from the Advanced Options in AppWizard.

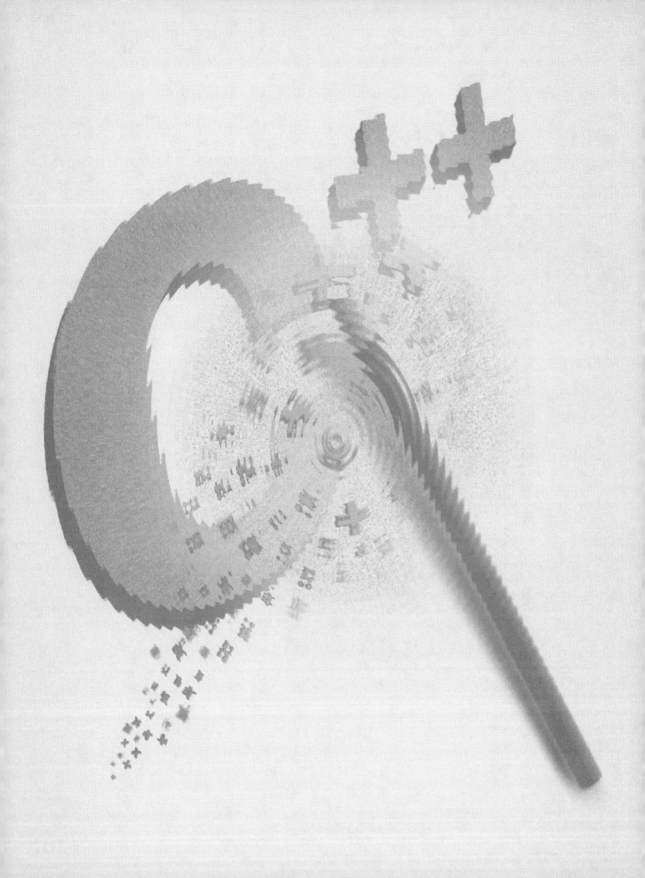

Working with Menus and Toolbars

In the last chapter, we saw how a simple framework application generated by the AppWizard is made up and how the parts interrelate. In this chapter, we'll start customizing our MDI framework application, Sketcher, with a view to making it into a useful program. The first step in this process is to understand how menus are defined in Visual C++, and how functions are created to service the application-specific menu items that we add to our program. We'll also see how to add toolbar buttons to the application. By the end of this chapter you'll have learned:

- How an MFC-based program handles messages
- What menu resources are, and how you can create and modify them
- What menu properties are, and how you can create and modify them
- How to create a function to service the message generated when a menu item is selected
- How to add handlers to update menu properties
- How to add toolbar buttons and associate them with existing menu items

Communicating with Windows

As we saw in Chapter 2, Windows communicates with your program by sending messages to it. Most of the drudgery of message handling in a Visual C++ program is taken care of by MFC, so you don't have to worry about providing a **WndProc()** function at all. MFC enables you to provide functions to handle the individual messages that you're interested in and to ignore the rest. These functions are referred to as **message handlers** or just **handlers**. Since your application is MFC-based, a message handler is always a member function of one of your application's classes.

The association between a particular message and the function in your program that is to service it is established by a **message map**—each class in your program that can handle Windows messages will have one. A message map for a class is simply a table of member functions that handle Windows messages. Each entry in the message map associates a function with a particular message; when a given message occurs, the corresponding function will be called. Only the messages that are relevant to a class will appear in the message map for the class.

A message map for a class is created automatically by AppWizard, or by ClassWizard when you add a class that handles messages to your program. Additions to, and deletions from, a message map are mainly managed by ClassWizard, but there are circumstances where you need to modify the message map manually. The start of a message map in your code is indicated by a **BEGIN_MESSAGE_MAP()** macro, and the end is marked by an **END_MESSAGE_MAP()** macro. Let's look into how a message map operates using our Sketcher example.

Understanding Message Maps

A message map is established by AppWizard for each of the main classes in your program. In the instance of an MDI program such as Sketcher, a message map will be defined for each of **CSketcherApp**, **CSketcherDoc**, **CSketcherView**, **CMainFrame** and **CChildFrame**. You can see the message map for a class in the **.cpp** file containing the implementation of the class. Of course, the functions that are included in the message map also need to be declared in the class definition, but they are identified here in a special way. Look at the definition for the **CSketcherApp** class shown here:

```
class CSketcherApp: public CWinApp
{
public:
    CSketcherApp();

// Overrides
    // ClassWizard generated virtual function overrides
    //{{AFX_VIRTUAL(CSketcherApp)
    public:
    virtual BOOL InitInstance();
    //}}AFX_VIRTUAL

// Implementation

    //{{AFX_MSG(CSketcherApp)
    afx_msg void OnAppAbout();
    // NOTE - the ClassWizard will add and remove member functions here.
    //    DO NOT EDIT what you see in these blocks of generated code!
    //}}AFX_MSG
    DECLARE_MESSAGE_MAP()
};
```

You can see the comments that indicate the start (**//{{AFX_MSG(CSketcherApp)**) and end (**// }}AFX_MSG**) of the lines in the class definition where ClassWizard will add declarations for the message handlers that you define in the class. The functions appearing here will also appear in a message map in the class implementation in the **.cpp** file for the class. In **CSketcherApp**, only one message handler, **OnAppAbout()**, is declared. The word **afx_msg** at the beginning of the line is just to distinguish a message handler from other member functions in the class. It will be converted to white space by the preprocessor, so it has no effect when the program is compiled.

The macro **DECLARE_MESSAGE_MAP()** indicates that the class can contain function members that are message handlers. In fact, any class that you derive from the MFC class **CCmdTarget** can potentially have message handlers, so such classes will have this macro included as part of the class definition by AppWizard or ClassWizard, depending on which was responsible for creating it. The diagram below shows the MFC classes derived from **CCmdTarget** that have been used in our examples so far:

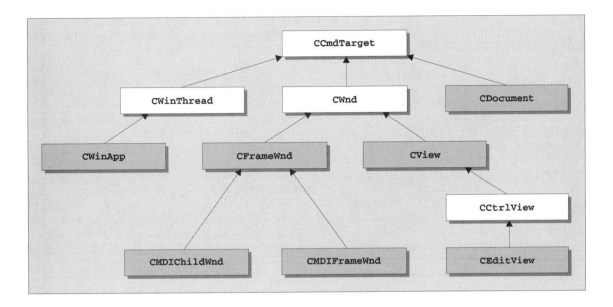

The classes that have been used directly, or as a direct base for our own application classes, are shown shaded. Thus, our class **CSketcherApp** has **CCmdTarget** as an indirect base class and, therefore, will always include the **DECLARE_MESSAGE_MAP()** macro. All of the view (and other) classes derived from **CWnd** will also have it.

If you are adding your own members to a class directly, it's best to leave the **DECLARE_MESSAGE_MAP()** macro as the last line in the class definition. If you do add members after **DECLARE_MESSAGE_MAP()**, you'll also need to include an access specifier for them: **public**, **protected**, or **private**.

Message Handler Definitions

If a class definition includes the macro **DECLARE_MESSAGE_MAP()**, the class implementation must include the macros **BEGIN_MESSAGE_MAP()** and **END_MESSAGE_MAP()**. If you look in **Sketcher.cpp**, you'll see the following code as part of the implementation of **CSketcherApp**:

```
BEGIN_MESSAGE_MAP(CSketcherApp, CWinApp)
   //{{AFX_MSG_MAP(CSketcherApp)
   ON_COMMAND(ID_APP_ABOUT, OnAppAbout)
      // NOTE - the ClassWizard will add and remove mapping macros here.
      //    DO NOT EDIT what you see in these blocks of generated code!
   //}}AFX_MSG_MAP
   // Standard file based document commands
   ON_COMMAND(ID_FILE_NEW, CWinApp::OnFileNew)
   ON_COMMAND(ID_FILE_OPEN, CWinApp::OnFileOpen)
   // Standard print setup command
   ON_COMMAND(ID_FILE_PRINT_SETUP, CWinApp::OnFilePrintSetup)
END_MESSAGE_MAP()
```

This is a message map. The **BEGIN_MESSAGE_MAP()** and **END_MESSAGE_MAP()** macros define the boundaries of the message map, and each of the message handlers in the class will appear between these macros. In the case above, the code is only handling one category of message, the type of **WM_COMMAND** message called a **command message**, which is generated when the user selects a menu option or accelerator keys. (If that seems clumsy, it's because there's another kind of **WM_COMMAND** message called a **control notification message**, as we shall see later in this chapter.)

The message map knows which menu or key is pressed by the identifier (ID) that's included in the message. There are four **ON_COMMAND** macros in the code above, one for each of the command messages to be handled. The first argument to this macro is an ID which is associated with one particular command, and the **ON_COMMAND()** macro ties the function name to the command specified by the ID. Thus, when a message corresponding to the identifier **ID_APP_ABOUT** is received, the function **OnAppAbout()** will be called. Similarly, for a message corresponding to the **ID_FILE_NEW** identifier, the function **OnFileNew()** will be called. This handler is actually defined in the base class, **CWinApp**, as are the two remaining handlers.

The **BEGIN_MESSAGE_MAP()** macro has two arguments. The first argument identifies the current class name for which the message map is defined and the second provides a connection to the base class for finding a message handler. If a handler isn't found in the class defining the message map, the message map for the base class is then searched.

Note that command IDs such as **ID_APP_ABOUT** are standard IDs defined in MFC. These correspond to messages from standard menu items and toolbar buttons. The prefix **ID_** is used to identify a command associated with a menu item or a toolbar button, as we'll see when we discuss resources later. For example, **ID_FILE_NEW** is the ID that corresponds to the File | New menu item being selected, and **ID_APP_ABOUT** corresponds to the Help | About menu option.

There are more symbols besides **WM_COMMAND** that Windows uses to identify standard messages. Each of them is prefixed with **WM_** for Windows Message. These symbols are defined in **Winuser.h**, which is included in **Windows.h**. If you want to look at them, you'll find **Winuser.h** in the **include** folder in the **VC** folder containing your Visual C++ system.

There's a nice shortcut for viewing a **.h** file. If the name of the file appears in the editor window, you can just right click on it, and select the menu item **Open "Filename.h"** from the pop-up.

Windows messages often have additional data values that are used to refine the identification of a particular message specified by a given ID. The message **WM_COMMAND**, for instance, is sent for a whole range of commands, including those originating from selecting a menu item or a toolbar button.

Note that you should not map a message (or in the case of command messages, a command ID) to more than one message handler in a class. If you do, it won't break anything, but the second message handler will never be called. Since one of the major uses of the ClassWizard is to define message handlers and make appropriate entries in the message maps in your program, this situation should not arise if you stick to using the ClassWizard. Only when you need to make message map entries manually will you need to take care not to assign more than one handler to a message.

Message Categories

There are three categories of messages that your program may be dealing with, and the category to which it belongs will determine how a message is handled. The message categories are:

Message category	Explanation
Windows messages	These are standard Windows messages that begin with the **WM_** prefix, with the exception of **WM_COMMAND** messages which we shall come to in a moment. Examples of Windows messages are **WM_PAINT**, which indicates that you need to redraw the client area of a window, and **WM_LBUTTONUP**, which signals that the left mouse button has been released.
Control notification messages	These are **WM_COMMAND** messages which are sent from controls (such as a list box) to the window that created the control, or from a child window to a parent window. Parameters associated with a **WM_COMMAND** message enable messages from the controls in your application to be differentiated.
Command messages	These are also **WM_COMMAND** messages that originate from the user interface elements, such as menu items and toolbar buttons. MFC defines unique identifiers for standard menu and toolbar command messages.

The standard Windows messages in the first category will be identified by the **WM_**-prefixed IDs that Windows defines. We'll be writing handlers for some of these messages in the next chapter. The messages in the second category are a particular group of **WM_COMMAND** messages that we'll see in Chapter 7 when we work with dialogs. We'll deal with the last category, messages originating from menus and toolbars, in this chapter. In addition to the message IDs defined by MFC for the standard menus and toolbars, you can define your own message IDs for the menus and toolbar buttons that you add to your program. If you don't supply IDs for these items, MFC will automatically generate IDs for you, based on the menu text.

Handling Messages in Your Program

You can't put a handler for a message anywhere you like. The permitted sites for a handler depend on what kind of message is to be processed. The first two categories of message that we saw above, that is, standard Windows messages and control notification messages, are always handled by objects of classes derived from **CWnd**. Frame window classes and view classes, for example, are derived from **CWnd**, so they can have member functions to handle Windows messages and control notification messages. Application classes, document classes and document template classes are not derived from **CWnd**, so they can't handle these messages.

Using the ClassWizard solves the headache of remembering where to place handlers, as it will only give you the options that are allowed. For example, if you select **CSketcherDoc** as the Class name:, you won't be offered any of the **WM_** messages.

For standard Windows messages, the class **CWnd** provides default message handling. Thus, if your derived class doesn't include a handler for a standard Windows message, it will be processed by the default handler defined in the base class. If you do provide a handler in your class, you'll sometimes still need to call the base class handler as well, so that the message will be processed properly. When you're creating your own handler, ClassWizard will provide a skeleton implementation of it, which will include a call to the base handler where necessary.

Handling command messages is much more flexible. You can put handlers for these in the application class, the document and document template classes, and of course in the window and view classes in your program. So, what happens when a command message is sent to your application, bearing in mind there are a lot of options as to where it is handled?

How Command Messages are Processed

All command messages are sent to the main frame window for the application. The main frame window then tries to get the message handled by routing it in a specific sequence to the classes in your program. If one class can't process the message, it passes it on to the next.

For an SDI program, the sequence in which classes are offered an opportunity to handle a command message is:

1 The view object

2 The document object

3 The document template object

4 The main frame window object

5 The application object

The view object is given the opportunity to handle a command message first and, if no handler has been defined, the next class object has a chance to process it. If none of the classes has a handler defined, default Windows processing takes care of it, essentially throwing the message away.

For an MDI program, things are only a little more complicated. Although we have the possibility of multiple documents, each with multiple views, only the active view and its associated document are involved in the routing of a command message. The sequence for routing a command message in an MDI program is:

1 The active view object

2 The document object associated with the active view

3 The document template object for the active document

4 The frame window object for the active view

5 The main frame window object

6 The application object

It's possible to alter the sequence for routing messages, but this is so rarely necessary that we won't go into it in this book.

Extending the Sketcher Program

We're going to add code to the Sketcher program we created in the last chapter to implement the functionality we need to create sketches. We'll provide code for drawing lines, circles, rectangles and curves with various colors and line thicknesses, and for adding annotations to a sketch. The data for a sketch will be stored in a document, and we'll also allow multiple views of the same document at different scales.

It will take us several chapters to add everything we need, but a good starting point would be to add menu items to deal with the types of elements that we want to be able to draw, and to select a color for drawing. We'll make both the element type and color selection persistent in the program, which means that having selected a color and an element type, both of these will remain in effect until we change one or other of them.

The steps that we'll work through to add menus to Sketcher are:

- Define the menu items to appear on the main menu bar and in each of the menus.
- Decide which of the classes in our application should handle the message for each menu item.
- Add message handling functions to the classes for our menu messages.
- Add functions to the classes to update the appearance of the menus to show the current selection in effect.
- Add a toolbar button complete with tooltips for each of our menu items.

Elements of a Menu

We'll be looking at two aspects of dealing with menus in Visual C++: the creation and modification of the menu as it appears in your application, and the processing that is necessary when a particular menu item is selected—the definition of a message handler for it. We can look at creating the menu items first.

Creating and Editing Menu Resources

Menus are defined external to the program code in a **resource file** and the specification of the menu is referred to as a **resource**. There are several other kinds of resources that you can include in your application, such as dialogs, toolbars and icons. You'll be seeing more on these as we extend our application.

Having a menu defined in a resource allows the physical appearance of the menu to be changed without affecting the code that processes menu events. For example, you could change your menu items from English to French, or Norwegian, or whatever, without having to modify or recompile the program code. The code to handle the message created when the user selects a menu item doesn't need to be concerned with how the menu looks, only with the fact that it was selected. Of course, if you *add* items to the menu, you'll need to add some code for each of them to ensure that they actually do something!

The Sketcher program already has a menu, which means that it already has a resource file. We can access the resource file contents for the Sketcher program by selecting the ResourceView in the workspace window, or if you have the FileView displayed, by double-clicking **Sketcher.rc**. This will switch you to the ResourceView and display the resources. If you expand the menu resource, you'll see that there are two menus defined, indicated by the identifiers **IDR_MAINFRAME** and **IDR_SKETCHTYPE**. The first of these applies when there are no documents open in the application, and the second when we have one or more documents open. MFC uses the prefix **IDR_** to identify a resource which defines a complete menu for a window.

We're only going to be modifying the menu which has the identifier **IDR_SKETCHTYPE**. We don't need to look at **IDR_MAINFRAME**, as our new menu items will only be relevant when a document is open. You can invoke a resource editor for the menu by double-clicking its menu ID. If you do this for **IDR_SKETCHTYPE**, you'll see the window shown here:

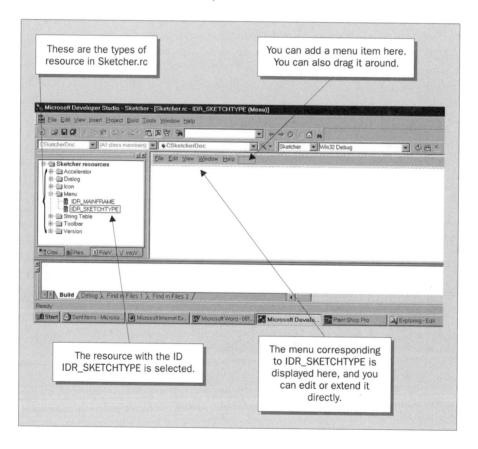

These are the types of resource in Sketcher.rc

You can add a menu item here. You can also drag it around.

The resource with the ID IDR_SKETCHTYPE is selected.

The menu corresponding to IDR_SKETCHTYPE is displayed here, and you can edit or extend it directly.

Adding a Menu Item to the Menu Bar

To add a new menu item, you can just click on the empty menu box to select it and type in the menu name. If you insert **&** in front of a letter in the menu item, the letter will be identified as a shortcut key to invoke the menu from the keyboard. Type the first menu item as E&lement. This will select l as the shortcut letter, so we can invoke the menu item by typing *Alt-l*. We can't use E because it's already used by Edit. As soon as you begin typing, the menu item properties box will appear, as shown here:

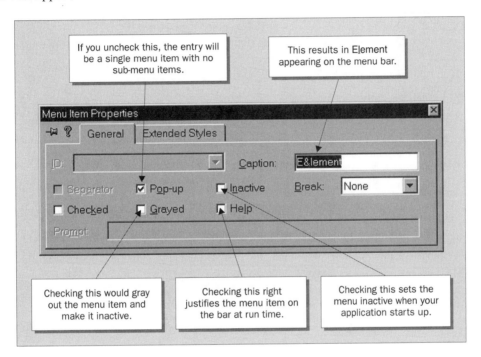

Properties are simply parameters that determine how the menu item will appear and behave. Since we want to create a menu containing the list of elements that we'll have in our program, we can leave everything as it is, so you can just press *Enter*. No ID is necessary for a pop-up menu item, since selecting it just displays the menu beneath. Note that you get a new blank menu box for the first item of the new menu, as well as one on the main menu bar.

It would be better if the Element menu appeared between the View and Window items, so place the cursor on the Element menu item and, with the left mouse button pressed, drag it to a position between the View and Window items. Then release the left mouse button. After positioning the new Element menu item, the next step is to add items on the menu beneath it.

Adding Items to the Element Menu

Select the first (currently empty) item in the Element menu by clicking on it, then type &Line as the Caption: in the Menu Item Properties dialog, as shown here:

117

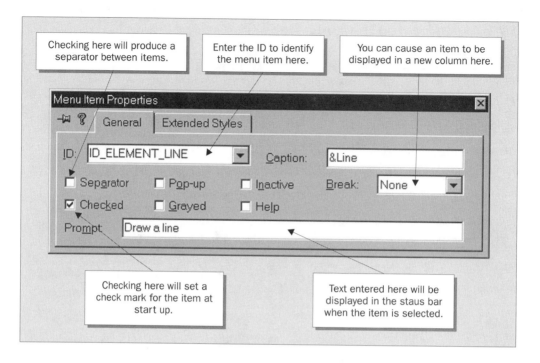

The properties modify the appearance of the menu item and also specify the ID of the message that will be passed to your program when the menu item is selected. Because this item is part of a pop-up menu, it isn't identified as a pop-up item by default, although you could make it another pop-up with a further list of items, in which case you would need to check the Pop-up box. Don't you love the way pop-ups pop up all over the place?

Defining Menu Item Properties

You can enter an ID for the menu item in the ID: box, as shown above. If you don't, one will be generated for you automatically, based on the menu item name. Sometimes, though, it's convenient to specify the ID yourself, such as when the generated ID is too long or its meaning is unclear. If you do choose to define your own ID, you should use the MFC convention of prefixing it with **ID_** to indicate that it's a command ID for a menu item. We can use the same format for each of the Element menu item IDs, in this case starting the ID with **ID_ELEMENT_**. The ID will identify the message created when the user selects the menu item, so you'll see it as an entry in the message map for the class handling the messages from the Element menu items.

In the Prompt: box, you can enter a text string that will appear in the status bar of your application when the menu item is highlighted. If you leave it blank, nothing is displayed in the status bar. We want the default element selected in the application at start up to be a line, so we can check the Checked box to get a check mark against the menu item to indicate this. We'll have to remember to add code to update check marks for the menu items when a different selection is made. The Break: entry can alter the appearance of the pop-up by shifting the item into a new column. We don't need that here, so leave it as it is. Press *Enter* to move to the next menu item.

Modifying Existing Menu Items

If you think that you may have made a mistake and want to change an existing menu item, or even if you just want to verify that you set the properties correctly, it's very easy to go back to an item. Just double-click the item you're interested in and the properties box for that item will be displayed. You can then change the properties in any way that you want and press *Enter* when you're done. If the item you want to access is in a menu that isn't displayed, just click on the item on the menu bar for the pop-up to be displayed.

Completing the Menu

Now go through the remaining Element menu items we need: &Rectangle, &Circle, and Cur&ve. Of course, none of these should have the Checked box checked. We can't use C as the hotkey for the last item, as hotkeys must be unique and we've already assigned C to the menu item for a circle. You can use the default IDs **ID_ELEMENT_RECTANGLE**, **ID_ELEMENT_CIRCLE**, and **ID_ELEMENT_CURVE** for these.

We also need a Color menu on the menu bar, with items for Black, Red, Green, and Blue. You can create these, starting at the empty menu entry on the menu bar, using the same procedure that we just went through. Set Black as checked, as that will be the default color. You can use the default IDs (**ID_COLOR_BLACK**, etc.) as the IDs for the menu items. You can also add the status bar prompt for each. Once you've finished that, if you drag Color so that it's just to the right of Element, the menu should appear as shown here:

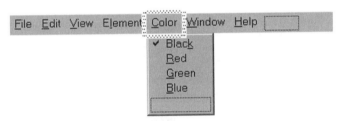

Note that you need to take care not to use the same letter more than once as a shortcut in the pop-up, or in the main menu for that matter. There's no check made as you create new menu items, but if you click the right mouse button with the cursor on the menu when you've edited it, you'll get a pop-up which contains an item Check Mnemonics. Selecting this will verify that you have no duplicate shortcut keys. It's a good idea to do this every time you edit a menu because it's very easy to create duplicates by accident.

That completes extending the menu for elements and colors. Don't forget to save the file to make sure that the additions are safely stored away. Next, we need to decide in which classes we want to deal with messages from our menu items, and add member functions to handle each of the messages. For that, we'll use the ClassWizard.

Using ClassWizard for Menu Messages

You're spoilt for choice for starting ClassWizard. You can invoke it from where we are (the Resource Editor for menus) by right-clicking in the right-hand pane and selecting ClassWizard... from the pop-up. Alternatively, you can enter *Ctrl-W* from the keyboard, or you can select it from the View menu. You'll see the ClassWizard window as shown here:

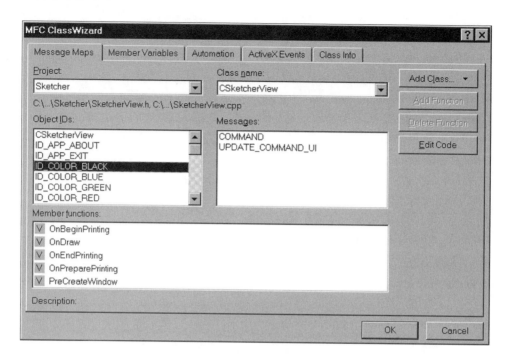

We'll concentrate on **Message Maps**, so ignore the other tabs for the moment. The contents of the five boxes on this tab are fairly self-explanatory:

Control	Use
Project:	Identifies the current project.
Class name:	Identifies the class that we're currently working on.
Object IDs:	Lists the IDs for which we can add handlers to the current class.
Messages:	Identifies the message types available for a particular object ID. (In the screenshot above, as we've selected a command ID, we have the option of choosing **COMMAND** or **UPDATE_COMMAND_UI**. We'll see the difference between these two message types later in this chapter.)
Member functions:	Lists the message handlers already defined in the current class.

You can see that the IDs we assigned to our menu items appear in the **Object IDs:** box. If you change to any of the other classes in the program by selecting from the drop-down list in the **Class name:** box, you'll see that the IDs for our new menu items appear there too. Because the menu items result in command messages, we can choose to handle them in any of the classes that are currently defined in the application. So how do we decide where we should process the messages?

Choosing a Class to Handle Menu Messages

Before we can decide which class should handle the messages for the menu items we've added, we must know what we want to do with the messages, so let's consider that.

We want the element type and the element color to be modal—that is, whatever is set for the element type and element color should remain in effect until one or other is changed. This will allow you to create as many blue circles as you want, and when you want red circles, you just change the color. We have two basic possibilities for handling the setting of a color and the selection of an element type: setting them by view or by document. We could set them by view, in which case, if there's more than one view of a document, each view will have its own color and element set. This would mean that we might draw a red circle in one view, switch to another view, and find that we're drawing a blue rectangle. This would be rather confusing, and in conflict with how we want them to work.

It would be better, therefore, to have the current color and element selection apply to a document. We can then switch from one view to another and continue drawing the same elements in the same color. There might be other differences between the views that we might implement, such as the scale at which the document is displayed perhaps, but the drawing operation will be consistent across multiple views.

This suggests that we should store the current color and element in the document object. These could then be accessed by any view object associated with the document object. Of course, if we had more than one document active, each document would have its own color and element type settings. It would, therefore, be sensible to handle the messages for our new menu items in the **CSketcherDoc** class and to store information about the current selections in an object of this class.

Creating Menu Message Functions

Switch the class shown in the ClassWizard Class name: box to CSketcherDoc and click on ID_COLOR_BLACK in the Object IDs: list. The window should appear as shown overleaf.

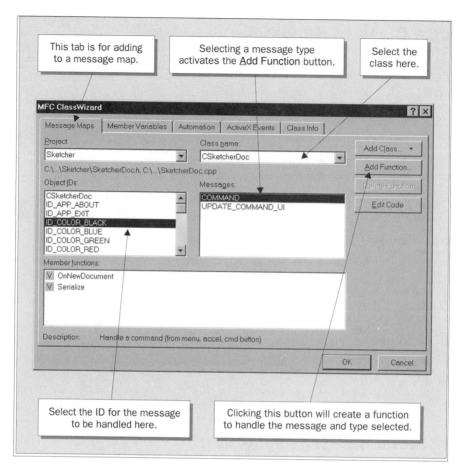

This tab is for adding to a message map.

Selecting a message type activates the Add Function button.

Select the class here.

Select the ID for the message to be handled here.

Clicking this button will create a function to handle the message and type selected.

The Messages: box in the window above shows, for a particular menu ID, the two kinds of message that can arise. They serve distinct purposes in dealing with a menu item:

Message	When Issued
COMMAND	This is issued when a particular menu item has been selected. The handler should provide the action appropriate to the menu item being selected, for example, setting the current color in the document object.
UPDATE_COMMAND_UI	This is issued when the menu should be updated—checked or unchecked, for example—depending on its status. This message occurs before a pop-up menu is displayed so you can set the appearance of the menu item before the user sees it.

The way these work is quite simple. When you click on a menu item in the menu bar, an UPDATE_COMMAND_UI message is sent for each item in that menu before the menu is displayed. This provides the opportunity to do any necessary updating of the menu items' properties. When these messages have been handled and any changes to the items' properties have been completed, the menu is drawn. When you then click on one of the items in the menu, a COMMAND message for that menu item is sent. We'll deal with the COMMAND messages for now, and come back to the UPDATE_COMMAND_UI messages a little later in this chapter.

With the ID_COLOR_BLACK object highlighted and COMMAND selected in the Messages: box, click on the button Add Function.... This is the window you'll see:

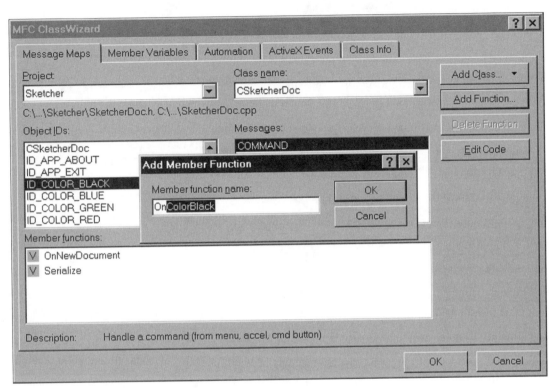

Here, the ClassWizard is about to generate a handler function in the class **CSketcherDoc** with the name shown. You have an opportunity to alter the function name, but this is a good choice so click on the OK button to accept it. This function will be added to the Member functions: box, and the message ID and the type of message that this handler will deal with will also be shown.

In the same way, add COMMAND message handlers for the other color menu IDs and all the element menu IDs. You can create each of the handler functions for the menu items with just four mouse clicks.

ClassWizard will have added the handlers to the class definition, which will now look like this:

```
class CSketcherDoc: public CDocument
{
...
   protected:

   // Generated message map functions
   protected:
```

```
        //{{AFX_MSG(CSketcherDoc)
        afx_msg void OnColorBlack();
        afx_msg void OnColorBlue();
        afx_msg void OnColorGreen();
        afx_msg void OnColorRed();
        afx_msg void OnElementCircle();
        afx_msg void OnElementCurve();
        afx_msg void OnElementLine();
        afx_msg void OnElementRectangle();
        //}}AFX_MSG
        DECLARE_MESSAGE_MAP()
    };
```

A declaration has been added for each of the handlers that we've specified in the ClassWizard dialog. Each of the function declarations has been prefixed with **afx_msg** to indicate that it is a message handler.

The ClassWizard also automatically updates the message map in your **CSketcherDoc** class with the new message handlers. If you take a look in the file **SketcherDoc.cpp**, you'll see the message map is as shown below:

```
    BEGIN_MESSAGE_MAP(CSketcherDoc, CDocument)
      //{{AFX_MSG_MAP(CSketcherDoc)
      ON_COMMAND(ID_COLOR_BLACK, OnColorBlack)
      ON_COMMAND(ID_COLOR_BLUE, OnColorBlue)
      ON_COMMAND(ID_COLOR_GREEN, OnColorGreen)
      ON_COMMAND(ID_COLOR_RED, OnColorRed)
      ON_COMMAND(ID_ELEMENT_CIRCLE, OnElementCircle)
      ON_COMMAND(ID_ELEMENT_CURVE, OnElementCurve)
      ON_COMMAND(ID_ELEMENT_LINE, OnElementLine)
      ON_COMMAND(ID_ELEMENT_RECTANGLE, OnElementRectangle)
      //}}AFX_MSG_MAP
    END_MESSAGE_MAP()
```

The ClassWizard has added an **ON_COMMAND()** macro for each of the handlers that you have identified. This associates the handler name with the message ID, so, for example, the member function **OnColorBlack()** will be called to service a COMMAND message for the menu item with the ID **ID_COLOR_BLACK**.

Each of the handlers generated by ClassWizard is just a skeleton. For example, take a look at the code provided for **OnColorBlack()**. This is also defined in the file **SketcherDoc.cpp**, so you can scroll down to find it, or go directly to it by switching to the ClassView and double-clicking the function name after expanding the tree for the class **CSketcherDoc** (make sure that the file is saved first):

```
    void CSketcherDoc::OnColorBlack()
    {
        // TODO: Add your command handler code here

    }
```

As you can see, the handler takes no arguments and returns nothing. It also does nothing at the moment, but this is hardly surprising since ClassWizard has no way of knowing what you want to do with these messages!

Coding Menu Message Functions

Let's consider what we should do with the COMMAND messages for our new menu items. We said earlier that we want to record the current element and color in the document, so we need a data member added to the **CSketcherDoc** class for each of these.

Adding Members to Store Color and Element Mode

You can add the data members that we need to the 'Attributes' section of the **CSketcherDoc** class definition, just by editing the class definition directly. Display the class definition by double-clicking the class name in the ClassView, then insert the code shown here:

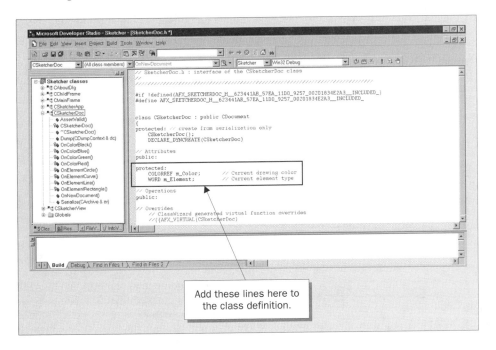

The three additional lines are shown in the box. The new data members are **m_Color** and **m_Element**. We've prefixed their names with **m_** to show that they are members of a class. **m_Element** is declared to be of type **WORD**, which is equivalent to **unsigned int**. We'll see why this is a good choice when we come to look into how to save a document in a file. The type for **m_Color** is **COLORREF**, a Windows-defined type that is used to represent color values. It's a 32-bit integer. We'll be able to use this value directly to set the color when we get to draw elements in a view. Both the new data members are **protected** because there is no need for them to be **public**. As we saw when we discussed classes, data members shouldn't be declared as **public** unless it's absolutely necessary, as this undermines the security of the class.

You could also have added these data members by right-clicking the class name in ClassView and selecting Add Member Variable... from the pop-up. You can add the information necessary to define these data members in the dialog box that is displayed. Of course, if you want to add comments—and it's a good idea to do so—you must still go back to the class definition to insert them.

Initializing the New Class Data Members

We need to decide how to represent a color and an element. We could just set them to numeric values, but this would introduce 'magic numbers' into the program, the significance of which would be less than obvious to anyone else looking at the code. A better way would be to define a set of constants that we can use to set values for the two member variables we have added. In this way, we can use a standard mnemonic to refer to a given type of element. We could define the element types with the following statements:

```
// Element type definitions
// Each type value must be unique
const WORD LINE = 101U;
const WORD RECTANGLE = 102U;
const WORD CIRCLE = 103U;
const WORD CURVE = 104U;
```

The constants initializing the element types are arbitrary unsigned integers. You can choose different values if you like, as long as they are all distinct. If we want to add further types in the future, it will obviously be very easy to add definitions here.

For the color values, it would be a good idea if we used constant variables that are initialized with the values that Windows uses to define the color in question. We can do this with the following lines of code:

```
// Color values for drawing
const COLORREF BLACK = RGB(0,0,0);
const COLORREF RED = RGB(255,0,0);
const COLORREF GREEN = RGB(0,255,0);
const COLORREF BLUE = RGB(0,0,255);
```

Each constant is initialized by **RGB()**, which is a standard macro defined in the file **Wingdi.h**, included as part of **Windows.h**. The three arguments define the red, green, and blue components of the color value respectively. Each parameter is an integer between 0 and 255, where these limits correspond to no color component and the maximum color component. **RGB(0,0,0)** corresponds to black, since there are no components of red, green, or blue. **RGB(255,0,0)** creates a color value with a maximum red component, and no green or blue contribution. Other colors can be created by combining red, green and blue components.

We need somewhere to put these constants, so let's create a new header file and call it **OurConstants.h**. You can create a new file by using the File | New menu option in Developer Studio, then entering the constant definitions as shown here:

```
//Definitions of constants

#if !defined(OurConstants_h)
#define OurConstants_h

   // Element type definitions
   // Each type value must be unique
   const WORD LINE = 101U;
   const WORD RECTANGLE = 102U;
   const WORD CIRCLE = 103U;
   const WORD CURVE = 104U;
   /////////////////////////////////////
```

```
   // Color values for drawing
   const COLORREF BLACK = RGB(0,0,0);
   const COLORREF RED = RGB(255,0,0);
   const COLORREF GREEN = RGB(0,255,0);
   const COLORREF BLUE = RGB(0,0,255);
   ////////////////////////////////////////

#endif //!defined(OurConstants.h)
```

As you'll recall, the pre-processor directive **#if !defined** is there to ensure that the definitions aren't included more than once. The block of statements down to **#endif** will only be included if **OurConstants_h** hasn't been defined previously.

After saving the file, you can add the following **#include** statement to the beginning of the file **Sketcher.h**:

```
#include "OurConstants.h"
```

Sketcher.h is included into the other **.cpp** files in the program, so our constants will be available to any of them. To ensure Developer Studio displays the new file in FileView, you need to add the file to the header files folder. Right click on Header Files in FileView and select Add Files to Folder... from the pop-up. Then enter the name **OurConstants.h** in the dialog. You can verify that our new constants are now part of the project by expanding Globals in the ClassView. You'll see the names of the color and element types that have been added, along with the global variable **theApp**.

Modifying the Class Constructor

It's important that we make sure that the data members we have added to the **CSketcherDoc** class are initialized when a document is created. You can add the code to do this to the class constructor as shown here:

```
CSketcherDoc::CSketcherDoc()
{
   // TODO: add one-time construction code here
   m_Element = LINE;   // Set initial element type
   m_Color = BLACK;    // Set initial drawing color
}
```

The element type is initialized with **LINE** and the color with **BLACK**, consistent with the initial check marks that we specified for the menus.

Now we're ready to add the code for the handler functions that we created. We can do this with the ClassView. Click on the name of the first handler function, **OnColorBlack()**. We just need to add one line to the function, so the code for it becomes:

```
void CSketcherDoc::OnColorBlack()
{
   m_Color = BLACK;           // Set the drawing color to black
}
```

The only job that the handler has to do is to set the appropriate color. In the interests of conciseness, the new line replaces the comment provided by ClassWizard. You can go through and add one line to each of the Color menu handlers.

The element menu handlers are much the same. The handler for the Element | Line menu item will be:

```
void CSketcherDoc::OnElementLine()
{
    m_Element = LINE;           // Set element type as a line
}
```

With this model, it's not too difficult to write the other handlers for the Element menu. That's eight message handlers completed. Let's rebuild the example and see how it works.

Running the Extended Example

Assuming that there are no typos, the compiled and linked program should run without error. When you run the program you should see the window shown here:

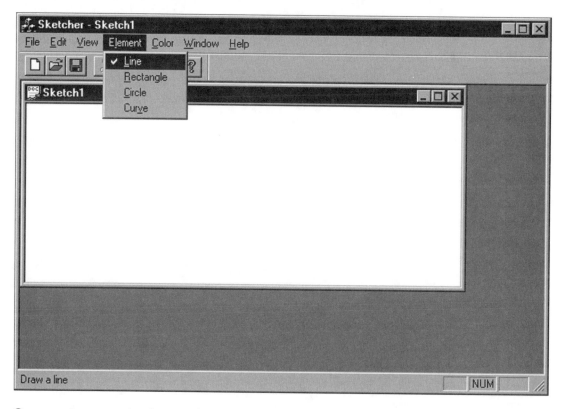

Our new menus are in place on the menu bar, and you can see that the items we have added in the Element menu are all there, as is the message in the status bar that we provided in the properties box. You could also verify that *Alt-C* and *Alt-l* work as well. The things that don't work are the check marks for the currently selected color and element, which remain firmly stuck to their initial defaults. Let's look at how we can fix that.

Adding Message Handlers to Update the User Interface

To set the check mark correctly for the new menus, we need to add the second kind of message handler, UPDATE_COMMAND_UI (or update command user interface), for each of the new menu items. This sort of message handler is specifically aimed at updating the menu item properties before the item is displayed.

Let's go back to the ClassWizard. Make sure that the Class name: box shows CSketcherDoc first, then select ID_COLOR_BLACK in the Object IDs: box and UPDATE_COMMAND_UI in the Messages: box. You'll be able to click on the Add Function... button and see the window shown below:

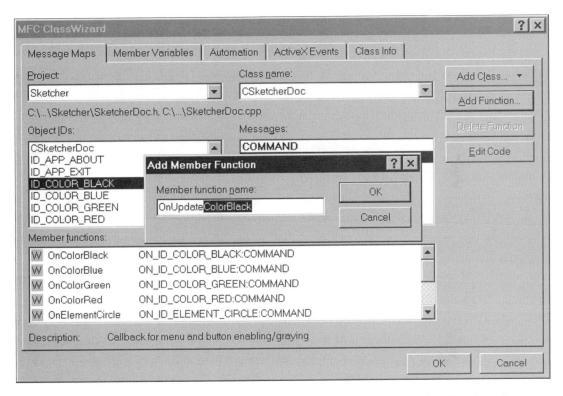

You can see the description of the purpose of the function below the Member functions: box. This description fits our requirement precisely. The name for an update function has been generated, **OnUpdateColorBlack()**, and since this seems a reasonable name for the function we want, click on the OK button and have ClassWizard generate it. As well as generating the skeleton function definition in **SketcherDoc.cpp**, its declaration will be added to the class definition. An entry for it will also be made in the message map:

```
ON_UPDATE_COMMAND_UI(ID_COLOR_BLACK, OnUpdateColorBlack)
```

This uses the macro **ON_UPDATE_COMMAND_UI()**, which identifies the function you have just generated as the handler to deal with update messages corresponding to the ID shown. You can now add command update handlers for each of the seven other menu items.

Coding a Command Update Handler

You can access the code for the handler, `OnUpdateColorBlack()`, by selecting the appropriate line in the Member functions box, and then clicking the Edit Code button. This is the skeleton code for the function:

```
void CSketcherDoc::OnUpdateColorBlack(CCmdUI* pCmdUI)
{
    // TODO: Add your command update UI handler code here

}
```

The argument passed to the handler is a pointer to an object of the `CCmdUI` class. This is an MFC class that is only used with update handlers. The pointer points to an object that identifies the particular menu item originating the update message and can be used to access members of the class object. The class has five member functions that act on user interface items. The purpose of each of these are:

Method	Purpose
`ContinueRouting()`	Pass the message on to the next priority handler.
`Enable()`	Enable or disable the relevant interface item.
`SetCheck()`	Set a check mark for the relevant interface item.
`SetRadio()`	Set a button in a radio group on or off.
`SetText()`	Set the text for the relevant interface item.

We'll use the third function, `SetCheck()`, as that seems to do what we want. The function is declared in the `CCmdUI` class as:

```
virtual void SetCheck(int nCheck = 1);
```

This function will set a menu item as checked if the argument passed is 1, and set it unchecked if the argument passed is 0. The parameter has a default value of 1, so if you just want to set a check mark for a menu item regardless, you can call this function without specifying an argument.

In our case, we want to set a menu item as checked if it corresponds with the current color. We can, therefore, write the update handler for `OnUpdateColorBlack()` as:

```
void CSketcherDoc::OnUpdateColorBlack(CCmdUI* pCmdUI)
{
    // Set menu item Checked if the current color is black
    pCmdUI->SetCheck(m_Color==BLACK);
}
```

The first part of the statement, `pCmdUI->SetCheck`, calls the `SetCheck()` function of the Color | Black menu item, while the comparison `m_Color==BLACK` results in 1 if `m_Color` is `BLACK`, or 0 otherwise. The effect, therefore, is to check the menu item only if the current color stored in `m_Color` is `BLACK`, which is precisely what we want.

Since the update handlers for all the menu items in a menu are always called before the menu is displayed, you can code the other handlers in the same way to ensure that only the item corresponding to the current color (or the current element) will be checked:

```
void CSketcherDoc::OnUpdateColorBlue(CCmdUI* pCmdUI)
{
   // Set menu item Checked if the current color is blue
   pCmdUI->SetCheck(m_Color==BLUE);
}

void CSketcherDoc::OnUpdateColorGreen(CCmdUI* pCmdUI)
{
   // Set menu item Checked if the current color is green
   pCmdUI->SetCheck(m_Color==GREEN);
}

void CSketcherDoc::OnUpdateColorRed(CCmdUI* pCmdUI)
{
   // Set menu item Checked if the current color is red
   pCmdUI->SetCheck(m_Color==RED);
}
```

A typical Element menu item update handler will be coded as:

```
void CSketcherDoc::OnUpdateElementCircle(CCmdUI* pCmdUI)
{
   // Set Checked if the current element is a circle
   pCmdUI->SetCheck(m_Element==CIRCLE);
}
```

You can now code all the other update handlers in a similar manner:

```
void CSketcherDoc::OnUpdateElementCurve(CCmdUI* pCmdUI)
{
   // Set Checked if the current element is a curve
   pCmdUI->SetCheck(m_Element==CURVE);
}

void CSketcherDoc::OnUpdateElementLine(CCmdUI* pCmdUI)
{
   // Set Checked if the current element is a line
   pCmdUI->SetCheck(m_Element==LINE);
}

void CSketcherDoc::OnUpdateElementRectangle(CCmdUI* pCmdUI)
{
   // Set Checked if the current element is a rectangle
   pCmdUI->SetCheck(m_Element==RECTANGLE);
}
```

Once you get the idea, it's easy, isn't it?

Exercising the Update Handlers

When you've added the code for all the update handlers, you can build and execute the Sketcher application again. Now, when you change a color or an element type selection, this will be reflected in the menu, as shown below:

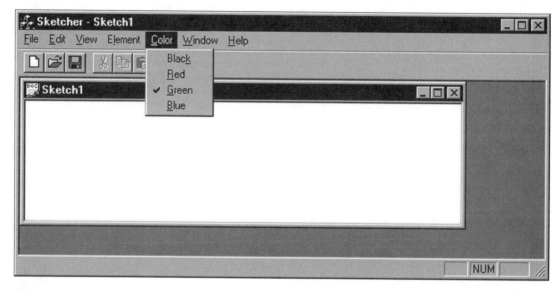

We've completed all the code that we need for our menu items. Make sure that you have saved everything before embarking on the next stage. These days, toolbars are a must in any Windows program of consequence, so we should now take a look at how we can add toolbar buttons to support our new menus.

Adding Toolbar Buttons

Select the ResourceView and extend the toolbar resource. You'll see that it has the same ID as the main menu, **IDR_MAINFRAME**. If you double-click this ID, the Resource Editor window will be as shown below:

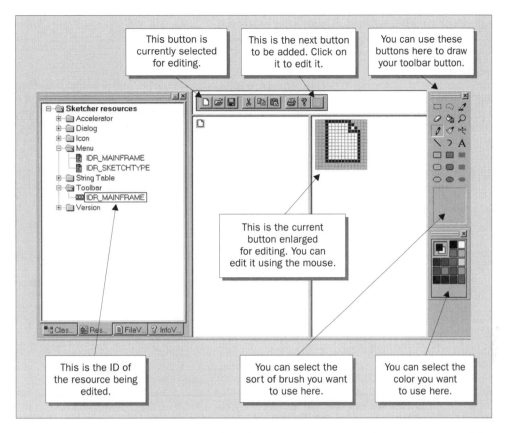

A toolbar button is a 16x15 array of pixels which contains a pictorial representation of the function it operates. You can see above that the resource editor provides an enlarged view of a toolbar button so that you can see and manipulate individual pixels. If you click on the new button at the right-hand end of the row as indicated, you'll be able to draw this button. Before starting the editing, drag the new button about half a button width to the right. It will separate from its neighbor on the left to start a new block.

We should keep the toolbar button blocks in the same sequence as the items on the menu bar, so we'll create the element type selection buttons first. We'll be using the following editing buttons provided by the resource editor:

Pencil for drawing individual pixels

Eraser for erasing individual pixels

Fill an area with the current color

Zoom the view of the button

Draw a rectangle

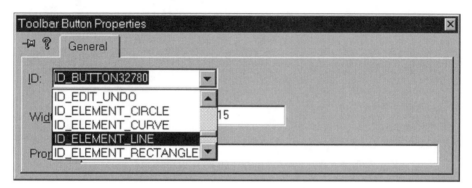

Draw an ellipse

Draw a curve

Make sure that the black color is selected and use the pencil tool to draw a diagonal line in the enlarged image of the new toolbar button. In fact, if you want it a bit bigger, you can use the 'zoom' editing button to enlarge it up to eight times its actual size. If you make a mistake, you can change to the eraser editing button, but you need to make sure that the color selected corresponds to the background color for the button you are editing. You can also erase individual pixels by clicking on them using the right mouse button, but again you need to be sure that the background color is set correctly when you do this. To set the background color, just click on the appropriate color using the right mouse button. Once you're happy with what you've drawn, the next step is to edit the toolbar button properties.

Editing Toolbar Button Properties

Double-clicking your new button in the toolbar will bring up its properties window:

The properties box will show a default ID for the button, but we want to associate the button with the menu item Element | Line that we've already defined, so select ID_ELEMENT_LINE from the drop-down box. You'll find that this will also cause the same prompt to appear in the status bar, because the prompt is recorded along with the ID. You can press *Enter* to complete the button definition.

You can now go on to designing the other three element buttons. You can use the rectangle editing button to draw a rectangle and the ellipse button to draw a circle. You can draw a curve using the pencil to set individual pixels, or use the curve button. You need to associate each button with the ID corresponding to the equivalent menu item that we defined earlier.

Now add the buttons for the colors. You should also drag the first button for selecting a color to the right, so that it starts a new group of buttons. You could keep the color buttons very simple and just color the whole button with the color it selects. You can do this by selecting the appropriate foreground color, then selecting the 'fill' editing button and clicking on the enlarged button image. Again you need to use **ID_COLOR_BLACK**, **ID_COLOR_RED**, etc., as IDs for the buttons. The toolbar editing window should look like the one shown here:

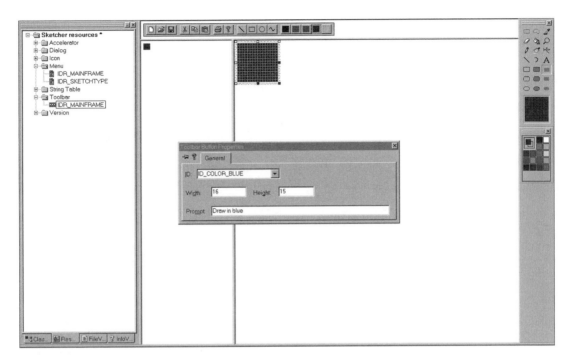

That's all we need for the moment, so save the resource file and give Sketcher another spin.

Exercising the Toolbar Buttons

Build the application once again and execute it. You should see the application window shown below:

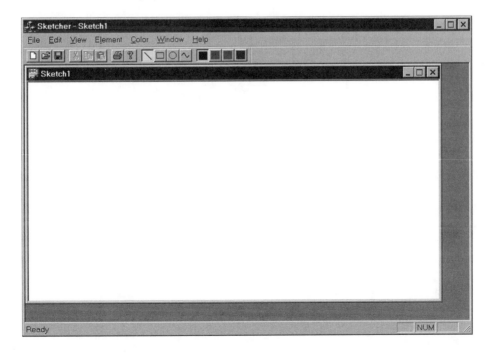

There are some amazing things happening here. The toolbar buttons that we added already reflect the default settings that we defined for the new menu items. If you let the cursor linger over one of the new buttons, the prompt for the button will appear in the status bar. The new buttons work as a complete substitute for the menu items and any new selection made, using either the menu or the toolbar, is reflected by showing the toolbar button depressed, as well as the check against the menu item.

If you close the document view window, Sketch1, you'll see that our toolbar buttons are automatically grayed and disabled. If you open a new document window, they will be automatically enabled once again. You can also try dragging the toolbar with the cursor. You can move it to either side of the application window, or have it free-floating. You can also enable or disable it through the View | Toolbar menu option. We got all this without writing a single additional line of code!

Adding Tooltips

There's one further tweak that we can add to our toolbar buttons which is remarkably easy: adding **tooltips**. A tooltip is a small box that appears adjacent to the toolbar button when you let the cursor linger on the button. The tooltip contains a text string which is an additional clue as to the purpose of the toolbar button.

To add tooltips, select the ResourceView and, after expanding the resource list, double-click on the String Table resource. This contains the IDs and prompt strings associated with menu items and toolbar buttons. You should see the IDs for the menus that we added earlier. Double-click on ID_ELEMENT_LINE to cause the String Properties dialog to be displayed. To add a tooltip, you just need to add **\n**, followed by the tooltip text to the end of the prompt text. For this ID, you could add **\nLine**, for example.

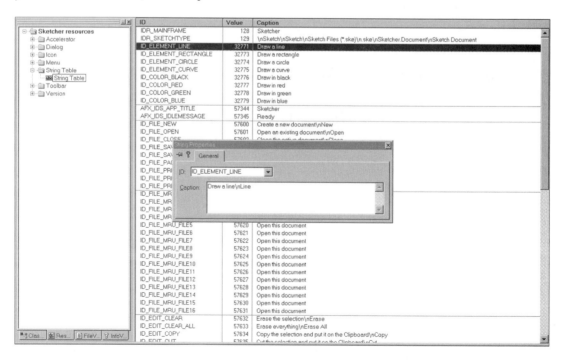

If you press *Enter*, the new prompt string with the tooltip text appended will be recorded against the ID. You can now go through the other menu IDs for elements and colors adding similar tooltips.

That's all you have to do. After saving the String Table resource, you can now rebuild the application and execute it. Placing the cursor over one of the new toolbar buttons will cause the tooltip to be displayed after a second or two.

Summary

In this chapter, you've learned how MFC connects a message with a class member function to process it, and you've written your first message handlers. Much of the work in writing a Windows program is writing message handlers, so it's important to have a good grasp of what happens in the process. When we get to consider other message handlers, you'll see that the process for adding them is just the same.

You have also extended the standard menu and the toolbar in the AppWizard-generated program, which provides a good base for the application code that we will add in the next chapter. Although there's no functionality under the covers yet, the menu and toolbar operation looks very professional, courtesy of the AppWizard-generated framework and ClassWizard.

The important points that we've seen in this chapter are:

▶ MFC defines the message handlers for a class in a message map which appears in the **.cpp** file for the class.

▶ Command messages which arise from menus and toolbars can be handled in any class that's derived from **CCmdTarget**. These include the application class, the frame and child frame window classes, the document class and the view class.

▶ Messages other than command messages can only be handled in a class derived from **CWnd**. This includes frame window and view classes, but not application or document classes.

▶ MFC has a predefined sequence for searching the classes in your program to find a message handler for a command message.

▶ You should always use ClassWizard to add message handlers to your program.

▶ The physical appearances of menus and toolbars are defined in resource files, which are edited by the built-in resource editor within the Developer Studio.

▶ Items in a menu that can result in command messages are identified by a symbolic constant with the prefix **ID_**. These IDs are used to associate a handler with the message from the menu item.

▶ To associate a toolbar button with a particular menu item, you give it the same ID as that of the menu item.

▶ To add a tooltip for a toolbar button corresponding to a menu item, you add the tooltip text to the entry for the ID for the menu item in the String Table resource. The tooltip text is separated from the menu prompt text by **\n**.

In the next chapter, you'll be adding the code necessary to draw elements in a view and, using the menus and toolbar buttons that we have created here, to select what is to be drawn and in which color. This is where the Sketcher program begins to live up to its name.

Exercises

Ex4-1: Add a menu item Ellipse to the Element pop-up.

Ex4-2: Implement the command and command update handlers for it in the document class.

Ex4-3: Add a toolbar button corresponding to the Ellipse menu item and add a tooltip for the button.

Ex4-4: Modify the command update handlers for the color menu items so that the currently selected item is displayed in upper case, and the others are displayed in lower case.

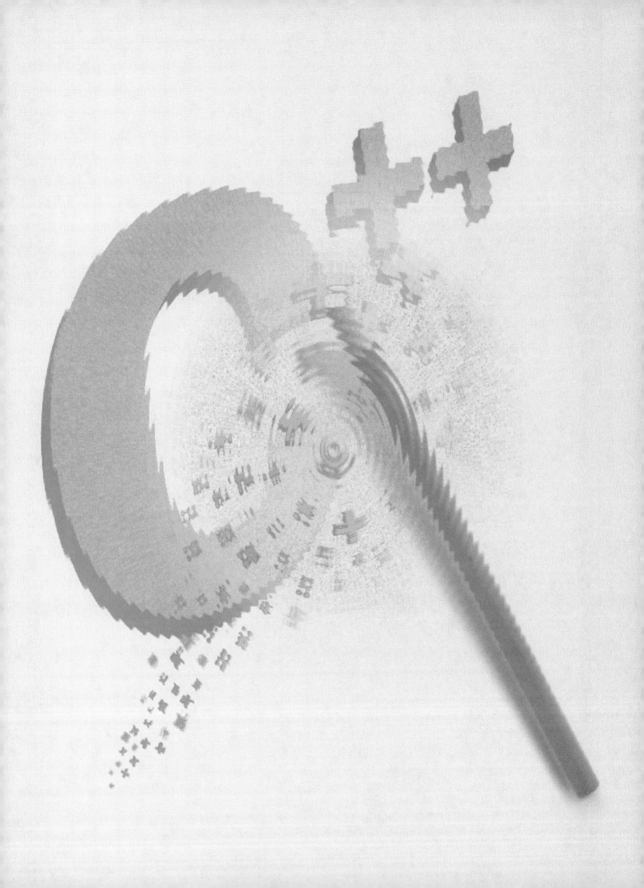

Drawing in a Window

In this chapter, we'll add some meat to our Sketcher application. We'll concentrate on understanding how you get graphical output displayed in the application window. Although we'll be able to draw all but one of the elements for which we have added menu items, we'll leave the problem of how to store them in a document until the next chapter. In this chapter, you will learn:

▶ What coordinate systems Windows provides for drawing in a window

▶ What a device context is and why it is necessary

▶ How and when your program draws in a window

▶ How to define handlers for mouse messages

▶ How to define your own shape classes

▶ How to program the mouse to draw your shapes in a window

▶ How to get your program to capture the mouse

Basics of Drawing in a Window

Before we go into drawing using MFC, it's useful to get an idea of what is happening under the covers of the Windows operating system. Like any other operation under Windows, writing to a window on your display screen is achieved through using Windows API functions. There's slightly more to it than that though; the way Windows works complicates the situation somewhat.

For a start, you can't just write to a window and forget it. There are many events that occur which mean that you must redraw the window—if the user resizes the window that you're drawing in, for instance, or if part of your window is exposed by the user moving another window.

Fortunately, you don't need to worry about the details of such occurrences because Windows actually manages all these events for you, but it does mean that you can only write permanent data to a window when your application receives a specific Windows message requesting that you do so. It also means that you need to be able to reconstruct everything that you've drawn in the window at any time.

When all, or part, of a window needs to be redrawn, Windows sends a **WM_PAINT** message to your application. This is intercepted by MFC, which passes the message to a function member of one of your classes. You'll see how to handle this a little later in this chapter.

The Window Client Area

A window doesn't have a fixed position on the screen, or even a fixed visible area, because a window can be dragged around using the mouse and resized by dragging its borders. How then do you know where to draw on the screen?

Fortunately, you don't. Because Windows provides you with a consistent way of drawing in a window, you don't have to worry about where it is on the screen. Otherwise, drawing in a window would be inordinately complicated. Windows does this by maintaining a coordinate system for the client area of a window that is local to the window. It always uses the top left corner of the client area as its reference point. All points within the client area are defined relative to this point, as shown here:

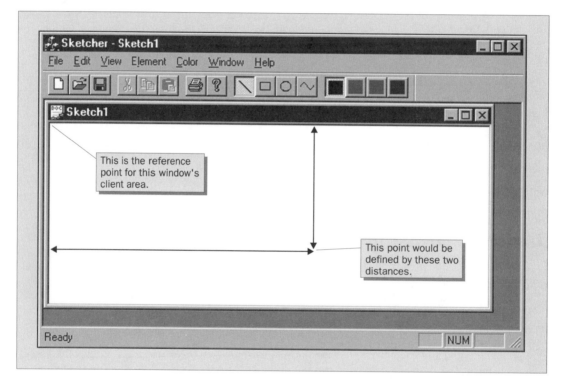

The horizontal and vertical distances of a point from the top left corner of the client area will always be the same, regardless of where the window is on the screen, or how big it is. Of course, Windows will need to keep track of where the window is, and when you draw something at a point in the client area, it will need to figure out where that actually is on the screen.

The Windows Graphical Device Interface

The final constraint Windows imposes is that you don't actually write data to the screen in any direct sense. All output to your display screen is graphical, regardless of whether it is lines and circles, or text. Windows insists that you define this output using the **Graphical Device Interface** (**GDI**). The GDI enables you to program graphical output independently of the hardware on which it will be displayed, meaning that your program will work on different machines with different display hardware. In addition to display screens, the Windows GDI also supports printers and plotters, so outputting data to a printer or a plotter involves essentially the same mechanisms as displaying information on the screen.

What is a Device Context?

When you want to draw something on a graphical output device such as the display screen, you must use a **device context**. A device context is a data structure that's defined by Windows and which contains information that allows Windows to translate your output requests, which are in the form of device-independent GDI function calls, into actions on the particular physical output device being used. A pointer to a device context is obtained by calling a Windows API function.

A device context provides you with a choice of coordinate systems called **mapping modes**, which will be automatically converted to client coordinates. You can also alter many of the parameters that affect the output to a device context by calling GDI functions; such parameters are called **attributes**. Examples of attributes that you can change are the drawing color, the background color, the line thickness to be used when drawing and the font for text output. There are also GDI functions that will provide information about the physical device you're working with. For example, you may need to be certain that the display on the computer executing your program can support 256 colors, or that a printer can support the output of bitmaps.

Mapping Modes

Each **mapping mode** in a device context is identified by an ID, in a manner similar to what we saw with Windows messages. Each symbol has the prefix **MM_** to indicate that it defines a mapping mode. The mapping modes provided by Windows are:

Mapping Mode	Definition
MM_TEXT	A logical unit is one device pixel with positive x from left to right, and positive y from top to bottom of the window client area.
MM_LOENGLISH	A logical unit is 0.01 inches with positive x from left to right, and positive y from the top of the client area upwards.
MM_HIENGLISH	A logical unit is 0.001 inches with the x and y directions as in **MM_LOENGLISH**.
MM_LOMETRIC	A logical unit is 0.1 millimeters with the x and y directions as in **MM_LOENGLISH**.
MM_HIMETRIC	A logical unit is 0.01 millimeters with the x and y directions as in **MM_LOENGLISH**.

Table Continued on Following Page

Mapping Mode	Definition
MM_ISOTROPIC	A logical unit is of arbitrary length, but the same along both the x and y axes. The x and y directions are as in **MM_LOENGLISH**.
MM_ANISOTROPIC	This mode is similar to **MM_ISOTROPIC**, but allows the length of a logical unit on the x axis to be different from that of a logical unit on the y axis.
MM_TWIPS	A logical unit is 0.05 of a point, which is $6.9*10^{-4}$ of an inch. (A **point** is a unit of measurement for fonts.) The x and y directions are as in **MM_LOENGLISH**.

We're not going to be using all of these mapping modes in this book. However, the ones we will be using form a good cross-section of those available, so you won't have any problem using the others when you need to.

MM_TEXT is the default mapping mode for a device context. If you need to use a different mapping mode, you'll have to take steps to change it. Note that the direction of the positive y axis in the **MM_TEXT** mode is opposite to what you will have seen in high school coordinate geometry, as you can see in the following drawing:

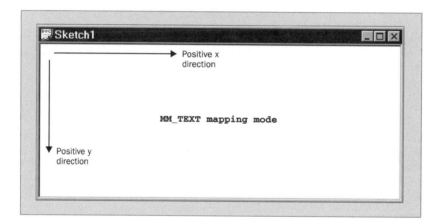

By default, the point at the top left corner of the client area has the coordinates (0,0) in *every* mapping mode, although it's possible to move the origin away from the top left corner of the client area if you want to. With the origin at the top left corner in **MM_TEXT** mode, a point 50 pixels from the left border and 100 pixels down from the top of the client area will have the coordinates (50,100). Of course, since the units are pixels, the point will be nearer the top left corner of the client area if your monitor is using the 800x600 SVGA resolution than if it's working with the 640x480 VGA resolution. An object drawn in this mapping mode will be smaller at the SVGA resolution than it would be at the VGA resolution.

Coordinates are always 16-bit signed integers in Windows 95, which is the same as in earlier 16-bit versions of Windows. (It's slightly different under Windows NT, where coordinates can be 32 bits, but we won't go into that here.) This limits the x and y values to ±32768. The maximum physical size of the total drawing varies with the physical length of a coordinate unit, which is determined by the mapping mode.

The directions of the x and y coordinate axes in **MM_LOENGLISH** and all the remaining mapping modes are the same as each other, but different from **MM_TEXT**. While positive y is consistent with what you learned in high school (y values increase as you move up the screen), **MM_LOENGLISH** is still slightly odd because the origin is at the top left corner of the client area, so for points within the visible client area, y is always negative.

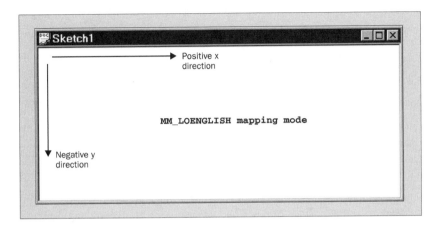

In the **MM_LOENGLISH** mapping mode, the units along the axes are 0.01 inches apiece, so a point at the position (50, -100) will be half an inch from the left border and one inch down from the top of the client area. An object will be the same size in the client area, regardless of the resolution of the monitor on which it is displayed. If you draw anything in the **MM_LOENGLISH** mode with negative x or positive y coordinates, it will be outside the client area and therefore invisible, since the reference point (0,0) is the top left hand corner by default. It's possible to move the position of the reference point though, by calling the Windows API function **SetViewportOrg()** (or the **SetViewportOrg()** member of the **CDC** MFC class, which we'll come to shortly).

The Drawing Mechanism in Visual C++

MFC encapsulates the Windows interface to your screen and printer and relieves you of the need to worry about much of the detail involved in programming graphical output. As we saw in the last chapter, your AppWizard generated application will already contain a class derived from the MFC class **CView** that's specifically designed to display document data on the screen.

The View Class in Your Application

AppWizard generated the class **CSketcherView** to display information from a document in the client area of a document window. The class definition includes overrides for several virtual functions, but the one we're particularly interested in here is the function **OnDraw()**, because this will be called whenever the client area of the document window needs to be redrawn. It's the function that's called by the application framework when a **WM_PAINT** message is received in your program.

The OnDraw() Member Function

The implementation of the **OnDraw()** member function that's created by AppWizard looks like this:

```
void CSketcherView::OnDraw(CDC* pDC)
{
    CSketcherDoc* pDoc = GetDocument();
    ASSERT_VALID(pDoc);

    // TODO: add draw code for native data here
}
```

A pointer to an object of the class **CDC** is passed to the **OnDraw()** member of the view class. This object has member functions that call the Windows API functions which allow you to draw in a device context.

Since you'll put all the code to draw the document in this function, the AppWizard has included a declaration for the pointer **pDoc** and initialized it using the function **GetDocument()**, which returns the address of the document object related to the current view:

```
CSketcherDoc* pDoc = GetDocument();
```

GetDocument() actually retrieves the pointer to the document from **m_pDocument**, an inherited data member of the view object. The function performs the important task of casting the pointer stored in this data member to the type corresponding to the document class in the application, **CSketcherDoc**. This is so that the compiler will have access to the members of the document class that you've defined. Otherwise, the compiler would only be able to access the members of the base class. Thus, **pDoc** will point to the document object in your application associated with the current view, and you will be using it to access the data that you've stored in the document object when you want to draw it.

The following line,

```
ASSERT_VALID(pDoc);
```

just makes sure that the pointer **pDoc** contains a valid address.

The object of the **CDC** class pointed to by the **pDC** argument that's passed to the **OnDraw()** function is the key to drawing in a window. It provides a device context, plus the tools we need to write graphics and text to it, so we clearly need to look at it in more detail.

The CDC Class

You should do all the drawing in your program using members of the **CDC** class. All objects of this class and classes derived from it contain a device context and the member functions you need for sending graphics and text to your display and your printer. There are also member functions for retrieving information about the physical output device that you are using.

Because **CDC** class objects can provide almost everything you're likely to need by way of graphical output, there are a lot of member functions of this class—in fact, well over a hundred. Therefore, we'll only look at the ones we're going to use in the Sketcher program here in this chapter, and go into others as we need them later on.

Note that MFC includes some more specialized classes for graphics output that are derived from **CDC**. For example, we'll be using objects of **CClientDC** which, because it is derived from **CDC**, also contains all the members we will discuss at this point. The advantage that **CClientDC** has over **CDC** is that it always contains a device context that represents only the client area of a window, and this is precisely what you want in most circumstances.

Displaying Graphics

In a device context, you draw entities such as lines, circles and text relative to a **current position**. A current position is a point in the client area that was set either by the previous entity that was drawn, or by calling a function to set it. For example, we could extend the **OnDraw()** function to set the current position as follows:

```
void CSketcherView::OnDraw(CDC* pDC)
{
    CSketcherDoc* pDoc = GetDocument();
    ASSERT_VALID(pDoc);

    pDC->MoveTo(50, 50);     // Set the current position as 50,50
}
```

The shaded line calls the function **MoveTo()** for the **CDC** object pointed to by **pDC**. This member function simply sets the current position to the x and y coordinates specified as arguments. As we saw earlier, the default mapping mode is **MM_TEXT**, so the coordinates are in pixels and the current position will be set to a point 50 pixels from the inside left border of the window, and 50 pixels down from the top of the client area.

The **CDC** class overloads the **MoveTo()** function to provide flexibility over how you specify the position that you want to set as the current position. There are two versions of the function, declared in the **CDC** class as:

```
CPoint MoveTo(int x, int y);      // Move to position x,y
CPoint MoveTo(POINT aPoint);      // Move to position defined by aPoint
```

The first version accepts the x and y coordinates as separate arguments. The second accepts one argument of type **POINT**, which is a structure defined as:

```
typedef struct tagPOINT
{
    LONG x;
    LONG y;
} POINT;
```

The coordinates are members of the **struct** and are of type **LONG**. You may prefer to use a class instead of a structure, in which case you can use objects of the class **CPoint** anywhere that a **POINT** object can be used. The class **CPoint** has data members **x** and **y** of type **LONG** (which is a 32 bit signed integer), and using **CPoint** objects has the advantage that the class also defines member functions that operate on **CPoint** and **POINT** objects. This may seem weird, since **CPoint** would seem to make **POINT** objects obsolete, but remember that the Windows API was built before MFC was around, and **POINT** objects are used in the Windows API and have to be dealt with sooner or later. We'll use **CPoint** objects in our examples, so you'll have an opportunity to see some of the member functions in action.

The return value from the **MoveTo()** function is a **CPoint** object that specifies the current position as it was *before* the move. You might think this a little odd, but consider the situation where you want to move to a new position, draw something, and then move back. You may not know the current position before the move, and once the move occurs it would be lost, so returning the position before the move makes sure it's available to you if you need it.

Drawing Lines

We can follow the call to **MoveTo()** in the **OnDraw()** function with a call to the function **LineTo()**, which will draw a line in the client area from the current position to the point specified by the arguments to the **LineTo()** function, as illustrated here:

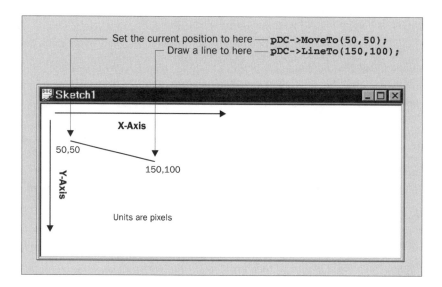

The class **CDC** also defines two versions of the **LineTo()** function with the prototypes:

```
BOOL LineTo(int x, int y); // Draw a line to position x,y
BOOL LineTo(POINT aPoint); // Draw a line to position defined by aPoint
```

This offers you the same flexibility in specifying the argument to the function as **MoveTo()**. You can use a **CPoint** object as an argument to the second version of the function. The function returns **TRUE** if the line was drawn, and **FALSE** otherwise.

When the **LineTo()** function is executed, the current position is changed to the point specifying the end of the line. This allows you to draw a series of connected lines by just calling the **LineTo()** function for each line. Look at the following version of the **OnDraw()** function:

```
void CSketcherView::OnDraw(CDC* pDC)
{
    CSketcherDoc* pDoc = GetDocument();
    ASSERT_VALID(pDoc);

    pDC->MoveTo(50,50);          // Set the current position
    pDC->LineTo(50,200);         // Draw a vertical line down 150 units
    pDC->LineTo(150,200);        // Draw a horizontal line right 100 units
```

```
        pDC->LineTo(150,50);        // Draw a vertical line up 150 units
        pDC->LineTo(50,50);         // Draw a horizontal line left 100 units
}
```

If you plug this into the Sketcher program and execute it, it will display the document window shown here:

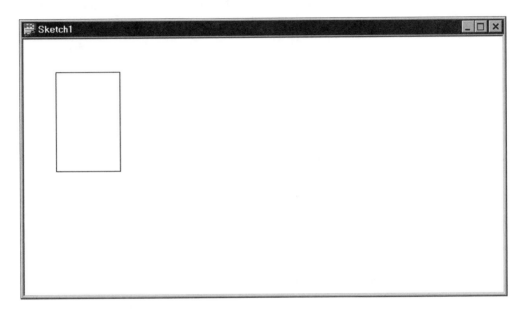

The four calls to the **LineTo()** function draw the rectangle shown counterclockwise, starting with the top left corner. The first call uses the current position set by the **MoveTo()** function; the succeeding calls use the current position set by the previous **LineTo()** function call. You can use this to draw any figure consisting of a sequence of lines, each connected to the previous line. Of course, you are also free to use **MoveTo()** to change the current position at any time.

Drawing Circles

You have a choice of several function members in the class **CDC** for drawing circles, but they're all designed to draw ellipses. As you will know from high school geometry, a circle is a special case of an ellipse, with the major and minor axes equal. You can, therefore, use the member function **Ellipse()** to draw a circle. Like other closed shapes supported by the **CDC** class, the **Ellipse()** function fills the interior of the shape with a color that you set. The interior color is determined by a **brush** that is selected into the device context. The current brush in the device context determines how any closed shape will be filled.

MFC provides a class **CBrush** which you can use to define a brush. You can set the color of a **CBrush** object and also define a pattern to be produced when filling a closed shape. If you want to draw a closed shape that isn't filled, you can use a null brush, which leaves the interior of the shape empty. We'll come back to brushes a little later in this chapter.

Another way to draw circles that aren't filled is to use the **Arc()** function, which doesn't involve brushes. This has the advantage that you can draw any arc of an ellipse, rather than the complete curve. There are two versions of this function in the **CDC** class, declared as:

```
BOOL Arc(int x1, int y1, int x2, int y2, int x3, int y3, int x4, int y4);
BOOL Arc(LPCRECT lpRect, POINT StartPt, POINT EndPt);
```

In the first version, (**x1,y1**) and (**x2,y2**) define the top left and bottom right corners of a rectangle enclosing the complete curve. If you make these coordinates into the corners of a square, the curve drawn will be a segment of a circle. The points (**x3,y3**) and (**x4,y4**) define the start and end points of the segment to be drawn. The segment is drawn counterclockwise. If you make (**x4,y4**) identical to (**x3,y3**), you'll generate a complete, apparently closed curve.

In the second version of **Arc()**, the enclosing rectangle is defined by a **RECT** object, and a pointer to this object is passed as the first argument. The function will also accept a pointer to an object of the class **CRect**, which has four public data members: **left**, **top**, **right**, and **bottom**. These correspond to the *x* and *y* coordinates of the top left and bottom right points of the rectangle respectively. The class also provides a range of function members which operate on **CRect** objects, and we shall be using some of these later.

The **POINT** objects **StartPt** and **EndPt** in the second version of **Arc()** define the start and end of the arc to be drawn.

Here's some code that exercises both versions of the **Arc()** function:

```
void CSketcherView::OnDraw(CDC* pDC)
{
  CSketcherDoc* pDoc = GetDocument();
  ASSERT_VALID(pDoc);

  pDC->Arc(50,50,150,150,100,50,150,100);  // Draw the 1st (large) circle

  // Define the bounding rectangle for the 2nd (smaller) circle
  CRect* pRect = new CRect(250,50,300,100);
  CPoint Start(275,100);                    // Arc start point
  CPoint End(250,75);                       // Arc end point
  pDC->Arc(pRect,Start, End);               // Draw the second circle
  delete pRect;
}
```

Note that we used a **CRect** class object instead of a **RECT** structure to define the bounding rectangle, and that we used **CPoint** class objects instead of **POINT** structures. We'll also be using **CRect** objects later, but they have some limitations, as you'll see. The **Arc()** function doesn't require a current position to be set, as the position and size of the arc are completely defined by the arguments you supply. The current position is unaffected by drawing an arc—it remains exactly wherever it was before the arc was drawn. Although coordinates can be ±32K, the maximum width or height of the rectangle bounding a shape is 32,767 because this is the maximum positive value that can be represented in a signed 16-bit integer.

Now try running Sketcher with this code in the **OnDraw()** function. You should get the results shown here:

Try re-sizing the borders. The client area is automatically redrawn as you cover or uncover the arcs in the picture. Remember that screen resolution will affect the scale of what is displayed. If you're using a VGA screen at 640x480 resolution, the arcs will be larger and further from the top left corner of the client area.

Drawing in Color

Everything that we've drawn so far has appeared on the screen in black. Drawing implies using a **pen object** which has a color and a thickness, and we've been using the default pen object that is provided in a device context. You're not obliged to do this, of course—you can create your own pen with a given thickness and color. MFC defines the class **CPen** to help you do this.

All closed curves that you draw are filled with the current brush in the device context. As we said, you can define a brush as an instance of the class **CBrush**. Let's take a look at some of the features of **CPen** and **CBrush** objects.

Creating a Pen

The simplest way to create a pen object is first to declare an object of the **CPen** class:

```
CPen aPen;                    // Declare a pen object
```

This object now needs to be initialized with the properties you want. You do this using the class member function **CreatePen()**, which is declared in the **CPen** class as:

```
BOOL CreatePen (int aPenStyle, int aWidth, COLORREF aColor);
```

The function returns **TRUE** as long as the pen is successfully initialized, and **FALSE** otherwise. The first argument defines the line style that you want to use when drawing. You must specify it with one of the following symbolic values:

Pen Style	Meaning
PS_SOLID	The pen draws a solid line.
PS_DASH	The pen draws a dashed line. This line style is valid only when the pen width is specified as 1.
PS_DOT	The pen draws a dotted line. This line style is valid only when the pen width is specified as 1.
PS_DASHDOT	The pen draws a line with alternating dashes and dots. This line style is valid only when the pen width is specified as 1.
PS_DASHDOTDOT	The pen draws a line with alternating dashes and double dots. This line style is valid only when the pen width is specified as 1.
PS_NULL	The pen doesn't draw anything.
PS_INSIDEFRAME	The pen draws a solid line, but unlike **PS_SOLID**, the points that specify the line occur on the edge of the pen rather than in the center, so that the drawn object never extends beyond the enclosing rectangle.

PS_SOLID   PS_INSIDEFRAME

The second argument to the **CreatePen()** function defines the line width. If **aWidth** has the value 0, the line drawn will be 1 pixel wide, regardless of the mapping mode in effect. For values of 1 or more, the pen width is in the units determined by the mapping mode. For example, a value of 2 for **aWidth** in **MM_TEXT** mode will be 2 pixels, while in **MM_LOENGLISH** mode the pen width will be 0.02 inches.

The last argument specifies the color to be used when drawing with the pen, so we could initialize a pen with the statement:

```
aPen.CreatePen(PS_SOLID, 2, RGB(255,0,0)); // Create a red solid pen
```

Assuming that the mapping mode is **MM_TEXT**, this pen will draw a solid red line which is 2 pixels wide.

Using a Pen

In order to use a pen, you must select it into the device context in which you are drawing. To do this, you use the **CDC** class member function **SelectObject()**. To select the pen you want to use, you call this function with a pointer to the pen object as an argument. The function returns a pointer to the previous pen object being used, so that you can save it and restore the old pen when you have finished drawing. A typical statement selecting a pen is:

```
CPen* pOldPen = pDC->SelectObject(&aPen);    // Select aPen as the pen
```

To restore the old pen when you're done, you simply call the function again, passing the pointer returned from the original call:

```
pDC->SelectObject(pOldPen);                  // Restore the old pen
```

We can demonstrate this in action by amending the previous version of the **OnDraw()** function in our view class to:

```
void CSketcherView::OnDraw(CDC* pDC)
{
   CSketcherDoc* pDoc = GetDocument();
   ASSERT_VALID(pDoc);

   // Declare a pen object and initialize it as
   // a red solid pen drawing a line 2 pixels wide
   CPen aPen;
   aPen.CreatePen(PS_SOLID, 2, RGB(255, 0, 0));

   CPen* pOldPen = pDC->SelectObject(&aPen); // Select aPen as the pen

   pDC->Arc(50,50,150,150,100,50,150,100);   // Draw the 1st circle

   // Define the bounding rectangle for the 2nd circle
   CRect* pRect = new CRect(250,50,300,100);
   CPoint Start(275,100);                     // Arc start point
   CPoint End(250,75);                        // Arc end point
   pDC->Arc(pRect,Start, End);                // Draw the second circle
   delete pRect;

   pDC->SelectObject(pOldPen);                // Restore the old pen
}
```

If you build and execute the Sketcher application with this version of the **OnDraw()** function, you will get the same arcs drawn as before, but this time the lines will be thicker and they'll be red. You could usefully experiment with this example by trying different combinations of arguments to the **CreatePen()** function and seeing their effects. Note that we have ignored the value returned from the **CreatePen()** function, so we run the risk of the function failing and not detecting it in the program. It doesn't matter here as the program is still trivial, but as we develop the program it will become important to check for failures of this kind.

Creating a Brush

An object of the **CBrush** class encapsulates a Windows brush. You can define a brush to be solid, hatched, or patterned. A brush is actually an 8x8 block of pixels that's repeated over the region to be filled.

To define a brush with a solid color, you can specify the color when you create the brush object. For example,

```
CBrush aBrush(RGB(255,0,0));      // Define a red brush
```

which defines a red brush. The value passed to the constructor must be of type **COLORREF**, which is the type returned by the **RGB()** macro, so this is a good way to specify the color.

Another constructor is available to define a hatched brush. It requires two arguments to be specified, the first defining the type of hatching, and the second specifying the color, as before. The hatching argument can be any of the following symbolic constants:

Hatching Style	Meaning
HS_HORIZONTAL	Horizontal hatching
HS_VERTICAL	Vertical hatching
HS_BDIAGONAL	Downward hatching from left to right at 45 degrees
HS_FDIAGONAL	Upward hatching from left to right at 45 degrees
HS_CROSS	Horizontal and vertical crosshatching
HS_DIAGCROSS	Crosshatching at 45 degrees

So, to obtain a red, 45-degree crosshatched brush, you could define the **CBrush** object with the statement:

```
CBrush aBrush(HS_DIAGCROSS, RGB(255,0,0));
```

You can also initialize a **CBrush** object in a similar manner to that for a **CPen** object, by using the **CreateSolidBrush()** member function of the class for a solid brush, and the **CreateHatchBrush()** member for a hatched brush. They require the same arguments as the equivalent constructors. For example, we could create the same hatched brush as before, with the statements:

```
CBrush aBrush;                    // Define a brush object
aBrush.CreateHatchBrush(HS_DIAGCROSS, RGB(255,0,0));
```

Using a Brush

To use a brush, you select the brush into the device context by calling the **SelectObject()** member of the **CDC** class in a parallel fashion to that used for a pen. This member function is overloaded to support selecting brush objects into a device context. To select the brush we defined previously, you would simply write:

```
pDC->SelectObject(aBrush);      // Select the brush into the device context
```

There are a number of standard brushes available. Each of the standard brushes is identified by a predefined symbolic constant, and there are seven that you can use. They are the following:

GRAY_BRUSH	LTGRAY_BRUSH	DKGRAY_BRUSH
BLACK_BRUSH	WHITE_BRUSH	
HOLLOW_BRUSH	NULL_BRUSH	

The names of these brushes are quite self-explanatory. To use one, you call the **SelectStockObject()** member of the **CDC** class, passing the symbolic name for the brush that you want to use as an argument. To select the null brush, which will leave the interior of a closed shape unfilled, you could write:

```
pDC->SelectStockObject(NULL_BRUSH);
```

Here, **pDC** is a pointer to a **CDC** object, as before. You can also use one of a range of standard pens through this function. The symbols for standard pens are **BLACK_PEN**, **NULL_PEN** (which doesn't draw anything), and **WHITE_PEN**. The **SelectStockObject()** function returns a pointer to the object being replaced in the device context. This is to enable you to save it for restoring later when you have finished drawing.

Because the function works with a variety of objects—we've seen pens and brushes in this chapter, but it also works with fonts—the type of the pointer returned is **CGdiObject***. The **CGdiObject** class is a base class for all the graphic device interface object classes and thus a pointer to this class can be used to store a pointer to any object of these types. However, you need to cast the pointer value returned to the appropriate type so that you can select the old object back to restore it. This is because the **SelectObject()** function you use to do this is overloaded for each of the kinds of object that can be selected. There's no version of **SelectObject()** that accepts a pointer to a **CGdiObject** as an argument, but there are versions that accept an argument of type **CBrush***, **CPen***, and pointers to other GDI objects.

The typical pattern of coding for using a stock brush and later restoring the old brush when you're done is:

```
CBrush* pOldBrush = (CBrush*)pDC->SelectStockObject(NULL_BRUSH);

// draw something

pDC->SelectObject(pOldBrush);                       // Restore the old brush
```

We'll be using this in our example later in the chapter.

155

Drawing Graphics in Practice

We now know how to draw lines and arcs, so it's about time we considered how the user is going to define what they want drawn. In other words, we need to decide how the user interface is going to work.

Since this program is to be a sketching tool, we don't want the user to worry about coordinates. The easiest mechanism for drawing is using just the mouse. To draw a line, for instance, the user could position the cursor and press the left mouse button where they wanted the line to start, and then define the end of the line by moving the cursor with the left button held down. It would be ideal if we could arrange that the line was continuously drawn as the cursor was moved with the left button down (this is known as 'rubber-banding' to graphic designers). The line would be fixed when the left mouse button was released. This process is illustrated in the diagram below:

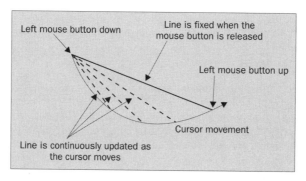

We could allow circles to be drawn in a similar fashion. The first press of the left mouse button would define the center and, as the cursor was moved with the button down, the program would track it. The circle would be continuously redrawn, with the current cursor position defining a point on the circumference of the circle. As with drawing a line, the circle would be fixed when the left mouse button was released. We can see this in the diagram here:

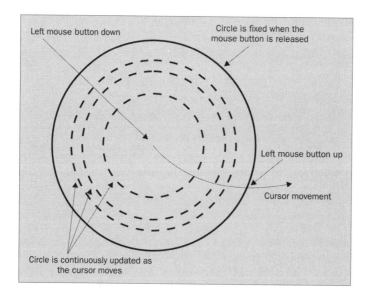

We can draw a rectangle as easily as we draw a line, as illustrated here:

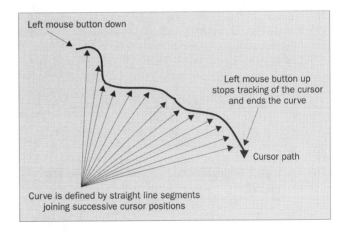

The first point is defined by the position of the cursor when the left mouse button is pressed. This is one corner of the rectangle. The position of the cursor when the mouse is moved with the left button held down defines the diagonal opposite corner of the rectangle. The rectangle actually stored is the last one defined when the left mouse button is released.

A curve will be somewhat different. An arbitrary number of points may define a curve. The mechanism we'll use is illustrated here:

As with the other shapes, the first point is defined by the cursor position when the left mouse button is pressed. Successive positions recorded when the mouse is moved are connected by straight line segments to form the curve, so the mouse track defines the curve to be drawn.

Now we know how the user is going to define an element, clearly our next step in understanding how to implement this is to get a grip on how the mouse is programmed.

Programming the Mouse

To be able to program the drawing of shapes in the way we've discussed, we need to know various things about the mouse:

▶ When a mouse button is pressed, since this signals the start of a drawing operation

▶ Where the cursor is when a button is pressed, because this defines a reference point for the shape

▶ When the mouse moves, and where the cursor moves to when it does. A mouse movement after detecting that a mouse button has been pressed is a cue to draw a shape, and the cursor position provides a defining point for the shape

▶ When the mouse button is released, and the cursor position at that instant, because this signals that the final version of the shape should be drawn

As you may have guessed, all this information is provided by Windows in the form of messages sent to your program. The implementation of the process for drawing lines and circles will consist almost entirely of writing message handlers.

Messages from the Mouse

When the user of our program is drawing a shape, they will be interacting with a particular document view. The view class is, therefore, the obvious place to put the message handlers for the mouse. Fire up the ClassWizard and take a look at the **Message Maps** tab for the **CSketcherView** class. We don't want the messages associated with **ID_**-specified objects; we need to get to the standard Windows messages sent to the class, which have IDs prefixed with **WM_**. You can see these if you select the class name in the **Object IDs:** box and scroll down the **Messages:** list, as shown here:

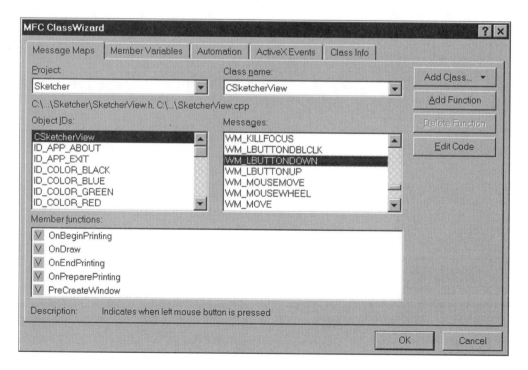

We're interested in three mouse messages at the moment:

Message	Occurs...
WM_LBUTTONDOWN	when the left mouse button is pressed.
WM_LBUTTONUP	when the left mouse button is released.
WM_MOUSEMOVE	when the mouse is moved.

These messages are quite independent of one another and are being sent to the document views in your program even if you haven't supplied handlers for them. It's quite possible for a window to receive a **WM_LBUTTONUP** message without having previously received a **WM_LBUTTONDOWN** message. This can happen if the button is pressed with the cursor over another window and then moved to your view window before being released.

If you scroll the Messages: box, you'll see there are other mouse messages that can occur. You can choose to process any or all of the messages, depending on your application requirements. Let's define in general terms what we want to do with the three messages that we're currently interested in, based on the process for drawing shapes that we saw earlier:

WM_LBUTTONDOWN

This starts the process of drawing an element. So we will:

1 Note that the element drawing process has started.

2 Record the current cursor position as the first point for defining an element.

WM_MOUSEMOVE

This is an intermediate stage where we want to create and draw a temporary version of the current element, but only if the left mouse button is down, so:

1 Check that the left button is down.

2 If it is, delete any previous version of the current element that was drawn.

3 If it isn't, then exit.

4 Record the current cursor position as the second defining point for the current element.

5 Cause the current element to be drawn using the two defining points.

WM_LBUTTONUP

This indicates that the process for drawing an element is finished, so all we need to do is:

1 Store the final version of the element defined by the first point recorded, together with the position of the cursor when the button is released for the second point.

2 Record the end of the process of drawing an element.

Let's now use ClassWizard to generate handlers for these three mouse messages.

Mouse Message Handlers

You can create the handlers for the mouse messages in the same way as you created the menu message handlers. Just open the ClassWizard dialog and click on the **Add Function** button with the message highlighted in the **Messages:** list box. Alternatively, you can use the Wizard Bar. If you display **CSketcherView** in the list box on the left and select the down arrow, you'll see that the pop-up menu contains an option **Add Windows Message Handler....** If you click on this you'll see the dialog shown here.

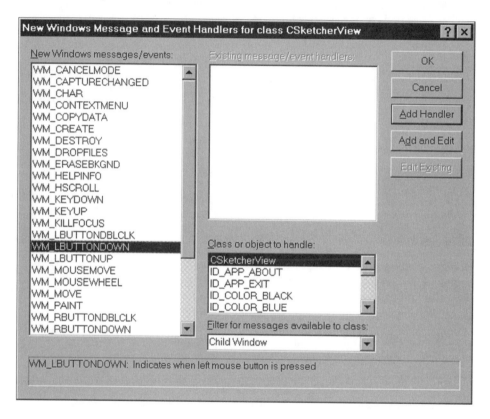

You select the message that you want to add a handler for from the list box on the left, and click on the **Add Handler** button. All the handlers defined for the class will be shown in the list box on the right. You can select any of these when you want to edit the implementation of a handler. Just double-click on the message, or click on the **Edit Existing** button with the appropriate message highlighted.

The functions generated will be **OnLButtonDown()**, **OnLButtonUp()** and **OnMouseMove()**. You don't get the option of changing the names of these functions because you're replacing versions that are already defined in the base class for your **CSketcherView** class. Let's look at how we implement these handlers.

The ClassWizard Generated Code

We can start by looking at the **WM_LBUTTONDOWN** message handler. Make sure that it's highlighted and click on the Edit Existing button. This is the skeleton code that's generated:

```
void CSketcherView::OnLButtonDown(UINT nFlags, CPoint point)
{
    // TODO: Add your message handler code here and/or call default

    CView::OnLButtonDown(nFlags, point);
}
```

You can see that ClassWizard has put a call to the base class handler in the skeleton version. This ensures that the base handler is called if you don't add any code here. In this case you don't need to call the base class handler when you handle the message yourself, although you can if you want to. Whether you need to call the base class handler for a message depends on the circumstances.

Generally, the comment indicating where you should add your own code is a good guide. Where it suggests, as in the present instance, that calling the base class handler is optional, you can omit it when you add your own message handling code. Note that the position of the comment in relation to the call of the base class handler is also important, as sometimes you must call the base class message handler before your code, and other times afterwards. The comment indicates where your code should appear in relation to the base class message handler call.

The handler in your class is passed two arguments: **nFlags**, which is of type **UINT** and contains a number of status flags indicating whether various keys are down, and the **CPoint** object **point**, which defines the cursor position when the left mouse button was pressed. The type **UINT** is a portable unsigned integer which corresponds to a 32-bit unsigned integer in Windows 95.

The value of **nFlags** which is passed to the function can be any combination of the following symbolic values:

Flag	Meaning
MK_CONTROL	Corresponds to the *Ctrl* key being pressed.
MK_LBUTTON	Corresponds to the left mouse button being down.
MK_MBUTTON	Corresponds to the middle mouse button being down.
MK_RBUTTON	Corresponds to the right mouse button being down.
MK_SHIFT	Corresponds to the *Shift* key being pressed.

Being able to detect if a key is down in the message handler allows you to support different actions depending on what you find. The value of **nFlags** may contain more than one of these indicators, each of which corresponds to a particular bit in the word, so you can test for a particular key using the bitwise AND operator. For example, to test for the *Ctrl* key being pressed, you could write:

```
if(nFlags & MK_CONTROL)
    // Do something...
```

The expression **nFlags & MK_CONTROL** will only have the value **TRUE** if the **nFlags** variable has the bit defined by **MK_CONTROL** set. In this way, you can have different actions when the left mouse button is pressed, depending on whether the *Ctrl* key is also pressed. We use the bitwise AND operator here, so corresponding bits are ANDed together. Don't confuse this with the logical AND, **&&**, which would not do what we want here.

The arguments passed to the other two message handlers are the same as those for the **OnLButtonDown()** function; the code generated by the ClassWizard for them is:

```
void CSketcherView::OnLButtonUp(UINT nFlags, CPoint point)
{
   // TODO: Add your message handler code here and/or call default

   CView::OnLButtonUp(nFlags, point);
}
```

```
void CSketcherView::OnMouseMove(UINT nFlags, CPoint point)
{
   // TODO: Add your message handler code here and/or call default

   CView::OnMouseMove(nFlags, point);
}
```

Apart from the function names, the skeleton code is the same for each. With an understanding of the information passed to the message handlers, we can start adding our own code.

Drawing Using the Mouse

For the **WM_LBUTTONDOWN** message, we want to record the cursor position as the first point defining an element. We also want to record the position of the cursor after a mouse move. The obvious place to store these is in the **CSketcherView** class, so we can add data members to the attributes section of the class for these as follows:

```
class CSketcherView: public CView
{
   protected: // create from serialization only
      CSketcherView();
      DECLARE_DYNCREATE(CSketcherView)

   // Attributes
   public:
      CSketcherDoc* GetDocument();

   protected:
      CPoint m_FirstPoint;      // First point recorded for an element
      CPoint m_SecondPoint;     // Second point recorded for an element

   ...
```

If you take a look a little further down the listing, you'll see that ClassWizard has added these three function declarations:

```
// Generated message map functions
protected:
```

```
        //{{AFX_MSG(CSketcherView)
    afx_msg void OnLButtonDown(UINT nFlags, CPoint point);
    afx_msg void OnLButtonUp(UINT nFlags, CPoint point);
    afx_msg void OnMouseMove(UINT nFlags, CPoint point);
        //}}AFX_MSG
    DECLARE_MESSAGE_MAP()
};
```

FYI Another way of adding a new variable to a class is to right-click on the class name in the ClassView and select **Add Variable...** from the context menu. You can then fill in the details of the variable in the dialog. However, there will be no comments explaining the new data member unless you add them separately.

The new data members are **protected** to prevent direct modification of them from outside the class. Both the data members need to be initialized, so you should add code to the class constructor to do this, as follows:

```
// CSketcherView construction/destruction

CSketcherView::CSketcherView()
{
    // TODO: add construction code here
    m_FirstPoint = CPoint(0,0);          // Set 1st recorded point to 0,0
    m_SecondPoint = CPoint(0,0);         // Set 2nd recorded point to 0,0
}
```

We can now implement the handler for the **WM_LBUTTONDOWN** message as:

```
void CSketcherView::OnLButtonDown(UINT nFlags, CPoint point)
{
    // TODO: Add your message handler code here and/or call default
    m_FirstPoint = point;                // Record the cursor position
}
```

All it does is to note the coordinates passed by the second argument. We can ignore the first argument in this situation altogether.

We can't complete this function yet, but we can have a stab at writing the code for the **WM_MOUSEMOVE** message handler in outline:

```
void CSketcherView::OnMouseMove(UINT nFlags, CPoint point)
{
    // TODO: Add your message handler code here and/or call default
    if(nFlags & MK_LBUTTON)
    {
        m_SecondPoint = point;      // Save the current cursor position

        // Test for a previous temporary element
        {
            // We get to here if there was a previous mouse move
            // so add code to delete the old element
        }
```

163

```
            // Add code to create new element
            // and cause it to be drawn
        }
    }
```

The first thing that the handler does (after verifying the left mouse button is down) is to save the current cursor position. This will be used as the second defining point for an element. The rest of the logic is clear in general terms, but there are major gaps in our knowledge of how to complete the function. We have no means of defining an element—we need to be able to define an element as an object of a class. Even if we could, we don't know how to delete an element or get one drawn when we have a new one. A brief digression is called for.

Getting the Client Area Redrawn

As we've already discovered, the client area gets drawn by the **OnDraw()** member function of the **CSketcherView** class, which is called when a **WM_PAINT** message is received. Along with the basic message to repaint the client area, Windows supplies information about the part of the client area that needs to be redrawn. This can save a lot of time when you're displaying complicated images, because only the area specified actually needs to be redrawn, which may be a very small proportion of the total area.

You can tell Windows that a particular area should be redrawn by calling the **InvalidateRect()** function, which is an inherited member of your view class. The function accepts two arguments, the first of which is a pointer to a **RECT** or **CRect** object that defines the rectangle in the client area to be redrawn. Passing **NULL** for this parameter causes the whole client area to be redrawn. The second parameter is a **BOOL** value which is **TRUE** if the background to the rectangle is to be erased, and **FALSE** otherwise. This argument has a default value of **TRUE** since you normally want the background erased before the rectangle is redrawn, so you can ignore it most of the time.

A typical situation in which you'd want to cause an area to be redrawn would be where something has changed which necessitates the contents of the area being recreated—moving a displayed entity might be an example. In this case, you want to erase the background to remove the old representation of what was displayed before you draw the new version. When you want to draw on top of an existing background, you just pass **FALSE** as the second argument to **InvalidateRect()**.

The **InvalidateRect()** function doesn't directly cause any part of the window to be redrawn; it just communicates to Windows the rectangle that you would like to have it redraw at some time. Windows maintains an **update region**—actually a rectangle—which identifies the area in a window that needs to be redrawn. The area specified in your call to **InvalidateRect()** is added to the current update region, so the new update region will enclose the old region plus the new rectangle you have indicated as invalid. Eventually a **WM_PAINT** message will be sent to the window and the update region will be passed to the window along with it. When processing of the **WM_PAINT** message is complete, the update region is reset to the empty state.

Thus, all you have to do to get a newly-created shape drawn is:

1 Make sure that the **OnDraw()** function in your view includes the newly-created item when it redraws the window.

2 Call **InvalidateRect()** with a pointer to the rectangle bounding the shape to be redrawn passed as the first argument.

Similarly, if you want a shape removed from the client area of a window, you need to do the following:

1 Remove the shape from the items that the **OnDraw()** function will draw.

2 Call **InvalidateRect()** with the first argument pointing to the rectangle bounding the shape that is to be removed.

Since the background to the rectangle specified is automatically erased, as long as the **OnDraw()** function doesn't draw the shape again, the shape will disappear. Of course, this means that we need to be able to obtain the rectangle bounding any shape that we create, so we'll include a function to provide this as a member of our classes that define the elements that can be drawn by Sketcher.

Defining Classes for Elements

Thinking ahead a bit, we'll need to store elements in a document in some way, and to be able to perform file operations with them. We'll deal with the details of file operations later on, but for now it's enough to know that the MFC class **CObject** includes the tools for us to do this, so we'll use **CObject** as a base class for our element classes.

We'll also have the problem that we don't know in advance what sequence of element types the user will create. Our program must be able to handle any sequence of elements. This suggests that using a base class pointer for selecting a particular element class function might simplify things a bit. For example, we won't need to know what an element is in order to draw it. As long as we're accessing the element through a base class pointer, we can always get an element to draw itself by using a virtual function. This is a good example of polymorphism at work. All we need to do to achieve this is to make sure that the classes defining specific elements share a common base class, and that in this class we declare as **virtual** all the functions we want to be selected automatically at run time. This indicates that our class structure should be like that shown in the diagram below:

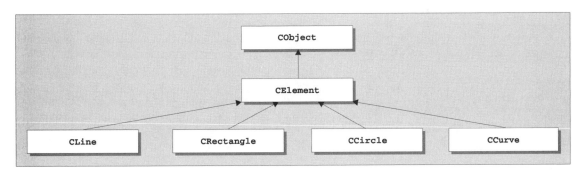

The arrows in the diagram point towards the base class in each case. If we need to add another element type, all we need to do is derive another class from **CElement**. Since these classes are closely related, we'll be putting the definitions for all these classes in a single new **.h** file that we can call **Elements.h**. Create a new source file and add the following skeleton code:

```
#if !defined(Elements_h)
#define Elements_h

// Generic element class
class CElement: public CObject
{
    // Add virtual function declarations here
};

// Class defining a line object
class CLine: public CElement
{
    // Add class definition here
};

// Class defining a rectangle object
class CRectangle: public CElement
{
    // Add class definition here
};

// Class defining a circle object
class CCircle: public CElement
{
    // Add class definition here
};

// Class defining a curve object
class CCurve: public CElement
{
    // Add class definition here
};

#endif //!defined(Elements_h)
```

You can save the file in the **Sketcher** folder as **Elements.h**. If you then add the file to the Header Files folder in FileView (right-click on Header Files to get the pop-up), the new classes will be displayed in ClassView. We've added the standard **#if !defined** command to protect against having the definitions for our element classes included more than once. Since we haven't involved the ClassWizard in this process, no **.cpp** file for any of these classes exists yet.

FYI
From time to time you might see the directive #ifndef in place of #if !defined. The two are completely equivalent, except that the label doesn't require brackets in the former case (e.g. #ifndef Elements_h).

Storing a Temporary Element in the View

When we discussed how shapes would be drawn, it was evident that as the mouse was dragged after pressing the left mouse button, a series of temporary element objects would be created and drawn. Now that we know that the base class for all the shapes is **CElement**, we can add a pointer to the view class to store the address of the temporary element. The class definition will become:

```
class CElement;

class CSketcherView: public CView
{
// other bits of the class definition as before...

// Attributes
public:
   CSketcherDoc* GetDocument();

protected:
   CPoint m_FirstPoint;        // First point recorded for an element
   CPoint m_SecondPoint;       // Second point recorded for an element
   CElement* m_pTempElement;   // Pointer to temporary element

// other bits of the class definition as before...
};
```

Of course, we should ensure that this is initialized when the view object is constructed, so we need to add the following line to the **CSketcherView** class constructor:

```
   m_pTempElement = 0;        // Set temporary element pointer to 0
```

We'll be able to use this pointer in the **WM_MOUSEMOVE** message handler as a test for previous temporary elements.

Since we'll be creating **CElement** class objects in the view class member functions, and we refer to the **CElement** class in defining the data member that points to a temporary element, we should ensure that the definition of the **CElement** class is included before the **CSketcherView** class definition wherever **SketcherView.h** is included into a **.cpp** file. You can do this for **CSketcherView** by adding a **#include** directive for **Elements.h** to the **SketcherView.cpp** file before the **#include** directive for **SketcherView.h**:

```
   #include "Elements.h"
```

Sketcher.cpp also has a **#include** directive for **SketcherView.h**, so you should add a **#include** for **Elements.h** to this file too.

The CElement Class

We need to fill out the element class definitions. We'll be doing this incrementally as we add more and more functionality to the Sketcher application, but what do we need right now? Some data members, such as color, are clearly common to all types of element; we'll put those in the **CElement** class so that they will be inherited in each of the derived classes. However, the data members in the classes which define specific element properties will be quite disparate, so we'll declare these members in the particular derived class to which they belong.

The **CElement** class will then only contain virtual functions that will be replaced in the derived classes, plus data and function members which are the same in all the derived classes. The virtual functions will be those that are selected automatically for a particular object through a pointer. For now, we can define the **CElement** class as:

```
   class CElement: public CObject
   {
```

```
    protected:
        COLORREF m_Color;                            // Color of an element

    public:
        virtual ~CElement(){}                        // Virtual destructor
        virtual void Draw(CDC* pDC) {}               // Virtual draw operation

        CRect GetBoundRect();    // Get the bounding rectangle for an element

    protected:
        CElement(){}                                 // Default constructor
};
```

The members to be inherited by the derived classes are a data member storing the color, **m_Color**, and a function member to calculate the rectangle bounding an element, **GetBoundRect()**. This function returns a value of type **CRect** which will be the rectangle bounding the shape.

We also have a virtual destructor—necessary to ensure that derived class objects are destroyed properly—and a virtual **Draw()** function which, in the derived classes, will draw the particular object in question. The default constructor is in the **protected** section of the class to ensure that it can't be used externally. The **Draw()** function will need a pointer to a **CDC** object passed to it in order to provide access to the drawing functions that we saw earlier.

You might be tempted to declare the **Draw()** member as a pure virtual function in the **CElement** class—after all, it can have no meaningful content in this class. This would also force its definition in any derived class. Normally you would do this, but our class inherits a facility from **CObject** called **serialization** that we'll use later for storing objects in a file, and this will require that an instance of our class be created. A class with a pure virtual function member is an abstract class, and instances of an abstract class can't be created. If you want to use MFC's serialization capability for storing objects, your classes mustn't be abstract.

You might also be tempted to declare the **GetBoundRect()** function as returning a *pointer* to a **CRect** object—after all, we're going to pass a pointer to the **InvalidateRect()** member function in the view class. However, this could lead to problems. You'll be creating the **CRect** object as local to the function, so the pointer would be pointing to a nonexistent object on return from the **GetBoundRect()** function. You could get around this by creating the **CRect** object on the heap, but then you'd need to take care that it's deleted after use, otherwise you'd be filling the heap with **CRect** objects—a new one for every call of **GetBoundRect()**. A further possibility is that you could store the bounding rectangle for an element as a class member and generate it when the element is created. This is a reasonable alternative, but if you changed an element subsequently, by moving it say, you would need to ensure the bounding rectangle was recalculated.

The CLine Class

We'll define the **CLine** class as:

```
class CLine: public CElement
{
    public:
        virtual void Draw(CDC* pDC);   // Function to display a line

        // Constructor for a line object
```

```
        CLine(CPoint Start, CPoint End, COLORREF aColor);

    protected:
        CPoint m_StartPoint;            // Start point of line
        CPoint m_EndPoint;              // End point of line

        CLine(){}                  // Default constructor - should not be used
};
```

The data members that define a line are **m_StartPoint** and **m_EndPoint**, both of which are **protected**. The class has a **public** constructor which has parameters for the values that define a line, and a default constructor declared as **protected** to prevent its use externally.

Implementing the CLine Class

We can place the implementation of the member functions in a new file called **Elements.cpp** that we can define in outline as:

```
// Implementations of the element classes
#include "stdafx.h"

#include "OurConstants.h"
#include "Elements.h"

// Add definitions for member functions here
```

We need the file **stdafx.h** to be included into this file to gain access to the definitions of the standard system header files. The other two files we've included are the ones we created containing definitions for our constants and for the classes we're implementing here. We may need to add **#include** statements for the files containing definitions for AppWizard-generated classes if we use any in our code.

We also need to add the **Elements.cpp** file to the Sketcher project, so once you have saved this file, you need to select the Project | Add To Project... menu item and add the file to the project. You can achieve the same result by right clicking in the editor window and selecting from the pop-up menu.

Of course, we'll have to add each of the member function definitions to this file manually, since ClassWizard wasn't involved in defining the classes. We're now ready to add the constructor for the **CLine** class to the **Elements.cpp** file.

The CLine Class Constructor

The code for this will be:

```
// CLine class constructor
CLine::CLine(CPoint Start, CPoint End, COLORREF aColor)
{
    m_StartPoint = Start;       // Set line start point
    m_EndPoint = End;           // Set line end point
    m_Color = aColor;           // Set line color
}
```

There's nothing too intellectually taxing here. We just store each of the values passed to the constructor in the appropriate data member.

Drawing a Line

The **Draw()** function isn't too difficult either, although we do need to take account of the color to be used when the line is drawn:

```
// Draw a CLine object
void CLine::Draw(CDC* pDC)
{
    // Create a pen for this object and
    // initialize it to the object color and line width of 1 pixel
    CPen aPen;
    if(!aPen.CreatePen(PS_SOLID, m_Pen, m_Color))
    {
        // Pen creation failed. Abort the program
        AfxMessageBox("Pen creation failed drawing a line", MB_OK);
        AfxAbort();
    }

    CPen* pOldPen = pDC->SelectObject(&aPen);   // Select the pen

    // Now draw the line
    pDC->MoveTo(m_StartPoint);
    pDC->LineTo(m_EndPoint);

    pDC->SelectObject(pOldPen);                  // Restore the old pen
}
```

We create a pen as we saw earlier, only this time we make sure that the creation works. If it doesn't, the most likely cause is that we're running out of memory, which is a serious problem. This will almost invariably be caused by an error in the program, so we have written the function to call **AfxMessageBox()**, which is a global function to display a message box, and then call **AfxAbort()** to terminate the program. The first argument to **AfxMessageBox()** specifies the message that is to appear, and the second specifies that it should have an OK button. You can get more information on either of these functions by placing the cursor within the function name in the editor window and then pressing *F1*.

After selecting the pen, we move the current position to the start of the line, defined in the **m_StartPoint** data member, and then draw the line from this point to the point **m_EndPoint**. Finally, we restore the old pen and we are done.

Creating Bounding Rectangles

At first sight, obtaining the bounding rectangle for a shape looks trivial. For example, a line is always a diagonal of its enclosing rectangle, and a circle is *defined* by its enclosing rectangle, but there are a couple of slight complications. Firstly, the shape must lie *completely* inside the rectangle, so we must allow for the thickness of the line used to draw the shape when we create the bounding rectangle. Secondly, how you work out adjustments to the coordinates defining the rectangle depends on the mapping mode, so we must take that into account too.

Look at the illustration below, relating to obtaining the bounding rectangle for a line and a circle:

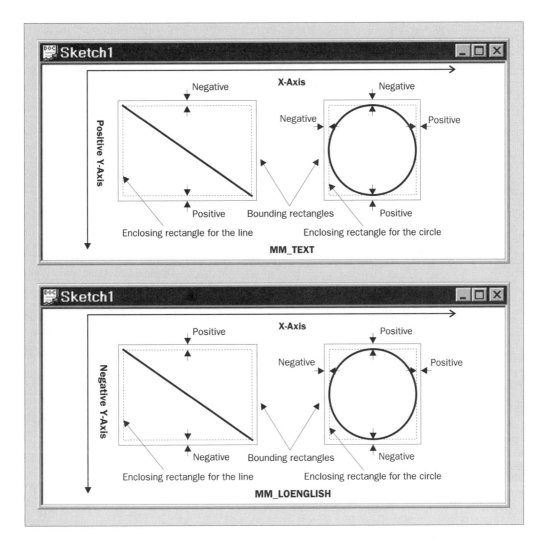

We'll call the rectangle that is used to draw a shape the 'enclosing rectangle', while the rectangle which takes into account the width of the pen we'll call the 'bounding rectangle'. The illustration shows the shapes with their enclosing rectangles, and their bounding rectangles offset by the line thickness. This is obviously exaggerated here so you can see what's happening.

The differences in how you calculate the coordinates for the bounding rectangle in different mapping modes only concern the *y* coordinates. To get the corners of the bounding rectangle in the **MM_TEXT** mapping mode, subtract the line thickness from the *y* coordinate of the top left corner of the defining rectangle, and add it to the *y* coordinate of the bottom right corner. However, in **MM_LOENGLISH** (and all the other mapping modes), the *y* axis increases in the opposite direction, so you need to *add* the line thickness to the *y* coordinate of the top left corner of the defining rectangle, and *subtract* it from the *y* coordinate of the bottom right corner. For all the mapping modes, you subtract the line thickness from the *x* coordinate of the top left corner of the defining rectangle, and add it to the *x* coordinate of the bottom right corner.

171

To implement our element types as consistently as possible, we could store an enclosing rectangle for each shape in a data element in the base class. This will need to be calculated when a shape is constructed. The job of the **GetBoundRect()** function in the base class will then be to calculate the bounding rectangle by offsetting the enclosing rectangle by the pen width. We can amend the **CElement** class definition by adding two data members, as follows:

```
class CElement: public CObject
{
   protected:
      COLORREF m_Color;                 // Color of an element
      CRect m_EnclosingRect;            // Rectangle enclosing an element
      int m_Pen;                        // Pen width

   public:
      virtual ~CElement(){}             // Virtual destructor
      virtual void Draw(CDC* pDC) {}    // Virtual draw operation

      CRect GetBoundRect();   // Get the bounding rectangle for an element

   protected:
      CElement(){}                      // Default constructor
};
```

You can add these by right clicking on the class name and selecting Add Member Variable... from the pop-up, or you can add the statements directly in the editor window along with the comments.

We must update the **CLine** constructor so that it has the correct pen width:

```
// CLine class constructor
CLine::CLine(CPoint Start, CPoint End, COLORREF aColor)
{
   m_StartPoint = Start;      // Set line start point
   m_EndPoint = End;          // Set line end point
   m_Color = aColor;          // Set line color
   m_Pen = 1;                 // Set pen width
}
```

We can now implement the **GetBoundRect()** member of the base class, assuming the **MM_TEXT** mapping mode:

```
// Get the bounding rectangle for an element
CRect CElement::GetBoundRect()
{
   CRect BoundingRect;               // Object to store bounding rectangle
   BoundingRect = m_EnclosingRect;   // Store the enclosing rectangle

   // Increase the rectangle by the pen width
   BoundingRect.InflateRect(m_Pen, m_Pen);
   return BoundingRect;              // Return the bounding rectangle
}
```

This will return the bounding rectangle for any derived class object. We define the bounding rectangle by modifying the coordinates of the enclosing rectangle stored in the base class data member so that it is enlarged all round by the pen width, using the **InflateRect()** method of the **CRect** class.

The **CRect** class provides an operator **+** for rectangles, which we could have used instead. For example, we could have written the statement before the **return** as:

```
BoundingRect = m_EnclosingRect + CRect(m_Pen, m_Pen, m_Pen, m_Pen);
```

Equally, we could have simply added (or subtracted) the pen width to each of the *x* and *y* values that make up the rectangle. We could have replaced the assignment with the following statements:

```
BoundingRect = m_EnclosingRect;
BoundingRect.top -= m_Pen;
BoundingRect.left -= m_Pen;
BoundingRect.bottom += m_Pen;
BoundingRect.right += m_Pen;
```

FYI   As a reminder, the individual data members of a **CRect** object are **left** and **top** (storing the *x* and *y* coordinates of the top left corner) and **right** and **bottom** (storing the coordinates of the bottom right corner). These are all **public** members, so we can access them directly. A commonly made mistake, especially by me, is to write the coordinate pair as (**top,left**) instead of in the correct order (**left,top**).

The hazard with both this and the **InflateRect()** option is that there is a built-in assumption that the mapping mode is **MM_TEXT**, which means that the positive *y* axis is assumed to run from top to bottom. If you change the mapping mode, neither of these will work properly, although it's not immediately obvious that they won't.

Normalized Rectangles

The **InflateRect()** function works by subtracting the values that you give it from the **top** and **left** members of the rectangle and adding the values to the **bottom** and **right**. This means that you may find your rectangle actually decreasing in size if you don't make sure that the rectangle is **normalized**. A normalized rectangle has a **left** value that is less than or equal to the **right** value, and a **top** value that is less than or equal to the **bottom** value. You can make sure that a **CRect** object is normalized by calling the **NormalizeRect()** member of the object. Most of the **CRect** member functions will require the object to be normalized in order for them to work as expected, so we need to make sure that when we store the enclosing rectangle in **m_EnclosingRect**, it is normalized.

Calculating the Enclosing Rectangle for a Line

All we need now is code in the constructor for a line to calculate the enclosing rectangle:

```
CLine::CLine(CPoint Start, CPoint End, COLORREF Color)
{
    m_StartPoint = Start;        // Set line start point
    m_EndPoint = End;            // Set line end point
    m_Color = Color;             // Set line color
    m_Pen = 1;                   // Set pen width

    // Define the enclosing rectangle
    m_EnclosingRect = CRect(Start, End);
```

173

```
        m_EnclosingRect.NormalizeRect();
    }
```

This simply calculates the coordinates of the top left and bottom right points, defining the rectangle from the start and end points of the line. We need to take care, though, that the bounding rectangle has the **top** value less than the **bottom** value, regardless of the relative positions of the start and end points of the line, so we call the **NormalizeRect()** member of the **m_EnclosingRect** object.

The CRectangle Class

Although we'll be defining a rectangle object by the same data we used to define a line, we don't need to store the defining points. The enclosing rectangle in the data member inherited from the base class completely defines the shape, so we don't need any data members:

```
// Class defining a rectangle object
class CRectangle: public CElement
{
    public:
        virtual void Draw(CDC* pDC);  // Function to display a rectangle

        // Constructor for a rectangle object
        CRectangle(CPoint Start, CPoint End, COLORREF aColor);

    protected:
        CRectangle(){}          // Default constructor - should not be used
};
```

The definition of the rectangle becomes very simple—just a constructor, the virtual **Draw()** function, and the default constructor in the **protected** section of the class.

The CRectangle Class Constructor

The code for the class constructor is somewhat similar to that for a **CLine** constructor:

```
// CRectangle class constructor
CRectangle:: CRectangle(CPoint Start, CPoint End, COLORREF aColor)
{
    m_Color = aColor;          // Set rectangle color
    m_Pen = 1;                 // Set pen width

    // Define the enclosing rectangle
    m_EnclosingRect = CRect(Start, End);
    m_EnclosingRect.NormalizeRect();
}
```

Since we created the class definition manually, there will be no skeleton definition for the constructor, so you need to add the definition directly to **Elements.cpp**.

This is cheap code. Some minor alterations to a subset of the **CLine** constructor, fix the comments, and we have a new constructor for **CRectangle**. It just stores the color and pen width and computes the enclosing rectangle from the points passed as arguments.

Drawing a Rectangle

There is a member of the class **CDC** to draw a rectangle, called **Rectangle()**. This draws a closed figure and fills it with the current brush. You may think that this isn't quite what we want, since we want to draw rectangles as outlines only, but by selecting a **NULL_BRUSH** this is exactly what we'll draw. Just so you know, there's also a function **PolyLine()**, which draws shapes consisting of multiple line segments from an array of points, or we could have used **LineTo()** again, but the easiest approach for us is to use the **Rectangle()** function:

```
// Draw a CRectangle object
void CRectangle::Draw(CDC* pDC)
{
   // Create a pen for this object and
   // initialize it to the object color and line width of 1 pixel
   CPen aPen;
   if(!aPen.CreatePen(PS_SOLID, m_Pen, m_Color))
   {
      // Pen creation failed
      AfxMessageBox("Pen creation failed drawing a rectangle", MB_OK);
      AfxAbort();
   }

   // Select the pen
   CPen* pOldPen = pDC->SelectObject(&aPen);
   // Select the brush
   CBrush* pOldBrush = (CBrush*)pDC->SelectStockObject(NULL_BRUSH);

   // Now draw the rectangle
   pDC->Rectangle(m_EnclosingRect);

   pDC->SelectObject(pOldBrush);           // Restore the old brush
   pDC->SelectObject(pOldPen);             // Restore the old pen
}
```

After setting up the pen and the brush, we can simply pass the whole rectangle directly to the **Rectangle()** function to get it drawn. All that then remains to do is to clear up after ourselves and restore the device context's old pen and brush.

The CCircle Class

The interface of the **CCircle** class is no different from that of the **CRectangle** class. We can define a circle solely by its enclosing rectangle, so the class definition will be:

```
// Class defining a circle object
class CCircle: public CElement
{
   public:
      virtual void Draw(CDC* pDC);  // Function to display a circle

      // Constructor for a circle object
      CCircle(CPoint Start, CPoint End, COLORREF aColor);

   protected:
      CCircle(){}              // Default constructor - should not be used
};
```

We have defined a public constructor, and the default constructor is declared as **protected** again.

Implementing the CCircle Class

As we discussed earlier, when you create a circle, the point where you press the left mouse button will be the center, and after moving the cursor with the left button down, the point where you release the cursor is a point on the circumference of the final circle. The job of the constructor will be to convert these points into the form used in the class to define a circle.

The CCircle Class Constructor

The point at which you release the left mouse button can be anywhere on the circumference, so the coordinates of the points specifying the enclosing rectangle need to be calculated, as illustrated below:

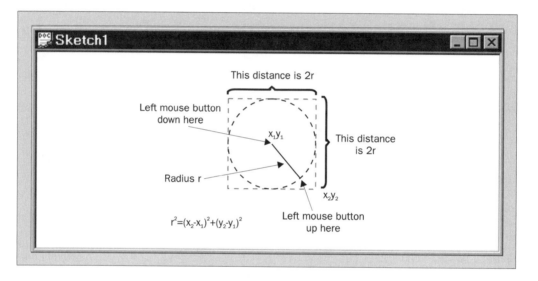

From this diagram, you can see that we can calculate the coordinates of the top left and bottom right points of the enclosing rectangle relative to the center of the circle (x_1, y_1), which is the point we record when the left mouse button is pressed. Assuming that the mapping mode is **MM_TEXT**, for the top left point we just subtract the radius from each of the coordinates of the center. Similarly, the bottom right point is obtained by adding the radius to the x and y coordinates of the center. We can, therefore, code the constructor as:

```
// Constructor for a circle object
CCircle::CCircle(CPoint Start, CPoint End, COLORREF aColor)
{
    // First calculate the radius
    // We use floating point because that is required by
    // the library function (in math.h) for calculating a square root.
    long Radius = (long) sqrt((double)((End.x-Start.x)*(End.x-Start.x)+
                                       (End.y-Start.y)*(End.y-Start.y)));

    // Now calculate the rectangle enclosing
    // the circle assuming the MM_TEXT mapping mode
```

```
    m_EnclosingRect = CRect(Start.x-Radius, Start.y-Radius,
                             Start.x+Radius, Start.y+Radius);

    m_Color = aColor;        // Set the color for the circle
    m_Pen = 1;               // Set pen width to 1
}
```

To use the **sqrt()** function, you should add the line **#include <math.h>** to the beginning of the file, after the include for **stdafx.h**. The maximum coordinate values are 16 bits, and the **CPoint** members **x** and **y** are declared as **long**, so evaluating the argument to the **sqrt()** function can safely be carried out as an integer. The result of the square root calculation will be of type **double**, so we cast it to **long** because we want to use it as an integer.

Drawing a Circle

We've already seen how to draw a circle using the **Arc()** function in the **CDC** class, so let's use the **Ellipse()** function here. The **Draw()** function in the **CCircle** class will be:

```
// Draw a circle
void CCircle::Draw(CDC* pDC)
{
   // Create a pen for this object and
   // initialize it to the object color and line width of 1 pixel
   CPen aPen;
   if(!aPen.CreatePen(PS_SOLID, m_Pen, m_Color))
   {
      // Pen creation failed
      AfxMessageBox("Pen creation failed drawing a circle", MB_OK);
      AfxAbort();
   }

   CPen* pOldPen = pDC->SelectObject(&aPen);   // Select the pen

   // Select a null brush
   CBrush* pOldBrush = (CBrush*)pDC->SelectStockObject(NULL_BRUSH);

   // Now draw the circle
   pDC->Ellipse(m_EnclosingRect);

   pDC->SelectObject(pOldPen);              // Restore the old pen
   pDC->SelectObject(pOldBrush);            // Restore the old brush
}
```

After selecting a pen of the appropriate color and a null brush, the circle is drawn by calling the **Ellipse()** function. The only argument is a **CRect** object which encloses the circle to be drawn. This is another example of code that's almost for free, as it's very similar to the code we wrote earlier to draw a rectangle.

The CCurve Class

The **CCurve** class is different from the others in that it needs to handle a variable number of defining points. This necessitates maintaining a list of some kind, and since we will look at how MFC can help with lists in the next chapter, we'll defer defining the detail of this class until then. For now, we'll include a class definition that provides dummy member functions so we can compile and link code that contains calls to them. In **Elements.h**, you should have:

```
class CCurve: public CElement
{
    public:
        virtual void Draw(CDC* pDC); // Function to display a curve

        // Constructor for a curve object
        CCurve(COLORREF aColor);

    protected:
        CCurve(){}               // Default constructor - should not be used
};
```

And in **Elements.cpp**:

```
// Constructor for a curve object
CCurve::CCurve(COLORREF aColor)
{
    m_Color = aColor;
    m_EnclosingRect = CRect(0,0,0,0);
    m_Pen = 1;
}

// Draw a curve
void CCurve::Draw(CDC* pDC)
{
}
```

Neither the constructor nor the **Draw()** member function does anything useful yet, and we have no data members to define a curve. The constructor just sets the color, sets **m_EnclosingRect** to an empty rectangle, and sets the pen width. We'll expand the class into a working version in the next chapter.

Completing the Mouse Message Handlers

We can now come back to the **WM_MOUSEMOVE** message handler and fill out the detail. You can get to it through the ClassWizard or by expanding **CSketcherView** in the ClassView and double-clicking the handler name, **OnMouseMove()**.

This handler will only be concerned with drawing a succession of temporary versions of an element as you move the cursor, because the final element will be created when you release the left mouse button. We can therefore treat the drawing of temporary elements to provide rubber-banding as being entirely local to this function, leaving the final version of the element being created to be drawn by the **OnDraw()** function member of the view. This approach will result in the drawing of the rubber-banded elements being reasonably efficient, as we won't involve the **OnDraw()** function, which ultimately will be responsible for drawing the entire document.

We can do this best with the help of a member of the **CDC** class that is particularly effective in rubber-banding operations: **SetROP2()**.

Setting the Drawing Mode

The **SetROP2()** function sets the **drawing mode** for all subsequent output operations in the device context associated with a **CDC** object. The 'ROP' bit of the function name stands for **R**aster **OP**eration, because the setting of drawing modes only applies to raster displays. In case you're wondering, 'What's SetROP1() then?'—there isn't one. The function name represents 'Set Raster OPeration to', not 2!

There are other kinds of graphic displays, called vector displays or directed beam displays, for which this mechanism does not apply, but you are unlikely to meet them these days—they have been largely rendered obsolete by raster displays.

The drawing mode determines how the color of the pen that you use for drawing is to combine with the background color to produce the color of the entity you are displaying. You specify the drawing mode with a single argument to the function which can be any of the following values:

Drawing Mode	Effect
R2_BLACK	All drawing is in black.
R2_WHITE	All drawing is in white.
R2_NOP	Drawing operations do nothing.
R2_NOT	Drawing is in the inverse of the screen color. This ensures the output will always be visible, since it prevents drawing in the same color as the background.
R2_COPYPEN	Drawing is in the pen color. This is the default drawing mode if you don't set it.
R2_NOTCOPYPEN	Drawing is in the inverse of the pen color.
R2_MERGEPENNOT	Drawing is in the color produced by ORing the pen color with the inverse of the background color.
R2_MASKPENNOT	Drawing is in the color produced by ANDing the pen color with the inverse of the background color.
R2_MERGENOTPEN	Drawing is in the color produced by ORing the background color with the inverse of the pen color.
R2_MASKNOTPEN	Drawing is in the color produced by ANDing the background color with the inverse of the pen color.
R2_MERGEPEN	Drawing is in the color produced by ORing the background color with the pen color.
R2_NOTMERGEPEN	Drawing is in the color that is the inverse of the **R2_MERGEPEN** color.
R2_MASKPEN	Drawing is in the color produced by ANDing the background color with the pen color.
R2_NOTMASKPEN	Drawing is in the color that is the inverse of the **R2_MASKPEN** color.
R2_XORPEN	Drawing is in the color produced by exclusive ORing the pen color and the background color.
R2_NOTXORPEN	Drawing is in the color that is the inverse of the **R2_XORPEN** color.

Each of these symbols is predefined and corresponds to a particular drawing mode. There are a lot of options here, but the one that can work some magic for us is the last of them, **R2_NOTXORPEN**.

When we set the mode as **R2_NOTXORPEN**, the first time you draw a particular shape on the default white background, it will be drawn normally in the pen color you specify. If you draw the same shape again, overwriting the first, the shape will disappear, because the color that the shape will be drawn in corresponds to that produced by exclusive ORing the pen color with itself. The drawing color that results from this will be white. You can see this more clearly by working through an example.

White is formed from equal proportions of the 'maximum' amounts of red, blue, and green. For simplicity, we can represent this as 1,1,1—the three values represent the RGB components of the color. In the same scheme, red is defined as 1,0,0. These combine as follows:

	R	G	B	
Background—white	1	1	1	
Pen—red	1	0	0	
XORed	0	1	1	
NOT XOR	1	0	0	which is red

So, the first time we draw a red line on a white background, it comes out red. If we draw the same line a second time, overwriting the existing line, the background pixels we are writing over are red. The resultant drawing color works out as follows:

	R	G	B	
Background—red	1	0	0	
Pen—red	1	0	0	
XORed	0	0	0	
NOT XOR	1	1	1	which is white

Since the rest of the background is white, the line will disappear.

You need to take care to use the right background color here. You should be able to see that drawing with a white pen on a red background is not going to work too well, as the first time you draw something it will be red, and therefore invisible. The second time it will appear as white. If you draw on a black background, things will appear and disappear, as on a white background, but they will not be drawn in the pen color you choose.

Coding the OnMouseMove() Handler

Let's start by adding the code that creates the element after a mouse move message. Since we are going to draw the element from the handler function, we need to create an object for the device context. The most convenient class to use for this is **CClientDC**, which is derived from **CDC**. As we said earlier, the advantage of using this class rather than **CDC** is that it will automatically take care of creating the device context for us and destroying it when we are done. The device context that it creates corresponds to the client area of a window, which is exactly what we want. Add the following code to the outline handler that we defined:

```
void CSketcherView::OnMouseMove(UINT nFlags, CPoint point)
{
    // Define a Device Context object for the view
    CClientDC aDC(this);
    aDC.SetROP2(R2_NOTXORPEN);      // Set the drawing mode
    if(nFlags & MK_LBUTTON)
    {
        m_SecondPoint = point;        // Save the current cursor position
        // Test for a previous temporary element
        {
            // We get to here if there was a previous mouse move
            // so add code to delete the old element
        }

        // Create a temporary element of the type and color that
        // is recorded in the document object, and draw it
        m_pTempElement = CreateElement();  // Create a new element
        m_pTempElement->Draw(&aDC);        // Draw the element
    }
}
```

The first new line of code creates a local **CClientDC** object. The **this** pointer that we pass to the constructor identifies the current view object, so the **CClientDC** object will have a device context that corresponds to the client area of the current view. As well as the characteristics we mentioned, this object has all the drawing functions we need, as they are inherited from the class **CDC**. The first member function we use is **SetROP2()**, which sets the drawing mode to **R2_NOTXORPEN**.

To create a new element, we save the current cursor position in the data member **m_SecondPoint**, and then call a view member function **CreateElement()**. (We'll define the **CreateElement()** function as soon as we have finished this handler.) This function should create an element using the two points stored in the current view object, with the color and type specification stored in the document object, and return the address of the element. We save this in **m_pTempElement**.

Using the pointer to the new element, we call its **Draw()** member to get the object to draw itself. The address of the **CClientDC** object is passed as an argument. Since we defined the **Draw()** function as virtual in the base class **CElement**, the function for whatever type of element **m_pTempElement** is pointing to will automatically be selected. The new element will be drawn normally with the **R2_NOTXORPEN** because we are drawing it for the first time on a white background.

We can use the pointer **m_pTempElement** as an indicator of whether a previous temporary element exists. The code for this part of the handler will be:

```
void CSketcherView::OnMouseMove(UINT nFlags, CPoint point)
{
    // Define a Device Context object for the view
    CClientDC aDC(this);               // DC is for this view
    aDC.SetROP2(R2_NOTXORPEN);         // Set the drawing mode
    if(nFlags&MK_LBUTTON)
    {
        m_SecondPoint = point;         // Save the current cursor position

        if(m_pTempElement)
```

181

```
        {
            // Redraw the old element so it disappears from the view
            m_pTempElement->Draw(&aDC);
            delete m_pTempElement;      // Delete the old element
            m_pTempElement = 0;         // Reset the pointer to 0
        }

        // Create a temporary element of the type and color that
        // is recorded in the document object, and draw it
        m_pTempElement = CreateElement();  // Create a new element
        m_pTempElement->Draw(&aDC);        // Draw the element
    }
}
```

A previous temporary element exists if the pointer **m_pTempElement** is not zero. We need to redraw the element it points to in order to remove it from the client area of the view. We then delete the element and reset the pointer to zero. The new element will then be created and drawn by the code that we added previously. This combination will automatically rubber-band the shape being created, so it will appear to be attached to the cursor position as it moves. We must remember to reset the pointer **m_pTempElement** back to 0 in the **WM_LBUTTONUP** message handler after we create the final version of the element.

Creating an Element

We need to add the **CreateElement()** function as a **protected** member to the 'Operations' section of the **CSketcherView** class:

```
class CSketcherView: public CView
{

    // Rest of the class definition as before...

    // Operations
public:

    protected:
        CElement* CreateElement(); // Create a new element on the heap

    // Rest of the class definition as before...

};
```

To do this you can either amend the class definition directly by adding the line shown above, or you can right-click on the class name, **CSketcherView**, in ClassView, and select Add Member Function... from the menu. This will open the following dialog:

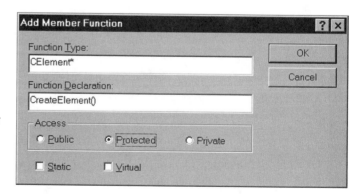

Add the specifications of the function, as shown, and click on OK, so that a declaration for the function member will be added to the class definition, and you will be taken directly to a skeleton for the function in **SketcherView.cpp**. If you added the declaration to the class definition manually, you'll need to add the complete definition for the function to the **.cpp** file. This is:

```
// Create an element of the current type
CElement* CSketcherView::CreateElement()
{
    // Get a pointer to the document for this view
    CSketcherDoc* pDoc = GetDocument();
    ASSERT_VALID(pDoc);                    // Verify the pointer is good

    // Now select the element using the type stored in the document
    switch(pDoc->GetElementType())
    {
        case RECTANGLE:
            return new CRectangle(m_FirstPoint, m_SecondPoint,
                                            pDoc->GetElementColor());

        case CIRCLE:
            return new CCircle(m_FirstPoint, m_SecondPoint,
                                        pDoc->GetElementColor());

        case CURVE:
            return new CCurve(pDoc->GetElementColor());

        case LINE:
            return new CLine(m_FirstPoint, m_SecondPoint,
                                    pDoc->GetElementColor());

        default:
            // Something's gone wrong
            AfxMessageBox("Bad Element code", MB_OK);
            AfxAbort();
            return NULL;
    }
}
```

The lines that aren't shaded are those that will have been supplied automatically if you added the function to the class using the Add Member Function dialog. The first thing we do here is to get a pointer to the document by calling **GetDocument()**, as we've seen before. For safety, the **ASSERT_VALID()** macro is used to ensure that a good pointer is returned. In the debug version of MFC that's used in the debug version of your application, this macro calls the **AssertValid()** member of the object which is specified as the argument to the macro. This checks the validity of the current object, and if the pointer is **NULL** or the object is defective in some way, an error message will be displayed. In the release version of MFC, the **ASSERT_VALID()** macro does nothing.

The **switch** statement selects the element to be created based on the type returned by a function in the document class, **GetElementType()**. Another function in the document class is used to obtain the current element color. We can add the definitions for both these functions directly to the **CSketcherDoc** class definition, because they are very simple:

```
class CSketcherDoc: public CDocument
{

    // Rest of the class definition as before...

    // Operations
    public:
        WORD GetElementType()          // Get the element type
            { return m_Element; }
        COLORREF GetElementColor()     // Get the element color
            { return m_Color; }

    // Rest of the class definition as before...

};
```

Each of the functions returns the value stored in the corresponding data member. Remember that putting a member function definition in the class definition is equivalent to a request to make the function **inline**, so as well as being simple, these should be fast.

Dealing with WM_LBUTTONUP Messages

The **WM_LBUTTONUP** message completes the process of creating an element. The job of this handler is to pass the final version of the element that was created to the document object, and then clean up the view object data members. You can access and edit the code for this handler in the same way as you did for the last one. Add the following lines to the function:

```
void CSketcherView::OnLButtonUp(UINT nFlags, CPoint point)
{
    // Make sure there is an element
    if(m_pTempElement)
    {
        // Call a document class function to store the element
        // pointed to by m_pTempElement in the document object

        delete m_pTempElement;   // This code is temporary
        m_pTempElement = 0;      // Reset the element pointer
    }
}
```

The **if** statement will test that **m_pTempElement** is not zero. It's always possible that the user could press and release the left mouse button without moving the mouse, in which case no element would have been created. As long as there is an element, the pointer to the element will be passed to the document object; we'll add the code for this in the next chapter. In the meantime, we'll just delete the element here so as not to pollute the heap. Finally, the **m_pTempElement** pointer is reset to 0, ready for the next time the user draws an element.

Exercising Sketcher

Before we can run the example with the mouse message handlers, we need to update the **OnDraw()** function in the **CSketcherView** class implementation to get rid of any old code that we added earlier.

To make sure that the **OnDraw()** function is clean, go to ClassView and double-click on the function name to take you to its implementation in **SketcherView.cpp**. Delete any old code that you added, but leave in the first two lines that AppWizard provided to get a pointer to the document object. We'll need this later to get to the elements when they're stored in the document. The code for the function should now be:

```
void CSketcherView::OnDraw(CDC* pDC)
{
   CSketcherDoc* pDoc = GetDocument();
   ASSERT_VALID(pDoc);
}
```

Since we have no elements in the document as yet, we don't need to add anything to this function at this point. When we start storing data in the document in the next chapter, we'll need to add code here to draw the elements in response to a **WM_PAINT** message. Without it, the elements will just disappear whenever you resize the view, as you'll see.

Running the Example

After making sure that you have saved all the source files, build the program. If you haven't made any mistakes entering the code, you'll get a clean compile and link, so you can execute the program. You can draw lines, circles and rectangles in any of the four colors the program supports. A typical window is shown below:

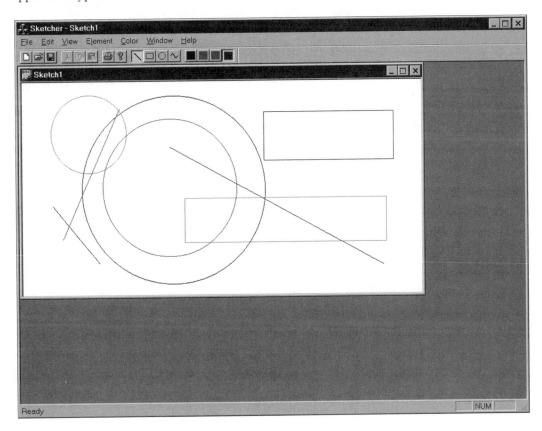

Try experimenting with the user interface. Note that you can move the window around, and that the shapes stay in the window as long as you don't move it so far that they're outside the borders of the application window. If you do, the elements do not reappear after you move it back. This is because the existing elements are never redrawn. When the client area is covered and uncovered, Windows will send a **WM_PAINT** message to the application, which will cause the **OnDraw()** member of the view object to be called. As you know, the **OnDraw()** function for the view doesn't do anything at present. This will get fixed when we use the document to store the elements.

When you resize the view window, the shapes disappear immediately, but when you move the whole view around, they remain (as long as they don't slide beyond the application window border). How come? Well, when you resize the window, Windows invalidates the whole client area and expects your application to redraw it in response to the **WM_PAINT** message. If you move the view around, Windows takes care of relocating the client area as it is. You can demonstrate this by moving the view so that a shape is partially obscured. When you slide it back, you still have a partial shape, with the bit that was obscured erased.

If you try drawing a shape while dragging the cursor outside the client view area, you'll notice some peculiar effects. Outside the view window, we lose track of the mouse, which tends to mess up our rubber-banding mechanism. What's going on?

Capturing Mouse Messages

The problem is caused by the fact that Windows is sending the mouse messages to the window under the cursor. As soon as the cursor leaves the client area of our application view window, the **WM_MOUSEMOVE** messages are being sent elsewhere. We can fix this by using some inherited members of **CSketcherView**.

Our view class inherits a function, **SetCapture()**, which tells Windows that we want our window to get *all* the mouse messages until such time as we say otherwise, by calling another inherited function in our view class, **ReleaseCapture()**. We can capture the mouse as soon as the left button is pressed by modifying the handler for the **WM_LBUTTONDOWN** message:

```
// Handler for left mouse button down message
void CSketcherView::OnLButtonDown(UINT nFlags, CPoint point)
{
    m_FirstPoint = point;            // Record the cursor position
    SetCapture();                    // Capture subsequent mouse messages
}
```

Now we must call the **ReleaseCapture()** function in the **WM_LBUTTONUP** handler. If we don't do this, other programs will not be able to receive any mouse messages as long as our program continues to run. Of course, we should only release the mouse if we've captured it earlier. The function **GetCapture()**, which our view class inherits, will return a pointer to the window that has captured the mouse, and this gives us a way of telling whether or not we have captured mouse messages. We just need to add the following to the handler for **WM_LBUTTONUP**:

```
void CSketcherView::OnLButtonUp(UINT nFlags, CPoint point)
{
    if(this == GetCapture())
        ReleaseCapture();            // Stop capturing mouse messages
```

```
    // Make sure there is an element
    if(m_pTempElement)
    {
       // Call a document class function to store the element
       // pointed to by m_pTempElement in the document object

       delete m_pTempElement;   // This code is temporary
          m_pTempElement = 0;      // Reset the element pointer
    }
}
```

If the pointer returned by the **GetCapture()** function is equal to the pointer **this**, our view has captured the mouse, so we release it.

The final alteration we should make is to modify the **WM_MOUSEMOVE** handler so that it only deals with messages that have been captured by our view. We can do this with one small change:

```
void CSketcherView::OnMouseMove(UINT nFlags, CPoint point)
{
    // Rest of the handler as before...

    if((nFlags & MK_LBUTTON) && (this == GetCapture()))
    {
        // Rest of the handler as before...
    }
}
```

The handler will now only process the message if the left button is down *and* the left button down handler for our view has been called, so that the mouse has been captured by our view window.

If you rebuild Sketcher with these additions, you'll find that the problems which arose earlier when the cursor was dragged off the client area no longer occur.

Summary

After completing this chapter, you should have a good grasp of how to write message handlers for the mouse, and how to organize drawing operations in your Windows programs. The important points that we have covered in this chapter are:

▶ By default, Windows addresses the client area of a window using a client coordinate system with the origin in the top left corner of the client area. The positive *x* direction is from left to right, and the positive *y* direction is from top to bottom.

▶ You can only draw in the client area of a window by using a device context.

▶ A device context provides a range of logical coordinate systems called mapping modes for addressing the client area of a window.

▶ The default origin position for a mapping mode is the top left corner of the client area. The default mapping mode is **MM_TEXT** which provides coordinates measured in pixels. The positive *x* axis runs from left to right in this mode, and the positive *y* axis from top to bottom.

▶ Your program should always draw the permanent contents of the client area of a window in response to a **WM_PAINT** message, although temporary entities can be drawn at other times. All the drawing for your application document should be controlled from the **OnDraw()** member function of a view class. This function is called when a **WM_PAINT** message is received by your application.

▶ You can identify the part of the client area you want to have redrawn by calling the **InvalidateRect()** function member of your view class. The area passed as an argument will be added by Windows to the total area to be redrawn when the next **WM_PAINT** message is sent to your application.

▶ Windows sends standard messages to your application for mouse events. You can create handlers to deal with these messages by using ClassWizard.

▶ You can cause all mouse messages to be routed to your application by calling the **SetCapture()** function in your view class. You must release the mouse when you're finished with it by calling the **ReleaseCapture()** function. If you fail to do this, other applications will be unable to receive mouse messages.

▶ You can implement rubber-banding when creating geometric entities by drawing them in the message handler for mouse movements.

▶ The **SetROP2()** member of the **CDC** class enables you to set drawing modes. Selecting the right drawing mode greatly simplifies rubber-banding operations.

Exercises

Ex5-1: Add the menu item and toolbar button for an element of type ellipse, as in the exercises from Chapter 4, and define a class to support drawing ellipses defined by two points on opposite corners of their enclosing rectangle.

Ex5-2: Which functions now need to be modified to support drawing an ellipse? Modify the program to draw an ellipse.

Ex5-3: Which functions must you modify in the example from the previous exercise so that the first point defines the center of the ellipse, and the current cursor position defines a corner of the enclosing rectangle? Modify the example to work this way. (Hint—look up the **CPoint** class members in Help.)

Ex5-4: Add a new menu pop-up to the **IDR_SKETCHTYPE** menu for Pen Style, to allow solid, dashed, dotted, dash-dotted, and dash-dot-dotted lines to be specified.

Ex5-5: Which parts of the program need to be modified to support the operation of the menu, and the drawing of elements in these line types?

Ex5-6: Implement support for the new menu pop-up and drawing elements in any of the line types.

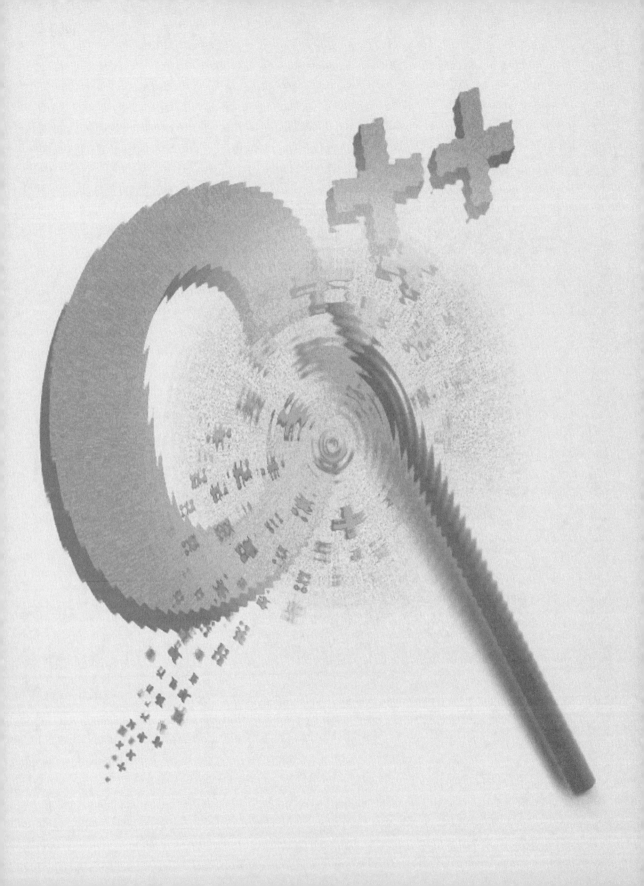

Creating the Document and Improving the View

In this chapter, we'll look into the facilities offered by MFC for managing collections of data items. We'll use these to complete the class definition and implementation for the curve element that we left open in the last chapter. We'll also extend the Sketcher application to store data in a document, and make the document view more flexible, introducing several new techniques in the process.

In this chapter, you'll learn:

▶ What collections are, and what you can do with them

▶ How to use a collection to store point data for a curve

▶ How to use a collection to store document data

▶ How to implement drawing a document

▶ How to implement scrolling in a view

▶ How to create a pop-up menu at the cursor

▶ How to highlight the element nearest the cursor to provide feedback to the user for moving and deleting elements

▶ How to program the mouse to move and delete elements

What are Collection Classes?

By the nature of Windows programming, you'll frequently need to handle collections of data items where you have no advance knowledge of how many items you will need to manage, or even what particular type they are going to be. This is clearly illustrated by our Sketcher application. The user can draw an arbitrary number of elements which can be lines, rectangles, circles and curves, and in any sequence. MFC provides a group of **collection classes** designed to handle exactly this sort of problem—a **collection** being an aggregation of an arbitrary number of data items organized in a particular way.

Types of Collection

MFC provides you with a large number of collection classes for managing data. We'll use just a couple of them in practice, but it would be helpful to understand the types of collections available. MFC supports three kinds of collections, differentiated by the way in which the data items are organized. The way a collection is organized is referred to as the **shape** of the collection. The three types of organization, or shape, are:

Shape	How information is organized
Array	An array in this context is just like an array in the C++ language. It's an ordered arrangement of elements, where any element is retrieved by using an integer index value. An array collection can automatically grow to accommodate more data items. However, one of the other collection types is generally preferred, since array collections can be rather slow in operation.
List	A list collection is an ordered arrangement of data items, where each item has two pointers associated with it which point to the next and previous items in the list. The list we have here is called a **doubly linked** list, because it has backward - as well as forward-pointing links. It can be searched in either direction and, like an array, a list collection grows automatically when required. A list collection is easy to use, and fast when it comes to adding items. Searching for an item can be slow, though, if there are a lot of data items in the list.
Map	A map is an unordered collection of data items, where each item is associated with a key that is used to retrieve the item from the map. A key is usually a string, but it can also be a numeric value. Maps are fast in storing data items and in searching, since a key will take you directly to the item you need. This sounds as though maps are always the ideal choice, and this is often the case, but for sequential access arrays will be faster. You also have the problem of choosing a key for your object that's unique for each item in the list.

MFC collection classes provide two approaches to implementing each type of collection. One approach is based on the use of class templates and provides you with **type-safe** handling of data in a collection. Type-safe handling means that the data passed to a function member of the collection class will be checked to ensure that it's of a type that can be processed by the function.

The other approach makes use of a range of collection classes (rather than templates), but these perform no data checking. If you want your collection classes to be type-safe, you have to include code yourself to assure this. These latter classes were available in older versions of Visual C++ under Windows, but the template collection classes were not. We'll concentrate on the template-based versions, since these will provide the best chance of avoiding errors in our application.

The Type-Safe Collection Classes

The template-based type-safe collection classes support collections of objects of any type, and collections of pointers to objects of any type. Collections of objects are supported by the template classes **CArray**, **CList** and **CMap**, and collections of pointers to objects are supported by the template classes **CTypedPtrArray**, **CTypedPtrList** and **CTypedPtrMap**. We won't go into the detail of all of these, just the two that we'll use in the Sketcher program. One will store objects and the other will store pointers to objects, so you'll get a feel for both sorts of collection.

Collections of Objects

The template classes for defining collections of objects are all derived from the MFC class **CObject**. They are defined this way so that they inherit the properties of the **CObject** class which are particularly useful for a number of things, including the file input and output operations (serialization, which we'll look at in Chapter 8).

These template classes can store and manage any kind of object, including all the C++ basic data types, plus any classes or structures that you or anybody else might define. Because these classes store objects, whenever you add an element to a list, an array, or a map, the class template object will need to make a copy of your object. Consequently, any class type that you want to store in any of these collections must have a copy constructor. The copy constructor for your class will be used to create a duplicate of the object that you wish to store in the collection.

Let's look at the general properties of each of the template classes providing type-safe management of objects. This is not an exhaustive treatment of all the member functions provided. Rather, it's intended to give you a sufficient flavor of how they work to enable you to decide if you want to use them or not. You can get information on all of the member functions by using <u>H</u>elp to get to the template class definition.

The CArray Template Class

You can use this template to store any kind of object in an array and have the array automatically grow to accommodate more elements when necessary. An array collection is illustrated below:

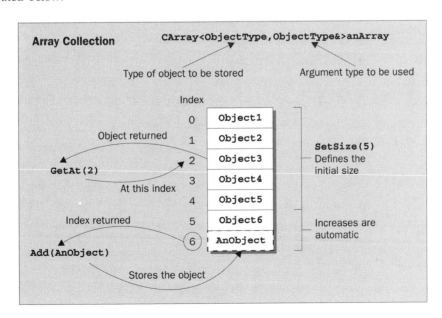

As with arrays in C++, elements in array collections are indexed from 0. The declaration of an array collection takes two arguments. The first argument is the type of the object to be stored so, if your array collection is to store objects of type **CPoint**, for example, you specify **CPoint** as the first argument. The second argument is the type to be used in member function calls. To avoid the overhead in copying objects when passed by value, this is usually a reference, so an example of an array collection declaration to hold **CPoint** objects is:

```
CArray<CPoint, CPoint&> PointArray;
```

This defines the array collection class object, **PointArray**, which will store **CPoint** objects. When you call function members of this object, the argument is a reference, so to add a **CPoint** object, you would write

```
PointArray.Add(aPoint);
```

and the argument **aPoint** will be passed as a reference.

If you declare an array collection, it's important to call the **SetSize()** member function to fix the initial number of elements that you require before you use it. It will still work if you don't do this, but the initial allocation of elements and subsequent increments will be small, resulting in inefficient operation and frequent reallocation of memory for the array. The initial number of elements that you should specify depends on the typical size of array you expect to need, and how variable the size is. If you expect the minimum your program will require to be of the order of 400 to 500 elements, for example, but with expansion up to 700 or 800, an initial size of 600 should be suitable.

To retrieve the contents of an element, you can use the **GetAt()** function, as shown in the diagram above. To store the third element of **PointArray** in a variable **aPoint**, you would write:

```
aPoint = PointArray.GetAt(2);
```

The class also overloads the **[]** operator, so you could retrieve the third element of **PointArray** by using **PointArray[2]**. For example, if **aPoint** is a variable of type **CPoint**, you could write:

```
aPoint = PointArray[2];          // Store a copy of the third element
```

For array collections that are not **const**, this notation can also be used instead of the **SetAt()** function to set the contents of an existing element. The following two statements are, therefore, equivalent:

```
PointArray.SetAt(3,NewPoint);    // Store NewObject in the 4th element
PointArray[3] = NewPoint;        // Same as previous line of code
```

Here, **NewPoint** is an object of the type used to declare the array. In both cases, the element must already exist. You cannot extend the array by this means. To extend the array, you can use the **Add()** function shown in the diagram, which adds a new element to the array. There is also a function **Append()** to add an *array* of elements to the end of the array.

Helper Functions

Whenever you call the **SetSize()** function member of an array collection, a global function, **ConstructElements()**, is called to allocate memory for the number of elements you want to store in the array collection initially. This is called a **helper function**, as it helps in the process of setting the size of the array collection. The default version of this function sets the contents of the allocated memory to zero and doesn't call a constructor for your object class, so you'll need to supply your own version of this helper function if this action isn't appropriate for your objects. This will be the case if space for data members of objects of your class is allocated dynamically, or if there is other initialization required. **ConstructElements()** is also called by the member function **InsertAt()**, which inserts one or more elements at a particular index position within the array.

Members of the **CArray** collection class that remove elements call the helper function **DestructElements()**. The default version does nothing so, if your object construction allocates any memory on the heap, you must override this function to release the memory properly.

The **CList** collection template makes use of a helper function when searching the contents of a list for a particular object. We'll discuss this further in the next section. Another helper function, **SerializeElements()**, is used by the array, list and map collection classes, but we'll discuss this when we come to look into how we can write a document to file.

The CList Template Class

A list collection is very flexible; you're likely to find yourself using lists more often than you use either arrays or maps. Let's look at the list collection template in some detail, as we'll apply it in our Sketcher program. The parameters to the **CList** collection class template are the same as those for the **CArray** template:

```
CList<ObjectType, ObjectType&> aList;
```

You need to supply two arguments to the template when you declare a list collection: the type of object to be stored, and the way an object is to be specified in function arguments. The example shows the second argument as a reference, since this is used most frequently. It doesn't necessarily have to be a reference, though—you could use a pointer, or even the object type (so objects would be passed by value), but this would be slow.

We can use a list to manage a curve in the Sketcher program. We could declare a list collection to store the points specifying a curve object with the statement:

```
CList<CPoint, CPoint&> PointList;
```

This declares a list called **PointList** that stores **CPoint** objects, which are passed to functions in the class by reference. We'll come back to this when we fill out more detail of the Sketcher program in this chapter.

Adding Elements to a List

You can add objects at the beginning or at the end of the list by using the **AddHead()** or **AddTail()** member functions, as shown in the following diagram:

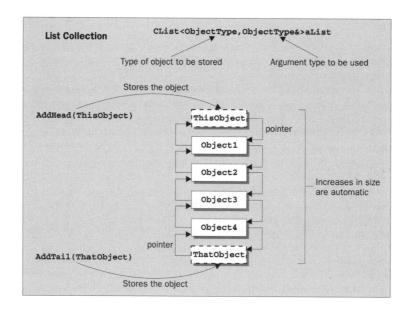

The diagram shows backward and forward pointers for each list element, which 'glue' the objects in the list together. These are internal links that you can't access in any direct way, but you can do just about anything you want by using the functions provided in the public interface to the class.

To add the object **aPoint** to the tail of the list **PointList**, you would write:

```
PointList.AddTail(aPoint);    // Add an element to the end
```

As new elements are added, the size of the list will increase automatically.

Both the **AddHead()** and **AddTail()** functions return a value of type **POSITION**, which specifies the position of the inserted object in the list. The way in which a variable of type **POSITION** is used is shown in the next diagram:

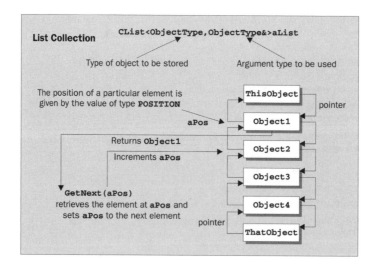

You can use a value of type **POSITION** to retrieve the object at a given position in the list by using the **GetNext()** function. Note that you can't perform arithmetic on values of type **POSITION**—you can only modify a position value through member functions of the list object. Furthermore, you can't set a position value to a specific numerical value. **POSITION** variables can only be set through member functions of the list object.

As well as returning the object, the **GetNext()** function increments the position variable passed to it, so that it points to the next object in the list. You can, therefore, use repeated calls to **GetNext()** to step through a list element by element. The position variable is set to **NULL** if you use **GetNext()** to retrieve the last object from the list, so you can use this to control your loop operation. You should always make sure that you have a valid position value when you call member functions of a list object.

You can insert an element in a list at a specific position as long as you have a **POSITION** value. To insert the object **ThePoint** in the list **PointList** immediately *before* an element at the position **aPosition**, you can use the statement:

```
PointList.InsertBefore(aPosition, ThePoint)
```

The function **InsertBefore()** will also return the position of the new object. To insert an element after the object at a given position, the function **InsertAfter()** is provided. These functions are often used with a list containing geometric elements to be displayed. Elements will be drawn on the screen in the sequence that you traverse the list. Elements that appear later in the list will overlay elements that are positioned earlier, so the order of elements determines what overlays what. You can therefore determine which of the existing elements a new element overlays by entering it at an appropriate position in the list.

When you need to set an existing object in a list to a particular value, you can use the function **SetAt()**, as long as you know the position value for the object:

```
PointList.SetAt(aPosition, aPoint);
```

There is no return value for this function. You must ensure that the **POSITION** value you pass to the function is valid. An invalid value will cause an error. You should, therefore, only pass a **POSITION** value to this function that was returned by one of the other member functions, and you must have verified that it isn't **NULL**.

Iterating through a List

If you want to get the **POSITION** value for the beginning or the end of the list, the class provides the member functions **GetHeadPosition()** and **GetTailPosition()**. Starting with the **POSITION** value for the head of the list, you can iterate through the complete list by calling **GetNext()** until the position value is **NULL**. We can illustrate the typical code to do this using the list of **CPoint** objects that we declared earlier:

```
CPoint CurrentPoint(0,0);

// Get the position of the first list element
POSITION aPosition = PointList.GetHeadPosition();

while(aPosition)                 // Loop while aPosition is not NULL
{
   CurrentPoint = PointList.GetNext(aPosition);
```

```
        // Process the current object...
    }
```

You can work through the list backwards by using another member function, **GetPrev()**, which retrieves the current object and then decrements the position indicator. Of course, in this case, you would start out by calling **GetTailPosition()**.

Once you know a position value for an object in a list, you can retrieve the object with the member function **GetAt()**. You specify the position value as an argument and the object is returned. An invalid position value will cause an error.

Searching a List

You can find the position of an element that's stored in a list by using the member function **Find()**:

```
    POSITION aPosition = PointList.Find(ThePoint);
```

This searches for the object specified as an argument by calling a global template function **CompareElements()** to compare the objects in the list with the argument. This is the helper function we referred to earlier that aids the search process. The default implementation of this function compares the address of the argument with the address of each object in the list. This implies that if the search is to be successful, the argument must actually be an element in the list—not a copy. If the object is found in the list, the position of the element is returned. If it isn't found, **NULL** is returned. You can specify a second argument to define a position value where the search should begin.

If you want to search a list for an object that is *equal* to another object, you must implement your own version of **CompareElements()** that performs a proper comparison. The function template is of the form:

```
    template<class TYPE, class ARG_TYPE> BOOL CompareElements(
                    const TYPE* pElement1, const ARG_TYPE* pElement2);
```

where **pElement1** and **pElement2** are pointers to the objects to be compared. For the **PointList** collection class object, the prototype of the function generated by the template would be:

```
    BOOL CompareElements(CPoint* pPoint1, CPoint* pPoint2);
```

To compare the **CPoint** objects, you could implement this as:

```
    BOOL CompareElements(CPoint* pPoint1, CPoint* pPoint2)
        { return *pPoint1 == *pPoint2; }
```

This uses the **operator==()** function implemented in the **CPoint** class. In general you would need to implement the **operator==()** function for your own class in this context. You could then use it to implement the helper function **CompareElements()**.

You can also obtain the position of an element in a list by using an index value. The index works in the same way as for an array, with the first element being at index 0, the second at index 1, and so on. The function **FindIndex()** takes an index value of type **int** as an argument and returns a value of type **POSITION** for the object at the index position in the list.

If you want to use an index value, you are likely to need to know how many objects there are in a list. The **GetCount()** function will return this for you:

```
int ObjectCount = PointList.GetCount();
```

Here, the integer count of the number of elements in the list will be stored in the variable **ObjectCount**.

Deleting Objects from a List

You can delete the first element in a list using the member function **RemoveHead()**. This function will return the object that is the new head of the list. To remove the last object, you can use the function **RemoveTail()**. Both of these functions require that there should be at least one object in the list, so you should use the function **IsEmpty()** first, to verify that the list is not empty. For example:

```
if(!PointList.IsEmpty())
   PointList.RemoveHead();
```

The function **IsEmpty()** returns **TRUE** if the list is empty, and **FALSE** otherwise.

If you know the position value for an object that you want to delete from the list, you can do this directly:

```
PointList.RemoveAt(aPosition);
```

There's no return value from this function. It's your responsibility to ensure that the position value you pass as an argument is valid. If you want to delete the entire contents of a list, you use the member function **RemoveAll()**:

```
PointList.RemoveAll();
```

This function will also free the memory that was allocated for the elements in the list.

Helper Functions for a List

We have already seen how the **CompareElements()** helper function is used by the **Find()** function for a list. Both the **ConstructElements()** and **DestructElements()** global helper functions are also used by members of a **CList** template class. These are template functions which will be declared using the object type you specify in your **CList** class declaration. The template prototypes for these functions are:

```
template< class TYPE > void ConstructElements(
                                   TYPE* pElements, int nCount);
template< class TYPE > void DestructElements(
                                   TYPE* pElements, int nCount);
```

To obtain the function that's specific to your list collection, you just plug in the type for the objects you are storing. For example, the prototypes for the **PointList** class for these will be:

```
void ConstructElements(CPoint* pPoint, int PointCount);
void DestructElements(CPoint* pPoint, int PointCount);
```

199

Note that the parameters here are pointers. We mentioned earlier that arguments to the **PointList** member functions would be references, but this doesn't apply to the helper functions. The parameters to both functions are the same: the first is a pointer to an array of **CPoint** objects, and the second is a count of the number of objects in the array.

The **ConstructElements()** function is called whenever you enter an object in the list, and the **DestructElements()** function is called when you remove an object. As for the **CArray** template class, you need to implement your versions of these functions if the default operation is not suitable for your object class.

The CMap Template Class

Because of the way they work, maps are particularly suited to applications where your objects obviously have a relatively dissimilar key associated with them, such as a customer class where each customer will have an associated customer number, or a name and address class where the name might be used as a key. The organization of a map is shown below:

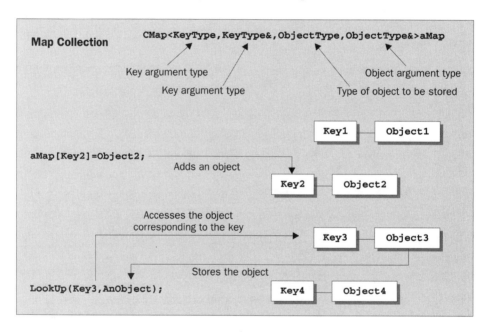

A map stores an object and key combination. The key is used to determine where in the block of memory allocated to the map the object is to be stored. The key, therefore, provides a means of going directly to an object stored, as long as the key is unique. The process of converting a key to an integer that can be used to calculate the address of an entry in a map is called **hashing**.

The hashing process applied to a key produces an integer called a hash value. This hash value is typically used as an offset to a base address to determine where to store the key and its associated object in the map. If the memory allocated to the map is at address **Base**, and each entry requires **Length** bytes, the entry producing the hash value **HashValue** will be stored at **Base+HashValue*Length**.

The hashing process may not produce a unique hash value from a key, in which case an element—the key together with the associated object—will be entered and linked to whatever element or elements were previously stored with the same hashed key value (often as a list). Of course, the fewer unique hash values that are generated, the less efficient the retrieval process from your map will be, because searching will typically be required to retrieve elements that have the same hash value.

There are four arguments necessary when you declare a map:

```
CMap<LONG, LONG&, CPoint, CPoint&> PointMap;
```

The first two specify the key type and how it is passed as an argument. Usually, it will be passed as a reference. The second pair of arguments specify the object type and how the object is passed as an argument, as we have seen previously.

You can store an object in a map by using the `[]` operator, as shown in the diagram above. You can also use a member function `SetAt()` to store an object, where you supply the key value and the object as arguments. Note that you cannot use the `[]` operator on the right-hand side of an assignment to retrieve an object, as this version of the operator is not implemented in the class.

To retrieve an object, you use the `LookUp()` function shown in the diagram. This will retrieve the object corresponding to the key specified; the function returns **TRUE** if the object was found, and **FALSE** otherwise. You can also iterate through all the objects in a map using a variable of type **POSITION**, although the sequence in which objects are retrieved is unrelated to the sequence in which they were added to the map. This is because objects are stored in a map in locations determined by the hash value, not by the sequence in which they were entered.

Helper Functions Used by CMap

As well as the helper functions that we have discussed in the context of arrays and lists, map collection classes also use a global function `HashKey()`, which is defined by this template:

```
template<class ARG_KEY>
   UINT HashKey(ARG_KEY key);
```

This function converts your key value to a hash value of type **UINT**. The default version does this by simply shifting your key value right by 4 bit positions. You need to implement your own version of this function if the default operation isn't suited to your key type.

There are different techniques used for hashing which vary depending on the type of data being used as a key, and the number of elements you are likely to want to store in your map. The likely number of elements to be stored indicates the number of unique hash values you need. A common method for hashing a numeric key value is to compute the hash value as the value of the key modulo N, where N is the number of different values you want. For reasons it would take too long to explain here, N needs to be prime for this to work well.

We can perhaps understand the principles of the mechanism used here with a simple example. Suppose you expect to store up to 100 different entries in a map using a key value, **Key**. You could hash the key with the statement:

```
HashValue = Key%101;
```

This will result in values for the **HashValue** between 0 and 100, which is exactly what you need to calculate the address for an entry. Assuming your map is stored at some location in memory, **Base**, and the memory required to store the object along with its key is **Length** bytes, then you can store an entry that produces the hash value **HashValue** at the location **Base+HashValue*Length**. With the hashing process as above, we can accommodate up to 101 entries at unique positions in the map.

Where a key is a character string, the hashing process is rather more complicated, particularly with long or variable strings. However, a method that is commonly used involves using numerical values derived from characters in the string. This typically involves assigning a numerical value to each character, so if your string was lower case letters plus spaces, you could assign each character a value between 0 and 26, with *space* as 0, *a* as 1, *b* as 2, and so on. The string can then be treated as the representation of a number to some base, 32 say. The numerical value for the string 'fred', for instance, would then be

$6*32^3+18*32^2+5*32^1+4*32^0$

and, assuming you expected to store 500 strings, you could calculate the hashed value of the key as:

$6*32^3+18*32^2+5*32^1+4*32^0 \bmod 503$

The value of 503 for N is the smallest prime greater than the likely number of entries. The base chosen to evaluate a hash value for a string is usually a power of 2 that corresponds to the minimum value that is greater than or equal to the number of possible different characters in a string. For long strings, this can generate very large numbers, so special techniques are used to compute the value modulo N. Detailed discussion of this is beyond the scope of this book.

The Typed Pointer Collections

The typed pointer collection class templates store pointers to objects, rather than objects themselves. This is the primary difference between these class templates and the template classes we have just discussed. We'll look at how the **CTypedPtrList** class template is used, because we'll use this as a basis for managing elements in our document class, **CSketcherDoc**.

The CTypedPtrList Template Class

You can declare a typed pointer list class with a statement of the form:

```
CTypedPtrList<BaseClass, Type*> ListName;
```

The first argument specifies a base class that must be one of two pointer list classes defined in MFC, either **CObList** or **CPtrList**. Your choice will depend on how your object class has been defined. Using the **CObList** class creates a list supporting pointers to objects derived from **CObject**, while **CPtrList** supports lists of **void*** pointers. Since the elements in our Sketcher example have **CObject** as a base class, we'll concentrate on how **CObList** is used.

The second argument to the template is the type of the pointers to be stored in the list. In our example, this is going to be **CElement***, since all our shapes have **CElement** as a base and **CElement** is derived from **CObject**. Thus, the declaration of a class for storing shapes is:

```
CTypedPtrList<CObList, CElement*> m_ElementList;
```

We could have used **CObList*** types to store the pointers to our elements, but then the list could contain an object of any class that has **CObject** as a base. The declaration of **m_ElementList** ensures that only pointers to objects of the class **CElement** can be stored. This provides a greatly increased level of security in the program.

CTypePtrList Operations

The functions provided in the **CTypedPtrList** based classes are similar to those supported by **CList**, except of course that all operations are with pointers to objects rather than with objects, so let's tabulate them. They fall into two groups: those that are defined in **CTypedPtrList**, and those that are inherited from the base class—**CObList** in this case.

Defined in **CTypedPtrList**:

Function	Remarks
GetHead()	Returns the pointer at the head of the list. You should use **IsEmpty()** to verify that the list is not empty before calling this function.
GetTail()	Returns the pointer at the tail of the list. You should use **IsEmpty()** to verify that the list is not empty before calling this function.
RemoveHead()	Removes the first pointer in the list. You should use **IsEmpty()** to verify that the list is not empty before calling this function.
RemoveTail()	Removes the last pointer in the list. You should use **IsEmpty()** to verify that the list is not empty before calling this function.
GetNext()	Returns the pointer at the position indicated by the variable of type **POSITION** passed as a reference argument. The variable is updated to indicate the next element in the list. When the end of the list is reached, the position variable is set to **NULL**. This function can be used to iterate forwards through all the pointers in the list.
GetPrev()	Returns the pointer at the position indicated by the variable of type **POSITION** passed as a reference argument. The variable is updated to indicate the previous element in the list. When the beginning of the list is reached, the position variable is set to **NULL**. This function can be used to iterate backwards through all the pointers in the list.
GetAt()	Returns the pointer stored at the position indicated by the variable of type **POSITION** passed as an argument, which isn't changed. Since the function returns a reference, as long as the list is not defined as **const**, this function can be used on the left of an assignment operator to modify a list entry.

Inherited from **CObList**:

Function	Remarks
AddHead()	Adds the pointer passed as an argument to the head of the list and returns a value of type **POSITION** that corresponds to the new element. There is another version of this function which can add another *list* to the head of the list.
AddTail()	Adds the pointer passed as an argument to the tail of the list and returns a value of type **POSITION** that corresponds to the new element. There is another version of this function which can add another *list* to the tail of the list.
RemoveAll()	Removes all the elements from the list. Note that this doesn't delete the objects pointed to by elements in the list. You need to take care of this yourself.
GetHeadPosition()	Returns the position of the element at the head of the list.
GetTailPosition()	Returns the position of the element at the tail of the list.
SetAt()	Stores the pointer specified by the second argument at the position in the list defined by the first argument. An invalid position value will cause an error.
RemoveAt()	Removes the pointer from the position in the list specified by the argument of type **POSITION**. An invalid position value will cause an error.
InsertBefore()	Inserts a new pointer specified by the second argument before the position specified by the first argument. The position of the new element is returned.
InsertAfter()	Inserts a new pointer specified by the second argument after the position specified by the first argument. The position of the new element is returned.
Find()	Searches for a pointer in the list that is identical to the pointer specified as an argument. Its position is returned if it is found. **NULL** is returned otherwise.
FindIndex()	Returns the position of a pointer in the list specified by a zero-based integer index argument.
GetCount()	Returns the number of elements in the list.
IsEmpty()	Returns **TRUE** if there are no elements in the list, and **FALSE** otherwise.

We'll see some of these member functions in action a little later in this chapter in the context of implementing the document class for the Sketcher program.

Using the CList Template Class

We can make use of the **CList** collection template in the definition of the curve object in our Sketcher application. A curve is defined by two or more points, so storing these in a list would be a good method of handling them. We first need to define a **CList** collection class object as a member of the **CCurve** class. We'll use this collection to store points. We've looked at the **CList** template class in some detail, so this should be easy.

The **CList** template class has two parameters, so the general form of declaring a collection class of this type is:

```
CList<YourObjectType, FunctionArgType> ClassName;
```

The first argument, **YourObjectType**, specifies the type of object that you want to store in the list. The second argument specifies the argument type to be used in function members of the collection class when referring to an object. This is usually specified as a reference to the object type to minimize copying of arguments in a function call. So let's declare a collection class object to suit our needs in the **CCurve** class as:

```
class CCurve: public CElement
{
// Rest of the class definition...

protected:
    // CCurve data members to go here
    CList<CPoint, CPoint&> m_PointList;  // Type safe point list

    CCurve(){}            // Default constructor - should not be used
};
```

The rest of the class definition is omitted here, since we're not concerned with it for now. The collection declaration is shaded. It declares the collection **m_PointList** which will store **CPoint** objects in the list, and its functions will use reference arguments to **CPoint** objects.

The **CPoint** class doesn't allocate memory dynamically, so we won't need to implement **ConstructElements()** or **DestructElements()**, and we don't need to use the **Find()** member function, so we can forget about **CompareElements()** as well.

Drawing a Curve

Drawing a curve is different from drawing a line or a circle. With a line or a circle, as we move the cursor with the left button down, we are creating a succession of different line or circle elements that share a common reference point— the point where the left mouse button was pressed. This is not the case when we draw a curve, as shown in the diagram below:

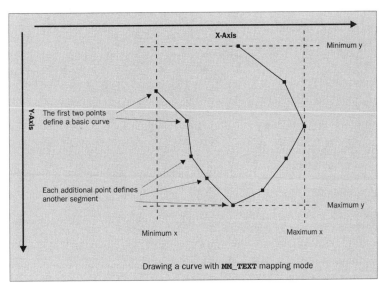

Drawing a curve with **MM_TEXT** mapping mode

When we move the cursor while drawing a curve, we're not creating a sequence of new curves, but extending the same curve, so each successive point adds another segment to the curve's definition. We therefore need to create a curve object as soon as we have the two points from the **WM_LBUTTONDOWN** message and the first **WM_MOUSEMOVE** message. Points defined with subsequent mouse move messages then define additional segments to the existing curve object. We'll need to add a function **AddSegment()** to the **CCurve** class to extend the curve once it has been created by the constructor.

A further point to consider is how we are to calculate the enclosing rectangle. This is defined by getting the minimum x and minimum y pair from all the defining points to establish the top left corner of the rectangle, and the maximum x and maximum y pair for the bottom right. This involves going through all the points in the list. We will, therefore, compute the enclosing rectangle incrementally in the **AddSegment()** function as points are added to the curve.

Defining the CCurve Class

With these features added, the complete definition of the **CCurve** class will be:

```
class CCurve: public CElement
{
public:
    virtual void Draw(CDC* pDC);             // Function to display a curve

    // Constructor for a curve object
    CCurve(CPoint FirstPoint, CPoint SecondPoint, COLORREF aColor);

    void AddSegment(CPoint& aPoint);         //Add a segment to the curve

protected:
    // CCurve data members to go here
    CList<CPoint, CPoint&> m_PointList;       // Type safe point list

    CCurve(){}                       // Default constructor - should not be used
};
```

You should modify the definition of the class in **Elements.h** to correspond with the above. The constructor has the first two defining points and the color as parameters, so it only defines a curve with one segment. This will be called in the **CreateElement()** function invoked by the **OnMouseMove()** function in the view class the first time a **WM_MOUSEMOVE** message is received for a curve, so don't forget to modify the **CreateElement()** function to call the constructor with the correct arguments. The statement using the **CCurve** constructor in the **switch** in this function should be changed to:

```
    case CURVE:
        return new CCurve(m_FirstPoint, m_SecondPoint,
                                pDoc->GetElementColor());
```

After the constructor has been called, all subsequent **WM_MOUSEMOVE** messages will result in the **AddSegment()** function being called to add a segment to the existing curve, as shown in the diagram below:

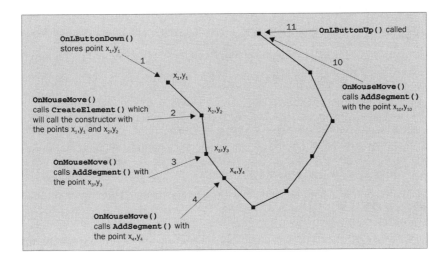

This shows the complete sequence of message handler calls for a curve composed of nine segments. The sequence is indicated by the numbered arrows. The code for the **OnMouseMove()** function in **CSketcherView** needs to be updated as follows:

```
void CSketcherView::OnMouseMove(UINT nFlags, CPoint point)
{
    CClientDC aDC(this);                   // Device context for the current view
    if((nFlags&MK_LBUTTON) && (this==GetCapture()))
    {
        m_SecondPoint = point;      // Save the current cursor position

        if(m_pTempElement)
        {
            if(CURVE == GetDocument()->GetElementType())    // Is it a curve?
            {   // We are drawing a curve
                // so add a segment to the existing curve
                ((CCurve*)m_pTempElement)->AddSegment(m_SecondPoint);
                m_pTempElement->Draw(&aDC);   // Now draw it
                return;                       // We are done
            }

            aDC.SetROP2(R2_NOTXORPEN);                   // Set drawing mode
            // Redraw the old element so it disappears from the view
            m_pTempElement->Draw(&aDC);
            delete m_pTempElement;               // Delete the old element
            m_pTempElement = 0;                  // Reset the pointer to 0
        }
        // Create an element of the type and color
        // recorded in the document object
        m_pTempElement = CreateElement();
        m_pTempElement->Draw(&aDC);
    }
}
```

We have to treat an element of type **CURVE** as a special case once it has been created, because on all subsequent calls of the **OnMouseMove()** handler, we want to call the **AddSegment()** function for the existing element, rather than construct a new one in place of the old, and we don't need to set the drawing mode since we don't need to erase the previous curve each time. We take care of this by moving the call to **SetROP2()** to a position after the code processing a curve.

Adding the curve segment and drawing the extended curve is taken care of within the **if** we have added. Note that we must cast the **m_pTempElement** pointer to type **CCurve*** in order to use it to call **AddSegment()** for the old element, because **AddSegment()** is not a virtual function. If we don't add the cast, we'll get an error, because the compiler will try to resolve the call statically to a member of the **CElement** class.

Implementing the CCurve Class

Let's first write the code for the constructor. This should be added to **Elements.cpp** in place of the temporary constructor that we used in the last chapter. It needs to store the two points passed as arguments in the **CList** data member, **m_PointList**:

```
CCurve::CCurve(CPoint FirstPoint,CPoint SecondPoint, COLORREF aColor)
{
   m_PointList.AddTail(FirstPoint);      // Add the 1st point to the list
   m_PointList.AddTail(SecondPoint);     // Add the 2nd point to the list
   m_Color = aColor;                     // Store the color
   m_Pen = 1;                            // Set the pen width

   // Construct the enclosing rectangle assuming MM_TEXT mode
   m_EnclosingRect = CRect(FirstPoint, SecondPoint);
   m_EnclosingRect.NormalizeRect();
}
```

The points are added to the list, **m_PointList**, by calling the **AddTail()** member of the **CList** template class. This function adds a copy of the point passed as an argument to the end of the list. The enclosing rectangle is defined in exactly the same way that we defined it for a line.

The next function we should add to **Elements.cpp** is **AddSegment()**. This function will be called when additional curve points are recorded, after the first version of a curve object has been created. This member function is very simple:

```
void CCurve::AddSegment(CPoint& aPoint)
{
   m_PointList.AddTail(aPoint);                    // Add the point to the end

   // Modify the enclosing rectangle for the new point
   m_EnclosingRect = CRect(min(aPoint.x, m_EnclosingRect.left),
                           min(aPoint.y, m_EnclosingRect.top),
                           max(aPoint.x, m_EnclosingRect.right),
                           max(aPoint.y, m_EnclosingRect.bottom));
}
```

The **min()** and **max()** functions we use here are standard macros that are the equivalent of using the conditional operator for choosing the minimum or maximum of two values. The new point is added to the tail of the list in the same way as in the constructor. It's important that each new point is added to the list in a way that is consistent with the constructor, because we'll draw the segments using the points in sequence, from the beginning to the end of the list. Each line segment will be drawn from the end point of the previous line to the new point. If the points are not in the right sequence, the line segments won't be drawn correctly. After adding the new point, the enclosing rectangle for the curve is redefined, taking account of the new point.

The last member function we need to define for the interface to the **CCurve** class is **Draw()**:

```
void CCurve::Draw(CDC* pDC)
{
    // Create a pen for this object and
    // initialize it to the object color and line width of 1 pixel
    CPen aPen;
    if(!aPen.CreatePen(PS_SOLID, m_Pen, m_Color))
    {
        // Pen creation failed. Close the program
        AfxMessageBox("Pen creation failed drawing a curve", MB_OK);
        AfxAbort();
    }

    CPen* pOldPen = pDC->SelectObject(&aPen);   // Select the pen

    // Now draw the curve
    // Get the position in the list of the first element
    POSITION aPosition = m_PointList.GetHeadPosition();

    // As long as it's good, move to that point
    if(aPosition)
        pDC->MoveTo(m_PointList.GetNext(aPosition));

    // Draw a segment for each of the following points
    while(aPosition)
        pDC->LineTo(m_PointList.GetNext(aPosition));

    pDC->SelectObject(pOldPen);                 // Restore the old pen
}
```

To draw the **CCurve** object, we need to iterate through all the points in the list from the beginning, drawing each segment as we go. We get a **POSITION** value for the first element by using the function **GetHeadPosition()** and then use **MoveTo()** to set the first point as the current position in the device context. We then draw line segments in the **while** loop as long as **aPosition** is not **NULL**. The **GetNext()** function, which appears as the argument to the **LineTo()** function, returns the current point and simultaneously increments **aPosition** to refer to the next point in the list.

Exercising the CCurve Class

With the changes we've just discussed added to the Sketcher program, we have implemented all the code necessary for the element shapes in our menu. In order to make use of the collection class templates, though, we must include the file **afxtempl.h**. The best place to put the **#include** statement would be in **StdAfx.h**, so that it will be added to the precompiled header file. Go to **StdAfx.h** in file mode and add the line shown below:

```
// stdafx.h: include file for standard system include files,
//  or project specific include files that are used frequently, but
//      are changed infrequently
//

#if _MSC_VER >= 1000
#pragma once
#endif // _MSC_VER >= 1000

#if!defined(AFX_STDAFX_H__623441A5_57EA_11D0_9257_00201834E2A3__INCLUDED_)
#define AFX_STDAFX_H__623441A5_57EA_11D0_9257_00201834E2A3__INCLUDED_

#define VC_EXTRALEAN        // Exclude rarely-used stuff from Windows headers

#include <afxwin.h>         // MFC core and standard components
#include <afxext.h>         // MFC extensions
#include <afxtempl.h>       // Collection templates
#ifndef _AFX_NO_AFXCMN_SUPPORT
#include <afxcmn.h>         // MFC support for Windows Common Controls
#endif // _AFX_NO_AFXCMN_SUPPORT

//{{AFX_INSERT_LOCATION}}
// Microsoft Developer Studio will insert additional declarations immediately
before the previous line.

#endif //!defined(AFX_STDAFX_H__623441A5_57EA_11D0_9257_00201834E2A3__INCLUDED_)
```

With the file included here, it will also be available to the implementation of **CSketcherDoc** when we get to use a collection class template there.

You can now build the Sketcher program once more, and execute it. You should be able to create curves in all four colors. A typical application window is shown below:

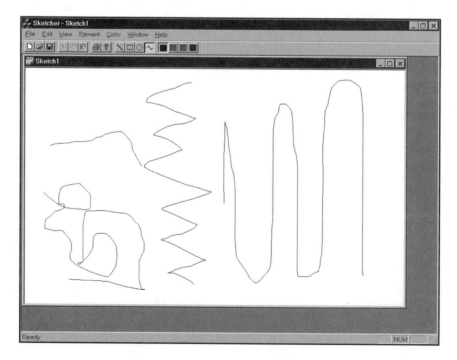

Of course, like the other elements you can draw, the curves are not persistent. As soon as you cause a **WM_PAINT** message to be sent to the application, by resizing the view for instance, they will disappear. Once we can store them in the document object for the application, though, they will be a bit more permanent, so let's take a look at that next.

Creating the Document

The document in the Sketcher application needs to be able to store an arbitrary collection of lines, rectangles, circles and curves in any sequence, and an excellent vehicle for handling this is a list. Because all the element classes that we've defined include the capability for the objects to draw themselves, drawing the document is easily accomplished by stepping through the list.

Using a CTypedPtrList Template

We can declare a **CTypedPtrList** that will store pointers to instances of our shape classes as **CElement** pointers. We just need to add the list declaration as a data member in the **CSketcherDoc** class definition:

```
class CSketcherDoc: public CDocument
{
protected: // create from serialization only
    CSketcherDoc();
    DECLARE_DYNCREATE(CSketcherDoc)

// Attributes
public:

protected:
    COLORREF m_Color;                       // Current drawing color
    WORD m_Element;                         // Current element type
    CTypedPtrList<CObList, CElement*> m_ElementList;  // Element list

// Operations
public:
    WORD GetElementType(){return m_Element;}   // Get the element type
    COLORREF GetElementColor(){return m_Color;}// Get the element color

// Rest of the class as before...

};
```

The **CSketcherDoc** class now refers to the **CElement** class. We need to make sure that all **#include** directives for **CSketcherDoc** in the **.cpp** files are preceded by a **#include** for **Elements.h**. Add a **#include** for **Elements.h** to **SketcherDoc.cpp**, and make sure the **#include** statements in **Sketcher.cpp** and **SketcherView.cpp** are in the right order.

We'll also need a member function to add an element to the list. **AddElement()** would be a good, if unoriginal, name for this. We create shape objects on the heap, so we can just pass a pointer to the function and, since all it does is add an element, we might just as well put the implementation in the class definition:

```
class CSketcherDoc: public CDocument
{

// Rest of the class as before...

// Operations
public:
    WORD GetElementType()                    // Get the element type
        { return m_Element; }
    COLORREF GetElementColor()               // Get the element color
        { return m_Color; }
    void AddElement(CElement* pElement)      // Add an element to the list
        { m_ElementList.AddTail(pElement); }

// Rest of the class as before...

};
```

Adding an element to the list only requires one statement which calls the **AddTail()** member function. That's all we need to create the document, but we need to consider what happens when a document is closed. We need to make sure that the list of pointers, and all the elements they point to, are destroyed properly. To do this, we need to add code to the destructor for **CSketcherDoc** objects.

Implementing the Document Destructor

In the destructor, we'll need to go through the list deleting the element pointed to by each entry. Once that is complete, we must delete the pointers from the list. The code to do this will be:

```
CSketcherDoc::~CSketcherDoc()
{
    // Get the position at the head of the list
    POSITION aPosition = m_ElementList.GetHeadPosition();

    // Now delete the element pointed to by each list entry
    while(aPosition)
        delete m_ElementList.GetNext(aPosition);

    m_ElementList.RemoveAll();    // Finally delete all pointers
}
```

We use the **GetHeadPosition()** function to obtain the position value for the entry at the head of the list, and initialize the variable **aPosition** with this value. We then use **aPosition** in the **while** loop to walk through the list and delete the object pointed to by each entry. The function **GetNext()** returns the current pointer entry and updates the **aPosition** variable to refer to the next entry. When the last entry is retrieved, **aPosition** will be set to **NULL** by the **GetNext()** function and the loop will end. Once we have deleted all the element objects pointed to by the pointers in the list, we just need to delete the pointers themselves. We can delete the whole lot in one go by calling the **RemoveAll()** function for our list object.

You should add this code to the definition of the destructor in **SketcherDoc.cpp**. You can go directly to the code for the destructor through the ClassView.

Drawing the Document

As the document owns the list of elements, and the list is **protected**, we can't use it directly from the view. The **OnDraw()** member of the view does need to be able to call the **Draw()** member for each of the elements in the list, though, so we need to consider how best to do this. Let's look at our options:

▶ We could make the list **public**, but this would rather defeat the object of maintaining protected members of the document class, as it would expose all the function members of the list object.

▶ We could add a member function to return a pointer to the list, but this would effectively make the list **public** and also incur overhead in accessing it.

▶ We could add a **public** function to the document which would call the **Draw()** member for each element. We could then call this member from the **OnDraw()** function in the view. This wouldn't be a bad solution, as it would produce what we want and would still maintain the privacy of the list. The only thing against it is that the function would need access to a device context, and this is really the domain of the view.

▶ We could make the **OnDraw()** function a friend of **CSketcherDoc**, but this would expose all of the members of the class, which isn't desirable, particularly with a complex class.

▶ We could add a function to provide a **POSITION** value for the first list element, and a second member to iterate through the list elements. This wouldn't expose the list, but it would make the element pointers available.

The last option looks to be the best choice, so let's go with that. We can extend the document class definition to:

```
class CSketcherDoc: public CDocument
{

// Rest of the class as before...

// Operations
public:
    WORD GetElementType()              // Get the element type
       { return m_Element; }
    COLORREF GetElementColor()         // Get the element color
       { return m_Color; }
    void AddElement(CElement* pElement)  // Add an element to the list
       { m_ElementList.AddTail(pElement); }
    POSITION GetListHeadPosition()        // return list head POSITION value
       { return m_ElementList.GetHeadPosition(); }
    CElement* GetNext(POSITION& aPos)     // Return current element pointer
       { return m_ElementList.GetNext(aPos); }

// Rest of the class as before...

};
```

By using the two functions we have added to the document class, the **OnDraw()** function for the view will be able to iterate through the list, calling the **Draw()** function for each element. The implementation of **OnDraw()** to do this will be:

```
void CSketcherView::OnDraw(CDC* pDC)
{
    CSketcherDoc* pDoc = GetDocument();
    ASSERT_VALID(pDoc);

    POSITION aPos = pDoc->GetListHeadPosition();
    while(aPos)                           // Loop while aPos is not null
    {
        pDoc->GetNext(aPos)->Draw(pDC);   // Draw the current element
    }
}
```

If we implement it like this, the function will always draw all the elements the document contains. The statement in the **while** loop first gets a pointer to an element from the document with the expression **pDoc->GetNext()**. The pointer that is returned is used to call the **Draw()** function for that element. The statement works this way without parentheses because of the left to right associativity of the **->** operator. The **while** loop plows through the list from beginning to end. We can do it better, though, and make our program more efficient.

Frequently, when a **WM_PAINT** message is sent to your program, only part of the window needs to be redrawn. When Windows sends the **WM_PAINT** message to a window, it also defines an area in the client area of the window, and only this area needs to be redrawn. The **CDC** class provides a member function, **RectVisible()**, which checks whether a rectangle that you supply to it as an argument overlaps the area that Windows requires to be redrawn. We can use this to make sure we only draw the elements that are in the area Windows wants redrawn, thus improving the performance of the application:

```
void CSketcherView::OnDraw(CDC* pDC)
{
    CSketcherDoc* pDoc = GetDocument();
    ASSERT_VALID(pDoc);

    POSITION aPos = pDoc->GetListHeadPosition();
    CElement* pElement = 0;               // Store for an element pointer
    while(aPos)                           // Loop while aPos is not null
    {
        pElement = pDoc->GetNext(aPos);   // Get the current element pointer
        // If the element is visible...
        if(pDC->RectVisible(pElement->GetBoundRect()))
            pElement->Draw(pDC);          // ...draw it
    }
}
```

We get the position for the first entry in the list and store it in **aPos**. This controls the loop, which retrieves each pointer entry in turn. The bounding rectangle for each element is obtained using the **GetBoundRect()** member of the object and is passed to the **RectVisible()** function in the **if** statement. As a result, only elements that overlap the area that Windows has identified as invalid will be drawn. Drawing on the screen is a relatively expensive operation in terms of time, so checking for just the elements that need to be redrawn, rather than drawing everything each time, will improve performance considerably.

Adding an Element to the Document

The last thing we need to do to have a working document in our program is to add the code to the **OnLButtonUp()** handler in the **CSketcherView** class to add the temporary element to the document:

```
void CSketcherView::OnLButtonUp(UINT nFlags, CPoint point)
{
   if(this == GetCapture())
      ReleaseCapture();        // Stop capturing mouse messages

   // If there is an element, add it to the document
   if(m_pTempElement)
   {
      GetDocument()->AddElement(m_pTempElement);
      InvalidateRect(0);         // Redraw the current window
      m_pTempElement = 0;       // Reset the element pointer
   }
}
```

Of course, we need to check that there really is an element before we add it to the document. The user might just have clicked the left mouse button without moving the mouse. After adding the element to the list in the document, we call **InvalidateRect()** to get the client area for the current view redrawn. The argument of 0 invalidates the whole of the client area in the view. Because of the way the rubber-banding process works, some elements may not be displayed properly if we don't do this. If you draw a horizontal line, for instance, and then rubber-band a rectangle with the same color so that its top or bottom edge overlaps the line, the overlapped bit of line will disappear. This is because the edge being drawn is XORed with the line underneath, so you get the background color back. We must also reset the pointer **m_pTempElement** to avoid confusion when another element is created.

Exercising the Document

After saving all the modified files, you can build the latest version of Sketcher and execute it. You'll now be able to produce art such as 'the happy programmer' shown below.

The program is now working more realistically. It stores a pointer to each element in the document object, so they're all automatically redrawn as necessary. The program also does a proper clean-up of the document data when it's deleted.

There are still some limitations in the program that we need to address. For instance:

▶ You can open another view window by using the <u>W</u>indow | <u>N</u>ew Window menu option in the program. This capability is built in to an MDI application and opens a new view to an existing document, not a new document. However, if you draw in one window, the elements are not drawn in the other window. Elements never appear in windows other than the one where they were drawn, unless the area they occupy needs to be redrawn for some other reason.

▶ We can only draw in the client area we can see. It would be nice to be able to scroll the view and draw over a bigger area.

▶ Neither can we delete an element, so if you make a mistake, you either live with it or start over with a new document.

These are all quite serious deficiencies which, together, make the program fairly useless as it stands. We'll overcome all of them before the end of this chapter.

Improving the View

The first item that we can try to fix is the updating of all the document windows that are displayed when an element is drawn. The problem arises because only the view in which an element is drawn knows about the new element. Each view is acting independently of the others and there is no communication between them. We need to arrange for any view that adds an element to the document to let all the other views know about it, and they need to take the appropriate action.

Updating Multiple Views

The document class conveniently contains a function **UpdateAllViews()** to help with this particular problem. This function essentially provides a means for the document to send a message to all its views. We just need to call it from the **OnLButtonUp()** function in the **CSketcherView** class, whenever we have added a new element to the document:

```
void CSketcherView::OnLButtonUp(UINT nFlags, CPoint point)
{
   if(this == GetCapture())
      ReleaseCapture();        // Stop capturing mouse messages

   // If there is an element, add it to the document
   if(m_pTempElement)
   {
      GetDocument()->AddElement(m_pTempElement);
      GetDocument()->UpdateAllViews(0,0,m_pTempElement);  // Tell all the views
      m_pTempElement = 0;          // Reset the element pointer
   }
}
```

When the **m_pTempElement** pointer is not **NULL**, the specific action of the function has been extended to call the **UpdateAllViews()** member of our document class. This function communicates with the views by causing the **OnUpdate()** member function in each view to be called. The three arguments to **UpdateAllViews()** are described below:

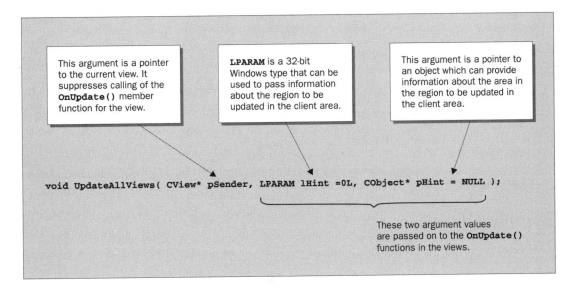

This argument is a pointer to the current view. It suppresses calling of the **OnUpdate()** member function for the view.

LPARAM is a 32-bit Windows type that can be used to pass information about the region to be updated in the client area.

This argument is a pointer to an object which can provide information about the area in the region to be updated in the client area.

```
void UpdateAllViews( CView* pSender, LPARAM lHint =0L, CObject* pHint = NULL );
```

These two argument values are passed on to the **OnUpdate()** functions in the views.

The first argument to the **UpdateAllViews()** function call will often be the **this** pointer for the current view. This suppresses the call of the **OnUpdate()** function for the current view. This is a useful feature when the current view is already up to date. In our case, because we are rubber-banding, we want to get the current view redrawn as well, so by specifying the first argument as 0, we get the **OnUpdate()** function called for all the views, including the current view. This removes the need to call **InvalidateRect()** as we did before.

We don't use the second argument to **UpdateAllViews()** here, but we do pass the pointer to the new element through the third argument. Passing a pointer to the new element will allow the views to figure out which bit of their client area needs to be redrawn.

In order to catch the information passed to the **UpdateAllViews()** function, we need to add the **OnUpdate()** member function to our view class. You can do this by opening ClassWizard and looking at the Message Maps tab for **CSketcherView**. If you select **CSketcherView** in the Object IDs: box, you'll be able to find OnUpdate in the Messages: box. Click on the Add Function button, then the Edit Code button. You only need to add the highlighted code below to the function definition:

```cpp
void CSketcherView::OnUpdate(CView* pSender, LPARAM lHint, CObject* pHint)
{
    // Invalidate the area corresponding to the element pointed to
    // if there is one, otherwise invalidate the whole client area
    if(pHint)
        InvalidateRect(((CElement*)pHint)->GetBoundRect());
    else
        InvalidateRect(0);
}
```

The three arguments passed to the **OnUpdate()** function in the view class correspond to the arguments that we passed in the **UpdateAllViews()** function call. Thus, **pHint** will contain the address of the new element. However, we can't assume that this is always the case. The **OnUpdate()** function is also called when a view is first created, but with a **NULL** pointer for the third argument. Therefore, the function checks that the **pHint** pointer isn't **NULL** and only then gets the bounding rectangle for the element passed as the third argument. It invalidates this area in the client area of the view by passing the rectangle to the **InvalidateRect()** function. This area will be redrawn by the **OnDraw()** function in this view when the next **WM_PAINT** message is sent to the view. If the **pHint** pointer is **NULL**, the whole client area is invalidated.

You might be tempted to consider redrawing the new element in the **OnUpdate()** function. This isn't a good idea. You should only do permanent drawing in response to the Windows **WM_PAINT** message. This means that the **OnDraw()** function in the view should be the only place that's initiating any drawing operations for document data. This ensures that the view is drawn correctly whenever Windows deems it necessary.

If you build and execute Sketcher with the new modifications included, you should find that all the views will be updated to reflect the contents of the document.

Scrolling Views

Adding scrolling to a view looks remarkably easy at first sight; the water is in fact deeper and murkier that it at first appears, but let's jump in anyway. The first step is to change the base class for **CSketcherView** from **CView** to **CScrollView**. This new base class has the scrolling functionality built in, so you can alter the definition of the **CSketcherView** class to:

```
class CSketcherView: public CScrollView
{
    // Class definition as before...
};
```

You must also modify two lines of code at the beginning of the **SketcherView.cpp** file which refer to the base class for **CSketcherView**. You need to replace **CView** with **CScrollView** as the base class:

```
IMPLEMENT_DYNCREATE(CSketcherView, CScrollView)

BEGIN_MESSAGE_MAP(CSketcherView, CScrollView)
```

However, this is still not quite enough. The new version of our view class needs to know some things about the area we are drawing on, such as the size and how far the view is to be scrolled when you use the scroller. This information has to be supplied before the view is first drawn. We can put the code to do this in the **OnInitialUpdate()** function in our view class.

We supply the information that is required by calling a function inherited from the **CScrollView** class: **SetScrollSizes()**. The arguments to this function are shown in the following diagram:

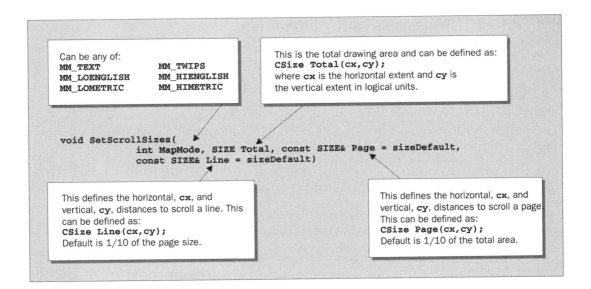

Scrolling a distance of one line occurs when you click on the up or down arrow on the scroll bar; a page scroll occurs when you click on the scrollbar itself. We have an opportunity to change the mapping mode here. **MM_LOENGLISH** would be a good choice for our application, but let's first get scrolling working in **MM_TEXT**, as there are still some difficulties to be uncovered.

To add the code to call **SetScrollSizes()**, you need to override the default version of the **OnInitialUpdate()** function in the view. Use ClassWizard to add the function to **CSketcherView** by double-clicking OnInitialUpdate in the Messages: box and clicking Edit Code. The version generated will call the default version in **CScrollView**. We just add our code to the function where indicated by the comment:

```
void CSketcherView::OnInitialUpdate()
{
    CScrollView::OnInitialUpdate();

    // Define document size
    CSize DocSize(20000,20000);

    // Set mapping mode and document size.
    SetScrollSizes(MM_TEXT,DocSize);
}
```

This maintains the mapping mode as **MM_TEXT** and defines the total extent that we can draw on as 20000 pixels in each direction.

This is enough to get the scrolling mechanism working. Build the program and execute it with these additions and you'll be able to draw a few elements and then scroll the view. However, although the window scrolls OK, if you try to draw more elements with the view scrolled, things don't work as they should. The elements appear in a different position from where you draw them and they're not displayed properly. What's going on?

Logical Coordinates and Client Coordinates

The problem is the coordinate systems that we're using—and that plural is deliberate. We've actually been using two coordinate systems in all our examples up to now, although you may not have noticed. As we saw in the previous chapter, when we call a function such as **LineTo()**, it assumes that the arguments passed are **logical coordinates**. The function is a member of the **CDC** class which defines a device context, and the device context has its own system of logical coordinates. The mapping mode, which is a property of the device context, determines what the unit of measurement is for the coordinates when you draw something.

The coordinate data that we receive along with the mouse messages, on the other hand, has nothing to do with the device context or the **CDC** object—and outside of a device context, logical coordinates don't apply. The points passed to our **OnLButtonDown()** and **OnMouseMove()** handlers have coordinates that are always in device units, that is, pixels, and are measured relative to the top left corner of the client area. These are referred to as **client coordinates**. Similarly, when we call **InvalidateRect()**, the rectangle is assumed to be defined in terms of client coordinates.

In **MM_TEXT** mode, the client coordinates and the logical coordinates in the device context are both in units of pixels, and so they're the same *as long as you don't scroll the window*. In all our previous examples there was no scrolling, so everything worked without any problems. With the latest version, it all works fine until you scroll the view, whereupon the logical coordinates origin (the 0,0 point) is moved by the scrolling mechanism, and so it's no longer in the same place as the client coordinates origin. The *units* for logical coordinates and client coordinates are the same here, but the *origins* for the two coordinates systems are different. This situation is illustrated below:

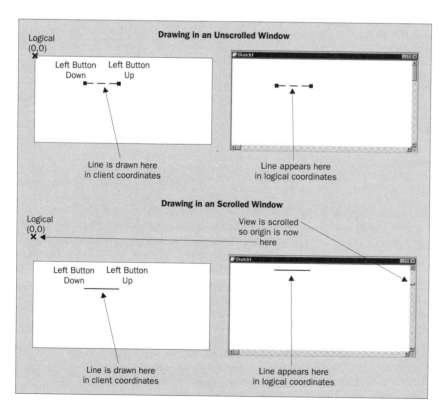

The left-hand side shows the position in the client area where you draw, and the points that are the mouse positions defining the line. These are recorded in client coordinates. The right-hand side shows where the line will actually be drawn. Drawing is in logical coordinates, but we have been using client coordinate values. In the case of the scrolled window, the line appears displaced, due to the logical origin being relocated.

This means that we are actually using the wrong values to define elements in our program, and when we invalidate areas of the client area to get them redrawn, the rectangles passed to the function are also wrong. Hence the weird behavior of our program. With other mapping modes it gets worse, because not only are the units of measurement in the two coordinate systems different, but also the *y* axes may be in opposite directions!

Dealing with Client Coordinates

Let's consider what we need to do to fix the problem. There are two things we may have to address:

1 We need to convert the client coordinates that we got with mouse messages to logical coordinates before we can use them to create our elements.

2 We need to convert a bounding rectangle that we created in logical coordinates back to client coordinates if we want to use it in a call to **InvalidateRect()**.

This amounts to making sure we always use logical coordinates when using device context functions, and always use client coordinates for other communications about the window. The functions we will have to apply to do the conversions are associated with a device context, so we need to obtain a device context whenever we want to convert from logical to client coordinates, or vice versa. We can use the coordinate conversion functions of the **CDC** class that are inherited by **CClientDC** to do the work.

The new version of the **OnLButtonDown()** handler incorporating this will be:

```
// Handler for left mouse button down message
void CSketcherView::OnLButtonDown(UINT nFlags, CPoint point)
{
    CClientDC aDC(this);        // Create a device context
    OnPrepareDC(&aDC);          // Get origin adjusted
    aDC.DPtoLP(&point);         // convert point to Logical
    m_FirstPoint = point;       // Record the cursor position
    SetCapture();               // Capture subsequent mouse messages
}
```

We obtain a device context for the current view by creating a **CClientDC** object and passing the pointer **this** to the constructor. The advantage of **CClientDC** is that it automatically releases the device context when the object goes out of scope. It's important that device contexts are not retained, as there are a limited number available from Windows and you could run out of them. If you use **CClientDC**, you're always safe.

As we're using **CScrollView**, the **OnPrepareDC()** member function inherited from that class must be called to set the origin for the logical coordinate system in the device context to correspond with the scrolled position. Once the origin is set by this call, the function **DPtoLP()**, which converts from **D**evice **P**oints **to L**ogical **P**oints, is used to convert the **point** value that's passed to the handler to logical coordinates. We then store the converted value, ready for creating an element in the **OnMouseMove()** handler.

The new code for the **OnMouseMove()** handler will be as follows:

```
void CSketcherView::OnMouseMove(UINT nFlags, CPoint point)
{
    CClientDC aDC(this);             // Device context for the current view
    OnPrepareDC(&aDC);               // Get origin adjusted

    if((nFlags&MK_LBUTTON)&&(this==GetCapture()))
    {
        aDC.DPtoLP(&point);          // convert point to Logical
        m_SecondPoint = point;       // Save the current cursor position

    // Rest of the function as before
}
```

The code for the conversion of the point value passed to the handler is essentially the same as in the previous handler, and that's all we need here for the moment. The last function that we must change is easy to overlook: the **OnUpdate()** function in the view class. This needs to be modified to:

```
void CSketcherView::OnUpdate(CView* pSender, LPARAM lHint, CObject* pHint)
{
    // Invalidate the area corresponding to the element pointed to
    // if there is one, otherwise invalidate the whole client area
    if(pHint)
    {
        CClientDC aDC(this);          // Create a device context
        OnPrepareDC(&aDC);            // Get origin adjusted

        // Get the enclosing rectangle and convert to client coordinates
        CRect aRect=((CElement*)pHint)->GetBoundRect();
        aDC.LPtoDP(aRect);
        InvalidateRect(aRect);        // Get the area redrawn
    }
    else
        InvalidateRect(0);            // Invalidate the client area
}
```

The modification here just creates a **CClientDC** object and uses the **LPtoDP()** function member to convert the rectangle for the area that's to be redrawn to client coordinates.

If you now compile and execute Sketcher with the modifications we have discussed and are lucky enough not to have introduced any typos, it will work correctly, regardless of the scroller position.

Using MM_LOENGLISH Mapping Mode

Let's now look into what we need to do to use the **MM_LOENGLISH** mapping mode. This will provide drawings in logical units of 0.01 inches, and will also ensure that the drawing size is consistent on displays at different resolutions. This will make the application much more satisfactory from the users' point of view.

We can set the mapping mode in the call to **SetScrollSizes()** made from the **OnInitialUpdate()** function in the view class. We also need to specify the total drawing area, so, if we define it as 3000 by 3000, this will provide a drawing area of 30 inches by 30 inches, which should be adequate for our needs. The default scroll distances for a line and a page will be satisfactory, so we don't need to specify those. You can use ClassView to get to the **OnInitialUpdate()** function and then change it to that shown below:

```
void CSketcherView::OnInitialUpdate()
{
   CScrollView::OnInitialUpdate();

   // Define document size as 30x30ins in MM_LOENGLISH
   CSize DocSize(3000,3000);

   // Set mapping mode and document size.
   SetScrollSizes(MM_LOENGLISH, DocSize);
}
```

We just alter the arguments in the call to **SetScrollSizes()** for the mapping mode and document the size that we want. That's all we need to enable the view to work in **MM_LOENGLISH**, but we still need to fix our dealings with rectangles.

Note that you are not limited to setting the mapping mode once and for all. You can change the mapping mode in a device context at any time and draw different parts of the image to be displayed using different mapping modes. A function **SetMapMode()** is used to do this, but we won't be going into this any further here. We'll stick to getting our application working just using **MM_LOENGLISH**. Whenever we create a **CClientDC** object for the view and call **OnPrepareDC()**, the device context that it owns will have the mapping mode we've set for the view.

The problem we have with rectangles is that our element classes all assume **MM_TEXT**, and in **MM_LOENGLISH** these will be upside-down because of the reversal of the y axis. When we apply **LPtoDP()** to a rectangle, it is assumed to be oriented properly with respect to the **MM_LOENGLISH** axes. Because ours are not, the function will mirror our rectangles in the x axis. This creates a problem when we call **InvalidateRect()** to invalidate an area of a view, as the mirrored rectangle in device coordinates will not be recognized by Windows as being inside the visible client area.

We have two options for dealing with this. We can modify the element classes so that the enclosing rectangles are the right way up for **MM_LOENGLISH**, or we can re-normalize the rectangle that we intend to pass to the **InvalidateRect()** function. The easiest course is the latter, since we only need to modify one member of the view class, **OnUpdate()**:

```
void CSketcherView::OnUpdate(CView* pSender, LPARAM lHint, CObject* pHint)
{
   // Invalidate the area corresponding to the element pointed to
   // if there is one, otherwise invalidate the whole client area
   if(pHint)
   {
      CClientDC aDC(this);            // Create a device context
      OnPrepareDC(&aDC);              // Get origin adjusted

      // Get the enclosing rectangle and convert to client coordinates
      CRect aRect=((CElement*)pHint)->GetBoundRect();
```

```
              aDC.LPtoDP(aRect);
              aRect.NormalizeRect();
              InvalidateRect(aRect);            // Get the area redrawn
          }
      else
              InvalidateRect(0);
      }
```

That should do it for the program as it stands. If you rebuild Sketcher, you should have scrolling working, with support for multiple views. We'll need to remember to re-normalize any rectangle that we convert to device coordinates for use with **InvalidateRect()** in the future. Any reverse conversion will also be affected.

Deleting and Moving Shapes

Being able to delete shapes is a fundamental requirement in a drawing program. One question relating to this that we'll need to find an answer for is how you're going to select the element you want to delete. Of course, once we decide how to select an element, this will apply equally well if you want to move an element, so we can treat moving and deleting elements as related problems. But let's first consider how we're going to bring move and delete operations into the program.

A neat way of providing move and delete functions would be to have a pop-up **context menu** appear at the cursor position when you click the right mouse button. We could then put Move and Delete as items on the menu. A pop-up that works like this is a very handy facility that you can use in lots of different situations.

How should the pop-up be used? The standard way that context menus work is that the user moves the mouse over a particular object and right-clicks on it. This selects the object and pops up a menu containing a list of items which relate to actions that can be performed on that object. This means that different objects can have different menus. You can see this in action in Developer Studio itself. When you right-click on a class icon in ClassView, you get a menu that's different to the one you get if you right-click on the icon for a member function. The menu that appears is sensitive to the context of the cursor, hence the term 'context menu'. We have two contexts to consider in Sketcher. You could right click with the cursor over an element, and you could right click when there is no element under the cursor.

So, how will we implement this functionality in the Sketcher application? We can do it simply by creating two menus: one for when we have an element under the cursor, and one for when we don't. We can check if there's an element under the cursor when the user presses the right mouse button. If there *is* an element under the cursor, we can highlight the element so that the user knows exactly which element the context pop-up is referring to.

Let's first take a look at how we can create a pop-up at the cursor and, once that works, come back to how we are going to implement the detail of the move and delete operations.

Implementing a Context Menu

The first step is to create a menu containing two pop-ups: one containing Move and Delete as items, the other a combination of the Element and Color menu items. So, change to ResourceView and expand the list of resources. Right-click on the Menu folder to bring up a context menu—another demonstration of what we are trying to create in our application. Select Insert Menu to create a new menu. This will have a default name **IDR_MENU1** assigned, but you can change this by right-clicking the new menu name and selecting Properties. You could change it to something more suitable, such as **IDR_CURSOR_MENU**, in the ID: box.

To add menu items to the menu, double-click **IDR_CURSOR_MENU**. Now create two new items on the menu bar. These can have any old caption, since they won't actually be seen by the user. They will represent the two context menus that we will provide with Sketcher, so we have named them element and no element, according to the situation in which the context menu will be used. Now you can add the Move and Delete items to the element pop-up.

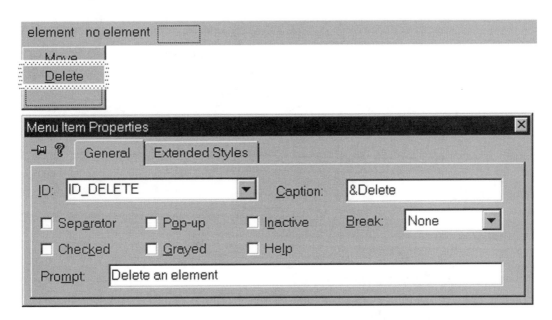

Make sure that you type sensible IDs rather than allowing the default, which is to use the junk name on the menu bar. Here, we have entered **ID_MOVE** and **ID_DELETE** as the IDs for the two items in the pop-up. The illustration shows the properties box for the Delete menu item.

The second menu contains the list of available elements and colors separated by a Separator. The IDs used should be the same as we applied to the **IDR_SKETCHTYPE** menu. The handler for a menu is associated with the menu ID. Menu items with the same ID will use the same handlers, so the same handler will be used for the Line menu item regardless of whether it's invoked from the main menu pop-up or from the context menu. To insert the separator, just double click on the empty menu item so the dialog is displayed.

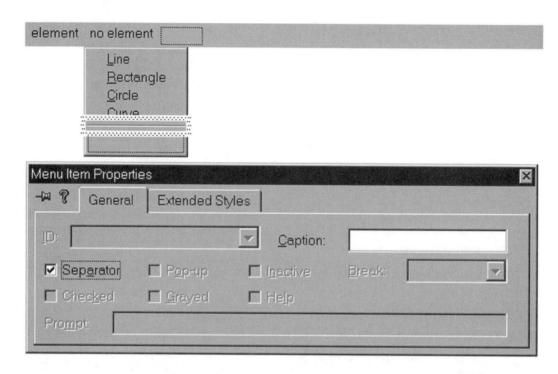

You can then click on the Separator check box and close the dialog without entering anything else.

Close the properties box and save the resource file. At the moment, all we have is the definition of the menu in a resource file. It isn't connected to the code in the Sketcher program. We now need to associate this menu and its ID, **IDR_CURSOR_MENU**, with our view class. This will enable us to create command handlers for the menu items in the pop-up corresponding to the IDs **ID_MOVE** and **ID_DELETE**.

Associating a Menu with a Class

To associate the new menu with the view class in Sketcher, you can use ClassWizard. With the cursor on the menu bar of our new menu, click the right mouse button and select ClassWizard from the pop-up. This will bring up a dialog which will ask whether you want to Create or Select a class. We want to Select an existing class, which is the default option, so just click OK. This will bring up a second dialog with a list of available classes to associate with the menu. Select CSketcherView from the Class list: and click the Select button.

Once you've done that, you'll be back to ClassWizard's standard window. Now, select ID_MOVE in the Object IDs: box, COMMAND in the Messages: box, and click the Add Function... button to create a handler for the menu item. Do the same for ID_DELETE and then close the ClassWizard dialog.

We don't have to do anything for the second context menu, as we already have handlers written for them in the document class. These will take care of the messages from the pop-up items automatically. We're now ready to write the code to allow the pop-up to be displayed.

Displaying a Pop-Up at the Cursor

MFC provides a class called **CMenu** for managing and processing menus. Whenever you want to do something with a new menu, you can create a local object of this class and use its member functions to do what you want. We want to be able to display the pop-up menu when the user presses (or more specifically, releases) the right mouse button, so clearly we need to add the code to do this to the handler for **WM_RBUTTONUP** in **CSketcherView**. You can add the handler for this message using ClassWizard in the same way that you added the handlers for the other mouse messages. Just fire up ClassWizard again and select the **WM_RBUTTONUP** message in the Messages: box for **CSketcherView**. Then create the handler and click the Edit Code button. The code you need to add is:

```
void CSketcherView::OnRButtonUp(UINT nFlags, CPoint point)
{
    // Create the cursor menu
    CMenu aMenu;
    aMenu.LoadMenu(IDR_CURSOR_MENU);      // Load the cursor menu
    ClientToScreen(&point);               // Convert to screen coordinates

    // Display the pop-up at the cursor position
    aMenu.GetSubMenu(0)->TrackPopupMenu(TPM_LEFTALIGN|TPM_RIGHTBUTTON,
                                         point.x, point.y, this);
}
```

We don't need to keep the call to the handler in the base class **CScrollView** that ClassWizard supplied. That was there to ensure that the message would be handled in the base class, even if you didn't add code to deal with it. As we said before, the comment left by ClassWizard to indicate where you should add your code is a clue to the fact that you can omit it in this case.

The handler first creates a local **CMenu** object, **aMenu**, then uses its member function **LoadMenu()** to load the menu that we have just created. The cursor position when the user presses the right button is passed to the handler in the argument **point**, which is in client coordinates. When we display the menu, we must supply the coordinates of where the menu is to appear in **screen coordinates**. Screen coordinates are in pixels and have the top left corner of the screen as position 0,0. As in the case of client coordinates, the positive y axis is from top to bottom. The inherited function **ClientToScreen()** in **CSketcherView** does the conversion for us.

To display the menu, we call two functions. The **GetSubMenu()** member of the object **aMenu** returns a pointer to a **CMenu** object. This object contains the pop-up from the menu owned by **aMenu**, which is the .**IDR_CURSOR_MENU** menu that we loaded previously. The argument to **GetSubMenu()** is an integer index specifying the pop-up, with index 0 referring to the first pop-up. The function **TrackPopupMenu()** for the **CMenu** object returned is then called. The arguments to **TrackPopupMenu()** are shown below:

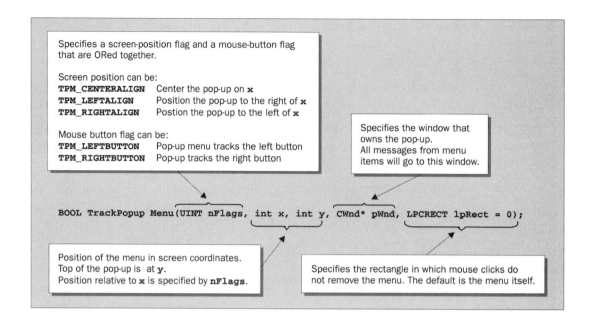

In our case, we have specified the pop-up as being associated with the right mouse button, and displayed it with the left side of the pop-up at the *x* coordinate passed to the function. The coordinates are the *x* and *y* coordinates of the cursor position specified by the **point** object after conversion to screen coordinates. The **this** pointer is used to specify the current view as the owning window.

We don't specify the fifth argument, so it defaults to 0. The rectangle is, therefore, the pop-up itself, so, if you click outside the pop-up, it will close the menu without selecting an item or causing a message to be sent to the view. Of course, if you click on a menu item, it will still close, but will also cause a message to be sent corresponding to the item clicked.

Choosing a Context Menu

At the moment, the **OnRButtonUp()** handler will only display the first context pop-up, no matter where the right button is clicked in the view. This isn't really what we want it to do. The first context menu applies specifically to an element, whereas the second context menu applies in general. We want to display the first menu if there is an element under the cursor, and to display the second menu if there isn't.

We need two things to fix this up. First, we need a mechanism to find out which (if any) element is at the current cursor position, and second, we need to save the address of this element somewhere so we can use it in the **OnRButtonUp()** handler. Let's deal with saving the address of the element first, as this is the easier bit.

When we find out which element is under the cursor, we'll store its address in a data member, **m_pSelected**, of the view class. This will be available to the right mouse button handler, since that's in the same class. You can add the declaration for this variable to the **protected** section of the **CSketcherView** class:

```
class CSketcherView: public CScrollView
{
  // Rest of the class as before...

  protected:
    CPoint m_FirstPoint;          // First point recorded for an element
    CPoint m_SecondPoint;         // Second point recorded for an element
    CElement* m_pTempElement;     // Pointer to temporary element
    CElement* m_pSelected;        // Currently selected element

    // Rest of the class as before...
};
```

Alternatively, you can right-click on the class name and select Add Member Variable... from the pop-up to open the dialog for adding a data member. It is, however, usually a good idea to go back and add some comments.

You also need to initialize this element in the class constructor, so add the code shown below:

```
CSketcherView::CSketcherView()
{
// TODO: add construction code here
   m_FirstPoint = CPoint(0,0);   // Set 1st recorded point to 0,0
   m_SecondPoint = CPoint(0,0);  // Set 2nd recorded point to 0,0
   m_pTempElement = 0;           // Set temporary element pointer to 0
   m_pSelected = 0;              // No element selected initially
}
```

We'll figure out how to decide when an element is under the cursor in a moment, but in the meantime we can use the **m_pSelected** member of the view in the implementation of the **OnRButtonUp()** handler:

```
void CSketcherView::OnRButtonUp(UINT nFlags, CPoint point)
{
    // Find the element under the cursor
    m_pSelected = SelectElement(point);

    // Create the cursor menu
    CMenu aMenu;
    aMenu.LoadMenu(IDR_CURSOR_MENU);  // Load the cursor menu
    ClientToScreen(&point);           // Convert to screen coordinates

    // Display the pop-up at the cursor position
    if(m_pSelected)
       aMenu.GetSubMenu(0)->TrackPopupMenu(TPM_LEFTALIGN|TPM_RIGHTBUTTON,
                                           point.x, point.y, this);
    else
       aMenu.GetSubMenu(1)->TrackPopupMenu(TPM_LEFTALIGN|TPM_RIGHTBUTTON,
                                           point.x, point.y, this);
}
```

To get things going, we first store the address of the element at the cursor position (if there is one) by calling the function **SelectElement()**, which accepts a **CPoint** object as an argument to indicate the current cursor position, and returns a pointer to the element at that position, or **NULL** if there isn't one. We'll implement this function in a moment. We will also come back a little later to consider whether this is the best place to find an element at the cursor, bearing in mind that you really can't be sure whether an element will be selected or not when you click the right mouse button.

We have used the data member **m_pSelected** to choose which context menu to display. If the address stored is not **NULL** we'll display the first context menu with the Move and Delete menu items. If **m_pSelected** is **NULL**, there's no element under the cursor, and so we display the second context menu with the color and element type choices.

Identifying a Selected Element

To find which element is selected, we need to implement the function **SelectElement()** to examine the elements in the document to see whether any of them are at the cursor position. We can add a function member to the view class called **SelectElement()**, which will have a **CPoint** object as a parameter containing the current cursor position in client coordinates.

A simple method we can use to decide whether a particular element is at the cursor position is to see if the current cursor position is inside the bounding rectangle for the element. We can use the functions that we added to the document class to iterate through the list of elements. As we retrieve the pointer to each element in turn, we can check whether the current cursor position is within the bounding rectangle for the element.

First, add the declaration of **SelectElement()** to the **protected** section of **CSketcherView** as follows:

```
CElement* SelectElement(CPoint aPoint);          // Select an element
```

There's no reason for the function to be **public** since it's only used internally. You can add the implementation of the function to **SketcherView.cpp**, like this:

```
// Find the element at the cursor
CElement* CSketcherView::SelectElement(CPoint aPoint)
{
    // Convert parameter aPoint to logical coordinates
    CClientDC aDC(this);
    OnPrepareDC(&aDC);
    aDC.DPtoLP(&aPoint);

    CSketcherDoc* pDoc=GetDocument();         // Get a pointer to the document
    CElement* pElement = 0;                   // Store an element pointer
    CRect aRect(0,0,0,0);                     // Store a rectangle
    POSITION aPos = pDoc->GetListTailPosition();  // Get last element posn

    while(aPos)                               // Iterate through the list
    {
        pElement = pDoc->GetPrev(aPos);
        aRect = pElement->GetBoundRect();
        // Select the first element that appears under the cursor
        if(aRect.PtInRect(aPoint))
            return pElement;
    }
    return 0;                                 // No element found
}
```

We first get a device context so that we can convert the parameter **aPoint** from client coordinates to logical coordinates, since all our element data is stored in logical coordinates. We then store a pointer to the document in **pDoc**, which we can use to call the document functions to retrieve elements. We declare local variables, **pElement** and **aRect**, which we will use to store an element pointer and the bounding rectangle for an element, respectively.

To find the element at the cursor we iterate through the list backwards, so we'll search from the most recently added element to the oldest. We get the **POSITION** value corresponding to the last element in the list by calling the function **GetListTailPosition()**, and store this value in **aPos**. We use this to run through the elements in the list by calling the function **GetPrev()** for the document. For each position value, we check whether the bounding rectangle for the corresponding element encloses the current cursor position that was passed in the parameter **aPoint**.

We determine whether **aPoint** is within the rectangle bounding an element in the **if** statement using the **PtInRect()** member of the **CRect** class. This function requires the rectangle to be normalized, which, of course, all ours are because we created them to be so. The function returns **TRUE** if the **CPoint** value passed as an argument is within the **aRect** object, and **FALSE** otherwise. As soon as we find a rectangle that encloses **aPoint**, we exit the function, returning the pointer to the corresponding element. If we manage to walk through the entire list without finding an element, which occurs when the cursor is not over an element, we return 0.

For **SelectElement()** to compile, we must add the **GetListTailPosition()** and **GetPrev()** functions to the document class. These are very similar to the **GetListHeadPosition()** and **GetNext()** functions we already have in **CSketcherDoc**. You can add the code for these to the class definition as follows:

```
POSITION GetListTailPosition()          // Return list tail POSITION value
   { return m_ElementList.GetTailPosition(); }
CElement* GetPrev(POSITION& aPos)        // Return current element pointer
   { return m_ElementList.GetPrev(aPos); }
```

The code is now in a state where we can test the context menus.

Exercising the Pop-Ups

We have added all the code we need to make the pop-ups operate, so you can build and execute Sketcher to try it out. If there are no elements under the cursor, the second context pop-up appears, allowing you to change the element type and color. These options work because they generate exactly the same messages as the main menu options and because we have already written handlers for them.

If there is an element under the cursor, the first context menu will appear with <u>M</u>ove and <u>D</u>elete on it. It won't do anything at the moment, as we've yet to handle the messages it generates. Try right button clicks outside of the view window. Messages for these are not passed to the document view window in our application, so the pop-up is not displayed.

Note that the context menu to select elements and colors isn't quite right—the check marks are not set properly. The document class handles the messages from the menu, but the **UPDATE_COMMAND_UI** messages don't apply to the context menu—they only work with the **IDR_SKETCHTYPE** menu. How do we fix that?

Checking the Context Menu Items

The **CMenu** class has a function designed to do exactly what we want. Its prototype is:

```
UINT CheckMenuItem(UINT nIDCheckItem, UINT nCheck);
```

This function will check or uncheck any item in the context menu. The first parameter selects which entry in the context pop-up is to be checked or unchecked; the second parameter is a combination of two flags, one of which determines how the first parameter specifies which item is to be checked, and the other specifies whether the menu item is to be checked or unchecked. Because each flag is a single bit in a **UINT** value, you combine the two using the bitwise OR.

The flag to determine how the item is identified can be one of two possible values:

MF_BYPOSITION   The first parameter is an index where 0 specifies the first item, 1 the second, and so on.

MF_BYCOMMAND   The first parameter is a menu ID.

We will use **MF_BYCOMMAND**, so we don't have to worry about the sequence in which the menu items appear in the pop-up, or even in which sub-menu they appear.

The possible flag values to check or uncheck an item are **MF_CHECKED** and **MF_UNCHECKED**, respectively.

The code for checking or unchecking a menu item will be essentially the same for all the menu items in the second context pop-up. Let's see how we can set the check for the menu item Black correctly. The first argument to the **CheckMenuItem()** function will be the menu ID, **ID_COLOR_BLACK**. The second argument will be **MF_BYCOMMAND** combined with either **MF_CHECKED** or **MF_UNCHECKED**, depending on the current color selected. We can obtain the current color from the document using the **GetElementColor()** function, with the following statement:

```
COLORREF Color = GetDocument()->GetElementColor();
```

We can use the **Color** variable to select the appropriate flag using the conditional operator, and then combine the result with the **MF_BYCOMMAND** flag to obtain the second argument to the **CheckMenuItem()** function, so the statement to set the check for the item will be:

```
aMenu.CheckMenuItem(ID_COLOR_BLACK,
                    (BLACK==Color?MF_CHECKED:MF_UNCHECKED)|MF_BYCOMMAND);
```

We don't need to specify the sub-menu here, since the menu item is uniquely defined in the menu by its ID. You just need to change the ID and the color value in this statement to obtain the statement to set the flags for each of the other color menu items.

Checking the element menu items is essentially the same. To check the Line menu item we can write:

```
WORD ElementType = GetDocument()->GetElementType();
aMenu.CheckMenuItem(ID_ELEMENT_LINE,
              (LINE==ElementType?MF_CHECKED:MF_UNCHECKED)|MF_BYCOMMAND);
```

The complete code for the **OnRButtonUp()** handler will therefore be:

```
void CSketcherView::OnRButtonUp(UINT nFlags, CPoint point)
{
   // Find the element under the cursor
   m_pSelected = SelectElement(point);

   // Create the cursor menu
   CMenu aMenu;
   aMenu.LoadMenu(IDR_CURSOR_MENU);       // Load the cursor menu
   ClientToScreen(&point);                // Convert to screen coordinates

   // Display the pop-up at the cursor position
   if(m_pSelected)
      aMenu.GetSubMenu(0)->TrackPopupMenu(TPM_LEFTALIGN|TPM_RIGHTBUTTON,
                                          point.x, point.y, this);
   else
   {
      // Check color menu items
      COLORREF Color = GetDocument()->GetElementColor();
      aMenu.CheckMenuItem(ID_COLOR_BLACK,
                   (BLACK==Color?MF_CHECKED:MF_UNCHECKED)|MF_BYCOMMAND);
      aMenu.CheckMenuItem(ID_COLOR_RED,
                   (RED==Color?MF_CHECKED:MF_UNCHECKED)|MF_BYCOMMAND);
      aMenu.CheckMenuItem(ID_COLOR_GREEN,
                   (GREEN==Color?MF_CHECKED:MF_UNCHECKED)|MF_BYCOMMAND);
      aMenu.CheckMenuItem(ID_COLOR_BLUE,
                   (BLUE==Color?MF_CHECKED:MF_UNCHECKED)|MF_BYCOMMAND);

      // Check element menu items
      WORD ElementType = GetDocument()->GetElementType();
      aMenu.CheckMenuItem(ID_ELEMENT_LINE,
              (LINE==ElementType?MF_CHECKED:MF_UNCHECKED)|MF_BYCOMMAND);
      aMenu.CheckMenuItem(ID_ELEMENT_RECTANGLE,
          (RECTANGLE==ElementType?MF_CHECKED:MF_UNCHECKED)|MF_BYCOMMAND);
      aMenu.CheckMenuItem(ID_ELEMENT_CIRCLE,
              (CIRCLE==ElementType?MF_CHECKED:MF_UNCHECKED)|MF_BYCOMMAND);
      aMenu.CheckMenuItem(ID_ELEMENT_CURVE,
              (CURVE==ElementType?MF_CHECKED:MF_UNCHECKED)|MF_BYCOMMAND);

      // Display the context pop-up
      aMenu.GetSubMenu(1)->TrackPopupMenu(TPM_LEFTALIGN|TPM_RIGHTBUTTON,
                                          point.x, point.y, this);
   }
}
```

Highlighting Elements

Ideally, the user will want to know which element is under the cursor *before* they right-click to get the context menu. When you want to delete an element, you want to know which element you are operating on. Equally, when you want to use the other context menu—to change color, for example—you need to be sure no element is under the cursor. To show precisely which element is under the cursor, we need to highlight it in some way before a right button click occurs.

We can do this in the **Draw()** member function for an element. All we need to do is pass an argument to the **Draw()** function to indicate when the element should be highlighted. If we pass the address of the currently-selected element that we save in the **m_pSelected** member of the view to the **Draw()** function, then we can compare it to the **this** pointer to see if it is the current element.

Highlights will all work in the same way, so we'll take the **CLine** member as an example. You can add similar code to each of the classes for the other element types. Before we start changing **CLine**, we must first amend the definition of the base class **CElement**:

```
class CElement:public CObject
{
   protected:
      COLORREF m_Color;        // Color of an element
      CRect m_EnclosingRect;   // Rectangle enclosing an element
      int m_Pen;                            // Pen width

   public:
      virtual ~CElement(){}    // Virtual destructor

      // Virtual draw operation
      virtual void Draw(CDC* pDC, CElement* pElement=0){}

      CRect GetBoundRect();    // Get the bounding rectangle for an element

   protected:
      CElement(){}             // Default constructor
};
```

The change is to add a second parameter to the virtual **Draw()** function. This is a pointer to an element. The reason for initializing the second parameter to zero is to allow the use of the function with just one argument; the second will be supplied as 0 by default.

You need to modify the declaration of the **Draw()** function in each of the classes derived from **CElement** in exactly the same way. For example, you should change the **CLine** class definition to:

```
class CLine: public CElement
{
   public:
      // Function to display a line
      virtual void Draw(CDC* pDC, CElement* pElement=0);

      // Constructor for a line object
      CLine(CPoint Start, CPoint End, COLORREF aColor);

   protected:
      CPoint m_StartPoint;        // Start point of line
      CPoint m_EndPoint;          // End point of line

      CLine(){}                   // Default constructor - should not be used
};
```

The implementation for each of the **Draw()** functions for the classes derived from **CElement** all need to be extended in the same way. The function for the **CLine** class will be:

```
void CLine::Draw(CDC* pDC, CElement* pElement)
{
    // Create a pen for this object and
    // initialize its color and set line width of 1 pixel
    CPen aPen;
    COLORREF aColor = m_Color;              // Initialize with element color
    if(this == pElement)                    // This element selected?
        aColor = SELECT_COLOR;              // Set highlight color
    if(!aPen.CreatePen(PS_SOLID, m_Pen, aColor))
    {                                       // Pen creation failed
        AfxMessageBox("Pen creation failed drawing a line", MB_OK);
        AfxAbort();
    }

    CPen* pOldPen = pDC->SelectObject(&aPen);  // Select the pen

    // Now draw the line
    pDC->MoveTo(m_StartPoint);
    pDC->LineTo(m_EndPoint);

    pDC->SelectObject(pOldPen);                 // Restore the old pen
}
```

This is a very simple change. We set the new local variable **aColor** to the current color stored in **m_Color**, and the **if** statement will reset the value of **aColor** to **SELECT_COLOR** when **pElement** is equal to **this**—which will be the case when the current element and the selected element are the same. You also need to add the definition for **SELECT_COLOR** to the **OurConstants.h** file:

```
// Element type definitions
// Each type value must be unique
const WORD LINE = 101U;
const WORD RECTANGLE = 102U;
const WORD CIRCLE = 103U;
const WORD CURVE = 104U;
/////////////////////////////////////

// Color values for drawing
const COLORREF BLACK = RGB(0,0,0);
const COLORREF RED = RGB(255,0,0);
const COLORREF GREEN = RGB(0,255,0);
const COLORREF BLUE = RGB(0,0,255);
const COLORREF SELECT_COLOR = RGB(255,0,180);
/////////////////////////////////////
```

We have nearly implemented the highlighting. The derived classes of the **CElement** class are now able to draw themselves as selected—we just need a mechanism to cause an element to *be* selected. So where should we do this? As we said, ideally, we want to have the element under the cursor always highlighted by default. We need to find a handler in the view that can take care of this all the time.

Is there a handler that always knows where the cursor is? **OnMouseMove()** would seem to fit the bill, since it will be called automatically whenever the cursor moves. We can put code in here to ensure that if there is an element under the cursor, it will always be highlighted. The amendments to this function are indicated below:

```
void CSketcherView::OnMouseMove(UINT nFlags, CPoint point)
{

// Rest of the function as before

    // Create a temporary element of the type and color that
    //  is recorded in the document object, and draw it
    m_pTempElement = CreateElement();    // Create a new element
    m_pTempElement->Draw(&aDC);          // Draw the element
  }
  else            // We are not drawing an element...
  {               // ...so do highlighting
    CRect aRect;
    CElement* pCurrentSelection = SelectElement(point);

    if(pCurrentSelection!=m_pSelected)
    {
      if(m_pSelected)              // Old elemented selected?
      {                            // Yes, so draw it unselected
        aRect = m_pSelected->GetBoundRect(); // Get bounding rectangle
        aDC.LPtoDP(aRect);                   // Conv to device coords
        aRect.NormalizeRect();               // Normalize
        InvalidateRect(aRect, FALSE);        // Invalidate area
      }
      m_pSelected = pCurrentSelection;       // Save elem under cursor
      if(m_pSelected)                        // Is there one?
      {                                      // Yes, so get it redrawn
        aRect = m_pSelected->GetBoundRect(); // Get bounding rectangle
        aDC.LPtoDP(aRect);                   // Conv to device coords
        aRect.NormalizeRect();               // Normalize
        InvalidateRect(aRect, FALSE);        // Invalidate area
      }
    }
  }
}
```

We only want to deal with highlighting elements when we aren't in the process of creating a new element. All the highlighting code can thus be added in an **else** clause for the main **if**. It starts by calling **SelectElement()** with the current cursor position as the argument, and stores the result in a local variable, **pCurrentSelection**. The remaining code is then only executed if the element under the cursor is different from the one that was there last time this function was called; there's no point changing the highlighting if the cursor has only moved within an element.

The remaining code does two things. If there is an element already highlighted, it invalidates the area it occupies to get it redrawn. Having done that, it stores the element now under the cursor in **m_pSelected** and (provided that there *is* an element) invalidates the bounding rectangle to get it redrawn. Notice how the calls to **InvalidateRect()** in this function are given a second parameter, **FALSE**. This parameter is optional and specifies that when we update the rectangle, we don't want to update the background as well. This is safe here because nothing is ever moved in this function, and will mean less flicker and faster update times—try omitting **FALSE** and you'll see what I mean.

Since we now do the highlighting here, you can delete the lines from the **OnRButtonUp()** handler:

```
    // Find the element under the cursor
    m_pSelected = SelectElement(point);
```

Drawing Highlighted Elements

We still need to arrange that the highlighted element is actually drawn highlighted. Somewhere, the **m_pSelected** pointer must be passed to the draw function for each element. The only place to do this is in the **OnDraw()** function in the view:

```
void CSketcherView::OnDraw(CDC* pDC)
{
    CSketcherDoc* pDoc = GetDocument();
    ASSERT_VALID(pDoc);

    POSITION aPos = pDoc->GetListHeadPosition();
    CElement* pElement = 0;                    // Store for an element pointer
    while(aPos)                                // Loop while aPos is not null
    {
        pElement = pDoc->GetNext(aPos);        // Get the current element pointer
        // If the element is visible...
        if(pDC->RectVisible(pElement->GetBoundRect()))
            pElement->Draw(pDC, m_pSelected);  // ...draw it
    }
}
```

We only need to change one line. The **Draw()** function for an element has the second argument added to communicate the address of the element to be highlighted.

Exercising the Highlights

This is all that's required for the highlighting to work all the time. You can build and execute Sketcher to try it out. Any time there is an element under the cursor, the element is drawn in magenta. This makes it obvious which element the context menu is going to act on before you right click the mouse, and means that you know in advance which context menu will be displayed.

Servicing the Menu Messages

The next step is to provide handlers for the Move and Delete menu items by adding some code to the skeleton functions we created back when we designed the pop-up menus. We'll add the code for Delete first, as that's the simpler of the two.

Deleting an Element

The code that you need to delete a selected element is very simple:

```
void CSketcherView::OnDelete()
{
    if(m_pSelected)
    {
        CSketcherDoc* pDoc = GetDocument();  // Get the document pointer
        pDoc->DeleteElement(m_pSelected);    // Delete the element
        pDoc->UpdateAllViews(0);             // Redraw all the views
```

237

```
            m_pSelected = 0;                    // Reset selected element ptr
      }
   }
```

The code to delete an element is only executed if **m_pSelected** contains a valid address, indicating that there is an element to be deleted. We get a pointer to the document and call the function **DeleteElement()** for the document object; we'll add this member to the **CSketcherDoc** class in a moment. When the element has been removed from the document, we call **UpdateAllViews()** to get all the views redrawn without the deleted element. Finally, we set **m_pSelected** to zero to indicate that there isn't an element selected.

You should add a declaration for **DeleteElement()** as a **public** member of the **CSketcherDoc** class:

```
   void DeleteElement(CElement* pElement);   // Delete an element
```

It accepts a pointer to the element to be deleted as an argument and returns nothing. You can implement it as:

```
   void CSketcherDoc::DeleteElement(CElement* pElement)
   {
      if(pElement)
      {
         // If the element pointer is valid,
         // find the pointer in the list and delete it
         POSITION aPosition = m_ElementList.Find(pElement);
         m_ElementList.RemoveAt(aPosition);
         delete pElement;            // Delete the element from the heap
      }
   }
```

You shouldn't have any trouble with this. After making sure that we have a non-null pointer, we find the **POSITION** value for the pointer in the list using the **Find()** member of the list object. We use this with the **RemoveAt()** member to delete the pointer from the list, then we delete the element pointed to by the parameter **pElement** from the heap.

That's all we need to delete elements. You should now have a Sketcher program in which you can draw in multiple scrolled views, and delete any of the elements in your sketch from any of the views.

Moving an Element

Moving the selected element is a bit more involved. As the element must move along with the mouse cursor, we must add code to the **OnMouseMove()** method to account for this behavior. As this function is also used to draw elements, we need a mechanism for indicating when we're in 'move' mode. The easiest way to do this is to have a flag in the view class, which we can call **m_MoveMode**. If we make it of type **BOOL**, we can use the value **TRUE** for when move mode is on, and **FALSE** for when it's off.

We'll also need to keep track of the cursor during the move, so we need another data member in the view for this. We can call it **m_CursorPos**, and it will be of type **CPoint**. Another thing we should provide for is the possibility of aborting a move. To do this we must remember the first position of the cursor, so we can move the element back. This will be another member of type **CPoint**, and we can call it **m_FirstPos**. Add the three new members to the **protected** section of the view class:

```
class CSketcherView: public CScrollView
{
   // Rest of the class as before...

   protected:
      CPoint m_FirstPoint;        // First point recorded for an element
      CPoint m_SecondPoint;       // Second point recorded for an element
      CElement* m_pTempElement;   // Pointer to temporary element
      CElement* m_pSelected;      // Currently selected element
      BOOL m_MoveMode;            // Move element flag
      CPoint m_CursorPos;         // Cursor position
      CPoint m_FirstPos;          // Original position in a move

   // Rest of the class as before...
};
```

We need to initialize these in the constructor for **CSketcherView** by adding the following statements:

```
CSketcherView::CSketcherView()
{
   m_FirstPoint = CPoint(0,0);      // Set 1st recorded point to 0,0
   m_SecondPoint = CPoint(0,0);     // Set 2nd recorded point to 0,0
   m_pTempElement = 0;              // Set temporary element pointer to 0
   m_pSelected = 0;                 // No elements selected initially
   m_MoveMode = FALSE;              // Set move mode off
   m_CursorPos = CPoint(0,0);       // Initialize as zero
   m_FirstPos = CPoint(0,0);        // Initialize as zero
}
```

The element move process starts when the Move menu item from the context menu is selected. Now we can add the code to the message handler for the Move menu item to set up the conditions necessary for the operation:

```
void CSketcherView::OnMove()
{
   CClientDC aDC(this);
   OnPrepareDC(&aDC);                   // Set up the device context
   GetCursorPos(&m_CursorPos);          // Get cursor position in screen coords
   ScreenToClient(&m_CursorPos);        // Convert to client coords
   aDC.DPtoLP(&m_CursorPos);            // Convert to logical
   m_FirstPos = m_CursorPos;            // Remember first position
   m_MoveMode = TRUE;                   // Start move mode
}
```

We are doing four things in this handler:

1 Getting the coordinate of the current position of the cursor, since the move operation starts from this reference point.

2 Converting the cursor position to logical coordinates, because our elements are defined in logical coordinates.

3 Remembering the initial cursor position in case the user wants to abort the move later.

4 Setting the move mode on as a flag for the **OnMouseMove()** handler to recognize.

The **GetCursorPos()** function is a Windows API function that will store the current cursor position in **m_CursorPos**. Note we pass a pointer to this function. The cursor position will be in screen coordinates, that is, coordinates relative to the top left hand corner of the screen. All operations with the cursor are in screen coordinates. We need the position in logical coordinates, so we must do the conversion in two steps. The **ScreentoClient()** function (which is an inherited member of the view class) converts from screen to client coordinates, and then we apply the **DPtoLP()** function member of the **aDC** object to the result to convert to logical coordinates.

After saving the initial cursor position in **m_FirstPos**, we set **m_MoveMode** to **TRUE** so that the **OnMouseMove()** handler can deal with moving the element.

Now we have set the move mode flag, it's time to update the mouse move message handler to deal with moving an element.

Modifying the WM_MOUSEMOVE Handler

Moving an element only occurs when move mode is on and the cursor is being moved. Therefore, all we need to do in **OnMouseMove()** is to add code to handle moving an element in a block which only gets executed when **m_MoveMode** is **TRUE**. The new code to do this is as follows:

```
void CSketcherView::OnMouseMove(UINT nFlags, CPoint point)
{
   CClientDC aDC(this);          // DC is for this view
   OnPrepareDC(&aDC);            // Get origin adjusted

   // If we are in move mode, move the selected element and return
   if(m_MoveMode)
   {
      aDC.DPtoLP(&point);        // Convert to logical coordinatess
      MoveElement(aDC, point);   // Move the element
      return;
   }

   // Rest of the mouse move handler as before...
}
```

This addition doesn't need much explaining really, does it? The **if** verifies that we're in move mode and then calls a function **MoveElement()**, which does what is necessary for the move. All we need to do now is to implement this function.

Add the declaration for **MoveElement()** as a **protected** member of the **CSketcherView** class by adding the following at the appropriate point in the class definition:

```
void MoveElement(CClientDC& aDC, CPoint& point);   // Move an element
```

As always, you can also right-click on the class name in ClassView to do this if you want to. The function will need access to the object owning a device context for the view, **aDC**, and the current cursor position, **point**, so both of these are reference parameters. The implementation of the function in the **.cpp** file will be:

```
void CSketcherView::MoveElement(CClientDC& aDC, CPoint& point)
{
   CSize Distance = point - m_CursorPos;   // Get move distance
   m_CursorPos = point;            // Set current point as 1st for next time

   // If there is an element, selected, move it
   if(m_pSelected)
   {
      aDC.SetROP2(R2_NOTXORPEN);
      m_pSelected->Draw(&aDC,m_pSelected); // Draw the element to erase it
      m_pSelected->Move(Distance);         // Now move the element
      m_pSelected->Draw(&aDC,m_pSelected); // Draw the moved element
   }
}
```

The distance to move the element currently selected is stored locally as a **CSize** object, **Distance**. The **CSize** class is specifically designed to represent a relative coordinate position and has two public data members, **cx** and **cy**, which correspond to the *x* and *y* increments. These are calculated as the difference between the current cursor position, stored in **point**, and the previous cursor position saved in **m_CursorPos**. This uses the – operator, which is overloaded in the **CPoint** class. The version we are using here returns a **CSize** object, but there is also a version which returns a **CPoint** object. You can usually operate on **CSize** and **CPoint** objects combined. We save the current cursor position in **m_CursorPos** for use the next time this function is called, which will occur if there is a further mouse move message during the current move operation.

Moving an element in the view is going to be implemented using the **R2_NOTXORPEN** drawing mode, because it's easy and fast. This is exactly the same as what we've been using during the creation of an element. We redraw the selected element in its current color (the selected color) to reset it to the background color, and then call the function **Move()** to relocate the element by the distance specified by **Distance**. We'll add this function to the element classes in a moment. When the element has moved itself, we simply use the **Draw()** function once more to display it highlighted at the new position. The color of the element will revert to normal when the move operation ends, as the **OnLButtonUp()** handler will redraw all the windows normally by calling **UpdateAllViews()**.

Getting the Elements to Move Themselves

We need to add the **Move()** function as a virtual member of the base class, **CElement**. Modify the class definition to:

```
class CElement:public CObject
{
   protected:
      COLORREF m_Color;                   // Color of an element
      CRect m_EnclosingRect;              // Rectangle enclosing an element
      int m_Pen;                          // Pen width

   public:
      virtual ~CElement(){}               // Virtual destructor

      // Virtual draw operation
      virtual void Draw(CDC* pDC, CElement* pElement = 0){}
      virtual void Move(CSize& aSize){}   // Move an element
      CRect GetBoundRect();     // Get the bounding rectangle for an element
```

```
      protected:
         CElement(){}                            // Default constructor
   };
```

As we discussed before in relation to the **Draw()** member, although an implementation of the **Move()** function here has no meaning, we can't make it a pure virtual function because of the requirements of serialization.

We need to add a declaration for the **Move()** function as a **public** member of each of the classes derived from **CElement**. It will be the same in each:

```
// Function to move an element
virtual void Move(CSize& aSize);
```

Now we can look at how we implement the **Move()** function in the **CLine** class:

```
void CLine::Move(CSize& aSize)
{
   m_StartPoint += aSize;          // Move the start point
   m_EndPoint += aSize;            // and the end point
   m_EnclosingRect += aSize;       // Move the enclosing rectangle
}
```

This is very easy because of the overloaded **+=** operators in the **CPoint** and **CRect** classes. They all work with **CSize** objects, so we just add the relative distance specified by **aSize** to the start and end points for the line, and to the enclosing rectangle.

Moving a **CRectangle** object is even easier:

```
void CRectangle::Move(CSize& aSize)
{
   m_EnclosingRect+= aSize;        // Move the rectangle
}
```

Because the rectangle is defined by the **m_EnclosingRect** member, that's all we need to move it.

The **Move()** member of **CCircle** is identical:

```
void CCircle::Move(CSize& aSize)
{
   m_EnclosingRect+= aSize;        // Move rectangle defining the circle
}
```

Moving a **CCurve** object is a little more complicated because it's defined by an arbitrary number of points. You can implement the function as follows:

```
void CCurve::Move(CSize& aSize)
{
   m_EnclosingRect += aSize;            // Move the rectangle

   // Get the 1st element position
   POSITION aPosition = m_PointList.GetHeadPosition();
```

```
      while(aPosition)
         m_PointList.GetNext(aPosition) += aSize; // Move each pt in the list
   }
```

There's still not a lot to it. We first move the enclosing rectangle stored in **m_EnclosingRect**, using the overloaded **+=** operator for **CRect** objects. We then iterate through all the points defining the curve, moving each one in turn with the overloaded **+=** operator in **CPoint**.

Dropping the Element

All that remains now is to drop the element in position once the user has finished moving it, or to abort the whole move. To drop the element in its new position, the user will click the left mouse button, so we'll manage this operation in the **OnLButtonDown()** handler. To abort the operation, the user will click the right mouse button—so we can add a handler for **OnRButtonDown()** to deal with this.

Let's deal with the left mouse button first. We need to provide for this as a special action when move mode is on. The changes are highlighted below:

```
void CSketcherView::OnLButtonDown(UINT nFlags, CPoint point)
{
   CClientDC aDC(this);            // Create a device context
   OnPrepareDC(&aDC);              // Get origin adjusted
   aDC.DPtoLP(&point);             // convert point to Logical

   if(m_MoveMode)
   {
      // In moving mode, so drop the element
      m_MoveMode = FALSE;                  // Kill move mode
      m_pSelected = 0;                     // De-select the element
      GetDocument()->UpdateAllViews(0);    // Redraw all the views
   }
   else
   {
      m_FirstPoint = point;         // Record the cursor position
      SetCapture();                 // Capture subsequent mouse messages
   }
}
```

The code is pretty simple. We must first make sure that we're in move mode. If this is the case, we just set the move mode flag back to **FALSE** and then de-select the element. This is all that's required because we've been tracking the element with the mouse, so it's already in the right place. Finally, to tidy up all the views of the document, we call the document's **UpdateAllViews()** function, causing all the views to be redrawn.

Add a handler for the **WM_RBUTTONDOWN** message to **CSketcherView** using ClassWizard. The implementation for this must do two things: move the element back to where it was, and the turn off move mode. The code to do this is:

```
void CSketcherView::OnRButtonDown(UINT nFlags, CPoint point)
{
   if(m_MoveMode)
   {
      // In moving mode, so drop element back in original position
      CClientDC aDC(this);
```

```
        OnPrepareDC(&aDC);                // Get origin adjusted
        MoveElement(aDC, m_FirstPos);     // Move element to orig position
        m_MoveMode = FALSE;               // Kill move mode
        m_pSelected = 0;                  // De-select element
        GetDocument()->UpdateAllViews(0); // Redraw all the views
        return;                           // We are done
    }
}
```

We first create a **CClientDC** object for use in the **MoveElement()** function. We then call the **MoveElement()** function to move the currently selected element the distance from the current cursor position to the original cursor position that we saved in **m_FirstPos**. Once the element has been repositioned, we just turn off move mode, deselect the element, and get all the views redrawn.

Exercising the Application

Everything is now complete for the context pop-ups to work. If you build Sketcher, you can select the element type and color from one context menu, or if you are over an element, then you can move or delete that element from the other context menu.

Dealing with Masked Elements

There's still a limitation that you might want to get over. If the element you want to move or delete is enclosed by the rectangle of another element that is drawn after the element you want, you won't be able to highlight it because the **SelectElement()** function will always find the outer element first. The outer element completely masks the element it encloses. This is a result of the sequence of elements in the list. You could fix this by adding a <u>S</u>end to Back item to the context menu that would move an element to the beginning of the list.

Add a separator and a menu item to the element drop down in the **IDR_CURSOR_MENU** resource as shown.

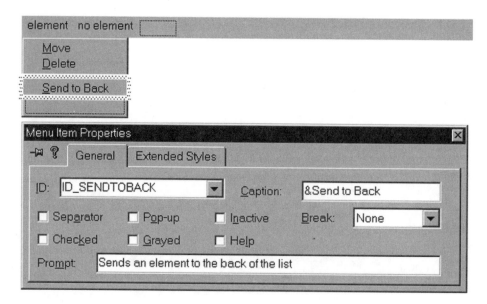

Once you've assigned a suitable ID, close the properties dialog and double click on the new menu item while holding down the *Ctrl* key. You can then add a handler for the item to the view class. We need to handle it in the view because that's where we record the selected element. We can implement the handler as:

```
void CSketcherView::OnSendtoback()
{
    GetDocument()->SendToBack(m_pSelected);        // Move element in list
}
```

We're going to get the document to do the work by passing the currently selected element pointer to a function **SendToBack()** that we will implement in the **CSketcherDoc** class. Add it to the class definition with a **void** return type, and a parameter of type **CElement***. We can implement this function as:

```
void CSketcherDoc::SendToBack(CElement* pElement)
{
    if(pElement)
    {
        // If the element pointer is valid,
        // find the pointer in the list and remove the element
        POSITION aPosition = m_ElementList.Find(pElement);
        m_ElementList.RemoveAt(aPosition);

        m_ElementList.AddHead(pElement);  // Put it back to the beginning
    }
}
```

Once we have the **POSITION** value corresponding to the element, we remove the element from the list by calling **RemoveAt()**. Of course, this does not delete the element from memory, it just removes the pointer to it from the list. Then we add the element pointer back at the beginning of the list using the **AddHead()** function.

With the element moved to the head of the list, it cannot mask any of the others because we search from the end. We will always find one of the other elements first if the applicable bounding rectangle encloses the current cursor position. The Send to Back menu option will always be able to resolve any element masking problem in the view.

Summary

In this chapter, you've seen how to apply MFC collection classes to the problems of managing objects and managing pointers to objects. Collections are a real asset in programming for Windows because the application data that you store in a document often originates in an unstructured and unpredictable way, and you need to be able traverse the data whenever a view needs to be updated.

You have also seen how to create document data and manage it in a pointer list in the document, and in the context of the Sketcher application, how the views and the document communicate with each other.

We've improved the view capability in Sketcher in several ways. We've added scrolling to the views using the MFC class **CScrollView**, and we've introduced a pop-up at the cursor for moving and deleting elements. We've also implemented an element highlighting feature to provide the user with feedback when moving or deleting elements.

We have covered quite a lot of ground in this chapter, and some of the important points you need to keep in mind are:

▶ If you need a collection class to manage your objects or pointers, the best choice is one of the template-based collection classes, since they provide type-safe operation in most cases.

▶ When you draw in a device context, coordinates are in logical units that depend on the mapping mode set. Points in a window that are supplied along with Windows mouse messages are in client coordinates. The two coordinate systems are usually not the same.

▶ Coordinates that define the position of the cursor are in screen coordinates which are measured in pixels relative to the top left corner of the screen.

▶ Functions to convert between client coordinates and logical coordinates are available in the **CDC** class.

▶ Windows requests that a view is redrawn by sending a **WM_PAINT** message to your application. This causes the **OnDraw()** member of the affected view to be called.

▶ You should always do any permanent drawing of a document in the **OnDraw()** member of the view class. This will ensure that the window is drawn properly when required by Windows.

▶ You can make your **OnDraw()** implementation more efficient by calling the **RectVisible()** member of the **CDC** class to check whether an entity needs to be drawn.

▶ To get multiple views updated when you change the document contents, you can call the **UpdateAllViews()** member of the document object. This causes the **OnUpdate()** member of each view to be called.

▶ You can pass information to the **UpdateAllViews()** function to indicate which area in the view needs to be redrawn. This will make redrawing the views faster.

▶ You can display a context menu at the cursor position in response to a right mouse click. This menu is created as a normal pop-up.

Exercises

Ex6-1: Implement the **CCurve** class so that points are added to the head of the list instead of the tail.

Ex6-2: Implement the **CCurve** class in the Sketcher program using a typed pointer list, instead of a list of objects to represent a curve.

Ex6-3: Look up the **CArray** template collection class in Help, and use it to store points in the **CCurve** class in the Sketcher program.

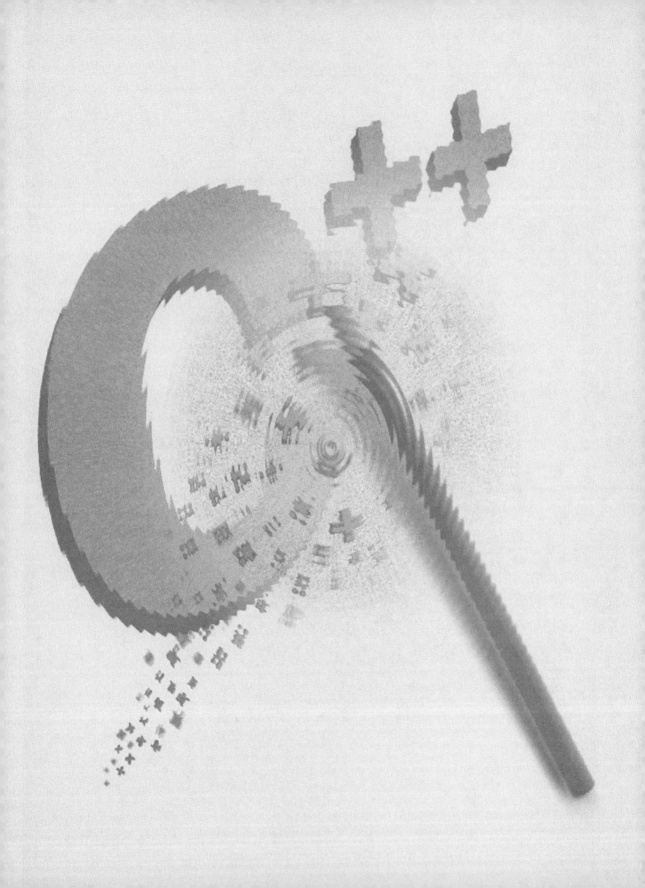

7

Working with Dialogs and Controls

Dialogs and controls are basic tools for user communications in the Windows environment. In this chapter, you'll learn how to implement dialogs and controls by applying them to extend the Sketcher program. As you do so, you'll see:

- What a dialog is and how you can create dialog resources
- What controls are and how to add them to a dialog
- What basic varieties of controls are available to you
- How to create a dialog class to manage a dialog
- How to program the creation of a dialog box and how to get information back from the controls in it
- What is meant by modal and modeless dialogs
- How to implement and use direct data exchange and validation with controls

Understanding Dialogs

Of course, dialogs are not new to you. Most Windows programs of consequence use dialogs to manage some of their data input. You click a menu item and up pops a **dialog box** with various **controls** that you use for entering information. Just about everything that appears in a dialog box is a control. A dialog box is actually a window and, in fact, each of the controls in a dialog is also a specialized window. Come to think of it, most things you see on the screen under Windows are windows!

Although controls have a particular association with dialog boxes, you can also create and use them in other windows if you want to. A typical dialog box is illustrated overleaf.

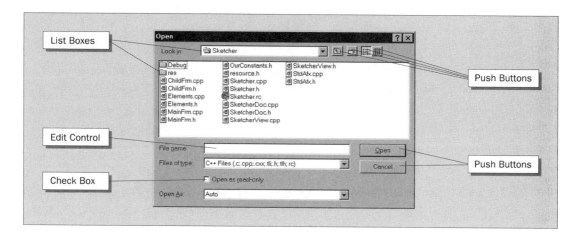

This is the <u>F</u>ile | <u>O</u>pen... dialog in Visual C++. The annotations show the variety of controls that are used, which combine to provide a very intuitive interface for selecting a file to be opened. This makes the dialog very easy to use, even though there's a whole range of possibilities here.

There are two things needed to create and use a dialog box in an MFC program. The physical appearance of the dialog box, which is defined in a resource file, and a dialog class object that's used to manage the operation of the dialog and its controls. MFC provides a class called **CDialog** for you to use, once you have defined your dialog resource.

Understanding Controls

There are many different controls available to you in Windows, and in most cases there's quite a bit of flexibility in how they look and operate. Most of them fall into one of six categories. We'll take a look at these and, for each category, see what a typical control looks like and what it does.

Type	Appearance	What they do
Static Controls	This is a static control	These provide static information, such as titles or instructions, or simply provide decoration in a dialog in the form of an icon or a filled rectangle.
Button Controls	○ A radio button	Buttons allow communication to the application with a single mouse button click. Radio buttons, named after the old car radios which used push buttons to select predefined stations, are usually grouped so that if one is checked, the others are unchecked.
	☐ A check box	Check boxes, on the other hand, can be individually checked, so more than one can be checked at one time.
	A push button	Push buttons, such as OK and Cancel buttons, are typically used to close a dialog.

Type	Appearance	What they do
Scroll Bars		We have already seen scroll bars attached to the edge of our view window. Scroll bar controls can be free-standing and are used inside a dialog box.
List Boxes	Items Listbox Sample	This presents a list from which you can choose predefined items The scroll bar need not appear in a short list. The list can also have multiple columns, and can be scrolled horizontally. A version of the list box is available that can display icons as well as text.
Edit Controls	You can edit this	In its simplest form, you can enter and edit a line of text. An edit control can be extended to allow sophisticated editing of multiple lines of text.
Combo Boxes	Choose this item Or choose this item Or enter one yourself	These combine the capability of a list box with the option of modifying a line or entering a complete line yourself. This is used to present a list of files in the Save As dialog.

A control may or may not be associated with a class object. Static controls don't do anything directly, so an associated class object may seem superfluous, but there's an MFC class, **CStatic**, that provides functions to enable you to alter the appearance of static controls. Button controls can also be handled by the dialog object in many cases, but again MFC does provide the **CButton** class for use in situations where you need a class object to manage a control. MFC also provides a full complement of classes to support the other controls. Since a control is a window, they are all derived from **CWnd**.

Common Controls

The set of standard controls that are supported by MFC and the Resource Editor under 32-bit versions of Windows are called **common controls**. Common controls include all of the controls we have just seen, as well as other more complex controls such as the **animate control**, for example, which has the capability to play an AVI (**A**udio **V**ideo **I**nterleaved) file, and the **tree control** which can display a hierarchy of items in a tree. The tree control is used in Explorer in Windows 95 to display your files and folders in a hierarchy, but it can be used to display anything you like that can usefully be represented by a tree.

Another useful control in the set of common controls is the **spin button**. You can use this to increment or decrement values in an associated edit control. To go into all of the possible controls that you might use is beyond the scope of this book, so we'll just take a few illustrative examples (including an example that uses a spin button) and implement them in the Sketcher program.

Creating a Dialog Resource

Let's take a concrete example. We can add a dialog to Sketcher to provide a choice of pen widths for drawing elements. This will ultimately involve modifying the current pen width in the document, as well as in **CElement**, and adding or modifying functions to deal with pen widths. We'll deal with all that, though, once we've got the dialog together.

First, change to the ResourceView, expand the resource tree for Sketcher and right-click on the Dialog folder in the tree. You'll see the pop-up shown here:

If you click on Insert Dialog, a new dialog resource is displayed with a default ID assigned. You can edit the ID by right-clicking on it and selecting Properties from the pop-up. Change the ID to something more meaningful, such as **IDD_PENWIDTH_DLG**. To the right of the ResourceView, you'll see a basic dialog box which already has an OK button and a Cancel button. There is also a Controls palette from which you can select the controls to be added. The palette includes 22 buttons, 21 of which select a Windows 95 common control.

Adding Controls to a Dialog Box

To provide a mechanism for entering a pen width, we're going to change the basic dialog that's initially displayed to the one shown below:

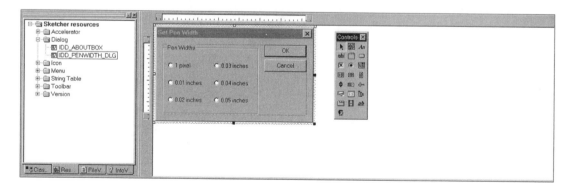

The dialog has six radio buttons which provide the pen width options. These are enclosed within a **group box** with the caption Pen Widths. Each radio button has an appropriate label to identify it.

The first step is to change the text in the title bar of the dialog box:

Make sure that the select button is active in the Controls window. You can now right-click on the dialog box to display its properties box and modify the caption text to Set Pen Width, as shown above. Each of the controls in a dialog will have their own set of properties that you can access and modify in the same way as for the dialog box itself.

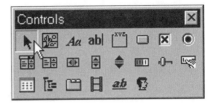

The next step is to add the group box:

We'll use the group box to enclose the radio buttons that will be used to select a pen width. The group box serves to associate the radio buttons in a group from an operational standpoint, and to provide a caption and a boundary for the group of buttons. Where you need more than one set of radio buttons, a means of grouping them is essential if they are to work properly.

Select the button corresponding to the group box from the common controls palette by clicking it with the left mouse button. Then move the cursor to the approximate position in the dialog box where you want the center of the group box to be and press the left mouse button once more. This will place a group box of default size on to the dialog. You can then drag the borders of the group box to enlarge it to accommodate the six radio buttons that we will add. To set the caption for the group box, you can just type the caption you want. In this case, type Pen Widths. The properties box will open automatically.

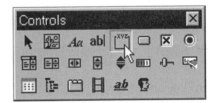

The last step is to add the radio buttons:

Select the radio button control as shown. You can now position the mouse cursor at the point where you want to position a radio button within the group box and click the left mouse button. Do the same for all six radio buttons. For each button, just type in the caption to change it; this will open the properties box as before—the width of the radio button will increase to accommodate the text. You can also drag the border of the button to set its size. You can change the ID for each radio button in the properties dialog to correspond better with its purpose: **IDC_PENWIDTH0** for the 1 pixel pen width, **IDC_PENWIDTH1** for the 0.01 inch width pen, **IDC_PENWIDTH2** for the 0.02 inch pen, and so on.

You can position individual controls by dragging them around with the mouse when the selection tool is active in the Controls window. You can also select a group of controls by selecting successive controls with the *Shift* key pressed, or by dragging the cursor with the left button pressed to create a rectangle enclosing them. To align a group of controls, select an item from the Layout menu, or use the toolbar which appeared at the bottom of the window when you opened this resource for editing. This toolbar is dockable, so you can drag it into the main window if you like.

Testing the Dialog

The dialog resource is now complete. You can test it by selecting the Layout | Test menu option, pressing *Ctrl-T*, or by using the leftmost dialog edit toolbar button that appears at the bottom of the Developer Studio window. This will display a dialog window with the basic operations of the controls available, so you can try clicking on the radio buttons. When you have a group of radio buttons, only one can be selected, so, as you select one, any other that was previously selected is reset. Click on the OK or Cancel button in the dialog to end the test. Once you have saved the dialog resource, we're ready to add some code to support it.

Programming for a Dialog

There are two aspects to programming for a dialog: getting it displayed and handling the effects of its controls. Before we can display the dialog corresponding to the resource we've just created, we first need to define a dialog class for it. ClassWizard will help us with this.

Adding a Dialog Class

With the cursor on the dialog box that we've just created, press the right mouse button and select ClassWizard... from the pop-up at the cursor. ClassWizard will then take you through a process to associate a class with the dialog. The first ClassWizard dialog will ask whether you want to associate the new resource with a new class or an existing class. We'll define a new dialog class derived from the MFC class **CDialog**, which you can call **CPenDialog** in the following dialog. Just click OK to bring it up.

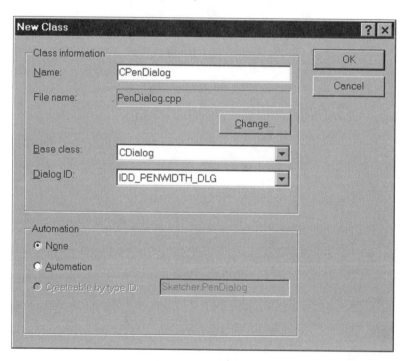

In the New Class dialog, type in **CPenDialog** in the Name: box. The Base Class: drop-down list will automatically show **CDialog**, which is fine for us. You may have to select the Dialog ID:, just make sure that it shows **IDD_PENWIDTH_DLG**. You can now click OK to create the new class.

The **CDialog** class is a window class (derived from the MFC class **CWnd**) that's specifically for displaying and managing dialogs. The dialog resource that we've created will automatically be associated with an object of our **CPenDialog** class, since the class definition includes a definition of a member **IDD** which is initialized with the ID of the dialog resource:

```
class CPenDialog : public CDialog
{
// Construction
public:
    CPenDialog(CWnd* pParent = NULL);   // standard constructor

// Dialog Data
    //{{AFX_DATA(CPenDialog)
    enum { IDD = IDD_PENWIDTH_DLG };
        // NOTE: the ClassWizard will add data members here
    //}}AFX_DATA

    // Plus the rest of the class definition...
};
```

The highlighted statement defines **IDD** as a symbolic name for the dialog ID in the enumeration. Incidentally, using an enumeration is the *only* way you can get an initialized data member into a class definition. If you try putting an initial value for any regular data member declaration it won't compile. You will get an error message about illegal use of pure syntax. It works here because an **enum** defines a symbolic name for an **int**. Unfortunately, you can only define values of type **int** in this way. It's not strictly necessary here, since the initialization for **IDD** could be done in the constructor, but this is how ClassWizard chose to do it. This technique is more commonly used to define a symbol for the dimension of an array which is a member of a class, in which case using an enumeration is your only option.

Having our own dialog class derived from **CDialog** also enables us to customize the dialog class by adding data members and functions to suit our particular needs. You'll often want to handle messages from controls within the dialog class, although you can also choose to handle them in a view or a document class if this is more convenient.

Modal and Modeless Dialogs

There two different types of dialog, which work in quite distinct ways. These are termed **modal** and **modeless** dialogs. While a modal dialog remains in effect, all operations in the other windows in the application are suspended until the dialog box is closed, usually by clicking on an OK or Cancel button. With a modeless dialog, you can move the focus back and forth between the dialog box and other windows in your application just by clicking on them with the mouse, and you can continue to use the dialog box at any time until you close it. ClassWizard is an example of a modal dialog, while the properties window is modeless.

A modeless dialog box is created by calling the **Create()** function defined in the **CDialog** class, but as we'll only be using modal dialogs in our example, we call the **DoModal()** function in the dialog object, as you'll see shortly.

Displaying a Dialog

Where you put the code to display a dialog in your program depends on the application. In the Sketcher program, we need to add a menu item which, when it's selected, will result in the pen width dialog being displayed. We'll put this in the **IDR_SKETCHTYPE** menu bar. As both the width and the color are associated with a pen, we'll rename the Color menu as Pen. You do this just by double-clicking the Color menu item to open its properties box and changing the Caption: entry to &Pen.

When we add the menu item Width... to the Pen menu, we should separate it from the colors in the menu. You can add a separator after the last color menu item by double-clicking the empty menu item and selecting the Separator check box. If you close the properties box, you can then enter the new Width... item as the next menu item after the separator. Double-click on the menu to display the menu properties for modification, as shown below:

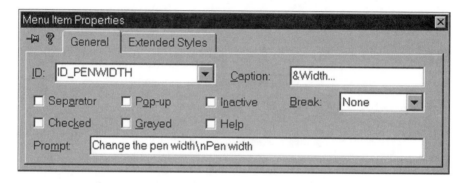

Enter **ID_PENWIDTH** as the ID for the menu item. You can also add a status bar prompt for it and, since we'll also add a toolbar button, you can include text for the tool tip as well. The menu will look like this:

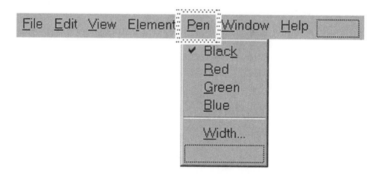

To add the toolbar button, open the toolbar resource by extending Toolbar in the ResourceView and double-clicking on **IDR_MAINFRAME**. You can add a toolbar button to represent a pen width. The one shown below tries to represent a pen drawing a line:

To associate the new button with the menu item that we just added, open the properties box for the button and specify its ID as **ID_PENWIDTH**, the same as that for the menu item.

Code to Display the Dialog

The code to display the dialog will go in the handler for the Pen | Width... menu item, so in which class should we implement this handler? We could consider the view class as a candidate for dealing with pen widths, but following our previous logic with colors and elements, it would be sensible to have the current pen width selection in the document, so we'll put the handler in the **CSketcherDoc** class. Open ClassWizard and create a function for the COMMAND message handler corresponding to **ID_PENWIDTH** in the **CSketcherDoc** class. Now edit this handler and enter the following code:

```
// Handler for the pen width menu item
void CSketcherDoc::OnPenwidth()
{
    CPenDialog aDlg;                    // Create a local dialog object

    // Display the dialog as modal
    aDlg.DoModal();
}
```

There are just two statements in the handler at the moment. The first creates a dialog object which is automatically associated with our dialog resource. We then display the dialog by calling the function **DoModal()** in the **aDlg** object. When the dialog box is closed, the function returns a value corresponding to the button used to close it. In our dialog, the value returned can be **IDOK** if the OK button is selected to close the dialog, or **IDCANCEL** if the dialog is closed using the Cancel button. We'll add code to use this return value a little later.

Because the handler declares a **CPenDialog** object, you must add a **#include** statement for **PenDialog.h** to the beginning of **SketcherDoc.cpp** (after the **#include**s for **stdafx.h** and **Sketcher.h**), otherwise you'll get compilation errors when you build the program. Once you've done that, you can build Sketcher and try out the dialog. It should appear when you click the toolbar button or the Pen | Width... menu item. Of course, if the dialog is to do anything, we still have to add the code to support the operation of the controls.

Supporting the Dialog Controls

For our pen dialog, we'll store the selected pen width in a data member, **m_PenWidth**, of the **CPenDialog** class. You can either add the data member by right-clicking the **CPenDialog** class name, or you can add it directly to the class definition as follows:

```
class CPenDialog : public CDialog
{
// Construction
public:
    CPenDialog(CWnd* pParent = NULL);   // standard constructor

// Dialog Data
    //{{AFX_DATA(CPenDialog)
    enum { IDD = IDD_PENWIDTH_DLG };
        // NOTE: the ClassWizard will add data members here
    //}}AFX_DATA
```

```
// Data stored in the dialog
public:
    int m_PenWidth;                    // Record the pen width

// Plus the rest of the class definition....

};
```

FYI   If you do use the context menu for the class to add **m_PenWidth**, be sure to add a comment to the class definition. This is a good habit to get into, even when the member name looks self-explanatory.

We'll use the data member **m_PenWidth** to set the radio button corresponding to the current pen width in the document as checked. We'll also arrange that the pen width selected in the dialog is stored in this member, so that we can retrieve it when the dialog closes.

Initializing the Controls

We can initialize the radio buttons by overriding the function **OnInitDialog()** which is defined in the base class, **CDialog**. This function is called in response to a **WM_INITDIALOG** message, which is sent during the execution of **DoModal()**, just before the dialog box is displayed. You can add the function to the class by selecting **WM_INITDIALOG** in the Messages: box in ClassWizard. The implementation for our version of **OnInitDialog()** will be:

```
BOOL CPenDialog::OnInitDialog()
{
    CDialog::OnInitDialog();

    // Check the radio button corresponding to the pen width
    switch(m_PenWidth)
    {
        case 1:
            CheckDlgButton(IDC_PENWIDTH1,1);
            break;
        case 2:
            CheckDlgButton(IDC_PENWIDTH2,1);
            break;
        case 3:
            CheckDlgButton(IDC_PENWIDTH3,1);
            break;
        case 4:
            CheckDlgButton(IDC_PENWIDTH4,1);
            break;
        case 5:
            CheckDlgButton(IDC_PENWIDTH5,1);
            break;
        default:
            CheckDlgButton(IDC_PENWIDTH0,1);
    }
    return TRUE;  // return TRUE unless you set the focus to a control
                  // EXCEPTION: OCX Property Pages should return FALSE
}
```

You should leave the call to the base class function there, as it does some essential setup for the dialog. The **switch** statement will check one of the radio buttons, depending on the value set in the **m_PenWidth** data member. This implies that we must arrange to set **m_PenWidth** before we execute **DoModal()**, since the **DoModal()** function causes the **WM_INITDIALOG** message to be sent and our version of **OnInitDialog()** to be called.

The **CheckDlgButton()** function is inherited indirectly from **CWnd** through **CDialog**. If the second argument is 1, it checks the button corresponding to the ID specified in the first argument. If the second argument is 0, the button is unchecked. This works with both check boxes and radio buttons.

Handling Radio Button Messages

Once the dialog box is displayed, every time you click on one or other of the radio buttons, a message will be generated and sent to the application. To deal with these messages, we can add handlers to our **CPenDialog** class. Open ClassWizard and create a handler for the **BN_CLICKED** message for each of the radio button IDs, **IDC_PENWIDTH0** through **IDC_PENWIDTH5**. The implementations of all of these are very similar, since they each just set the pen width in the dialog object. As an example, the handler for **IDC_PENWIDTH0** will be:

```
void CPenDialog::OnPenwidth0()
{
    m_PenWidth = 0;
}
```

You need to add the code for all six handlers to the **CPenDialog** class implementation, setting **m_PenWidth** to 1 in **OnPenWidth1()**, 2 in **OnPenWidth2()**, and so on.

Completing Dialog Operations

We need to modify the **OnPenwidth()** handler in **CSketcherDoc** to make the dialog effective. Add the following code to the function:

```
// Handler for the pen width menu item
void CSketcherDoc::OnPenwidth()
{
    CPenDialog aDlg;        // Create a local dialog object

    // Set the pen width in the dialog to that stored in the document
    aDlg.m_PenWidth = m_PenWidth;

    // Display the dialog as modal
    // When closed with OK, get the pen width
    if(aDlg.DoModal() == IDOK)
        m_PenWidth = aDlg.m_PenWidth;
}
```

The **m_PenWidth** member of the **aDlg** object is passed a pen width stored in the **m_PenWidth** member of the document; we've still to add this member to **CSketcherDoc**. The call of the **DoModal()** function now occurs in the condition of the **if** statement, which will be **TRUE** if the **DoModal()** function returns **IDOK**. In this case, we retrieve the pen width stored in the **aDlg** object and store it in the **m_PenWidth** member of the document. If the dialog box is closed using the Cancel button, **IDOK** won't be returned by **DoModal()** and the value of **m_PenWidth** in the document will not be changed.

Note that even though the dialog box is closed when **DoModal()** returns a value, the **aDlg** object still exists, so we can call its member functions without any problem. The object **aDlg** is destroyed automatically on return from **OnPenwidth()**.

All that remains to do to support variable pen widths in our application is to update the affected classes: **CSketcherDoc**, **CElement**, and the four shape classes derived from **CElement**.

Adding Pen Widths to the Document

We need to add the member **m_PenWidth** to the document, and the function **GetPenWidth()** to allow external access to the value stored. You should add the shaded statements below to the **CSketcherDoc** class definition:

```
class CSketcherDoc : public CDocument
{
// the rest as before...

protected:
// the rest as before...
   int m_PenWidth;                      // Current pen width

// Operations
public:
// the rest as before...
   int GetPenWidth()                    // Get the current pen width
      { return m_PenWidth; }

// the rest as before...
};
```

Because it's trivial, we can define the **GetPenWidth()** function in the definition of the class and gain the benefit of it being implicitly **inline**. We do need to add initialization for **m_PenWidth** to the constructor for **CSketcherDoc**, so add the line,

```
   m_PenWidth = 0;      // Set 1 pixel pen
```

to the constructor definition in **SketcherDoc.cpp**.

Adding Pen Widths to the Elements

We have a little more to do to the **CElement** class and the shape classes derived from it. We already have a member **m_Pen** in **CElement** to store the width to be used when drawing an element, and we must extend each of the constructors for elements to accept a pen width as an argument, and set the member in the class accordingly. The **GetBoundRect()** function in **CElement** must be altered to deal with a pen width of zero. Let's deal with **CElement** first. The new version of **GetBoundRect()** in the **CElement** class will be:

```
// Get the bounding rectangle for an element
CRect CElement::GetBoundRect()
```

```
{
    CRect BoundingRect;                      // Object to store the bounding rectangle
    BoundingRect = m_EnclosingRect;          // Initialize with the enclosing rectangle

    //Increase bounding rectangle by the pen width
    int Offset = m_Pen == 0? 1:m_Pen;   // Width must be at least 1
    BoundingRect.InflateRect(Offset, Offset);
    return BoundingRect;
}
```

We use the local variable **Offset** to ensure that we pass the **InflateRect()** function a value of 1 if the pen width is zero (a pen width of 0 will always draw a line one pixel wide), and we pass the actual pen width in all other cases.

Each of the constructors for **CLine**, **CRectangle**, **CCircle** and **CCurve** needs to be modified to accept a pen width as an argument, and to store it in the **m_Pen** member of the class. The declaration for the constructor in each class definition needs to be modified to add the extra parameter. For example, in the **CLine** class, the constructor declaration will become,

```
CLine(CPoint Start, CPoint End, COLORREF aColor, int PenWidth);
```

and the constructor implementation should be modified to:

```
CLine::CLine(CPoint Start, CPoint End, COLORREF aColor, int PenWidth)
{
    m_StartPoint = Start;              // Set line start point
    m_EndPoint = End;                  // Set line end point
    m_Color = aColor;                  // Set line color
    m_Pen = PenWidth;                  // Set pen width

    // Define the enclosing rectangle
    m_EnclosingRect = CRect(Start, End);
    m_EnclosingRect.NormalizeRect();
}
```

You should modify each of the class definitions and constructors for the shapes in the same way.

Creating Elements in the View

The last change we need to make is to the **CreateElement()** member of **CSketcherView**. Since we've added the pen width as an argument to the constructors for each of the shapes, we must update the calls to the constructors to reflect this. Change the definition of **CSketcherView::CreateElement()** to:

```
CElement* CSketcherView::CreateElement()
{
    // Get a pointer to the document for this view
    CSketcherDoc* pDoc = GetDocument();
    ASSERT_VALID(pDoc);                        // Verify the pointer is good

    // Now select the element using the type stored in the document
    switch(pDoc->GetElementType())
    {
```

```
         case RECTANGLE:
            return new CRectangle(m_FirstPoint, m_SecondPoint,
                           pDoc->GetElementColor(), pDoc->GetPenWidth());
         case CIRCLE:
            return new CCircle(m_FirstPoint, m_SecondPoint,
                           pDoc->GetElementColor(), pDoc->GetPenWidth());
         case CURVE:
            return new CCurve(m_FirstPoint, m_SecondPoint,
                           pDoc->GetElementColor(), pDoc->GetPenWidth());
         case LINE:                        // Always default to a line
            return new CLine(m_FirstPoint, m_SecondPoint,
                        pDoc->GetElementColor(), pDoc->GetPenWidth());
      default:                          // Something's gone wrong
         AfxMessageBox("Bad Element code", MB_OK);
         AfxAbort();
   }
}
```

Each constructor call now passes the pen width as an argument. This is retrieved from the document using the **GetPenWidth()** function that we added to the document class.

Exercising the Dialog

You can now build and run the latest version of Sketcher to see how our dialog works out. Selecting the Pen | Width... menu option will display the dialog box so that you can select the pen width. The following screen is typical of what you might see when the program is executing:

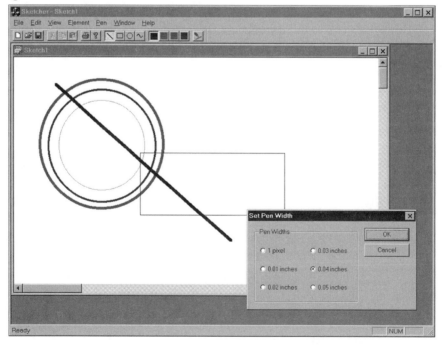

Note that the dialog box is a completely separate window. You can drag it around to position it where you want. You can even drag it outside the Sketcher application window.

Using a Spin Button Control

Now let's move on to looking at how the spin button can help us in the Sketcher application. The spin button is particularly useful when you want to constrain an input within a given integer range. It's normally used in association with another control, called a **buddy control**, which displays the value that the spin button modifies. The associated control is usually an edit control, but it doesn't have to be. We could apply the spin control to managing scaling in a document view. A drawing scale would be a view-specific property, and we would want the element drawing functions to take account of the current scale for a view.

Altering the existing code to deal with view scaling will require rather more work than setting up the control, so let's first look at how we can create a spin button and make it work.

Adding the Scale Menu Item and Toolbar Button

Let's begin by providing a means of displaying the scale dialog. Go to ResourceView and open the **IDR_SKETCHTYPE** menu. We'll add a S̲cale... menu item to the end of the V̲iew menu. First, add a separator to the end of that menu by checking the Separator check box in the properties window for a new item. Now fill in the properties window for the next item, as shown below. This item will bring up the scale dialog, so we end the caption with an ellipsis (three periods) to indicate that it displays a dialog. This is a standard Windows convention.

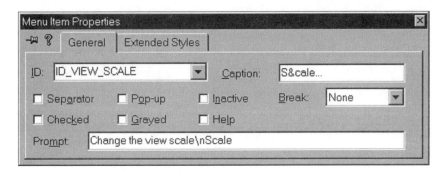

The menu should now look like this:

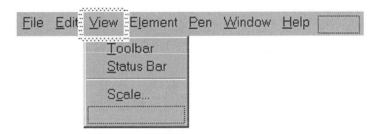

You can also add a toolbar button for this menu item. All you need to do is make sure that the ID for the button is also set to **ID_VIEW_SCALE**.

Creating the Spin Button

We've got the menu item; we'd better have a dialog to go with it. In ResourceView, add a new dialog by right-clicking the Dialog folder on the tree and selecting Insert Dialog. Change the ID to **IDD_SCALE_DLG**.

Click on the spin control in the palette and then click on the position in the dialog where you want it to be placed. Next, right-click on the spin control to display its properties. Change its ID to something more meaningful than the default, such as **IDC_SPIN_SCALE**. Now take at look at the Styles tab in the spin button properties. It's shown below:

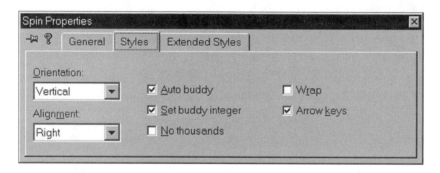

The Arrow keys check box will be automatically selected, enabling you to operate the spin button by using arrow keys on the keyboard. You should also check the box Set buddy integer, which specifies the buddy control value as an integer, and Auto buddy, which provides for automatic selection of the buddy control. The control selected as the buddy will automatically be the previous control defined in the dialog. At the moment, this is the Cancel button, which is not exactly ideal, but we'll see how to change this in a moment. The Alignment: list determines how the spin button will be displayed in relation to its buddy. You should set this to Right so that the spin button is attached to the right edge of its buddy.

Next, add an edit control at the side of the spin button by selecting the edit control from the palette and clicking in the dialog where you want it positioned. Change the ID for the edit control to **IDC_SCALE**.

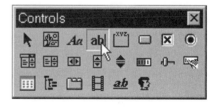

To make the contents of the edit control quite clear, you could add a static control just to the left of the edit control in the palette and enter View Scale: as the caption. You can select all three controls by clicking on them while holding down the *Shift* key. Clicking the right mouse button will pop up a menu at the cursor with options you can use for aligning the controls tidily, or you can use the Layout menu.

The Controls' Tab Sequence

Controls in a dialog have what is called a **tab sequence**. This is the sequence in which the focus shifts from one control to the next, determined initially by the sequence in which controls are added to the dialog. You can see the tab sequence for the current dialog box by selecting Layout | Tab Order from the main menu, or by pressing *Ctrl-D*.

The tab order will be displayed as shown. Because the Cancel button immediately precedes the spin button in sequence, the Auto buddy property for the spin button will select it as the buddy control. We want the edit control to precede the spin button in the tab sequence, so you need to select the controls by clicking on them with the left mouse button in the sequence: OK button; Cancel button; edit control; spin button; and finally the static control. Now the edit control will be selected as the buddy to the spin button.

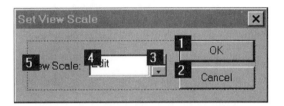

Generating the Scale Dialog Class

After saving the resource file, you can click the right mouse button on the dialog and select ClassWizard from the pop-up at the cursor. This will take you through a dialog to define the new class associated with the dialog resource that you have created. You should name the class **CScaleDialog**.

We need to define a variable in the dialog class that will store the value returned from the edit control, so switch to the Member Variables tab in ClassWizard and select the **IDC_SCALE** ID which identifies the edit control. Click on Add Variable... and enter the variable name as **m_Scale**. We'll be storing an integer scale value, so select **int** as the variable type and click OK.

The ClassWizard will display boxes at the bottom of the Member Variables tab where you can enter maximum and minimum values for the variable **m_Scale**. For our application, a minimum of 1 and a maximum of 8 would be good values. Note that this constraint only applies to the edit box; the spin control is independent of it. The definition which ClassWizard will produce when you click on the OK button is as follows:

```
class CScaleDialog : public CDialog
{
// Construction
public:
    CScaleDialog(CWnd* pParent = NULL);   // standard constructor

// Dialog Data
    //{{AFX_DATA(CScaleDialog)
    enum { IDD = IDD_SCALE_DLG };
    int m_Scale;
    //}}AFX_DATA

// Overrides
    // ClassWizard generated virtual function overrides
```

```
//{{AFX_VIRTUAL(CScaleDialog)
protected:
virtual void DoDataExchange(CDataExchange* pDX);    // DDX/DDV support
//}}AFX_VIRTUAL

// Implementation
protected:

    // Generated message map functions
    //{{AFX_MSG(CScaleDialog)
        // NOTE: the ClassWizard will add member functions here
    //}}AFX_MSG
    DECLARE_MESSAGE_MAP()
};
```

The interesting bits are shaded. The class is associated with the dialog resource through the **enum** statement initializing **IDD** with the ID of the resource. It contains the variable **m_Scale**, which is specified as a **public** member of the class, so we can set and retrieve its value directly.

Dialog Data Exchange and Validation

A virtual function called **DoDataExchange()** has been included in the class by ClassWizard. If you take a look in the **ScaleDialog.cpp** file, you'll find the implementation looks like this:

```
void CScaleDialog::DoDataExchange(CDataExchange* pDX)
{
    CDialog::DoDataExchange(pDX);
    //{{AFX_DATA_MAP(CScaleDialog)
    DDX_Text(pDX, IDC_SCALE, m_Scale);
    DDV_MinMaxInt(pDX, m_Scale, 1, 8);
    //}}AFX_DATA_MAP
}
```

This function is called by the framework to carry out the exchange of data between variables in a dialog and the dialog's controls. This mechanism is called **Dialog Data Exchange**, usually abbreviated to **DDX**. This is a very powerful mechanism that can provide automatic transfer of information between a dialog and its controls in most circumstances, thus saving you the effort of programming to get the data yourself, as we did with the radio buttons in the pen width dialog.

In our scale dialog, DDX handles data transfers between the edit control and the variable **m_Scale** in the **CScaleDialog** class. The variable **pDX** passed to the function controls the direction in which data is transferred. After calling the base class **DoDataExchange()** function, the **DDX_Text()** function is called, which actually moves data between the variable, **m_Scale**, and the edit control.

The call to the **DDV_MinMaxInt()** function verifies that the value transferred is within the limits specified. This mechanism is called **Dialog Data Validation**, or **DDV**. The **DoDataExchange()** function will be called automatically before the dialog is displayed, to pass the value stored in **m_Scale** to the edit control. When the dialog is closed with the OK button, it will be automatically called again to pass the value in the control back to the variable **m_Scale** in the dialog object. All this is taken care of for you. You only need to ensure that the right value is stored in **m_Scale** before the dialog box is displayed, and arrange to collect the result when the dialog box closes.

Initializing the Dialog

To initialize the dialog, we'll use the **OnInitDialog()** function, just as we did for the pen width dialog. This time we'll use it to set up the spin control. We'll initialize the **m_Scale** member a little later, when we create the dialog in the handler for a S<u>c</u>ale... menu item, because we'll want to set it to the value of the scale stored in the view. For now, add the handler for the **WM_INITDIALOG** message to the **CScaleDialog** class, using the same mechanism that you used for the previous dialog, and add code to initialize the spin control as follows:

```
BOOL CScaleDialog::OnInitDialog()
{
    CDialog::OnInitDialog();

    // First get a pointer to the spin control
    CSpinButtonCtrl* pSpin;
    pSpin = (CSpinButtonCtrl*)GetDlgItem(IDC_SPIN_SCALE);

    // If you have not checked the auto buddy option in
    // the spin control's properties, set the buddy control here

    // Set the spin control range
    pSpin->SetRange(1, 8);

    return TRUE;  // return TRUE unless you set the focus to a control
                  // EXCEPTION: OCX Property Pages should return FALSE
}
```

There are only three lines of code added, along with four lines of comments. The first line of code creates a pointer to an object of the MFC class **CSpinButtonCtrl**. This class is specifically for managing spin buttons, and is initialized in the next statement to point to the control in our dialog. The function **GetDlgItem()** is inherited from **CWnd** via **CDialog**, and it will retrieve the address of any control from the ID passed as an argument. Since, as we saw earlier, a control is just a specialized window, the pointer returned is of type **CWnd***, so we have to cast it to the type appropriate to the particular control, which is **CSpinButtonCtrl*** in this case. The third statement that we've added sets the upper and lower limits for the spin button by calling the **SetRange()** member of the spin control object. Although we've set the range limits for the edit control, this doesn't affect the spin control directly. If we don't limit the values in the spin control here, we would be allowing the spin control to insert values in the edit control that were outside the limits, so there would be an error message from the edit control. You can demonstrate this by commenting out the **SetRange()** statement here and trying out Sketcher without it.

If you want to set the buddy control using code rather than using the <u>A</u>uto buddy option in the spin button's properties, the **CSpinButtonCtrl** class has a function member to do this. You would need to add the statement,

```
pSpin->SetBuddy(GetDlgItem(IDC_SCALE));
```

at the point indicated by the comments.

267

Displaying the Spin Button

The dialog will be displayed when the Sc̲ale... menu option (or its associated toolbar button) is selected, so you need to use ClassWizard's Message Maps tab to add a COMMAND handler to the **CSketcherView** class corresponding to the **ID_VIEW_SCALE** message. Then you can select the E̲dit Code button and add code as follows:

```
void CSketcherView::OnViewScale()
{
    CScaleDialog aDlg;          // Create a dialog object
    aDlg.m_Scale = m_Scale;     // Pass the view scale to the dialog
    if(aDlg.DoModal() == IDOK)
    {
        m_Scale = aDlg.m_Scale;    // Get the new scale
        InvalidateRect(0);         // Invalidate the whole window
    }
}
```

The dialog is created as modal, in the same way as the pen width dialog. Before the dialog box is displayed by the **DoModal()** call, we store the scale value provided by the **CSketcherView** member, **m_Scale**, in the dialog member with the same name, which ensures that the control will display the current scale value when the dialog is displayed. If the dialog is closed with the OK button, we store the new scale from the dialog member **m_Scale**, in the view member **m_Scale**. Since we have changed the view scale, we need to get the view redrawn with the new scale value applied. The call to **InvalidateRect()** will do this for us.

Of course, we must add **m_Scale** to the definition of **CSketcherView**, so add the following line at the end of the other data members in the class definition:

```
    int m_Scale;          // Current view scale
```

You should also add a line to the **CSketcherView** constructor to initialize **m_Scale** to 1. This will result in a view always starting out with a scale of one to one. If you forget to do this, it's unlikely that your program will work properly.

As we're using the **CScaleDialog** class, we need to add an include statement for **ScaleDialog.h** to the beginning of the **SketcherView.cpp** file. That's all we need to get the scale dialog and its spin control operational. You can build and run Sketcher to give it a trial spin before we add the code to use a view scale factor.

Using the Scale Factor

Scaling with Windows usually involves using one of the scaleable mapping modes, **MM_ISOTROPIC** or **MM_ANISOTROPIC**. By using one or other of these mapping modes, you can get Windows to do most of the work. Unfortunately, it's not as simple as just changing the mapping mode, because neither of these mapping modes is supported by **CScrollView**. However, if we can get around that, we're home and dry. We'll use **MM_ANISOTROPIC**, so let's first understand what's involved in using this mapping mode.

Scaleable Mapping Modes

As we've said, there are two mapping modes that allow the mapping between logical coordinates and device coordinates to be altered. These are **MM_ISOTROPIC** and **MM_ANISOTROPIC**. **MM_ISOTROPIC** has the property that Windows will force the scaling factor for both the x and y axes to be the same, which has the advantage that your circles will always be circles, but the disadvantage that you can't map a document to fit into a rectangle of a different shape. **MM_ANISOTROPIC**, on the other hand, permits scaling of each axis independently. Because it's the more flexible, we'll use **MM_ANISOTROPIC** for scaling operations in Sketcher.

The way in which logical coordinates are transformed to device coordinates is dependent on the following parameters, which you can set:

Parameter	Description
Window Origin	The logical coordinates of the top left corner of the window. This is set by calling the function **CDC::SetWindowOrg()**.
Window Extent	The size of the window specified in logical coordinates. This is set by calling the function **CDC::SetWindowExt()**.
Viewport Origin	The coordinates of the top left corner of the window in device coordinates (pixels). This is set by calling the function **CDC::SetViewportOrg()**.
Viewport Extent	The size of the window in device coordinates (pixels). This is set by calling the function **CDC::SetViewportExt()**.

The *viewport* referred to here has no physical significance by itself; it serves only as a parameter for defining how coordinates are transformed from logical coordinates to device coordinates.

Remember that:

Logical coordinates (also referred to as *page coordinates*) are determined by the mapping mode. For example, the **MM_LOENGLISH** mapping mode has logical coordinates in units of 0.01 inches, with the origin in the top left corner of the client area, and the positive y axis direction running from bottom to top. These are used by the device context drawing functions.

Device coordinates (also referred to as *client coordinates* in a window) are measured in pixels in the case of a window, with the origin at the top left corner of the client area, and with the positive y axis direction from top to bottom. These are used outside of a device context, for example for defining the position of the cursor in mouse message handlers.

Screen coordinates are measured in pixels and have the origin at the top left corner of the screen, with the positive y axis direction from top to bottom. These are used when getting or setting the cursor position.

The formulae that are used by Windows to convert from logical coordinates to device coordinates are:

$$xDevice = (xLogical - xWindowOrg) * \frac{xViewPortExt}{xWindowExt} + xViewPortOrg$$

$$yDevice = (yLogical - yWindowOrg) * \frac{yViewPortExt}{yWindowExt} + yViewPortOrg$$

With coordinate systems other than **MM_ISOTROPIC** and **MM_ANISOTROPIC**, the window extent and the viewport extent are fixed by the mapping mode and you can't change them. Calling the functions **SetWindowExt()** or **SetViewportExt()** in the **CDC** object to change them will have no effect, although you can still move the position of (0,0) in your logical reference frame by calling **SetWindowOrg()** or **SetViewportOrg()**. However, for a given document size which will be expressed by the window extent in logical coordinate units, we can adjust the scale at which elements are displayed by setting the viewport extent appropriately. By using and setting the window and viewport extents, we can get the scaling done automatically.

Setting the Document Size

We need to maintain the size of the document in logical units in the document object. Add a **protected** data member, **m_DocSize**, to the **CSketcherDoc** class definition:

```
CSize m_DocSize;                          // Document size
```

We will also need to access this data member from the view class, so add a **public** function to the **CSketcherDoc** class definition as follows:

```
CSize GetDocSize()
   { return m_DocSize; }                  // Retrieve the document size
```

We must initialize the **m_DocSize** member in the constructor for the document, so modify the implementation of **CSketcherDoc()** as follows:

```
CSketcherDoc::CSketcherDoc()
{
   // TODO: add one-time construction code here
   m_Element = LINE;            // Set initial element type
   m_Color = BLACK;             // Set initial drawing color
   m_PenWidth = 0;              // Set 1 pixel pen
   m_DocSize = CSize(3000,3000); // Set initial document size 30x30 inches
}
```

We'll be using notional **MM_LOENGLISH** coordinates, so we can treat the logical units as 0.01 inches, and the value set will give us an area of 30 inches square to draw on.

Setting the Mapping Mode

We'll set the mapping mode to **MM_ANISOTROPIC** in the **OnPrepareDC()** member of **CSketcherView**. This is always called for any **WM_PAINT** message, and we've arranged to call it when we draw temporary objects in the mouse message handlers. However, we must do a little more than just set the mapping mode. The implementation of **OnPrepareDC()** will be:

```
void CSketcherView::OnPrepareDC(CDC* pDC, CPrintInfo* pInfo)
{
    CScrollView::OnPrepareDC(pDC, pInfo);
    CSketcherDoc* pDoc = GetDocument();
    pDC->SetMapMode(MM_ANISOTROPIC);          // Set the map mode
    CSize DocSize = pDoc->GetDocSize();       // Get the document size

    // y extent must be negative because we want MM_LOENGLISH
    DocSize.cy = -DocSize.cy;                 // Change sign of y
    pDC->SetWindowExt(DocSize);               // Now set the window extent

    // Get the number of pixels per inch in x and y
    int xLogPixels = pDC->GetDeviceCaps(LOGPIXELSX);
    int yLogPixels = pDC->GetDeviceCaps(LOGPIXELSY);

    // Calculate the viewport extent in x and y
    long xExtent = (long)DocSize.cx*m_Scale*xLogPixels/100L;
    long yExtent = (long)DocSize.cy*m_Scale*yLogPixels/100L;

    pDC->SetViewportExt((int)xExtent, (int)-yExtent); // Set viewport extent
}
```

You'll need to create the handler for this before you can add the code. The easiest way is to open the ClassWizard dialog by right clicking in the edit window and selecting ClassWizard... from the pop-up, and then to select OnPrepareDC from the Messages: drop-down list on the Message Maps tab for the **CSketcherView** class. If you click on the Add Function button and then the Edit Code button, you can type the code straight in.

Our override of the base class function is unusual in that we have left the call to **CScrollView::OnPrepareDC()** in, and added our modifications after it. If our class was derived from **CView**, we would replace the call to the base class version because it does nothing, but in the case of **CScrollView** this isn't the case. We need the base class function to set some attributes before we set the mapping mode. Don't make the mistake of calling the base class function at the end though—if you do, scaling won't work.

After setting the mapping mode and obtaining the document extent, we set the window extent with the *y* extent negative. This is just to be consistent with the **MM_LOENGLISH** mode that we were using previously—remember that the origin is at the top, so *y* values in the client area are negative with this mapping mode.

The **CDC** member function **GetDeviceCaps()** supplies information about the device that the device context is associated with. You can get various kinds of information about the device, depending on the argument you pass to the function. In our case, the arguments **LOGPIXELSX** and **LOGPIXELSY** return the number of pixels per logical inch in the *x* and *y* directions. These values will be equivalent to 100 units in our logical coordinates.

We use these values to calculate the *x* and *y* values for the viewport extent, which we store in the local variables **xExtent** and **yExtent**. The document extent along an axis in logical units, divided by 100, gives the document extent in inches. If this is multiplied by the number of logical pixels per inch for the device, we get the equivalent number of pixels for the extent. If we then use this value as the viewport extent, we will get the elements displayed at a scale of 1 to 1. If we simplify the equations for converting between device and logical coordinates by assuming the window origin and the viewport origin are both (0,0), they become:

$$xDevice = xLogical * \frac{xViewPortExt}{xWindowExt} \qquad yDevice = yLogical * \frac{yViewPortExt}{yWindowExt}$$

If we multiply the viewport extent values by the scale (in **m_Scale**), the elements will be drawn according to the value of **m_Scale**. This logic is exactly represented by the expressions for the *x* and *y* viewport extents in our code. The simplified equations with the scale included will be:

$$xDevice = xLogical * \frac{xViewPortExt * m\_Scale}{xWindowExt} \qquad yDevice = yLogical * \frac{yViewPortExt * m\_Scale}{yWindowExt}$$

You should be able the see from this that a given pair of device coordinates will vary in proportion to the scale value. The coordinates at a scale of 3 will be three times the coordinates at a scale of 1. Of course, as well as making elements larger, increasing the scale will also move them away from the origin.

That's all we need to scale the view. Unfortunately, at the moment the scrolling won't work with scaling, so let's see what we can do about that.

Implementing Scrolling with Scaling

CScrollView just won't work with **MM_ANISOTROPIC**, so clearly we must use another mapping mode to set up the scrollbars. The easiest way to do this is to use **MM_TEXT**, because in this case the logical coordinates are the same as the client coordinates—pixels, in other words. All we need to do, then, is to figure out how many pixels are equivalent to our logical document extent for the scale at which we are drawing, which is easier than you might think. We can add a function to **CSketcherView** to take care of the scrollbars and implement everything in there. Right-click on the **CSketcherView** class name and add a **public** function **ResetScrollSizes()** with a **void** return type. Add the code to the implementation, as follows:

```
void CSketcherView::ResetScrollSizes()
{
    CClientDC aDC(this);
    OnPrepareDC(&aDC);                              // Set up the device context
    CSize DocSize = GetDocument()->GetDocSize();    // Get the document size
    aDC.LPtoDP(&DocSize);                           // Get the size in pixels
    SetScrollSizes(MM_TEXT, DocSize);               // Set up the scrollbars
}
```

After creating a local **CClientDC** object for the view, we call **OnPrepareDC()** to set up the **MM_ANISOTROPIC** mapping mode. Because this takes account of the scaling, the **LPtoDP()** member of **aDC** will convert the document size stored in the local variable **DocSize** to the correct number of pixels for the current logical document size and scale. The total document size in pixels defines how large the scrollbars must be in **MM_TEXT** mode—remember **MM_TEXT** logical coordinates are in pixels. We can then get the **SetScrollSizes()** member of **CScrollView** to set up the scrollbars based on this by specifying **MM_TEXT** as the mapping mode.

It may seem strange that we can change the mapping mode in this way, but it's important to keep in mind that the mapping mode is nothing more than a definition of how logical coordinates are to be converted to device coordinates. Whatever mode (and therefore coordinate conversion algorithm) you've set up will apply to all subsequent device context functions until you change it, and you can change it whenever you want. When you set a new mode, subsequent device context function calls just use the conversion algorithm defined by the new mode. We figure how big the document is in pixels with **MM_ANISOTROPIC**, since this is the only way we can get the scaling into the process, and then switch to **MM_TEXT** to set up the scrollbars because we need units for this in pixels for it to work properly. Simple really, when you know how.

Setting Up the Scrollbars

We must set up the scrollbars initially for the view in the **OnInitialUpdate()** member of **CSketcherView**. Change the previous implementation of the function to:

```
void CSketcherView::OnInitialUpdate()
{
    ResetScrollSizes();                 // Set up the scrollbars
    CScrollView::OnInitialUpdate();
}
```

All we need to do is call the function that we just added to the view. This takes care of everything—well, almost. The **CScrollView** object needs an initial extent to be set for **OnPrepareDC()** to work properly, so we need to add one statement to the **CSketcherView** constructor:

```
CSketcherView::CSketcherView()
{
    m_FirstPoint = CPoint(0,0);         // Set 1st recorded point to 0,0
    m_SecondPoint = CPoint(0,0);        // Set 2nd recorded point to 0,0
    m_pTempElement = 0;                 // Set temporary element pointer to 0
    m_pSelected = 0;                    // No element selected initially
    m_MoveMode = FALSE;                 // Set move mode off
    m_CursorPos = CPoint(0,0);          // Initialize as zero
    m_FirstPos = CPoint(0,0);           // Initialize as zero
    m_Scale = 1;                        // Set scale to 1:1
    SetScrollSizes(MM_TEXT, CSize(0,0)); // Set arbitrary scrollers
}
```

This just calls **SetScrollSizes()** to an arbitrary extent to get the scrollbars initialized before the view is drawn. When the view is drawn for the first time, the **ResetScrollSizes()** function call in **OnInitialUpdate()** will set up the scrollbars properly.

Of course, each time the view scale changes, we need to update the scrollbars before the view is redrawn. We can take care of this in the **OnViewScale()** handler in **CSketcherView**:

```
void CSketcherView::OnViewScale()
{
    CScaleDialog aDlg;                  // Create a dialog object
    aDlg.m_Scale = m_Scale;             // Pass the view scale to the dialog
    if(aDlg.DoModal() == IDOK)
    {
        m_Scale = aDlg.m_Scale;         // Get the new scale
        ResetScrollSizes();             // Adjust scrolling to the new scale
        InvalidateRect(0);              // Invalidate the whole window
    }
}
```

Using our function **ResetScrollSizes()**, taking care of the scrollbars isn't complicated. Everything is covered by the one additional line of code.

Now you can build the project and run the application. You'll see that the scrollbars work just as they should. Note that each view maintains its own scale factor, independently of the other views.

Creating a Status Bar

With each view now being scaled independently, it becomes necessary to have some indication of what the current scale in a view is. A convenient way to do this would be to display the scale in a status bar. Windows 95 style conventions indicate that the status bar should appear at the bottom of the window, below the scroll bar if there is one. Also, there tends to be only one status bar attached to the main application window, which you can see in the following screen showing Sketcher at its current stage of development:

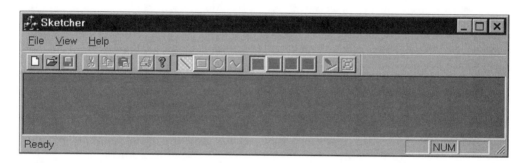

The status bar is divided into segments, called **panes**. The status bar in the previous screen has four panes. The one on the left contains the text Ready, and the other three are the recessed areas on the right. It's possible for you to write to this status bar, but you need to get access to the **m_wndStatusBar** member of **CMainFrame**, as this represents it. As it's a **protected** member of the class, you must add a public member function to modify the status bar. You could add a **public** function member to **CMainFrame** as follows:

```
void CMainFrame::SetPaneText(int Pane, LPCTSTR Text)
{
   m_wndStatusBar.SetPaneText(Pane, Text);
}
```

This function sets the text in the pane specified by **Pane** in the status bar represented by **m_wndStatusBar** to the text, **Text**. The status bar panes are indexed from the left, starting at 0. Now we could write from anywhere outside the **CMainFrame** class:

```
CMainFrame* pFrame = (CMainFrame*)AfxGetApp()->m_pMainWnd;
pFrame->SetPaneText(0, "Goodbye cruel world");
```

This gets a pointer to the main window of the application and outputs the text string you see to the leftmost pane in the status bar. This is fine, but the main application window is no place for a view scale. We may well have several views, so we really want to associate displaying the scale with each view. The answer is to give each child window its own status bar. The **m_wndStatusBar** in **CMainFrame** is an instance of the **CStatusBar** class. We can use the same class to implement our own status bars.

Adding a Status Bar to a Frame

The **CStatusBar** class defines a control bar with multiple panes in which you can display information. Objects of type **CStatusBar** can also provide the same functionality as the Windows common status bar control through a member function **GetStatusBarCtrl()**. There is an MFC class that specifically encapsulates each of the Windows common controls—the one for the common status bar control is **CStatusBarCtrl**. However, using this directly involves quite a bit of work to integrate it with the other MFC classes, as the raw Windows control doesn't connect to MFC. Using **CStatusBar** in our program is easier and safer. The **GetStatusBarCtrl()** function will return a reference to a **CStatusBarCtrl** object that provides all the functionality of the common control, and the **CStatusBar** object will take care of the communications to the rest of the MFC.

The first step to utilizing it is to add a data member for the status bar to the definition of **CChildFrame**, which is the frame window for a view, so add the following declaration to the **public** section of the class:

```
CStatusBar m_StatusBar;      // Status bar object
```

> *A word of advice is required at this point. Status bars should be part of the frame, not part of the view. We don't want to be able to scroll the status bars or draw over them. They should just remain anchored to the bottom of the window. If you added a status bar to the view, it would appear inside the scrollbars and would be scrolled whenever we scrolled the view. Any drawing over the part of the view containing the status bar would cause the bar to be redrawn, leading to an annoying flicker. Having the status bar as part of the frame avoids these problems.*

We need to initialize this data member just before the visible view window is displayed. So, using ClassWizard, add a function to the class that will be called in response to the **WM_CREATE** message, which is sent to the application when the window is to be created. Add the following code to the **OnCreate()** handler:

```
int CChildFrame::OnCreate(LPCREATESTRUCT lpCreateStruct)
{
    if (CMDIChildWnd::OnCreate(lpCreateStruct) == -1)
        return -1;

    // Create the status bar
    m_StatusBar.Create(this);

    // Work out the width of the text we want to display
    CRect textRect;
    CClientDC aDC(&m_StatusBar);
    aDC.SelectObject(m_StatusBar.GetFont());
    aDC.DrawText("View Scale:99", -1, textRect, DT_SINGLELINE|DT_CALCRECT);

    // Setup a part big enough to take the text
    int width = textRect.Width();
    m_StatusBar.GetStatusBarCtrl().SetParts(1, &width);
```

```
    // Initialize the text for the status bar
    m_StatusBar.GetStatusBarCtrl().SetText("View Scale:1", 0, 0);

    return 0;
}
```

The ClassWizard generated the code that isn't shaded. It has inserted a call to the base class version of the **OnCreate()** function, which takes care of creating the definition of the view window. It's important not to delete this function call, otherwise the window will not be created.

The actual creation of the status bar is done with the **Create()** function in the **CStatusBar** object. The **this** pointer for the current **CChildFrame** object is passed to the **Create()** function, setting up a connection between the status bar and the window that owns it. Let's look into what's happening in the code that we have added to the **OnCreate()** function.

Defining the Status Bar Parts

A **CStatusBar** object has an associated **CStatusBarCtrl** object with one or more **parts**. Parts and panes in the context of status bars are equivalent terms—**CStatusBar** refers to panes and **CStatusBarCtrl** refers to parts. You can display a separate item of information in each part.

We can define the number of parts and their widths by a call to the **SetParts()** member of the **CStatusBarCtrl** object. This function requires two arguments. The first argument is the number of parts in the status bar, and the second is an array specifying the right-hand edge of each part in client coordinates. If you omit the call to **SetParts()**, the status bar will have one part by default, which stretches across the whole bar. We could use this, but it looks untidy. A better approach is to size the part so that the text to be displayed fits nicely, and this is what we will do.

The first thing we do in the **OnCreate()** function is to create a temporary **CRect** object in which we'll store the enclosing rectangle for the text that we want to display. We then create a **CClientDC** object which will contain a device context with the same extent as the status bar. This is possible because the status bar, like other controls, is just a window.

Next, the font used in the status bar (set up as part of the desktop properties) is selected into the device context by calling the **SelectObject()** function. The **GetFont()** member of **m_StatusBar** returns a pointer to a **CFont** object that represents the current font. Obviously, the particular will determine how much space the text we want to display will take up.

The **DrawText()** member of the **CClientDC** object is called to calculate the enclosing rectangle for the text we want to display. This function has four arguments:

1 The text string to be drawn. We have passed a string containing the maximum number of characters we would ever want to display, **"View Scale:99"**.

2 The count of the number of characters in the string. We have specified this as -1, which indicates we are supplying a null-terminated string. In this case the function will work out the character count.

3 Our rectangle, **textRect**. The enclosing rectangle for the text will be stored here in logical coordinates.

4 One or more flags controlling the operation of the function.

We have specified a combination of two flags. **DT_SINGLELINE** specifies that the text is to be on a single line, and **DT_CALCRECT** specifies that we want the function to calculate the size of the rectangle required to display the string and store it in the rectangle pointed to by the third argument. The **DrawText()** function is normally used to output text, but in this instance the **DT_CALCRECT** flag stops the function from actually drawing the string. There are a number of other flags that you can use with this function; you can find details of them by looking up this function with Help.

The next statement sets up the parts for the status bar:

```
m_StatusBar.GetStatusBarCtrl().SetParts(1, &width);
```

The expression **m_StatusBar.GetStatusBarCtrl()** returns a reference to the **CStatusBarCtrl** object that belongs to **m_StatusBar**. The reference returned is used to call the function **SetParts()** for the object. The first argument to **SetParts()** defines the number of parts for the status bar—which is 1 in our case. The second argument is typically the address of an array of type **int** containing the *x* coordinate of the right hand edge of each part in client coordinates. The array will have one element for each part in the status bar. Since we have only one part we pass the address of the single variable, **width**, which contains the width of the rectangle we stored in **textRect**. This will be in client coordinates, since our device context uses **MM_TEXT** by default.

Lastly, we set the initial text in the status bar with a call to the **SetText()** member of **CStatusBarCtrl**. The first argument is the text string to be written, the second is the index position of the part which is to contain the text string, and the third argument specifies the appearance of the part on the screen. The third argument can be any of the following:

Style Code	Appearance
0	The text will have a border such that it appears recessed into the status bar.
SBT_NOBORDERS	The text is drawn without borders.
SBT_OWNERDRAW	The text is drawn by the parent window.
SBT_POPOUT	The text will have a border such that it appears to stand out from the status bar.

In our code, we specify the text with a border so that it appears recessed into the status bar. You could try the other options to see how they look.

Updating the Status Bar

If you build and run the code now, the status bars will appear but they will only show a scale factor of 1, no matter what scale factor is actually being used. Not very useful. What we need to do is to change the text each time a different scale is chosen. This means modifying the **OnViewScale()** handler in **CSketcherView** to change the status bar for the frame. We need to add only four lines of code:

```
void CSketcherView::OnViewScale()
{
   CScaleDialog aDlg;                // Create a dialog object
   aDlg.m_Scale = m_Scale;          // Pass the view scale to the dialog
```

```
if(aDlg.DoModal() == IDOK)
{
    m_Scale = aDlg.m_Scale;      // Get the new scale

    // Get the frame window for this view
    CChildFrame* viewFrame = (CChildFrame*)GetParentFrame();

    // Build the message string
    CString StatusMsg("View Scale:");
    StatusMsg += (char)('0' + m_Scale);

    // Write the string to the status bar
    viewFrame->m_StatusBar.GetStatusBarCtrl().SetText(StatusMsg, 0, 0);

    ResetScrollSizes();          // Adjust scrolling to the new scale
    InvalidateRect(0);           // Invalidate the whole window
}
}
```

As we refer to the **CChildFrame** object here, you must add a **#include** directive for **ChildFrm.h** to the beginning of **SketcherView.cpp** after the **#include** for **Sketcher.h**.

The first line calls the **GetParentFrame()** member of **CSketcherView** that's inherited from the **CScrollView** class. This returns a pointer to a **CFrameWnd** object to correspond to the frame window, so it has to be cast to **CChildFrame*** for it to be of any use to us.

The next two lines build the message that is to be displayed in the status bar. The **CString** class is used simply because it is more flexible than using a **char** array. **CString**s will be discussed in greater depth a bit later when we add a new element type to Sketcher. We get the character for the scale value by adding the value of **m_Scale** (which will be from 1 to 8) to the character **'0'**. This will generate characters from **'1'** to **'8'**.

Finally, we use the pointer to the child frame to get at the **m_StatusBar** member that we added earlier. We can then get its status bar control and use the **SetText()** member of the control to change the displayed text. The rest of the **OnViewScale()** function remains unchanged.

That's all we need for the status bar. If you build Sketcher again, you should have multiple, scrolled windows, each at different scales, with the scale displayed in a status bar in each view.

Using a List Box

Of course, you don't have to use a spin button to set the scale. You could also use a list box, for example. The logic for handling a scale factor would be exactly the same, and only the dialog box and the code to extract the value for the scale factor from it would change. If you want to try this out without messing up the development of the Sketcher program, you can copy the complete Sketcher project to another folder and make the modifications to the copy. Deleting part of a ClassWizard managed program can be a bit messy, so it's a useful experience for when you really need to do it.

Removing the Scale Dialog

You first need to delete the definition and implementation of **CScaleDialog** from the new Sketcher project, as well as the resource for the scale dialog. To do this, go to FileView, select **ScaleDialog.cpp** and press *Delete*, and then select **ScaleDialog.h** and press *Delete* to remove them from the project. Then go to ResourceView, expand the Dialog folder, click on IDD_SCALE_DLG and hit *Delete* to remove the dialog resource. Now, delete the **#include** statement for **ScaleDialog.h** from **SketcherView.cpp**. At this stage, all references to the original dialog class will have been removed from the project, but the files are still in your project directory so you must remove or delete them. All done yet? Not by a long chalk. The IDs for the resources are still around. To delete these, select the View | Resource Symbols... menu item, and select and delete **IDC_SCALE** and **IDC_SPIN_SCALE** from the list. If you haven't deleted the resources they represent, then they will still be checked and you won't be able to delete them.

In spite of all the deletions so far, ClassWizard will still think that the **CScaleDialog** class exists. To get around this, you need to start ClassWizard and attempt to choose **CScaleDialog** as the Class name:. After an initial warning, you'll see the following dialog:

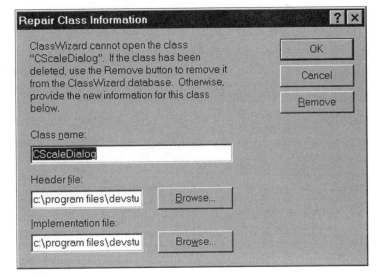

You should select Remove to remove the class from the project completely. You'll need to go through this rigmarole every time that you want to delete a class from an AppWizard-generated project. Believe it or not, we're still not done!

Select the Build | Clean menu item to remove any intermediate files from the project that may contain references to **CScaleDialog**, then close the project workspace by selecting the File | Close Workspace menu item, then re-open it again. Once that's done, we can start by recreating the dialog resource for entering a scale value.

Creating a List Box Control

Right-click on Dialog in ResourceView and add a new dialog with a suitable ID and caption. You could use the same ID as before, **IDD_SCALE_DLG**.

Select the list box button in the controls palette as shown, and click on where you want the list box positioned in the dialog box. You can enlarge the list box and adjust its position in the dialog by dragging it appropriately.

Right-click on the list box and select <u>P</u>roperties from the pop-up. You can set the ID to something suitable, such as **IDC_SCALELIST**. Next, select the Styles tab and set it to the options shown below:

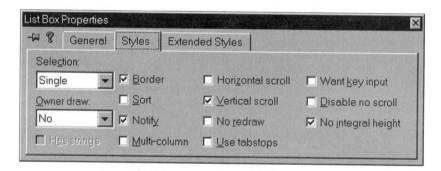

The <u>S</u>ort option box will be checked by default, so make sure you uncheck it. This will mean that strings that we add to the list box will not be automatically sorted. Instead, they'll be appended to the end of the list in the box, and so will be displayed in the sequence in which they are entered. Since we'll use the position in the list of the selected item to indicate the scale, it's important not to have the sequence changed. The list box will have a vertical scroll bar for the list entries by default, which is very useful, and we can ignore the other options. If you want to look into the effects of the other options, you can click the question mark button to display a help screen explaining them.

Now that the dialog is complete you can save it, and you're ready to create the class for the dialog.

Creating the Dialog Class

Right-click on the dialog and select Class<u>W</u>izard... from the pop-up. Again, you'll be taken through the dialog to create a new class. Give it an appropriate name, such as the one we used before: **CScaleDialog**. Once you've completed that, all you need to do is add a **public** member variable from ClassWizard's Member Variables tab, called **m_Scale**, corresponding to the list box ID, **IDC_SCALELIST**. The default type will be **int**, which is fine. ClassWizard will implement DDX for this data member and store an index to the selected entry in the list box in it.

We need to add some code to the **OnInitDialog()** member of **CScaleDialog** to initialize the list box, so you'll have to create a handler for **WM_INITDIALOG** using ClassWizard. Add code as follows:

```
BOOL CScaleDialog::OnInitDialog()
{
   CDialog::OnInitDialog();
```

```
        CListBox* pListBox = (CListBox*)GetDlgItem(IDC_SCALELIST);
        pListBox->AddString("Scale 1");
        pListBox->AddString("Scale 2");
        pListBox->AddString("Scale 3");
        pListBox->AddString("Scale 4");
        pListBox->AddString("Scale 5");
        pListBox->AddString("Scale 6");
        pListBox->AddString("Scale 7");
        pListBox->AddString("Scale 8");
```

```
    return TRUE;  // return TRUE unless you set the focus to a control
                  // EXCEPTION: OCX Property Pages should return FALSE
}
```

The first line that we have added obtains a pointer to the list box control by calling the **GetDlgItem()** member of the dialog class. This is inherited from the MFC class **CWnd**. It returns a pointer of type **CWnd***, so we need to cast this to the type **CListBox***, which is a pointer to the MFC class defining a list box.

Using the pointer to our dialog's **CListBox** object, we then use the **AddString()** member to add the lines defining the list of scale factors. These will appear in the list box in the order that we enter them, so that the dialog will be displayed as shown below:

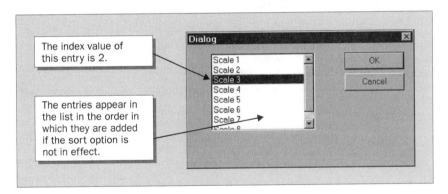

Each entry is associated with a zero-based index value that will be automatically stored in the **m_Scale** member of **CScaleDialog** through the DDX mechanism. Thus, if the third entry in the list is selected, **m_Scale** will be set to 2.

Displaying the Dialog

The dialog will be displayed by the **OnViewScale()** handler that we added to **CSketcherView** in the previous version of Sketcher. You just need to amend this to deal with the new dialog using a list box. The code for it will be as follows:

```
void CSketcherView::OnViewScale()
{
    CScaleDialog aDlg;              // Create a dialog object
    aDlg.m_Scale = m_Scale;        // Pass the view scale to the dialog
    if(aDlg.DoModal() == IDOK)
    {
        m_Scale = 1 + aDlg.m_Scale;  // Get the new scale
```

```
        // Get the frame that wraps this view
        CChildFrame* childFrame = (CChildFrame*)GetParentFrame();

        // Build the message string
        CString StatusMsg("View Scale:");
        StatusMsg += (char)('1' + m_Scale - 1);
        // Set the status bar
        childFrame->m_StatusBar.GetStatusBarCtrl().SetText(StatusMsg, 0, 0);

        ResetScrollSizes();          // Adjust scrolling to the new scale
        InvalidateRect(0);           // Invalidate the whole window
    }
}
```

Because the index value for the entry selected from the list is zero-based, we just need to add 1 to it to get the actual scale value to be stored in the view. The code to display this value in the view's status bar is exactly as before. The rest of the code to handle scale factors is already complete and requires no changes. Once you've added back the `#include` statement for `ScaleDialog.h`, you can build and execute this version of Sketcher to see the list box in action.

Using an Edit Box Control

We could use an edit box control to add annotations in Sketcher. We'll need a new element type, **CText**, that will correspond to a text string, and an extra menu item to set a **TEXT** mode for creating elements. Since a text element will only need one reference point, we can create it in the **OnLButtonDown()** handler. We'll also need a new menu item in the Element pop-up to set the **TEXT** mode. We'll add this text capability to Sketcher in the following sequence:

1 Create the dialog box resource and its associated class.

2 Add the new menu item.

3 Add the code to open the dialog for creating an element.

4 Add the support for a **CText** class.

Creating an Edit Box Resource

Create a new dialog resource in ResourceView by right-clicking the Dialog folder and selecting Insert Dialog from the pop-up. Change the ID for the new dialog to **IDD_TEXT_DLG** and the caption text to Enter Text.

To add an edit box, select the edit box icon from the control palette as shown, and then click the position in the dialog where you want to place it. You can adjust the size of the edit box by dragging its borders, and you can alter its position in the dialog by dragging the whole thing around.

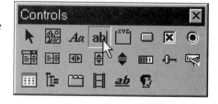

You can display the properties for the edit box by right-clicking it and selecting Properties from the pop-up. You could first change its ID to **IDC_EDITTEXT**, then select the Styles tab, which is shown below:

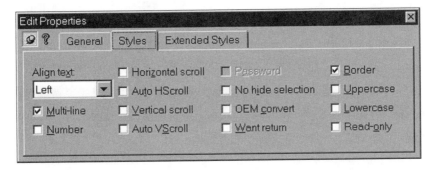

Some of the options here are of interest at this point. First, select the Multi-line option. This creates a multi-line edit box, where the text entered can span more than one line. This enables quite a long line of text to be entered and still remain visible in its entirety in the edit box.

The Align text: option determines how the text is to be positioned in the multi-line edit box. Left is fine for us, since we'll be displaying the text as a single line anyway, but you also have the options for Center and Right.

If you select the Want return option, pressing *Enter* on the keyboard would enter a return character in the text string. This would allow you to analyze the string if you wanted to break it into multiple lines for display. We don't want this effect, so leave it unselected. In this state, pressing *Enter* has the effect of the default control (which is the OK button) being selected, so pressing *Enter* will close the dialog.

If Auto HScroll is unselected, there will be an automatic spill to the next line in the edit box when you reach the end of a line of text. However, this is just for visibility in the edit box—it has no effect on the contents of the string.

When you've finished setting the styles for the edit box, you can press *Enter* to close it. You should make sure that the edit box is first in the tab order by selecting the Tab Order menu item from the Layout pop-up. You can then test the dialog by selecting the Test menu item. The dialog is shown below:

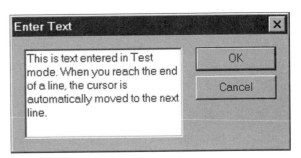

You can even enter text into the dialog in test mode to see how it works. Pressing *Enter* or clicking on the OK button will close the dialog.

Creating the Dialog Class

After saving the dialog resource, you can go to ClassWizard to create a suitable dialog class corresponding to the resource, which you could call **CTextDialog**. Next, switch to the Member Variables tab in ClassWizard, select the **IDC_EDITTEXT** control ID and click the Add Variable... button. Call the new variable **m_TextString** and select its type as **Cstring**—we'll take a look at this class once we've finished the dialog class. Having added the variable you can also specify a maximum length for it, as shown here:

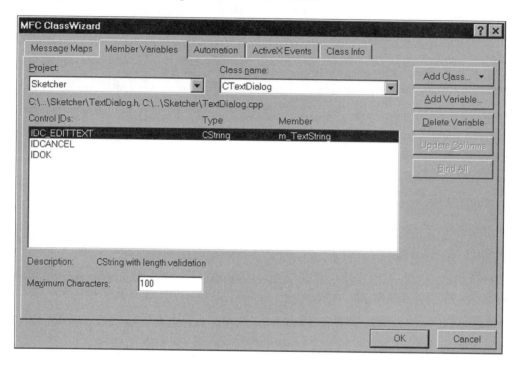

A length of 100 will be more than adequate for our needs. The variable that we have added here will be automatically updated from the data entered into the control by the DDX mechanism. You can click on OK to save the dialog class and close ClassWizard.

The CString Class

The **Cstring** class provides a very convenient and easy-to-use mechanism for handling strings that you can use just about anywhere a string is required. To be more precise, you can use a **Cstring** object in place of strings of type **const char***, which is the usual type for a character string in C++, or of type **LPCTSTR**, which is a type that comes up frequently in Windows API functions.

The **Cstring** class provides several overloaded operators which make it easy to process strings:

Operator	Usage
=	Copies one string to another, as in:

```
Str1 = Str2;               // Copies contents of Str1 to Str2
Str1 = "A normal string";  // Copies the RHS string to Str1
```

+	Concatenates two or more strings, as in:

```
Str1 = Str2 + Str3 + " more";    // Forms Str1 from 3 strings
```

+=	Appends a string to an existing **CString** object
==	Compares two strings for equality, as in:

```
if(Str1 == Str2)

        // do something
```

< <=	Tests if one string is less than, or less than or equal to, another.
> >=	Tests if one string is greater than, or greater than or equal to, another.

The variables **Str1** and **Str2** above are **CString** objects. **CString** objects automatically grow as necessary, such as when you add an additional string to the end of an existing object. For example, in the statements,

```
CString Str = "A fool and your money ";
Str += "are soon partners.";
```

the first statement declares and initializes the object **Str**. The second statement appends an additional string to **Str**, so the length of **Str** will automatically increase.

> *Generally, you should avoid creating **CString** objects on the heap as far as possible. The memory management necessary for growing them means that operations will be rather slow.*

Adding the Text Menu Item

Adding a new menu item should be easy by now. You just need to open the menu resource with the ID **IDR_SKETCHTYPE** by double-clicking it, and add a new menu item Text to the Element menu. The default ID, **ID_ELEMENT_TEXT**, will be fine so you can accept that. You can add a prompt to be displayed on the status bar corresponding to the menu item, and since we'll also want to add an additional toolbar button corresponding to this menu item, you can add a tool tip to the end of the prompt line, using \n to separate the prompt and the tool tip.

Don't forget the context menu. You can copy the menu item from **IDR_SKETCHTYPE**. Right click on the Text menu item and select Copy from the pop-up. Open the menu **IDR_CURSOR_MENU**, extend the no element menu, and you can right click on the empty item at the bottom and select Paste. All you then need to do is to drag the item to the appropriate position - before the separator—and save the resource file.

Add the toolbar button to the **IDR_MAINFRAME** toolbar and set its ID to the same as that for the menu item, **ID_ELEMENT_TEXT**. You can drag the new button so that it's positioned at the end of the block defining the other types of element. When you've saved the resources, we need to add a handler for the menu item.

Go to ClassWizard and add a COMMAND handler to **CSketcherDoc** corresponding to **ID_ELEMENT_TEXT**. Click the Edit Code button and add code as follows:

```
void CSketcherDoc::OnElementText()
{
    m_Element = TEXT;
}
```

Only one line of code is necessary to set the element type in the document to **TEXT**. You must also add a line to the **OurConstants.h** file:

```
const WORD TEXT = 105U;
```

This statement can be added at the end of the other element type definitions. You also need to add a function to check the menu item if it is the current mode, so use ClassWizard to add an **UPDATE_COMMAND_UI** handler corresponding to the **ID_ELEMENT_TEXT** ID, and implement the code for it as follows:

```
void CSketcherDoc::OnUpdateElementText(CCmdUI* pCmdUI)
{
    // Set checked if the current element is text
    pCmdUI->SetCheck(m_Element == TEXT);
}
```

This operates in the same way as the other Element pop-up menu items. We can now define the **CText** class for an object of type **TEXT**.

Defining a Text Element

We can derive the class **CText** from the **CElement** class as follows:

```
// Class defining a text object
class CText: public CElement
{
   public:
      // Function to display a text element
      virtual void Draw(CDC* pDC, CElement* pElement=0);

      // Constructor for a text element
      CText(CPoint Start, CPoint End, CString aString, COLORREF aColor);
      virtual void Move(CSize& aSize);        // Move a text element

   protected:
      CPoint m_StartPoint;                    // position of a text element
      CString m_String;                       // Text to be displayed
      CText(){}                               // Default constructor
};
```

You can put this definition at the end of the **Elements.h** file (but before the **#endif** statement, of course). This class definition declares the virtual **Draw()** and **Move()** functions, as the other element classes do. The data member **m_String** of type **CString** stores the text to be displayed, and **m_StartPoint** specifies the position of the string in the client area of a view.

We should now look at the constructor declaration in a little more detail. The **CText** constructor declaration defines four parameters which provide the following essential information:

Argument	Defines
CPoint Start	The position of the text in logical coordinates.
CPoint End	The corner opposite **Start** that defines the rectangle enclosing the text.
CString aString	The text string to be displayed as a **CString** object.
COLORREF aColor	The color of the text.

The pen width doesn't apply to an item of text, since the appearance is determined by the font. Although we do not need to pass a pen width as an argument to the constructor, the constructor will need to initialize the **m_PenWidth** member inherited from the base class, because it will be used in the computation of the bounding rectangle for the text.

Implementing the CText Class

We have three functions to implement for the **CText** class:

1 The constructor for a **CText** object.

2 The virtual **Draw()** function to display it.

3 The **Move()** function to support moving a text object by dragging it with the mouse.

You can add these to the **Elements.cpp** file.

The CText Constructor

The constructor for a **CText** object needs to initialize the class and base class data members:

```
CText::CText(CPoint Start, CPoint End, CString aString, COLORREF aColor)
{
   m_Pen = 1;                        // Pen width only for bounding rectangle
   m_Color = aColor;                 // Set the color for the text
   m_String = aString;               // Make a copy of the string
   m_StartPoint = Start;             // Start point for string

   m_EnclosingRect = CRect(Start, End);
   m_EnclosingRect.NormalizeRect();
}
```

This is all standard stuff, just like we've seen before for the other elements.

Drawing a CText Object

Drawing text in a device context is different to drawing a geometric figure. The **Draw()** function for a **CText** object is as follows:

```
void CText::Draw(CDC* pDC, CElement* pElement)
{
   COLORREF Color(m_Color);               // Initialize with element color

   if(this==pElement)
      Color = SELECT_COLOR;               // Set selected color

   // Set the text color and output the text
   pDC->SetTextColor(Color);
   pDC->TextOut(m_StartPoint.x, m_StartPoint.y, m_String);
}
```

We don't need a pen to display text. We just need to specify the text color using the **SetTextColor()** function member of the **CDC** object, and then use the **TextOut()** member to output the text string. This will display the string using the default font.

Since the **TextOut()** function doesn't use a pen, it won't be affected by setting the drawing mode of the device context. This means that the raster operations (ROP) method that we use to move the elements will leave temporary trails behind when applied to text. Remember that we used the **SetROP2()** function to specify the way in which the pen would logically combine with the background. By choosing **R2_NOTXORPEN** as the drawing mode, we could cause a previously drawn element to disappear by redrawing it—it would then revert to the background color and thus become invisible. Fonts aren't drawn using a pen, so it won't work with our text elements. We'll see how to fix this problem in the next chapter.

Moving a CText Object

The **Move()** function for a **CText** object is very simple:

```
void CText::Move(CSize& aSize)
{
   m_StartPoint += aSize;                 // Move the start point
   m_EnclosingRect += aSize;              // Move the rectangle
}
```

All we need to do is alter the point defining the position of the string, and the data member defining the enclosing rectangle, by the distance specified in the **aSize** parameter.

Creating a Text Element

Once the element type has been set to **TEXT**, a text object should be created at the cursor position whenever you click the left mouse button and enter the text you want to display. We therefore need to open the dialog to enter text in the **OnLButtonDown()** handler. Add the following code to this handler in **CSketcherView**:

```
void CSketcherView::OnLButtonDown(UINT nFlags, CPoint point)
{
   CClientDC aDC(this);              // Create a device context
   OnPrepareDC(&aDC);               // Get origin adjusted
```

```
    aDC.DPtoLP(&point);              // convert point to Logical
    // In moving mode, so drop the element
    if(m_MoveMode)
    {
        m_MoveMode = FALSE;          // Kill move mode
        m_pSelected = 0;             // De-select element
        GetDocument()->UpdateAllViews(0);   // Redraw all the views
    }
    else
    {
        CSketcherDoc* pDoc = GetDocument();   // Get a document pointer
        if(pDoc->GetElementType() == TEXT)
        {
            CTextDialog aDlg;
            if(aDlg.DoModal() == IDOK)
            {
                // Exit OK so create a text element
                CSketcherDoc* pDoc = GetDocument();
                CSize TextExtent = aDC.GetTextExtent(aDlg.m_TextString);

                // Get bottom right of text rectangle - MM_LOENGLISH
                CPoint BottomRt(point.x+TextExtent.cx, point.y-TextExtent.cy);
                CText* pTextElement = new CText(point, BottomRt,
                                    aDlg.m_TextString, pDoc->GetElementColor());

                // Add the element to the document
                pDoc->AddElement(pTextElement);

                // Get all views updated
                pDoc->UpdateAllViews(0,0,pTextElement);
            }
            return;
        }

        m_FirstPoint = point;        // Record the cursor position
        SetCapture();                // Capture subsequent mouse messages
    }
}
```

The code to be added is shaded. It creates a **CTextDialog** object and then opens the dialog using the **DoModal()** function call. The **m_TextString** member of **aDlg** will be automatically set to the string entered in the edit box, so we can just use this data member to pass the string entered back to the **CText** constructor if the OK button is used to close the dialog. The color is obtained from the document using the **GetElementColor()** member that we have used previously. The position of the text is the **point** value holding the cursor position that is passed to the handler.

We also need to calculate the opposite corner of the rectangle that bounds the text. Because the size of the rectangle for the block of text depends on the font used in a device context, we use the **GetTextExtent()** function in the **CClientDC** object, **aDC**, to initialize the **CSize** object, **TextExtent**, with the width and height of the text string in logical coordinates.

Calculating the rectangle for the text in this way is a bit of a cheat, which could cause a problem once we start saving documents in a file, since it's conceivable that a document could be read back into an environment where the default font in a device context is larger than that in effect when the rectangle was calculated. This shouldn't arise very often, so we won't worry about it here, but as a hint—if you want to pursue it—you could use an object of the class **CFont** in the **CText** definition to define a specific font to be used. You could then use the characteristics of the font to calculate the enclosing rectangle for the text string.

You could also use **CFont** to change the font size so that the text is also zoomed when the scale factor is increased. However, you also need to devise a way to calculate the bounding rectangle based on the font size currently being used, which will vary with the view scale.

The **CText** object is created on the heap because the list in the document only maintains pointers to the elements. We add the new element to the document by calling the **AddElement()** member of **CSketcherDoc**, with the pointer to the new text element as an argument. Finally, **UpdateAllViews()** is called with the first argument 0, which specifies that all views are to be updated.

For the program to compile successfully, you need to add a **#include** statement for **TextDialog.h** to the **SketcherView.cpp** file. You should now be able to produce annotated sketches using multiple scaled and scrolled views, such as the ones shown below:

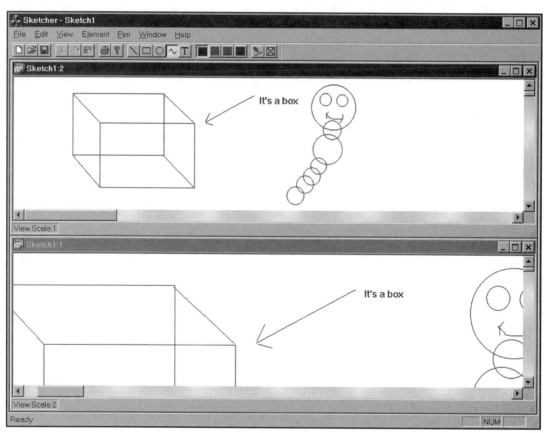

Summary

In this chapter, you've seen several different dialogs using a variety of controls. Although we haven't created dialogs involving several different controls at once, the mechanism for handling them is the same as we have seen, since each control can operate independently of the others.

The most important points that you've seen in this chapter are:

- A dialog involves two components: a resource defining the dialog box and its controls, and a class that will be used to display and manage the dialog.

- Information can be extracted from controls in a dialog using the DDX mechanism. The data can be validated using the DDV mechanism. To use DDX/DDV you need only to use ClassWizard to define variables in the dialog class associated with the controls.

- A modal dialog retains the focus in the application until the dialog box is closed. As long as a modal dialog is displayed, all other windows in an application are inactive.

- A modeless dialog allows the focus to switch from the dialog box to other windows in the application and back again. A modeless dialog can remain displayed as long as the application is executing, if required.

- Common Controls are a set of standard Windows 95 controls that are supported by MFC and the resource editing capabilities of Developer Studio.

- Although controls are usually associated with a dialog, you can add controls to any window if you want to.

Exercises

Ex7-1: Implement the scale dialog using radio buttons.

Ex7-2: Implement the pen width dialog using a list box.

Ex7-3: Implement the pen width dialog as a combo box with the drop list type selected on the Styles tab in the properties box. (The drop list type allows the user to select from a drop-down list, but not to key alternative entries in the list.)

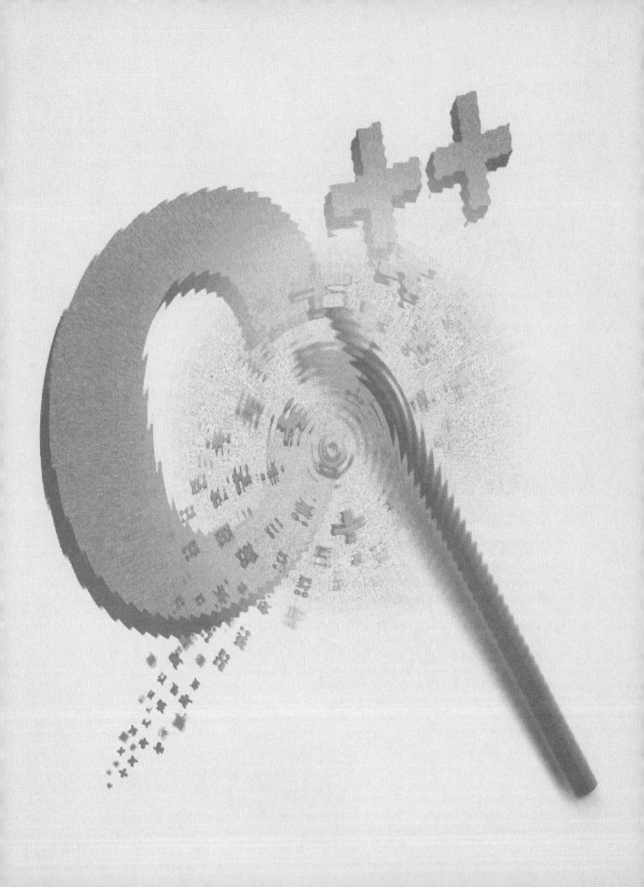

Storing and Printing Documents

With what we have accomplished so far in our Sketcher program, we can create a reasonably comprehensive document with views at various scales, but the information is transient since we have no means of saving a document. In this chapter, we'll remedy that by seeing how we can store a document on disk. We'll also see how we can output a document to a printer.

In this chapter, you will learn:

> What serialization is and how it works

> What you need to do to make objects of a class serializable

> The role of a **CArchive** object in serialization

> How to implement serialization in your own classes

> How to implement serialization in the Sketcher application

> How printing works with MFC

> What view class functions you can use to support printing

> What a **CPrintInfo** object contains and how it's used in the printing process

> How to implement multipage printing in the Sketcher application

Understanding Serialization

A document in an MFC-based program is not a simple entity—it's a class object that can be very complicated. It typically contains a variety of objects, each of which may contain other objects, each of which may contain still more objects... and that structure may continue for a number of levels.

We need to be able to save a document in a file, but writing a class object to a file represents something of a problem, as it isn't the same as a basic data item like an integer or a character string. A basic data item consists of a known number of bytes, so to write it to a file only requires that the appropriate number of bytes be written. Conversely, if you know an **int** was written to a file, then to get it back you just read the appropriate number of bytes.

Writing objects is different. Even if you write away all the data members of an object, that's not enough to be able to get the original object back. Class objects contain function members as well as data members, and all the members, both data and functions, will have access specifiers. Therefore, to record objects in an external file, the information written to the file must contain complete specifications of all the class structures involved. The read process must also be clever enough to synthesize the original objects completely from the data in the file. MFC supports a mechanism called **serialization** to help you to implement input from and output to disk of your class objects with a minimum of time and trouble.

The basic idea behind serialization is that any class that's serializable must take care of storing and retrieving itself. This means that for your classes to be serializable—in the case of the Sketcher application this will include **CElement** and the shape classes we have derived from it—they must be able to write themselves to a file. This implies that for a class to be serializable, all the class types that are used to declare data members must be serializable too.

Serializing a Document

This all sounds like it might be rather tricky, but the basic capability for serializing your document was built into the application by AppWizard right at the outset. The handlers for File | Save, File | Save As..., and File | Open all assume that you want serialization implemented for your document, and already contain the code to support it. Let's take a look at the parts of the definition and implementation of **CSketcherDoc** that relate to creating a document using serialization.

Serialization in the Document Class Definition

The code in the definition of **CSketcherDoc** that enables serialization of a document object is shown shaded in the following fragment:

```
class CSketcherDoc : public CDocument
{
protected: // create from serialization only
    CSketcherDoc();
    DECLARE_DYNCREATE(CSketcherDoc)

// Rest of the class...

// Overrides
    // ClassWizard generated virtual function overrides
    //{{AFX_VIRTUAL(CSketcherDoc)
    public:
    virtual BOOL OnNewDocument();
    virtual void Serialize(CArchive& ar);
    //}}AFX_VIRTUAL

// Rest of the class...

};
```

There are three items here relating to serializing a document object:

1 The **DECLARE_DYNCREATE()** macro.

2 The **Serialize()** member function.

3 The default class constructor.

DECLARE_DYNCREATE() is a macro which enables objects of the **CSketcherDoc** class to be created dynamically by the application framework during the serialization input process. It's matched by a complementary macro, **IMPLEMENT_DYNCREATE()**, in the class implementation. These macros only apply to classes derived from **CObject**, but as we shall see shortly, they aren't the only pair of macros that can be used in this context. For any class that you want to serialize, **CObject** must be a direct or indirect base, since it adds the functionality that enables serialization to work. This is why we took the trouble to derive our **CElement** class from **CObject**. Almost all MFC classes are derived from **CObject** and, as such, are serializable.

 The **Hierarchy Chart** in the **Microsoft Foundation Class Reference** of **Visual C++**, which you can access from InfoView, shows those classes which aren't derived from **CObject**. Note that **CArchive** is in this list.

The class definition also includes a declaration for a virtual function **Serialize()**. Every class that's serializable must include this function. It's called to perform both input and output serialization operations on the data members of the class. The object of type **CArchive** that's passed as an argument to this function determines whether the operation that is to occur is input or output. We'll look into this in more detail when we consider the implementation of serialization for the document class.

Note that the class explicitly defines a default constructor. This is also essential for serialization to work, as the default constructor will be used by the framework to synthesize an object when reading from a disk file, which is then filled out with the data from the file to set the values of the data members of the object.

Serialization in the Document Class Implementation

There are two bits of the file containing the implementation of **CSketcherDoc** that relate to serialization. The first is the macro **IMPLEMENT_DYNCREATE()** that complements the **DECLARE_DYNCREATE()** macro:

```
// SketcherDoc.cpp : implementation of the CSketcherDoc class
//

#include "stdafx.h"
#include "Sketcher.h"
#include "PenDialog.h"

#include "Elements.h"
#include "SketcherDoc.h"

#ifdef _DEBUG
```

```
#define new DEBUG_NEW
#undef THIS_FILE
static char THIS_FILE[] = __FILE__;
#endif


/////////////////////////////////////////////////////////////////////////////
// CSketcherDoc

IMPLEMENT_DYNCREATE(CSketcherDoc, CDocument)

// Message maps and the rest of the file...
```

All this macro does is to define the base class for **CSketcherDoc** as **CDocument**. This is required for the proper dynamic creation of a **CSketcherDoc** object, including members inherited from the base class.

The Serialize() Function

The class implementation also includes the definition of the **Serialize()** function:

```
void CSketcherDoc::Serialize(CArchive& ar)
{
   if (ar.IsStoring())
   {
      // TODO: add storing code here
   }
   else
   {
      // TODO: add loading code here
   }
}
```

This function serializes the data members of the class. The argument passed to the function is a reference to an object of the **CArchive** class, **ar**. The **IsStoring()** member of this class object returns **TRUE** if the operation is to store data members in a file, and **FALSE** if the operation is to read back data members from a previously stored document.

Since AppWizard can have no knowledge of what data your document contains, the process of writing and reading this information is up to you, as indicated by the comments. To understand how this is done, we need to look a little more closely at the **CArchive** class.

The CArchive Class

The **CArchive** class is the engine that drives the serialization mechanism. It provides an MFC-based equivalent of the stream operations in C++ that we used for reading from the keyboard and writing to the screen in our console program examples. An object of the MFC class **CArchive** provides a mechanism for streaming your objects out to a file, or recovering them again as an input stream, automatically reconstituting the objects of your class in the process.

A **CArchive** object has a **CFile** object associated with it which provides disk input/output capability for binary files, and provides the actual connection to the physical file. Within the serialization process, the **CFile** object takes care of all the specifics of the file input and output operations, and the **CArchive** object deals with the logic of structuring the object data to be written or reconstructing the objects from the information read. You only need to worry about the details of the associated **CFile** object if you are constructing your own **CArchive** object. With our document in Sketcher, the framework has already taken care of it and passes the **CArchive** object **ar**, that it constructs, to the **Serialize()** function in **CSketcherDoc**. We'll be able to use the same object in each of the **Serialize()** functions we add to the shape classes when we implement serialization for them.

CArchive overloads the extraction and insertion operators (**>>** and **<<**) for input and output operations respectively on objects of classes derived from **CObject**, plus a range of basic data types. These overloaded operators will work with the following types of objects:

Type	Definition
float	Standard single precision floating point.
double	Standard double precision floating point.
BYTE	8-bit unsigned integer.
int	16-bit signed integer.
LONG	32-bit signed integer.
WORD	16-bit unsigned integer.
DWORD	32-bit unsigned integer.
CObject*	Pointer to **CObject**.
CString	A **CString** object defining a string.
SIZE and **CSize**	An object defining a size as a **cx**, **cy** pair.
POINT and **CPoint**	An object defining a point as an **x**, **y** pair.
RECT and **CRect**	An object defining a rectangle by its top left and bottom right corners.
CTime	A **CTime** object defines a time and a date.
CTimeSpan	A **CTimeSpan** object contains a time interval in seconds, usually the difference between two **CTime** objects.

For basic data types in your objects, you use the insertion and extraction operators to serialize the data. To read or write an object of a serializable class which you have derived from **CObject**, you can either call the **Serialize()** function for the object, or use the extraction or insertion operator. Whichever way you choose must be used consistently for both input and output, so you mustn't output an object using the insertion operator and then read it back using the **Serialize()** function, or vice versa.

Where you don't know the type of an object when you read it, as in the case of the pointers in the list of shapes in our document, for example, you must *only* use the **Serialize()** function. This brings the virtual function mechanism into play, so the appropriate **Serialize()** function for the type of object pointed to is determined at run time.

A **CArchive** object is constructed either for storing objects or for retrieving objects. The **CArchive** function **IsStoring()** will return **TRUE** if the object is for output, and **FALSE** if the object is for input. We saw this used in the **if** statement in the **Serialize()** member of the **CSketcherDoc** class.

There are many other member functions of the **CArchive** class which are concerned with the detailed mechanics of the serialization process, but you don't usually need to know about them to use serialization in your programs.

Functionality of CObject-Based Classes

There are three levels of functionality available in your classes when they're derived from the MFC class **CObject**. The level you get in your class is determined by which of three different macros you use in the definition of your class:

Macro	Functionality
DECLARE_DYNAMIC()	Support for run-time class information.
DECLARE_DYNCREATE()	Support for run-time class information and dynamic object creation.
DECLARE_SERIAL()	Support for run-time class information, dynamic object creation and serialization of objects.

Each of these requires a complementary macro, named with the prefix **IMPLEMENT_** instead of **DECLARE_**, to be placed in the file containing the class implementation. As the table indicates, the macros provide progressively more functionality, so we'll concentrate on the third macro, **DECLARE_SERIAL()**, since it provides everything that the preceding macros do and more. This is the macro you should use to enable serialization in your own classes. It requires the macro **IMPLEMENT_SERIAL()** to be added to the file containing the class implementation.

You may be wondering why the document class uses **DECLARE_DYNCREATE()** and not **DECLARE_SERIAL()**. The **DECLARE_DYNCREATE()** macro provides the capability for dynamic creation of the objects of the class in which it appears. The **DECLARE_SERIAL()** macro provides the capability for serialization of the class, plus the dynamic creation of objects of the class, so it incorporates the effects of **DECLARE_DYNCREATE()**. Your document class doesn't need serialization, since the framework only has to synthesize the document object and then restore the values of its data members. However, the data members of a document *do* need to be serializable, as this is the process used to store and retrieve them.

The Macros Adding Serialization to a Class

With the **DECLARE_SERIAL()** macro in the definition of your **CObject**-based class, you get access to the serialization support provided by **CObject**. This includes special **new** and **delete** operators that incorporate memory leak detection in debug mode. You don't need to do anything to use this, as it works automatically.

The macro requires the class name to be specified as an argument, so for serialization of the **CElement** class, you would add the following line to the class definition:

```
DECLARE_SERIAL(CElement)
```

There's no semicolon required here since this is a macro, not a C++ statement.

It doesn't matter where you put the macro within the class definition (as long as it's not in a section that ClassWizard maintains), but if you always put it as the first line, then you'll always be able to verify that it's there, even when the class definition involves a lot of lines of code.

The macro **IMPLEMENT_SERIAL()**, which you need to place in the implementation file for your class, requires three arguments to be specified. The first argument is the name of your class, the second is the direct base class, and the third argument is an unsigned 32-bit integer identifying a **schema number**, or version number, for your program. This schema number allows the serialization process to guard against problems that can arise if you write objects with one version of a program and read them with another, in which the classes may be different.

For example, we could add the following line to the implementation of the **CElement** class:

```
IMPLEMENT_SERIAL(CElement, CObject, 1)
```

If we subsequently modified the class definition, we would change the schema number to 2, say. If the program attempts to read data that was written with a different schema number from that in the currently active program, an exception will be thrown. The best place for this macro is as the first line following the **#include**s and any initial comments in the **.cpp** file.

Where **CObject** is an indirect base of a class, as in the case of our **CLine** class, for example, each class in the hierarchy must have the serialization macros added for serialization to work in the top level class. For serialization in **CLine** to work, the macros must also be added to **CElement**.

How Serialization Works

The overall process of serializing a document is illustrated in a simplified form below:

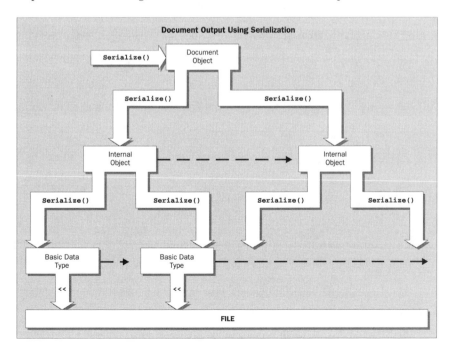

The **Serialize()** function in the document object needs to call the **Serialize()** function (or use an overloaded insertion operator) for each of its data members. Where a member is a class object, the **Serialize()** function for that object will serialize each of its data members in turn, until ultimately basic data types are written to the file. Since most classes in MFC ultimately derive from **CObject**, they contain serialization support, so you can almost always serialize objects of MFC classes.

The data that you'll deal with in the **Serialize()** member functions of your classes and the application document object will in each case be just the data members. The structure of the classes involved, and any other data necessary to reconstitute your original objects, is automatically taken care of by the **CArchive** object.

Where you derive multiple levels of classes from **CObject**, the **Serialize()** function in a class must call the **Serialize()** member of its direct base class to ensure that the direct base class data members are serialized. Note that serialization doesn't support multiple inheritance, so there can only be one base class for each class defined in a hierarchy.

How to Implement Serialization for a Class

From the previous discussion, we can summarize the actions that you need to take to add serialization to a class:

1 Make sure that the class is derived directly or indirectly from **CObject**.

2 Add the **DECLARE_SERIAL()** macro to the class definition (and to the direct base class if the direct base is not **CObject**).

3 Declare the function **Serialize()** as a member function of your class.

4 Add the **IMPLEMENT_SERIAL()** macro to the file containing the class implementation.

5 Implement the **Serialize()** function for your class.

Let's now see how we can implement serialization for documents in our Sketcher program.

Applying Serialization

To implement serialization in the Sketcher application, we need to complete the **Serialize()** function in **CSketcherDoc** to deal with all of the data members of that class. We need then to add serialization to each of the classes which specify objects that may be included in a document. Before we start adding serialization to our application classes, let's make some small changes to the program to record when we change the document. This isn't absolutely necessary, but it is highly desirable, since it will enable the program to guard against the document being closed without saving changes.

Recording Document Changes

There's already a mechanism for noting when a document changes; it uses an inherited member of **CSketcherDoc**, **SetModifiedFlag()**. By calling this function consistently whenever the document changes, you record the fact that the document has been altered in a data member of the document class object. This will cause a prompt to be displayed automatically when you try to exit the application without saving the modified document. The argument to the function **SetModifiedFlag()** is a value of type **BOOL**, and the default value is **TRUE**. If you have occasion to specify that the document was unchanged, you can call this function with the argument **FALSE**, although circumstances where this is necessary are rare.

There are only three occasions when we alter a document object:

1 When we call the **AddElement()** member of **CSketcherDoc** to add a new element.

2 When we call the **DeleteElement()** member of **CSketcherDoc** to delete an element.

3 When we move an element.

All three situations are very easy to deal with. All we need to do is add a call to **SetModifiedFlag()** to each of the functions involved in these operations. The definition of **AddElement()** appears in the class definition. You can extend this to:

```
void AddElement(CElement* pElement)        // Add an element to the list
{
   m_ElementList.AddTail(pElement);
   SetModifiedFlag();                      // Set the modified flag
}
```

You can get to the definition of **DeleteElement()** by clicking on its member name in the ClassView. You should add one line to it, as follows:

```
void CSketcherDoc::DeleteElement(CElement* pElement)
{
   if(pElement)
   {
      // If the element pointer is valid,
      // find the pointer in the list and delete it
      SetModifiedFlag();                  // Set the modified flag
      POSITION aPosition = m_ElementList.Find(pElement);
      m_ElementList.RemoveAt(aPosition);
      delete pElement;                    // Delete the element from the heap
   }
}
```

Note that we must only set the flag if **pElement** is not **NULL**, so you can't just stick the function call anywhere.

In a view object, moving an element occurs in the **MoveElement()** member called by the handler for the **WM_MOUSEMOVE** message, but we only actually change the document when the left mouse button is pressed. If there's a right button click, the element is put back to its original position, so you only need to add the call to the **SetModifiedFlag()** function for the document to the **OnLButtonDown()** function, as follows:

```
void CSketcherView::OnLButtonDown(UINT nFlags, CPoint point)
{
    CClientDC aDC(this);                    // Create a device context
    OnPrepareDC(&aDC);                      // Get origin adjusted
    aDC.DPtoLP(&point);                     // convert point to Logical

    if(m_MoveMode)
    {
        // In moving mode, so drop the element
        m_MoveMode = FALSE;                 // Kill move mode
        m_pSelected = 0;                    // De-select element
        GetDocument()->UpdateAllViews(0);   // Redraw all the views
        GetDocument()->SetModifiedFlag();   // Set the modified flag
    }
    // Rest of the function as before...
}
```

We just need to call the inherited member of our view class, **GetDocument()**, to get access to a pointer to the document object, and then use this pointer to call the **SetModifiedFlag()** function. We now have all the places where we change the document covered.

If you build and run Sketcher, and modify a document or add elements to it, you'll now get a prompt to save the document when you exit the program. Of course, the File | Save menu option doesn't do anything yet except clear the modified flag and save an empty file to disk. We need to implement serialization to get the document written away to disk properly, and that's the next step.

Serializing the Document

The first step is the implementation of the **Serialize()** function for the **CSketcherDoc** class. Within this function, we must add code to serialize the data members of **CSketcherDoc**. The data members that we have declared in the class are as follows:

```
class CSketcherDoc : public CDocument
{
protected: // create from serialization only
    CSketcherDoc();
    DECLARE_DYNCREATE(CSketcherDoc)

// Attributes
public:

protected:
    COLORREF m_Color;                                     // Current drawing color
    WORD m_Element;                                       // Current element type
    CTypedPtrList<CObList, CElement*> m_ElementList;      // Element list
    int m_PenWidth;                                       // Current pen width
    CSize m_DocSize;                                      // Document size
```

```
        // Rest of the class...
    };
```

All we need to do is to insert the statements to store and retrieve these five data members in the **Serialize()** member of the class. We can do this with the following code:

```
    void CSketcherDoc::Serialize(CArchive& ar)
    {
        m_ElementList.Serialize(ar);        // Serialize the element list

        if (ar.IsStoring())
        {
            ar << m_Color                   // Store the current color
               << m_Element                 // the current element type,
               << m_PenWidth                // and the current pen width
               << m_DocSize;                // and the current document size
        }
        else
        {
            ar >> m_Color                   // Retrieve the current color
               >> m_Element                 // the current element type,
               >> m_PenWidth                // and the current pen width
               >> m_DocSize;                // and the current document size
        }
    }
```

For four of the data members, we just use the extraction and insertion operators overloaded by **CArchive**. This works for the data member **m_Color**, even though its type is **COLORREF**, because type **COLORREF** is the same as type **long**. We can't use the extraction and insertion operators for **m_ElementList** because its type isn't supported by the operators, but as long as the **CTypedPtrList** class is defined from the collection class template using **CObList**, as we've done in the declaration of **m_ElementList**, the class will automatically support serialization. We can, therefore, just call the **Serialize()** function for the object.

We don't need to place calls to the **Serialize()** member of the object **m_ElementList** in the **if-else** statement because the kind of operation to be performed will be determined automatically by the **CArchive** argument **ar**. The single statement calling the **Serialize()** member of **m_ElementList** will take care of both input and output.

That's all we need for serializing the document class data members, but serializing the element list, **m_ElementList**, will cause the **Serialize()** functions for the element classes to be called to store and retrieve the elements themselves, so we also need to implement serialization for those classes.

Serializing the Element Classes

All the shape classes are serializable because we derived them from their base class **CElement**, which in turn is derived from **CObject**. The reason that we specified **CObject** as the base for **CElement** was solely to get support for serialization. We can now add support for serialization to each of the shape classes by adding the appropriate macros to the class definitions and implementations, and adding the code to the **Serialize()** function member of each class to serialize its data members. We can start with the base class, **CElement**, where you need to modify the class definition as follows:

```
class CElement: public CObject
{
    DECLARE_SERIAL(CElement)

protected:
    COLORREF m_Color;                   // Color of an element
    CRect m_EnclosingRect;              // Rectangle enclosing an element
    int m_Pen;                          // Pen width

public:
    virtual ~CElement(){}                           // Virtual destructor

    // Virtual draw operation
    virtual void Draw(CDC* pDC, CElement* pElement=0){}
    virtual void Move(CSize& aSize){}   // Move an element
    CRect GetBoundRect();               // Get the bounding rectangle for an element

    virtual void Serialize(CArchive& ar);   // Serialize function for CElement

protected:
    CElement(){}                                    // Default constructor
};
```

We have added the **DECLARE_SERIAL()** macro and a declaration for the virtual function **Serialize()**.

We already had the default constructor defined as **protected** in the class, although in fact it doesn't matter what its access specification is, as long as it appears explicitly in the class definition. It can be **public**, **protected**, or **private**, and serialization will still work. If you forget to include it, though, you'll get an error message when the **IMPLEMENT_SERIAL()** macro is compiled.

You should add the **DECLARE_SERIAL()** macro to each of the classes **CLine**, **CRectangle**, **CCircle**, **CCurve** and **CText**, with the relevant class name as the argument. You should also add a declaration for the **Serialize()** function as a **public** member of each class.

In the file **Elements.cpp**, you must add the following macro at the beginning:

```
IMPLEMENT_SERIAL(CElement, CObject, VERSION_NUMBER)
```

You can define the constant **VERSION_NUMBER** in the **OurConstants.h** file by adding the lines:

```
// Program version number for use in serialization
const UINT VERSION_NUMBER = 1;
```

You can then use the same constant when you add the macro for each of the other shape classes. For instance, for the **CLine** class you should add the line,

```
IMPLEMENT_SERIAL(CLine, CElement, VERSION_NUMBER)
```

and similarly for the other shape classes. When you modify any of the classes relating to the document, all you need to do is change the definition of **VERSION_NUMBER** in the **OurConstants.h** file, and the new version number will apply in all your **Serialize()**

functions. You can put all the **IMPLEMENT_SERIAL()** statements at the beginning of the file if you like. The complete set is:

```
IMPLEMENT_SERIAL(CElement, CObject, VERSION_NUMBER)
IMPLEMENT_SERIAL(CLine, CElement, VERSION_NUMBER)
IMPLEMENT_SERIAL(CRectangle, CElement, VERSION_NUMBER)
IMPLEMENT_SERIAL(CCircle, CElement, VERSION_NUMBER)
IMPLEMENT_SERIAL(CCurve, CElement, VERSION_NUMBER)
IMPLEMENT_SERIAL(CText, CElement, VERSION_NUMBER)
```

The Serialize() Functions for the Shape Classes

We need to implement the **Serialize()** member function for each of the shape classes. We can start with the **CElement** class:

```
void CElement::Serialize(CArchive& ar)
{
   CObject::Serialize(ar);          // Call the base class function

   if (ar.IsStoring())
   {
      ar << m_Color              // Store the color,
         << m_EnclosingRect      // and the enclosing rectangle,
         << m_Pen;               // and the pen width
   }
   else
   {
      ar >> m_Color              // Retrieve the color,
         >> m_EnclosingRect      // and the enclosing rectangle,
         >> m_Pen;               // and the pen width
   }
}
```

This function is of the same form as the one supplied for us in the **CSketcherDoc** class. All of the data members defined in **CElement** are supported by the overloaded extraction and insertion operators, and so everything is done using those operators. Note that we must call the **Serialize()** member for the **CObject** class to ensure that the inherited data members are serialized.

For the **CLine** class, you can code the function as:

```
void CLine::Serialize(CArchive& ar)
{
   CElement::Serialize(ar);        // Call the base class function

   if (ar.IsStoring())
   {
      ar << m_StartPoint         // Store the line start point,
         << m_EndPoint;          // and the end point
   }
   else
   {
      ar >> m_StartPoint         // Retrieve the line start point,
         >> m_EndPoint;          // and the end point
   }
}
```

Again, the data members are all supported by the extraction and insertion operators of the **CArchive** object **ar**. We call the **Serialize()** member of the base class **CElement** to serialize its data members, and this will call the **Serialize()** member of **CObject**. You can see how the serialization process cascades through the class hierarchy.

The **Serialize()** function member of the **CRectangle** class is very simple:

```
void CRectangle::Serialize(CArchive& ar)
{
   CElement::Serialize(ar);           // Call the base class function
}
```

All it does is to call the direct base class function, since the class has no additional data members.

The **CCircle** class doesn't have additional data members beyond those inherited from **CElement** either, so its **Serialize()** function also just calls the base class function:

```
void CCircle::Serialize(CArchive& ar)
{
   CElement::Serialize(ar);           // Call the base class function
}
```

For the **CCurve** class, we have surprisingly little work to do. The **Serialize()** function is coded as follows:

```
void CCurve::Serialize(CArchive& ar)
{
   CElement::Serialize(ar);           // Call the base class function
   m_PointList.Serialize(ar);         // Serialize the list of points
}
```

After calling the base class **Serialize()** function, we just call the **Serialize()** function for the **CList** object, **m_PointList**. Objects of any of the **CList**, **CArray**, and **CMap** classes can be serialized in this way, since once again, these classes are all derived from **CObject**.

The last class for which we need to add an implementation of **Serialize()** to **Elements.cpp** is **CText**:

```
void CText::Serialize(CArchive& ar)
{
   CElement::Serialize(ar);           // Call the base class function

   if (ar.IsStoring())
   {
      ar << m_StartPoint             // Store the start point
         << m_String;                // and the text string
   }
   else
   {
      ar >> m_StartPoint             // Retrieve the start point
         >> m_String;                // and the text string
   }
}
```

After calling the base class function, we serialize the two data members using the insertion and extraction operators in **ar**. The class **CString**, although not derived from **CObject**, is still fully supported by **CArchive** with these overloaded operators.

Exercising Serialization

That's all we need for storing and retrieving documents in our program! The save and restore menu options in the file menu are now fully operational without adding any more code. If you build and run Sketcher after incorporating the changes we've discussed in this chapter, you'll be able to save and restore files, and be automatically prompted to save a modified document when you try to close it or exit from the program, as shown here:

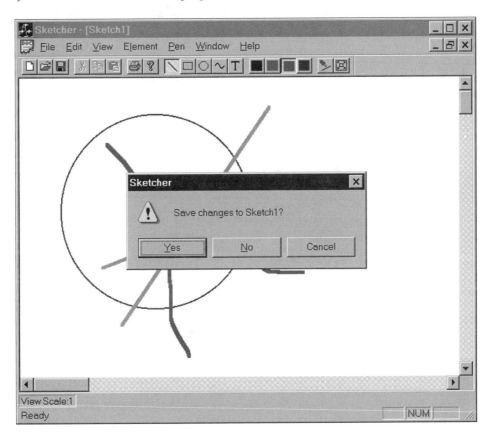

This works because of the **SetModifiedFlag()** calls that we added everywhere we update the document. If you click on the Yes button in the screen above, you'll see the File | Save As... dialog shown on the following page.

This is the standard dialog for this menu item under Windows 95. It's all fully working, supported by code supplied by the framework. The file name for the document has been generated from that assigned when the document was first opened, and the file extension is automatically defined as **.ske**. Our application now has full support for file operations on documents. Easy, wasn't it?

Moving Text

Now it's time to take a brief digression to go back and fix a problem that we created in the last chapter. You'll remember that whenever you try to move a text element, it leaves a trail behind it until the text is positioned on the document again. This is caused by our reliance on ROP drawing in the **MoveElement()** member of the view:

```
void CSketcherView::MoveElement(CClientDC& aDC, CPoint& point)
{
   CSize Distance = point - m_CursorPos;   // Get move distance
   m_CursorPos = point;            // Set current point as 1st for next time

   // If there is an element, selected, move it
   if(m_pSelected)
   {
     aDC.SetROP2(R2_NOTXORPEN);
     m_pSelected->Draw(&aDC,m_pSelected); // Draw the element to erase it
     m_pSelected->Move(Distance);         // Now move the element
     m_pSelected->Draw(&aDC,m_pSelected); // Draw the moved element
   }
}
```

As we mentioned, setting the drawing mode of the device context to **R2_NOTXORPEN** won't remove the trail left by moving the text. We could get around this by using a method of invalidating the rectangles that are affected by the moving elements so that they redraw themselves. This can, however, cause some annoying flicker when the element is moving fast. A better solution would be to use the invalidation method only for the text elements, and our original ROP method for all the other elements, but how are we to know which class the selected element belongs to? This is surprisingly simple: we can use an **if** statement, as follows:

```
if (m_pSelected->IsKindOf(RUNTIME_CLASS(CText)))
{
    // Code here will only be executed if the selected element is of class CText
}
```

This uses the **RUNTIME_CLASS** macro to get a pointer to an object of type **CRuntimeClass**, then passes this pointer to the **IsKindOf()** member function of **m_pSelected**. This returns a non-zero result if **m_pSelected** is of class **CText**, and returns zero otherwise. The only proviso is that the class we're checking for must be declared using **DECLARE_DYNCREATE** or **DECLARE_SERIAL** macros, which is why we left this fix until now.

The final code for **MoveElement()** will be as follows:

```
void CSketcherView::MoveElement(CClientDC& aDC, CPoint& point)
{
    CSize Distance = point - m_CursorPos;   // Get move distance
    m_CursorPos = point;            // Set current point as 1st for next time

    // If there is an element, selected, move it
    if(m_pSelected)
    {
        // If the element is text use this method...
        if (m_pSelected->IsKindOf(RUNTIME_CLASS(CText)))
        {
            CRect OldRect=m_pSelected->GetBoundRect();  // Get old bound rect
            m_pSelected->Move(Distance);                // Move the element
            CRect NewRect=m_pSelected->GetBoundRect();  // Get new bound rect
            OldRect.UnionRect(&OldRect,&NewRect);       // Combine the bound rects
            aDC.LPtoDP(OldRect);                        // Convert to client coords
            OldRect.NormalizeRect();                    // Normalize combined area
            InvalidateRect(&OldRect);                   // Invalidate combined area
            UpdateWindow();                             // Redraw immediately
            m_pSelected->Draw(&aDC,m_pSelected);        // Draw highlighted

            return;
        }

        // ...otherwise, use this method
        aDC.SetROP2(R2_NOTXORPEN);
        m_pSelected->Draw(&aDC,m_pSelected); // Draw the element to erase it
        m_pSelected->Move(Distance);            // Now move the element
        m_pSelected->Draw(&aDC,m_pSelected); // Draw the moved element
    }
}
```

You can see that the code for invalidating the rectangles that we need to use for moving the text is much less elegant than the ROP code that we use for all the other elements. It works, though, as you'll be able to see for yourself if you make this modification and build and run the application.

Printing a Document

Now let's look at printing the document. We already have a basic printing capability implemented in the Sketcher program, courtesy of AppWizard and the framework. The File | Print..., File | Print Setup..., and File | Print Preview menu items all work. The File | Print Preview will display a window showing the current Sketcher document on a page, as shown below:

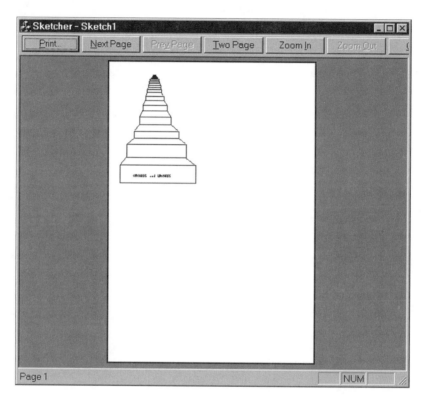

Whatever is in the current document is placed on a single sheet of paper at the current view scale. If the document's extent is beyond the boundary of the paper, the section of the document off the paper won't be printed. If you select the Print... button, this page will be sent to your printer.

As a basic capability which you get for free, it's quite impressive, but it's not adequate for most purposes. A typical document in our program may well not fit on a page, so you would either want to scale the document to fit, or perhaps more conveniently, print the whole document over as many pages as necessary. You can add your own print processing code to extend the capability of the facilities provided by the framework, but to implement this you first need to understand how printing has been implemented in MFC.

The Printing Process

Printing a document is controlled by the current view. The process is inevitably a bit messy, since printing is inherently a messy business, and it potentially involves you in implementing your own versions of quite a number of inherited functions in your view class.

The logic of the process and the functions involved are shown in the diagram below:

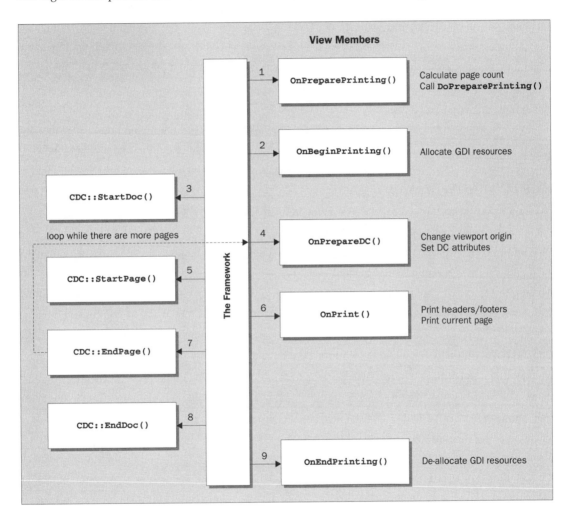

The diagram shows how the sequence of events is controlled by the framework and involves calling five inherited members of your view class, which you may need to override. The **CDC** member functions shown on the left side of the diagram communicate with the printer device driver and are called automatically by the framework.

The typical role of each of the functions in the current view during a print operation is specified in the notes alongside it. The sequence in which they are called is indicated by the numbers on the arrows. In practice, you don't necessarily need to implement all of these functions, only those that you want to for your particular printing requirements. Typically, you'll want at least to implement your own versions of **OnPreparePrinting()**, **OnPrepareDC()** and **OnPrint()**. You'll see an example of how these functions can be implemented in the context of the Sketcher program a little later in this chapter.

The output of data to a printer is done in the same way as outputting data to the display—through a device context. The GDI calls that you use to output text or graphics are device-independent, so they work just as well for a printer as they do for a display. The only difference is the device that the **CDC** object applies to.

The **CDC** functions in the process diagram communicate with the device driver for the printer. If the document to be printed requires more than one printed page, the process loops back to call the **OnPrepareDC()** function for each successive new page, as determined by the **EndPage()** function.

All the functions in your view class that are involved in the printing process are passed a pointer to an object of type **CPrintInfo** as an argument. This object provides a link between all the functions that manage the printing process, so let's take a look at the **CPrintInfo** class in more detail.

The CPrintInfo Class

A **CPrintInfo** object has a fundamental role in the printing process, since it stores information about the print job being executed and details of its status at any time. It also provides functions for accessing and manipulating this data. This object is the means by which information is passed from one view function to another during printing, and between the framework and your view functions.

An object of the **CPrintInfo** class is created whenever you select the File | Print... or File | Print Preview menu options. After being used by each of the functions in the current view that are involved in the printing process, it's automatically deleted when the print operation ends.

All the data members of **CPrintInfo** are **public**. They are:

Member	Usage
m_pPD	A pointer to the **CPrintDialog** object which displays the print dialog box.
m_bDirect	This is set to **TRUE** by the framework if the print operation is to bypass the print dialog box, and **FALSE** otherwise.
m_bPreview	A member of type **BOOL** which has the value **TRUE** if File	Print Preview was selected, and **FALSE** otherwise.
m_bContinuePrinting	A member of type **BOOL**. If this is set to **TRUE**, the framework will continue the printing loop shown in the diagram. If it's set to **FALSE**, the printing loop will end. You only need to set this variable if you don't pass a page count for the print operation to the **CPrintInfo** object (using the **SetMaxPage()** member function). In this case, you'll be responsible for signaling when you're finished by setting this variable to **FALSE**.
m_nCurPage	A value of type **UINT** which stores the page number of the current page. Pages are usually numbered starting from 1.

Member	Usage
m_nNumPreviewPages	A value of type **UINT** which specifies the number of pages displayed in the print preview window. This can be 1 or 2.
m_lpUserData	This is of type **LPVOID** and stores a pointer to an object that you create. This is to allow you to create an object to store additional information about the printing operation and associate it with the **CPrintInfo** object.
m_rectDraw	A **CRect** object which defines the usable area of the page in logical coordinates.
m_strPageDesc	A **CString** object containing a format string used by the framework to display page numbers during print preview.

A **CPrintInfo** object will have the following **public** member functions:

SetMinPage(UINT nMinPage)
The argument specifies the number of the first page of the document. There is no return value

SetMaxPage(UINT nMaxPage);
The argument specifies the number of the last page of the document. There is no return value

GetMinPage() const
Returns the number of the first page of the document as type **UINT**.

GetMaxPage() const
Returns the number of the last page of the document as type **UINT**.

GetFromPage() const
Returns the number of the first page of the document to be printed as type **UINT**. This value would be set through the print dialog.

GetToPage() const
Returns the number of the last page of the document to be printed as type **UINT**. This value would be set through the print dialog.

When you're printing a document consisting of several pages, you need to figure out how many printed pages the document will occupy, and store this information in the **CPrintInfo** object to make it available to the framework. You can do this in your version of the **OnPreparePrinting()** member of the current view.

To set the number of the first page in the document, you need to call the function **SetMinPage()** in the **CPrintInfo** object, which accepts the page number as an argument of type **UINT**. There's no return value. To set the number of the last page in the document, you call the function **SetMaxPage()**, which also accepts the page number as an argument of type **UINT** and doesn't return a value. If you later need to retrieve these values, you can use the functions **GetMinPage()** and **GetMaxPage()** in the **CPrintInfo** object.

The page numbers that you supply will be stored in the **CPrintDialog** object pointed to by the **m_pPD** member of **CPrintInfo**, and displayed in the dialog box which pops up when you select File | Print... from the menu. The user will then be able to specify the numbers of the first and last pages that are to be printed, which you can retrieve by calling the **GetFromPage()** and **GetToPage()** members of the **CPrintInfo** object. In each case, the values returned are of type **UINT**. The dialog will automatically verify that the numbers of the first and last pages to be printed are within the range you supplied by specifying the minimum and maximum pages of the document.

We now know what functions in our view class we can implement to manage printing for ourselves, with the framework doing most of the work. We also know what information is available through the **CPrintInfo** object passed to the functions concerned with printing. We can get a much clearer understanding of the detailed mechanics of printing if we implement a basic multipage print capability for Sketcher documents.

Implementing Multipage Printing

In the Sketcher program, we use the **MM_LOENGLISH** mapping mode to set things up and then switch to **MM_ANISOTROPIC**. This means that our shapes and the view extent are measured in terms of hundredths of an inch. Of course, with the unit of size a fixed physical measure, ideally we will want to print objects at their actual size.

With the document size specified as 3000 by 3000 units, we can create documents up to 30 inches square, which spreads over quite a few sheets of paper if we fill the whole area. It will require a little more effort to work out the number of pages necessary to print a sketch than with a typical text document, because in most instances we'll need a two-dimensional array of pages to print a complete sketch document.

To avoid overcomplicating the problem, let's assume that we're printing on something like a normal sheet of paper (either A4 size or 8½ by 11 inches) and in portrait orientation (which means the long edge is vertical). With either paper size, we'll print the document in a central portion of the paper measuring 6 inches by 9 inches. With these assumptions, we don't need to worry about the actual paper size, we just need to chop the document into 600 by 900 unit chunks. For a document larger than one page, we'll divide up the document as illustrated in the example below:

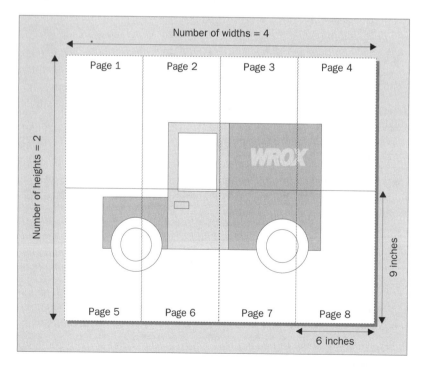

As you can see, we'll be numbering the pages row-wise, so in this case pages 1 to 4 are in the first row and pages 5 to 8 are in the second.

Getting the Overall Document Size

In order to figure out how many pages a particular document occupies, we're going to need to calculate the rectangle that encloses everything in the document. We can do this quite easily by adding a function **GetDocExtent()** to the document class **CSketcherDoc**. Add the following declaration to the **public** interface for **CSketcherDoc**:

```
CRect GetDocExtent();   // Get the bounding rectangle for the whole document
```

The implementation is no great problem. The code for it will be:

```
// Get the rectangle enclosing the entire document
CRect CSketcherDoc::GetDocExtent()
{
   CRect DocExtent(0,0,1,1);     // Initial document extent
   CRect ElementBound(0,0,0,0); // Space for element bounding rectangle

   POSITION aPosition = m_ElementList.GetHeadPosition();

   while(aPosition)         // Loop through all the elements in the list
   {
      // Get the bounding rectangle for the element
      ElementBound=(m_ElementList.GetNext(aPosition))->GetBoundRect();

      // Make coordinates of document extent the outer limits
      DocExtent.UnionRect(DocExtent, ElementBound);
   }
   DocExtent.NormalizeRect();
   return DocExtent;
}
```

You should add this function definition to the **SketcherDoc.cpp** file. The process loops through every element in the document, using the **aPosition** variable to step through the list and getting the bounding rectangle for each element. The **UnionRect()** member of the **CRect** class calculates the smallest rectangle that contains the two rectangles passed as arguments, and puts that value in the **CRect** object for which the function is called. Therefore, **DocExtent** will keep increasing in size until all the elements are contained within it. Note that we have to initialize **DocExtent** with **(0,0,1,1)**, as the **UnionRect()** function doesn't work properly with rectangles that have zero height or width.

Storing Print Data

The **OnPreparePrinting()** function in the view class is called by the application framework to enable you to initialize the printing process for your document. The basic initialization that's required is to provide information about how many pages are in the document for the print dialog that will be displayed. We'll need to store information about the pages that our document requires so that we can use it later in the other view functions involved in the printing process, so we'll originate this in the **OnPreparePrinting()** member of the view class too, store it in an object of our own class that we'll define for this purpose, and then store a pointer to the object in the **CPrintInfo** object that the framework makes available. This is largely to show you how this mechanism works, since in most cases you'll find it easier just to store the data in your view object, mainly because it makes the notation for referencing the data much simpler.

We'll need to store the number of pages running the width of the document, **m_nWidths**, and the number of rows of pages down the length of the document, **m_nLengths**. We'll also store the top-left corner of the rectangle enclosing the document data as a **CPoint** object, **m_DocRefPoint**, because we'll use this when we need to work out the position of a page to be printed from its page number. We can also store the file name for the document in a **CString** object, **m_DocTitle**, so that we can add it as a title to each page. The definition of our class to accommodate these will be:

```
class CPrintData
{
   public:
      UINT m_nWidths;        // No. of pages for the width of the document
      UINT m_nLengths;       // No. of pages for the length of the document
      CPoint m_DocRefPoint;  // Top left corner of the document contents
      CString m_DocTitle;    // The name of the document
};
```

You need to create a new file and add the class definition to it. Save the file as **PrintData.h** and add the file to the Header Files folder in FileView by right clicking the folder and selecting from the pop-up.

We don't need an implementation file for this class. The default constructor (which is automatically generated) will be quite adequate here. Since an object of this class is only going to be used transiently, we don't need to use **CObject** as a base, or to consider any other complication.

The printing process starts with a call to the view member **OnPreparePrinting()**, so let's see how we should implement that.

Preparing to Print

AppWizard added versions of **OnPreparePrinting()**, **OnBeginPrinting()** and **OnEndPrinting()** to **CSketcherView** at the outset. The base code provided for **OnPreparePrinting()** calls **DoPreparePrinting()** in the **return** statement, as you can see:

```
BOOL CSketcherView::OnPreparePrinting(CPrintInfo* pInfo)
{
   // default preparation
   return DoPreparePrinting(pInfo);
}
```

The **DoPreparePrinting()** function displays the print dialog using information about the number of pages to be printed that's defined in the **CPrintInfo** object. Whenever possible, you should calculate the number of pages to be printed and store it in the **CPrintInfo** object before this call occurs. Of course, in many circumstances you may need information from the device context for the printer before you can do this—when you're printing a document where the number of pages is going to be affected by the size of font to be used, for example—in which case it won't be possible to get the page count before you call **OnPreparePrinting()**. In this case, you can compute the number of pages in the **OnBeginPrinting()** member, which receives a pointer to the device context as an argument. This function is called by the framework after **OnPreparePrinting()**, so the information entered in the print dialog is available. This means that you can also take account of the paper size selected by the user in the print dialog.

We're assuming that the page size is large enough to accommodate a 6 inch by 9 inch area to draw the document data, so we can calculate the number of pages in **OnPreparePrinting()**. The code for it will be as follows:

```
BOOL CSketcherView::OnPreparePrinting(CPrintInfo* pInfo)
{
    pInfo->m_lpUserData = new CPrintData;   // Create a print data object
    CSketcherDoc* pDoc = GetDocument();     // Get a document pointer

    // Get the whole document area
    CRect DocExtent = pDoc->GetDocExtent();

    // Save the reference point for the whole document
    ((CPrintData*)(pInfo->m_lpUserData))->m_DocRefPoint =
                            CPoint(DocExtent.left, DocExtent.bottom);

    // Get the name of the document file and save it
    ((CPrintData*)(pInfo->m_lpUserData))->m_DocTitle = pDoc->GetTitle();

    // Calculate how many printed page widths of 600 units are required
    // to accommodate the width of the document
    ((CPrintData*)(pInfo->m_lpUserData))->m_nWidths =
                        (UINT)ceil(((double)(DocExtent.Width()))/600.0);

    // Calculate how many printed page lengths of 900 units are required
    // to accommodate the document length
    ((CPrintData*)(pInfo->m_lpUserData))->m_nLengths =
                        (UINT)ceil(((double)(DocExtent.Height()))/900.0);

    // Set the first page number as 1 and
    // set the last page number as the total number of pages
    pInfo->SetMinPage(1);
    pInfo->SetMaxPage(((CPrintData*)(pInfo->m_lpUserData))->m_nWidths *
                    ((CPrintData*)(pInfo->m_lpUserData))->m_nLengths);

    if(!DoPreparePrinting(pInfo))
    {
        delete (CprintData8)(pInfo->m lpUserData);
        return FALSE
    }

    return TRUE;
}
```

We first create a **CPrintData** object on the heap and store its address in the pointer **m_lpUserData** in the **CPrintInfo** object passed to the function via the pointer **pInfo**. After getting a pointer to the document, we get the rectangle enclosing all of the elements in the document by calling the function **GetDocExtent()** that we added to the document class earlier in this chapter. We then store the corner of this rectangle in the **m_DocRefPoint** member of the **CPrintData** object and put the name of the file containing the document in **m_DocTitle**.

Referencing the **CPrintData** object through the pointer in the **CPrintInfo** object is rather cumbersome. We get to the pointer with the expression **pInfo->m_lpUserData**, but because the pointer is of type **void**, we must add a cast to type **CPrintData*** in order to get to the **m_DocRefPoint** member of the object. The full expression to access the reference point for the document is therefore:

```
((CPrintData*)(pInfo->m_lpUserData))->m_DocRefPoint
```

We have to use this approach for all references to members of the **CPrintData** object, so any expression using them will be festooned with this notation. If we put the data in the view class, we would only need to use the name of the data member. Don't forget to add a **#include** directive for **PrintData.h** to the **SketcherView.cpp** file.

The next two lines of code calculate the number of pages across the width of the document, and the number of pages required to cover the length. The number of pages to cover the width is computed by dividing the width of the document by the width of the print area of a page, which is 600 units or 6 inches, and rounding up to the next highest integer using the **ceil()** library function from **math.h**. A **#include** for this file also needs to be added to **SketcherView.cpp**. For example, **ceil(2.1)** will return **3.0**, **ceil(2.9)** will also return **3.0**, and **ceil(-2.1)** will return **-2.0**. A similar calculation to that for the number of pages across the width of a document produces the number to cover the length. The product of these two values is the total number of pages to be printed, and this is the value that we'll supply for the maximum page number.

Finally we call **DoPreparePrinting()** to show the print dialog. We have to check the returned value from this call, just in case the user hits Cancel. If this is the case we must clean up our **CPrintData** otherwise we'll leak the memory.

Cleaning Up After Printing

Because we created the **CPrintData** object on the heap, we need to ensure that it's deleted when we're done with it. We do this by adding code to the **OnEndPrinting()** function:

```
void CSketcherView::OnEndPrinting(CDC* /*pDC*/, CPrintInfo* pInfo)
{
    // Delete our print data object
    delete (CPrintData*)(pInfo->m_lpUserData);
}
```

That's all we need to do for this function in the Sketcher program, but in some cases you'll need to do more. All your one-time final clean up should be done here. Make sure that you remove the comment delimiters (**/* */**) from the second parameter name, otherwise your function won't compile. The default implementation comments the parameter names out because you may not need to refer to them in your code. Since we use the **pInfo** parameter we must uncomment it, otherwise the compiler will report it as undefined.

We don't need to add anything to the **OnBeginPrinting()** function in the Sketcher program, but you'd need to add code to allocate any GDI resources, such as pens, if they were required throughout the printing process. You would then delete these as part of the clean up process in **OnEndPrinting()**.

Preparing the Device Context

At the moment, our program calls **OnPrepareDC()**, which sets up the mapping mode as **MM_ANISOTROPIC** to take account of the scaling factor. We need to make some additional changes so that the device context is properly prepared in the case of printing:

```
void CSketcherView::OnPrepareDC(CDC* pDC, CPrintInfo* pInfo)
{
    int Scale = m_Scale;              // Store the scale locally
    if(pDC->IsPrinting())
        Scale = 1;                    // If we are printing, set scale to 1

    CScrollView::OnPrepareDC(pDC, pInfo);
    CSketcherDoc* pDoc = GetDocument();
    pDC->SetMapMode(MM_ANISOTROPIC);            // Set the map mode
    CSize DocSize = pDoc->GetDocSize();         // Get the document size

    // y extent must be negative because we want MM_LOENGLISH
    DocSize.cy = -DocSize.cy;                   // Change sign of y
    pDC->SetWindowExt(DocSize);                 // Now set the window extent

    // Get the number of pixels per inch in x and y
    int xLogPixels = pDC->GetDeviceCaps(LOGPIXELSX);
    int yLogPixels = pDC->GetDeviceCaps(LOGPIXELSY);

    // Calculate the viewport extent in x and y
    long xExtent = (long)DocSize.cx*Scale*xLogPixels/100L;
    long yExtent = (long)DocSize.cy*Scale*yLogPixels/100L;

    pDC->SetViewportExt((int)xExtent, (int)-yExtent); // Set viewport extent
}
```

This function is called by the framework for output to the printer as well as to the screen. We need to make sure that when we're printing, a scale of 1 is used to set the mapping from logical coordinates to device coordinates. If you left everything as it was, the output would be at the current view scale, but you'd need to take account of the scale when calculating how many pages you needed, and how you set the origin for each page.

We can determine whether we have a printer device context or not by calling the **IsPrinting()** member of the current **CDC** object, which returns **TRUE** if we are printing. All we need to do when we have a printer device context is to set the scale to 1. Of course, we need to change the statements lower down which use the scale value, so that they use the local variable **Scale**, rather than the **m_Scale** member of the view. The values returned by the calls to **GetDeviceCaps()** with the arguments **LOGPIXELSX** and **LOGPIXELSY** return the number of logical points per inch in the x and y directions for your printer when we're printing, and the equivalent values for your display when we're drawing to the screen, so this automatically adapts the viewport extent to suit the device to which you're sending the output.

Printing the Document

We can write the data to the printer device context in the **OnPrint()** function. This is called once for each page to be printed. You will need to add this function to **CSketcherView**, using ClassWizard. Select OnPrint from the Messages: list on the Message Maps tab.

We can obtain the page number of the current page from the **m_nCurPage** member of the **CPrintInfo** object, and use this value to work out the coordinates of the position in the document that corresponds to the top-left corner of the current page. The way to do this is best understood using an example, so let's suppose that we're printing page seven of an eight-page document, as illustrated in the diagram on the following page.

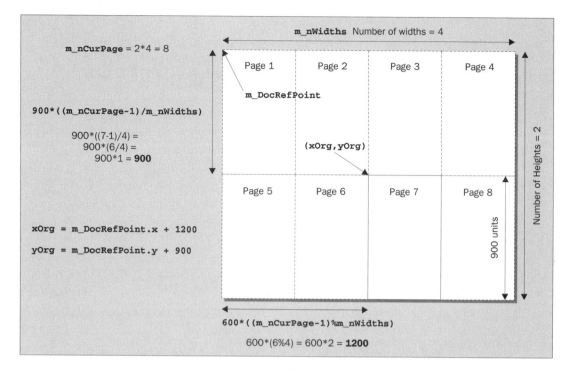

We can get an index to the horizontal position of the page by decrementing the page number by 1 and taking the remainder after dividing by the number of page widths required for the width of the printed area of the document. Multiplying the result by 600 produces the *x* coordinate of the top-left corner of the page, relative to the top-left corner of the rectangle enclosing the elements in the document. Similarly, we can determine the index to the vertical position of the document by dividing the current page number reduced by 1 by the number of page widths required for the horizontal width of the document. By multiplying the remainder by 900 you get the relative *y* coordinate of the top-left corner of the page. We can express this in two statements as follows:

```
int xOrg = ((CPrintData*)(pInfo->m_lpUserData))->m_DocRefPoint.x +
           600*((pInfo->m_nCurPage - 1)%
               (((CPrintData*)(pInfo->m_lpUserData))->m_nWidths));
int yOrg = ((CPrintData*)(pInfo->m_lpUserData))->m_DocRefPoint.y -
           900*((pInfo->m_nCurPage - 1)/
               (((CPrintData*)(pInfo->m_lpUserData))->m_nWidths));
```

The statements look complicated, but that's mostly because of the need to access the information stored in our **CPrintData** object through the pointer in the **CPrintInfo** object.

We want to print the file name of the document at the top of each page, and we want to be sure we don't print the document data over the file name. We also want to center the printed area on the page. We can do this by moving the origin of the coordinate system in the printer device context *after* we have printed the file name. This is illustrated in the diagram below:

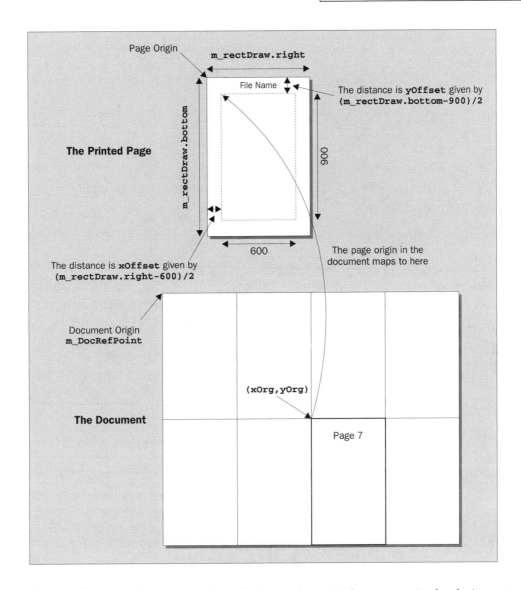

The diagram illustrates the correspondence between the printed page area in the device context and the page to be printed in the reference frame of the document data. Remember that these are in logical coordinates—the equivalent of **MM_LOENGLISH** in Sketcher—so y is increasingly negative from top to bottom. The page shows the expressions for the offsets from the page origin for the 600 by 900 area where we are going to print the page. We want to print the information from the document in the dashed area shown on the page, so we need to map the **xOrg**, **yOrg** point in the document to the position in the printed page shown, which is displaced from the page origin by the offset values **xOffset** and **yOffset**.

By default, the origin in the coordinate system that we use to define elements in the document is mapped to the origin of the device context, but we can change this. The **CDC** object provides a function **SetWindowOrg()** for this purpose. This enables you to define a point in the document's logical coordinate system that you want to correspond to the origin in the device context. It's important to save the old origin that's returned as a **CPoint** object from the **SetWindowOrg()** function. You must restore the old origin when you've finished drawing the current page, otherwise the **m_rectDraw** member of the **CPrintInfo** object will not be set up correctly when you come to print the next page.

The point in the document that we want to map to the origin of the page has the coordinates **xOrg-xOffset**, **yOrg+yOffset**. This may not be easy to visualize, but remember that by setting the window origin, we're defining the point that maps to the viewport origin. If you think about it, you should see that the **xOrg**, **yOrg** point in the document is where we want it on the page.

The complete code for printing a page of the document will be:

```
// Print a page of the document
void CSketcherView::OnPrint(CDC* pDC, CPrintInfo* pInfo)
{
   // Output the document file name
   pDC->SetTextAlign(TA_CENTER);              // Center the following text
   pDC->TextOut(pInfo->m_rectDraw.right/2, -20,
                      ((CPrintData*)(pInfo->m_lpUserData))->m_DocTitle);
   pDC->SetTextAlign(TA_LEFT);                // Left justify text

   // Calculate the origin point for the current page
   int xOrg = ((CPrintData*)(pInfo->m_lpUserData))->m_DocRefPoint.x +
              600*((pInfo->m_nCurPage - 1)%
                 (((CPrintData*)(pInfo->m_lpUserData))->m_nWidths));

   int yOrg = ((CPrintData*)(pInfo->m_lpUserData))->m_DocRefPoint.y -
              900*((pInfo->m_nCurPage - 1)/
                 (((CPrintData*)(pInfo->m_lpUserData))->m_nWidths));

   // Calculate offsets to center drawing area on page as positive values
   int xOffset = (pInfo->m_rectDraw.right - 600)/2;
   int yOffset = -(pInfo->m_rectDraw.bottom + 900)/2;

   // Change window origin to correspond to current page & save old origin
   CPoint OldOrg = pDC->SetWindowOrg(xOrg-xOffset, yOrg+yOffset);

   // Define a clip rectangle the size of the printed area
   pDC->IntersectClipRect(xOrg,yOrg,xOrg+600,yOrg-900);

   OnDraw(pDC);                          // Draw the whole document
   pDC->SelectClipRgn(NULL);             // Remove the clip rectangle
   pDC->SetWindowOrg(OldOrg);            // Restore old window origin
}
```

The first step is to output the file name that we squirreled away in the **CPrintInfo** object. The **SetTextAlign()** function member of the **CDC** object allows you to define the alignment of subsequent text output in relation to the reference point you supply for the text string in the **TextOut()** function. The alignment is determined by the constant passed as an argument to the function. You have three possibilities for specifying the alignment of the text:

Constant	Alignment
TA_LEFT	The point is at the left of the bounding rectangle for the text, so the text is to the right of the point specified. This is default alignment.
TA_RIGHT	The point is at the right of the bounding rectangle for the text, so the text is to the left of the point specified.
TA_CENTER	The point is at the center of the bounding rectangle for the text.

We define the x coordinate of the file name on the page as half the page width, and the y coordinate as 20 units, which is 0.2 inches, from the top of the page. After outputting the name of the document file as centered text, we reset the text alignment to the default, **TA_LEFT**, for the text in the document.

The **SetTextAlign()** function also allows you to change the position of the text vertically by ORing a second flag with the justification flag. The second flag can be any of the following:

Constant	Alignment
TA_TOP	Aligns the top of the rectangle bounding the text with the point defining the position of the text. This is the default.
TA_BOTTOM	Aligns the bottom of the rectangle bounding the text with the point defining the position of the text.
TA_BASELINE	Aligns the baseline of the font used for the text with the point defining the position of the text.

The next action in **OnPrint()** uses the method that we've just discussed for mapping an area of the document to the current page. We get the document drawn on the page by calling the **OnDraw()** function that is used to display the document in the view. This potentially draws the entire document, but we can restrict what appears on the page by defining a **clip rectangle**. A clip rectangle encloses a rectangular area in the device context within which output appears. Outside the clip rectangle, output is suppressed. It's also possible to define irregularly shaped areas for clipping called **regions**.

The initial default clipping area defined in the print device context is the page boundary. We define a clip rectangle which corresponds to the 600 by 900 area centered in the page. This ensures that we will only draw in this area, and the file name will not be overwritten.

After the current page has been drawn, we call **SetClipRgn()** with a **NULL** argument to remove the clip rectangle. If we don't do this, output of the document title is suppressed on all pages after the first because it lies outside the clip rectangle, which would otherwise remain in effect in the print process until the next time **IntersectClipRect()** gets called.

Our final action is to call **SetWindowOrg()** again to restore the window origin to its original location, as we discussed earlier.

Getting a Printout of the Document

To get your first printed Sketcher document, you just need to build the project and execute the program (once you've fixed any typos). If you try File | Print Preview, you should get something similar to the window shown below:

We get print preview functionality completely for free. The framework uses the code that you've supplied for the normal multipage printing operation to produce page images in the print preview window. What you see in the print preview window should be exactly the same as appears on the printed page.

Summary

In this chapter, we've seen how to get a document stored on disk in a form that allows us to read it back and reconstruct its constituent objects using the serialization process supported by MFC. To implement serialization for classes defining document data, you must:

- Derive your class directly or indirectly from **CObject**.
- Specify the **DECLARE_SERIAL()** macro in your class implementation.

🔹 Specify the **IMPLEMENT_SERIAL()** macro in your class definition.

🔹 Implement a default constructor in your class.

🔹 Declare the **Serialize()** function in your class.

🔹 Implement the **Serialize()** function in your class to serialize all the data members.

The serialization process uses a **CArchive** object to perform the input and output. You use the **CArchive** object passed to the **Serialize()** function to serialize the data members of the class.

Implementing classes for serialization also has the side-effect that it allows us access to run-time class information using the **RUNTIME_CLASS** macro and the **IsKindOf()** function.

We have also seen how MFC supports output to a printer. To add to the basic printing capability provided by default, you can implement your own versions of the view class functions involved in printing a document. The principal roles of each of these functions are:

Function	Role
OnPreparePrinting()	Determine the number of pages in the document and call the view member **DoPreparePrinting()**.
OnBeginPrinting()	Allocate the resources required in the printer device context which are needed throughout the printing process, and determine the number of pages in the document, where this is dependent on information from the device context.
OnPrepareDC()	Set attributes in the printer device context as necessary.
OnPrint()	Print the document.
OnEndPrinting()	Delete any GDI resources created in **OnBeginPrinting()** and do any other necessary clean-up.

Information relating to the printing process is stored in an object of type **CPrintInfo** that's created by the framework. You can store additional information in the view, or in another object of your own. If you use your own class object, you can keep track of it by storing a pointer to it in the **CPrintInfo** object.

Exercises

Ex8-1: Add some code to the **OnPrint()** function so that the page number is printed at the bottom of each page of the document in the form 'Page *n*'. If you use the features of the **CString** class, you can do this with just 3 extra lines!

Ex8-2: As a further enhancement to the **CText** class, change the implementation so that scaling works properly. (Hint—look up the **CreatePointFont()** function in the online help.)

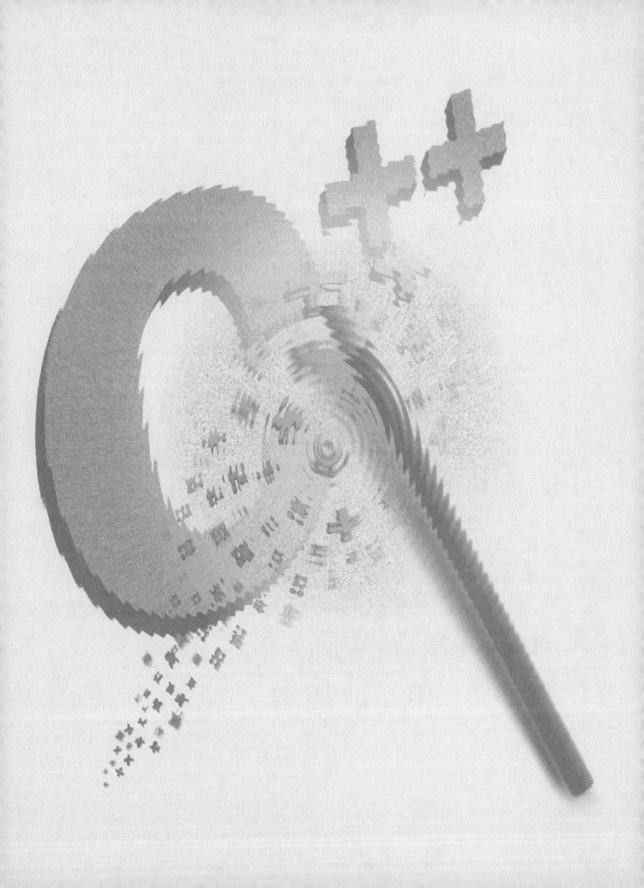

Writing Your Own DLLs

In this chapter, we'll be investigating a different kind of library from the static libraries that contain standard C++ functions such as **sqrt()** or **rand()**. These libraries are called **dynamic-link libraries**, or **DLLs**, and they provide a very powerful way of storing and managing standard library functions that is integral to the Windows environment. They also provide much more flexibility than static libraries.

A complete discussion of DLLs is outside the scope of a beginner's book, but they are important enough to justify including an introductory chapter on them. In this chapter, you will learn:

▶ What a DLL is and how it works

▶ When you should consider implementing a DLL

▶ What varieties of DLL are possible and what they are used for

▶ How you can extend MFC using a DLL

▶ How to define what is accessible in a DLL

▶ How to access the contents of a DLL in your programs

Understanding DLLs

Almost all programming languages support libraries of standard code modules for commonly used functions. In C++ we've been using lots of functions stored in standard libraries, such as the **ceil()** function that we used in the previous chapter, which is declared in the **math.h** header file. The code for this function is stored in a library file with the extension **.lib**, and when the executable module for the Sketcher program was created, the linker retrieved the code for this standard function from the library file and integrated a copy of it into the **.exe** file for the Sketcher program.

If you write another program and use the same function, it too will have its own copy of the **ceil()** function. The **ceil()** function is **statically linked** to each application, and is an integral part of each executable module, as illustrated here:

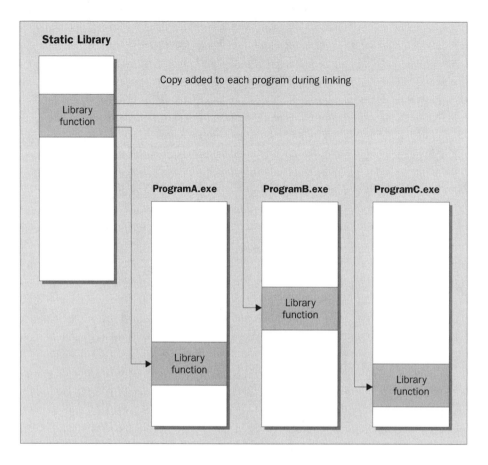

While this is a very convenient way of using standard functions with minimal effort on your part, it does have its disadvantages as a way of sharing common functions in the Windows environment. Since Windows can execute several programs simultaneously, a statically linked standard function being used by more than one program concurrently will be duplicated in memory for each program using it. This may not seem to matter very much for the `ceil()` function, but some functions—input and output, for instance—will invariably be common to most programs and are likely to occupy sizable chunks of memory. Having these statically linked would be extremely inefficient.

Another consideration is that a standard function from a static library may be linked into hundreds of programs in your system, so identical copies of the code for them will be occupying disk space in the `.exe` file for each program. For these reasons, an additional library facility is supported by Windows for standard functions. It's called a **dynamic link library**, and it's usually abbreviated to **DLL**. This allows one copy of a function to be shared among several concurrently executing programs and avoids the need to incorporate a copy of the code for a library function into a program that uses it.

How DLLs Work

A dynamic link library is a file containing a collection of modules that can be used by any number of different programs. The file usually has the extension **.dll**, but this isn't obligatory. When naming a DLL, you can assign any extension that you like, but this can affect how they're handled by Windows. Windows automatically loads dynamic link libraries that have the extension **.dll**. If they have some other extension, you will need to load them explicitly by adding code to do this to your program. Windows itself uses the extension **.exe** for some of its DLLs. You're also likely to have seen the extensions **.vbx** and **.ocx**, which are applied to DLLs containing specific kinds of controls.

You might imagine that you have a choice about whether or not you use dynamic-link libraries in your program, but you don't. The Win32 API is used by every Windows 95 program, and the API is implemented in a set of DLLs. DLLs really are fundamental to Windows programming.

Connecting a function in a DLL to a program is achieved differently from the process used with a statically linked library, where the code is incorporated once and for all when the program is linked to generate the executable module. A function in a DLL is only connected to a program that uses it when the application is run, and this is done on each occasion the program is executed, as illustrated here:

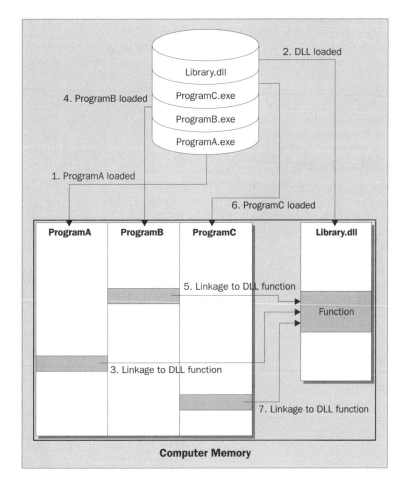

This illustrates what happens when three programs that use a function in a DLL are started successively, and then all execute concurrently. No code from the DLL is included in the executable module of any of the programs. When one of the programs is executed, the program is loaded into memory, and if the DLL it uses isn't already present, it too is loaded separately. The appropriate links between the program and the DLL are then established. If, when a program is loaded, the DLL is already there, all that needs to be done is to link the program to the required function in the DLL.

Note particularly that when your program calls a function in a DLL, Windows will automatically load the DLL into memory. Any program that's subsequently loaded into memory which uses the same DLL can use any of the capabilities provided by the *same copy* of the DLL, since Windows recognizes that the library is already in memory and just establishes the links between it and the program. Windows keeps track of how many programs are using each DLL that is resident in memory so that the library will remain in memory as long as at least one program is still using it. When a DLL is no longer used by any executing program, Windows will automatically delete it from memory.

MFC is provided in the form of a number of DLLs that your program can link to dynamically, as well as a library which your program can link to statically. By default, AppWizard generates programs that link dynamically to the DLL form of MFC.

Having a function stored in a DLL introduces the possibility of changing the function without affecting the programs that use it. As long as the interface to the function in the DLL remains the same, the programs can use a new version of the function quite happily, without the need for recompiling or re-linking them. Unfortunately, this also has a downside: it's very easy to end up using the wrong version of a DLL with a program. This can be a particular problem with applications which install DLLs in the Windows **System** folder. Some commercial applications arbitrarily write the DLLs associated with the program to this folder without regard to the possibility of a DLL with the same name being overwritten. This can interfere with other applications you've already installed and, in the worst case, can render them inoperable.

Run-Time Dynamic Linking

The DLL that we'll create in this chapter will be automatically loaded into memory when the program that uses it is loaded into memory for execution. This is referred to as **load-time dynamic linking** or **early binding**, because the links to the functions used are established as soon as the program and DLL have been loaded into memory. This kind of operation was illustrated in the previous diagram.

However, this isn't the only choice available. It's also possible to cause a DLL to be loaded after execution of a program has started. This is called **run-time dynamic linking,** or **late binding**. The sequence of operations that occurs with this is illustrated in the diagram below:

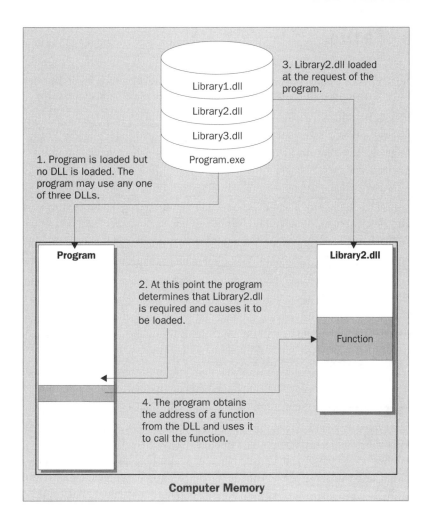

3. Library2.dll loaded at the request of the program.

Library1.dll

Library2.dll

Library3.dll

Program.exe

1. Program is loaded but no DLL is loaded. The program may use any one of three DLLs.

Program

Library2.dll

2. At this point the program determines that Library2.dll is required and causes it to be loaded.

Function

4. The program obtains the address of a function from the DLL and uses it to call the function.

Computer Memory

Run-time dynamic linking enables a program to defer linking of a DLL until it's certain that the functions in a DLL are required. This will allow you to write a program that can choose to load one or more of a number of DLLs based upon input to the program, so that only those functions that are necessary are actually loaded into memory. In some circumstances, this can drastically reduce the amount of memory required to run a program.

A program implemented to use run-time dynamic linking calls a function **LoadLibrary()** to load the DLL when it's required. The address of a function within the DLL can then be obtained using a function **GetProcAddress()**. When the program no longer has a need to use the DLL, it can detach itself from the DLL by calling the **FreeLibrary()** function. If no other program is using the DLL, it will be deleted from memory. We won't be going into further details of how this works in this book.

Contents of a DLL

A dynamic-link library isn't limited to storing code for functions. You can also put resources into a DLL, including such things as bitmaps and fonts. The Solitaire game that comes with Windows uses a dynamic-link library called **Cards.dll** which contains all the bitmap images of the cards and functions to manipulate them. If you wanted to write your own card game, you could conceivably use this DLL as a base and save yourself the trouble of creating all the bitmaps needed to represent the cards. Of course, in order to use it, you would need to know specifically which functions and resources are included in the DLL.

You can also define static global variables in a DLL, including C++ class objects, so that these can be accessed by programs using it. The constructors for global static class objects will be called automatically when such objects are created. You should note that each program using a DLL will get its own copy of any static global objects defined in the DLL, even though they may not necessarily be used by a program. For global class objects, this will involve the overhead of calling a constructor for each. You should, therefore, avoid introducing such objects into a DLL unless they are absolutely essential.

The DLL Interface

You can't access just anything that's contained in a DLL. Only items specifically identified as **exported** from a DLL are visible to the outside world. Functions, classes, global static variables and resources can all be exported from a DLL, and those that are make up the **interface** to it. Anything that isn't exported can't be accessed from the outside. We'll see how to export items from a DLL later in this chapter.

The DllMain() Function

Even though a DLL isn't executable as an independent program, it does contain a special variety of the **main()** function, called **DllMain()**. This is called by Windows when the DLL is first loaded into memory to allow the DLL to do any necessary initialization before its contents are used. Windows will also call **DllMain()** just before it removes the DLL from memory to enable the DLL to clean up after itself if necessary. There are also other circumstances where **DllMain()** is called, but these situations are outside the scope of this book.

Varieties of DLL

There are three different kinds of DLL that you can build with Visual C++ using MFC: an MFC extension DLL, a regular DLL with MFC statically linked, and a regular DLL with MFC dynamically linked.

MFC Extension DLL

You build this kind of DLL whenever it's going to include classes that are derived from the MFC. Your derived classes in the DLL effectively extend the MFC. The MFC must be accessible in the environment where your DLL is used, so all the MFC classes are available together with your derived classes—hence the name 'MFC extension DLL'. However, deriving your own classes from the MFC isn't the only reason to use an MFC extension DLL. If you're writing a DLL that includes functions which pass pointers to MFC class objects to functions in a program using it, or which receive such pointers from functions in the program, then you must create it as an MFC extension DLL

Accesses to classes in the MFC by an extension DLL are always resolved dynamically by linking to the shared version of MFC that is itself implemented in DLLs. An extension DLL is created using the shared DLL version of the MFC, so when you use an extension DLL, the shared version of MFC must be available. An MFC extension DLL can be used by a normal AppWizard generated application. It requires the option Use MFC in a Shared Dll to be selected under the General tab of the project settings, which you access through the Project | Settings... menu option. This is the default selection with an AppWizard-generated program. Because of the fundamental nature of the shared version of the MFC in an extension DLL, an MFC extension DLL can't be used by programs that are statically linked to MFC.

Regular DLL - Statically Linked to MFC

This is a DLL that uses MFC classes which are linked statically. Use of the DLL doesn't require MFC to be available in the environment in which it is used because the code for all the classes it uses will be incorporated into the DLL. This will bulk up the size of the DLL, but the big advantage is that this kind of DLL can be used by any Win32 program, regardless of whether it uses MFC.

Regular DLL - Dynamically Linked to MFC

This is a DLL that uses dynamically linked classes from MFC but doesn't add classes of its own. This kind of DLL can be used by any Win32 program regardless of whether it uses MFC itself, but use of the DLL does require the MFC to be available in the environment.

You can use the AppWizard to build all three types of DLL that use MFC. You can also create a project for a DLL that doesn't involve MFC at all, by selecting the project type as Dynamic-Link Library.

Deciding What to Put in a DLL

How do you decide when you should use a DLL? In most cases, the use of a DLL provides a solution to a particular kind of programming problem, so if you have the problem, a DLL can be the answer. The common denominator is often sharing code between a number of programs, but there are other instances where a DLL provides advantages. The kinds of circumstance where putting code or resources in a DLL provides a very convenient and efficient approach include the following:

- You have a set of functions or resources on which you want to standardize and which you will use in several different programs. The DLL is a particularly good solution for managing these, especially if some of the programs using your standard facilities are likely to be executing concurrently.

- You have a complex application which involves several programs and a lot of code, but which has sets of functions or resources that may be shared among several of the programs in the application. Using a DLL for common functionality or common resources enables you to manage and develop these with a great deal of independence from the program modules that use them and can simplify program maintenance.

- You have developed a set of standard application-oriented classes derived from MFC which you anticipate using in several programs. By packaging the implementation of these classes in an extension DLL, you can make using them in several programs very straightforward, and in the process provide the possibility of being able to improve the internals of the classes without affecting the applications that use them.

▶ You have developed a brilliant set of functions which provide an easy-to-use but amazingly powerful tool kit for an application area which just about everybody wants to dabble in. You can readily package your functions in a regular DLL and distribute them in this form.

There are also other circumstances where you may choose to use DLLs, such as when you want to be able to dynamically load and unload libraries, or to select different modules at run-time. You could even use them to ease the development and updating of your applications generally.

The best way of understanding how to use a DLL is to create one and try it out. Let's do that now.

Writing DLLs

There are two aspects to writing a DLL that we'll look at: how you actually write a DLL, and how you define what's to be accessible in the DLL to programs that use it. As a practical example of writing a DLL, we'll create an extension DLL to add a set of application classes to the MFC. We'll then extend this DLL by adding variables that will be available to programs using it.

Writing and Using an Extension DLL

We can create an MFC extension DLL to contain the shape classes for the Sketcher application. While this will not bring any major advantages to the program, it will demonstrate how you can write an extension DLL without involving you in the overhead of entering a lot of new code.

The starting point is AppWizard, so create a new project workspace by using the File | New... menu option, selecting the Projects tab and choosing MFC AppWizard (dll), as shown here:

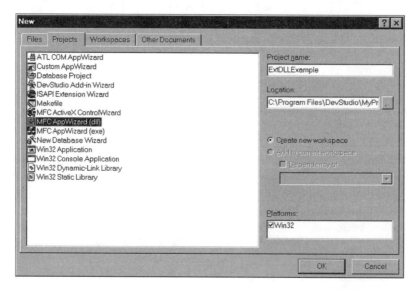

This selection identifies that we are creating an MFC-based DLL and will invoke the AppWizard. The option Win 32 Dynamic-Link Library that you see a little lower down the list is for creating DLLs that don't involve MFC. You need to make sure that the Location: entry corresponds to the folder where you want the folder containing the code for the DLL to be placed. Once this is done, and you've entered a suitable name for the DLL (as shown above), you can click on the OK button to go to the next step:

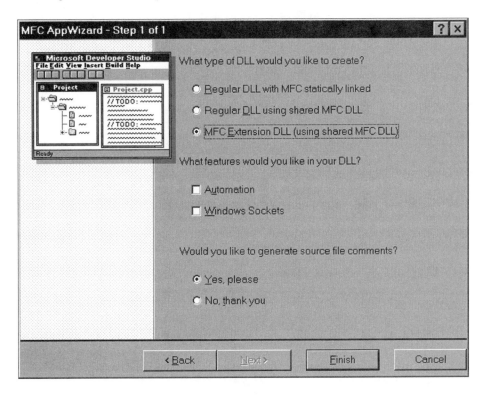

Here, you can see three radio buttons corresponding to the three types of MFC-based DLL that we discussed earlier. You should choose the third option, as shown above.

The two check boxes below the first group of three radio buttons allow you to include code to support Automation and Windows Sockets in the DLL. These are both advanced capabilities within a Windows program, so we don't need either of them here. **Automation** provides the potential for hosting objects created and managed by one application inside another, and we'll be taking a tentative look into this before the end of the book. **Windows Sockets** provides classes and functionality to enable your program to communicate over a network, but we won't be getting into this as it's beyond the scope of the book. The default choice to include comments is OK, so you can click on the Finish button and complete creation of the project.

Now that AppWizard has done its stuff, we can look into the code that has been generated on our behalf. If you look at the contents of the project using Windows Explorer, you'll see that AppWizard has generated a total of eleven files in the project folder, including a **.txt** file which contains a description of the other files, and one further resource file in the subfolder **Res**. You can read what they're all for in the **.txt** file, but the following two are the ones of immediate interest in implementing our DLL:

Filename	Contents
`ExtDLLExample.cpp`	This contains the function **DllMain()** and is the primary source file for the DLL.
`ExtDLLExample.def`	The information in this file is used by Visual C++ during compilation. It contains the name of the DLL, and you can also add to it the definitions of those items in the DLL that are to be accessible to a program using the DLL. We'll use an alternative and somewhat easier way of identifying such items in our example.

When your DLL is loaded, the first thing that happens is that **DllMain()** is executed, so perhaps we should take a look at that first.

Understanding DllMain()

If you take a look at the contents of **ExtDLLExample.cpp**, you will see that AppWizard has generated a version of **DllMain()** for us, as shown here:

```cpp
extern "C" int APIENTRY
DllMain(HINSTANCE hInstance, DWORD dwReason, LPVOID lpReserved)
{
   // Remove this if you use lpReserved
   UNREFERENCED_PARAMETER(lpReserved);

   if (dwReason == DLL_PROCESS_ATTACH)
   {
      TRACE0("EXTDLLEXAMPLE.DLL Initializing!\n");

      // Extension DLL one-time initialization
      if (!AfxInitExtensionModule(ExtDLLExampleDLL, hInstance))
         return 0;

      // Insert this DLL into the resource chain
      // NOTE: If this Extension DLL is being implicitly linked to by
      //   an MFC Regular DLL (such as an ActiveX Control)
      //   instead of an MFC application, then you will want to
      //   remove this line from DllMain and put it in a separate
      //   function exported from this Extension DLL.  The Regular DLL
      //   that uses this Extension DLL should then explicitly call that
      //   function to initialize this Extension DLL.  Otherwise,
      //   the CDynLinkLibrary object will not be attached to the
      //   Regular DLL's resource chain, and serious problems will
      //   result.

      new CDynLinkLibrary(ExtDLLExampleDLL);
   }
   else if (dwReason == DLL_PROCESS_DETACH)
   {
      TRACE0("EXTDLLEXAMPLE.DLL Terminating!\n");
      // Terminate the library before destructors are called
      AfxTermExtensionModule(ExtDLLExampleDLL);
   }
   return 1;   // ok
}
```

There are three arguments passed to **DllMain()**. The first argument, **hInstance**, is a handle which has been created by Windows to identify the DLL. Every task under Windows 95 has an instance handle which identifies it uniquely. The second argument, **dwReason**, indicates the reason why **DllMain()** is being called. You can see this argument being tested in the **if** statements in **DllMain()**. The first **if** tests for the value **DLL_PROCESS_ATTACH**, which indicates that a program is about to use the DLL, and the second **if** tests for the value **DLL_PROCESS_DETACH**, which indicates that a program is finished using the DLL. The third argument is a pointer that's reserved for use by Windows, so you can ignore it.

When the DLL is first used by a program, it's loaded into memory and the **DllMain()** function will be executed with the argument **dwReason** set to **DLL_PROCESS_ATTACH**. This will result in the function **AfxInitExtensionModule()** being called to initialize the DLL and an object of the class **CDynLinkLibrary** created on the heap. Windows uses objects of this class to manage extension DLLs. If you need to add initialization of your own, you can add it to the end of this block. Any clean-up you require for your DLL can be added to the block for the second **if** statement.

Adding Classes to the Extension DLL

We're going to use the DLL to contain the implementation of our shape classes, so move the files **Elements.h** and **Elements.cpp** from the folder containing the source for Sketcher to the folder containing the DLL. Be sure that you move rather than copy the files. Since the DLL is going to supply the shape classes for Sketcher, we don't want to leave them in the source code for Sketcher.

You'll also need to remove **Elements.cpp** from the Sketcher project. To do this, simply change to the FileView, highlight Elements.cpp by clicking on the file, then press *Delete*. If you don't do this, Visual C++ will complain that it couldn't find the file when you try to compile the project. Follow the same procedure to get rid of **Elements.h** from the Header Files folder.

The shape classes use the constants that we have defined in the file **OurConstants.h**, so *copy* this file from Sketcher to the folder containing the DLL. Note that the variable **VERSION_NUMBER** is used exclusively by the **IMPLEMENT_SERIAL()** macros in the shape classes, so you could delete it from the **OurConstants.h** file used in the Sketcher program.

We need to add **Elements.cpp** containing the implementation of our shape classes to the extension DLL project, so select the menu option Project | Add To Project | Files... and choose the file **Elements.cpp** from the list box in the dialog, as shown here:

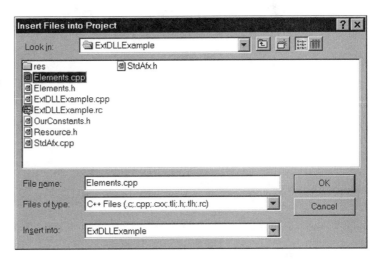

To make sure that the project includes the files containing the definitions of the shape classes and our constants, you need to add these to the project. To add **Elements.h** to the project, right click on Header Files in FileView, and select Add Files to Folder... from the pop-up. You can then select the **.h** file in the dialog. To add **OurConstants.h**, repeat the process, or if you like you can select both files at once by holding down the *Ctrl* key. This will make sure that all the classes are displayed in ClassView.

Exporting Classes from the Extension DLL

The names of the classes that are defined in the DLL and are to be accessible in programs that use it must be identified in some way, so that the appropriate links can be established between a program and the DLL. As we saw earlier, one way of doing this is by adding information to the **.def** file for the DLL. This involves adding what are called **decorated names** to the DLL and associating the decorated name with a unique identifying numeric value called an **ordinal**. A decorated name for a object is a name generated by the compiler, which adds an additional string to the name you gave to the object. This additional string provides information about the type of the object or, in the case of a function for example, information about the types of the parameters to the function. Among other things, it ensures that everything has a unique identifier and enables the linker to distinguish overloaded functions from each other.

Obtaining decorated names and assigning ordinals to export items from a DLL is a lot of work, and isn't the best or the easiest approach with Windows 95. A much easier way to identify the classes that we want to export from the DLL is to modify the class definitions in **Elements.h** to include the keyword **AFX_EXT_CLASS** before each class name, as shown below for the **CLine** class:

```
// Class defining a line object
class AFX_EXT_CLASS CLine: public CElement
{
DECLARE_SERIAL(CLine)

public:
   virtual void Draw(CDC* pDC, CElement* pElement=0);  // Function to display a
line
   virtual void Move(CSize& aSize);                    // Function to move an
element

   // Constructor for a line object
   CLine(CPoint Start, CPoint End, COLORREF aColor, int PenWidth);

   virtual void Serialize(CArchive& ar);  // Serialize function for CLine

protected:
   CPoint m_StartPoint;       // Start point of line
   CPoint m_EndPoint;         // End point of line

   CLine(){}             // Default constructor - should not be used
};
```

The keyword **AFX_EXT_CLASS** indicates that the class is to be exported from the DLL. This has the effect of making the complete class available to any program using the DLL and automatically allows access to any of the data and functions in the public interface of the class. The collection of things in a DLL that are accessible by a program using it is referred to as the **interface** to the DLL. The process of making an object part of the interface to a DLL is referred to as **exporting** the object.

You need to add the keyword **AFX_EXT_CLASS** to all of the other shape classes, including the base class **CElement**. Why is it necessary to export **CElement** from the DLL? After all, programs will only create objects of the classes derived from **CElement**, and not objects of the class **CElement** itself. The reason is that we have declared **public** members of **CElement** which form part of the interface to the derived shape classes, and which are almost certainly going to be required by programs using the DLL. If we don't export the **CElement** class, functions such as **GetBoundRect()** will not be available.

The final modification needed is to add the directive:

```
#include <afxtempl.h>
```

to **StdAfx.h** in the DLL project so that the definition of **CList** is available.

We've done everything necessary to add the shape classes to the DLL. All you need to do is compile and link the project to create the DLL.

Building a DLL

You build the DLL in exactly the same way as you build any other project—by using the Build | Build menu option. The output produced is somewhat different, though. You can see the files that are produced in the **Debug** subfolder of the project folder. The executable code for the DLL is contained in the file **ExtDLLExample.dll**. This file needs to be available to execute a program that uses the DLL. The file **ExtDLLExample.lib** is an import library file that contains the definitions of the items that are exported from the DLL, and it must be available to the linker when a program using the DLL is linked.

Using the Extension DLL in Sketcher

We now have no information in the Sketcher program on the shape classes, because we moved the files containing the class definitions and implementations to the DLL project. However, the compiler will still need to know where the shape classes are coming from in order to compile the code for the program. The Sketcher program needs to include a **.h** file defining the classes that are to be imported from the DLL. We can just copy the file **Elements.h** from the DLL project to the folder containing the Sketcher source. It would be a good idea to identify this file as specifying the imports from the DLL in the Sketcher source code. You could do this by changing its name to **DllImports.h**, in which case you'll need to change the **#include** statements that are already in the Sketcher program for **Elements.h** to refer to the new file name (these occur in **Sketcher.cpp**, **SketcherDoc.cpp**, and **SketcherView.cpp**).

When the Sketcher source has been recompiled, the linker will need to know where to find the DLL in order to include information that will trigger loading of the DLL when the Sketcher program is executed, and to allow the links to the class implementations in the DLL to be established. We must, therefore, add the location of the DLL to the project settings for the link operation. Select Project | Settings..., choose the Link tab of the Project Settings dialog, and enter the name of the **.lib** file for the DLL, **ExtDLLExample.lib** (including the full path to it), as shown here:

 FYI Be aware that if the complete path to the **.lib** file contains spaces (as in the example here), you'll need to enclose it within quotation marks for the linker to recognize it correctly.

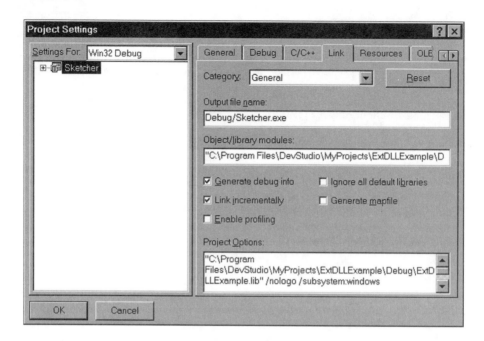

This shows the entry for the debug version of Sketcher. The **.lib** file for the DLL will be in the **Debug** folder within the DLL project folder, as you can see from the entry under Object/library modules: in the dialog box shown. If you create a release version of Sketcher, you'll also need the release version of the DLL available to the linker, so you'll have to enter the fully qualified name of the **.lib** file for the release version of the DLL, corresponding to the release version of Sketcher. The file to which the Link tab applies is selected in the Settings For: drop-down list box in the dialog above.

You can now build the Sketcher application once more, and everything should compile and link as usual. However, if you try to execute the program, this happens:

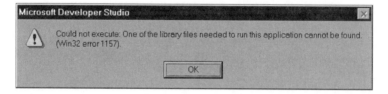

This is one of the less cryptic error messages—it's fairly clear what's gone wrong. To enable Windows to load a DLL for a program, it's usual to place the DLL in your **\Windows\System** folder. Since you probably don't want to clutter up this folder unnecessarily, you can copy **ExtDllExample.dll** from the **Debug** folder of the DLL project to the **Debug** folder for Sketcher. Sketcher should execute exactly as before, except that now it will use the shape classes in the DLL we have created.

Files Required to Use a DLL

From what we've just seen in the context of using the DLL we created in the Sketcher program, we conclude that three files must be available to use a DLL in a program:

Extension	Contents
`.h`	Defines those items that are exported from a DLL and enables the compiler to deal properly with references to such items in the source code of a program using the DLL. The `.h` file needs to be added to the source code for the program using the DLL.
`.lib`	Defines the items exported by a DLL in a form which enables the linker to deal with references to exported items when linking a program that uses a DLL.
`.dll`	Contains the executable code for the DLL which is loaded by Windows when a program using the DLL is executed.

If you plan to distribute program code in the form of a DLL for use by other programmers, you need to distribute all three files in the package. For users, just the `.dll` is required.

Exporting Variables and Functions from a DLL

You've seen how you can export classes from an extension DLL using the **AFX_EXT_CLASS** keyword. You can also export *objects* of classes that are defined in a DLL, as well as ordinary variables and functions. These can be exported from any kind of DLL by using the attribute **dllexport** to identify them. By using **dllexport** to identify class objects, variables or functions that are to be exported from a DLL, you avoid getting involved in the complications of modifying the **.def** file and, as a consequence, you make defining the interface to the DLL a straightforward matter.

Don't be misled into thinking that the approach we're taking to exporting things from our DLL makes the **.def** file method redundant. The **.def** file approach is more complicated—which is why we're taking the easy way out—but it offers distinct advantages in many situations over the approach we're taking. This is particularly true in the context of products that are distributed widely, and are likely to be developed over time. One major plus is that a **.def** file enables you to define the ordinals that correspond to your exported functions. This allows you to add more exported functions later and assign new ordinals to them, so the ordinals for the original set of functions remain the same. This means that someone using a new version of the DLL with a program built to use the old version doesn't have to relink their application.

You must use the **dllexport** attribute in conjunction with the keyword **_declspec** when you identify an item to be exported. For example, the statement

```
_declspec(dllexport) double aValue = 1.5;
```

defines the variable **aValue** of type **double** with an initial value of 1.5, and identifies it as a variable that is to be available to programs using the DLL. To export a function from a DLL, you use the **dllexport** attribute in a similar manner. For example:

```
_declspec(dllexport) CString FindWinner(CString* Teams);
```

This statement exports the function **FindWinner()** from the DLL.

To avoid the slightly cumbersome notation for specifying the **dllexport** attribute, you can simplify it by using a preprocessor directive:

```
#define DllExport _declspec(dllexport)
```

With this definition, the two previous examples can be written alternatively as:

```
DllExport double aValue = 1.5;
DllExport CString FindWinner(CString* Teams);
```

This notation is much more economical, as well as being easier to read, so you may wish to adopt this approach when coding your DLLs.

Obviously, only symbols which represent objects with global scope can be exported from a DLL. Variables and class objects that are local to a function in a DLL cease to exist when execution of a function is completed, in just the same way as in a function in a normal program. Attempting to export such symbols will result in a compile-time error.

Importing Symbols into a Program

The **dllexport** attribute identifies the symbols in a DLL that form part of the interface. If you want to use these in a program, you must make sure that they are correspondingly identified as being imported from the DLL. This is done by using the **dllimport** keyword in declarations for the symbols to be imported in a **.h** file. We can simplify the notation by using the same technique we applied to the **dllexport** attribute. Let's define **DllImport** with the directive:

```
#define DllImport _declspec(dllimport)
```

We can now import the **aValue** variable and the **FindWinner()** function with the declarations:

```
DllImport double aValue;
DllImport CString FindWinner(CString* Teams);
```

These statements would appear in a **.h** file which would be included into the **.cpp** files in the program that referenced these symbols.

Implementing the Export of Symbols from a DLL

We could extend the extension DLL to make the symbols defining shape types and colors available in the interface to it. We can then remove the definitions that we have in the Sketcher program and import the definitions of these symbols from the extension DLL.

We can first modify the source code for the DLL to add the symbols for shape element types and colors to its interface. To export the element types and colors, they must be global variables. As global variables, it would be better if they appeared in a **.cpp** file, rather than a **.h** file, so move the definitions of these out of the **OurConstants.h** file to the beginning of **Elements.cpp** in the DLL source. You can then apply the **dllexport** attribute to their definitions in the **Elements.cpp** file, as follows:

```
// Definitions of constants and identification of symbols to be exported

#define DllExport __declspec(dllexport)

// Element type definitions
// Each type value must be unique
DllExport extern const WORD LINE = 101U;
DllExport extern const WORD RECTANGLE = 102U;
DllExport extern const WORD CIRCLE = 103U;
DllExport extern const WORD CURVE = 104U;
DllExport extern const WORD TEXT = 105U;
//////////////////////////////////////

// Color values for drawing
DllExport extern const COLORREF BLACK = RGB(0,0,0);
DllExport extern const COLORREF RED = RGB(255,0,0);
DllExport extern const COLORREF GREEN = RGB(0,255,0);
DllExport extern const COLORREF BLUE = RGB(0,0,255);
DllExport extern const COLORREF SELECT_COLOR = RGB(255,0,180);
//////////////////////////////////////
```

Add these to the beginning of **Elements.cpp**, after the **#include** directives. We first define the symbol **DllExport** to simplify the specification of the variables to be exported, as we saw earlier. We then assign the attribute **dllexport** to each of the element types and colors.

You will notice that the **extern** specifier has also been added to the definitions of these variables. The reason for this is the effect of the **const** modifier, which indicates to the compiler that the values are constants and shouldn't be modified in the program, which was what we wanted. However, by default, it also specifies the variables as having internal linkage, so they are local to the file in which they appear. We want to export these variables to another program, so we have to add the modifier **extern** to override the default linkage specification due to the **const** modifier and ensure that they have external linkage. Symbols that are assigned external linkage are global and so can be exported. Of course, if the variables didn't have the **const** modifier applied to them, we wouldn't need to add **extern**, since they would be global automatically as long as they appeared at global scope.

The **OurConstants.h** file now only contains one definition:

```
// Definitions of constants

#if !defined(OurConstants_h)
#define OurConstants_h

   // Define the program version number for use in serialization
   UINT VERSION_NUMBER = 1;

#endif // !defined(OurConstants_h)
```

Of course, this is still required because it is used in the **IMPLEMENT_SERIAL()** macros in **Elements.cpp**. You can now build the DLL once again, so it's ready to use in the Sketcher program. Don't forget to copy the latest version of the **.dll** file to the Sketcher **Debug** folder.

Using Exported Symbols

To make the symbols exported from the DLL available in the Sketcher program, you need to specify them as imported from the DLL. You can do this by adding the identification of the imported symbols to the file **DllImports.h** which contains the definitions for the imported classes. In this way, we'll have one file specifying all the items imported from the DLL. The statements that appear in this file will be as follows:

```
// Variables defined in the shape DLL ExtDLLExample.dll
#if !defined(DllImports_h)
#define DllImports_h

#define DllImport __declspec( dllimport )

// Import element type declarations
// Each type value must be unique
DllImport extern const WORD LINE;
DllImport extern const WORD RECTANGLE;
DllImport extern const WORD CIRCLE;
DllImport extern const WORD CURVE;
DllImport extern const WORD TEXT;
//////////////////////////////////

// Import color values for drawing
DllImport extern const COLORREF BLACK;
DllImport extern const COLORREF RED;
DllImport extern const COLORREF GREEN;
DllImport extern const COLORREF BLUE;
DllImport extern const COLORREF SELECT_COLOR;
//////////////////////////////////
```

```
// Plus the definitions for the element classes...
```

```
#endif // !defined(DllImports_h)
```

This defines and uses the **DllImport** symbol to simplify these declarations, in the way that we saw earlier. This means that the **OurConstants.h** file in the Sketcher project is now redundant, so we can delete it, along with the **#include** for it in **Sketcher.h**. It's a good idea to close and reopen the project after deleting the file from the project, as Visual C++ can be a little reluctant to let go of dependencies. This usually forces it to let go, though.

That looks as though we've done everything necessary to use the new version of the DLL with Sketcher, but we haven't. If you try to recompile Sketcher, you'll get error messages for the **switch** statement in the **CreateElement()** member of **CSketcherView**.

The values in the case statements must be constant, but although we've given the element type variables the attribute **const**, the compiler has no access to these values because they are defined in the DLL, not in the Sketcher program. The compiler, therefore, can't determine what these constant case values are, and flags an error. The simplest way round this problem is to replace the **switch** statement in the **CreateElement()** function by a series of **if** statements, as follows:

```
// Create an element of the current type
CElement* CSketcherView::CreateElement()
{
```

```
// Get a pointer to the document for this view
CSketcherDoc* pDoc = GetDocument();
ASSERT_VALID(pDoc);                           // Verify the pointer is good

// Now select the element using the type stored in the document
WORD ElementType = pDoc->GetElementType();
if(ElementType == RECTANGLE)
   return new CRectangle(m_FirstPoint, m_SecondPoint,
                         pDoc->GetElementColor(), pDoc->GetPenWidth());


if(ElementType == CIRCLE)
   return new CCircle(m_FirstPoint, m_SecondPoint,
                      pDoc->GetElementColor(), pDoc->GetPenWidth());


if(ElementType == CURVE)
   return new CCurve(m_FirstPoint, m_SecondPoint,
                     pDoc->GetElementColor(), pDoc->GetPenWidth());
else
   // Always default to a line
   return new CLine(m_FirstPoint, m_SecondPoint,
                    pDoc->GetElementColor(), pDoc->GetPenWidth());
}
```

We've added a local variable **ElementType** to store the current element type retrieved from the document. This is then tested against the element types imported from the DLL in the series of **if** statements. This does exactly the same job as the **switch** statement, but has no requirement for the element type constants to be known explicitly. If you now build Sketcher with these changes added, it will execute using the DLL, using the exported symbols as well as the exported shape classes.

Summary

In this chapter, you've learned the basics of how to construct and use a dynamic link library. The most important points we've looked at in this context are:

▶ Dynamic link libraries provide a means of linking to standard functions dynamically when a program executes, rather than incorporating them into the executable module for a program.

▶ An AppWizard-generated program links to a version of MFC stored in DLLs by default.

▶ A single copy of a DLL in memory can be used by several programs executing concurrently.

▶ An **extension** DLL is so called because it extends the set of classes in MFC. An extension DLL must be used if you want to export MFC-based classes or objects of MFC classes from a DLL. An extension DLL can also export ordinary functions and global variables.

▶ A **regular** DLL can be used if you only want to export ordinary functions or global variables that aren't instances of MFC classes.

▶ You can export classes from an extension DLL by using the keyword **AFX_EXT_CLASS** preceding the class name in the DLL.

➤ You can export ordinary functions and global variables from a DLL by assigning the **dllexport** attribute to them using the **_declspec** keyword.

➤ You can import the classes exported from an extension DLL by using including the **.h** file from the DLL that contains the class definitions using the **AFX_EXT_CLASS** keyword.

➤ You can import ordinary functions and global variables that are exported from a DLL by assigning the **dllimport** attribute to their declarations in your program by using the **_declspec** keyword.

Exercises

Ex9-1: This is the last time we'll be amending this version of the Sketcher program, so try this. Using the DLL we've just created, implement a Sketcher document viewer—in other words, a program which simply opens a document created by Sketcher and displays the whole thing in a window at once. You needn't worry about editing, scrolling or printing, but you will have to work out the scaling required to make a big picture fit in a little window!

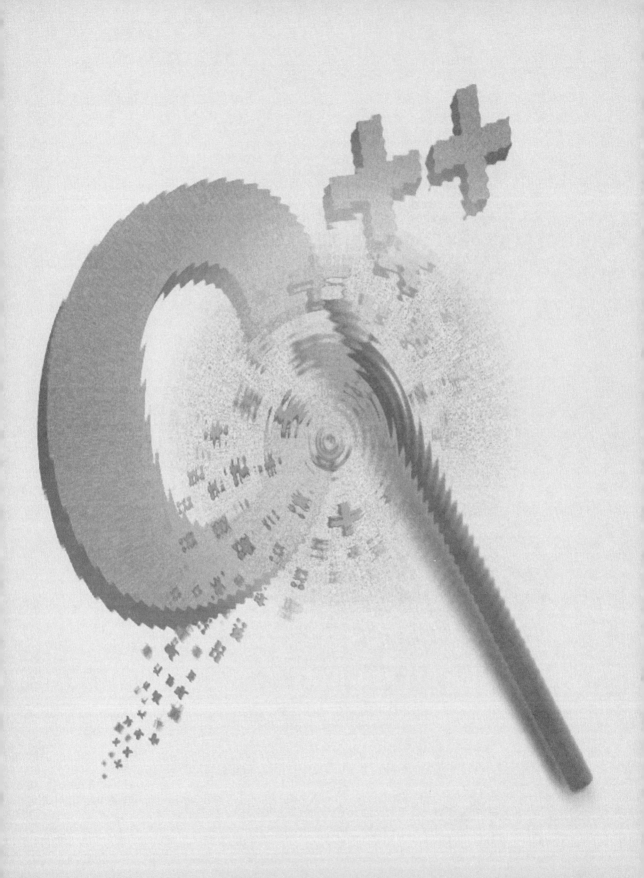

Connecting to Data Sources

In this chapter, we'll show you to how to interface to a database using Visual C++ and MFC. This is by no means a comprehensive discussion of the possibilities, since we'll only address retrieving data, but at least you'll take a few steps down this particular path.

In this chapter you will learn:

- What SQL is, and how it is used
- How to retrieve data using the SQL **SELECT** operation
- What a recordset object is, and how it links to a relational database table
- How a recordset object can retrieve information from a database
- How a record view can display information from a recordset
- How to create a database program using AppWizard
- How to add recordsets to your program
- How to handle multiple record views

Database Basics

This is not the place for a detailed dissertation on database technology, but we do need to make sure that we have a common understanding of database terminology. Databases come in a variety of flavors, but the majority these days are **relational databases**. It is relational databases that we will be talking about throughout this chapter.

In a database, your data is organized into one or more **tables**. You can think of a database table as being like a spreadsheet table, made up of rows and columns. Each row contains information about a single item, and each column contains the information about the same characteristic from every item.

A **record** is equivalent to a row in the spreadsheet. Each record consists of elements of data that make up that record. These elements of data are known as **fields**. A field is a cell in the table identified by the column heading. The term *field* can also represent the whole column.

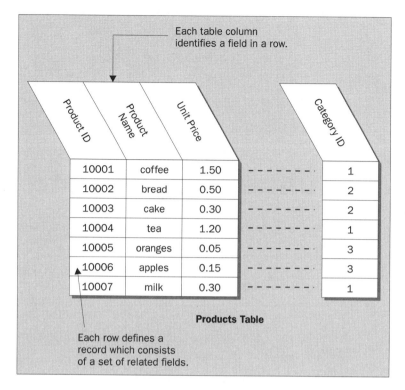

Each table column
identifies a field in a row.

Product ID | Product Name | Unit Price | | Category ID

We can best see the
structure of a table with a
diagram:

Product ID	Product Name	Unit Price		Category ID
10001	coffee	1.50	- - - - - - - -	1
10002	bread	0.50	- - - - - - - -	2
10003	cake	0.30	- - - - - - - -	2
10004	tea	1.20	- - - - - - - -	1
10005	oranges	0.05	- - - - - - - -	3
10006	apples	0.15	- - - - - - - -	3
10007	milk	0.30	- - - - - - - -	1

Products Table

Each row defines a
record which consists
of a set of related fields.

Here you can see that this table is being used to store information on a line of products. Unsurprisingly then, the table is called **Products**. Each record in the table, represented by a row in the diagram, contains the data for one product. The description of a product is separated into fields in the table, each storing information about one aspect of a product: **Product Name**, **Unit Price**, and so on.

Although the fields in this table store only relatively simple information (character strings or numeric values), the type of data you decide to put in a particular field can be virtually anything you want. You could store times, dates, pictures or even binary objects in a database.

A table will usually have at least one field that can be used to identify each record uniquely and in the example above the **Product ID** is a likely candidate. A field in a table that serves to identify each record within the table is called a **key**; a key which uniquely identifies each record in a table is referred to as a **primary key**. In some cases, a table may have no single field that uniquely identifies each record. In this circumstance, two or more key fields may be used. A key composed of two or more fields is called a **multivalue key**.

The relational aspect of a database, and the importance of keys, comes into play when you store related information in separate tables. You define relationships between the tables, using keys, and use the relationships to find associated information stored in your database. Note that the tables themselves don't know about relationships, just as the table doesn't understand the bits of data stored in it. It is the program that accesses the data which must use the information in the tables to pull together related data, whether that program is Access, SQL Server, or your own program written in Visual C++. These are known collectively as **relational database management systems** or **RDBMSs**.

A real-world, well-designed relational database will usually consist of a large number of tables. Each table usually has only several fields and many records. The reason for only having a few fields in each table is to increase query performance. Without going into the details of database optimization, have faith that it's much faster to query many tables with a few fields each than to query a single table with many fields.

We can extend the example shown in the previous diagram to illustrate a relational database with two tables: **Products** and **Categories**.

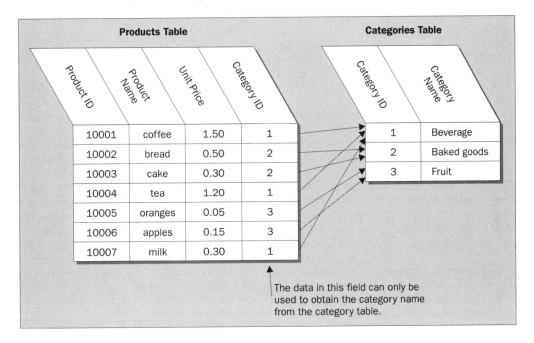

As you can see from the diagram, the **Category ID** field is used to relate the information stored in the two tables. **Category ID** uniquely identifies a category record in the **Categories** table, so it is a primary key for that table. In the **Products** table, the **Category ID** field is used to relate a product record to a category, so the field is termed a **foreign key** for that table.

Relational databases can be created and manipulated in numerous ways. There are a large number of RDBMSs on the market that provide a wide range of facilities for creating and manipulating database information. Obviously, it's possible for you to add and delete records in a database table, and to update the fields in a record, although typically there are controls within the RDBMS to limit such activities, based on the authorization level of the user. As well as accessing information from a single table in a database, you can combine records from two or more tables into a new table, based on their relationships, and retrieve information from that. Combining tables in this way is called a **table join**. To program all these kinds of operations for a relational database, you can use a language known as **SQL**, which is supported by most RDBMSs and programming languages.

A Little SQL

SQL (often pronounced 'sequel') stands for **S**tructured **Q**uery **L**anguage. It's a relatively simple language, designed specifically for accessing and modifying information in relational databases. It was originally developed at IBM in a mainframe environment, but is now used throughout the computing world. SQL doesn't actually exist as a software package by itself—it's usually hosted by some other environment, whether that's an RDBMS or a programming language, such as COBOL, C or C++. The environment hosting SQL provides for mundane things such as regular I/O and talking to the operating system, while SQL is used to query the database.

MFC support for databases uses SQL to specify queries and other operations on database tables. These operations are provided by a set of specialized classes. You'll see how to use some of these in the example that we'll write later in this chapter.

SQL has statements to retrieve, sort and update records from a table, to add and delete records and fields, to join tables and to compute totals, as well as a lot of other capabilities for creating and managing database tables. We won't be going into all the possible programming options available in SQL, but we'll discuss the details sufficiently to enable you to understand what's happening in the examples that we write, even though you may not have seen any SQL before.

When we use SQL in an MFC-based program, we won't need to write complete SQL statements for the most part because the framework takes care of assembling a complete statement and supplying it to the database engine you're using. Nevertheless, we'll look here at how typical SQL statements are written in their entirety, so that you get a feel for how the language statements are structured.

SQL statements are written with a terminating semicolon (just like C++ statements), and keywords in the language are written in capital letters. Let's take a look at a few examples of SQL statements and see how they work.

Retrieving Data Using SQL

To retrieve data, you use the **SELECT** statement. In fact, it's quite surprising how much of what you want to do with a database is covered by the **SELECT** statement, which operates on one or more tables in your database. The result of executing a **SELECT** statement is always a **recordset**, which is a collection of data produced using the information from the tables you supply in the detail of the statement. The data in the recordset is organized in the form of a table, with named columns that are from the tables you specified in the **SELECT** statement, and rows or records that are selected, based on conditions specified in the **SELECT** statement. The recordset generated by a **SELECT** statement might have only one record, or might even be empty.

Perhaps the simplest retrieval operation on a database is to access all the records in a single table, so given that our database includes a table called **Products**, we can obtain all the records in this table with the following SQL statement:

```
SELECT * FROM Products;
```

The `*` indicates that we want all the fields in the database. The parameter following the keyword **FROM** defines the table from which the fields are to be selected. We haven't constrained the records that are returned by the **SELECT** statement, so we'll get all of them. A little later we'll see how to constrain the records that are selected.

If you wanted all the records, but only needed to retrieve specific fields in each record, you could specify these by using the field names separated by commas in place of the asterisk in the previous example. An example of a statement that would do this is:

```
SELECT ProductID,UnitPrice FROM Products;
```

This statement selects all the records from the **Products** table, but only the **ProductID** and **UnitPrice** fields for each record. This will produce a table having just the two fields specified here.

The field names that we've used don't contain spaces, but they could. Where a name contains spaces, standard SQL says that it has to be written between double quotes. If the fields had the names **Product ID** and **Unit Price**, we would write the **SELECT** statement as:

```
SELECT "Product ID","Unit Price" FROM Products;
```

Using double quotes with names, as we have done here, is a bit inconvenient in the C++ context, as we need to be able to pass SQL statements as strings. In C++, double quotes are already used as character string delimiters, so there would be confusion if we tried to enclose the names of database objects (tables or fields) in double quotes.

For this reason, when you reference database table or field names which include spaces in the Visual C++ environment, you should enclose them within square brackets rather than double quotes. Thus, you would write the field names from the example as **[Product ID]** and **[Unit Price]**. You'll see this notation in action in the database program that we write later in this chapter.

Choosing Records

Unlike fields, records in a table don't have names. The only way to choose particular records is by applying some condition or restriction on the contents of one or more of the fields in a record, so that only records meeting the condition are selected. This is done by adding a **WHERE** clause to the **SELECT** statement. The parameter following the **WHERE** keyword defines the condition that is to be used to select records.

We could select the records in the **Products** table that have a particular value for the **Category ID** field, with the statement:

```
SELECT * FROM Products WHERE [Category ID] = 1;
```

This selects just those records where the **Category ID** field has the value 1, so from the table we illustrated earlier, we would get the records for coffee, tea and milk. Note that a single equals sign is used to specify a check for equality in SQL, not **==** as we use in C++.

You can use other comparison operators, such as **<**, **>**, **<=** and **>=**, to specify the condition in a **WHERE** clause. You can also combine logical expressions with **AND** and **OR**. To place a further restriction on the records selected in the last example, we could write:

```
SELECT * FROM Products WHERE [Category ID] = 1 AND [Unit Price] > 0.5;
```

In this case, the resulting table would just contain two records, because milk would be out as it's too cheap. Only records with a **Category ID** of 1 and a **Unit Price** value greater than 0.5 are selected by this statement.

Joining Tables Using SQL

You can also use the **SELECT** statement to join tables together, although it's a little more complicated than you might imagine. Suppose we have two tables: **Products** with three records and three fields, and **Orders** with three records and four fields. These are illustrated below:

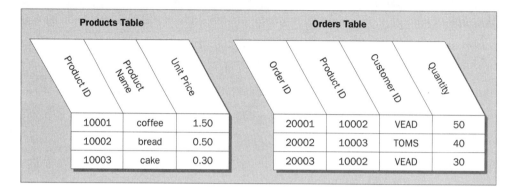

Here, we have a meager product set in the **Products** table, consisting of just coffee, bread and cake, and we have three orders as shown in the **Orders** table—but we haven't managed to sell any coffee.

We could join these tables together with the **SELECT** statement:

```
SELECT * FROM Products,Orders;
```

This statement creates a recordset using the records from both the tables specified. The recordset will have seven fields, three from the **Products** table and four from the **Orders** table, but how many records does it have? The answer is illustrated in the diagram here:

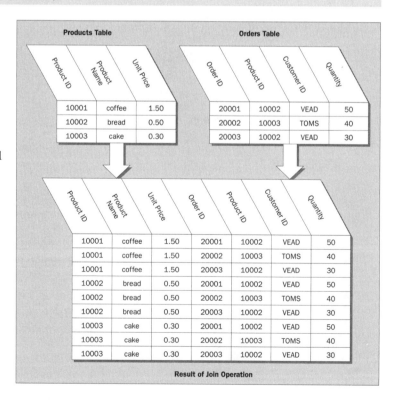

The recordset produced by the **SELECT** statement has nine records that are created by combining each record from the **Products** table with every record from the **Orders** table, so all possible combinations are included. This may not be exactly what is required, or what you expected. Arbitrarily including all combinations of records from one table with another is of limited value. The meaning of a record containing details of the bread product and an order for cake is hard to fathom. You could also end up with an incredibly big table in a real situation. If you combine a table containing 100 products with one containing 500 orders and you don't constrain the join operation, the resulting table will contain 50,000 records!

To get a useful join, you usually need to add a **WHERE** clause to the **SELECT** statement. With the tables we've been using, one condition that would make sense would be to only allow records where the **Product ID** from one table matched the same field in the other table. This would combine each record from the **Products** table with the records from the **Orders** table that related to that product. The statement to do this would be:

```
SELECT * FROM Products,Orders WHERE Products.[Product ID] = Orders.[Product ID];
```

Notice how a specific field for a particular table is identified here. You add the table name as a prefix and separate it from the field name with a period. This qualification of the field name is essential where the same field name is used in both tables. Without the table name, there's no way to know which of the two fields you mean. With this **SELECT** statement and the same table contents we used previously, we'll get the recordset shown here:

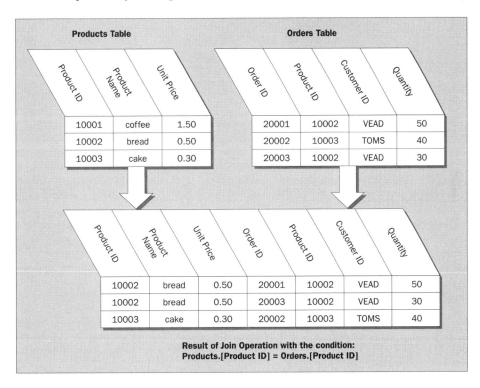

Result of Join Operation with the condition:
Products.[Product ID] = Orders.[Product ID]

Of course, this may still be unsatisfactory in that we have two fields containing the **Product ID**, but you could easily remove this by specifying the field names you want, instead of the ***** in the **SELECT** statement. However, the columns with the same name could be distinguished here by being qualified with the name of their original table when they appear in the recordset.

Sorting Records

When you retrieve data from a database using the **SELECT** statement, you'll often want the records sorted in a particular order. With the previous example, the tables shown are already ordered, but in practice this isn't necessarily the case. You might want to see the output of the last example sorted in a different way, depending on the circumstances. At one time, it might be convenient to have the records ordered by **Customer ID**, and on another occasion perhaps ordered by **Quantity** within **Product ID**. The **ORDER BY** clause added to the **SELECT** statement will do this for you. For example, we could refine the last **SELECT** statement by adding an **ORDER BY** clause:

```
SELECT * FROM Products,Orders WHERE Products.[Product ID] = Orders.[Product ID]
                    ORDER BY [Customer ID];
```

The result of this will be the same records that we obtained with the last example, but with the records arranged so that the **Customer ID** field is in ascending sequence. Since the kind of data stored in a given field is known, the records will be ordered according to the data type applicable to the field. In our case the ordering will be alphabetical.

If you wanted to sort on two fields, **Customer ID** and **Product ID** say, and you wanted the records arranged in descending sequence, you would write:

```
SELECT * FROM Products,Orders
            WHERE Products.[Product ID] = Orders.[Product ID]
            ORDER BY [Customer ID] DESC, Products.[Product ID] DESC;
```

We need to use the qualified name, **Products.[Product ID]**, in the **ORDER BY** clause to avoid ambiguity, as we do in the **WHERE** clause. The keyword **DESC** at the end of each field in the **ORDER BY** statement specifies descending sequence for the sort operation. There's a complementary keyword, **ASC**, for ascending sequence, although this is usually omitted because it is the default condition.

This is by no means all there is to SQL, or even all there is to the **SELECT** statement, but it's enough to get you through the database example that we will write.

FYI — If you need to know more about SQL, there's an excellent book written by Joe Celko and published by Wrox Press entitled *Instant SQL Programming*. ISBN 1-874416-50-8.

Database Support in MFC

You're spoilt for choice when you use MFC for database application development, since two distinct approaches are supported, each of which uses its own set of MFC classes.

One approach is to use **Data Access Objects (DAO)**. These objects provide an interface to the **Jet database engine**. The Jet database engine is a generalized piece of software that provides the ability to store data in, and retrieve data from, a range of database management systems. Jet is the engine used by Microsoft's Access DBMS. Whenever you manipulate a database in Access, you're actually getting Jet to do all the hard work. Jet is optimized for accessing Access (**.mdb**) database files directly, but will also enable you to attach to any database that supports the **O**pen **D**ata**B**ase **C**onnectivity interface, better known as **ODBC**. This allows you to manipulate databases in any format for which you have the appropriate ODBC driver. Databases that you can access using Jet, in addition to Microsoft Access, include Oracle, dBase 5, Btrieve 6.0, and FoxPro.

The other approach is ODBC-specific, but since ODBC drivers are also available for **.mdb** files, both approaches cover essentially the same range of database formats. How do you choose between them?

The first consideration is whether you're accessing your database in a client/server environment. If you are, you need to use ODBC. If you're not in a client/server situation, perhaps the most significant factor is whether you are going to use your program primarily with **.mdb** databases. If you are, the DAO-based approach will be more efficient than the ODBC approach. On the other hand, if you use the DAO approach with databases other than those in Microsoft Access format, which don't use the Microsoft Jet engine to drive them, you'll be working through the ODBC interface included within the DAO implementation, and this will be less efficient than using the ODBC specific approach directly. The DAO-based classes also provide a more comprehensive range of capabilities than the ODBC classes, so you need to consider this aspect as well.

If you want to take a simplistic view, you could decide on the basis that if you intend to use Microsoft Access databases and you're not in a client/server situation, you should program using DAO, otherwise you use ODBC.

DAO vs. ODBC

DAO uses objects for accessing and manipulating a database. There are objects representing tables, queries and the database itself. These objects insulate you from the detail of the specific database system implementation you are concerned with and provide you with a programming interface that is consistent with the object-oriented approach to programming.

ODBC, on the other hand, is a system-independent interface to a database environment that requires an **ODBC driver** to be provided for each database system from which you want to manipulate data. ODBC defines a set of function calls for database operations that are system-neutral. You can only use a database with ODBC if you have the DLL that contains the driver to work with that database application's file format. The purpose of the driver is to interface the standard set of system-independent calls for database operations that will be used in your program to the specifics of a particular database implementation.

While the concept here is rather different from that of DAO, the programming approach in Visual C++ is very similar with both methodologies. MFC packages the ODBC interface in a set of classes that are structured in a very similar way to the classes that apply with DAO. The application of MFC classes for ODBC closely parallels the use of the equivalent DAO classes.

It would be useful now to take a broad view of the classes supporting DAO and ODBC in MFC. We won't go into detail at this point, but will use a programming example to understand the basic mechanics of how the ODBC classes can be used.

Classes Supporting DAO

The following eight classes are used with the DAO approach:

Class	What it does
CDaoWorkspace	An object of this class manages a database session from start to finish. A **CDaoDatabase** object requires a **CDaoWorkspace** object to be available, and if you don't create one, the framework will supply one automatically when your **CDaoDatabase** object is created. A workspace object can contain several database objects.
CDaoDatabase	An object of this class implements a connection to a specific database. An object of this class will always be created when you access a database, but you don't necessarily have to create a database object explicitly. It can be created implicitly when you create a **CDaoRecordset** object.
CDaoRecordset	An object of a class derived from this class represents the result of an SQL **SELECT** operation, which is a set of records. The object makes available one record of the table produced by the **SELECT** at a time, and provides a range of functions to enable you to move backwards and forwards through the records available, and to search for records conforming to a set of search criteria.
CDaoRecordView	An object of a class derived from this class is used to display the current record from an associated recordset object. The record view object uses a child dialog to display data items from the DAO recordset object. There are automatic mechanisms for updating the controls in the dialog with current data from the DAO recordset object.
CDaoFieldExchange	This class supports the exchange of data between your database and a DAO recordset object. You can use objects of this class yourself, but AppWizard and ClassWizard will implement and maintain the use of these objects automatically.
CDaoQueryDef	An object of this class defines a query on your database that is usually predefined in the database. These are typically standard queries that are used frequently in a particular database. A **CDaoQueryDef** object can be used to create a **CDaoRecordset** object that represents a particular **SELECT** statement. An object of this class can also be used to execute SQL statements explicitly, by using its **Execute()** member function.
CDaoTableDef	An object of this class defines a table in your database. It can represent an existing table, or can be used to construct a new table.
CDaoException	An object of this class is constructed when an exception condition arises from a DAO database operation. All DAO errors cause exceptions and result in objects of this class being created. The **CDaoException** class members enable you to determine the cause of the exception.

The most essential classes that you'll use in DAO programming are a **CDaoDatabase** class that will represent your database, one or more classes derived from **CDaoRecordset** that will represent **SELECT** operations on your database, and one or more classes derived from **CDaoRecordView** that will display data made available by your **CDaoRecordset**-based classes. As we shall see, an ODBC application involves a similar set of basic classes with the same sort of functionality. The **CDaoTableDef** and **CDaoQueryDef** classes provide capability that is not available within MFC support for ODBC.

Classes Supporting ODBC

MFC support for ODBC is implemented through five classes:

Class	What it does
CDatabase	An object of this class represents a connection to your database. This connection must exist before you can carry out any operations on the database. No workspace class is used with an ODBC database.
CRecordset	An object of a class derived from this class represents the result of an SQL **SELECT** operation. This is the same concept that we saw with the **CDaoRecordset** class.
CRecordView	An object of a class derived from this class is used to display current information from an associated recordset object. This is the same concept that we saw with the **CDaoRecordView** class.
CFieldExchange	This class provides for the exchange of data between the database and a recordset object, in the same manner that we saw for DAO databases.
CDBException	Objects of this class represent exceptions that occur within ODBC database operations.

The ODBC classes look very much like a subset of the DAO classes and, in the sense that the interface they provide is similar to that of the equivalent DAO classes, they are. Of course, the underlying process for accessing the database is rather different.

We can best understand how database operations with MFC work by creating an example. We will use the ODBC approach, but apply it to accessing a Microsoft Access database. The database that we'll use is supplied on the Visual C++ CD. It has the merit of containing a considerable variety of tables that are populated by realistic numbers of records. This will give you a lot of scope for experimentation, as well as providing some feel for how well your code will work in practice. It's easy to be lulled into a false sense of security by running your program against a test database where the numbers of tables and records within a table is trivial. It can be quite a surprise to find out how long transactions can take in a real world context.

Creating a Database Application

For our example, we'll show how to use three related tables in the database contained in the **sampdata.mdb** file. You'll find this file in the **\DevStudio\VC\Samples\mfc\database\daoctl** folder on the Visual C++ CD. Copy the file to a suitable folder on your hard disk and make sure that it's no longer set to read-only. (In Windows 95, you can alter this by right-clicking the file, selecting Properties from the pop-up menu and making sure that the Read-only attribute box is unchecked.) Since you'll always have the read-only version of the database on the CD to go back to if something goes wrong, you won't need to worry about messing it up, so feel free to experiment as we go along.

In the first step, we'll create a program to display records from the **Products** table in the database. We'll then add code to allow us to examine all the orders for a given product using two other tables. Finally, we'll access the **Customers** table to enable the customer details for an order to be displayed. Before we can start with the code, we need to identify the database to the operating system.

Registering an ODBC Database

Before you can use an ODBC database, it needs to be registered. You do this through the Control Panel that you access by selecting Settings from the Start menu. In the Control Panel, select the 32bit ODBC icon. The procedure may vary depending on which release of Windows 95 you're using, but if you have a recent version, you should see the dialog shown here:

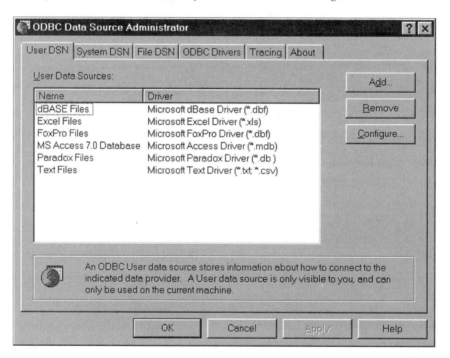

The User DSN tab shows you the data sources you already have configured on your system, which may differ from the ones in the diagram. Click on the Add... button to add a new data source. You should see the next dialog:

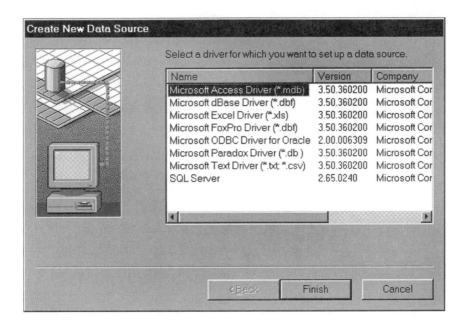

Here you must select from the list of ODBC drivers the one that we're going to use: **Microsoft Access Driver(*.mdb)**. This was automatically installed with the typical setup when you installed Windows. If you don't see this driver, you need to go back to Windows setup to install it. When you've selected the driver, click on the Finish button. This will take you to yet another dialog, as shown:

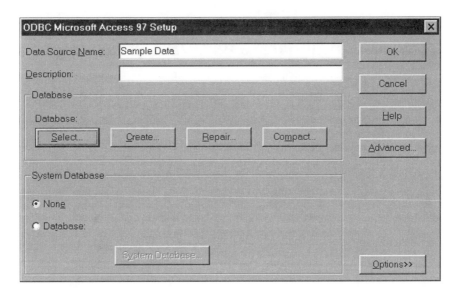

Enter **Sample Data** as the Data Source Name:. We'll use this name to identify the database when we generate our application using AppWizard. You now need to click on the Select... button to go to the final, Select Database dialog, in which you can select the **sampdata.mdb** file in whichever directory it now sits:

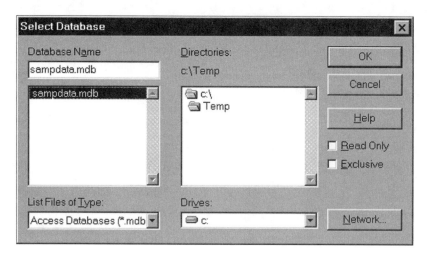

Finally, click on three successive OK buttons, and you've registered the database. If this procedure isn't the same on your PC, you'll need to resort to Help for your operating system, or just experiment with the ODBC option on Control Panel. The truth is in there.

Once you've succeeded, we can go ahead with our database application and, as ever, the starting point is AppWizard.

Using AppWizard to Generate an ODBC Program

Create a new project workspace in the usual way and give it a suitable name, such as **DBSample**. Choose the SDI interface for document support, since that will be sufficient for our needs. The document is somewhat incidental to operations in a database application, since most things are managed by recordset and record view objects. As you'll see, the main use of the document is to store recordset objects, so you won't need more than one of them. Click on the Next > button to move to the next step.

In Step 2 you have a choice as to whether you include file support with the database view option. File support refers to serializing the document, which isn't normally necessary since any database input and output that you need will be taken care of using the recordset objects in your application. Therefore, you should choose the option without file support, as shown here:

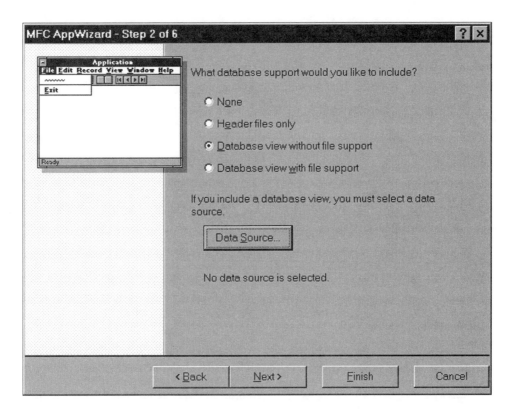

When you select either of the database options, the Data Source... button is activated. You now need to click on this button to specify the database that your application is going to use. This will display the dialog shown here:

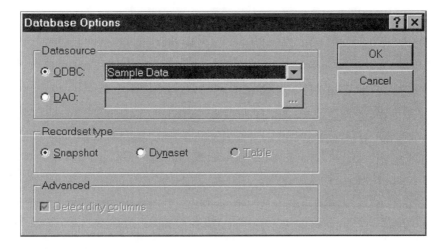

ODBC is already selected as the database option and, if you expand the drop-down list, you should find Sample Data as one of the data sources available to you (provided you've registered it correctly beforehand). In the dialog above, it has already been selected.

AppWizard will automatically equip your program with a recordset class and a record view class, and the dialog also shows a choice for the recordset your program will use. The grayed Table option only applies if you're using DAO. For ODBC, you have a choice between Snapshot and Dynaset for your initial recordset class. There's a significant difference between these options, so let's look at what they mean.

Snapshot vs. Dynaset Recordsets

Your recordset object will provide you with the result of a **SELECT** operation on the database. In the case of a **snapshot** recordset, the query is executed once and the result is stored in memory. Your recordset object can then make available to you any of the records in the table that result from the query, so a snapshot is essentially static in nature. Any changes that might occur in the database due to other users updating the database will not be reflected in the data you have obtained with your snapshot recordset. If you need to see changes that may have been made, you'll need to rerun the **SELECT** statement.

There's another feature of snapshot recordsets that depends on whether you're using DAO or ODBC. A DAO snapshot can't be changed by your program—it's read-only. However, an ODBC snapshot can be either read-only or updatable. An updatable snapshot writes any modifications that you make to the table straight back to the underlying database, and your program can see the change. Other programs with a snapshot of the database will not, however, see the changes until they requery the database.

With the **dynaset** option, your recordset object will automatically refresh the current record from the database when you move from one record to another in the table generated by the query for the recordset. As a consequence, the record available in the recordset will reflect the up-to-date status of the database when you accessed the record, not when you first opened the recordset. Be aware that the refresh only occurs when your recordset object accesses a record. If the data in the current record is modified by another user, this will not be apparent in your recordset object unless you move to another record and then return to the original record. A dynaset recordset uses an index to the database tables involved to generate the contents of each record dynamically.

Since we have no other users accessing the Sample Data database, you can choose the Snapshot option for our example. This will be adequate here because we'll only be implementing the retrieval of data from the database. If you want to try to add some update capability yourself, you should use the Dynaset option.

Choosing Tables

Once Snapshot has been chosen, you can click on the OK button to display the dialog which will determine the tables that the recordset class in your application will relate to. Here, you are effectively specifying the tables parameter for the **SELECT** statement that will be applied for the recordset. The dialog is shown here:

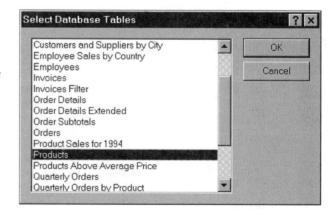

The dialog lists all the tables in the Sample Data database and, as you can see, there are quite a few. You could select several tables to be associated with the recordset by holding down the *Shift* key as you click on entries in the list box, but here we only need one, so just select the Products table, as shown, and then click on the OK button.

You have now specified the operation for the recordset class that AppWizard will generate as:

```
SELECT * FROM Products;
```

The use of * for all fields is determined by the framework. It just uses the table names you choose here to form the SQL operation that will be applied for the recordset.

You can now move through the remaining steps for generating the project workspace without changing any of the options, until you get to the dialog displaying the class and filenames to be used, which is Step 6, as shown here:

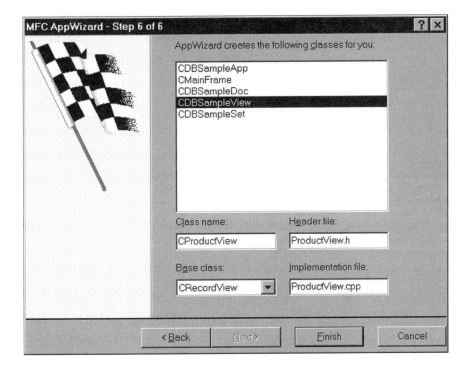

As well as the changes shown above for the **CDBSampleView** class, you should also change the **CDBSampleSet** class name to **CProductSet**, and the associated **.h** and **.cpp** file names to be consistent with the class name. Once that's done, you can click on Finish and generate the program.

Understanding the Program Structure

The basic structure of the program is as we've seen before, comprising an application class **CDBSampleApp**, a frame window class **CMainFrame**, a document class **CDBSampleDoc**, and a view class **CProductView**. A document template object is responsible for creating and relating the frame window, the document and the view objects. This is done in a standard manner in the **InitInstance()** member of the application object.

The document class is quite standard, except that AppWizard has added a data member, **m_productSet** which is an object of the **CProductSet** class. As a consequence, a recordset object will be automatically created when the document object is created in the **InitInstance()** function member of the application object. The significant departures from a non-database program arise in the detail of the **CRecordset** class, and in the **CRecordView** class, so let's take a look at those.

Understanding Recordsets

We can look at the definition of the **CProductSet** class that AppWizard has generated piecemeal and see how each piece works. The bits under discussion are shaded.

Recordset Creation

The first segment of the class definition that is of interest is:

```
class CProductSet : public CRecordset
{
public:
    CProductSet(CDatabase* pDatabase = NULL);
    DECLARE_DYNAMIC(CProductSet)

// Plus more of the class definition...

// Overrides
    // ClassWizard generated virtual function overrides
    //{{AFX_VIRTUAL(CProductSet)
    public:
    virtual CString GetDefaultConnect();    // Default connection string
    virtual CString GetDefaultSQL();        // default SQL for Recordset
    virtual void DoFieldExchange(CFieldExchange* pFX);// RFX support
    //}}AFX_VIRTUAL

// Plus some more standard stuff

};
```

The class has **CRecordset** as a base class and provides the functionality for retrieving data from the database. The constructor for the class accepts a pointer to a **CDatabase** object that is set to **NULL** as a default. The parameter to the constructor allows a **CProductSet** object to be created for a **CDatabase** object that already exists, which allows an existing connection to a database to be reused. Opening a connection to a database is a lengthy business, so it's advantageous to reuse a database connection when you can.

If no pointer is passed to the constructor, as will be the case for the **m_productSet** member of the document class **CDBSampleDoc**, the framework will automatically create a **CDatabase** object for you and call the **GetDefaultConnect()** function member of **CProductSet** to define the connection. The implementation of this function provided by AppWizard is as follows:

```
CString CProductSet::GetDefaultConnect()
{
    return _T("ODBC;DSN=Sample Data");
}
```

This function is a pure virtual function in the base class, and so must always be implemented in a derived recordset class. The implementation provided by AppWizard will return the text string shown to the framework. This identifies our database by name and enables the framework to create a **CDatabase** object to provide the database connection automatically.

In practice, it's usually necessary to supply a user ID and a password before access to a database is permitted. You can add this information to the string returned by the **GetDefaultConnect()** function. Where this is necessary, you specify your user ID by adding **UID=** and your ID following the **DSN=** part of the string, and you specify the password by adding **PWD=** followed by your password. Each piece of the string is separated from the next by a semicolon. For example, if your user ID is Reuben and your password is Hype, you could specify these in the **return** statement from **GetDefaultConnect()** as:

```
    return _T("ODBC;DSN=Sample Data;UID=Reuben;PWD=Hype");
```

You can also make the framework pop up a dialog for the user to select the database name from the list of registered database sources by writing the return as:

```
    return _T("ODBC;");
```

Querying the Database

The **CProductSet** class includes a data member for each field in the **Products** table. AppWizard obtains the field names from the database and uses these to name the corresponding data members of the class. They appear in the block of code delimited by the **AFX_FIELD** comments in the following:

```
class CProductSet : public CRecordset
{
public:
    CProductSet(CDatabase* pDatabase = NULL);
    DECLARE_DYNAMIC(CProductSet)

// Field/Param Data
    //{{AFX_FIELD(CProductSet, CRecordset)
    long    m_ProductID;
    CString m_ProductName;
    long    m_SupplierID;
    long    m_CategoryID;
    CString m_QuantityPerUnit;
    CString m_UnitPrice;
    int     m_UnitsInStock;
    int     m_UnitsOnOrder;
    int     m_ReorderLevel;
    BOOL    m_Discontinued;
    //}}AFX_FIELD
```

```
// Overrides
   // ClassWizard generated virtual function overrides
   //{{AFX_VIRTUAL(CProductSet)
   public:
   virtual CString GetDefaultConnect();  // Default connection string
   virtual CString GetDefaultSQL();       // default SQL for Recordset
   virtual void DoFieldExchange(CFieldExchange* pFX);  // RFX support
   //}}AFX_VIRTUAL

// Implementation
#ifdef _DEBUG
   virtual void AssertValid() const;
   virtual void Dump(CDumpContext& dc) const;
#endif

};
```

The type of each data member is set to correspond with the field type for the corresponding field in the **Products** table. You may not want all these fields in practice, but you shouldn't delete them willy-nilly in the class definition. As you will see shortly, they are referenced in other places, so always use ClassWizard to delete fields that you don't want. A further caveat is that you must not delete primary keys. If you do, the recordset won't work, so you need to be sure which fields are primary keys before chopping out what you don't want.

The SQL operation which applies to the recordset to populate these data members is specified in the **GetDefaultSQL()** function. The implementation that AppWizard has supplied for this is:

```
CString CProductSet::GetDefaultSQL()
{
   return _T("[Products]");
}
```

The string returned is obviously obtained from the table you selected during the creation of the project. The square brackets have been included to provide for the possibility of the table name containing blanks. If you had selected several tables in **Step 2** of the project creation process, they would all be inserted here, separated by commas, with each table name enclosed within square brackets.

The **GetDefaultSQL()** function is called by the framework when it constructs the SQL statement to be applied for the recordset. The framework slots the string returned by this function into a skeleton SQL statement with the form:

```
SELECT * FROM < String returned by GetDefaultSQL() >;
```

This looks very simplistic, and indeed it is, but we can add **WHERE** and **ORDER BY** clauses to the operation, as you'll see later.

Data Transfer between the Database and the Recordset

The transfer of data from the database to the recordset, and vice versa, is accomplished by the **DoFieldExchange()** member of the **CProductSet** class. The implementation of this function provided by AppWizard is:

```
void CProductSet::DoFieldExchange(CFieldExchange* pFX)
{
```

```
   //{{AFX_FIELD_MAP(CProductSet)
   pFX->SetFieldType(CFieldExchange::outputColumn);
   RFX_Long(pFX, _T("[ProductID]"), m_ProductID);
   RFX_Text(pFX, _T("[ProductName]"), m_ProductName);
   RFX_Long(pFX, _T("[SupplierID]"), m_SupplierID);
   RFX_Long(pFX, _T("[CategoryID]"), m_CategoryID);
   RFX_Text(pFX, _T("[QuantityPerUnit]"), m_QuantityPerUnit);
   RFX_Text(pFX, _T("[UnitPrice]"), m_UnitPrice);
   RFX_Int(pFX, _T("[UnitsInStock]"), m_UnitsInStock);
   RFX_Int(pFX, _T("[UnitsOnOrder]"), m_UnitsOnOrder);
   RFX_Int(pFX, _T("[ReorderLevel]"), m_ReorderLevel);
   RFX_Bool(pFX, _T("[Discontinued]"), m_Discontinued);
   //}}AFX_FIELD_MAP
}
```

This function is called automatically by the framework to store data in and retrieve data from the database. It works in a similar fashion to the **DoDataExchange()** function we have seen with dialog controls, in that the **pFX** parameter determines whether the operation is a read or a write. Each time it's called, it moves a single record to or from the recordset object.

The first function called is **SetFieldType()**, which sets a mode for the **RFX_()** function calls that follow. In this case, the mode is specified as **outputColumn**, which indicates that data is to be exchanged between the database field and the corresponding argument specified in each of the following **RFX_()** function calls.

There are a whole range of **RFX_()** functions for various types of database field. The function call for a particular field will correspond with the data type applicable to that field. The first argument to an **RFX_()** function call is the **pFX** object which determines the direction of data movement. The second argument is the table field name and the third is the data member that is to store that field for the current record.

Understanding the Record View

The purpose of the view class is to display information from the recordset object in the application window, so we need to understand how this works. The bits of the class definition for the **CProductView** class produced by AppWizard that are of primary interest are shaded:

```
class CProductView : public CRecordView
{
protected: // create from serialization only
   CProductView();
   DECLARE_DYNCREATE(CProductView)

public:
   //{{AFX_DATA(CProductView)
   enum{ IDD = IDD_DBSAMPLE_FORM };
   CProductSet* m_pSet;
      // NOTE: the ClassWizard will add data members here
   //}}AFX_DATA

// Attributes
public:
   CDBSampleDoc* GetDocument();

// Operations
public:
```

```
    // Overrides
      // ClassWizard generated virtual function overrides
      //{{AFX_VIRTUAL(CProductView)
      public:
      virtual CRecordset* OnGetRecordset();
      virtual BOOL PreCreateWindow(CREATESTRUCT& cs);
      protected:
      virtual void DoDataExchange(CDataExchange* pDX);    // DDX/DDV support
      virtual void OnInitialUpdate(); // called first time after construct
      virtual BOOL OnPreparePrinting(CPrintInfo* pInfo);
      virtual void OnBeginPrinting(CDC* pDC, CPrintInfo* pInfo);
      virtual void OnEndPrinting(CDC* pDC, CPrintInfo* pInfo);
      //}}AFX_VIRTUAL

      // plus implementation and generated message maps
      // that we have seen with standard view classes...
    };
```

The view class for a recordset always needs to be derived because the class has to be customized to display the particular fields from the recordset that we want. The base class, **CRecordView**, includes all the functionality required to manage communications with the recordset. All we need to do is use ClassWizard to tailor our record view class to suit our application. We'll get to that in a moment.

Note that the constructor is **protected**. This is because objects of this class are expected to be created from serialization, which is a default assumption for record view classes. When we add further record views to our application, we'll need to change the default access for their constructors to **public** because we'll be creating the views ourselves.

In the block bounded by the comments containing **AFX_DATA**, the enumeration adds the ID **IDD_DBSAMPLE_FORM** to the class. This is the ID for a blank dialog that AppWizard has included in the program. We'll need to add controls to this dialog to display the database fields from the **Products** table that we want displayed. The dialog ID is passed to the base class, **CRecordView**, in the initialization list of the constructor for our view class:

```
CProductView::CProductView() : CRecordView(CProductView::IDD)
{
    //{{AFX_DATA_INIT(CProductView)
       // NOTE: the ClassWizard will add member initialization here
    m_pSet = NULL;
    //}}AFX_DATA_INIT
    // TODO: add construction code here
}
```

This action links the view class to the dialog, which is necessary to enable the mechanism which transfers data between the recordset object and the view object to work.

There is also a pointer to a **CProductSet** object, **m_pSet**, in the **AFX_DATA** block of the class definition, which is initialized to **NULL** in the constructor. A more useful value for this pointer is set in the **OnInitialUpdate()** member of the class, which has been implemented as:

```
void CProductView::OnInitialUpdate()
{
    m_pSet = &GetDocument()->m_productSet;
    CRecordView::OnInitialUpdate();
}
```

This function is called when the record view object is created and sets **m_pSet** to the address of the **m_productSet** member of the document, thus tying the view to the product set object.

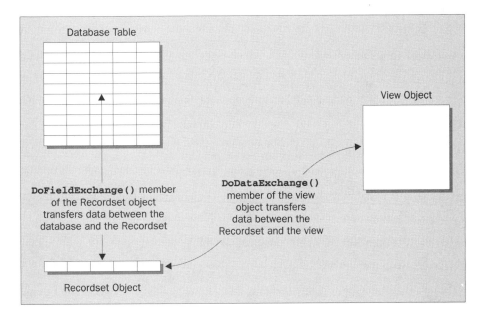

The transfer of data between the data members in the **CProductSet** object that correspond to fields in the **Products** table, and the controls in the dialog associated with the **CProductView** object, will be managed by the **DoDataExchange()** member of **CProductView**. The code in this function to do this isn't in place yet, since we first need to add the controls to the dialog that are going to display the data, and then use ClassWizard to link the controls to the recordset data members. Let's do that next.

Creating the View Dialog

The first step is to place the controls on the dialog, so go to ResourceView, expand the list of Dialog resources and double-click on **IDD_DBSAMPLE_FORM**. You can delete the static text object with the TODO message from the dialog. If you right-click on the dialog, you can choose to view its Properties, as shown here:

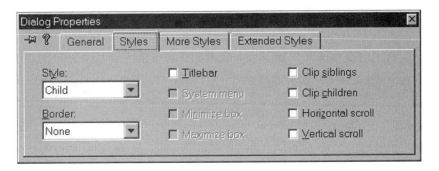

The Style: option has been set to Child because the dialog is going to be a child window and will fill the client area. The Border: option has been set to None because if it fills the client area, the dialog doesn't need a border.

We'll add a static text control to identify each field from the recordset that we want to display, plus an edit control to display it. The tab order of the text control should be such that each static text control immediately precedes the corresponding control displaying the data in sequence. This is because ClassWizard will determine the data member name to be associated with each control that is to display a field from the text in the static control immediately preceding it. The text you choose for the static control is, therefore, most important if this is to work.

You can add each static control, followed immediately by the corresponding edit control, to create the tab order that you want, or you can simply fix the tab order at the end using the Layout | Tab Order menu option.

You can enlarge the dialog by dragging its borders. Then, place controls on the dialog as shown here:

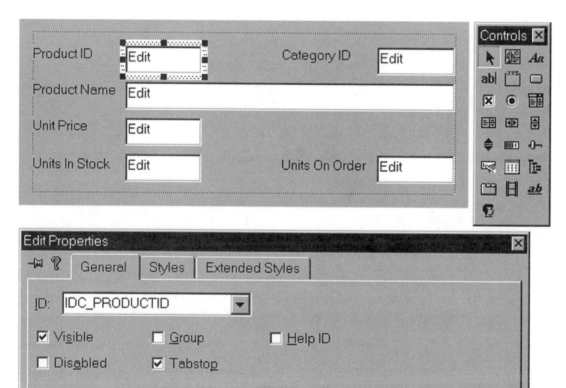

You can add the text to each static control by just typing it as soon as the control has been placed on the dialog. The Properties dialog box will open automatically. As you see, the text for each static control corresponds to the field name in the database. You need to make sure that all the edit controls have different IDs. It's helpful to use the field name as part of the control ID, as shown in the Properties dialog above. You need not worry about the IDs for the static controls, since they aren't referenced in the program. After you have arranged the controls, you should check the tab order to make sure that each static control has a sequence number one less than its corresponding edit control.

You can add other fields to the dialog if you want. The one that is most important for the rest of our example is the **Product ID**, so you *must* include that. Save the dialog and then we can move on to the last step, which is to link the controls to the variables in the recordset class.

Linking the Controls to the Recordset

Linking the controls to the data members of **CProductSet** is simplicity itself. Just double-click on the **Product ID** edit control while holding down the *Ctrl* key and you'll see the dialog box shown here:

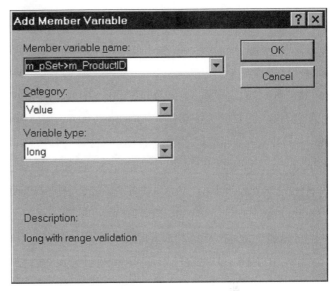

ClassWizard has filled in all the required values for you using the text from the preceding static control and the information from **CProductSet**. All you need to do is to verify that the variable name is correct—it should be if you put the right text in the static control—and click on OK. You then need to repeat this for the other edit controls on your dialog. This will enable ClassWizard to fill out the code for the **DoDataExchange()** function in the **CProductView** class, which will now be implemented as:

```
void CProductView::DoDataExchange(CDataExchange* pDX)
{
    CRecordView::DoDataExchange(pDX);
    //{{AFX_DATA_MAP(CProductView)
    DDX_FieldText(pDX, IDC_PRODUCTID, m_pSet->m_ProductID, m_pSet);
    DDX_FieldText(pDX, IDC_PRODUCTNAME, m_pSet->m_ProductName, m_pSet);
    DDX_FieldText(pDX, IDC_UNITPRICE, m_pSet->m_UnitPrice, m_pSet);
    DDX_FieldText(pDX, IDC_UNITSINSTOCK, m_pSet->m_UnitsInStock, m_pSet);
    DDX_FieldText(pDX, IDC_CATEGORYID, m_pSet->m_CategoryID, m_pSet);
    DDX_FieldText(pDX, IDC_UNITSONORDER, m_pSet->m_UnitsOnOrder, m_pSet);
    //}}AFX_DATA_MAP
}
```

This function works in the same way you've seen previously with dialog controls. Each **DDX_()** function transfers data between the control and the corresponding data member of the **CProductSet** class, which is accessed through the pointer **m_pSet**.

The complete mechanism for data transfer between the database and the dialog owned by the **CProductView** object is illustrated here:

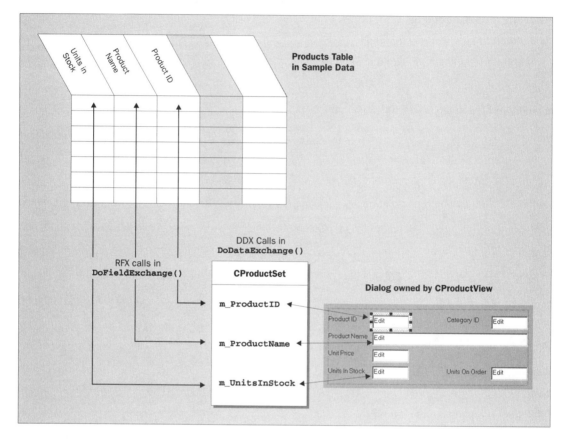

The recordset class and the record view class cooperate to enable data to be transferred between the database and the controls in the dialog. The **CProductSet** class handles transfers between the database and its data members and **CProductView** deals with transfers between the data members of **CProductSet** and the controls in the dialog.

Exercising the Example

Believe it or not, you can now run the example. Just build it in the normal way and then execute it. The application should display a window similar to this one:

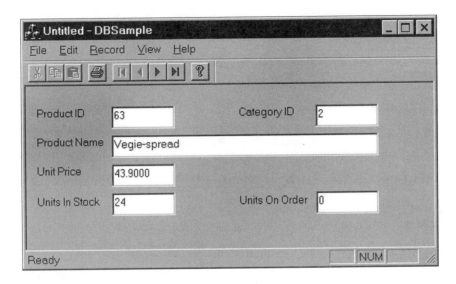

The **CRecordView** base class automatically implements toolbar buttons that step from one record in the recordset to the next or to the previous record. There are also toolbar buttons to move directly to the first or last record in the recordset. You'll notice that the products are not completely in order. It would be nice to have them sorted in **Product ID** sequence, so let's see how we can do that.

Sorting a Recordset

As we saw earlier, the data is retrieved from the database by the recordset, using an SQL **SELECT** statement which is generated by the framework using the **GetDefaultSQL()** member. We can add an **ORDER BY** clause to the statement generated by setting a value in the **m_strSort** member of **CProductSet**, which is inherited from **CRecordSet**. This will cause the output table from the query to be sorted, based on the string stored in **m_strSort**. We only need to set the **m_strSort** member to a string that contains the field name that we want to sort on; the framework will provide the **ORDER BY** keywords. But where should we add the code to do this?

The transfer of data between the database and the recordset occurs when the **Open()** member of the recordset object is called. In our program, the **Open()** function member of the recordset object is called by the **OnInitialUpdate()** member of the base class to our view class, **CRecordView**. We can, therefore, put the code for setting the sort specification in the **OnInitialUpdate()** member of the **CProductView** class, as follows:

```
void CProductView::OnInitialUpdate()
{
    m_pSet = &GetDocument()->m_productSet;
    m_pSet->m_strSort = "[ProductID]";        // Set the sort fields
    CRecordView::OnInitialUpdate();
}
```

We just set **m_strSort** in the recordset to the name of the **ProductID** field. Square brackets are useful, even when there are no blanks in a name, because they differentiate strings containing these names from other strings, so you can immediately pick out the field names. They are, of course, optional if there are no blanks in the field name.

If there was more than one field that you wanted to sort on here, you would just include each of the field names in the string, separated by commas.

Modifying the Window Caption

There's one other thing we could add to this function at this point. The caption for the window would be better if it showed the name of the table being displayed. We can fix this by adding code to set the title in the document object:

```
void CProductView::OnInitialUpdate()
{
    m_pSet = &GetDocument()->m_productSet;
    m_pSet->m_strSort = "[ProductID]";       // Set the sort fields
    CRecordView::OnInitialUpdate();

    // Set the document title to the table name
    if (m_pSet->IsOpen())                      // Verify the recordset is open
    {
        CString strTitle = _T("Table Name"); // Set basic title string
        CString strTable = m_pSet->GetTableName();
        if (!strTable.IsEmpty())               // Verify we have a table name
            strTitle += _T(":") + strTable;    // and add to basic title
        GetDocument()->SetTitle(strTitle);     // Set the document title
    }
}
```

After checking that the recordset is indeed open, we initialize a local **CString** object with a basic title string. We then get the name of the table from the recordset object by calling its **GetTableName()** member. In general, you should check that you do get a string returned from the **GetTableName()** function. Various conditions can arise that will prevent a table name from being set—for instance, there may be more than one table involved in the recordset. After appending a colon followed by the table name we have retrieved to the basic title in **strTitle**, we set the result as the document title by calling the document's **SetTitle()** member.

If you rebuild the application and run it again, it will work as before, but with a new window caption and with the product IDs in ascending sequence.

Using a Second Recordset Object

Now that we can view all the products in the database, a reasonable extension of the program would be to add the ability to view all the orders for any particular product. To do this, we'll add another recordset class to handle order information from the database, and a complementary view class to display some of the fields from the recordset. We'll also add a button to the **Products** dialog to enable you to switch to the **Orders** dialog when you want to view the orders for the current product. This will enable us to operate with the arrangement shown in the next diagram:

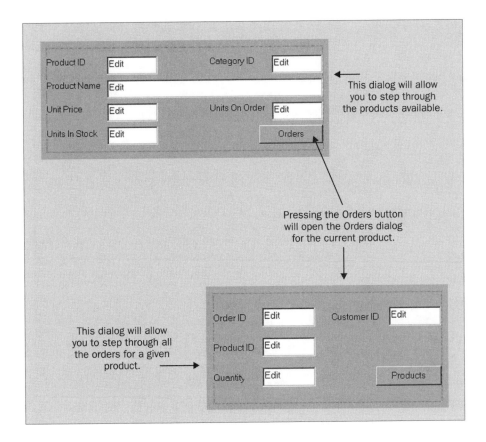

The **Products** dialog will be the starting position. You will be able to step backwards and forwards through all the available products. Clicking the Orders button will switch you to the dialog where you'll be able to view all the orders for the current product. You will be able to return to the **Products** dialog by clicking the Products button.

Adding a Recordset Class

We start by adding the recordset class using ClassWizard, so bring that into view by right clicking in the editor window and selecting from the pop-up. Then, click on the Add Class... button in the ClassWizard dialog and select New... from the pop-up. In the dialog, enter the name of the class as **COrderSet** and select the base class from the drop-down list box, as shown here:

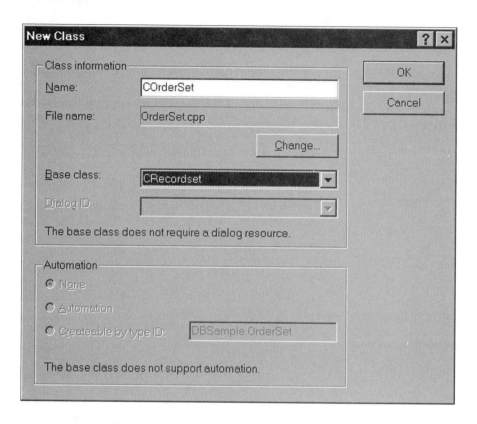

If you now select the OK button, ClassWizard will take you to the dialog to select the database for the recordset class. Select Sample Data from the list box and leave the Recordset type as Snapshot, as before. Then click on the OK button to move to the table selection dialog shown here:

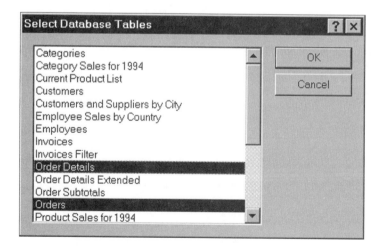

We'll select two tables to associate with the **COrderSet** class, so select the Orders and Order Details table names. You can then click the OK button to complete the process.

You can examine what has been created through ClassWizard. If you switch to the Member Variables tab, you'll see the dialog shown here:

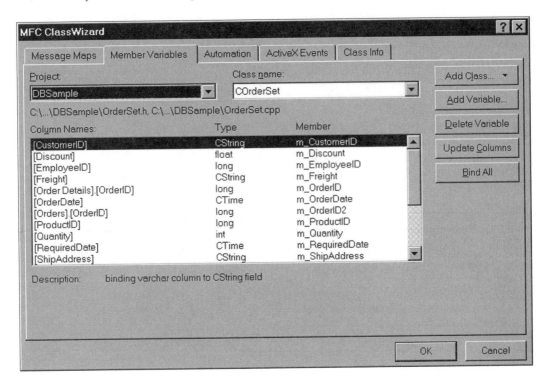

ClassWizard has created a data member for every field in each of the tables. Note that the **OrderID** field appears in both tables, so ClassWizard identifies these by prefixing the field names with the table name in each case. The data member for the **OrderID** field in the **Orders** table is differentiated from the member for the corresponding field in the **Order Details** table by adding a **2** to the name created from the field name.

If you don't want all these fields, you can delete any of them by selecting the appropriate record in the list and then clicking the Delete Variable button. You should, however, take care not to delete any variables that are primary keys. When you delete a data member for a table field, ClassWizard will take care of deleting the initialization for it in the class constructor and the **RFX_()** call for it in the **DoFieldExchange()** member function. The variables that we need are: **m_OrderID**, **m_OrderID2**, **m_ProductID**, **m_Quantity** and **m_CustomerID**.

You can now close ClassWizard by clicking the OK button. To hook the new recordset to the document, you need to add a data member to the definition of the **CDBSampleDoc** class, so right-click the class name in ClassView and select Add Member Variable... from the pop-up. Specify the type as **COrderSet** and the variable name as **m_OrderSet**. You can leave it as a **public** member of the class. After clicking OK to finish adding the data member to the document, you need to be sure the compiler understands that **COrderSet** is a class before it gets to compiling the **CBSampleDoc** class. If you take a look at the definition of **CBDSampleDoc**, you'll see that a **#include** statement has already been added to the top of **DBSampleDoc.h**:

```
#include "OrderSet.h"    // Added by ClassView
...
class CDBSampleDoc : public CDocument
{ // Rest of class definition }
```

Adding a Record View Class

Now you need to create another dialog resource. This must be done before you create the view class so that ClassWizard can automatically connect the dialog to the class for you.

Creating the Dialog Resource

Switch to ResourceView, right-click on the Dialog folder and select Insert Dialog from the pop-up. You can delete both of the default buttons from the dialog. Now change the name and styles for the dialog, so right-click on it and display the Properties box. Change the dialog ID to **IDD_ORDERS_FORM**. You also need to change the dialog style to Child and the border style to None. You do this on the Styles tab, as shown here:

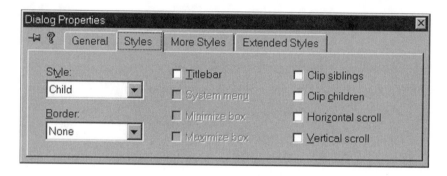

You're now ready to populate the dialog with controls for the fields that you want to display from the **Orders** and **Order Details** tables. If you switch to ClassView and extend the **COrderSet** part of the classes tree, you'll be able to see the names of the variables concerned while you're working on the dialog. Add controls to the dialog as shown here:

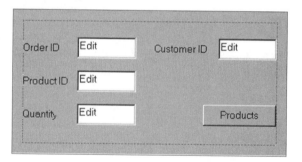

Here, we have four edit controls for the **OrderID**, **CustomerID**, **ProductID**, and **Quantity** fields from the tables associated with the **COrderSet** class, together with static controls to identify them. You can add a few more if you wish. Don't forget to modify the IDs for the edit controls so that they are representative of the purpose of the control. You can use the table field names as we did previously. You also need to check the tab order and verify that each static control immediately precedes the associated edit control in sequence. If they don't, just click on them in the sequence that you want.

The button control labeled Products will be used to return to the **Products** table view, so modify the ID for this button to **IDC_PRODUCTS**. When everything is arranged to your liking, save the dialog resource.

Creating the Record View Class

To create the view class for the recordset, right-click on the dialog and select ClassWizard... from the pop-up. You will then see a dialog offering you two options for identifying a class to associate with the dialog. If you elect to create a new class, you'll see the dialog for creating a New Class:

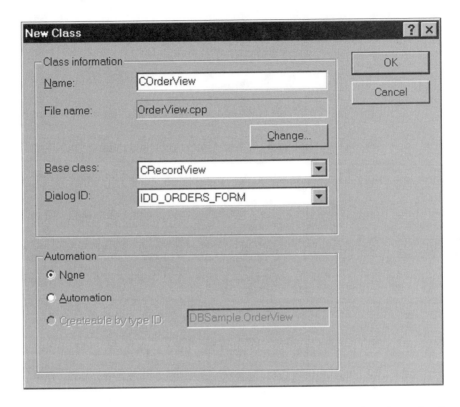

You need to enter the class name as **COrderView** and select the base class from the drop-down list box as **CRecordView**. You also need to select the ID for the dialog you have just created, **IDD_ORDERS_FORM**, from the Dialog ID: list box.

When you click on the OK button, ClassWizard will automatically choose **COrderSet** as the recordset class to be associated with the view class, so all you have to do is click this OK button as well.

You can see what the characteristics of the **COrderView** class are if you look at the Class Info tab shown here:

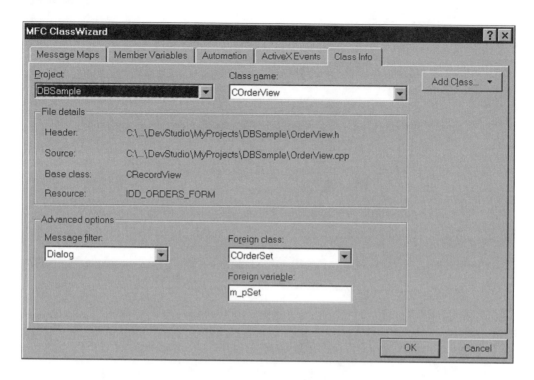

This tells you everything you need to know. The view class, which is derived from **CRecordView**, is hooked to the dialog resource you created with the ID **IDD_ORDERS_FORM** and has the **COrderSet** class associated with it. A data member **m_pSet** has also been added to hold the address of the associated **COrderSet** object. The class **COrderSet** is called a **foreign class** in the dialog above because **DDX** normally links data members of a dialog class and a view class. In this case, a third, 'foreign', class (which is **COrderSet**) is also involved, since this is the source of the data being exchanged.

Strangely, ClassWizard adds an unorthodox **#include** statement to the beginning of the **.h** file for **COrderView** which specifies a fully qualified name for the **OrderSet.h** file, even if the file is in the project directory. This can be a nuisance, particularly if you move the folder containing the project to somewhere else. It can also cause you to have multiple definitions of the **COrderSet** class in your program, about which the compiler will certainly complain by issuing an error message. I suggest that you simply alter the **#include** statement so that it contains only the name of the **OrderSet.h** file, as shown here:

```
#include "OrderSet.h"
```

This is preferable to the fully qualified version, which probably looks something like this:

```
#include "C:\Program Files\DevStudio\MyProjects\DBSample\OrderSet.h"
```

Check out the destructor for the **COrderView** class, which will have been implemented by ClassWizard with the following code:

```
COrderView::~COrderView()
{
```

```
        if (m_pSet)
            delete m_pSet;
    }
```

Remove the **if** and the **delete** statement. They aren't necessary in our example because the **COrderSet** object will be created and deleted by the framework, so we shouldn't delete it in the view. If you leave the code in you'll get assertion failures when you close the application, because an attempt will be made to delete the object twice.

Linking the Dialog Controls to the Recordset

To link the controls to the recordset, you follow the same procedure as we did for the **CProductView** class. Go back to the dialog **IDD_ORDERS_FORM** and double-click each edit control while holding down the *Ctrl* key.

Customizing the Record View Class

As it stands, the SQL **SELECT** operation for a **COrderSet** object will produce a table which will contain all combinations of records from the two tables involved. This could be a lot of records, so we must add the equivalent of a **WHERE** clause to the query to restrict the records selected to those that make sense. But there's another problem too: when we switch from the **Products** table display, we don't want to look at just any old orders. We want to see precisely those orders for the product ID we were looking at, which amounts to selecting only those orders that have the same product ID as that contained in the current **CProductSet** record. This is also effected through a **WHERE** clause. In the MFC context, the **WHERE** clause for a **SELECT** operation for a recordset is called a **filter**.

Adding a Filter to the Recordset

Adding a filter to the query is accomplished by assigning a string to the **m_strFilter** member of the recordset object. This member is inherited from the base class, **CRecordSet**. As with the **ORDER BY** clause, which we added by assigning a value to the **m_strSort** member of the recordset, the place to implement this is in the **OnInitialUpdate()** member of the record view class, just before the base class function is called.

We want to set two conditions in the filter. One is to restrict the records generated in the recordset to those where the **OrderID** field in the **Orders** table is equal to the field with the same name in the **Order Details** table. We can write this condition as:

```
    [Orders].[OrderID] = [Order Details].[OrderID]
```

The other condition we want to apply is that, for the records meeting the first condition, we only want those with a **ProductID** field that is equal to the **ProductID** field in the current record in the recordset object displaying the **Products** table. This means that we need to have the **ProductID** field from the **COrderSet** object compared to a variable value. The variable in this operation is called a parameter, and the condition in the filter is written in a special way:

```
    ProductID = ?
```

The question mark represents a parameter value for the filter, and the records that will be selected are those where the **ProductID** field equals the parameter value. The value that is to replace the question mark will be set in the **DoFieldExchange()** member of the recordset. We'll implement this in a moment, but first let's complete the specification of the filter.

383

We can define the string for the filter variable that incorporates both the conditions that we need with the statement:

```
// Set the filter as Product ID field with equal Order IDs
m_pSet->m_strFilter =
    "[ProductID] = ? AND [Orders].[OrderID] = [Order Details].[OrderID]";
```

We'll insert this into the **OnInitialUpdate()** member of the **COrderView** class, but before that, let's finish setting the parameter for the filter.

Defining the Filter Parameter

We need to add a data member to the **COrderSet** class that will store the current value of the **ProductID** field from the **CProductSet** object, and will also act as the parameter to substitute for the ? in our filter for the **COrderSet** object. So, right-click on the **COrderSet** class name in ClassView and select Add Member Variable... from the pop-up. The variable type needs to be the same as that of the **m_ProductID** member of the **CProductSet** class, which is **long**, and you can specify the name as **m_ProductIDparam**. You can also leave it as a **public** member. Now we need to initialize this data member in the constructor and set the parameter count, so add the code shown below:

```
COrderSet::COrderSet(CDatabase* pdb) : CRecordset(pdb)
{
    //{{AFX_FIELD_INIT(COrderSet)
    m_OrderID = 0;
    m_ProductID = 0;
    m_Quantity = 0;
    m_OrderID2 = 0;
    m_CustomerID = _T("");
    m_nFields = 5;
    //}}AFX_FIELD_INIT

    m_ProductIDparam = 0L;    // Set initial parameter value
    m_nParams = 1;            // Set number of parameters

    m_nDefaultType = snapshot;
}
```

All of the unshaded code was supplied by ClassWizard to initialize the data members corresponding to the fields in the recordset and to specify the type as **snapshot**. Our code initializes the parameter to zero and sets the count of the number of parameters to 1. The **m_nParams** variable is inherited from the base class, **CRecordSet**. Since there is a parameter count, evidently you can have more than one parameter in the filter for the recordset. The application framework requires the count of the number of parameters in your recordset to be set to reflect the number of parameters you're using, otherwise it won't work correctly.

To identify the **m_ProductIDparam** variable in the class as a parameter to be substituted in the filter for the **COrderSet** object, we must also add some code to the **DoFieldExchange()** member of the class:

```
void COrderSet::DoFieldExchange(CFieldExchange* pFX)
{
    //{{AFX_FIELD_MAP(COrderSet)
    pFX->SetFieldType(CFieldExchange::outputColumn);
    RFX_Long(pFX, _T("[Order Details].[OrderID]"), m_OrderID);
```

```
RFX_Long(pFX, _T("[ProductID]"), m_ProductID);
RFX_Int(pFX, _T("[Quantity]"), m_Quantity);
RFX_Long(pFX, _T("[Orders].[OrderID]"), m_OrderID2);
RFX_Text(pFX, _T("[CustomerID]"), m_CustomerID);
//}}AFX_FIELD_MAP

    // Set the field type as parameter
    pFX->SetFieldType(CFieldExchange::param);
    RFX_Long(pFX, _T("ProductIDParam"), m_ProductIDparam);
}
```

The ClassWizard has provided code to transfer data between the database and the field variables
it has added to the class. There is one **RFX_()** function call for each data member of the
recordset.

Other than the comment, we only needed to add two lines to the code that ClassWizard has
generated to specify **m_ProductIDparam** as a filter. The first line of code calls the
SetFieldType() member of the **pFX** object to set the mode for the following **RFX_()** calls to
param. The effect of this is to cause the third argument in any succeeding **RFX_()** calls to be
interpreted as a parameter that is to replace a ? in the filter for the recordset. If you have more
than one parameter, the parameters substitute for the question marks in the **m_strFilter** string
in sequence from left to right, so it's important to ensure that the **RFX_()** calls are in the right
order. With the mode set to **param**, the second argument in the **RFX_()** call is ignored, so you
could put **NULL** here, or some other string if you want.

Initializing the Record View

We now need to add the code to the **OnInitialUpdate()** member of the **COrderView** class.
As well as specifying the filter, we can also define a value for **m_strSort** to sort the records in
OrderID sequence, and add code to change the window caption to match the tables we're
dealing with:

```
void COrderView::OnInitialUpdate()
{
    BeginWaitCursor();       // This could take time so start the wait cursor
    CDBSampleDoc* pDoc = (CDBSampleDoc*)GetDocument();   // Get doc pointer
    m_pSet = &pDoc->m_OrderSet;          // Get a pointer to the recordset

    // Use the DB that is open for products recordset
    m_pSet->m_pDatabase = pDoc->m_productSet.m_pDatabase;

    // Set the current product ID as parameter
    m_pSet->m_ProductIDparam = pDoc->m_productSet.m_ProductID;

    // Set the filter as product ID field
    m_pSet->m_strFilter =
      "[ProductID] = ? AND [Orders].[OrderID] = [Order Details].[OrderID]";

    GetRecordset();                          // Get the recordset

    // Now fix the caption
    if (m_pSet->IsOpen())
    {
        CString strTitle = "Table Name:";
        CString strTable = m_pSet->GetTableName();      // Get the table name
```

```
            //If the recordset uses 2 or more tables, the name will be empty
        if (!strTable.IsEmpty())
            strTitle += _T(":") + strTable;       // It isn't so use the name
        else
            strTitle += _T("Orders - Multiple Tables"); // Use generic name

        GetDocument()->SetTitle(strTitle);         // Set the document title
    }

    CRecordView::OnInitialUpdate();
    EndWaitCursor();
}
```

The version of the **COrderSet** class that has been implemented by ClassWizard doesn't override the **GetDocument()** member because it isn't associated with the document class. As a result, we need to cast the pointer from the base class **GetDocument()** member to a pointer to a **CDBSampleDoc** object. Alternatively, you could add an overriding version of **GetDocument()** to **COrderSet** to do the cast. Clearly, we need a pointer to our document object because we need to access the members of the object.

Because we refer to the **CDBSampleDoc** class, you need to add three **#include** statements to the beginning of the **OrderView.cpp** file:

```
#include "ProductSet.h"
#include "OrderSet.h"
#include "DBSampleDoc.h"
```

The **BeginWaitCursor()** call added by ClassWizard at the start of the **OnInitialUpdate()** function displays the hourglass cursor while this function is executing. The reason for this is that, especially when multiple tables are involved, this function can take an appreciable time to execute. The processing of the query and the transfer of data to the recordset all takes place in here. The cursor is returned to normal by the **EndWaitCursor()** call at the end of the function.

The first thing that our code does is to set the **m_pDatabase** member of the **COrderSet** object to the same as that for the **CProductSet** object. If we don't do this, the framework will re-open the database when the orders recordset is opened. Since the database has already been opened for the products recordset, this would waste a lot of time.

Next, we set the value for the parameter variable to the current value in the **m_ProductID** member of the products recordset. This value will replace the question mark in the filter when the orders recordset is opened and so select the records we want. We then set the filter for the orders recordset to the string we saw earlier.

Next, the **GetRecordSet()** call supplied by ClassWizard is executed. This in turn calls the **OnGetRecordSet()** member, which creates a recordset object if there isn't one—in our case there is one because we added it to the document object—and then calls the **Open()** function for the recordset.

Finally, we have the code we saw earlier to define the caption for the window. The test for an empty table name isn't strictly necessary—we know that the table name will be empty, because the recordset has two tables specified for it. You could just use the code to explicitly define the caption, but the code we've implemented serves to demonstrate that the table name is indeed empty in this case.

Accessing Multiple Tables

Since we have implemented our program with the single document interface, we have one document and one view. The availability of just one view might appear to be a problem, but we can arrange for the frame window object in our application to create an instance of our **COrderView** class, and switch the current window to that when the orders recordset is to be displayed.

We'll need to keep track of what the current window is, which we can do by assigning a unique ID to each of the record view windows in our application. At the moment there are two: the product view and the order view. To do this, create a new file called **OurConstants.h** and add the following code to define the window IDs:

```
// Definition of our constants

#if !defined(OUR_CONSTANTS_H)
#define OUR_CONSTANTS_H

// Arbitrary constants to identify record views
const UINT PRODUCT_VIEW = 1U;
const UINT ORDER_VIEW = 2U;

/////////////////////////////////////////////////////

#endif // !defined(OUR_CONSTANTS_H)
```

We can now use one of these constants to identify each view and to record the ID of the current view in the frame window object. To do this, add a **public** data member to the **CMainFrame** class of type **UINT** and give it the name **m_CurrentViewID**. Once you've done that, you can initialize it in the constructor for **CMainFrame**, by adding code as follows:

```
CMainFrame::CMainFrame()
{
    m_CurrentViewID = PRODUCT_VIEW;        // We always start with this view
}
```

Now add a **#include** statement for **OurConstants.h** to the beginning of **MainFrm.cpp** so that the definition of **PRODUCT_VIEW** is available here.

Switching Views

To enable the view switching mechanism, we're going to add a public function member called **SelectView()** to the **CMainFrame** class, which will have a parameter defining a view ID. This function will switch from the current view to whatever view is specified by the ID passed as an argument.

Right-click on **CMainFrame** and select Add Member Function... from the pop-up. You can enter the return type as **void** and the Function Declaration: entry as **SelectView(UINT ViewID)**. The implementation of the function is as follows:

```
void CMainFrame::SelectView(UINT ViewID)
{
    CView* pOldActiveView = GetActiveView();        // Get current view

    // Get pointer to new view if it exists
```

```
      // if it doesn't the pointer will be null
      CView* pNewActiveView = (CView*)GetDlgItem(ViewID);

      // If this is 1st time around for the new view,
      // the new view won't exist, so we must create it
      if (pNewActiveView == NULL)
      {
        switch(ViewID)
        {
          case ORDER_VIEW:       // Create an Order view
            pNewActiveView = (CView*)new COrderView;
            break;
          default:
            AfxMessageBox("Invalid View ID");
            return;
        }

        // Switching the views
        // Obtain the current view context to apply to the new view
        CCreateContext context;
        context.m_pCurrentDoc = pOldActiveView->GetDocument();
        pNewActiveView->Create(NULL, NULL, 0L, CFrameWnd::rectDefault,
                                                 this, ViewID, &context);
        pNewActiveView->OnInitialUpdate();
      }
      SetActiveView(pNewActiveView);                // Activate the new view
      pOldActiveView->ShowWindow(SW_HIDE);          // Hide the old view
      pNewActiveView->ShowWindow(SW_SHOW);          // Show the new view
      pOldActiveView->SetDlgCtrlID(m_CurrentViewID); // Set the old view ID
      pNewActiveView->SetDlgCtrlID(AFX_IDW_PANE_FIRST);
      m_CurrentViewID = ViewID;                     // Save the new view ID
      RecalcLayout();
    }
```

The operation of the function falls into three distinct parts:

1 Getting pointers to the current view and the new view.

2 Creating the new view if it doesn't exist.

3 Swapping to the new view in place of the current view.

The address of the current active view is supplied by the **GetActiveView()** member of the **CMainFrame** object. To get a pointer to the new view, we call the **GetDlgItem()** member of the frame window object. If a view with the ID specified in the argument to the function exists, it returns the address of the view, otherwise it returns **NULL** and we need to create the new view.

Since we'll create a **COrderView** object on the heap here, we need access to the constructor for the class. The default access specification for the constructor **COrderView()** in the class definition is **protected**, so change it to **public** to make creating the view object legal, as in the following code:

```
class COrderView : public CRecordView
{
```

```
public:
   COrderView();           // we changed this to public
```

```
protected:
   DECLARE_DYNCREATE(COrderView)

   // rest of class definition
};
```

After creating a view object, we define a **CCreateContext** object, **context**. A **CCreateContext** object is only necessary when you're creating a window for a view that is to be connected to a document. A **CCreateContext** object contains data members that can tie together a document, a frame window and a view, and for MDI applications, a document template as well. When we switch between views, we'll create a new window for the new view to be displayed in. Each time we create a new view window, we will use the **CCreateContext** object to establish a connection between the view and our document object. All we need to do is store a pointer to our document object in the **m_pCurrentDoc** member of **context**. In general you may need to store additional data in the **CCreateContext** object before you create; it depends on the circumstances and the kind of window you're creating.

In the call to the **Create()** member of the view object which creates the window for the new view, we pass the object, **context**, as an argument. This will establish a proper relationship with our document and will validate the document pointer. The argument **this** in the call to **Create()** specifies the current frame as the parent window, and the **ViewID** argument specifies the ID of the window. This ID enables the address of the window to be obtained with a subsequent call to the **GetDlgItem()** member of the parent window.

To make the new view the active view, we call the **SetActiveView()** member of **CMainFrame**. The new view will then replace the current active view. To remove the old view window, we call the **ShowWindow()** member of the view with the argument **SW_HIDE** using the pointer to the old view. To display the new view window, we call the same function with the argument **SW_SHOW** using the pointer to the new view.

```
SetActiveView(pNewActiveView);              // Activate the new view
pOldActiveView->ShowWindow(SW_HIDE);        // Hide the old view
pNewActiveView->ShowWindow(SW_SHOW);        // Show the new view
pOldActiveView->SetDlgCtrlID(m_CurrentViewID); // Set the old view ID
pNewActiveView->SetDlgCtrlID(AFX_IDW_PANE_FIRST);
m_CurrentViewID = ViewID;                   // Save the new view ID
```

We restore the ID of the old active view to the ID value that we've defined for it in the **m_CurrentViewID** member of the **CMainFrame** class that we added earlier. We also set the ID of the new view to **AFX_IDW_PANE_FIRST** to identify it as the first window for the application. This is necessary because our application has but one view, so the first view is the only view. Lastly, we save our ID for the new window in the **m_CurrentViewID** member, so it's available the next time the current view is replaced. The call to **RecalcLayout()** causes the view to be redrawn when the new view is selected.

You must add a **#include** statement for the **OrderView.h** file to beginning of the **MainFrm.cpp** file, so that the **COrderView** class definition is available here. Once you have saved **MainFrm.cpp**, we can move on to adding a button control to the **Products** dialog to link to the **Orders** dialog, and adding handlers for this button and its partner on the **Orders** dialog to call the **SelectView()** member of **CMainFrame**.

Enabling the Switching Operation

To implement the view switching mechanism, go back to ResourceView and open the **IDD_DBSAMPLE_FORM** dialog. You need to add a button control to the dialog, as shown here:

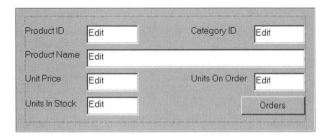

You can set the ID for the button to **IDC_ORDERS**, consistent with the naming for the other controls in the dialog.

After saving the resource, you can create a handler for the button by double-clicking it while holding down the *Ctrl* key. ClassWizard will add the function **OnOrders()** to the **CProductView** class, and this handler will be called when the button is clicked. You only need to add one line of code to complete the handler:

```
void CProductView::OnOrders()
{
    ((CMainFrame*)GetParentFrame())->SelectView(ORDER_VIEW);
}
```

The **GetParentFrame()** member of the view object is inherited from **CWnd**, which is an indirect base class of **CMainFrame**. This function returns a pointer to the parent frame window and we use it to call the **SelectView()** function that we've just added to the **CMainFrame** class. The argument **ORDER_VIEW** will cause the frame window to switch to the **Orders** dialog window. If this is the first time this has occurred, it will create the view object and the window. On the second and subsequent occasions that a switch to the orders view is selected, the existing **Orders** view will be reused.

You must add the following **#include** statements to the beginning of the **ProductView.cpp** file:

```
#include "OurConstants.h"
#include "MainFrm.h"
```

The next task is to add the handler for the button we previously placed on the **IDD_ORDERS_FORM** dialog. Double-click the button with the *Ctrl* key pressed, as before, and add the following code to the **OnProducts()** handler that is generated in the **COrderView** class:

```
void COrderView::OnProducts()
{
    ((CMainFrame*)GetParentFrame())->SelectView(PRODUCT_VIEW);
}
```

This works in the same way as the previous button control handler. Again, you must add **#include** statements for the **OurConstants.h** and **MainFrm.h** files to the beginning of the **.cpp** file, and then save it.

Handling View Activation

When we switch to a view that already exists, we need to ensure that the recordset is refreshed and that the dialog is re-initialized, so that the correct information is displayed. When an existing view is activated or deactivated, the framework calls the **OnActivateView()** member of the class. We need to override this function in each of our view classes. You can do this using the Message Maps tab in the ClassWizard dialog. With the class name selected in the Object IDs list box, extend the Messages list box and double click on OnActivateView. You need to add the handler to both view classes.

You can add the following code to complete the implementation of the function:

```
void COrderView::OnActivateView(BOOL bActivate,
                                CView* pActivateView, CView* pDeactiveView)
{
    if(bActivate)
    {
        // Get a pointer to the document
        CDBSampleDoc* pDoc = (CDBSampleDoc*)GetDocument();

        // Get a pointer to the frame window
        CMainFrame* pMFrame = (CMainFrame*)GetParentFrame();

        // If the last view was the product view, we must re-query
        // the recordset with the product ID from the product recordset
        if(pMFrame->m_CurrentViewID==PRODUCT_VIEW)
        {
            if(!m_pSet->IsOpen())      // Make sure the recordset is open
                return;
            // Set current product ID as parameter
            m_pSet->m_ProductIDparam = pDoc->m_productSet.m_ProductID;
            m_pSet->Requery();         // Get data from the DB

            // If we are past the EOF there are no records
            if(m_pSet->IsEOF())
                AfxMessageBox("No orders for the current product ID");
        }

        // Set the window caption
        CString strTitle = _T("Table Name:");
        CString strTable = m_pSet->GetTableName();
        if(!strTable.IsEmpty())
            strTitle += strTable;
        else
            strTitle += _T("Orders - Multiple Tables");
        pDoc->SetTitle(strTitle);
        CRecordView::OnInitialUpdate();          // Update values in dialog
    }

    CRecordView::OnActivateView(bActivate, pActivateView, pDeactiveView);
}
```

We only execute our code if the view is being activated; if this is the case, the **bActivate** argument will be **TRUE**. After getting pointers to the document and the parent frame, we verify that the previous view was the product view, before re-querying the order set. This check isn't necessary at present, since the previous view is always the product view, but if and when we add another view to our application, this will not always be true, so we might as well put the code in now.

To requery the database, we set the parameter member of **COrderSet**, **m_ProductIDparam**, to the current value of the **m_ProductID** member of the product recordset. This will cause the orders for the current product to be selected. We don't need to set the **m_strFilter** member of the recordset here because that will have been set in the **OnInitialUpdate()** function when the **CRecordView** object was first created. The **IsEOF()** function member of the **COrderSet** object is inherited from **CRecordSet** and will return **TRUE** if the recordset is empty when it is requeried.

You now need to add the **OnActivateView()** function to the **CProductView** class as well, and code it as follows:

```
void CProductView::OnActivateView(BOOL bActivate,
                                  CView* pActivateView, CView* pDeactiveView)
{
    if(bActivate)
    {
        // Update the window caption
        CString strTitle = _T("Table Name");
        CString strTable = m_pSet->GetTableName();
        strTitle += _T(":") + strTable;
        GetDocument()->SetTitle(strTitle);
    }
    CRecordView::OnActivateView(bActivate, pActivateView, pDeactiveView);
}
```

In this case, all we need to do if the view has been activated is to update the window caption. Since the product view is the driving view for the rest of the application, we always want to return the view to its state before it was deactivated. If we do nothing apart from updating the window caption, the view will be displayed in its previous state.

Viewing Orders for a Product

You are now ready to try to build the executable module for the new version of the example. When you run the example, you should be able to see the orders for any product just by clicking the Orders button on the products dialog. A typical view of an order is shown here:

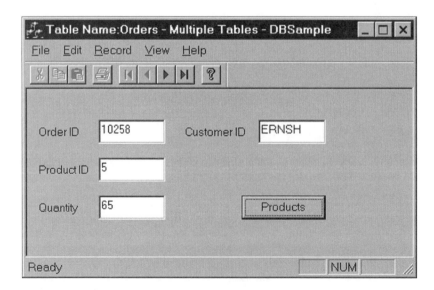

Clicking the Products button will return you to the products dialog, so you can browse further through the products. In this dialog, you can use the toolbar buttons to browse all the orders for the current product.

The Customer ID is a bit cryptic. We could add one more view to display the details of the customer's name and address. It won't be too difficult because we've built the mechanism to switch between views already.

Viewing Customer Details

The basic mechanism that we'll add will work through another button control on the order dialog, which will switch to a new dialog for customer data. As well as controls to display customer data, we'll add two buttons to the customer dialog: one to return to the order view, and the other to return to the product view. We'll need another view ID corresponding to the customer view, which we can add with the following line in the **OurConstants.h** file:

```
const UINT CUSTOMER_VIEW = 3U;
```

Let's now add the recordset for the customer details.

Adding the Customer Recordset

The process is exactly the same as we followed for the **COrderSet** class. You use the Add Class... button in ClassWizard to define the **CCustomerSet** class, with **CRecordSet** specified as the base class. You select the database as Sample Data, as before, and select the Customers table for the recordset. The class should then be created with the data members shown here:

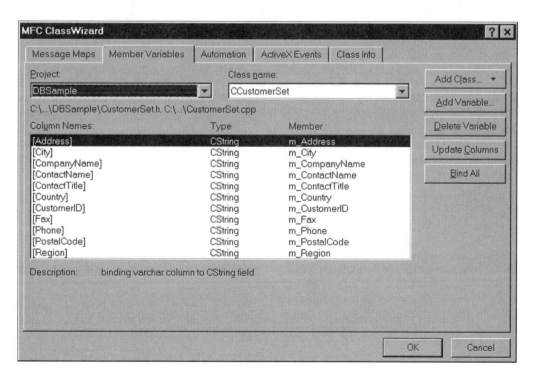

You can click on the OK button to store the class. At this point, you could add a **CCustomerSet** member to the document so that it will be created when the document object is created. Right-click on the **CDBSampleDoc** class name in ClassView and add a variable of type **CCustomerSet** with the name **m_CustomerSet**. You can leave the access specifier as **public**.

You will find that ClassView has already added an **#include** directive for **CustomerSet.h** into **DBSampleDoc.h**. After saving all the files you have modified, you can move next to creating the customer dialog resource.

Creating the Customer Dialog Resource

This process is also exactly the same as the one you went through for the orders dialog. Change to ResourceView and create a new dialog resource with the ID **IDD_CUSTOMER_FORM**, not forgetting to set the style to Child and the border to None in the Properties box for the dialog. After deleting the default buttons, add controls to the dialog to correspond to the field names for the **Customers** table, as shown here:

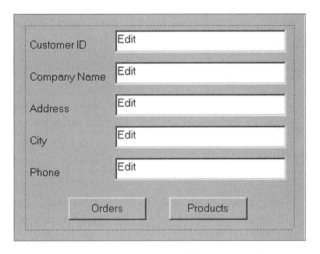

The two buttons enable you to switch to either the Orders dialog, which will be how you got here, or directly back to the Products dialog.

Specify the IDs for the controls, using the field names as a basis. You can get help with this by expanding the list of members of **CCustomerSet** in ClassView and keeping that visible while you work on the dialog. You can set the button IDs as **IDC_ORDERS** and **IDC_PRODUCTS**. Remember to check the tab order is as required and then save the dialog resource. Now we're ready to create the view class for the recordset.

Creating the Customer View Class

Right-click the dialog and select Class<u>W</u>izard... from the pop-up. Create a new class based on **CRecordView** with the name **CCustomerView**, and select the **IDD_CUSTOMER_FORM** as the ID for the dialog to be associated with the class. ClassWizard should automatically choose **CCustomerSet** as the recordset for the view class. Complete the process and click on OK in ClassWizard. You can then associate the edit controls with variables in the recordset.

To tie the controls to the recordset data members, double-click on each edit control in turn with the *Ctrl* key held down. If the tab order for the controls is correct, all the variables should be selected automatically.

You can also process the button controls in the same way to add the **OnOrders()** and **OnProducts()** functions to the class. The code for these is very similar to the corresponding functions in the other views. The code you need to add to **OnOrders()** is:

```
void CCustomerView::OnOrders()
{
   ((CMainFrame*)GetParentFrame())->SelectView(ORDER_VIEW);
}
```

You can add a similar line of code to the **OnProducts()** function:

```
void CCustomerView::OnProducts()
{
   ((CMainFrame*)GetParentFrame())->SelectView(PRODUCT_VIEW);
}
```

Once again, the destructor for **CCustomerView** will contain code to delete the object pointed to by **m_pSet**, as follows:

```
CCustomerView::~CCustomerView()
{
   if (m_pSet)
      delete m_pSet;
}
```

Delete the highlighted lines, since the framework will delete the record set object without our intervention.

We now need to add code to specify a filter for the customer recordset so that we only get the customer details displayed that correspond to the customer ID field from the current order in the **COrderSet** object.

Adding a Filter

We can define the filter in the **OnInitialUpdate()** member of **CCustomerView**. Since we only anticipate one record being returned corresponding to each customer ID, we don't need to worry about sorting. The code you need to add to this function is as follows:

```
void CCustomerView::OnInitialUpdate()
{
   BeginWaitCursor();

   CDBSampleDoc* pDoc = (CDBSampleDoc*)GetDocument();
   m_pSet = &pDoc->m_CustomerSet;       // Initialize the recordset pointer

   // Set the DB for the customer recordset
   m_pSet->m_pDatabase = pDoc->m_productSet.m_pDatabase;

   // Set the current customer ID as the filter parameter value
   m_pSet->m_CustomerIDparam = pDoc->m_OrderSet.m_CustomerID;
   m_pSet->m_strFilter ="CustomerID = ?";    // Filter on CustomerID field

   GetRecordset();
   CRecordView::OnInitialUpdate();
   if (m_pSet->IsOpen())
   {
      CString strTitle = m_pSet->m_pDatabase->GetDatabaseName();
      CString strTable = m_pSet->GetTableName();
      if (!strTable.IsEmpty())
         strTitle += _T(":") + strTable;
```

```
        GetDocument()->SetTitle(strTitle);
    }
    EndWaitCursor();
}
```

After getting a pointer to the document, we store the address of the **CCustomerSet** object member of the document in the **m_pSet** member of the view. We know the database is already open, so we can set the database pointer in the customer recordset to that stored in the **CProductSet** object.

The parameter for the filter will be defined in the **m_CustomerIDparam** member of **CCustomerSet**. We'll add this member to the class in a moment. It's set to the current value of the **m_CustomerID** member of the **COrderSet** object owned by the document. The filter is defined in such a way that the customer recordset will only contain the record with the same customer ID as that in the current order.

To handle activation of the customer view, you must add the **OnActivateView()** function using ClassWizard, as before. You can implement it as follows:

```
void CCustomerView::OnActivateView(BOOL bActivate,
                                    CView* pActivateView, CView* pDeactiveView)
{
    if(bActivate)
    {
        if(!m_pSet->IsOpen())
            return;
        CDBSampleDoc* pDoc = (CDBSampleDoc*)GetDocument();

        // Set current customer ID as parameter
        m_pSet->m_CustomerIDparam = pDoc->m_OrderSet.m_CustomerID;
        m_pSet->Requery();                 // Get data from the DB
        CRecordView::OnInitialUpdate();    // Redraw the dialog

        // Check for empty recordset
        if(m_pSet->IsEOF())
            AfxMessageBox("No customer details for the current customer ID");

        CString strTitle = _T("Table Name:");
        CString strTable = m_pSet->GetTableName();
        if (!strTable.IsEmpty())
            strTitle += strTable;
        else
            strTitle += _T("Multiple Tables");
        pDoc->SetTitle(strTitle);
    }
    CRecordView::OnActivateView(bActivate, pActivateView, pDeactiveView);
}
```

If this function is called because the view has been activated (rather than deactivated), **bActivate** will have the value **TRUE**. In this case, we set the filter parameter from the order recordset and re-query the database.

The **m_CustomerIDparam** member for the **CCustomerSet** recordset object that's associated with this view object is set to the customer ID from the orders recordset object that's stored in the document. This will be the customer ID for the current order. The call to the **Requery()**

function for the **CCustomerSet** object will retrieve records from the database using the filter we've set up. The result will be that the details for the customer for the current order will be stored in the **CCustomerSet** object, and then passed to the **CCustomerView** object for display in the dialog.

You will need to add the following **#include** statements to the beginning of the **CustomerView.cpp** file:

```
#include "ProductSet.h"
#include "OrderSet.h"
#include "CustomerSet.h"
#include "DBSampleDoc.h"
#include "OurConstants.h"
#include "MainFrm.h"
```

The first three are required because of classes used in the definition of the document class. We need **DBSampleDoc.h** because of the **CDBSampleDoc** class reference in **OnInitialUpdate()**, and the remaining two **.h** files contains definitions that are referred to in the button handlers in the **CCustomerView** class.

At this point, you can save the current file and return to the definition of the **CCustomerView** class. Delete the full path from **#include** that has been added to the **.h** file for **CustomerSet.h**. You'll also need to change the constructor from **protected** access specification to **public** because we need to be able to create a customer view object in the **SelectView()** member of **CMainFrame**.

Implementing the Filter Parameter

Add a **public** variable of type **CString** to the **CCustomerSet** class to correspond with the type of the **m_CustomerID** member of the recordset, and give it the name **m_CustomerIDparam**. You can initialize this in the constructor and set the parameter count as follows:

```
CCustomerSet::CCustomerSet(CDatabase* pdb) : CRecordset(pdb)
{
   //{{AFX_FIELD_INIT(CCustomerSet)
   m_CustomerID = _T("");
   m_CompanyName = _T("");
   m_ContactName = _T("");
   m_ContactTitle = _T("");
   m_Address = _T("");
   m_City = _T("");
   m_Region = _T("");
   m_PostalCode = _T("");
   m_Country = _T("");
   m_Phone = _T("");
   m_Fax = _T("");
   m_nFields = 11;
   //}}AFX_FIELD_INIT
   m_CustomerIDparam = _T("");      // Initial customer ID parameter
   m_nParams = 1;                   // Number of parameters
   m_nDefaultType = snapshot;
}
```

ClassWizard uses the comments containing **AFX_FIELD_INIT** as markers for updating the constructor when data members for table fields are added or deleted, so we add our initialization code outside that block. We set the parameter to an empty string and the parameter count in **m_nParams** to 1.

To set up the parameter, you add statements to the **DoFieldExchange()** member, as before:

```
void CCustomerSet::DoFieldExchange(CFieldExchange* pFX)
{
   //{{AFX_FIELD_MAP(CCustomerSet)
   pFX->SetFieldType(CFieldExchange::outputColumn);
   RFX_Text(pFX, _T("[CustomerID]"), m_CustomerID);
   RFX_Text(pFX, _T("[CompanyName]"), m_CompanyName);
   RFX_Text(pFX, _T("[ContactName]"), m_ContactName);
   RFX_Text(pFX, _T("[ContactTitle]"), m_ContactTitle);
   RFX_Text(pFX, _T("[Address]"), m_Address);
   RFX_Text(pFX, _T("[City]"), m_City);
   RFX_Text(pFX, _T("[Region]"), m_Region);
   RFX_Text(pFX, _T("[PostalCode]"), m_PostalCode);
   RFX_Text(pFX, _T("[Country]"), m_Country);
   RFX_Text(pFX, _T("[Phone]"), m_Phone);
   RFX_Text(pFX, _T("[Fax]"), m_Fax);
   //}}AFX_FIELD_MAP
   pFX->SetFieldType(CFieldExchange::param);      // Set parameter mode
   RFX_Text(pFX, _T("CustomerIDParam"), m_CustomerIDparam);
}
```

After setting the **param** mode by calling the **SetFieldType()** member of the **pFX** object, we call the **RFX_Text()** function to pass the parameter value for substitution in the filter. We use **RFX_Text()** because the parameter variable is of type **CString**. There are various **RFX_()** functions supporting a range of parameter types.

Once you've completed this modification, you can save the **CustomerSet.cpp** file.

Linking the Order Dialog to the Customer Dialog

To permit a switch to the customer dialog, we require a button control on the **IDD_ORDERS_FORM** dialog, so open it in ResourceView and add an extra button, as shown here:

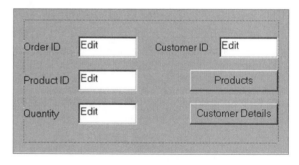

You can define the ID for the new button control as **IDC_CUSTOMER**. After you save the dialog, you can add a handler for the button by double-clicking on it while keeping the *Ctrl* key pressed. The handler only requires one line of code to be added to it, as follows:

```
void COrderView::OnCustomer()
{
    ((CMainFrame*)GetParentFrame())->SelectView(CUSTOMER_VIEW);
}
```

This obtains the address of the frame window and uses it to call the **SelectView()** member of **CMainFrame** to switch to a customer view. The final step to complete the program is to add the code to the **SelectView()** function that will deal with the **CUSTOMER_VIEW** value being passed to it. This requires just three additional lines of code, as follows:

```
void CMainFrame::SelectView(UINT ViewID)
{
   CView* pOldActiveView = GetActiveView();       // Get current view

   // Get pointer to new view if it exists
   // if it doesn't the pointer will be null
   CView* pNewActiveView = (CView*)GetDlgItem(ViewID);

   // If this is 1st time around for the new view,
   // the new view won't exist, so we must create it
   if (pNewActiveView == NULL)
   {
      switch(ViewID)
      {
         case ORDER_VIEW:       // Create an Order view
            pNewActiveView = (CView*)new COrderView;
            break;
         case CUSTOMER_VIEW:    // Create a customer view
            pNewActiveView = (CView*)new CCustomerView;
            break;
         default:
            AfxMessageBox("Invalid View ID");
            return;
      }

      CCreateContext context;
      context.m_pCurrentDoc = pOldActiveView->GetDocument();
      pNewActiveView->Create(NULL, NULL, 0L, CFrameWnd::rectDefault,
                                          this, ViewID, &context);
      pNewActiveView->OnInitialUpdate();
   }
   SetActiveView(pNewActiveView);                     // Activate the new view
   pNewActiveView->ShowWindow(SW_SHOW);               // Hide the old view
   pOldActiveView->ShowWindow(SW_HIDE);               // Show the new view
   pOldActiveView->SetDlgCtrlID(m_CurrentViewID); // Set the old view ID
   pNewActiveView->SetDlgCtrlID(AFX_IDW_PANE_FIRST);
   m_CurrentViewID = ViewID;                          // Save the new view ID
   RecalcLayout();
}
```

The only change necessary is the addition of a **case** statement in the **switch** to create a **CCustomerView** object when one doesn't exist. Each view object will be re-used next time around, so they only get created once. The code to switch between views works with any number of views, so if you want this function to handle more views, you just need to add another **case** in the **switch** for each new view that you want. Although we are creating view objects dynamically here, we don't need to worry about deleting them. Because they are associated with a document object, they will be deleted by the framework when the application closes.

Because we reference the **CCustomerView** class in the **SelectView()** function, you must add a **#include** statement for the **CustomerView.h** file to the block at the beginning of **MainFrm.cpp**.

Exercising the Database Viewer

At this point, the program is complete. You can build the application and execute it. As before, the main view of the database is the products view. Clicking on Orders will, as before, take you to the orders view. The second button on this form should now be active, and clicking on it takes you to the details of the customer:

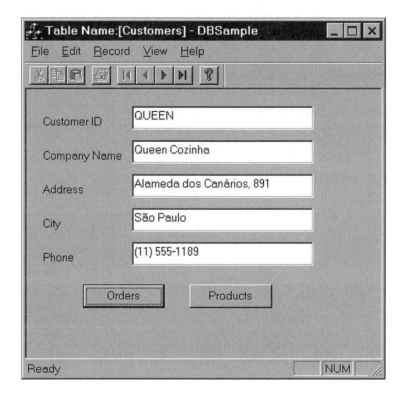

The two buttons take you back to the Orders view or the Products view respectively.

Summary

You should now be comfortable with the basics of how MFC links to your database. The fundamentals of the recordset and the record view are the same, whether you use the DAO or the ODBC classes. Although we haven't covered adding records to tables or deleting them in our example, you should have little difficulty implementing this as the recordset already has the functions you need built-in.

The key points we've seen in this chapter are:

▶ MFC provides DAO and ODBC support for accessing databases.

▶ To use a database with ODBC the database must be registered.

▶ A connection to a database is represented by a **CDatabase** or a **CDaoDatabase** object.

▶ A recordset object represents an SQL **SELECT** statement applied to a defined set of tables. Where necessary, the framework will automatically create a database object representing a connection to a database when a recordset object is created.

▶ A **WHERE** clause can be added for a recordset object through its **m_strFilter** data member.

▶ An **ORDER BY** clause can be defined for a recordset through its **m_strSort** data member.

▶ A record view object is used to display the contents of a recordset object.

Exercises

Ex10-1: Using the **Products** table again, add a 'stock control' dialog to the application. This should be reachable through a button on the products dialog, and must itself contain a button to go back to the products dialog. The fields it should display are the product ID, product name, reorder level, unit price and units in stock. Don't worry about filtering or sorting at the moment; just get the basic mechanism working.

Ex10-2: Refine the above project so that the stock control dialog automatically displays information about the product that was being shown in the products dialog when the button was pressed.

Ex10-3: Implement a system whereby the user of the database is warned in the stock control dialog about the present stock being near or below the reorder level. You'll have noticed by now that some of the stock reorder levels are set to zero; don't display a warning in those cases.

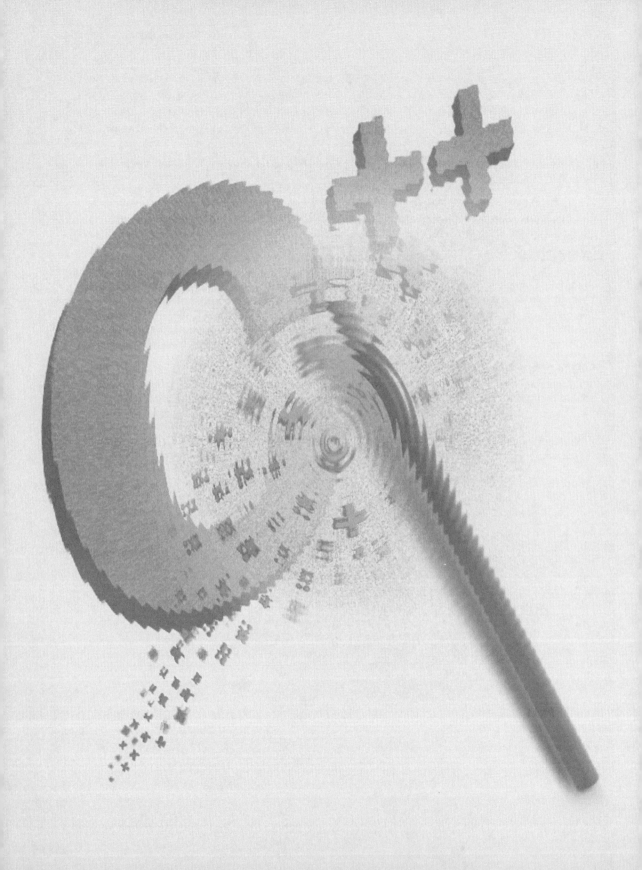

Understanding OLE Documents

OLE is a complex topic which many would argue is out of place in a beginners' programming book. However, because of the advantages it brings, more and more applications are making the most of OLE, so it's important to have a basic understanding of how it works.

There are whole books dedicated to OLE, so we'll only scratch the surface in this chapter. Fortunately, MFC hides most of the complexity, and with the help you get from AppWizard you shouldn't find it difficult to implement some examples that use OLE. By the end of this chapter you will have learnt:

▶ What OLE is and how it can be used

▶ How the OLE mechanism works

▶ What OLE containers and OLE servers are

▶ How to write a simple OLE container using AppWizard

▶ How to write an OLE server using AppWizard

Object Linking and Embedding

Before we launch into writing code, we first need to get the ideas and terminology straight. **Object Linking and Embedding**, perhaps better known as **OLE** (and sometimes pronounced 'olé'), is a mechanism which enables you to write a program—a text editor, say—that will allow other applications to edit data within it that it can't handle itself, like graphics. OLE also allows an application that you write to handle data contained within other applications. This isn't the whole story, but it's what we'll concentrate on.

Once you've allowed your program to contain these data objects, you can have any kind of object you like, and as many of them as you like. This is a pretty incredible capability when you think about it: the program hosting these alien objects has no knowledge of what they are, but you can still edit and manipulate them as though they were handled by the same program. In fact, there's a different program involved for each type of alien object you're working with.

An object from one program can appear in another in two different ways. An object from an external document can be **linked** to the document of another program, in which case the external object isn't stored as part of the document for the current program, but just as a reference allowing it to be retrieved from wherever it is. Alternatively, an external document can be **embedded** in the current document, in which case it's actually stored within it. A document that contains an embedded or linked OLE object is called a **compound document**.

A linked object has the advantage that it can be modified independently of the compound document, so that when you open a document containing a linked object, the latest version of the object will automatically be incorporated. However, if you delete the file containing the linked object, or even move it to another folder, the compound document will not know about this and won't be able to find the linked object. With an embedded object, the object only exists in the context of the compound document and is, therefore, not independently accessible. The compound document with all its embedded OLE objects is a single file, so there's no possibility of the embedded objects getting lost. These provisions aside, to the user there appears to be no difference between the appearances of the compound documents.

Containers and Servers

Clearly, to enable OLE to work, a program must contain special code supporting this sort of functionality. A program that can handle embedded objects is called an **OLE container** and a program that creates objects that can be embedded in an OLE container is referred to as an **OLE server**. OLE servers also come in two flavors. A **full server** can operate as an independent program, or just servicing an object embedded in a compound document. A **mini-server** can't operate in stand-alone mode—its sole function is to support objects in a compound document.

It's possible for an application to be both an OLE server and an OLE container. The AppWizard can generate programs which have OLE container and/or OLE server functionality built in. All you have to do is to choose the appropriate options when creating an OLE project.

Compound Documents

A compound document is illustrated here:

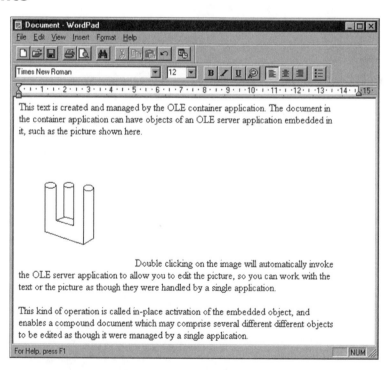

When you work with an embedded object in a program, the code for the application that generated the embedded object can be automatically invoked to allow you to edit the object in the container application window. This is referred to as **in-place activation**. With an OLE server that supports in-place activation, you can edit an embedded object in an OLE container application just by double-clicking it. The menus and toolbars for the container application will then change to incorporate those required to use the server application to edit the object. More than that, if there are several different embedded objects, the menus and toolbars in the container will change to incorporate the menus and toolbars for whatever embedded object you're working with, all completely automatically.

With in-place activation, the appearance of the compound document comprising the natively-supported object and the embedded object or objects is seamless, and generally hides the fact that several different programs may be involved in manipulating what you see in the application window.

If an OLE server doesn't support in-place activation, double-clicking the embedded object will open a separate window for the server application, allowing you to edit the embedded object. When you've finished editing the embedded object, you only need to close the server application window to resume work with the container application. Obviously, in-place activation is a much more attractive way of handling compound documents, as it appears to the user as a single application. Most containers also allow you to edit an embedded object in a server window, even when the server does support in-place activation. Double-clicking an object while holding down the *Ctrl* or the *Alt* key often initiates this mode of server operation. In-place activation is only possible with embedded, not linked, items.

Activating an Embedded Object

Once an object has been embedded in a container, the server supporting it can be in two basic states. When the server has been activated in-place for editing, the object is shown with a shaded border in the client area of the container. If you click once outside the object, the server will be deactivated and the shaded border will not be displayed. You can see both of these states in the following screen:

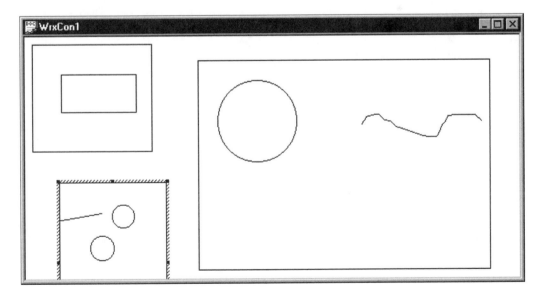

There are three embedded objects here. Only the object at the bottom left is in-place activated, and in fact only one object can be in this state at a time. The user interface is under the control of the server. The other two embedded objects are inactive, and no communication between the container and server is necessary for them. To change an inactive object to the fully in-place activated state, you just double-click on it. With the fully activated object, the server will advise the container each time the area occupied by the embedded object needs to be redrawn. This could be because the contents have changed, or because a larger area is required.

If you *single*-click on an inactive object, the appearance of the object will be as for an inactive object but with resize handles on the borders. In this situation, you can't edit the object, but you can resize the area it occupies by dragging the border. You can also move the object around in the client area. The container signals the server whenever the contents of the object need to be redrawn because of changes to the size or position of the area occupied by the embedded object.

How Does OLE Work?

The communications between an OLE server application for an embedded object and the OLE container application are concerned primarily with the area occupied by the object, when it needs to be redrawn, and the resources the server needs to make available in the container for editing, such as menus and toolbars. The container has no knowledge of what is to be displayed by the server. All it knows is that an area in its view is going to be used by the server and the server is going to sort out what needs to be displayed. Neither does the container know which menus or toolbars are required to use the server—all it does is provide space for them within its own menus and toolbars. It's a bit like the owner of a market hall renting a stall to someone. The person who runs the stall does what they want, within an agreed set of rules. The owner doesn't get involved in what goes on at the stall or what they sell. As long as the rent is paid and the rules are obeyed, everybody's happy.

As you've probably guessed, the communication between an OLE container and the servers supporting the embedded objects uses the Windows operating system as a go-between. Each OLE program uses a common OLE DLL which is part of Windows, and the functions in the DLL provide the means of passing information between them. Thus, the key to the operation of OLE is a **standard interface**. The standard interface that enables OLE to work is specified by the **Component Object Model**, or **COM**. This is essentially a definition of the appearance of an embedded object and how a container communicates with it. COM is a big topic, and we won't be delving into the detail. We'll just be looking close enough to understand the ideas involved.

The OLE Component Object Model

The Component Object Model has sets of standard functions that are used for OLE communications, packaged in named groups called **interfaces**. This is analogous to a C++ class which defines an interface through its **public** function members. A complete discussion of COM is far beyond the scope of this book, but its operation is hidden in the framework that we get with an AppWizard-generated program, so you won't need to deal with the details. However, we'll look far enough into it to give you a feel for what's happening when we implement an OLE container and a server later in this chapter.

For a COM object such as an OLE server, at least one interface (or group of functions), called **IUnknown**, is always implemented. The **IUnknown** interface contains three standard functions:

Interface names usually start with 'I', just as class names usually begin with 'C'.

Function	Usage
`QueryInterface()`	Tests whether a particular interface is supported by the object. If an interface that is queried is supported, a pointer to it is returned. The calling function can then access the functions in the queried interface through the pointer.
`AddRef()`	Increments a count of the number of clients using the interface. This count enables the object owning the interface to know when it is no longer required.
`Release()`	Decrements the count of the number of clients using the interface. When the count is zero, the object knows that it is no longer in use and can remove itself from memory.

You can do almost anything with these three functions. Since the `QueryInterface()` function allows you to ask about other interfaces, you can access any interface that an object supports, as long as you know about it. OLE defines a set of standard interfaces, each identified by an **interface ID**, or **IID**, which is passed as an argument in the `QueryInterface()` call. It's also possible to define your own custom interfaces which will also need to be identified by a unique IID. We won't need to look into the detail of these interface functions, since for the most part MFC takes care of using them.

`IUnknown` is by no means all there is to the component object model. There are several other interfaces involved, concerned with transferring data, managing memory and so on, but we can create a container and a server without knowing any more about COM, so let's press on.

The Registry

In order to use an OLE server, it must be identified in some way. When you run an OLE container, you wouldn't want to be just rummaging around your hard disk to see if any of the applications on your PC might support OLE, so how are OLE programs identified?

An **OLE object** can be a program, a document type, or indeed any kind of object that supports OLE. Each OLE object in your system is identified by a unique 128-bit numeric value, called a **class ID** or **CLSID**. CLSIDs and IIDs are in turn particular types of **globally unique ID**s, or **GUID**s. The IDs are called 'globally unique' because they are generated by an algorithm that ensures within reason that they are unique throughout the world. Information about every OLE object in your system, including its CLSID, is stored on your hard disk in a database called the **system registry**.

You can look at the registry by executing the program **Regedit.exe**. A typical window is shown here:

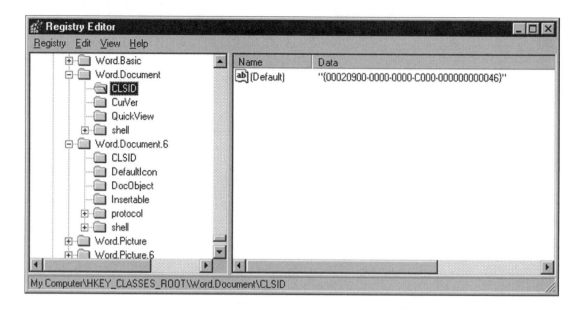

It's not advisable to start messing around with the values in the registry, as you can very quickly render Windows unusable. The registry is definitely a case for looking with your eyes and not your hands!

This shows the Word.Document entry for the word processing package, Microsoft Word, and its class ID. You can see that there is also a key (it looks like a folder) for Word.Picture, which represents a different document type. Because it is also an OLE object, this also has its own CLSID. An OLE server can't be used until it has been entered in the system registry with all the information necessary to identify it.

MFC Classes Supporting OLE

MFC has a set of classes that represent OLE objects, as well as classes that represent documents that can contain OLE objects. The relationships between these classes are illustrated here:

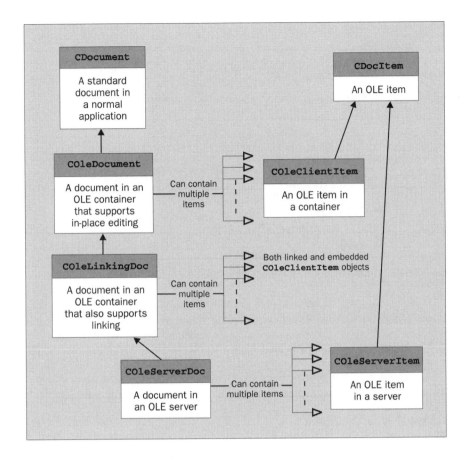

The arrows in the diagram point from a derived class towards a base class, so the **COleServerDoc** class, for example, inherits the functionality of its base class **COleLinkingDoc**, as well as its indirect base classes, which are **CDocument** and **COleDocument**.

OLE Object Classes

The two classes that are shown derived from the class **CDocItem**, **COleClientItem** and **COleServerItem**, represent different perspectives of an OLE object corresponding to the points of view of a container and a server respectively, as shown here:

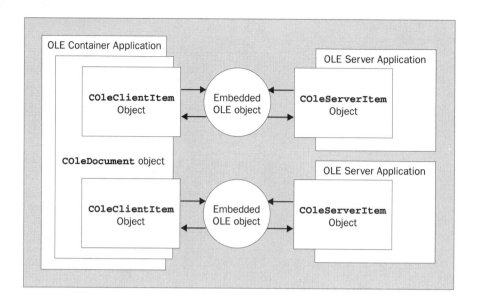

This shows two different OLE objects embedded in a container application. The class objects in the container corresponding to the embedded objects will both be included in the container document object. Each embedded object will have its own server application, and each server will have a **COleServerItem** object corresponding to the object in the container for which it is responsible. This is a simplified representation, since the OLE DLL is involved in the communications.

An Embedded Object in a Container

The class **COleClientItem** provides the interfaces required by a container to manage an embedded item. This involves a large number of functions which enable the object to be queried and manipulated, as well as functions which enable communications between the container and the server. The most important of these are the ones you will need to implement, which are as follows:

Function to implement	Usage
OnChange()	This function is called by the framework when a change to an embedded item is signaled by the item's server. The typical action is to invalidate the embedded object to get it redrawn in the container.
OnGetItemPosition()	This function is called by the framework to obtain the rectangle in the client area of the container where the OLE object is to be displayed.
OnChangeItemPosition()	This function is called by the framework to indicate to the container that the extent of the embedded object has changed during editing.
Serialize()	If you add any members to the object in the container, you will need to serialize them in this function.

The drawing of an embedded object and any modifications made by the user is carried out by the server, but the object is displayed in an area in a window that is owned and managed by the container. Thus, the communications between the container and the server are fundamental to proper OLE operation.

An Embedded Object in a Server

An OLE object embedded in a server application is represented by an object of the class **COleServerItem** in the server. The interface supporting a server in **COleServerItem** also involves a large number of functions, but the most important of these are:

Function to implement	Usage
OnDraw()	This function is responsible for drawing the embedded object in the container when it's not being edited, so it's essential to implement it. When the object is in-place active, the object is drawn by the **OnDraw()** function in the server's view class. Drawing in the container has to be done by the server because the container has no knowledge of the internals of the embedded object. When the server runs stand-alone, the **OnDraw()** function in the view object is of course also responsible for drawing the object in the normal way.
Serialize()	This function is responsible for serializing the embedded object when required to do so by the container. This is usually implemented by calling the **Serialize()** function for the document object in the server.
OnGetExtent()	This function is called by the framework to get the actual extent of the embedded object. This is communicated to the container application.
NotifyChanged()	This function is called by the server application when it changes the embedded object. This signals the change to the framework which will call the **OnChange()** function in the corresponding **COleClientItem** object in the container.

OLE Document Classes

Specialized document classes are necessary for OLE applications because the documents must include the ability to deal with the added complexity of OLE objects. There are two document classes that are used in OLE container applications: **COleDocument** and **COleLinkingDoc**. **COleDocument** supports embedded objects that are edited in-place by a server. It represents the embedded objects as instances of a class derived from **COleClientItem**. The class **COleLinkingDoc** is derived from **COleDocument** and adds support for linked objects that are stored separately from the container document. The document class in a container application is typically derived from either **COleDocument** or **COleLinkingDoc**. The container example that we'll implement later in this chapter will use the **COleDocument** class as a base.

A document in a server application is derived from the class **COleServerDoc**. When the server is supporting an embedded object, the OLE object is represented by a class derived from the **COleServerItem** class that we saw earlier. Of course, a server document will only include one instance of this class, which will represent the whole document when it is embedded in a container document.

A document class for an OLE server must implement the member **OnGetEmbeddedItem()**, because this is a pure virtual function in the **COleServerDoc** class. If you don't implement it, your code won't compile. This function is called by the framework to get a pointer to the OLE object supported by the server and is used by the framework to call function members of the object.

Implementing an OLE Container

AppWizard makes it very easy to create an OLE container application, so let's try it out. Create a new project of type MFC AppWizard (exe). You could call it something meaningful, like WrxContainer. Select the OK button to create it, then click on the Next > button to accept the default MDI implementation, and another Next > without electing for database support. The next step is shown here:

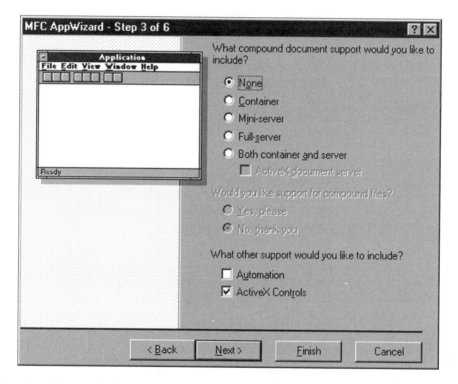

Select the Container radio button here to generate an OLE container. When you click on this, the option for compound files will be activated and selected automatically. The other options on this dialog are all the variations on a server that we referred to earlier: the Mini-server is just a server that can't be used independently of a container; the Full-server can operate as a stand-alone application or as a server to a container. We'll implement a full server a little later in this chapter. The third possibility, Both container and server, generates a program that can run stand-alone, can run as a server and can itself act as a container for other embedded objects. This raises the possibility of an embedded object containing embedded objects.

The other two options, Automation and ActiveX Controls, provide additional levels of functionality. Automation adds a programmable interface to your application so that other applications which have provision for doing so can make use of functions within your application. Selecting ActiveX Controls adds the capability for your program to incorporate and use ActiveX controls. We'll be looking at creating an ActiveX control in the next chapter.

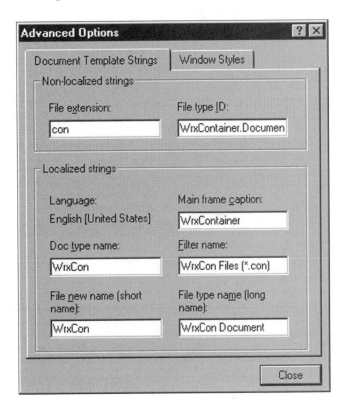

Click on Next > to go to Step 4 and select the Advanced... button. Change the File extension field to con as shown (the Filter name field will adjust automatically).

The entry in the File type ID: box, WrxContainer.Document, will appear in the registry.

The only other change to make is on Step 6 when you get to the list of classes that AppWizard plans to generate. Select the class CWrxContainerCntrItem, and shorten it to CWrxContainerItem, and also change the names of the files that this class will live in to WrxContainerItem.h and WrxContainerItem.cpp. This is just for our convenience. You can then proceed to the end and generate the program.

If you look at the classes in the program by selecting the ClassView tab, you'll see that we have the standard set of classes supporting the MFC document/view architecture. If you look at the definition of **CWrxContainerApp**, you'll see that it is perfectly standard. The differences really start to become apparent in the initialization of the application object.

Initializing a Container Application

The initialization is done in the **InitInstance()** member of the application class **CWrxContainerApp**. The code generated for it by AppWizard is as follows:

```
BOOL CWrxContainerApp::InitInstance()
{
    // Initialize OLE libraries
    if (!AfxOleInit())
    {
        AfxMessageBox(IDP_OLE_INIT_FAILED);
        return FALSE;
    }

    AfxEnableControlContainer();

    // Standard initialization
    // If you are not using these features and wish to reduce the size
    //  of your final executable, you should remove from the following
    //  the specific initialization routines you do not need.

#ifdef _AFXDLL
    Enable3dControls();           // Call this when using MFC in a shared DLL
#else
    Enable3dControlsStatic();   // Call this when linking to MFC statically
#endif

    // Change the registry key under which our settings are stored.
    // You should modify this string to be something appropriate
    // such as the name of your company or organization.
    SetRegistryKey(_T("Local AppWizard-Generated Applications"));

    LoadStdProfileSettings();  // Load standard INI file options (including MRU)

    // Register the application's document templates.  Document templates
    //  serve as the connection between documents, frame windows and views.

    CMultiDocTemplate* pDocTemplate;
    pDocTemplate = new CMultiDocTemplate(
        IDR_WRXCONTYPE,
        RUNTIME_CLASS(CWrxContainerDoc),
        RUNTIME_CLASS(CChildFrame), // custom MDI child frame
        RUNTIME_CLASS(CWrxContainerView));
    pDocTemplate->SetContainerInfo(IDR_WRXCONTYPE_CNTR_IP);
    AddDocTemplate(pDocTemplate);

    // The rest of the function definition is
    //  is as in a normal application that we have seen before...

}
```

This time we've used shading to highlight the differences between this code and that generated in a standard application. We'll just discuss these differences. The call to the global function **AfxOleInit()** initializes the system DLL that supports OLE operations. This establishes the links between the application and the DLL. If the initialization fails for some reason, perhaps because the version of the DLL required by the application is not installed, a message will be displayed and the container will terminate.

The call to the member function **SetContainerInfo()** of the document template object transfers the ID of the menu to be used when an OLE object is embedded and in-place active. The container has three different menu resources that are shown in the diagram below:

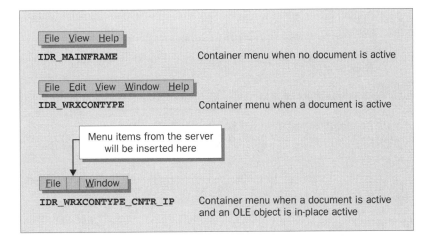

The menu corresponding to the ID passed to the **SetContainerInfo()** function has separator bars to identify where the menu items supplied by the server are to be inserted. The additional menu items are inserted automatically by the framework when the embedded object is active. We'll look at the specific menu items that are inserted when we implement an OLE server, but it is essentially the set required to interact with the in-place object.

The CWrxContainerItem Class

Another differentiating feature of our container application is the class **CWrxContainerItem**, which is derived from **COleClientItem**. As we have seen, an object of this class refers to an embedded OLE object which is supported by a server application. When you introduce an object into the container application, a **CWrxContainerItem** object is constructed and will only be destroyed when the container document is closed or the embedded item it corresponds to is deleted from the container. When a **CWrxContainerItem** is constructed, the constructor requires a pointer to the container's document object, so that the object being constructed is associated with the container document. The definition of the class provided by AppWizard is:

```
class CWrxContainerItem : public COleClientItem
{
  DECLARE_SERIAL(CWrxContainerItem)

// Constructors
public:
  CWrxContainerItem(CWrxContainerDoc* pContainer = NULL);
    // Note: pContainer is allowed to be NULL to enable IMPLEMENT_SERIALIZE.
    //  IMPLEMENT_SERIALIZE requires the class have a constructor with
    //  zero arguments.  Normally, OLE items are constructed with a
    //  non-NULL document pointer.

// Attributes
public:
  CWrxContainerDoc* GetDocument()
    { return (CWrxContainerDoc*)COleClientItem::GetDocument(); }
  CWrxContainerView* GetActiveView()
    { return (CWrxContainerView*)COleClientItem::GetActiveView(); }
```

```
        // ClassWizard generated virtual function overrides
        //{{AFX_VIRTUAL(CWrxContainerItem)
        public:
        virtual void OnChange(OLE_NOTIFICATION wNotification, DWORD dwParam);
        virtual void OnActivate();
        protected:
        virtual void OnGetItemPosition(CRect& rPosition);
        virtual void OnDeactivateUI(BOOL bUndoable);
        virtual BOOL OnChangeItemPosition(const CRect& rectPos);
        //}}AFX_VIRTUAL

   // Implementation
   public:
        ~CWrxContainerItem();
   #ifdef _DEBUG
        virtual void AssertValid() const;
        virtual void Dump(CDumpContext& dc) const;
   #endif
        virtual void Serialize(CArchive& ar);
   };
```

As the note in the code indicates, the constructor will normally be called with a pointer to a container document as an argument. The default value of **NULL** for the parameter is only there because the serialization mechanism requires a default constructor.

One addition to the **CWrxContainerItem** class definition that we can make straight away is a data member to store the rectangle defining the position of the embedded object. Add the following declaration to the **public** section of the class definition:

```
    CRect m_Rect;      // Item position in the document object
```

You can do this by right-clicking the class name in ClassView and selecting Add Member Variable... from the pop-up. Now each item can record where it is in the container document. You should also add initialization for the **m_Rect** member to the constructor:

```
   CWrxContainerItem::CWrxContainerItem(CWrxContainerDoc* pContainer)
     : COleClientItem(pContainer)
   {
       m_Rect.SetRect(10, 10, 100, 100);      // Set initial item position
   }
```

The statement initializes **m_Rect** by calling the **SetRect()** member of the **CRect** class. This sets an arbitrary position which will be overridden when an object is added to the container document. Note that the constructor explicitly calls the base class constructor in the initialization list for our constructor and passes the pointer to the document object to it.

We should also arrange to store and retrieve **m_Rect** by adding the following code to the implementation of the **Serialize()** function for the embedded object:

```
   void CWrxContainerItem::Serialize(CArchive& ar)
   {
       ASSERT_VALID(this);

       // Call base class first to read in COleClientItem data.
       // Since this sets up the m_pDocument pointer returned from
```

```
    //  CWrxContainerItem::GetDocument, it is a good idea to call
    //  the base class Serialize first.
    COleClientItem::Serialize(ar);

    // now store/retrieve data specific to CWrxContainerItem
    if (ar.IsStoring())
    {
        ar << m_Rect;
    }
    else
    {
        ar >> m_Rect;
    }
}
```

The base class **Serialize()** function takes care of everything else, so we don't need to add anything further.

AppWizard has provided an implementation of **GetDocument()** which returns a pointer to the document object, and **GetActiveView()** which returns a pointer to the active view belonging to the document containing the embedded object. The next member function that we're interested in is **OnChange()**, which is called when an embedded object is fully open for editing and is modified in some way.

Reacting to OLE Object Modification

When the server modifies an embedded object, it calls a function to notify the framework that a change has occurred. The framework reacts by calling the **OnChange()** member of the object in the container application. The container owns the window in which the object is displayed, so it's up to the container to do something about the change.

The reason for calling the **OnChange()** function is indicated by the first argument passed, the two arguments being of type **OLE_NOTIFICATION** (**nCode**) and **DWORD** (**dwParam**). We need to deal with two possibilities: when **nCode** has the value **OLE_CHANGED**, which indicates that the object has been modified, and when **nCode** has the value **OLE_CHANGED_STATE**, which indicates the object has changed in some other way. You should add the code for this to the implementation of the **OnChange()** member, as follows:

```
void CWrxContainerItem::OnChange(OLE_NOTIFICATION nCode, DWORD dwParam)
{
    ASSERT_VALID(this);

    COleClientItem::OnChange(nCode, dwParam);

    // When an item is being edited (either in-place or fully open)
    //  it sends OnChange notifications for changes in the state of the
    //  item or visual appearance of its content.

    switch(nCode)
    {
        case OLE_CHANGED:                // Item appearance has been changed
            InvalidateItem();            // Invalidate the current item
            GetServerSize();             // Update to the size from the server
            break;
        case OLE_CHANGED_STATE:          // Item state has changed
```

```
                // Pass a hint to update all views in the document
                InvalidateItem();
                break;
        }
    }
```

Our code replaces the call to **UpdateAllViews()** in the default implementation. We will update selectively, depending on what is happening to the embedded object. Where the value of **nCode** indicates that there was a change to the content of the server, we need to get the object redrawn. We initiate this by calling the function **InvalidateItem()**, which we'll add to the **CWrxContainerItem** class in a moment. We also need to deal with the possibility that the size of the object may be altered by the server, and we may want to record the area it occupies in the **m_Rect** member and resize it in the container document view. This will be done in the second function that we'll add to the **CWrxContainerItem** class, **GetServerSize()**.

The second value of **nCode** reflects a change in state such as occurs when an object is active but not being edited, and the user double-clicks the object in the document view to edit it. In this case, we just need to get the object redrawn by calling the **InvalidateItem()** function. You'll need to add this function, so right-click the CWrxContainerItem class name in ClassView and select the Add Member Function... menu item from the pop-up. Specify the return type as **void** and enter the function name as **InvalidateItem()**. You can leave its access specification as **public**. Click on the OK button, then add the following code to its implementation:

```
void CWrxContainerItem::InvalidateItem()
{
    // Pass a hint to update all views in the document
    GetDocument()->UpdateAllViews(0, HINT_UPDATE_ITEM, this);
}
```

This calls the **UpdateAllViews()** function member of the document object to get all the views redrawn. The second argument value, **HINT_UPDATE_ITEM**, indicates that there is a hint passed in the third argument which is the address of the current object. This will be used when the **OnUpdate()** function in the container document view is called as a consequence of the call to **UpdateAllViews()**. We'll be extending the implementation of the view a little later in this chapter.

We can define the value of the symbol **HINT_UPDATE_ITEM** within the definition file for the **CWrxContainerItem** class. Add it at the beginning of the **WrxContainerItem.h** file with the directive:

```
#define HINT_UPDATE_ITEM 1    // Indicates a hint is present
```

When you have entered this definition, you can add the **GetServerSize()** function next. Just right-click the **CWrxContainerItem** class name again and select Add Member Function... from the pop-up. Enter the return type as **void** and the function name as **GetServerSize()**. You can implement the function as follows:

```
void CWrxContainerItem::GetServerSize()
{
    CSize aSize;                        // Create a size object
    if (GetCachedExtent(&aSize))       // Get the size of the current item
    {
        // Size is specified by OLE in HIMETRIC units
        CClientDC aDC(0);              // Get a device context
```

```
        aDC.HIMETRICtoDP(&aSize); // Convert size to device coordinates

        // Verify that size has changed and item is not in-place active
        if (aSize != m_Rect.Size() && !IsInPlaceActive())
        {
            InvalidateItem();          // Invalidate old item

            // Change the rectangle for the item to the new size
            m_Rect.right = m_Rect.left + aSize.cx;
            m_Rect.bottom = m_Rect.top + aSize.cy;

            InvalidateItem();          // Invalidate the item with the new size
        }
    }
}
```

The size of the OLE object is stored in the **aSize** object by the **GetCachedExtent()** member function that is inherited from the base class, **COleClientItem**. If the object is blank, this function will return **FALSE** and we will do nothing.

Whenever size information about an OLE object is passed to or from the framework, it is always in **HIMETRIC** units to ensure that such information is handled uniformly. This provides a standard unit for specifying size information that has more precision than any of the other possible choices, such as **LOMETRIC**, **HIENGLISH** or **LOENGLISH**. This means that whenever you pass size information to the framework, you must convert it from whatever units you're using to **HIMETRIC**. Whenever you receive size information, you need to convert it to whatever units you require, if they are different from **HIMETRIC**. In the container, we need the rectangle to be in device units, which are pixels, so we get a **CClientDC** object which provides a conversion function from **HIMETRIC** to device coordinate units.

After converting **aSize** to pixels, we then check that the size is actually different from that recorded in **m_Rect** for the item and that the object is not still in-place active. We don't want to do anything if the size hasn't changed. If the item *is* in-place active and a change occurs, the framework will call **OnChangeItemPosition()**. We'll come to this shortly, so we don't need to handle that situation here.

The **Size()** member of the **CRect** class returns the size of the rectangle stored in **m_Rect**. The **IsInPlaceActive()** function inherited from **COleClientItem** returns **TRUE** if the object is currently being edited, and **FALSE** otherwise. With a new size, we invalidate the object with its old extent, create a new extent, then invalidate the object with the new extent. We define the new extent corresponding to the new size by leaving the top left point of the rectangle in **m_Rect** in the same position and creating the bottom right point coordinates by adding the **cx** and **cy** components of **aSize** to the top left point coordinates.

Dealing with the Position of an Object in the Container

There are two members of the **CWrxContainerItem** class concerned with the position of the object in the view: **OnGetItemPosition()** and **OnChangeItemPosition()**.

As we noted earlier, the function **OnGetItemPosition()** is called by the framework when it needs to know where the object is to be displayed in the document view in the container. This occurs each time an item is in-place activated. A reference to a **CRect** object is passed as an argument, in which you need to store the required information. You can do this quite simply by modifying the default implementation to correspond with the following:

```
void CWrxContainerItem::OnGetItemPosition(CRect& rPosition)
{
   ASSERT_VALID(this);

   rPosition = m_Rect;
}
```

We just set the **rPosition** variable that is passed as a parameter to the value we have in the **m_Rect** member of the object. This replaces the previous line of code . Since we update the rectangle in **m_Rect** whenever we get a change signaled by the server, this will always be the current rectangle appropriate to the object.

The **OnChangeItemPosition()** member is called when you move the embedded object in the view, when you resize the borders of the object in the view, or when the server requests that the size of the object be altered. We therefore need to change the default implementation to the following:

```
BOOL CWrxContainerItem::OnChangeItemPosition(const CRect& rectPos)
{
   ASSERT_VALID(this);

   if (!COleClientItem::OnChangeItemPosition(rectPos))
     return FALSE;

   InvalidateItem();               // Invalidate the item at the old position
   m_Rect = rectPos;               // Set the item rectangle to the new position
   InvalidateItem();               // Invalidate the item in the new position
   GetDocument()->SetModifiedFlag();    // Mark the document as changed

   return TRUE;
}
```

Since we're moving the object or altering its extent, we first invalidate it in its old position. After that, we set **m_Rect** for the object to the new extent passed in the parameter **rectPos**, and then invalidate the object in its new position. Finally, we call the **SetModifiedFlag()** member of the document to indicate that the document in the container has been changed.

Managing Multiple Embedded Objects

The container program generated by AppWizard assumes that there's only one embedded object. To manage more than one, we must add functionality to the **CWrxContainerView** class to enable a user to switch from one embedded object to another. This means keeping track of a current active object, processing a single mouse click in a view to switch to the object at the cursor position, and responding to a double mouse click by activating the object at the cursor position. The view class already contains a data member **m_pSelection** that is a pointer to an embedded item, so we can store the currently active item in this variable. AppWizard has already added statements to set this member to **NULL** in the constructor for the view class and in the **OnInitialUpdate()** member of the view, so we don't need to worry about initializing it.

Let's take a look at how we handle a single mouse click.

Selecting an Object

We need to add a handler for the **WM_LBUTTONDOWN** message to **CWrxContainerView**, so right-click on CWrxContainerView in ClassView and select Add Windows Message Handler.... Now select WM_LBUTTONDOWN in the New Windows messages/events list and click the Add and Edit button. Add code to the handler as follows:

```
void CWrxContainerView::OnLButtonDown(UINT nFlags, CPoint point)
{
    // Get address of item hit
    CWrxContainerItem* pHitItem = HitTestItems(point);
    SelectItem(pHitItem);                   // Now select the item

    if (pHitItem)      // As long as an item was selected
    {
        CRectTracker aTracker;              // Create a tracker rectangle

        // Set the tracker rectangle to the item selected
        SetupTracker(pHitItem, &aTracker);
        UpdateWindow();                     // Get the window redrawn

        // Enable the rectangle to be resized
        // TRUE is returned from Track() if rectangle is changed
        if (aTracker.Track(this, point))
        {
            pHitItem->InvalidateItem();     // Invalidate the old item

            // Set the item rectangle to the new tracker rectangle
            pHitItem->m_Rect = aTracker.m_rect;
            // Invalidate the item with the new tracker rect
            pHitItem->InvalidateItem();
            GetDocument()->SetModifiedFlag();// Mark document as changed
        }
    }

    CView::OnLButtonDown(nFlags, point);
}
```

The handler uses several helper functions that we will add once we've discussed how it works in general terms. The first helper function, **HitTestItems()**, is used to initialize the pointer **pHitItem**. This function iterates over all the OLE objects in the container until it finds one that has the **point** object within its bounding rectangle. The **point** object is passed to the handler as an argument and contains the current cursor position, so the item containing it will be the item the user has clicked on. Its address is returned and stored in the local pointer **pHitItem**. If no item was hit, a null pointer will be returned from **HitTestItems()**.

If the user has clicked on an embedded item, we create an object of the class **CRectTracker**. An object of this class is a rectangle called a **tracker** that can be displayed in different ways to provide visual clues to different situations. A tracker can be set to display its border as solid, dotted or hatched. The interior of the tracker can be hatched, and it can also have resize handles. You can use a **CRectTracker** object anywhere you need this kind of capability. The first thing we do with our tracker, **aTracker**, is to initialize it using the helper function **SetupTracker()**. This will set the tracker rectangle to be the same size as the rectangle stored in the embedded object pointed to by **pHitItem** and set its appearance according to the state of the object. Two examples of trackers appear in this window:

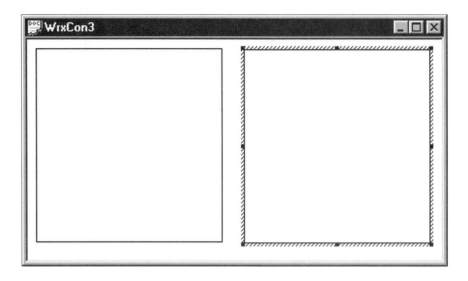

The one on the left represents an inactive object and the one on the right, with the hatched border and the resize handles, represents an active item.

After initializing the tracker, we call the **UpdateWindow()** member function of **CWrxContainerView**. This is a function that is inherited indirectly from the **CWnd** class which causes the window to be redrawn immediately and will result in the tracker being displayed.

In the succeeding **if** statement, the **Track()** member of the tracker object is called. This is quite a sophisticated function that provides for the possibility that this **WM_LBUTTONDOWN** message was triggered by the user re-sizing the border of the embedded object. The arguments are a pointer to the current window and the current cursor position, **point**. The function captures the mouse and allows the user to resize the tracker rectangle by dragging its borders. As the border is dragged, the cursor is tracked and the border updated as long as the left mouse button is held down. The **Track()** function stores the modified rectangle in the tracker object and returns **TRUE** if the tracker was re-sized, and **FALSE** otherwise.

If the tracker rectangle was changed, the current item with its old extent is invalidated to get the area it occupies redrawn. The **m_rect** member of the tracker object contains the new rectangle, which is stored in the **m_Rect** member of the embedded object. Finally, the item with the new extent is invalidated to get it redrawn.

Finding the Object Selected

The helper function **HitTestItems()** searches through the embedded items in the document to find the one the user is clicking on. You can add this function to the class by right-clicking on CWrxContainerView in the ClassView. Specify the **private** function's return type as **CWrxContainerItem***, and the name as **HitTestItems(CPoint aPoint)**. Select the OK button and enter its code as follows:

```
CWrxContainerItem* CWrxContainerView::HitTestItems(CPoint aPoint)
{
    CWrxContainerDoc* pDoc = GetDocument();
    CWrxContainerItem* pItem = 0;       // Place to store an item pointer
```

```
    // Get position of the first item
    POSITION aPosition = pDoc->GetStartPosition();

    while(aPosition)    // Iterate over items until one is hit
    {
       pItem = (CWrxContainerItem*)pDoc->GetNextItem(aPosition);
       if (pItem->m_Rect.PtInRect(aPoint))
          return pItem;    // Return pointer to item hit
    }
    return 0;               // No item hit
}
```

After getting a pointer to the document object, we create a pointer, **pItem**, to store the address of the item hit. We get a position value for the first item in the document by calling the **GetStartPosition()** member of the document object. The value returned from this function is of type **POSITION** because pointers to the items stored in the document are maintained in a list. This is used in the same way as you've seen with the lists we used in the Sketcher application. We iterate through the list of embedded objects by calling the **GetNextItem()** member of the document object.

In the loop, the **m_Rect** member of each embedded object is tested using the **PtInRect()** member of **CRect** to see whether the **aPoint** object is inside the rectangle. As soon as an object is found where this is the case, the address of the embedded object is returned. If we reach the end of the list, **aPosition** will be zero and the **while** loop will end. In this case we haven't hit an item, so we return a null pointer value. This situation arises when the user clicks on a point in the view that is outside of all the embedded objects. This might be done to deactivate the current object, for instance, so that another object can be embedded in the document.

Setting an Object as Selected

When the user clicks on an item, we must deactivate any active item and activate the new item. This is carried out by the **SelectItem()** helper function that we used in the **OnLButtonDown()** handler. You can add this function by right-clicking on CWrxContainerView in ClassView and selecting Add Member Function... from the pop-up. You can specify the return type as **void** and enter the name as **SelectItem(CWrxContainerItem* pItem)**. You can then add the code for the function as follows:

```
void CWrxContainerView::SelectItem(CWrxContainerItem * pItem)
{
    if (m_pSelection != 0 && m_pSelection != pItem)
       m_pSelection->Close();      // De-activate current selected item

    if (m_pSelection != pItem)      // Only update view for a new selection
    {
       if (m_pSelection)            // Check there is an old selection
          // Update area for the old
          OnUpdate(0, HINT_UPDATE_ITEM, m_pSelection);

       m_pSelection = pItem;   // Set the current selection to the new item
       if (m_pSelection)         // Check there is a new selection
          // Update area for the new
          OnUpdate(0, HINT_UPDATE_ITEM, m_pSelection);
    }
}
```

The first **if** statement deactivates the currently selected object (which has its address stored in the **m_pSelection** member of the view) provided there's a current selection that's different from the new item to be selected (which has its address passed in the parameter **pItem**). Note that we won't deactivate the current item if it's the same as the new item.

The next **if** tests whether the address of the new item is different from that of the old. If they are the same, we have nothing further to do. Otherwise, we verify that the address of the current selected item is not zero before using it as the hint argument in the call to the **OnUpdate()** member of the view.

Finally, we store the address of the new embedded object in the **m_pSelection** member of the view. If *it* isn't zero, we use it as a hint in the call to the **OnUpdate()** function once more.

Setting the Tracker Style

The last helper function sets the style for the tracker which determines its appearance. You can add this function in the same way as the others by right-clicking on CWrxContainerView in ClassView. Set the return type as **void** and the name of the function as **SetupTracker(CWrxContainerItem* pItem, CRectTracker* pTracker)**. The code for the function is as follows:

```
void CWrxContainerView::SetupTracker(CWrxContainerItem* pItem,
                                             CRectTracker* pTracker)
{
    pTracker->m_rect = pItem->m_Rect;

    if (pItem == m_pSelection)       // Check if the item is selected
        pTracker->m_nStyle |= CRectTracker::resizeInside;

    if (pItem->GetType() == OT_LINK)       // Test for linked item
        // Item is linked so dotted border
        pTracker->m_nStyle |= CRectTracker::dottedLine;
    else
        // Item is embedded so solid border
        pTracker->m_nStyle |= CRectTracker::solidLine;

    // If the item server window is open or activated in-place,
    // hatch over the item
    if (pItem->GetItemState() == COleClientItem::openState ||
                    pItem->GetItemState() == COleClientItem::activeUIState)
        pTracker->m_nStyle |= CRectTracker::hatchInside;
}
```

The **m_rect** member of the tracker object stores the rectangle representing the tracker in device coordinates. This is set up by storing the rectangle in the **m_Rect** member of the object, which has its address passed as the parameter **pItem**.

The style of the tracker object is stored in the member **m_nStyle**. This can consist of a number of different flags, so the style is set by ORing flags with **m_nStyle**. The symbols corresponding to possible values for the flags are defined in an enumeration within the definition of the **CRectTracker** class, so you must prefix them with **CRectTracker::**. The symbols defining valid flags are:

Flag	Meaning
solidLine	Specifies the border of the rectangle as solid. This is used for an embedded object that is inactive.
dottedLine	Specifies the border of the rectangle as dotted. This is used to identify a linked object. We won't be dealing with linked objects.
hatchedBorder	Specifies the border of the rectangle as hatched. This identifies an embedded object as active, with the server menus displayed in the container.
resizeInside	Specifies that resize handles appear inside the border.
resizeOutside	Specifies that resize handles appear outside the border.
hatchInside	Specifies that the interior of the rectangle is to be hatched. This is used to identify an object that can't be edited in its present state.

The first **if** statement in the **SetupTracker()** function checks whether the object indicated by **pItem** is actually the current selection. If it is, the **resizeInside** style is set to allow the border to be resized. The next **if** checks whether the item is linked by calling the **GetType()** member of the object. If it is, the flag **dottedLine** is added, otherwise we assume that it is embedded and set the **solidLine** flag. The last **if** statement checks the state of the item by calling its **GetItemState()** member. The states that are tested for reflect conditions under which the item can't be edited, so the **hatchInside** style is set.

Setting the Cursor

Although we've implemented the capability to resize an object by dragging the tracker rectangle, the user has no indication of when this is possible. We really need to ensure that the cursor representation provides a cue for this by switching its appearance to a double arrow to indicate when a border can be dragged, or to a four-way arrow showing that the object can be moved in the view, as is usual for Windows applications.

To do this, we must add a handler for the **WM_SETCURSOR** message. As long as the mouse hasn't been captured, this message is sent to the application whenever the cursor is moved. All we need to do is implement the handler to check where the cursor is in relation to the tracker for the currently selected object.

You can use the ClassView context menu to add the Windows message handler and then code it as follows:

```
BOOL CWrxContainerView::OnSetCursor(CWnd* pWnd, UINT nHitTest, UINT message)
{
    if (pWnd == this && m_pSelection)
    {
        CRectTracker aTracker;                  // Create a tracker rectangle
        SetupTracker(m_pSelection, &aTracker);  // Set the tracker style

        // Change the cursor if it is over the currently selected item
        // Check if the last hit was in the tracker rectangle
        if (aTracker.SetCursor(this, nHitTest))
            return TRUE;                         // and if so return TRUE
    }

    return CView::OnSetCursor(pWnd, nHitTest, message);
}
```

425

The first parameter passed to the handler is a pointer to the window that currently contains the cursor. The second parameter is a numeric value that identifies the area in the window where the cursor is. The third parameter, which we will ignore, is a mouse message number.

After verifying that the cursor is in the view window and that there is an object selected, we create a **CRectTracker** object and set its style to correspond to the state of the selected object. We then use the **SetCursor()** member of the tracker object, **aTracker**, which will take care of setting the cursor appropriately if it is over the tracker. If the cursor was not set, the **SetCursor()** function will return 0 and the message will be passed to the handler in the **CView** class to give it a chance to set the cursor.

Activating an Embedded Object

An object is activated by double-clicking it, so we need to add a handler for the **WM_LBUTTONDBLCLK** message to **CWrxContainerView**. You can use the ClassView context menu to add the Windows message handler and implement it with the following code:

```
void CWrxContainerView::OnLButtonDblClk(UINT nFlags, CPoint point)
{
    OnLButtonDown(nFlags, point);
    if (m_pSelection)
        m_pSelection->DoVerb((GetKeyState(VK_CONTROL) < 0) ?
                        OLEIVERB_OPEN:OLEIVERB_PRIMARY, this);
    CView::OnLButtonDblClk(nFlags, point);
}
```

Because the left button has been clicked, we first call the **OnLButtonDown()** handler. If **m_pSelection** is not zero, we use the pointer to call the **DoVerb()** member of the embedded item selected.

The word **verb** has been given a special meaning in the context of OLE. A **verb** specifies an action that an embedded object is to take, usually in response to some action by the user. The first argument to the **DoVerb()** function specifies a verb, which in our case is given by:

```
(GetKeyState(VK_CONTROL) < 0) ? OLEIVERB_OPEN:OLEIVERB_PRIMARY
```

This is a conditional expression which will result in the verb **OLEIVERB_OPEN** if the function **GetKeyState()** returns a negative value, and the verb **OLEIVERB_PRIMARY** if it doesn't. The **GetKeyState()** function tests the status of keys, in this case the *Ctrl* key. If the *Ctrl* key is pressed, the function will return a negative value. If you double-click with the *Ctrl* key pressed, the verb **OLEIVERB_OPEN** will be selected, otherwise the other verb will be selected.

The verb **OLEIVERB_OPEN** opens the item for editing in a separate server window, although the object will remain embedded in the container. You will see that the object in the container window will be cross-hatched, because opening the server window modifies the style of the tracker for the object to do this. The verb **OLEIVERB_PRIMARY** activates the server and makes the item available for in-place editing in the container in the normal way. The second argument to **DoVerb()** identifies the current view in the container where the double-click occurred.

Drawing Multiple Embedded Objects

To draw objects in the container document, you must extend the **OnDraw()** handler in **CWrxContainerView**. The version provided by AppWizard assumes that there is only one object. We need it to iterate over all the objects in the document and draw each of them with an appropriate tracker. Change the code to the following:

```
void CWrxContainerView::OnDraw(CDC* pDC)
{
    CWrxContainerDoc* pDoc = GetDocument();
    ASSERT_VALID(pDoc);

    // Get the first item position
    POSITION aPosition = pDoc->GetStartPosition();

    while (aPosition)      // For each item in the list
    {
        // Get the pointer to the current item
        CWrxContainerItem* pItem =
                        (CWrxContainerItem*)pDoc->GetNextItem(aPosition);
        pItem->Draw(pDC, pItem->m_Rect);    // Now draw the item

        // Now create a suitable tracker for the item
        CRectTracker aTracker;              // Create a tracker rectangle
        SetupTracker(pItem, &aTracker);     // Set the style for current item
        aTracker.Draw(pDC);                 // Draw the tracker rectangle
    }
}
```

This is very straightforward. We iterate through all the items embedded in the document in the **while** loop, using the **GetNextItem()** function member of the document object that you saw earlier. For each item in the list, we call the **Draw()** function to get it to draw itself, passing the **m_Rect** member of the item as the second argument. This function is inherited from the base class, **COleClientItem**. We didn't implement a **Draw()** function for the **CWrxContainerItem** class; you'll remember that we saw at the beginning of this chapter that the server, not the container, draws embedded objects.

The object will be drawn by the **OnDraw()** member of the OLE object in the server. This drawing operation will generate the picture in an internal format called a **metafile**, which is a way of storing all the function calls you make to draw the image to produce a device-independent representation of the image. This can then be replayed in a specific device context. The **Draw()** function member of **COleClientItem** will access the metafile generated by the server and display it in the device context here.

After drawing an item, we create a tracker with a style based on the state of the current item and get it to draw itself by calling its **Draw()** member. Each time a tracker needs to be displayed for an item, we can just generate a new one because it's only a visual aid to interaction. It doesn't need to be permanently saved with the item.

We have no local data in the container document. If the container application has its own document data, you would need to display that in the **OnDraw()** function as well.

Dealing with Object Insertion

AppWizard already provided the mechanism for handling the insertion of a new object into the container. This is in the implementation of the handler **OnInsertObject()** in the **CWrxContainerView** class. We can make two additions to improve it a little, though. We'll add code to update the rectangle for a new object to that corresponding to the size from the server, and replace the default code that redraws all the views in the container with code that only redraws the area occupied by the new object:

```
void CWrxContainerView::OnInsertObject()
{
    // Invoke the standard Insert Object dialog box to obtain information
    //  for new CWrxContainerItem object.
    COleInsertDialog dlg;
    if (dlg.DoModal() != IDOK)
      return;

    BeginWaitCursor();

    CWrxContainerItem* pItem = NULL;
    TRY
    {
        // Create new item connected to this document.
        CWrxContainerDoc* pDoc = GetDocument();
        ASSERT_VALID(pDoc);
        pItem = new CWrxContainerItem(pDoc);
        ASSERT_VALID(pItem);

        // Initialize the item from the dialog data.
        if (!dlg.CreateItem(pItem))
            AfxThrowMemoryException();  // any exception will do
        ASSERT_VALID(pItem);

        pItem->UpdateLink();            // Update the item display
        pItem->GetServerSize();         // Update the item size

        // If item created from class list (not from file) then launch
        //  the server to edit the item.
        if (dlg.GetSelectionType() == COleInsertDialog::createNewItem)
            pItem->DoVerb(OLEIVERB_SHOW, this);

        ASSERT_VALID(pItem);

        // As an arbitrary user interface design, this sets the selection
        //  to the last item inserted.

        // TODO: reimplement selection as appropriate for your application
        SelectItem(pItem);             // Select last inserted item
        pItem->InvalidateItem();       // then invalidate the item
    }
    CATCH(CException, e)
    {
        if (pItem != NULL)
        {
            ASSERT_VALID(pItem);
            pItem->Delete();
        }
        AfxMessageBox(IDP_FAILED_TO_CREATE);
    }
    END_CATCH

    EndWaitCursor();
}
```

In the **TRY** block, the default code creates a new **CWrxContainerItem** object associated with the document and stores its address in **pItem**. This is then initialized to the new embedded object through the **CreateItem()** member of the dialog object **dlg**, which manages the selection of the type of object to be embedded. As long as everything works OK, the first two lines of code we've added are executed. The call to the **UpdateLink()** member of the new **CWrxContainerItem** object causes the contents of the embedded object to be drawn. We then call our **SetServerSize()** helper function to update the size to that required for the server.

The next **if** statement in the default code checks for a new embedded item being created, rather than one being loaded from a file. If it's a new item, it executes the **DoVerb()** member of the object to open it for editing. Our new code follows, which calls our **SelectItem()** function to select the new item and causes the area occupied by the new object to be redrawn. These lines replace the two default lines which set **m_pSelection** and called **UpdateAllViews()**.

Trying Out the OLE Container

The container is ready to run. You can build it in the normal way and, if you haven't made any typos, it should execute. You may well have applications installed on your system which are OLE servers, in which case you'll see a list of them when you select the Edit | Insert New Object... menu option:

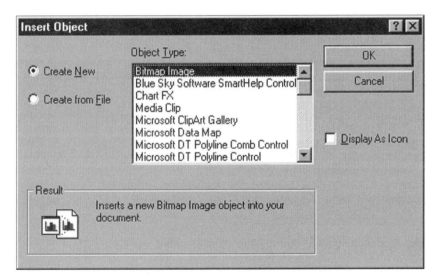

This shows some of the OLE servers that are around in my system. If you want to load a file, you should check the radio button Create from File on the left. Of course, you can add more than one embedded object, as shown in the following screen:

429

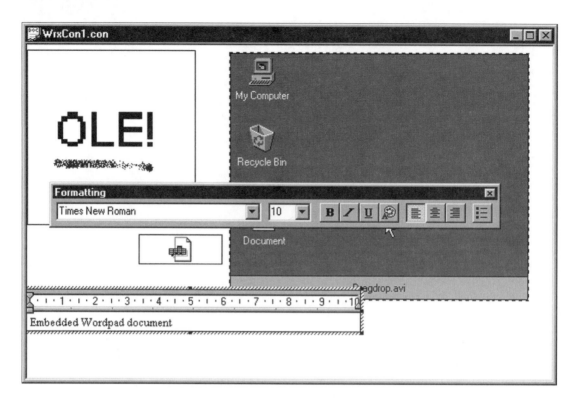

Here you can see inactive bitmap, AVI and MIDI objects, and an in-place active WordPad document towards the bottom. The Formatting toolbar shown here is supplied by the WordPad server application.

Implementing an OLE Server

It would be nice to have the Sketcher application working as a server. If we had chosen the options in AppWizard at the beginning, we would have the basics built in now, but that would have meant carrying a lot of excess baggage around in the early stages, which we really didn't want. However, we can quite quickly reconstruct a skeleton version of Sketcher to act as a full server. For this exercise, we'll just add the bare bones drawing capability that we had in the early versions of Sketcher, plus serialization of the document object. We'll go through the code that you need to add to the AppWizard-generated base program, but you should be able to steal a lot of it from versions of Sketcher that you have already. Of course, if you want to, you can add any of the other functionality that we implemented in earlier chapters, but here we'll just discuss the minimum we need to get an operational server going that we can exercise in our container.

The first step is to recreate the basic Sketcher application as an OLE server using AppWizard.

Generating a Server Application

Create a new project of type MFCAppWizard (exe) and call it Sketcher. Make sure that it's in a different folder from any of the other versions of Sketcher you may have around. The process is almost identical to the one we used to generate the program in the first instance—it should be an MDI application, and the only differences from the default options are in Step 3 and Step 4. In Step 3, make sure that you select the Full-server option as the type of application. In Step 4, select the Advanced button to bring up the Advanced Options dialog, then set the entries as you see here:

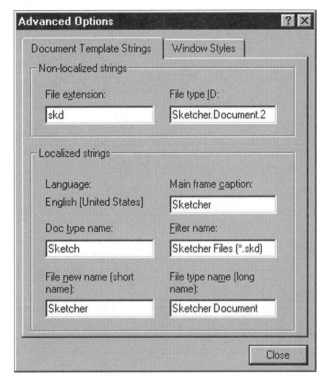

You can see that we have used a different File extension and File type ID for this version of the Sketcher application. Once this information has been filled in, you can click Close and then Finish to create the new project. You may find that you get the following message displayed, in which case, you should click No to ensure that a unique ID is used for your documents.

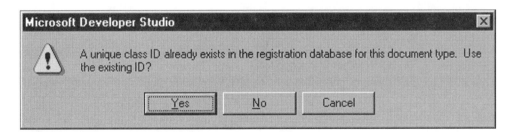

Adding Sketcher Application Functionality

The first step to recreating Sketcher is to copy the **Elements.h**, **Elements.cpp** and **OurConstants.h** files from an earlier version of Sketcher to the folder containing the current version. Make sure that it's a version containing serialization of the elements; the one you had at the end of Chapter 8 will do nicely. Then, add the **Elements.cpp** file to the current project by using the Project | Add To Project | Files... menu option.

We'll attempt to keep the code simple in this version of Sketcher, so we won't implement scrolling, text, different pen widths or the context menu. The only change that you'll need to make to the elements as we used them in Chapter 8 is to remove the **PenWidth** parameter from the constructors, both in the class definitions and in the implementations, and set the **m_Pen** member to 1 in each element constructor. The easiest way to do this is to search for **', int PenWidth'** in both the **Elements.h** and **Elements.cpp** files and replace this string with nothing using the Edit | Replace... menu item. Once that's done, go back to the **.cpp** file and replace all occurrences of **PenWidth** with **1**.

You can now follow what should be a well-trodden path to add the basic drawing functionality to the project. You can do it in the following steps:

Document Data and Interface Functions

Add the **protected** data members to the **CSketcherDoc** class:

```
WORD m_Element;
COLORREF m_Color;
CSize m_DocSize;
```

To do this, you can right-click on the class name in ClassView, or just copy the code from an earlier implementation. The third data item is a record of the document size, which we'll use extensively when Sketcher is operating as an OLE server.

Next, you can add the **protected** data member for storing the list of elements:

```
CTypedPtrList<CObList, CElement*> m_ElementList;  // Element list
```

Note that you have to add this explicitly, and that you must remember to add a **#include** for **afxtempl.h** to **StdAfx.h**. (Put it after the **#include** for **afxole.h**).

The first three data members must be initialized in the constructor for the document:

```
CSketcherDoc::CSketcherDoc()
{
   // Use OLE compound files
   EnableCompoundFile();

   // TODO: add one-time construction code here
   m_Element = LINE;            // Set initial element type
   m_Color = BLACK;             // Set initial drawing color
   m_DocSize = CSize(200,200);  // Set document size
}
```

Because we refer to the constants that we've defined for the element types and colors, you must add a **#include** directive for **OurConstants.h** to the beginning of **SketcherDoc.cpp**. We must also remember to clean up the **m_ElementList** object in the destructor for the document:

```
CSketcherDoc::~CSketcherDoc()
{
   // Get the position at the head of the list
   POSITION aPosition = m_ElementList.GetHeadPosition();

   // Now delete the element pointed to by each list entry
```

```
        while (aPosition)
            delete m_ElementList.GetNext(aPosition);

        m_ElementList.RemoveAll();   // Finally delete all pointers
    }
```

You can copy the **public** interface functions for the document class directly from the Chapter 8 version of Sketcher. The ones that you need are:

```
WORD GetElementType()                 // Get the element type
    { return m_Element; }

COLORREF GetElementColor()            // Get the element color
    { return m_Color; }

void AddElement(CElement* pElement)   // Add an element to the list
    { m_ElementList.AddTail(pElement); }

POSITION GetListHeadPosition()        // return list head POSITION value
    { return m_ElementList.GetHeadPosition(); }

CElement* GetNext(POSITION& aPos)     // Return current element pointer
    { return m_ElementList.GetNext(aPos); }

CSize GetDocSize()                    // Return the current document size
    { return m_DocSize; }
```

Because we refer to the **CElement** class here, you should add an **#include** statement for **Elements.h** to the **SketcherDoc.h** file.

You also need to implement the **Serialize()** member of the document:

```
void CSketcherDoc::Serialize(CArchive& ar)
{
    m_ElementList.Serialize(ar);      // Serialize the element list
    if (ar.IsStoring())
    {
        ar << m_Color                 // Store the current color
            << m_Element              // the current element type,
            << m_DocSize;             // and the document size
    }
    else
    {
        ar >> m_Color                 // Retrieve the current color
            >> m_Element              // the current element type,
            >> m_DocSize;             // and the document size
    }
}
```

The reason that you need serialization implemented for your server is that, when an embedded object is deactivated, the framework uses it to save the document. When you reactivate the object, it is restored using serialization. This is necessary because your server may be servicing several embedded objects at one time.

Adding the Menus

Now you need to add the E|ement and Color menus that we had in earlier versions of Sketcher (Chapter 4 and later). You should add them to the **IDR_SKETCHTYPE** menu, just as we did before. You'll see that this version of Sketcher contains a couple of menu resources in addition to **IDR_SKETCHTYPE** and **IDR_MAINFRAME** which are for use when the program is operating as a server, but ignore these for now—we'll get to them later. For each menu item, use the same IDs and captions that we used before.

There is a shortcut you can use here to transfer your menus across from a previous version of Sketcher. First, close all the open windows in Developer Studio, then open the **.rc** file for the menu you want to copy. Double-click on the **IDR_SKETCHTYPE** menu resource for the newly opened file to display the menu. Open **IDR_SKETCHTYPE** for the current project, then use the Window | Tile Horizontally to view both menus simultaneously. You can copy the menu items that you want by dragging them with the mouse while holding down the *Ctrl* key.

Now you should add the COMMAND and UPDATE_COMMAND_UI handlers for each menu item to the **CSketcherDoc** class, exactly as you did way back in Chapter 4. You can use ClassWizard to add these handlers, then copy the code for the command handlers (**OnColorBlack()**, etc.) and update handlers (**OnUpdateColorBlack()**, etc.) from an earlier version of Sketcher into the current one, or you can just enter the code—the functions are very simple. The typical command handler for an element is:

```
void CSketcherDoc::OnElementCircle()
{
    // TODO: Add your command handler code here
    m_Element = LINE;        // Set element type as a line
}
```

A typical update command handler is:

```
void CSketcherDoc::OnUpdateElementLine(CCmdUI* pCmdUI)
{
    // TODO: Add your command update UI handler code here
    // Set Checked if the current element is a line
    pCmdUI->SetCheck(m_Element==LINE);
}
```

All the command and command update handlers are of a similar form.

Adding the Toolbar Buttons

You can also add the toolbar buttons for the menu items exactly as before. All you need are the buttons for the four element types and the four colors. You add these to the toolbar **IDR_MAINFRAME** and set the IDs to the same as those for the corresponding menu item.

If you like, you can also take a shortcut to this process. In the same way that you did for the menus, display the current project **IDR_MAINFRAME** toolbar and one containing the toolbar buttons you need—any version of Sketcher from the end of Chapter 4 onwards will be OK. You can then drag toolbar buttons from one toolbar to the other by holding down the *Ctrl* key. You only need the four buttons for colors and the four for element types.

Adding the View Application Functionality

The **protected** data items you need in the **CSketcherView** class definition are:

```
CPoint m_FirstPoint;      // First point recorded for an element
CPoint m_SecondPoint;     // Second point recorded for an element
CElement* m_pTempElement; // Pointer to temporary element
```

Since the class definition uses the **CElement** class, we ought to add an **#include** statement for **Elements.h** to **SketcherView.h**.

The data members must be initialized in the constructor, so add the code to the constructor implementation to do this:

```
CSketcherView::CSketcherView()
{
    m_FirstPoint = CPoint(0,0);      // Set 1st recorded point to 0,0
    m_SecondPoint = CPoint(0,0);     // Set 2nd recorded point to 0,0
    m_pTempElement = 0;              // Set temporary element pointer to 0
}
```

The only message handling functions you need to add to the view class at this point are the handlers for **WM_LBUTTONDOWN**, **WM_LBUTTONUP** and **WM_MOUSEMOVE**. Add these as before by using ClassWizard or the context menu from ClassView.

You can use simple implementations of the handlers, similar to those from Chapter 6 without the context menu support, but with the proper conversion from client coordinates to logical coordinates. The handler for **WM_LBUTTONDOWN** is:

```
void CSketcherView::OnLButtonDown(UINT nFlags, CPoint point)
{
    CClientDC aDC(this);        // Create a device context
    OnPrepareDC(&aDC);          // Prepare the device context
    aDC.DPtoLP(&point);         // Convert point to Logical
    m_FirstPoint = point;       // Record the cursor position
    SetCapture();               // Capture subsequent mouse messages
}
```

The implementation of the handler for **WM_LBUTTONUP** messages will be:

```
void CSketcherView::OnLButtonUp(UINT nFlags, CPoint point)
{
    CSketcherDoc* pDoc = GetDocument();     // Get the document pointer

    if (this == GetCapture())
        ReleaseCapture();                   // Stop capturing mouse messages

    // If there is an element, add it to the document
    if (m_pTempElement)
    {
        pDoc->AddElement(m_pTempElement);   // Add the element

        // Tell the other views about it
        pDoc->UpdateAllViews(0, 0, m_pTempElement);
        m_pTempElement = 0;                 // Reset the element pointer
    }
}
```

Finally, the code for the **WM_MOUSEMOVE** handler will be:

```
void CSketcherView::OnMouseMove(UINT nFlags, CPoint point)
{
    // Define a Device Context object for the view
    CClientDC aDC(this);
    OnPrepareDC(&aDC);                  // Prepare the device context

    if ((nFlags & MK_LBUTTON) && (this == GetCapture()))
    {
        aDC.DPtoLP(&point);             // Convert point to logical
        m_SecondPoint = point;          // Save the current cursor position

        if(m_pTempElement)
        {
            if(CURVE == GetDocument()->GetElementType())    // Is it a curve?
            {   // We are drawing a curve
                // so add a segment to the existing curve
                ((CCurve*)m_pTempElement)->AddSegment(m_SecondPoint);
                m_pTempElement->Draw(&aDC);   // Now draw it
                return;                       // We are done
            }

            aDC.SetROP2(R2_NOTXORPEN);        // Set drawing mode

            // Redraw the old element so it disappears from the view
            m_pTempElement->Draw(&aDC);
            delete m_pTempElement;      // Delete the old element
            m_pTempElement = 0;         // Reset the pointer to 0
        }

        // Create a temporary element of the type and color that
        // is recorded in the document object, and draw it
        m_pTempElement = CreateElement();  // Create a new element
        m_pTempElement->Draw(&aDC);        // Draw the element
    }
}
```

All of this should be quite familiar to you now, so these additions shouldn't take very long. We also need the **CreateElement()** function to create elements on the heap. Add a **protected** declaration for this function to the view class and implement it as:

```
CElement* CSketcherView::CreateElement()
{
    // Get a pointer to the document for this view
    CSketcherDoc* pDoc = GetDocument();
    ASSERT_VALID(pDoc);                     // Verify the pointer is good

    // Now select the element using the type stored in the document
    switch (pDoc->GetElementType())
    {
    case RECTANGLE:
        return new CRectangle(m_FirstPoint, m_SecondPoint,
                    pDoc->GetElementColor());
    case CIRCLE:
        return new CCircle(m_FirstPoint, m_SecondPoint,
                    pDoc->GetElementColor());
```

```
      case CURVE:
        return new CCurve(m_FirstPoint, m_SecondPoint,
                          pDoc->GetElementColor());
      case LINE:
        return new CLine(m_FirstPoint, m_SecondPoint,
                          pDoc->GetElementColor());

      default:                       // Something's gone wrong
        AfxMessageBox("Bad Element code", MB_OK);
        AfxAbort();
        return NULL;
    }
}
```

This is like the code you've seen in earlier chapters.

Drawing the Document

As you well know by now, we'll draw the document in the **OnDraw()** member of the view class. The implementation is:

```
void CSketcherView::OnDraw(CDC* pDC)
{
    CSketcherDoc* pDoc = GetDocument();
    ASSERT_VALID(pDoc);

    POSITION aPos = pDoc->GetListHeadPosition();
    CElement* pElement = 0;                 // Store for an element pointer
    while (aPos)                            // Loop while aPos is not null
    {
      pElement = pDoc->GetNext(aPos);    // Get the current element pointer
      // If the element is visible...
      if (pDC->RectVisible(pElement->GetBoundRect()))
        pElement->Draw(pDC);               // ...draw it
    }
}
```

This is identical code to that in earlier versions of Sketcher, so you can copy it from one of those if you like.

We must add the **OnUpdate()** function to respond to the **UpdateAllViews()** call that occurs when we add an element to the document, so add this handler to **CSketcherView** using ClassWizard or the WizardBar. The implementation for it will be:

```
void CSketcherView::OnUpdate(CView* pSender, LPARAM lHint, CObject* pHint)
{
    // Invalidate the area corresponding to the element pointed to
    // if there is one, otherwise invalidate the whole client area
    if (pHint)
    {
      CClientDC aDC(this);                // Create a device context
      OnPrepareDC(&aDC);                  // Prepare the device context

      // Get the enclosing rectangle and convert to client coordinates
      CRect aRect = ((CElement*)pHint)->GetBoundRect();
      aDC.LPtoDP(aRect);
```

```
        aRect.NormalizeRect();
        InvalidateRect(aRect);          // Get the area redrawn
    }
    else
        InvalidateRect(0);
}
```

Once again, this is very similar to the code we've used in previous versions of Sketcher. Finally, you need to add a **#include** statement for **OurConstants.h** to **SketcherView.cpp** after the **#include** for **Sketcher.h**.

Now that you've added **OnDraw()**, **OnUpdate()**, the mouse handlers, the **CreateElement()** function and the **#include** statements, you should have a basic working version of Sketcher with the OLE server mechanism built in. You can build it and run it as a stand-alone application to check out all is well. Any omissions or errors should come out during the compilation. When it works stand-alone, you can try it out in the container.

Running Sketcher as a Server

Start the WrxContainer application and select Insert New Object... from the Edit menu. The list of OLE servers available should include Sketcher Document, if that is how you identified the file type name in Step 4 of the AppWizard dialog to create the OLE version of Sketcher. If you select this, a Sketcher object will be loaded ready for editing.

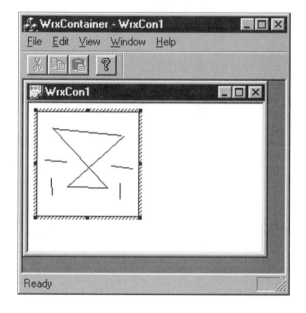

Unfortunately, we have no Sketcher menus or toolbars in the container, but at least you can draw black lines. However, there's another little problem: if you click outside the object to deactivate it, the contents of the object disappear. We clearly have a little more work to do on our server.

Server Resources

Let's go back to the Sketcher server and take a look at the menus. If you extend the Menu part of the resource tree, you'll see that there are two extra menu resources included in the server beyond the two menus that are used when Sketcher is running stand-alone. The contents of these are shown here:

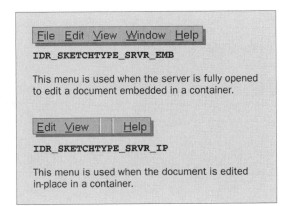

The menu corresponding to **IDR_SKETCHTYPE_SRVR_EMB** is used when you open the server to edit an object embedded in a container by double-clicking the object while holding down the *Ctrl* key. This will appear in a server window separate from the container, so this menu should contain all the items that appear in Sketcher when it's running stand-alone.

The **IDR_SKETCHTYPE_SRVR_IP** menu applies when you're editing an object in-place, which occurs when you just double-click on an object embedded in a container. The server menu will be merged with the menu in the container to enable you to interact with the server during editing, while still providing access to the essential container menus. The segments of the menus in the server and the container that are delineated by the separators will be merged in a predetermined sequence, as we shall see.

If you extend the Toolbar resources in the ResourceView, you'll see that there's also an extra toolbar with the ID **IDR_SKETCHTYPE_SRVR_IP**. This will replace the container's toolbar when you're editing an object in-place. We can copy the menu and toolbar resources that we need in the extra menus from the **IDR_SKETCHTYPE** menu and the **IDR_MAINFRAME** toolbar in the project.

Updating Menu Resources

The first step is to arrange to display the **IDR_SKETCHTYPE** and **IDR_SKETCHTYPE_SRVR_EMB** menus together. The easiest way to do this is to close all the windows in the project, then, with ResourceView displayed in the Project Window, extend the Menu resource tree and double-click on **IDR_SKETCHTYPE** and **IDR_SKETCHTYPE_SRVR_EMB** to open both windows. Finally, select Tile Horizontally from the Window menu.

You can now simply copy each menu that you need in turn from **IDR_SKETCHTYPE** to **IDR_SKETCHTYPE_SRVR_EMB** by dragging it with *Ctrl* held down as we did before. You need to copy the Color and Element menus. That completes the **IDR_SKETCHTYPE_SRVR_EMB** menu, so you can save it. All the links to the handlers for the menu items are already in place because they are the ones that are used normally.

After saving **IDR_SKETCHTYPE_SRVR_EMB**, you can close the window for this menu and open the menu **IDR_SKETCHTYPE_SRVR_IP**. Select Window | Tile Horizontally so that this menu and **IDR_SKETCHTYPE** are both visible. You can then copy the Element and Color menu items from **IDR_SKETCHTYPE** to **IDR_SKETCHTYPE_SRVR_IP**. The new menu should look like this:

The combined menu is now in a state where it will merge with the container menu to provide a composite menu in the container application for in-place editing of a Sketcher object.

How Container and Server Menus are Merged

If we assume the context of the container that we created earlier in this chapter, the menu for our server will be merged into the container's menu, as shown here:

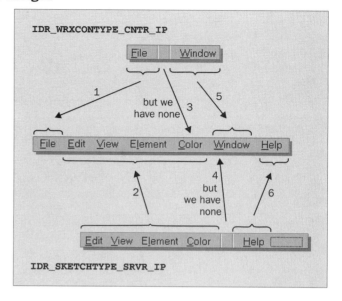

The diagram shows the composite menu in the center that is produced in the container by merging the menus from the container and the server. The numbers on the arrows indicate the sequence in which segments of the two menus are added to form the composite menu. There's actually more scope here than we're using, as we have no items between the separators in either the server or the container. The resulting menu has the File and Window menu items from the container, since a save operation will apply to the container document with its embedded objects, and the window in which the object is displayed is owned by the container application. The application menu items and the Help menu item are contributed by the server.

Updating Toolbar Resources

You need to open both toolbars in the current project corresponding to the IDs **IDR_MAINFRAME** and **IDR_SKETCHTYPE_SRVR_IP** in the same way that you opened the menus previously. Then modify the toolbar with the ID **IDR_SKETCHTYPE_SRVR_IP** as shown here:

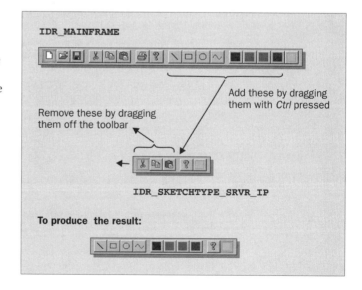

As we saw earlier, you can copy toolbar buttons using the same mechanism that you used for copying menu items. Just drag each button while holding down the *Ctrl* key. We need to remove the buttons indicated because these apply to server editing operations and, in the container context, the container operations will apply. We haven't implemented these functions in Sketcher anyway.

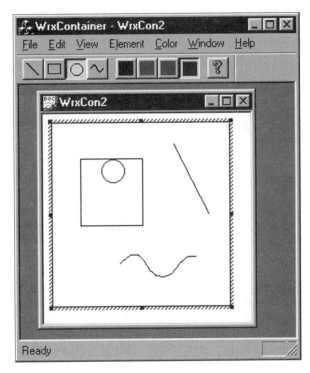

That completes updating the resources for the Sketcher project. Now would be a good time to save the resources if you haven't done so already. You can build Sketcher at this point to see how menu merging works out. If you run the container application and insert an object of the latest version of the Sketcher server, you should get something like the next screen:

All the menus and toolbar buttons from Sketcher should work OK. You can draw any of the elements in any color. The problem of the picture not staying around when the object is deactivated remains, but we're getting there.

Adding Server Functionality

As we discussed earlier on in this chapter, a server object is an instance of the class **COleServerItem** in the server application. It's this object that's responsible for drawing the embedded item when it isn't active. In Sketcher, AppWizard has provided the class **CSketcherSrvrItem**, which is derived from **COleServerItem**, so this class represents the embedded object in Sketcher. Whenever the embedded object is being edited, the drawing is being done by the **OnDraw()** function in **CSketcherView** and is being transferred to the container to be displayed. When the embedded object isn't active, the container is asking the **CSketcherSrvrItem** object to draw it, but we haven't provided the capability to do this. This is what we need to do now.

Implementing the Embedded Object

A **CSketcherSrvrItem** object has two essential jobs to do. It must draw the object when the object is embedded but isn't being edited in-place, and it must be able to supply the extent of the document when requested by the framework on behalf of the container. Drawing is done by the **OnDraw()** member of the **CSketcherSrvrItem** class and the document extent is supplied by the **OnGetExtent()** member.

Scaleable Mapping Modes

There are some complications arising from Sketcher being a server. We can no longer draw the document in the same way as before. You already know that there are two places in the Sketcher program where an embedded document will be drawn: in the **OnDraw()** function in the view object when it's being edited, and in the **OnDraw()** function of the **CSketcherSrvrItem** object when it isn't. Further complications arise because we'll be drawing the embedded document in a rectangle within a view of a container. This rectangle is inevitably small. After all, the whole point of embedding objects is that they should coexist with other objects. It may also be moved about and varied in size, so we need to use a flexible mapping mode.

There are two mapping modes that allow the mapping between logical coordinates and device coordinates to be altered: **MM_ISOTROPIC** and **MM_ANISOTROPIC**. We discussed these mapping modes back in Chapter 7, but it won't hurt to go over things again. The **MM_ISOTROPIC** mapping mode has the property that Windows will force the scaling factor to be the same for both the x and y axes, which has the advantage that your circles will always be circles, but you can't map a document to fit into a rectangle of a different shape—you will always leave part of the rectangle empty. **MM_ANISOTROPIC**, on the other hand, permits scaling of each axis independently, so that you can map an object to fit exactly into a rectangle of any shape, but, of course, shapes will deform in the process. Because it's the more flexible, we will use **MM_ANISOTROPIC** in our server version of Sketcher. This is necessary in the view class, as well as in the class representing the embedded object.

You'll remember that we saw the following equations which express device coordinates in terms of logical coordinates:

$$xDevice = (xLogical - xWindowOrg) * \frac{xViewPortExt}{xWindowExt} + xViewPortOrg$$

$$yDevice = (yLogical - yWindowOrg) * \frac{yViewPortExt}{yWindowExt} + yViewPortOrg$$

With a bit of algebraic juggling, you'll see that the conversion from device coordinates to logical coordinates will use the formulae:

$$xLogical = (xDevice - xViewPortOrg) * \frac{xWindowExt}{xViewPortExt} + xWindowOrg$$

$$yLogical = (yDevice - yViewPortOrg) * \frac{yWindowExt}{yViewPortExt} + yWindowOrg$$

With coordinate systems other than **MM_ISOTROPIC** and **MM_ANISOTROPIC**, the window extent and the viewport extent are fixed by the mapping mode, and you can't change them. Calling the functions **SetWindowExt()** or **SetViewportExt()** in the **CDC** object to change them will have no effect, although you can still move the position of (0, 0) in your logical reference frame around by calling **SetWindowOrg()** or **SetViewportOrg()**. With **MM_ISOTROPIC** and **MM_ANISOTROPIC**, you can mess everything around to your heart's content.

Updating the View

We need to adjust how the document is drawn by the view to take account of the implications of the server mode of operation. This means using a mapping mode that allows for flexibility in the way the conversion from logical to device coordinates occurs. In other words, we need to work with the **MM_ANISOTROPIC** mode. We can best do this by adding the **OnPrepareDC()** function to **CSketcherView** and setting up the mapping mode there, as we did in Chapter 7.

Changing the Mapping Mode

With the server version of Sketcher, we must define our logical units for drawing in the **MM_ANISOTROPIC** mapping mode so that Windows can determine the mapping to pixels. This is a bit more complicated than it seems at first sight, and requires a little more thought than our Chapter 7 exercise. You must take account of the scaling between the size at which you're drawing a document and the size of the document when it's displayed in the container.

The measure of this scaling between the server and the container is called a **zoom factor**. We'll use this zoom factor to provide true WYSIWYG drawing for embedded objects. If you don't adjust for the zoom factor, the size of a document object will vary depending on whether it's being edited or not. The **GetZoomFactor()** member of **COleDocument** provides a value for the zoom factor that you can use to adjust the viewport extent in the device context to get the correct mapping.

We'll set up the mapping mode and the parameters that determine how our logical coordinates are converted in the **OnPrepareDC()** function member of **CSketcherView**. Of course, you'll need to add the function to the view class using ClassWizard. Its implementation will be as follows:

```
void CSketcherView::OnPrepareDC(CDC* pDC, CPrintInfo* pInfo)
{
    CView::OnPrepareDC(pDC, pInfo);
    CSketcherDoc* pDoc = GetDocument();
    pDC->SetMapMode(MM_ANISOTROPIC);
    CSize DocSize = pDoc->GetDocSize();

    // y extent must be negative because document assumes MM_LOENGLISH
    DocSize.cy = -DocSize.cy;   // Change sign of y
    pDC->SetWindowExt(DocSize); // Now set the window extent

    // Get the zoom factor for the server compared to the container
    // If the server isn't in-place active, zoom factor will be 1 to 1
    CSize SizeNum, SizeDenom;           // Places to store zoom factors
    pDoc->GetZoomFactor(&SizeNum, &SizeDenom);

    int xLogPixels = pDC->GetDeviceCaps(LOGPIXELSX);
    int yLogPixels = pDC->GetDeviceCaps(LOGPIXELSY);

    long xExtent = ((long)DocSize.cx*xLogPixels*SizeNum.cx)/(100*SizeDenom.cx);
    long yExtent = ((long)DocSize.cy*yLogPixels*SizeNum.cy)/(100*SizeDenom.cy);
    pDC->SetViewportExt((int)xExtent, (int)-yExtent);
}
```

Note that we add our code *after* the call to the base class function that was supplied in the default implementation. After setting the mapping mode to **MM_ANISOTROPIC**, we set the window extent to correspond to the size of the document, not forgetting that the *y* extent must be negative because we're assuming **MM_LOENGLISH** compatibility, with the origin at the top-left corner of the client area. As we saw earlier, the conversion to device coordinates is determined by the ratio of the window extent to the viewport extent, so we need to set the viewport extent to be the number of pixels that are equivalent to the window extent we've specified, adjusted for the zoom factor.

As you've seen previously, the number of pixels in a logical inch is returned by the **GetDeviceCaps()** member of the **CDC** object. By using the argument **LOGPIXELSX** we get the number of pixels in a logical inch on the *x* axis, and perform a similar operation for the *y* axis. A logical inch is a Windows invention which is an inch enlarged to make characters readable. For every 100 logical units, we want to set the viewport extent to a logical inch's worth of pixels, so the number of pixels for the viewport's *x*-extent, before adjustment for the zoom factor, is:

$$\frac{DocSize.cx * xLogPixels}{100}$$

The zoom factor is returned as two **CSize** values—**SizeNum** and **SizeDenom**—corresponding to the numerator and denominator in the factor respectively. The ratio of the **cx** members of these apply to the *x*-extent for the viewport and the ratio of the **cy** members apply to the *y*-extent. Thus, the *x*-extent, for example, is calculated by the expression:

$$\frac{DocSize.cx * xLogPixels * SizeNum.cx}{100 * SizeDenom.cx}$$

This is what we have in the code for the function above.

Drawing the Embedded Object

To draw the embedded object, we need to add code to the **OnDraw()** member of **CSketcherSrvrItem** as follows:

```
BOOL CSketcherSrvrItem::OnDraw(CDC* pDC, CSize& rSize)
{
   // Remove this if you use rSize
   UNREFERENCED_PARAMETER(rSize);

   CSketcherDoc* pDoc = GetDocument();
   ASSERT_VALID(pDoc);

   // TODO: set mapping mode and extent
   //  (The extent is usually the same as the size returned from OnGetExtent)
   pDC->SetMapMode(MM_ANISOTROPIC);
   CSize DocSize = pDoc->GetDocSize(); // Get the current document size

   DocSize.cy = -DocSize.cy;          // Invert the y axis for MM_LOENGLISH
   pDC->SetWindowOrg(0,0);
   pDC->SetWindowExt(DocSize);

   // TODO: add drawing code here.  Optionally, fill in the HIMETRIC extent.
   //  All drawing takes place in the metafile device context (pDC).
```

```
      POSITION aPos = pDoc->GetListHeadPosition();
      CElement* pElement = 0;        // Store for an element pointer
      while (aPos)                   // Loop while aPos is not null
      {
         pElement = pDoc->GetNext(aPos);  // Get the current element pointer

         // If the element is visible...
         if (pDC->RectVisible(pElement->GetBoundRect()))
            pElement->Draw(pDC);          // ...draw it
      }
```

```
   return TRUE;
}
```

This is relatively straightforward. After setting the mapping mode, we retrieve the size of the document and use this to set the window extent. We make sure that the value for the *y* extent is negative. All our code in Sketcher assumes **MM_LOENGLISH** with the origin at the top-left corner of the client area. We must, therefore, specify the *y* extent and set the origin here to be consistent with that assumption. Note that AppWizard already supplied the statement to set the mapping mode to **MM_ANISOTROPIC**. This is the standard approach to drawing an embedded server object.

After setting up the mapping mode and the window extent, we draw the document using the same code we used in the **OnDraw()** function in the view. Drawing here is not directly to the screen. The GDI function calls that create the document image are stored in a metafile, which is a device-independent representation of the image. The viewport extent will be adjusted by the framework to map this metafile into the rectangle in the container view before the metafile is replayed to draw the document. This will result in the image being deformed if the rectangle enclosing the item in the container has been resized. If you want to prevent this, you need to include code here to do so. One possibility is to use **MM_ISOTROPIC** to force consistent scaling of the axes.

We haven't set the value of the second parameter, **rSize**, in the **OnDraw()** function. If you set this value it should be the size of the document in **MM_HIMETRIC** units. If you don't set it (we haven't here), the framework will call the **OnGetExtent()** function in the **COleServerItem** class object to get it from there. We'll implement that next.

Getting the Extent of an Embedded Object

The framework calls the **OnGetExtent()** member of the embedded object class in the server to get the size of the document that is to be displayed in the container. We need to implement this to return the size of the document object in Sketcher. The code to do this is as follows:

```
BOOL CSketcherSrvrItem::OnGetExtent(DVASPECT dwDrawAspect,
                                                  CSize& rSize)
{
   // Most applications, like this one, only handle drawing the content
   //  aspect of the item.  If you wish to support other aspects, such
   //  as DVASPECT_THUMBNAIL (by overriding OnDrawEx), then this
   //  implementation of OnGetExtent should be modified to handle the
   //  additional aspect(s).

   if (dwDrawAspect != DVASPECT_CONTENT)
      return COleServerItem::OnGetExtent(dwDrawAspect, rSize);
```

```
// CSketcherSrvrItem::OnGetExtent is called to get the extent in
//  HIMETRIC units of the entire item.  The default implementation
//  here simply returns a hard-coded number of units.

CSketcherDoc* pDoc = GetDocument();
ASSERT_VALID(pDoc);

// TODO: replace this arbitrary size
rSize = pDoc->GetDocSize();          // Get the document size

CClientDC aDC(0);                    // Get device context for conversion
aDC.SetMapMode(MM_ANISOTROPIC);      // Set map mode that is scaleable

// Set window extent to 1 inch in each direction in MM_LOENGLISH
aDC.SetWindowExt(100, -100);         // Set window extent with negative y

// Set viewport extent to the number of pixels in 1 inch
aDC.SetViewportExt(aDC.GetDeviceCaps(LOGPIXELSX),
                   aDC.GetDeviceCaps(LOGPIXELSY));

aDC.LPtoHIMETRIC(&rSize);            // Convert document size to HIMETRIC

return TRUE;
}
```

The comments explain what the framework expects from this function. Here, we take a simplistic approach and just retrieve the document size that is stored in the document. Ideally, the value returned should reflect the physical extent of the object to be drawn, not just the arbitrarily assigned extent for the document, but this will suffice to get our server working. The size must be returned in **HIMETRIC** units because this is the standard unit of measure set by the framework. Our document size is in **LOENGLISH** units, so we need to set up a mapping that will ensure that the logical unit in the device context is equivalent to this. We do this by setting the window extent to 100, which is the equivalent of 1 inch in each direction in **LOENGLISH** units, and then setting the viewport extent to the number of logical pixels per inch in each direction.

The number of logical pixels per inch is obtained by calling the **GetDeviceCaps()** member of the **CClientDC** object with the arguments shown. You will remember we used this in Chapter 7 when we were implementing scaling, and in Chapter 8 to get the number of points per inch for the printer. By using suitable arguments, you can use this function to get at a vast range of parameters that apply to the device context. You can get the complete list of these through the Help menu option. Finally, having set the scaling in the device context appropriately, we call the function **LPtoHIMETRIC()** to convert the document size to **HIMETRIC** units.

Add a **#include** directive for **Elements.h** to the beginning of the **SrvrItem.cpp** file because of the references to the **CElement** class in the **OnDraw()** member function.

Notifying Changes

To communicate to the framework that we've altered the document, we need to call the functions **NotifyChanged()** and **SetModifiedFlag()** whenever we do so. This is because both the container and the server need to know the document has changed. Both functions are members of the document class that is inherited from the base class, **COleDocument**.

We need to call the functions in the **WM_LBUTTONUP** handler in the view class:

```
void CSketcherView::OnLButtonUp(UINT nFlags, CPoint point)
{
   CSketcherDoc* pDoc = GetDocument();   // Get the document pointer

   if (this == GetCapture())
      ReleaseCapture();                   // Stop capturing mouse messages

   // If there is an element, add it to the document
   if (m_pTempElement)
   {
      pDoc->AddElement(m_pTempElement);    // Add the element
      pDoc->SetModifiedFlag();             // Note the modification
      // Tell the other views about it
      pDoc->UpdateAllViews(0, 0, m_pTempElement);
      m_pTempElement = 0;                  // Reset the element pointer
      pDoc->NotifyChanged();               // Tell the container...
      pDoc->SetModifiedFlag();             // ...and the server
   }
}
```

For the cut-down version of the Sketcher application, this is the only place where we change the document. The two new lines are highlighted in the above code.

Executing the Server

Sketcher should now be ready to run as a server. You can try it out stand-alone first, to make sure nothing has been overlooked. To run as a server, Sketcher needs to be entered in the registry, but this will be done automatically for you when you build the application.

You can run Sketcher with the container we created at the beginning of this chapter. Run the container application and select Edit | Insert New Object... from the menu. Then choose Sketcher Document from the list box in the dialog and click the OK button. You should then get an embedded Sketcher object, ready for editing.

You aren't limited to Sketcher. You can try embedding objects of other server applications. There are sure to be some on your system. Below, you can see an example of the container running with a Paintbrush object and a Sketcher object embedded:

Here, the Sketcher object is in-place active and currently being edited, as you can see from the hatched tracker border and the toolbar and menu items. You may also like to try editing an embedded object in a server window. You'll remember that you do this by double-clicking the object while you hold down the *Ctrl* key.

Summary

In this chapter, we've taken a brief look into how to implement an OLE container and a server based on AppWizard-generated base code. The significant points that we have discussed in this chapter are:

▶ A program that can host OLE objects that are maintained and edited by an independent program is called an **OLE container**. An OLE container can typically accommodate multiple embedded objects of different types.

▶ OLE objects in a container can be **linked**, in which case they are stored separately from the container document, or **embedded**, in which case they are stored within the container document.

▶ A program that can provide an object embedded in an OLE container application is called an **OLE server**. A server can also be a container.

▶ There are two kinds of server that you can create with AppWizard: a **mini-server** which can only operate in support of embedded objects, and a **full server** which can operate as a stand-alone application as well as a server.

▶ Embedded objects in a container are represented by instances of a class derived from the class **COleClientItem**. A server document that is embedded in a container is represented in the server application by an instance of a class derived from **COleServerItem**.

▶ Embedded objects are drawn in the container view by the server application. When an embedded object is being edited, it is drawn by the **OnDraw()** member of the document view object in the server, otherwise it is drawn by the **OnDraw()** member of the class derived from **COleServerItem**.

▶ An object is subjected to a scaling effect when it is displayed embedded in a container. Consequently, the server must use a mapping mode to allow the drawing operation to take account of the effect of this. This typically involves using **MM_ANISOTROPIC** as the mapping mode in the server.

Exercises

Ex11-1: Add a menu item to the Edit menu of WrxContainer that allows you to delete the selected item from the container. (Hint—look in the online documentation at the class members of **COleClientItem**. You'll find the function you need under General Operations.)

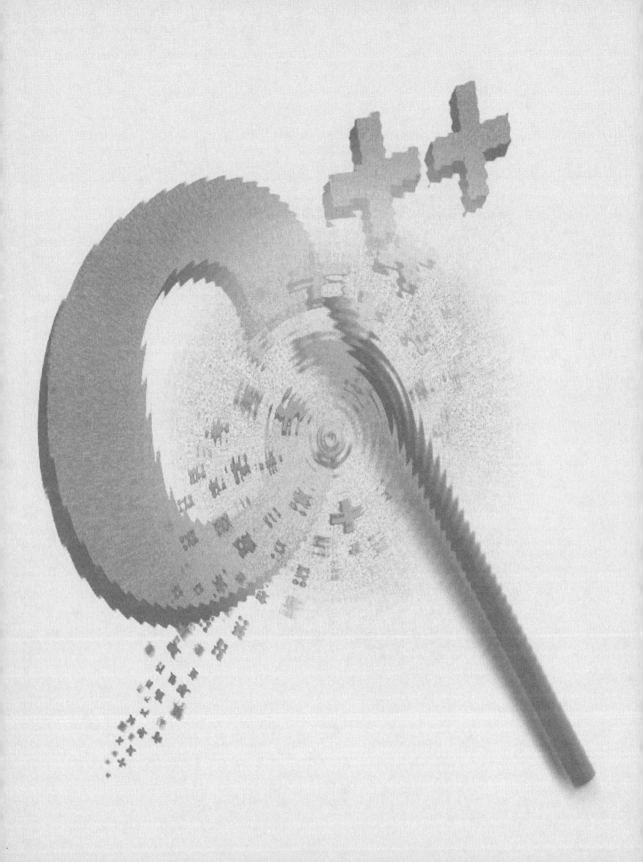

ActiveX Controls

ActiveX controls are another powerful innovation and are becoming very important in the development of applications. This chapter, therefore, ventures a few steps into the basic concepts of ActiveX controls and how they work. We'll create a simple ActiveX control example that you'll be able to exercise using the test container provided with Visual C++.

By the end of this chapter, you will have learned:

- What OLE controls are
- What ActiveX controls are
- What properties are and how they are used
- What ambient and stock properties are
- What methods in an ActiveX control are
- What events are and how they are used
- How to use Developer Studio to implement an ActiveX control
- How to add properties to a control
- How to add events to a control
- How to provide constants for use with your control
- How to embed an ActiveX control in a Web page

ActiveX and OLE

Perhaps the most important point to keep in mind is that OLE and ActiveX are marketing terms. Clearly, they do correspond to things in the real world, but they are subject to change over time. Marketing has always fully embraced the notion, first expressed by Humpty Dumpty, that words mean whatever you want them to mean.

The term OLE, which we discussed in the last chapter, predates ActiveX. OLE originally related just to the ability to embed a document created by one application within a document created by another. The archetypal example of this is an Excel spreadsheet embedded in a Word document. The original concept of OLE changed substantially over time and eventually spawned the notion of the Component Object Model, COM, which we outlined in the last chapter. COM transcends the original OLE concept in that it's a general interface specification for creating software components that you can connect together in virtually any context.

ActiveX is a term coined by Microsoft to identify their technologies that can be applied to the Internet. Since these, like OLE, are COM-based, there is an inevitable overlap between what OLE and ActiveX relate to, to the extent that you will find the terms used interchangeably in many contexts. For the moment there seems to be a distinction between OLE and ActiveX, although this could conceivably be eliminated completely in time. Let's explore what the terms OLE and ActiveX mean when they are applied to controls.

What Are OLE Controls?

Just like the Windows controls that we have seen in previous chapters, an OLE control is a facility for a programmer to use someone else's code. For instance, a Visual Basic programmer could use your C++ control in his code. An OLE control is often referred to as an **OCX**, because the extension to the name of the executable module for an OLE control is usually **.ocx**.

OLE controls provide a way to implement component-based software, and they achieve this by using COM as the means of communication. With the ever-increasing complexity of applications, there's a growing need to be able to assemble applications from sets of components which, although written completely independently of one another, can be slotted together as required. An OLE document server goes a little way along that path, in that an OLE container can use any OLE server that's written to conform to the OLE standard. The primary limitation of an OLE server is that it's anonymous as far as the container is concerned—the container has no knowledge of what the server does and has no real mechanism for communicating with it. An OLE control is different. It can communicate extensively with the container, so a greater degree of integration is possible between the container and the control.

What About ActiveX Controls?

You've almost certainly heard about **ActiveX controls** as part of the huge amount of discussion and interest in ActiveX, but you're probably wondering exactly what they are and how they relate to OLE controls.

An ActiveX control is defined simply as a control which meets two conditions: it must communicate with its container using the COM interface **IUnknown**, and it must be able to create its own entries in the System Registry. We mentioned in the previous chapter that every COM object must implement the interface known as **IUnknown**, so this is the minimum requirement for something to be a COM object, but many COM objects (such as OLE servers and containers) will also implement other interfaces. An ActiveX control, however, is only *required* to implement **IUnknown** to qualify. Therefore, other COM controls that may implement other interfaces are also ActiveX controls, as long as they can create their own Registry entries.

Although we didn't look beneath the MFC code to see what interfaces were necessary to implement an OLE server or container, you can rest assured that each OLE server or container is required to implement a certain set of interfaces that interact with each other in a particular way. Similarly, an OLE control must, by definition, implement a particular set of interfaces. Since

OLE document servers and OLE controls are COM objects, they must (and do) implement **IUnknown**; since they are also able to create their own Registry entries, they qualify as ActiveX controls. Thus we can say that all OLE controls are ActiveX controls, but not all ActiveX controls are OLE controls (because an ActiveX control doesn't have to implement the interfaces necessary to make it an OLE control).

It follows that anywhere you see 'OLE control' in this chapter, you can read it as 'ActiveX control'. Indeed, in the Visual C++ documentation you'll see it stated that OLE controls have been renamed ActiveX controls. We'll still use the term OLE control in this chapter because much of the current documentation, as well as the MFC class names, still uses this terminology.

A detailed discussion of ActiveX is outside the scope of this book, but we'll get far enough into how to create a control to give you a solid base for learning more. In this chapter, the ActiveX control that we'll develop will, in fact, be a full-blown OLE control that supports rather more than the minimum required for an ActiveX control. In the next chapter we'll take a look at how the **Active Template Library** (**ATL**) can be used to create an ActiveX component that's implemented rather differently from this chapter's control.

How OLE Controls Work

First and foremost, an OLE control communicates with the environment that's using it through a set of standard OLE interfaces, specific to OLE controls. The standard for OLE controls is an extension of the standard relating to OLE compound documents that we discussed in Chapter 20. You can easily reuse an OLE control in different application contexts, since a program that is to use an OLE control uses the same interfaces, regardless of what the control does.

A program that uses an OLE control is called an **OLE control container**, which implies that it supports the standard interfaces necessary to communicate with the OLE control. Obviously, an OLE control container is typically an application in its own right, which uses one or more OLE controls in its implementation. Because an OLE control uses the OLE interface, it's extremely portable, in that it can be used in any program designed to act as an OLE control container. An OLE control that you write using Visual C++ can be used in applications implemented in other programming languages, as long as they also support the standard OLE control interface.

The major advantage of an OLE control over an OLE server is its potential for integrating with its container. There are three ways in which an OLE control and its container can interact. As well as being able to accommodate the transfer of data to and from an OLE container, an OLE control supports a programmable interface through which its container can alter the behavior of the control, and the control can send messages to its container. The names for the mechanisms corresponding to these three capabilities are **properties**, **methods** and **events**. Let's take a look at what each of these involves.

Properties

Properties are variables which specify things about an OLE control. Although they have names, properties are specifically identified by integer values called **DispIDs**, which is an abbreviation for **Dispatch IDs**. In the case of **standard properties**, which are properties defined within the OLE standard, the DispIDs are negative values.

There are three kinds of property used in communications between an OLE control and its container:

▶ **Ambient properties**, which specify information about the environment provided by the container.

▶ **Control properties**, which are values determining aspects of the control and are set by the control.

▶ **Extended properties**, which are parameters that affect a control, such as the position where it is displayed, but which are set by the container.

Ambient Properties

Ambient properties are values that the container makes available to a control. A control cannot alter ambient properties, but it can use the values to provide better integration with the container. Through having access to such things as the screen's current background and foreground colors, the control can adjust its appearance to look consistent with that of the current container. More than that, a control may be displayed from various points in the code which goes to make up a container application, and the ambient properties may vary from place to place. The control can be programmed to automatically adapt to the conditions prevailing whenever it is displayed.

In order for ambient properties to be of any use, before you create a control you need to know which ambient properties are likely to be available. If you know what they are, you can incorporate code in your control to react to them. For this reason, there is a standard set of ambient properties. There are eighteen standard ambient properties defined in all, and they all have negative DispID values. MFC defines symbols for these in the **Olectl.h** file. We won't look at them all, but some of the more common ambient properties are:

Ambient Property Symbol	Purpose
`BackColor`	Specifies the background color, in RGB values, used by the container.
`DisplayName`	Specifies the name of the control for use in error messages.
`Font`	Specifies the font used by the container.
`ForeColor`	Specifies the foreground color, in RGB values, used by the container for the display of text and graphics.
`ScaleUnits`	Specifies the name of the coordinate units being used by container.
`TextAlign`	Specifies how the container would like text displayed in a control to be aligned. A value of 0 indicates general alignment, which 1 means text left justified and numbers right justified. A value of 1 is left justified, 2 means text should be centered, 3 means right justified, and 4 is full justification.

These are the ones that you're likely to use most often, but you can get the complete set by looking at the contents of **Olectl.h**. Each of the DispIDs for these is represented by a symbol which is obtained by preceding the name in upper case with **DISPID_AMBIENT_**, so the symbol corresponding to the DispID for **ForeColor** is **DISPID_AMBIENT_FORECOLOR**. You're not obliged to do anything about any of the ambient properties when you write an OLE control, and a container isn't obliged to provide any of them, but your control will look more professional if you react to those that are available and relevant.

Control Properties

Control properties are attributes which are set by, and give information about, the control. They can be any kind of attribute that's relevant to your control, but there's a standard set of these too, corresponding to control parameters that are also of interest to a container. If (as we shall in our example) you create your control using the MFC ActiveX ControlWizard, the base class for your control will be **COleControl**. This class implements nine standard control properties, which are referred to as **stock properties**. They are:

Stock Property	Purpose
BackColor	Specifies the background color for the control in RGB values.
Appearance	Specifies whether the control appears flat (with the value **FALSE**), or has a 3D appearance (with the value **TRUE**).
BorderStyle	Determines whether a control is displayed with a border.
Font	Defines the current font for the control.
ForeColor	Specifies, in RGB values, the foreground color for the control that's used to display text and graphics.
Enabled	When this has the value **TRUE**, it indicates that the control is enabled.
HWnd	Specifies the handle of the control's main window.
Text	Value for a text box, list box, or combo box in the control.
Caption	Defines the caption for the control.

The DispIDs for these properties can be specified by symbols consisting of the name for the property in capital letters with a prefix of **DISPID_**, so the symbol for the font property is **DISPID_FONT**. These symbols are also defined in **Olectl.h**.

It's possible to arrange for a container to be notified automatically when a stock property is modified by a control. It is also possible to arrange that the control seeks permission from the container before a certain stock property is changed. You are under no obligation to implement support for any particular stock property in a control, although it makes sense to support some of the basic stock properties that relate to the control's appearance. The usual approach is to synchronize them with the corresponding ambient properties.

You'll certainly be defining non-standard properties for your control, and these are referred to as **custom properties**. Custom properties can be anything you need to provide as a means of adapting the behavior of your control.

Extended Properties

Extended properties are properties that apply to a control, but which are set by the container for the control. A control is able to access the extended properties defined by the container, but it is not usually necessary to do so. There are only four extended properties defined, with the names, **Visible**, **Parent**, **Cancel**, and **Default**. We won't dwell on these, as we won't be concerned with them in this book, but you should avoid giving your own properties names that are the same as these.

Property Pages

A **property page** is a dialog that's used to display an interface for modifying a group of properties so that the values assigned to them can be altered by the programmer.

With a complicated control, several property pages may be used, with a group of related properties being assigned to each page. A series of property pages like this is organized into a **property sheet**, which has the appearance of a tabbed dialog box. You've used such tabbed dialog boxes many times in Developer Studio, so they'll be nothing new to you.

MFC includes the class **CPropertySheet** to define a property sheet, and the class **CPropertyPage** to define individual tabbed pages within a property sheet. Each property page will use controls such as edit boxes, list boxes or radio buttons for the setting of individual property values. We'll see how to use controls on a property page to set values for properties when we come to implement an ActiveX control later in this chapter.

Methods

In this context, a method is a function in a control that can be invoked to perform some action in response to an external request. There are two stock methods defined by the **COleControl** class:

Method Name	Purpose
Refresh()	Causes the control to be redrawn.
DoClick()	Simulates the control being clicked with the left mouse button.

Of course, you can also add your own custom methods to a control that will execute when some specific action occurs. We'll be adding custom methods to an OLE control example later in this chapter.

The ability of an OLE control to react to ambient properties, and the ability of a container to call control methods which affect the operation of the control, is referred to as **Automation**, although it is not limited to OLE controls. You can, for example, implement Automation in an OLE server to provide a programmable mechanism for a container to interact with the server.

Events

Events are signals that an OLE control sends to a container as a consequence of some action by the user on the control, or when some Windows message is received by the control. A control event can have parameters associated with it that provide additional information about the event. The container needs to implement functions to service these events in an appropriate way. The most common standard OLE control events are:

Event Name	Purpose
Click	Occurs when a mouse button is pressed and then released over a control.
DblClick	Occurs when the control is double-clicked.
KeyDown	Occurs when a key is pressed and the control has the focus.
KeyPress	Occurs when a **WM_CHAR** message is received.
KeyUp	Occurs when a key is released and the control has the focus.
MouseDown	Occurs when a mouse button is pressed while the cursor is over the control.
MouseMove	Occurs when the cursor moves over the control.
MouseUp	Occurs when a mouse button is released over the control.
Error	Signals the container when some kind of error has occurred.

All the standard events noted above are supported by the class **COleControl**.

The Interface to an OLE Control

In order to make the properties, events and methods of a control available to a container program, there needs to be an external description of what they are. Controls developed using the MFC ActiveX ControlWizard in Developer Studio make the external description available in a **type library** file, which has the extension **.tlb**. This file is produced from the definitions of the interface elements expressed in the **Object Description Language**, or **ODL**, which is stored in a source file with the extension **.odl**. ODL is also sometimes referred to as the **Object Definition Language**.

ODL was originated with OLE as a means of defining interfaces, but in the next chapter we'll see that COM interfaces can also be defined using the **Interface Definition Language**, or **IDL** for short. The Microsoft implementation of IDL incorporates ODL, so the Microsoft IDL processor, **MIDL**, will handle either ODL or IDL. IDL is more recent and more general than ODL, and will almost certainly render ODL obsolete in time.

You don't need to worry about the detail of the object description language, since this is all taken care of by ClassWizard when you add properties and other interface elements to your control. In the **.odl** file, you will find statements that associate the DispIDs for particular control properties with the variables in the code for your control which represent them. The same applies to the DispIDs for methods in your control that you make available to a container, and the events that you implement. The appropriate entries will be added to the **.odl** file as you develop the source code for your control, and the type library file for your control will be generated automatically when you build the executable module.

Implementing an ActiveX Control

We can implement a model of a traffic signal as an ActiveX control. We'll expose properties for the period of time for which the stop or go light operates, and for the starting condition of the signal, to make it possible to change these externally.

The starting point for our example is a basic ActiveX (OLE) control that we can create using ControlWizard in Developer Studio.

Creating a Basic ActiveX Control

Create a new project and workspace with the type set to MFC ActiveX ControlWizard, as shown below:

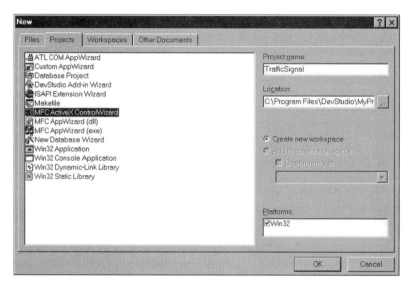

You can name the project as shown, or choose your own name if you wish. ControlWizard will use the name you supply as the name of the directory containing the project files, and as a basis for naming the classes in the project. Now click on the OK button to move to the next step.

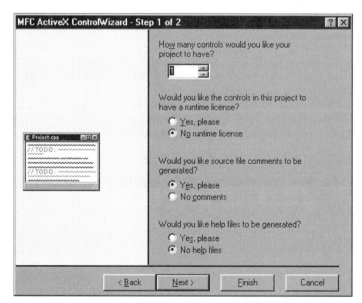

We're going to leave all these options at their default settings, but let's take a brief run-through of what they are.

The first choice allows you to specify up to 99 controls within a single project. This is in case you're developing a package of controls that will be used or distributed as a unit. Since we're just starting out, trying to get one working will provide us with enough entertainment.

Next, you have the option of including a run-time license. This is a program mechanism for controlling where your control can be used. Your control can be used in an application that is licensed—which implies that the application was developed with a suitable `.lic` license file available—but a user of the application won't be able to use your control in another context.

The last two options here hardly need explanation. It goes without saying that we want the code to be commented, and we don't want help files to be generated because we don't need the overhead of creating their contents at this point. For a production control that would be used extensively, the help files would most likely be a must.

The second and final ActiveX ControlWizard step is shown here:

The first option allows you to change the names of files and classes relating to the project, and if you click on the Edit Names... button you can see what you can alter in our project. The Type IDs for the control and the property page classes will be entered in the registry eventually, so you need to avoid conflicts. Before the code is generated, ControlWizard will check for conflicts with the existing registry entries and let you know if there's a potential problem. If you leave everything as it is for the moment, there shouldn't be any.

The control features that are selected by the check boxes are quite straightforward. We do want our control to be activated when it's visible and we might as well have an 'About' box. If you extend the drop-down list box you'll see that you can base the control on an existing Windows control, such as a button or an edit box, but that doesn't apply in our case. The last option here, for advanced ActiveX enhancements, we'll leave unexposed and move on to accept all the default settings on this step. If you click on the Finish button, ControlWizard will go ahead and create all the files for the project.

Structure of the Program

If you look at ClassView and extend the contents, you'll see that we have a new icon used with **_DTrafficSignal** and **_DTrafficSignalEvents**. This icon indicates these are COM interface elements. The green icon used with **AboutBox()** indicates that it's an interface method. All these interface specifications appear in the **TrafficSignal.odl** file. We'll look into this in more detail later in the chapter.

There are just three classes defined: the application class **CTrafficSignalApp**, the control class **CTrafficSignalCtrl**, and the property page class **CTrafficSignalPropPage**.

The Application Class

The application class **CTrafficSignalApp** is very simple, containing just two members: the **InitInstance()** function, in which you can include any initialization code you want to add, and the **ExitInstance()** function, in which you can do any necessary clean-up when the control is terminated.

This external simplicity hides a good deal of internal sophistication. The base class for our application class is **COleControlModule** which in turn is derived from **CWinApp**, which provides all of the functionality of any other Windows application. The default version of the **InitInstance()** function calls the version in **COleControlModule**, which initializes the control.

The Control Class

The class **CTrafficSignalCtrl** is derived from the MFC class **COleControl** and provides the interface to the control container. The definition provided by ControlWizard is as follows:

```
class CTrafficSignalCtrl : public COleControl
{
   DECLARE_DYNCREATE(CTrafficSignalCtrl)

// Constructor
public:
   CTrafficSignalCtrl();
```

```
// Overrides
   // ClassWizard generated virtual function overrides
   //{{AFX_VIRTUAL(CTrafficSignalCtrl)
   public:
   virtual void OnDraw(CDC* pdc, const CRect& rcBounds, const CRect& rcInvalid);
   virtual void DoPropExchange(CPropExchange* pPX);
   virtual void OnResetState();
   //}}AFX_VIRTUAL

// Implementation
protected:
   ~CTrafficSignalCtrl();

   DECLARE_OLECREATE_EX(CTrafficSignalCtrl)    // Class factory and guid
   DECLARE_OLETYPELIB(CTrafficSignalCtrl)      // GetTypeInfo
   DECLARE_PROPPAGEIDS(CTrafficSignalCtrl)     // Property page IDs
   DECLARE_OLECTLTYPE(CTrafficSignalCtrl)      // Type name and misc status

// Message maps
   //{{AFX_MSG(CTrafficSignalCtrl)
      // NOTE - ClassWizard will add and remove member functions here.
      //    DO NOT EDIT what you see in these blocks of generated code !
   //}}AFX_MSG
   DECLARE_MESSAGE_MAP()

// Dispatch maps
   //{{AFX_DISPATCH(CTrafficSignalCtrl)
      // NOTE - ClassWizard will add and remove member functions here.
      //    DO NOT EDIT what you see in these blocks of generated code !
   //}}AFX_DISPATCH
   DECLARE_DISPATCH_MAP()

   afx_msg void AboutBox();

// Event maps
   //{{AFX_EVENT(CTrafficSignalCtrl)
      // NOTE - ClassWizard will add and remove member functions here.
      //    DO NOT EDIT what you see in these blocks of generated code !
   //}}AFX_EVENT
   DECLARE_EVENT_MAP()

// Dispatch and event IDs
public:
   enum {
   //{{AFX_DISP_ID(CTrafficSignalCtrl)
      // NOTE: ClassWizard will add and remove enumeration elements here.
      //    DO NOT EDIT what you see in these blocks of generated code !
   //}}AFX_DISP_ID
   };
};
```

You'll need to add application-specific data and function members to this class to customize the control to your requirements.

The **OnDraw()** function is called when a **WM_PAINT** message is sent to the control, so you add the drawing operations for your control to this function.

The **DoPropExchange()** member handles serialization of the properties for the control. ClassWizard will automatically extend this function for stock properties that you add, but if your control requires custom properties, you must add code to serialize these yourself. It may not be immediately obvious why you would want to serialize the properties of a control, but think about what might be involved in setting up a complicated control that you are using in a program. There could be a significant number of properties that you need to set to achieve the behavior that you want, and without serialization someone using your program would need to set every single one each time your application was executed. This could get very tedious very quickly.

The **OnResetState()** member is called by the framework when the control properties need to be set to their default values. The default implementation of this member calls the **DoPropExchange()** function to do this. If your control needs special initialization, you can add it to the **OnResetState()** member.

The group of four macros starting with **DECLARE_OLECREATE_EX()** are included by ControlWizard to set up essential mechanisms required for the operation of an ActiveX control, and we'll mention a little more about them shortly when we discuss the implementation of the class.

This class will eventually include the code to support the specifics of the interface to a container. You can see that there are three blocks at the end of the class, relating to **message maps**, **dispatch maps** and **event maps** definitions, that are maintained by ClassWizard. The message maps are the same as the ones we have seen previously in ordinary Windows programs, providing Windows message handlers for the class. The dispatch maps specify the connection between internal and external names for properties and methods which are accessible by a container. The event maps will include the specification of the class function that's responsible for firing each event that the control can send to its container. Entries in all these maps are all handled automatically by ClassWizard as and when you specify elements of the interface.

Implementation of the Control Class

The default implementation of the control class provided by ControlWizard in **TrafficSignalCtl.cpp** has the definitions of the maps we've just discussed, plus a lot of other stuff that's essential to the operation of the control. With the exception of the list of property pages, all of these are maintained by ClassWizard, so you can safely ignore their detailed contents. We'll just give the briefest indication of what they are, so that you get a basic understanding of what they do.

The maps are followed by the block that contains the list of property pages for the control. There is just one at present, but if you need to add more property pages to your control, then for each page you must add an additional line which applies the **PROPPAGEID()** macro to the property page class name. You must also increase the count of the number of property pages to correspond to the total number of property pages that you have.

The next macro in the implementation of **CTrafficSignalCtrl** is:

```
IMPLEMENT_OLECREATE_EX(CTrafficSignalCtrl,
                "TRAFFICSIGNAL.TrafficSignalCtrl.1",
                0x261d8be5, 0x6938, 0x11d0, 0xab, 0x3a,
                0, 0x20, 0xaf, 0x71, 0xe4, 0x33)
```

The purpose of this macro is to create a **class factory** for the control. A class factory is an object that has the ability to create COM objects and, in this case, the objects it will be able to create are instances of our control. Instances of our control are identified by the CLSID which is specified here in the last eleven arguments to the macro. This is a unique identifier for our control that has been generated automatically by ControlWizard. The class factory object implements another standard COM interface, known as the **IClassFactory** interface, but you need not be concerned with the detailed mechanics of this—it's all handled by the framework.

The **IMPLEMENT_OLETYPELIB()** macro which follows creates a member of the control class that's used to retrieve information about the interface to a container that's supported by the control. The detail of this is also taken care of by the framework.

We then have definitions of two global constants, which are **struct**s that define unique identifiers for the interfaces to a container supported by our control. These identifiers are used to reference the interfaces. They are followed by a global constant which defines miscellaneous characteristics of the control's behavior, and a macro which implements these characteristics.

The definition of **UpdateRegistry()** overrides the base class implementation. The purpose of this member is to cause the control to be entered in the system registry. The control cannot be used until it has been registered. Note that **UpdateRegistry()** is a member of the factory class **CTrafficSignalCtrlFactory**, not **COleControl**. It isn't obvious where the factory class is defined—there's no definition evident in the **.h** files for our control—so where does it come from? If you look back at the definition of **CTrafficSignalCtrl**, you'll see that it contains the line:

```
DECLARE_OLECREATE_EX(CTrafficSignalCtrl)    // Class factory and guid
```

DECLARE_OLECREATE_EX() is a macro that creates a factory class definition for our control class. The class name appearing between the parentheses is used in the macro to create the definition for **CTrafficSignalCtrlFactory**. This is all handled by the preprocessor and the compiler, so you never see the source code for the class definition. Because the definition that's created for the factory class is *nested* within the **CTrafficSignalCtrl** control class, its members must be referenced using fully qualified names. Hence the need for both class names being used as qualifiers when referring to **UpdateRegistry()**.

The remainder of the implementation of **CTrafficSignalCtrl** contains simple default implementations of the class members, some of which we'll extend when we customize the control to behave as we want.

The Property Page Class

The class **CTrafficSignalPropPage** implements the ability to set control properties through property pages. Each property page that is created for your control is managed by an instance of this class. The definition of this class provided by ControlWizard is:

```
class CTrafficSignalPropPage : public COlePropertyPage
{
    DECLARE_DYNCREATE(CTrafficSignalPropPage)
    DECLARE_OLECREATE_EX(CTrafficSignalPropPage)

// Constructor
public:
    CTrafficSignalPropPage();
```

```
   // Dialog Data
      //{{AFX_DATA(CTrafficSignalPropPage)
      enum { IDD = IDD_PROPPAGE_TRAFFICSIGNAL };
         // NOTE - ClassWizard will add data members here.
         //    DO NOT EDIT what you see in these blocks of generated code !
      //}}AFX_DATA

   // Implementation
   protected:
      virtual void DoDataExchange(CDataExchange* pDX);    // DDX/DDV support

   // Message maps
   protected:
      //{{AFX_MSG(CTrafficSignalPropPage)
         // NOTE - ClassWizard will add and remove member functions here.
         //    DO NOT EDIT what you see in these blocks of generated code !
      //}}AFX_MSG
      DECLARE_MESSAGE_MAP()

   };
```

The main activity supported by this class is the transfer of data that is set through a property page to update the variables that represent the properties in your ActiveX control implementation. The data is entered through controls, such as buttons and list boxes that you place on a property page, and the **DoDataExchange()** function handles the exchange of data between the controls collecting the input and the variables in the control.

Implementation of the Property Page Class

If you look in the **TrafficSignalPpg.cpp** file for the property page class, you'll see that it contains code for defining a CLSID and an implementation of the **UpdateRegistry()** member function. This is because each property page is a COM object in its own right and has its own class factory and entry in the system registry.

The class constructor doesn't contain any code at present, but ClassWizard will add code to initialize any properties that we add to the property page. Similarly, the **DoDataExchange()** function will be extended by ClassWizard when we add variables to receive the values for properties from controls on the property page.

Defining a Traffic Signal Object

We can define the basic representation of a traffic signal in a class. To add this class to the project, select New Class... from the Insert menu. Select Generic Class for the Class type and give the class the name **CTrafficSignal**. Now Change... the filenames to be used for the class to **OurTrafficSignal.h** and **OurTrafficSignal.cpp**. Finally, click OK to create the new class.

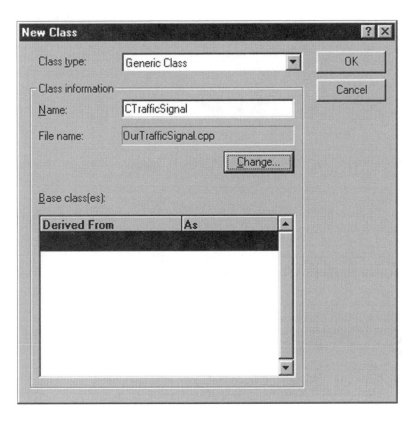

The first thing we should consider is what we want the traffic signal to do. That will give us an idea of what function members we'll need to provide a satisfactory interface to the class.

A traffic signal object will represent the signal in a particular state. The change of state will be triggered externally to the class. We'll need the ability to set the initial state of the signal and step the signal from one state to another, keeping our traffic signal object very simple.

We can build in the ability for the signal to draw itself, but it would be useful if the size of the signal could adapt to the size of the control when it's displayed. If we decide that the signal will be the same height as the control, and will be positioned in the center of it, we can pass sufficient information to a signal such that it can draw itself to fit the control with just two functions in the class interface: one to set the position of the control, the other to set the height. We can calculate a value for the width based on the height.

With these considerations in mind, we can define the traffic signal class as follows. Add the highlighted code to the new class definition in **OurTrafficSignal.h**.

```
class CTrafficSignal
{
public:
   CTrafficSignal();
   virtual ~CTrafficSignal();
```

```
   // Class interface
   void SetPosition(CPoint ptPosition)
      { m_ptPosition = ptPosition; }
   void SetHeight(int nHeight)
      { m_nHeight =nHeight; }
   void SetSignalState(int nState)
      { m_nSignalState = nState; }
   void Draw(CDC* pDC);                  // Draw the traffic signal
   int NextState();                      // Change to the next state

private:
   CPoint m_ptPosition;   // Bottom center of signal
   int m_nHeight;         // Height of signal
   int m_nSignalState;    // State of signal
};
```

We have five functions defining the class interface to provide the capability we've just outlined, and three **private** data members for the position of the signal, the height of the signal and the state of the signal, which will determine which light is lit. The reference point for the position is arbitrarily the center point on the bottom edge of the signal.

The only functions that we haven't defined in the class definition are the **Draw()** function which will draw the signal using the **m_ptPosition** and **m_nHeight** values, and the **NextState()** function which will change the signal to the next state in sequence by setting the value of **m_nSignalState** appropriately. All we need to complete the class is to add the definitions for these.

Implementing the NextState() Function

Before we can implement the **NextState()** function, we need to define what we mean by a state. The signal has three different states: it can be at 'stop', at 'go', or it can be at 'get-ready-to-stop'. (British signals have an extra state, 'get-ready-to-go', between stop and go, but we won't implement that.) We can define these states by a set of **const** variables that we can put in another file, so create a new source file and save it in the control project folder as **OurConstants.h**, then add the following code:

```
// Definition of constants

#if !defined(__OURCONSTANTS_H__)
#define __OURCONSTANTS_H__

const int STOP         = 101;
const int GO           = 103;
const int READY_TO_STOP = 104;

#endif // !defined(__OURCONSTANTS_H__)
```

After saving the file, you can add it to the project by right-clicking in the project window and selecting Insert File into Project from the pop-up. The file should then appear in the FileView immediately.

Now add **#include "OurConstants.h"** to the top of **OurTrafficSignal.cpp** just below all the other **#include**s, since we're going to define the **NextState()** function using these constants. Add the following code to the end of **OurTrafficSignal.cpp**.

```
// Change the signal state to the next in sequence
int CTrafficSignal::NextState()
{
   switch (m_nSignalState)
   {
      case STOP:
        m_nSignalState = GO;
        break;
      case GO:
        m_nSignalState = READY_TO_STOP;
        break;
      case READY_TO_STOP:
        m_nSignalState = STOP;
        break;
      default:
        m_nSignalState = STOP;
        AfxMessageBox("Invalid signal state");
   }
   return m_nSignalState;
}
```

This is very straightforward. The three cases in the **switch** correspond to the three possible states of the signal, and each sets the **m_nSignalState** variable to the next state in sequence. The action for the default case, which would only arise if an invalid state were set somewhere, is to arbitrarily set the signal state to **STOP** and to display a message.

Implementing the Draw() Function

To draw the signal, we need a feel for how the width is set in relation to the height, and the positioning of the lights relative to the reference point **m_ptPosition**. The dimensions determining this are shown in the diagram below:

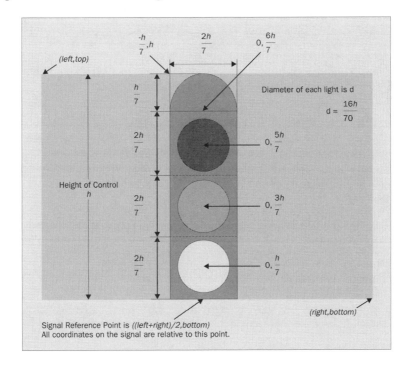

Signal Reference Point is *((left+right)/2,bottom)*
All coordinates on the signal are relative to this point.

The overall height of the signal is the same as that of the control. All the other dimensions for the signal have been defined in terms of the height to produce a consistently proportioned representation of it. All the coordinates for the centers of the lights and the top semicircular section are defined relative to the reference point for the signal which is set at the center of the base. The reference point is positioned at the midpoint on the bottom edge of the control.

There are several steps to drawing the complete signal, so let's build up the code for the **Draw()** function incrementally. Using the drawing above and the coordinates of the reference point for the signal stored in the data member **m_ptPosition**, we can draw the basic outline of the signal with the following code, which you should add to the **OurTrafficSignal.cpp** file:

```
// Draw the signal
void CTrafficSignal::Draw(CDC* pDC)
{
   // Set the pen and brush to draw the signal
   CBrush* pOldBrush = (CBrush*)pDC->SelectStockObject(GRAY_BRUSH);
   CPen* pOldPen = (CPen*)pDC->SelectStockObject(BLACK_PEN);

   // Define the main body of the signal
   int nLeft = m_ptPosition.x - m_nHeight/7;
   int nTop = m_ptPosition.y - (long)m_nHeight*6L/7L;
   int nRight = m_ptPosition.x + m_nHeight/7;
   int nBottom = m_ptPosition.y;

   pDC->Rectangle(nLeft, nTop, nRight, nBottom);  // Draw the body

   // Define the semi-circular top of the signal
   CRect rect(nLeft, nTop - m_nHeight/7, nRight, nTop + m_nHeight/7);
   CPoint ptStart(nRight, nTop);
   CPoint ptEnd(nLeft, nTop);

   pDC->Chord(rect, ptStart, ptEnd);

   // Code to create brushes for the lights will go here...
   // Code to actually draw the lights will go here...

   pDC->SelectObject(pOldBrush);        // Put the old brush back
   pDC->SelectObject(pOldPen);          // Put the old pen back
}
```

We use the **SelectStockObject()** member of the **CDC** class to select a standard gray brush and a standard black pen into the device context, saving the old objects in each case so we can restore them when we're done. The brush is used to fill the interior of any closed shapes we draw subsequently. We need to cast the pointer returned from **SelectStockObject()** to the appropriate type, as it returns a **void*** pointer.

The next step is to calculate the coordinates of the upper left and bottom right corners of the rectangle making up the main body of the signal. We won't change the mapping mode so the default **MM_TEXT** will apply, with positive y from top to bottom, and positive x from left to right. With these coordinates, we draw a closed rectangle with the **Rectangle()** member of the **CDC** class. The interior of the rectangle will automatically be filled with the current brush color.

To draw the semicircle on the top of the signal, we calculate a **CRect** object corresponding to the coordinates of the top left and bottom right corners of the rectangle enclosing a full circle, together with the end points of the semicircular section that we want. The **Chord()** member of

CDC will draw a closed figure corresponding to the segment of the circle from **StartPt** to **EndPt** plus the chord, and fill the interior with the current brush color.

To draw the lights, we'll need to define the colors that we're going to use for them. We can add the definitions for the colors in the **OurConstants.h** file with the following code:

```
const COLORREF RED    = RGB(255, 0, 0);
const COLORREF ORANGE = RGB(200, 100, 0);
const COLORREF GREEN  = RGB(0, 255, 0);
const COLORREF GRAY   = RGB(100, 100, 100);
```

The red, orange and green colors are the colors for the lights when they are on, and the gray color will be used for a light when it's off. If you don't like the way the colors come out, you can always mess around with the RGB values for them!

For each light, we'll need to create a brush to fill its interior depending on the state of the signal stored in **m_nSignalState**. We can do this by adding code to the **Draw()** function, as follows:

```
// Draw the signal
void CTrafficSignal::Draw(CDC* pDC)
{
    // Drawing code as before...

    // Create brushes for the lights
    CBrush brStop;              // A brush to fill the stop light
    CBrush brReady;             // A brush to fill the ready light
    CBrush brGo;                // A brush to fill the go light

    switch (m_nSignalState)
    {
        case STOP:                              // Red only
            brStop.CreateSolidBrush(RED);
            brReady.CreateSolidBrush(GRAY);
            brGo.CreateSolidBrush(GRAY);
            break;
        case GO:                                // Green only
            brStop.CreateSolidBrush(GRAY);
            brReady.CreateSolidBrush(GRAY);
            brGo.CreateSolidBrush(GREEN);
            break;
        case READY_TO_STOP:                     // Orange only
            brStop.CreateSolidBrush(GRAY);
            brReady.CreateSolidBrush(ORANGE);
            brGo.CreateSolidBrush(GRAY);
            break;
        default:
            brStop.CreateSolidBrush(GRAY);
            brReady.CreateSolidBrush(GRAY);
            brGo.CreateSolidBrush(GRAY);
    }

    // Code to actually draw the lights will go here...

    pDC->SelectObject(pOldBrush);       // Get the old brush back
    pDC->SelectObject(pOldPen);         // Get the old pen back
}
```

We create a **CBrush** object for each light, which we'll use later to fill the interior of the lights. We set the color for each **CBrush** object in the **switch** by calling the **CreateSolidBrush()** member of the object. The colors are determined by the state set in **m_nSignalState**. If **m_nSignalState** doesn't contain a valid state, all the lights will be out.

With the brush colors set, we're ready to draw the three lights. We can do this by adding the following code to the **Draw()** function:

```
// Draw the signal
void CTrafficSignal::Draw(CDC* pDC)
{
    // Code to draw the outline of the signal as before...
    // Code to create brushes for the three lights as before...

    // Define the rectangle bounding the stop light
    int nMargin = (long)m_nHeight * 2L/70L;    // Ten percent of the width
    nLeft += nMargin;                          // Left side of stop light
    nTop += nMargin;                           // Top of stop light
    nRight -= nMargin;                         // Right side of stop light
    int nStep = (long)m_nHeight * 2L/7L;       // Distance between lights
    nBottom = nTop + nStep - 2 * nMargin;      // Bottom of stop light

    // Draw the stop light
    pDC->SelectObject(&brStop);
    pDC->Ellipse(nLeft, nTop, nRight, nBottom);

    // Set the position of the ready light
    nTop += nStep;
    nBottom += nStep;

    // Draw the ready light
    pDC->SelectObject(&brReady);
    pDC->Ellipse(nLeft, nTop, nRight, nBottom);

    // Set the position of the go light
    nTop += nStep;
    nBottom += nStep;

    // Draw the go light
    pDC->SelectObject(&brGo);
    pDC->Ellipse(nLeft, nTop, nRight, nBottom);

    pDC->SelectObject(pOldBrush);      // Get the old brush back
    pDC->SelectObject(pOldPen);        // Get the old pen back
}
```

To draw the lights, we'll be using the **Ellipse()** member of the class **CDC**. This requires an enclosing rectangle for the figure to be drawn, so we need to construct the coordinates of the top left and bottom right corners of the square enclosing each light. If we construct the square enclosing the red light, we can just displace this down by the appropriate amount to draw the orange light, and again by the same amount for the green light.

The diameter of each light is 20% less than the width of the signal, so we first calculate 10% of the width and store it in the local variable **nMargin**. We'll use this value to decrease the size of the bounding rectangle for a light, all round. At this point, the coordinates stored in **nLeft** and

nTop are the top left corner of the rectangle defining the main body of the signal. We can offset these by the value of **nMargin** to get the top left corner of the square enclosing the red light. We can obtain the *x* coordinate of the bottom right corner of the square by subtracting the value of **nMargin** from **nRight**; to get the *y* coordinate, we increment **nTop** by the value of **nStep**, which we have set to the width of the signal, and subtract twice the value of **nMargin**, that is, 20% of the width. All we then have to do to draw the red light is select the appropriate brush into the device context and use the **Ellipse()** function with the coordinates we have calculated.

Drawing the orange and green lights is simple. The orange light is the same size as the red one, just displaced in the *y* direction by the width of the signal which we've stored in **nStep**. The green light is displaced from the position of the orange light by a further distance **nStep** in the *y* direction.

Adding a Constructor

We need to add the implementation of the constructor to the file **OurTrafficSignal.cpp**. All this needs to do is to set some default values for the data members of the class:

```
CTrafficSignal::CTrafficSignal()
{
    m_ptPosition = CPoint(0, 0);  // Set arbitrary position
    m_nHeight = 1000;             // Set arbitrary height
    m_nSignalState = STOP;        // Set initial state to STOP
}
```

All the data member values will eventually be set by the control, so the values given here are arbitrary.

Using a CTrafficSignal Object

To add a traffic signal object to the control, we need to add a **protected** member to the class **CTrafficSignalCtrl**. You can do this either by right-clicking the class name in ClassView and following the dialog after selecting Add Member Variable... from the pop-up, or by adding the following code directly to the class definition in **TrafficSignalCtl.h**:

```
protected:
    CTrafficSignal* m_pSignal;    // Pointer to a traffic signal object
```

The merit of adding the code directly is that you can organize the class definition sensibly. Adding members using the dialog can put members of the class in rather bizarre places in the class definition.

Add a line just before the beginning of the **CTrafficSignalCtrl** class definition to inform the compiler that **CTrafficSignal** is a class:

```
class CTrafficSignal;
```

We now need to create an object in the constructor, so amend the default constructor definition in the file **TrafficSignalCtl.cpp** by adding a line of code to it, as follows:

```
CTrafficSignalCtrl::CTrafficSignalCtrl()
{
    InitializeIIDs(&IID_DTrafficSignal, &IID_DTrafficSignalEvents);

    m_pSignal = new CTrafficSignal;        // Create a signal
}
```

The first line of code in the constructor that was included by ControlWizard passes information to the base class about the interface to a container. This enables properties and events that we add to the control to be properly identified. Since we create a **CTrafficSignal** object on the heap, we should arrange to delete it in the class destructor, so modify the destructor as follows:

```
CTrafficSignalCtrl::~CTrafficSignalCtrl()
{
    delete m_pSignal;                      // Delete the signal
}
```

If we now add some code to the **OnDraw()** function, we can try out the control to make sure that our traffic signal object displays as we expect it to. The default **OnDraw()** function in the control draws an ellipse, so you need to delete that code and add code to draw the traffic signal, like this:

```
void CTrafficSignalCtrl::OnDraw(
            CDC* pdc, const CRect& rcBounds, const CRect& rcInvalid)
{
    pdc->FillRect(rcBounds,
                CBrush::FromHandle((HBRUSH)GetStockObject(WHITE_BRUSH)));

    // Set the height of the signal
    m_pSignal->SetHeight(abs(rcBounds.Height()));

    // The reference point for the signal is the middle of its base
    // so set the position of the signal at the midway point
    // along the bottom of the bound rectangle
    CPoint ptPosition(((long)rcBounds.right + rcBounds.left)/2L, rcBounds.bottom);
    m_pSignal->SetPosition(ptPosition);
    m_pSignal->Draw(pdc);                  // Draw the signal
}
```

The first statement in the default version fills the whole rectangle occupied by the control using a white brush. We'll be amending this later to use the background color defined by the ambient property, but for now you can leave it as it is.

The **rcBounds** parameter passed to the function defines the rectangle that the control occupies. We calculate the midpoint of the base of this rectangle and use this to set the position of the reference point in the traffic signal object. We then call the **Draw()** member of the object to get the traffic signal to draw itself.

Finally, we need to add **#include** statements to the beginning of the **TrafficSignalCtl.cpp** file for the **.h** files containing the definition of the **CTrafficSignal** class and the constants we have defined:

```
#include "OurTrafficSignal.h"
#include "OurConstants.h"
```

Testing the Control

If you build the control, it should be ready to run. It won't do much, since we haven't built in any ability to interact with a container, or to sequence the traffic signal, but at least you can verify that it looks like a traffic signal and that it re-sizes itself satisfactorily.

Of course, you need a container to exercise the control and, conveniently, Developer Studio has one available in the Tools menu. Just select the ActiveX Control Test Container option. The control needs to be in the system registry before you can use it, but if it compiled and linked OK, it will have been registered automatically.

Once the test container is running, select Edit | Insert OLE Control..., or click the first toolbar button on the left, to bring up a dialog displaying a list of controls that you can use. Select TrafficSignal Control from the list to get our control displayed in the container.

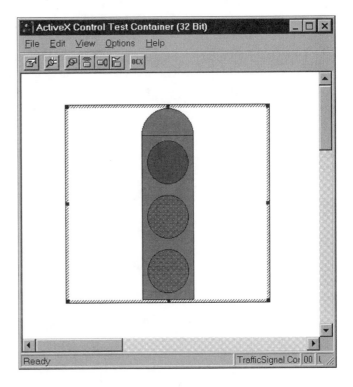

If you want to add another instance of our control, you can just click the toolbar button on the right, labeled OCX. You can resize the control and the signal should automatically alter its height and width. The hatching around the control indicates that it is currently active. You can render it inactive by clicking anywhere outside it. A single-click in the control will reactivate it again.

Now that the basic drawing code works, we should think about extending the control to add some properties and to get the signal working.

Using Stock and Ambient Properties

We can see how to introduce stock properties into our control by using the **BackColor** property as an example. You use ClassWizard to add stock properties to the control. With the control project open, select View | ClassWizard... in Developer Studio, and select the Automation tab.

Make sure that **CTrafficSignalCtrl** is shown in the Class name: list box and click on the Add Property... button.

If you extend the External name: list box, you'll see a list of stock properties. When you select BackColor, the other three list boxes will be set to appropriate values and grayed to indicate that you can't change them. The Stock radio button is also selected automatically. The resulting dialog is shown below:

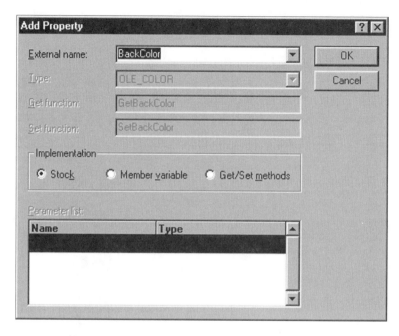

If you now select the OK button, you'll return to the ClassWizard dialog shown below:

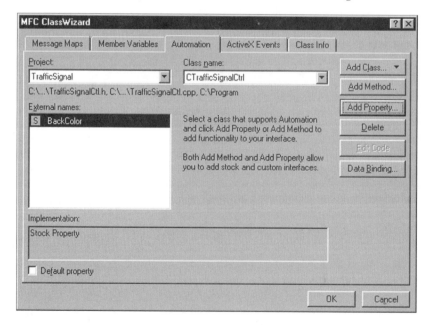

The list of External names: now includes the name BackColor. The prefix S indicates that it's a stock property. Custom properties will be prefixed with C, as you'll see when we add some a little later. If you look in the implementation file for **CTrafficSignalCtrl**, you'll see that the dispatch map has been modified by ClassWizard to become the following:

```
BEGIN_DISPATCH_MAP(CTrafficSignalCtrl, COleControl)
   //{{AFX_DISPATCH_MAP(CTrafficSignalCtrl)
   DISP_STOCKPROP_BACKCOLOR()
   //}}AFX_DISPATCH_MAP
   DISP_FUNCTION_ID(CTrafficSignalCtrl, "AboutBox", DISPID_ABOUTBOX,
                    AboutBox, VT_EMPTY, VTS_NONE)
END_DISPATCH_MAP()
```

This extra line of code ensures that the **BackColor** property is made available to the world outside our control. With this code in place, users will be able to set and retrieve the value for the **BackColor** of our control, but if we don't add any drawing code that actually makes use of this property, there would be little point in having it. We must add some code to the **OnDraw()** function so that our control actually uses the value of the **BackColor** property for its background:

```
void CTrafficSignalCtrl::OnDraw(
           CDC* pdc, const CRect& rcBounds, const CRect& rcInvalid)
{
    // Set the background using the control's BackColor property
    CBrush brBack(TranslateColor(GetBackColor()));
    pdc->FillRect(rcBounds, &brBack);           // Fill the background

    // Set the height of the signal
    m_pSignal->SetHeight(abs(rcBounds.Height()));

    // The reference point for the signal is the middle of its base
    // so set the position of the signal at the midway point
    // along the bottom of the base rectangle
    CPoint ptPosition(((long)rcBounds.right + rcBounds.left)/2L, rcBounds.bottom);
    m_pSignal->SetPosition(ptPosition);
    m_pSignal->Draw(pdc);                        // Draw the signal
}
```

You should replace the default code that filled the background with the shaded lines of code above. The **GetBackColor()** function, which is inherited from **COleControl**, returns the color stored in the stock property in the control as type **OLE_COLOR**. The **OLE_COLOR** type defines a standard way of representing color values when they are transferred between COM objects. The **OLE_COLOR** value is converted to a **COLORREF** value (RGB value) by the **TranslateColor()** function.

There are functions defined in the **COleControl** class for each of the stock properties that you may include in your control. Examples of these are **GetForeColor()** which returns the foreground color, and **GetScaleUnits()** which returns the type of units used in the container.

The implementation for the stock property provided by **COleControl** uses the ambient **BackColor** property of the container to initialize the **BackColor** property for the control. This means that the background color of the container and control should be the same when the control is first added to the container. If the background color in the container later changes for some reason, the stock property in the container won't be updated. If you want to find out the current background color in the container, you can use the **AmbientBackColor()** function inherited from **COleControl**.

475

You can easily see the difference between the effects of **GetBackColor()** and **AmbientBackColor()** by trying two versions of the control in the test container. First, build the current version of the control that uses **GetBackColor()** in its drawing code. Start the Test Container by selecting it from the <u>T</u>ools menu. You can load the control by selecting <u>I</u>nsert OLE Control... from the <u>E</u>dit menu and selecting the control from the list available in the dialog. There is also a toolbar button that you can use corresponding to this menu item.

You can change the ambient background color by selecting Set Ambient Properties... from the <u>E</u>dit menu, or by selecting the second toolbar button from the left. You can choose the property that you want to set from the drop-down list box in the dialog, as shown:

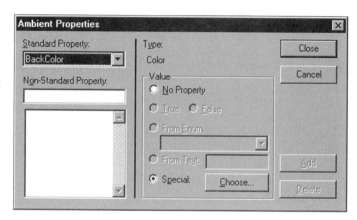

To select a color, click on the <u>C</u>hoose... button in the dialog. Even though you change it, the new background color will have no effect on the control. However, if you load another instance of the control, it will use the new background color. Once you've added one instance of a control, you can add another just by clicking on the toolbar button labeled OCX. Note that the visible background of the test container is always white, even when you change the ambient property to another color. Although most containers will keep their actual background color and the ambient background color in synch, it doesn't have to be that way.

Now let's see what happens if we use the ambient background color to draw the background of our control. Change the code in **CTrafficSignalCtrl::OnDraw()** as shown:

```
void CTrafficSignalCtrl::OnDraw(
        CDC* pdc, const CRect& rcBounds, const CRect& rcInvalid)
{
    // Set the background using the control's BackColor property
    // CBrush brBack(TranslateColor(GetBackColor()));
    // Set the background using the container's ambient BackColor property
    CBrush brBack(TranslateColor(AmbientBackColor()));

    pdc->FillRect(rcBounds, &brBack);          // Fill the background

    // Set the height of the signal
    m_pSignal->SetHeight(abs(rcBounds.Height()));

    // The reference point for the signal is the middle of its base
    // so set the position of the signal at the midway point
    // along the bottom of the bound rectangle
    CPoint ptPosition(((long)rcBounds.right + rcBounds.left)/2L, rcBounds.bottom);
    m_pSignal->SetPosition(ptPosition);
    m_pSignal->Draw(pdc);                      // Draw the signal
}
```

If you build the new version of the control and insert it in the Test Container, you'll see the difference in the way the background is drawn. This version of the control will always use the ambient background color, even when you change it in the test container. If you do change the ambient back color of the container, you'll need to get the control to redraw itself—by moving it, for example—in order to see it use the new color.

When you've finished experimenting with the control, comment out the line that uses **AmbientBackColor()** and uncomment the line that uses **GetBackColor()** to get back to the original scheme. Then we can look at adding custom properties to the control.

Adding Custom Properties to the Control

There are actually four different flavors of custom property that you can define for an ActiveX control. They reflect different ways in which the properties can operate:

▶ The simplest variety of custom property is of type **DISP_PROPERTY**. This is represented by a data member of the control class and is usually made available just for information. Because the property is freely accessible, this is referred to as **direct exposure** of the property.

▶ The **DISP_PROPERTY_NOTIFY** type of property is represented by a data member of the control class, and has a function in the control class which is called if the property value is altered. This allows the control to adapt its operation to the new value for the control immediately. The notification function will typically cause the control to be redrawn.

▶ The **DISP_PROPERTY_EX** type of property is supported with functions accessible by a container both to set the value of the property and to retrieve its current value. These are usually referred to as **Get/Set** functions. This type of property is referred to as being **indirectly exposed**.

▶ The **DISP_PROPERTY_PARAM** type of property is similar to the **DISP_PROPERTY_EX** type in that it has **Get/Set** functions to manipulate it, but in addition can involve multiple parameter values stored in an array.

We'll try out custom properties by adding two to our control. One property that we might want to add is the duration of the stop or go period when the signal is running. A real signal might well operate so that the time that the signal was at red and green could vary, depending on traffic conditions. Another property could be the start-up conditions when the signal runs. Let's suppose that we'll allow it to start on either red or green. We can provide the option for the user to set this through a custom property.

Using ClassWizard to Add Custom Properties

First, we'll add the property to define which light is 'on' when the signal runs. We can make this a logical value which will make the signal start on red if the property value is **TRUE**, and green otherwise.

With the control project open, start up ClassWizard and select the Automation tab. Make sure the **CTrafficSignalCtrl** class is shown in the Class name: list box and click on the Add Property... button. You can enter **StartRed** as the External name, **m_bStartRed** as the Variable name and select **BOOL** from the Type: drop-down list box, as shown below:

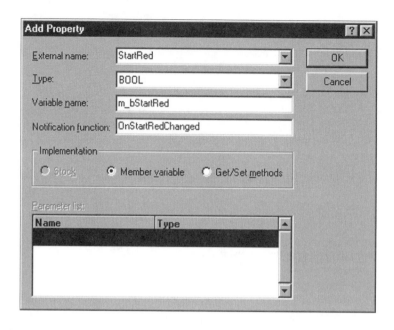

The type of the member variable for a property must be one of those from the list. You can't use your own types here. ClassWizard will generate a variable and a notification function with the names shown, so here our property is of type **DISP_PROPERTY_NOTIFY**. The Member variable radio button has also been selected by default.

You can select the OK button to close this dialog and return to the Automation tab. You'll see that the list of External names now includes StartRed, which is shown with the prefix C because it is a custom property. We can now add the second custom property which will determine the time period for stop and go conditions for the signal, so select the Add Property... button once more.

We'll make this property of type **DISP_PROPERTY_EX**, just for the experience, so select the Get/Set methods radio button. You can enter the external name as **StopOrGoTime**, and select **long** from the Type: drop-down list box. The dialog will appear as shown:

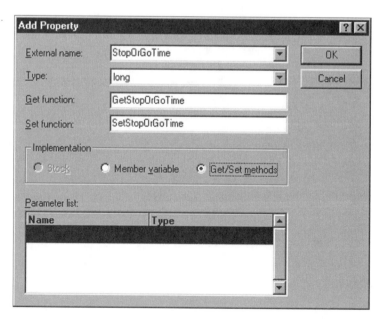

Remember that we have a diminished set of types available, so although **long** isn't the most convenient for a time interval, it will have to do. Note that there are edit boxes showing the names that ClassWizard has assigned to the **Get** and **Set** functions. You can change these if you want, but the defaults seem to be reasonable.

If you were specifying a property of type **DISP_PROPERTY_PARAM**, you would need to specify parameters to the **Get**/**Set** functions in the Parameter list: box at the bottom of the dialog.

You can select the OK button to return to the Automation tab. We now have two custom properties listed in addition to our stock property. The two functions that have been added to **CTrafficSignalCtrl** are also noted, and we could go directly to them by selecting the Edit Code button, but we're not ready to do that yet. We've finished with ClassWizard for the moment, though, so click the OK button.

If you take a look at the dispatch map in the implementation of **CTrafficSignalCtrl**, you'll see that the custom properties have been added and the types have been set based on the options we selected:

```
BEGIN_DISPATCH_MAP(CTrafficSignalCtrl, COleControl)
    //{{AFX_DISPATCH_MAP(CTrafficSignalCtrl)
    DISP_PROPERTY_NOTIFY(CTrafficSignalCtrl, "StartRed", m_bStartRed,
                    OnStartRedChanged, VT_BOOL)
    DISP_PROPERTY_EX(CTrafficSignalCtrl, "StopOrGoTime", GetStopOrGoTime,
                    SetStopOrGoTime, VT_I4)
    DISP_STOCKPROP_BACKCOLOR()
    //}}AFX_DISPATCH_MAP
    DISP_FUNCTION_ID(CTrafficSignalCtrl, "AboutBox", DISPID_ABOUTBOX,
                    AboutBox, VT_EMPTY, VTS_NONE)
END_DISPATCH_MAP()
```

Initializing Custom Properties

We need initial values to be set for both our custom properties, but the **StopOrGoTime** property has no variable defined for it. This is because the **Get**/**Set** functions are the interface between the container and the property, and you must fill in the detail. You can add a data member to the **CTrafficSignalCtrl** class definition directly by including the line:

```
long m_lStopOrGoTime;              // Duration of stop period, or go period
```

You can put this in the **protected** section since there's no reason to make it **public**. We can initialize this property and **m_bStartRed** by adding code to the **DoPropExchange()** member of the control class, which has the job of serializing properties:

```
void CTrafficSignalCtrl::DoPropExchange(CPropExchange* pPX)
{
    ExchangeVersion(pPX, MAKELONG(_wVerMinor, _wVerMajor));
    COleControl::DoPropExchange(pPX);

    // TODO: Call PX_ functions for each persistent custom property.
    PX_Bool(pPX, _T("StartRed"), m_bStartRed, TRUE);
    PX_Long(pPX, _T("StopOrGoTime"), m_lStopOrGoTime, 5000);

    // Set the signal state from the StartRed property
    if(m_bStartRed)
```

```
      m_pSignal->SetSignalState(STOP);
   else
      m_pSignal->SetSignalState(GO);
}
```

There's a global **PX_** function for each data type that can be used. They come in two versions. One version has three parameters and the other has an extra parameter; we're using the latter kind here. The parameters to the functions are, from left to right:

▶ A pointer to a **CPropExchange** object which determines whether the function is storing or retrieving property values.

▶ The external name of the property. The **_T()** macro, which is used here, takes care of converting the text if the control is used in an environment using the Unicode character set. It must be used for all literal strings that are to be transferred across the COM interface.

▶ A reference to the class data member that represents the property.

▶ A default value for the property which is used if the serialization process fails. The first time you use the control the process will fail, of course, since the properties haven't previously been saved.

The **PX_** function versions with three parameters omit the default value for the property. However, it's usually desirable to ensure that a value is set for all properties, so if you used this method, you'd need to ensure that a value was set elsewhere. Of course, on the second and subsequent times your control is used, the properties will be initialized to the values that were last set. We need the **if** statement following the **PX_** functions that import the property values because the signal state is dependent on the **StartRed** property. This sets the signal state to **STOP** if **m_bStartRed** is **TRUE**, and **GO** otherwise.

By default we set **m_bStartRed** to **TRUE** and **m_lStopOrGoTime** to 5000 initially. Time intervals are measured in milliseconds, therefore we're setting the default red and green signal intervals to 5 seconds, so you need to be ready to floor the pedal!

Making the Signal Work

To get the signal running, we need three more data members in our **CTrafficSignalCtrl** class. Add the following lines to the **protected** section of the class definition:

```
UINT m_nChangeTime;        // Duration of orange period
BOOL m_bSignalGo;          // TRUE indicates the signal is running
UINT m_nTimerID;           // Timer event ID
```

The first will define the duration of the transient state of the signal between red and green, the second is a flag which will be **TRUE** when the signal is running and **FALSE** when it is not, and the third is a variable identifying the timer we will use to control stepping the signal from one state to the next.

We can initialize these three members in the class constructor as follows:

```
CTrafficSignalCtrl::CTrafficSignalCtrl()
{
   InitializeIIDs(&IID_DTrafficSignal, &IID_DTrafficSignalEvents);
```

```
     m_pSignal = new CTrafficSignal;   // Create a signal
     m_bSignalGo = FALSE;              // Signal not running initially
     m_nChangeTime = 1500U;            // Change over time in milliseconds
     m_nTimerID = 10;                  // Timer ID
   }
```

Initially, the signal is not running since we have set **m_bSignalGo** to **FALSE**. The change-over time is set to 1.5 seconds and the timer ID is set to an arbitrary integer value of 10.

Starting and Stopping the Signal

We need some external means of starting and stopping the signal and, for demonstration purposes, a convenient way to do this is using a mouse click. We can get it to operate like a flip-flop, so that clicking the control when the signal is not running will start it, and vice versa.

Add a handler for the **WM_LBUTTONDOWN** message to **CTrafficSignalCtrl** using ClassWizard, and implement it as follows:

```
   void CTrafficSignalCtrl::OnLButtonDown(UINT nFlags, CPoint point)
   {
      // If the signal is stopped, start it
      // If the signal is running, stop it
      m_bSignalGo = !m_bSignalGo;
      if (m_bSignalGo)
         StartSignal();
      else
         StopSignal();

      COleControl::OnLButtonDown(nFlags, point);
   }
```

Since we want mouse clicks in the control to flip its operating state, the first action in the handler is to invert the value stored in **m_bSignalGo**. If this value is now **TRUE**, we call a member function **StartSignal()** to start the signal, and if it is **FALSE**, we invoke the function **StopSignal()** to stop the signal.

Starting the Signal

You can add the **StartSignal()** member by right-clicking the CTrafficSignalCtrl class name in ClassView and selecting Add Member Function... from the context menu. Enter the return type as **void** and the name as **StartSignal()**. The code for this **private** function will be:

```
   void CTrafficSignalCtrl::StartSignal()
   {
      // Setup a timer with the required interval
      m_nTimerID = SetTimer(m_nTimerID, (UINT)m_lStopOrGoTime, NULL);
      if (!m_nTimerID)
      {
         AfxMessageBox("No Timer!");
         exit(1);
      }
      InvalidateControl();   // Get the control redrawn
   }
```

We obtain a timer by calling the **SetTimer()** member of our class inherited from **CWnd**. The first argument is an ID for the timer which must be non-zero, and the second argument is the time interval we want, expressed in milliseconds as a **UINT** value. The third argument can be a pointer to a function that will be called when the time interval is up, but if it's **NULL**, as we've specified here, a **WM_TIMER** message will be sent. We'll add a handler for this in a moment.

There are a limited number of timers available, so we need to make sure that we got one. If none are available, the **SetTimer()** function returns **FALSE**, in which case we display a message and end the program. If a timer is available, **SetTimer()** returns the ID of the timer. Once we have a timer, we get the control redrawn so that it always starts with the state determined by the **StartRed** property. This will be set in the notification function for this property which we'll complete shortly.

Stopping the Signal

Add the **StopSignal()** function, which also has a **void** return type, and implement it as follows:

```
void CTrafficSignalCtrl::StopSignal()
{
    KillTimer(m_nTimerID);      // Destroy the timer
    InvalidateControl();        // Redraw the control
}
```

The **KillTimer()** function kills the timer event specified by the ID passed as an argument and removes any **WM_TIMER** messages that have been queued for it. The function returns **TRUE** if it finds the specified event, and **FALSE** otherwise, so it copes with a non-existent timer event without any problem. We get the control redrawn to return it to its initial state.

Handling WM_TIMER Messages

Add a handler for the **WM_TIMER** message using ClassWizard. The process is exactly the same as for any other message handler. Add code to the handler as follows:

```
void CTrafficSignalCtrl::OnTimer(UINT nIDEvent)
{
    UINT nInterval = 0;    // Interval in milliseconds

    // Step to the next state and set the time interval
    // based on the new state
    switch (m_pSignal->NextState())
    {
      case STOP: case GO:
        nInterval = (UINT)m_lStopOrGoTime;       // Stop or Go interval
        break;
      default:
        nInterval = m_nChangeTime;               // Transient interval
    }

    InvalidateControl();                         // Redraw the signal

    // Make sure the old timer is dead
    KillTimer(m_nTimerID);

    // Set a new timer event
    m_nTimerID = SetTimer(m_nTimerID, nInterval, NULL);
    if (!m_nTimerID)
    {
```

```
        AfxMessageBox("No Timer!");
        exit(1);
    }
}
```

The signal is stepped to the next state by calling the **NextState()** member of the
CTrafficSignal object. The new state is used to select the appropriate time interval for it.
Having stored the time interval in the local variable **nInterval**, we call
InvalidateControl() to get the signal drawn in its new state and start a new timer period.

Implementing the Notify Function for the Control

The notify function, **OnStartRedChanged()** will be called when the **StartRed** property is
modified externally, so we must add code to deal with this change, as follows:

```
void CTrafficSignalCtrl::OnStartRedChanged()
{
    // Stop the signal if necessary
    if (m_bSignalGo)
    {
       m_bSignalGo = FALSE;   // Set signal not running
       StopSignal();          // Stop the signal
    }
    // Set the signal object to the appropriate state
    if (m_bStartRed)
       m_pSignal->SetSignalState(STOP);
    else
       m_pSignal->SetSignalState(GO);

    InvalidateControl();   // Get the control redrawn

    SetModifiedFlag();
}
```

Other than at initialization when the control is loaded, this is the only place the **StartRed**
property change is acted upon. We need to take account of the possibility that the signal is
already running when the property is changed. We first check for this and stop the signal, since
we're assuming that the user changed the starting condition because it will be restarted (there
would be little point in changing it otherwise). To set the signal state, we use the
SetSignalState() member of **CTrafficSignal** with a parameter determined by the value of
the property. We then call **InvalidateControl()** to get the signal drawn in its latest state.

Implementing the Property Get/Set Functions

The **Get** function for the **StopOrGoTime** property is extremely simple since all we need to do is
return the current property value:

```
long CTrafficSignalCtrl::GetStopOrGoTime()
{
    return m_lStopOrGoTime;   // Return the current interval
}
```

The **Set** function requires a little more work:

```
void CTrafficSignalCtrl::SetStopOrGoTime(long nNewValue)
{
    // Only alter the control if the value is different
    if (m_1StopOrGoTime != nNewValue)
    {
        m_1StopOrGoTime = nNewValue;        // Set the new stop or go time

        OnStartRedChanged();                // Set the initial state
        SetModifiedFlag();
    }
}
```

The value passed to the function is the new value for the property, but we don't want to do anything drastic unless it's different from the old value. If we have a new value, we store it in the **m_1StopOrGoTime** member that we added for the purpose. We then set the signal state back to its initial starting state, according to the value of the property **StartRed**, by calling **OnStartRedChanged()**.

Using the Property Page

Now let's move on to adding some controls to the property page that ControlWizard conveniently provided for us, to allow us to modify the values of the control's custom properties. To add controls to the property page, you need to be in ResourceView. Extend the Dialog part of the resource set, and double-click on IDD_PROPPAGE_TRAFFICSIGNAL to display the property page dialog. You can remove the static text control that has been added to the dialog by selecting it and pressing the *Delete* key.

We need to add two controls to the property page corresponding to the **StartRed** property, which is Boolean, and the **StopOrGoTime** property, which is a **long** integer. The former we can handle with a check box control and for the latter we can use an edit box.

From the control palette, select a check box and place it at a suitable point on the property page. Bring up its properties and enter the text as Start with Red Light. You may also like to check the Left te<u>x</u>t check box on the Styles tab. Next, you can add a static text control and place it on the property page. Display its properties and change the text to Stop or Go Period:. Next, add an edit box to the property page and place it to the right of the static text box. Your property page should look something like this:

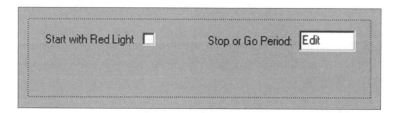

We've finished laying out the property page, so you can save the resource. Now we need to connect the controls that we've added to the properties in our ActiveX control.

Connecting Controls to Properties

First, we'll connect the check box to the **StartRed** property. Double-click on the check box control with the *Ctrl* key held down. You'll then see the Add Member Variable dialog box. You can complete the name for the variable to be added to the **CTrafficSignalPropPage** class as **m_bStartRed**, and the property name in the bottom list box as **StartRed**. The category and variable type boxes will already have been set as we are using a check box, so the dialog box will be as shown:

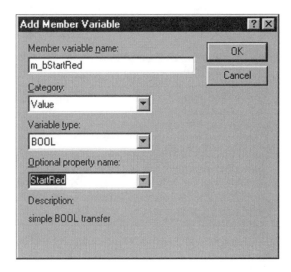

The drop-down list for property names provides stock property names for when you are adding these to a property page. You can click on the OK button to complete the addition of the data member to the class.

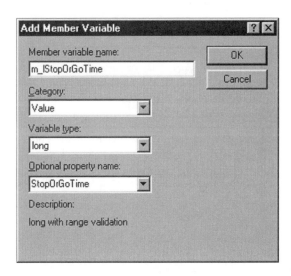

Next, you should double-click the edit box while holding the *Ctrl* key down to add the data member to receive the value of the **StopOrGoTime** property from the control. Enter the information in the dialog box as shown below:

Here you must set the Variable type: to **long** to be consistent with what we have specified previously for this value. Make sure the Category: entry is Value. As well as adding this data member, ClassWizard will make provision for range validation of the value entered, as indicated by the note at the bottom. You can click on the OK button to complete this operation and then save the property page.

In fact, ClassWizard has done rather more than just adding two data members to the **CTrafficSignalPropPage** class. It has also included initialization for them in the class constructor:

485

```
CTrafficSignalPropPage::CTrafficSignalPropPage() :
    COlePropertyPage(IDD, IDS_TRAFFICSIGNAL_PPG_CAPTION)
{
    //{{AFX_DATA_INIT(CTrafficSignalPropPage)
    m_bStartRed = FALSE;
    m_lStopOrGoTime = 0;
    //}}AFX_DATA_INIT
}
```

However, neither of these are good values for us, so set the initial value for **m_bStartRed** to **TRUE**, and the value for **m_lStopOrGoTime** to 5000.

The transfer of data between the controls and the variables we've added is accomplished using the **DDX** macros in the **DoPropExchange()** member of the property page class. These are exactly the same macros that we have seen used for controls in ordinary dialog boxes. ClassWizard has also added the code to do this, so the function implementation has already been created, as follows:

```
void CTrafficSignalPropPage::DoDataExchange(CDataExchange* pDX)
{
    //{{AFX_DATA_MAP(CTrafficSignalPropPage)
    DDP_Check(pDX, IDC_CHECK1, m_bStartRed, _T("StartRed") );
    DDX_Check(pDX, IDC_CHECK1, m_bStartRed);
    DDP_Text(pDX, IDC_EDIT1, m_lStopOrGoTime, _T("StopOrGoTime") );
    DDX_Text(pDX, IDC_EDIT1, m_lStopOrGoTime);
    //}}AFX_DATA_MAP
    DDP_PostProcessing(pDX);
}
```

The **DDP** macros you see here are specific to properties. They do the job of synchronizing the property values in the control with the values in the data members of the property page class, so all the updating of the property values is taken care of.

The last thing you need to do is to set the range limits for the **m_lStopOrGoTime** value. For this, you can add a **DDV** macro at the end of the block of **DDX** and **DDP** macros in the **DoDataExchange()** member, as follows:

```
void CTrafficSignalPropPage::DoDataExchange(CDataExchange* pDX)
{
    //{{AFX_DATA_MAP(CTrafficSignalPropPage)
    DDP_Check(pDX, IDC_CHECK1, m_bStartRed, _T("StartRed") );
    DDX_Check(pDX, IDC_CHECK1, m_bStartRed);
    DDP_Text(pDX, IDC_EDIT1, m_lStopOrGoTime, _T("StopOrGoTime") );
    DDX_Text(pDX, IDC_EDIT1, m_lStopOrGoTime);
    //}}AFX_DATA_MAP
    DDV_MinMaxUInt(pDX, m_lStopOrGoTime, 1000, 30000);
    DDP_PostProcessing(pDX);
}
```

You should add this line immediately before the **DDP_PostProcessing** macro to prevent values less than 1000 milliseconds or greater than 30000 milliseconds being accepted for the **StopOrGoTime** property. This is the same macro that's used for range checking values for controls in an ordinary dialog box.

Using the Control

You can now build the control once more, and exercise it using the test container. The window shows three instances of the control running in the container, each having a different interval set for the **StopOrGoTime** property:

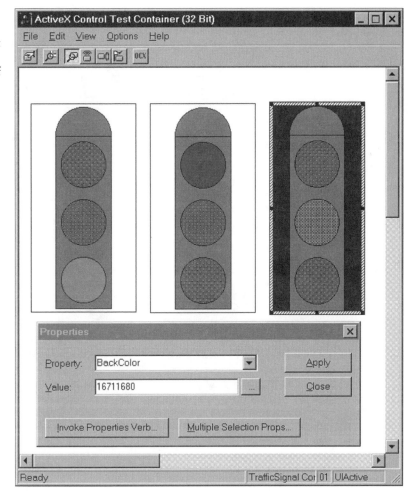

The Properties dialog box shown above is displayed when you select the View | Properties... menu option in the container, or the equivalent toolbar button. To display the property page for the control, you should click on the Invoke Properties Verb... button in the dialog box. Try setting the **StopOrGoTime** outside the permitted range. Whenever you set a property value, it only applies to the control that is currently active. An instance of the control which is running will continue to run when it isn't active, so several can run simultaneously.

Adding Events to a Control

You'll recall that events are used to tell a container that something has occurred in an ActiveX control. It might conceivably be useful for a container using our traffic signal control to know when the signal has changed and to know what state the signal has changed to.

487

You can add events to the control using ClassWizard. Open ClassWizard and select the ActiveX Events tab. After making sure **CTrafficSignalCtrl** is the class name selected, click on the Add Event... button. Enter the external name for the event as **SignalChanged** and add a parameter called **lNewState** of type **long**. This parameter will indicate to the container the new state of the control.

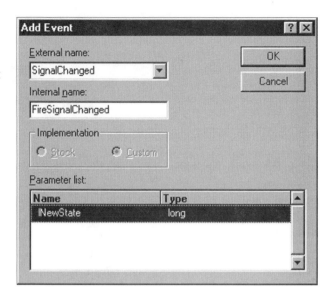

The drop-down list for the External name: list box contains names for standard events, but we don't need them here because we're creating a custom event. ClassWizard will fill in the internal name field. This will be the name of the function you call when you want to fire the event.

Click the OK button to create the event. The ActiveX Events tab will now show the new custom event. This event will have been entered in **CTrafficSignalCtrl**'s event map and the definition for the function **FireSignalChanged()** will also have been created. All we have to do is to use it.

The best place to fire this event is from the handler for the **WM_TIMER** message, because it is here that we change the state of the signal object. Close ClassWizard by clicking the OK button and switch to the **OnTimer()** function implementation from ClassView. Alter the code in it as follows:

```
void CTrafficSignalCtrl::OnTimer(UINT nIDEvent)
{
    UINT nInterval = 0;    // Interval in milliseconds

    // Step to the next state and set the time interval
    // based on the new state
    int nNewState = m_pSignal->NextState();
    switch (nNewState)
    {
        case STOP: case GO:
            nInterval = (UINT)m_lStopOrGoTime;    // Stop or Go interval
            break;
        default:
            nInterval = m_nChangeTime;            // Transient interval
    }
    FireSignalChanged(nNewState);

    InvalidateControl();                          // Redraw the signal

    // Make sure the old timer is dead
```

```
      KillTimer(m_nTimerID);
      // Set a new timer event
      m_nTimerID = SetTimer(m_nTimerID, nInterval, NULL);
      if (!m_nTimerID)
      {
         AfxMessageBox("No Timer!");
         exit(1);
      }
   }
```

Here, we're keeping track of the precise state of the traffic signal and passing it as a parameter to the event. The rest of the handler remains as before.

With the event added, you can compile the control and see how it runs in the test container. You can view the event log by selecting the <u>V</u>iew | <u>E</u>vent log... menu option in the container. The event log is shown below:

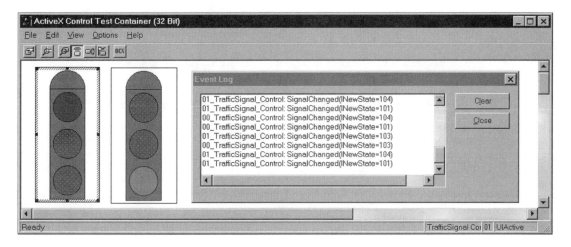

Here, two controls are running with different values assigned for the **StopOrGoTime** property. The individual instances of the control are indicated in the event log by the two digit prefix to the record of an event, the first instance of the control being numbered 00. You can also see the value that is being passed as the parameter to indicate the new state.

Of course, the control will also be usable from more functional control container applications, including Visual Basic or Visual C++ itself. In fact, since Visual Basic is such an important container when writing professional controls, it's a good idea to make your controls as easy as possible to use from that environment. We can enhance the ease in which our control can be used by changing some of the code in the **.odl** file. Remember that the **.odl** file is compiled into a type library that container applications can use to find information about an ActiveX control. We will make some simple changes to the file so that users of the control can use named constants for the values passed to the **SignalChanged** event.

The ODL File

First, open **TrafficSignal.odl** in Developer Studio. This file defines a **type library** for our control using ODL, which we alluded to earlier. The type library defines what's in the control by way of interfaces and data types that can be accessed externally. Although you're probably unfamiliar with ODL and the file may seem a bit confusing at first sight, ODL is actually relatively straightforward. In fact, you should be able to see that the file contains definitions for four items.

```
[ uuid(A833B927-78FF-11D0-9257-00201834E2A3), version(1.0),
  helpfile("TrafficSignal.hlp"),
  helpstring("TrafficSignal ActiveX Control module"),
  control ]
library TRAFFICSIGNALLib
{
    importlib(STDOLE_TLB);
    importlib(STDTYPE_TLB);

    //  Primary dispatch interface for CTrafficSignalCtrl

    [ uuid(A833B928-78FF-11D0-9257-00201834E2A3),
        helpstring("Dispatch interface for TrafficSignal Control"), hidden ]
    dispinterface _DTrafficSignal
    {
        properties:
            // NOTE - ClassWizard will maintain property information here.
            //    Use extreme caution when editing this section.
            //{{AFX_ODL_PROP(CTrafficSignalCtrl)
            [id(DISPID_BACKCOLOR), bindable, requestedit] OLE_COLOR BackColor;
            [id(1)] boolean StartRed;
            [id(2)] long StopOrGoTime;
            //}}AFX_ODL_PROP

        methods:
            // NOTE - ClassWizard will maintain method information here.
            //    Use extreme caution when editing this section.
            //{{AFX_ODL_METHOD(CTrafficSignalCtrl)
            //}}AFX_ODL_METHOD

            [id(DISPID_ABOUTBOX)] void AboutBox();
    };

    //  Event dispatch interface for CTrafficSignalCtrl

    [ uuid(A833B929-78FF-11D0-9257-00201834E2A3),
      helpstring("Event interface for TrafficSignal Control") ]
    dispinterface _DTrafficSignalEvents
    {
        properties:
            //  Event interface has no properties

        methods:
            // NOTE - ClassWizard will maintain event information here.
            //    Use extreme caution when editing this section.
            //{{AFX_ODL_EVENT(CTrafficSignalCtrl)
            [id(1)] void SignalChanged(long lNewState);
            //}}AFX_ODL_EVENT
    };

    //  Class information for CTrafficSignalCtrl
```

```
[ uuid(A833B92A-78FF-11D0-9257-00201834E2A3),
  helpstring("TrafficSignal Control"), control ]
coclass TrafficSignal
{
   [default] dispinterface _DTrafficSignal;
   [default, source] dispinterface _DTrafficSignalEvents;
};


//{{AFX_APPEND_ODL}}
//}}AFX_APPEND_ODL}}
};
```

The definition for the type library, which has the name **TRAFFICSIGNALLib**, is delimited by a pair of braces. The opening brace is immediately after the **library** statement, and the closing brace is at the end of the file. These braces enclose the definitions for three items in the type library: the primary dispatch interface, the event interface and the control. Each definition consists of some information between square brackets followed by a further set of information specific to the type of the item contained between braces. The whole structure looks rather like a set of nested classes.

The two **importlib** statements add all the standard OLE interfaces, types, and dispatch IDs to the type library for our control. Note that each definition in the ODL file is uniquely identified by a **uuid** tag. **UUID** stands for **u**niversally **u**nique **id**entifier, because it's a number that uniquely identifies the item. The UUID for an item should be different from any other UUID worldwide, so your UUIDs will certainly be different from those shown here.

For the control, the number given after **uuid** is the CLSID. You can see that it's the same number as was used in the ControlWizard-generated **IMPLEMENT_OLECREATE_EX** statement in **TrafficSignalCtl.cpp**.

```
IMPLEMENT_OLECREATE_EX( CTrafficSignalCtrl,
                "TRAFFICSIGNAL.TrafficSignalCtrl.1",
                0xa833b92a, 0x78ff, 0x11d0, 0x92, 0x57,
                0, 0x20, 0x18, 0x34, 0xe2, 0xa3 )
```

Each of the items we've provided in the interface to our control appears within the definitions in the type library. You can use a type library with an object browser, such as the OLE-COM Object Viewer (provided with Visual C++ in the **DevStudio\VC\bin** directory as **Oleview.exe**), to determine what interfaces are supported by a control, and the information provided by a type library can be used to build applications that will use a control. The type library information is recorded in the system registry, including the UUIDs for the library itself and the interface items it defines. Because a UUID, rather than a name, is used to identify an interface, there's no possibility of an interface to one control being confused with that for another.

Adding an Enumeration

We're going to change the ODL file so that it defines an enumeration for the state parameter of the **SignalChanged** event for our control. This will allow Visual Basic users to determine the state of our control in a very simple way. They'll be able to make use of the named constants that we will define to represent the status of the signal after a change has occurred. First, add the following code to the **.odl** file just below the **importlib** statements:

```
importlib(STDTYPE_TLB);
```

```
typedef [ uuid(/* Need to add a valid ID here */),
         helpstring("Signal state constants") ]
         enum { [helpstring ("Stop")] IsStop = 101,
               [helpstring ("Go")] IsGo = 103,
               [helpstring ("Ready to stop")] IsReadyToStop = 104
             } SignalState;
```

```
// Primary dispatch interface for CTrafficSignalCtrl
```

This code simply defines an enumeration called **SignalState** containing the named constants **IsStop**, **IsGo** and **IsReadyToStop**. These correspond to the values that could be passed via the **SignalChanged** event. It's a common ActiveX control convention to use mixed case constants with a two or three letter prefix to ensure that they're unique.

The one thing that's missing from this definition is a valid ID to use in the **uuid** statement. The ID needs to take a particular form and it needs to be unique, so we can't just type in anything here. Instead, we have to use the GUID generator utility, **Guidgen.exe**, that's supplied with Visual C++; **GUID** stands for **G**lobally **U**nique **ID**. This utility is also known as Uuidgen for obvious reasons, and you'll see references to both Guidgen and Uuidgen in the documentation. The reason that there are two names for the same thing is that there are two groups dealing with it. GUID comes from Microsoft, and UUID comes from the Open Software Foundation.

The easiest way to access Guidgen is through the Components and Controls Gallery, which you can get to by selecting Add to Project | Components and Controls... on the Project menu. You can also make the Components and Controls Gallery available as a toolbar button by right-clicking on one of the Developer Studio toolbars and selecting Customize... from the resulting menu.

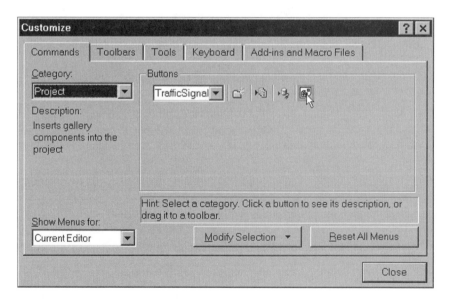

Change the Category to Project and drag the icon shown on to your favorite toolbar or create a new toolbar for it. Now close the Customize dialog and you can use the new toolbar button to display the Components and Controls Gallery.

If you do this now, you'll see a dialog showing a list of folders. Select the folder Developer Studio Components from the list. You'll see the dialog shown:

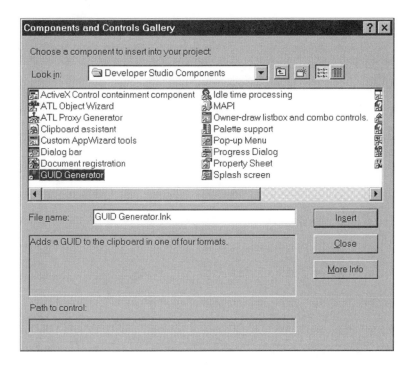

Select GUID Generator from the list and hit Insert. Now you'll be presented with a dialog that allows you to generate GUIDs in a variety of formats and copy them to the clipboard so that you can paste the results wherever they are needed:

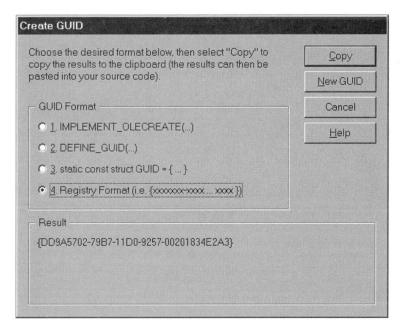

We want an ID in Registry Format, so select the radio button, click Copy to copy the GUID to the clipboard, then close the Gallery and return to the `.odl` file. Of course, the ID generated when you run GUID Generator will be different to the one shown here, since the whole point of the GUID Generator is that it produces unique IDs!

Now paste the generated ID between the parentheses of the **uuid** term in the definition of the enumeration by keying *Ctrl-V*, and remove the braces from around the ID. The last step to enable the enumeration to be used for determining the result of the event is to change the type of the event parameter from **long** to **SignalState**:

```
[ uuid(261D8BE4-6938-11D0-AB3A-0020AF71E433),
            helpstring("Event interface for TrafficSignal Control") ]
dispinterface _DTrafficSignalEvents
{
   properties:
       //  Event interface has no properties

   methods:
       // NOTE - ClassWizard will maintain event information here.
       //    Use extreme caution when editing this section.
       //{{AFX_ODL_EVENT(CTrafficSignalCtrl)
       [id(1)] void SignalChanged(SignalState lNewState);
       //}}AFX_ODL_EVENT
};
```

Now you can compile the control and test it out once more. If you use the test container, you won't see any differences in the control, but if you use Visual Basic (4 or later), you'll see that you can make use of the new constants we defined in the enumeration.

```
' Example Visual Basic code
Private Sub TrafficSignal1_SignalChanged(ByVal lNewState As Long)
   If lNewState = IsStop Then
       Print "Stop Light"
   End If
End Sub
```

The Visual Basic routine shown will be executed each time the **SignalChanged** event is fired by the control. The status stored in **lNewState** is compared with the **IsStop** value defined in the enumeration that we added to the `.odl` file. Whenever the signal state is **IsStop**, a message will be displayed.

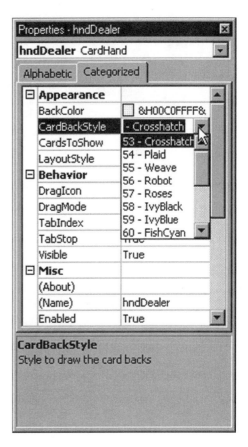

Enumerations like the one we've just defined are even more useful when used in conjunction with properties that should only accept a limited number of specific values. Visual Basic can use the constants defined in an enumeration and offer them to the user through the Properties window that it provides for all controls, as you can see in this sample:

Embedding an ActiveX Control in a Web Page

To get the next section to work, you'll need to have an ActiveX-aware browser installed on your PC. Internet Explorer 3.0 or later from Microsoft will do, or any other browser that supports ActiveX. If you can access the Internet but don't have an ActiveX capable browser, you can download Internet Explorer for free, courtesy of those nice folks at Microsoft. You'll find it on their web site at **http://www.microsoft.com**. While you're there, you might like to take a look at another freebie: the ActiveX Control Pad. This is a very nice tool that will help you to create web pages and embed ActiveX controls in them.

You define web pages using something called the **H**yper**T**ext **M**arkup **L**anguage, commonly known as **HTML**. The elements of a web page are specified by HTML tags, which usually occur in pairs, and are delimited by angled brackets. Fire up the ActiveX Control Pad and you'll see a new, basic document specified with the following HTML tags:

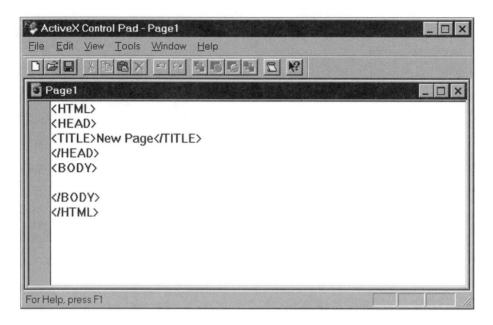

Each pair of tags enclose a particular kid of entity. The Microsoft ActiveX Control Pad creates this for you automatically. To customize it, you could start by changing the title to something more appropriate. If you want some text to appear on the page, you just add it between the **BODY** tags. To add our ActiveX control to the page, we use a pair of **<OBJECT>** tags, as follows:

```
<HTML>
<HEAD>
<TITLE> A Page with a Traffic Signal</TITLE>
</HEAD>
<BODY>
<OBJECT ID="TrafficSignal1" WIDTH=100 HEIGHT=50
  CLASSID="CLSID:A833B92A-78FF-11D0-9257-00201834E2A3">
</OBJECT>
</BODY>
</HTML>
```

Again, inserting an ActiveX control is very easy using Microsoft ActiveX Control Pad. All you have to do is select the control you want from the list presented by the menu item Edit | Insert ActiveX Control... and all the detail is taken care of. ActiveX Control Pad knows about all the controls in your system because they are entered in the registry, so you get the choice of inserting any of them.

In the page definition above, the specification of the name of object to be inserted, and the **CLASSID** for the object which identifies what kind of object it is, both appear in the opening **<OBJECT>** tag along with the width and height of the control. We've specified the **CLASSID** between quotes as the characters **CLSID:**, followed by the hexadecimal digits for the CLSID that appeared in the arguments to the **IMPLEMENT_OLECREATE_EX** macro that we saw earlier in **TrafficSignalCtrl.cpp**. This was:

```
IMPLEMENT_OLECREATE_EX( CTrafficSignalCtrl,
                "TRAFFICSIGNAL.TrafficSignalCtrl.1",
```

```
0xa833b92a, 0x78ff, 0x11d0, 0x92, 0x57,
0, 0x20, 0x18, 0x34, 0xe2, 0xa3)
```

Note that the sixth argument is a byte, so it actually has two hexadecimal digits, **0x00**.

 Don't worry if you don't have the ActiveX Control Pad. Just save the HTML segment into a file, and provided you make sure the CLSID is correct, the control will be displayed by your browser. The Control Pad doesn't do anything special, it just makes life a little easier.

That's all you need to include the control in the page, but there are a myriad of other possibilities available to you through HTML. You can assign values to parameters for the control for example, or determine its position on the page when it is displayed. Since we just want to see that it works, we'll ignore these and go with what we've got.

If you save the HTML above in a file with the extension **.htm—TrafficSignal.htm**, for example—you should then be able to open it in your web browser to see the control. The **<OBJECT>** tag is relatively new to HTML, and not all web browsers support it, so if the control doesn't appear, it probably isn't your code that's at fault. The page is shown here in a Microsoft Internet Explorer window:

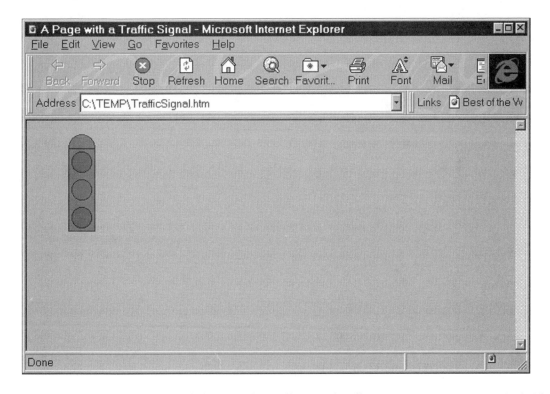

The control works, too. If you click on it, the traffic signal will start operating—amazing isn't it? Now it's up to you to discover what use you can put your new-found knowledge to.

Summary

In this chapter, we've dug a little into the how and why of OLE and ActiveX controls. You should have a good idea now of how a control communicates with its container, and how the basic features of an ActiveX control can be implemented. You also know that an OLE control *is* an ActiveX control.

The important ideas we have explored in this chapter are:

▶ An OLE control is a reusable software component. An OLE control is also an ActiveX control.

▶ ActiveX controls can be executed in any ActiveX container and can be embedded within a Web page.

▶ A control communicates with a container through properties, methods, and events.

▶ There are three kinds of properties for a control: ambient properties, control properties, and extended properties.

▶ A method is a function in a control that can be called from outside the control.

▶ Events are signals that a control sends to a container as a consequence of some action by the user.

▶ You can create an ActiveX control in Visual C++ by using the MFC ActiveX ControlWizard. The controls that it produces are also OLE controls.

▶ You can manipulate the **.odl** file to provide the users of your control with useful constants.

Of course, there is much more to learn about many of the topics we have covered, but we have scratched the surface sufficiently for you to see the gleam of gold underneath. ActiveX controls are an extremely powerful mechanism for reusing and distributing code, and there's no doubt that you will be seeing more and more of them. COM is more general though, and we'll look at that in the next chapter.

Exercises

Ex12-1: Explain the limitations of the **StartRed** property and say how the control could be improved by adding a new **StartState** property to define the starting state of the signal.

Ex12-2: Implement the new **StartState** property and use an enumeration for its possible values.

Ex12-3: (Advanced) Explain what difference it would have made to your implementation if there were already many users of the existing control. How could you ensure compatibility with the existing control? How could you discourage use of legacy functions? (Hints—investigate **CPropExchange::GetVersion()** (and **COleControl::ExchangeVersion()**). Also, ODL provides a **hidden** keyword.)

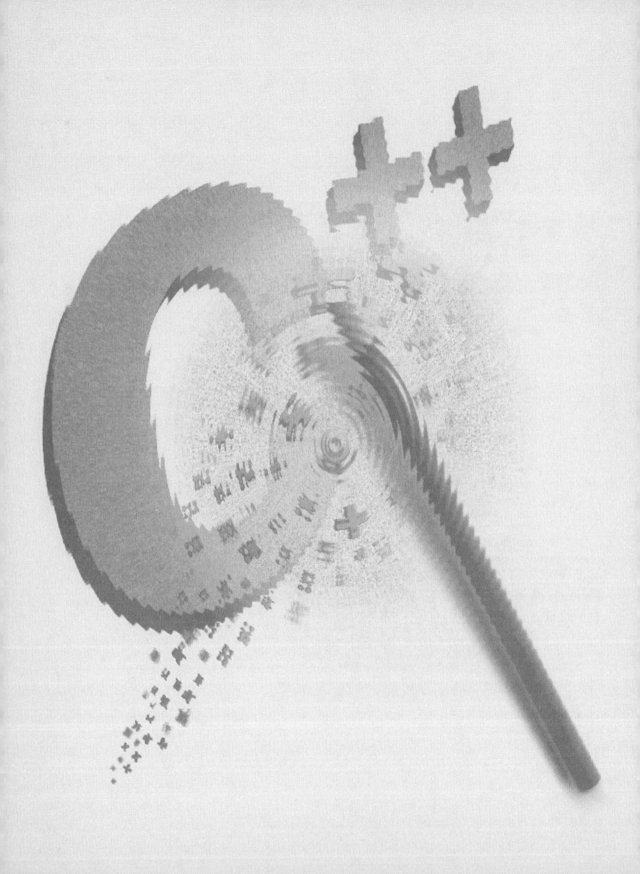

Using the Active Template Library

The **Active Template Library**, known as **ATL**, provides you with another means of creating COM components, including simple and full ActiveX controls, but using a very different approach from that of the previous chapter.

In this chapter you will learn:

- More about how COM works
- What the Active Template Library is
- How to use the ATL Object Wizard
- How to implement a simple COM component
- How you can use a COM component in Visual Basic
- How you can use a COM component in a C++ program
- How to implement a full ActiveX control using ATL

More About COM

Using ATL takes you much closer to COM than the example in the previous chapter, so we need to understand a little more about what COM involves. It's cards on the table time: COM is actually quite complicated. When you consider what COM achieves, it was inevitable, wasn't it? Defining a mechanism which allows program modules to be written in almost any language such that they can always be connected together—even when they're on different computers—is no mean achievement. The basic concepts are quite easy, but the devil is in the details. Fortunately, you can get by with an understanding of the basics, at least for the purposes of getting started with using ATL to create simple COM components.

You already know that COM is an interface specification for reusable software components. The COM interface isn't dependent on C++ or any other programming language in particular; provided a programming language has the capability to implement a COM interface, you can use it to create a COM component. COM doesn't require an object-oriented approach and classes aren't necessary to implement COM components, but they do make it easier. As we saw in the last chapter, all ActiveX controls are COM components, because they implement a COM interface.

A COM component is called a **server**, and a program that uses a COM component is called a **client**. A single COM component can be used by several clients simultaneously, rather like a function in a DLL. In fact, as we shall see later, we can store a COM component in a **.dll** file. To use a COM component, a client must create an **instance** of the component. An instance of a component is referred to as a **COM object**, although this term is also used to describe a COM component in general.

A COM interface contains only functions (often referred to as methods). A component can have properties—parameters that can be set for a component or have their values retrieved—as we saw with our TrafficSignal control, but these are accessed through **get** and **put** functions in the interface. A COM component has at least one interface, and can have several.

COM and Interfaces

The basis of COM is the interface called **IUnknown**. All COM component interfaces must support the minimum **IUnknown** capability, since **IUnknown** allows a client to find out what other interfaces the component has. This is the key to unlimited flexibility in what a COM interface can include. The **IUnknown** interface contains three functions:

Function Name	Description
QueryInterface()	You call this function to determine whether the component supports a particular interface and to get a pointer to the interface if it does.
AddRef()	A COM object that's being shared keeps track of the number of clients that are using the interface. Calling **AddRef()** increments the reference count.
Release()	Called by a client when it ceases using a component interface. Calling **Release()** decrements the reference count for an interface. When the interface count is zero, the object knows that there are no clients using the interface.

Since the client and the COM server may be implemented in completely different programming languages—indeed, the server and the client can be running on completely different computers—the interface functions aren't accessed directly by a client. Instead, they're accessed indirectly through a table of pointers to functions.

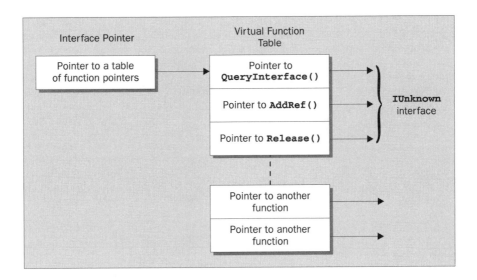

An interface pointer contains the address of a table containing the addresses of the functions in the interface. This table of addresses is called a **virtual function table** (or **vtable**); virtual functions in C++ work through a similar mechanism. An interface function is called indirectly through its address in the table. A particular function is referenced through the base address for the table, plus an offset for the particular entry required. In C++ terms, the entries in the vtable are pointers to functions, and the interface pointer is of type pointer to pointer, usually **void****.

COM defines its own data types. These are independent of C++, but they do of course map to C++ types. The parameters to a COM interface function can only be of the types that COM supports, and there are restrictions on how information is passed to and from an interface function. We shall see more of the detail of this when we come to put a COM component together.

The basic **IUnknown** interface is just a platform—the absolute minimum necessary to get communications working between a COM server and a client. In practice, other interfaces can be added that will be specific to the sort of capability implemented in a component. **IUnknown** provides the means by which a client can find out about these additional interfaces. In C++, **IUnknown** can be represented very easily as a class, and extending it then becomes a matter of deriving a new class that inherits the functions in **IUnknown**. Since the notion of virtual functions is fundamental to C++, accessing a COM interface is a relatively straightforward matter. The way in which **IUnknown** works is not always the most convenient in other environments, and some are just not comfortable with having to work through a virtual function table. An important COM interface that can overcome such difficulties, and that was first defined for use in the Visual Basic environment, is called a **dispatch interface** (or **dispinterface**).

Dispatch Interfaces

A dispatch interface is an interface that's based on a standard interface called **IDispatch**. **IDispatch** inherits the functions from **IUnknown**, and implements additional functions that make calling interface functions easier. In particular, the **IDispatch** interface adds a function called **Invoke()** that you can use to call different functions depending on an argument passed to it. The argument is a positive 32-bit integer value called a **DispID** (**Disp**atch **ID**) that identifies the function. To get the DispIDs for the functions implemented in a dispatch interface you call another function called **GetIDsOfNames()**. You can pass an array of function names to it and get back an array of corresponding DispIDs for the functions.

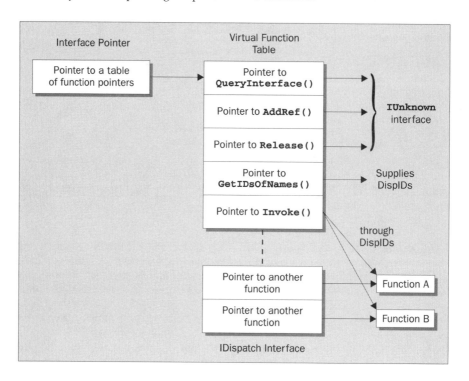

Note that the functions that are part of the dispatch interface and callable through **Invoke()** do not necessarily appear in the virtual function table. When they do, the interface is referred to as a **dual interface**, because the functions can be called through **Invoke()** using DispIDs, or they can be called directly through the virtual function table pointers. Calling functions through the vtable pointers is faster than calling them through **Invoke()**.

COM Interfaces and Class Interfaces

Don't confuse a COM interface with a class interface. Being immersed in C++ classes all the time makes it easy to mix them up, but when you write a COM component in C++ you will be involved with both kinds. The COM interface will be defined in a file using **IDL**, the Interface Description Language that we referred to in the last chapter. IDL looks quite similar to C++ but it most certainly isn't C++ and there are many differences. Keep in mind that IDL isn't a programming language in the normal sense; it's a language for defining interfaces and other information that will be stored in a type library—that is, in a **.tlb** file. When you build a COM component, the MIDL compiler processes the **.idl** file and the C++ compiler processes the **.cpp** files. The two are interrelated but they aren't the same.

Of course, a COM component will need to be implemented in C++. A C++ class will represent the COM object, and the implementation of the COM interface will require class functions to be declared corresponding to the COM interface functions. Since these are called from outside the

COM object, potentially from a client written in another programming language, the declaration and implementation of the interface functions must be made in a special way to accommodate this. The default C++ calling convention for functions isn't acceptable to COM. We'll see how we specify the calling convention to suit COM in an example.

Understanding the Active Template Library

Believe it or not, the Active Template Library is a library of class templates that support ActiveX—in other words, COM components. The ATL class templates enable you to create classes that form a basis for an ActiveX component that doesn't involve the overhead implicit in using the MFC. In fact, ATL is completely independent of the MFC. Such a component will therefore require substantially less memory than the MFC-based ActiveX control that we produced in the previous chapter.

Being able to produce a COM component in racing trim by using ATL is a major plus, but where there's a plus, there's often a minus or two. One minus in this case is that if your component needs any kind of visual representation that the user can see or interact with, you must program it yourself. This isn't necessarily as big a problem as it sounds, but it does mean that you'll be calling Windows API functions directly. Another minus is that you can't use ClassWizard with ATL programs—ClassWizard just doesn't support them. It's possible to use the MFC and ATL together, but there's really no point in doing so. If you intend to use the MFC, you don't need ATL at all.

We can deduce from this that ATL is aimed squarely at the development of components that are lightweight in memory requirements, but with the flexibility to add whatever capability you want. One context in which ATL excels is the development of lightweight, invisible controls.

Invisible Controls

'Invisible' and 'lightweight' suggest we could be dealing with vaporware here, but that certainly isn't the case. Why would you want such a component? Well, there are a couple of reasons. Firstly, consider a hypothetical COM component that provides a computation function of some kind. When you need the function it supplies, you can plug it into your application. It doesn't need a visual representation, and the lighter it is on memory requirements, the better. Secondly, we saw in the previous chapter that ActiveX controls can be used in web pages on the Internet. Clearly, the growing requirement for Internet web pages to contain active code implies a need for components in this context, and because Internet communications bandwidth is a critical resource, such components need to be as lightweight as possible. Clumping several heavyweight MFC-based ActiveX controls in your web page would most likely mean that nobody will be prepared to wait for it to download.

This second example is where ATL components come riding to the rescue, although it isn't immediately obvious how. Lightweight components are all very well, but an ATL-based, invisible one doesn't seem right—after all, if you can't see it, how do you know it's there, and what's more, how do you use it? The current facilities you have available to you for defining web pages can help. There are scripting languages such as VBScript and JavaScript that you can use within the description of a web page in HTML. From these scripting languages you can get and set component properties and call functions, so you can use them to interface with invisible components. You can even tie multiple components together so they work in an integrated way.

We can get a clearer idea of how an ATL-based COM component is developed by creating one. After we've done that we can see how to use it. We'll start with the simplest kind (it has no visual appearance implemented), but later we'll see how we can use ATL to implement the traffic signal control we created in the previous chapter without incurring the overhead of MFC.

Using the ATL COM AppWizard

We need something simple as an example of a COM component. Let's create a component that can figure out the maximum refresh rate for a monitor, given the monitor's horizontal scanning frequency. The horizontal scanning frequency is a measure of how many lines your monitor can draw in one second, so if you know how many lines there are on the screen, you can divide this into the scanning frequency to get how many times the screen will be redrawn in a second. The number of lines on the screen is just the vertical resolution, and we can get the component to figure that out. In reality, the refresh rate is also limited by the vertical scan rate that your monitor can sustain, but we'll ignore that for the purposes of this exercise.

Visual C++ 5 provides a special Wizard for projects using ATL, so we can jump right in with that. Start a new ATL COM AppWizard project called **RefreshRate**, as shown here.

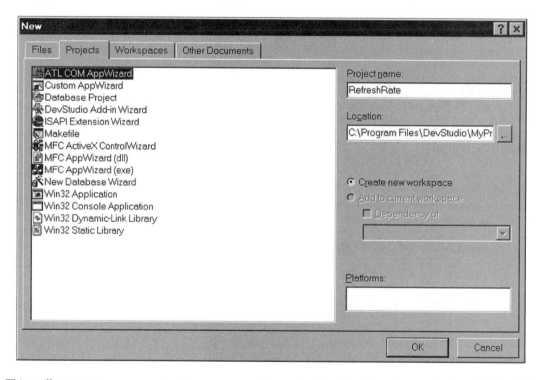

This will generate a new project in a new workspace in the directory shown in the edit box. If you click on the OK button you'll move on to the first (and only) step in the ATL COM AppWizard process:

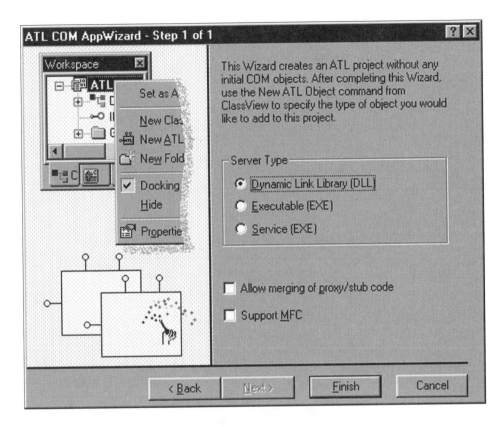

As you see, you can create a component as a DLL or as a `.exe` file. When you think about it, there's no reason why an application in a `.exe` file shouldn't have a COM interface—after all, that's essentially what you're using when you embed an Excel worksheet in a Word document. A COM component in a DLL is called an **in-process server**, because it shares the address space of a client. A COM component implemented in a `.exe` file is called an **out-of-process server** because it runs in its own address space. The default DLL Server Type option is what we want for our example.

When your COM component is in one address space and the client program using it is in another, the client clearly can't call the interface functions in the COM component directly. Some extra software is necessary in each process to manage the transfer of data and provide the interface between the client and the component.

The software that sits in the client process is called a **proxy**, because it represents the interface to the COM server component. The client communicates with the proxy, and the proxy communicates with the server process via a piece of software in that process called a **stub**. This calls the interface functions in the component on behalf of the client.

The process the proxy goes through when it gathers the arguments together for an interface function call is called **marshaling**; the process of sorting them out at the component end, which is carried out by the stub, is called **unmarshaling**. The proxy and stub code is generated from the `.idl` file by the MIDL compiler and is usually placed in a separate DLL. We have the option here of including this code within the same DLL as the component, but we'll leave it unchecked.

If you want to use the MFC classes, you can check the Support <u>M</u>FC box. This will add an application class to the project derived from **CWinApp**, and the program will contain an application object. It will also increase the size of the component considerably, but it does mean that you would be able to use *any* of the MFC classes in your project. We don't need it here, so leave this box unchecked as well.

If you click on the <u>F</u>inish button you'll see the last dialog which, as usual, shows you the details of the files that will be generated, and gives you a last chance to back out.

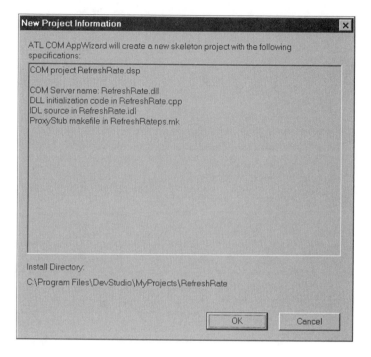

Don't weaken now! Click on the OK button to complete the operation. We can then take a look at the code that's generated for us.

Basic COM AppWizard Code

If you switch to ClassView and extend the tree, you'll see that there's very little there, especially compared with what we've been used to in the last few chapters:

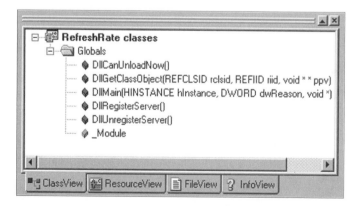

There are no classes defined at all. We have five global functions and a global object, **_Module**, defined. At the moment there's no COM object and no COM interface implemented.

Two of the global functions, **DllRegisterServer()** and **DllUnregisterServer()**, will provide the ability to register and unregister our COM component, as you can probably guess from the function names. The **DllMain()** function is called when the DLL is loaded into memory and, as we saw in Chapter 9, initializes the DLL. The function **DllCanUnloadNow()** determines whether the DLL is still in use, and is called to decide when to remove the DLL from memory. Lastly, the **DllGetClassObject()** function is used to retrieve the COM object from the DLL when you create an instance of the component in a client program. You don't usually call this function directly, though—we'll see how we can create an instance of a COM component later in this chapter.

The global object **_Module** is an instance of the class **CComModule**, which represents the COM server module we're creating. The COM server module will contain functions to manage all the class objects in the module and provides the mechanism for entering information about the COM components in the system registry. **DllRegisterServer()** and **DllUnregisterServer()** call functions belonging to the **_Module** object to perform the registration and unregistration operations. So where does our COM object implementation come from?

Adding a COM object to the Project

To add a COM object, you can either select the Insert | New ATL Object... menu item, or display the ATL toolbar and click on the button. A dialog will be displayed that gives you a selection of COM objects that you can add to your project:

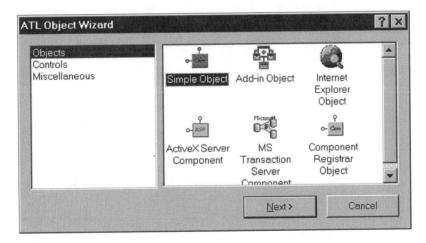

The dialog offers three sets of COM components to choose from: Objects, Controls and Miscellaneous. We'll be creating another COM component later in this chapter which will be an ActiveX control, but for now we will just add a Simple Object. Highlight that by clicking it, as shown, and click on the Next> button.

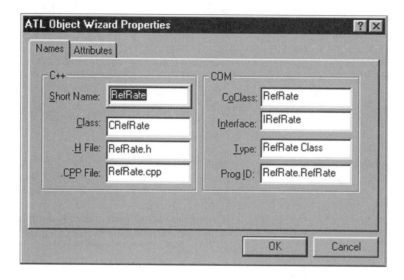

Here you need to enter the name for the COM component, **RefRate**. This is used as the basis for the C++ class name that implements the component, and for the names of the files containing the C++ code. It is also the basis for the names of the CoClass, which is the component class, the name of the interface, **IRefRate**, that the component will support, the type name and the Prog ID that will appear in the registry. Note that the component class is not a C++ class—it's a COM class which identifies the interfaces that the component supports.

The other tab on the dialog provides options as to how the component will be implemented:

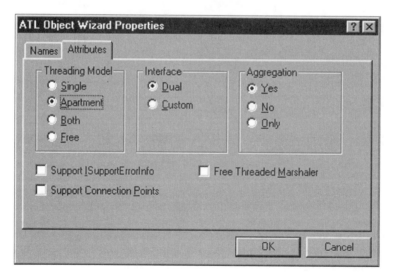

The threading options relate to the degree of concurrency of executing processes within a component and are beyond the scope of this book, so we'll ignore that here. Dual interfaces, on the other hand, we have mentioned previously. This option provides for interface functions to be callable through a dispatch interface (using the **Invoke()** function) as well as through the virtual function table. **Aggregation** refers to the capability of one COM component to make use of another, making the contained component's interfaces available as well as its own. All the defaults are fine for our example, so click on the OK button to add the object to our project. Let's see what we've got now.

ATL Object Code

The ATL-based component is very different from the ActiveX control we saw in the previous chapter. If you extend all the trees in ClassView, you can see that we have one class defined, **CRefRate**, and one interface, **IRefRate**, in addition to the five global functions and the global object **_Module** that we had before:

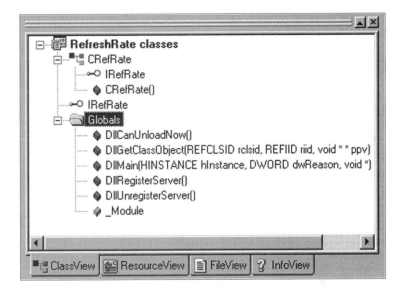

The class **CRefRate** represents our COM object, and **IRefRate** is the definition of the COM interface for this object. **IRefRate** is defined in the **RefreshRate.idl** file, and is implemented by the class **CRefRate**, which has its definition in **RefRate.h** and its implementation in **RefRate.cpp**, as you might expect. If you look at the files in the project in FileView, you will see a file of a type that we haven't met before: **RefRate.rgs**. This contains the information that will be entered in the system registry when we successfully build our COM project.

The COM Object Class

The definition of the class **CRefRate** is short, but there's quite a lot there nonetheless, because it has no less than three base classes. Notice that while MFC relies on single inheritance, ATL capitalizes on using multiple inheritance:

```
class ATL_NO_VTABLE CRefRate :
    public CComObjectRootEx<CComSingleThreadModel>,
    public CComCoClass<CRefRate, &CLSID_RefRate>,
    public IDispatchImpl<IRefRate, &IID_IRefRate, &LIBID_REFRESHRATELib>
{
```

```
public:
   CRefRate()
   {
   }

DECLARE_REGISTRY_RESOURCEID(IDR_REFRATE)

BEGIN_COM_MAP(CRefRate)
   COM_INTERFACE_ENTRY(IRefRate)
   COM_INTERFACE_ENTRY(IDispatch)
END_COM_MAP()

// IRefRate
public:
};
```

The base classes add the basic COM infrastructure that our COM object needs. As you can see, they're all generated from templates. The first base class, **CComObjectRootEx**, implements the basic COM interface, **IUnknown**. It takes cares of the reference counting through the **AddRef()** and **Release()** functions, and it implements the **QueryInterface()** function. The argument to the template, **CComSingleThreadModel**, makes the generated class applicable to single thread operations. This is a consequence of accepting the default threading model on the Attributes tab of the ATL Object Wizard.

The second base class, **CComCoClass**, defines the factory class for our component. The factory class enables an instance of the COM component to be created. You need to create an instance of a component before you can call any of its interface functions. The template for **CComCoClass** uses the class name, **CRefRate**, and the CLSID for the component as parameters to define the factory class.

The last base class, **IDispatchImpl**, will provide the dual interface for our control. We'll have **IUnknown** by default, plus the **IDispatch** interface functions to allow interface methods to be called using **Invoke()**. The three parameters to the template are our component interface, **IRefRate**, a pointer to the corresponding interface ID, and a pointer to the GUID for the type library. These aren't defined in the C++ code yet, but code will be added to define them when the **.idl** file is processed.

We will be extending the interface **IRefRate** by adding our own functions to the **.idl** file. When we do, we'll also need to add declarations for these functions to the **CRefRate** class definition. These will go after the **public** keyword at the end of the class definition.

The interfaces defined for the class are identified following the **BEGIN_COM_MAP()** macro. We have an entry for **IRefRate** in addition to the standard **IDispatch** interface, since this will contain our application-specific interface functions. The COM map makes the methods in these interfaces accessible to a container through the **QueryInterface()** method in **IUnknown**.

The Interface Definition

The IDL file, **RefreshRate.idl**, has two **import** statements for the files **oaidl.idl** and **ocidl.idl** at the beginning. These add all the standard definitions for the interfaces supported by ATL. The file also contains two main definitions: a definition of the interface **IRefRate**, and a definition of what will go into the type library which records information about the COM component. In each case there's a set of attributes appearing between square brackets, followed by the details of the definition. The IDL code defining the **IRefRate** interface is:

```
[
    object,
    uuid(B34EF5CF-7B79-11D0-96FE-002018349816),
    dual,
    helpstring("IRefRate Interface"),
    pointer_default(unique)
]
interface IRefRate : IDispatch
{
};
```

The **object** attribute indicates that this is a custom COM interface, and we'll be adding our own methods to this interface definition. The second attribute defines the UUID for the interface. This is the 128-bit universally unique ID we discussed in the previous chapter that identifies the interface, so the UUID you have in your version of the project will undoubtedly be different from the one here. The **dual** attribute determines that this is a dual interface, which as you know means that you can access functions directly through the vtable, or indirectly through **IDispatch::Invoke()**. **helpstring** can be used by applications that make use of the type library to describe the interface. The **pointer_default(unique)** dictates that if pointers to pointers are used as parameters in interface functions, they must each provide a unique access route to the data they point to—that is, to access any particular data item, only one pointer can be used. This enables the code that accesses the data to be simplified.

At the moment the interface contains no custom interface functions at all. We'll be adding ours between the braces following the **interface** statement. The basic COM requirement for **IUnknown** is taken care of with this, since **IRefRate** inherits from **IDispatch** which inherits from **IUnknown**.

The type library is specified with the following IDL code:

```
[
    uuid(B34EF5C2-7B79-11D0-96FE-002018349816),
    version(1.0),
    helpstring("RefreshRate 1.0 Type Library")
]
library REFRESHRATELib
{
    importlib("stdole32.tlb");

    [
        uuid(B34EF5D0-7B79-11D0-96FE-002018349816),
        helpstring("RefRate Class")
    ]
    coclass RefRate
    {
        [default] interface IRefRate;
    };
};
```

The standard OLE type library is imported with the **importlib** statement. The **coclass** definition statement incorporates our custom interface **IRefRate** which was defined previously, so that this will be part of each instance of the COM component implemented by the C++ class **CRefRate**.

Extending the Interface

The basic function our component will perform is to calculate the refresh rate for a monitor, given the horizontal scan frequency. We will therefore need an interface function we can call **RefreshRate()** that will accept an argument specifying the horizontal scan frequency in kilohertz (of type **long**, say) and return the refresh rate in hertz as another **long** value. If we were declaring this as a regular C++ function, it would have a prototype something like

```
long RefreshRate(long HScan);
```

However, we're defining a COM interface function here, and there are some constraints. A COM interface function should return a value of type **HRESULT**. This is a 32-bit value containing fields indicating success or failure of the operation. This is necessary because of the diversity of contexts in which a component might be used. Bearing in mind that the client may be on a different machine from the COM server, a lot can go wrong in the general case, so the **HRESULT** return type provides a rich set of possible return codes.

A consequence of all this is that if you want to return a data value to the client, such as the refresh rate we plan to calculate, you must return it through a parameter to the function. This complicates the specification of interface function parameters somewhat. In addition to the constraint that they must be of a type supported by COM, we also have the requirement that you must indicate in the interface definition which parameters to a function are inputting data and which are outputting data. You must also specify which, if any, of the output parameters is passing a return value back to the client.

Because of all this, the definition of our interface function in the IDL file turns out to be:

```
HRESULT RefreshRate([in] long HScan, [out, retval] long* retval);
```

The return type is **HRESULT**, and each parameter is preceded by attributes defined between square brackets. A parameter will have the attribute **in** if a value is being passed by the client to the function, the attribute **out** if a value is being passed from the function to the client, and the attributes **out** and **retval** if a value is being passed from the function to the client as a return value. A parameter that is specified as **in** can also have the attribute **out** if the function will use the parameter to return a value. A parameter with the attribute **out** must always be specified as a pointer; this means that the memory for storing the value is owned by the client. A parameter with the attribute **retval** must also have the attribute **out**, and therefore must be a pointer. Note that a parameter with the attribute **retval** must also be named **retval**.

Since we'll need to obtain the current vertical display resolution in order to calculate the refresh rate, we might as well include functions to supply the horizontal and vertical resolution of the display independent of the refresh rate. You will therefore need to modify the interface definition in **RefreshRate.idl** by adding the following statements:

```
[
    object,
    uuid(B34EF5CF-7B79-11D0-96FE-002018349816),
    dual,
    helpstring("IRefRate Interface"),
    pointer_default(unique)
]
interface IRefRate : IDispatch
{
```

```
            HRESULT RefreshRate([in] long HScan, [out, retval] long* retval);
            HRESULT GetVRes([out, retval] long* retval);
            HRESULT GetHRes([out, retval] long* retval);
      };
```

Both the **GetVRes()** and **GetHRes()** functions have a single parameter that has the **retval** attribute. Since we'll get the values to be returned by using the Windows API, no input parameters are necessary.

Implementing the Interface Functions

We must first add the functions we have defined as part of the interface to the class definition for our COM object:

```
class ATL_NO_VTABLE CRefRate :
    public CComObjectRootEx<CComSingleThreadModel>,
    public CComCoClass<CRefRate, &CLSID_RefRate>,
    public IDispatchImpl<IRefRate, &IID_IRefRate, &LIBID_REFRESHRATELib>
{
public:
    CRefRate()
    {
    }

DECLARE_REGISTRY_RESOURCEID(IDR_REFRATE)

BEGIN_COM_MAP(CRefRate)
    COM_INTERFACE_ENTRY(IRefRate)
    COM_INTERFACE_ENTRY(IDispatch)
END_COM_MAP()

// IRefRate
public:
    HRESULT __stdcall RefreshRate(long MaxHScan, long* retval);
    HRESULT __stdcall GetVRes(long* retval);
    HRESULT __stdcall GetHRes(long* retval);
};
```

The **__stdcall** qualifier that appears in front of each function name specifies that the function uses the **WINAPI** (or **PASCAL**) calling convention. This prescribes how the parameters are handled when the function is called, and differs from the standard C++ calling convention. All COM interface functions with a fixed number of parameters use this. We must now add the implementations for these functions to the **RefRate.cpp** file. Let's implement **RefreshRate()** first:

```
// Calculate the refresh rate
HRESULT __stdcall CRefRate::RefreshRate(long MaxHScan, long* retval)
{
    int ScreenY = GetSystemMetrics(SM_CYSCREEN); // Get vertical
    ScreenY = (int)(1.04 * ScreenY);             // Allow for overscan areas
    *retval = MaxHScan * 1000 / ScreenY;         // Return to client
    return S_OK;                                 // Return to COM
}
```

Getting the current screen resolution is easy. We just call the Windows API function **GetSystemMetrics()** with an argument that specifies the kind of information we want. The argument value **SM_CXSCREEN** would give the number of pixels in the horizontal direction, and the argument we have used, **SM_CYSCREEN**, results in the number of pixels on the screen vertically being returned. This function can supply a large number of other items of information, on which you can find details by placing the cursor on the function name and pressing *F1*.

There is usually some time lost between ending one screen scan and starting the next, so we compensate for this by effectively increasing the number of screen pixels in the *y* direction by 4%. We then divide the result into the value for the horizontal scan frequency to get the refresh rate, the 1000 multiplier being necessary because the units are kilohertz. We need to dereference **retval** to store the result. When the function is called by a client, the value (rather than a pointer to the value) will be returned, as we shall see. Here we are storing the result in the location pointed to by the **retval** argument.

Finally, we return the **HRESULT** value **S_OK** to the COM environment. **HRESULT** is quite a complex value: packed into its 32 bits are four different fields indicating the status on return from the function. We don't need to get into the detail of these, since most of it is intended for the operating system. Returning **S_OK** indicates the function succeeded; **E_FAIL** indicates an unspecified failure. There are in fact a variety of return codes for success beginning with **S_**, and similarly a range of error return codes beginning with **E_**. Because there are multiple codes for success and failure, you should not test an **HRESULT** value by comparing it with specific return codes such as **S_OK** or **E_FAIL**. You should use the macro **SUCCEEDED()** to test for success and the macro **FAILED()** to test for failure. For example, if the **HRESULT** value returned is **hR**, you could write:

```
if(SUCCEEDED(hR))
   // Do something for success...
else
   // Oh dear, it didn't work...
```

Implementing the other two interface functions is very easy:

```
HRESULT __stdcall CRefRate::GetVRes(long* retval)
{
   *retval = GetSystemMetrics(SM_CYSCREEN); // Return horizontal resolution
   return S_OK;                             // Return to COM environment
}

HRESULT __stdcall CRefRate::GetHRes(long* retval)
{
   *retval = GetSystemMetrics(SM_CXSCREEN); // Return vertical resolution
   return S_OK;                             // Return to COM environment
}
```

They both work in the same way. Each stores the result to be returned to the client in the location pointed to by **retval**, and then returns the **S_OK** value.

Building the Component

Build the component in exactly the same way as any other project. First, the MIDL compiler will process the **.idl** file to produce the **.tlb** file containing the type library, then the C++ compiler will compile the C++ source, the link step will generate the `.dll`, and finally the component will be registered. This presumes, of course, that there are no errors in the code you have added.

If you look at the External Dependencies folder in FileView, you'll see that the MIDL compiler has produced three new files:

File	Description
`atliface.h`	Contains declarations for the `IRegistrar` interface containing ATL functions that provide access to the system registry.
`RefreshRate.tlb`	Contains the type library for the program.
`RefreshRate_i.c`	Contains definitions for the IIDs for the `IRefRate` interface and the type library, and the CLSID for the COM component.

It has also added code to `RefreshRate.h`, which previously only contained a comment but now contains the code defining the virtual function table for our custom interface `IRefRate`. The virtual function table contains a pointer to each function in the interface. There's one version of the vtable that's selected if the symbol `__cplusplus` is defined (the C++ version), and one for when it isn't. In our context, the former applies.

You'll notice the macro `__RPC_FAR` applied to the type of the parameters in the pointer definitions for our interface functions in the virtual function table in `RefreshRate.h`. This macro only applies to 16-bit environments and is removed by the preprocessor in Windows 95 and other Win32 environments. That's why we didn't need it in our declarations in `CRefRate` class, but you should add it if you plan to compile the code for a 16-bit environment. The `STDMETHODCALLTYPE` macro that also appears is equivalent to the `__stdcall` specifier that we used in the `CRefRate` class and in the implementations of the functions.

If you're unsure what the prototypes in C++ for functions you have added to the interface in the `.idl` file are, you can always build the project to get the MIDL compiler to generate the `.h` file. There will be a lot of errors, since you won't have declared these functions in the component class, but you can copy the function declarations that appear in the interface definition in the `.h` file generated by the MIDL compiler. For example, if you look in the `Refresh.h` file you will see it has an interface entry for the `RefreshRate()` function as follows:

```
virtual HRESULT STDMETHODCALLTYPE RefreshRate(
    /* [in] */ long HScan,
    /* [retval][out] */ long __RPC_FAR *retval) = 0;
```

All you need to do is remove the `=0` at the end to get a declaration to put in your class:

```
virtual HRESULT STDMETHODCALLTYPE RefreshRate(
    /* [in] */ long HScan,
    /* [retval][out] */ long __RPC_FAR *retval);
```

You could then put this as the declaration in the class definition verbatim. The `STDMETHODCALLTYPE` is a macro that generates `__stdcall`, so you can leave that. The `__RPC_FAR` macro is for 16-bit environments and is ignored under Windows 95. The comments aren't particularly tidy, so you could remove those if you wanted to, but they don't do any harm.

Using the Component

Our component should be usable in any environment that supports COM. Using our COM component is easiest in Visual Basic, so let's give that a try first. After that, we'll see how we can incorporate **RefRate** into a C++ program. If you don't have or use Visual Basic, you can skip the next section and go straight to using **RefRate** in a C++ program.

Visual Basic Access to the COM Component

The first thing to establish, once you've started a new Visual Basic project, is that Visual Basic is aware of our COM component. Select the menu item <u>R</u>eferences... in the <u>T</u>ools menu to display the dialog shown here:

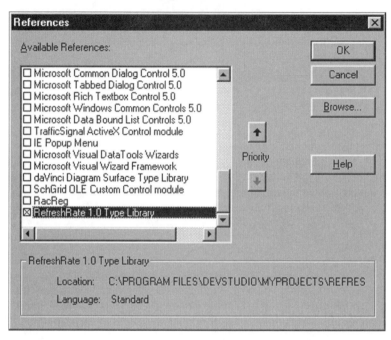

This lists the references that are identified in the system. All those checked are available to your Visual Basic program. If the type library for **RefreshRate** appears in the list, just click the check box and click on the OK button to make it available in your program. If it doesn't appear in the list, you can add it by clicking the <u>B</u>rowse... button, going to the directory containing the **RefreshRate** code, and selecting the type library file, **RefreshRate.tlb**.

The first step is to design a form that we can use to exercise our COM component. All we need are some text boxes and a few labels, as shown:

Four text boxes have been added to the form. You can assign names to the text boxes in the property list that reflect their purpose. Running from top to bottom, I used the names **txtHScanMax**, **txtRRate**, **txtHRes** and **txtVRes** respectively. The last three are output only, so you could set the Locked property to **TRUE** to prevent them from being edited. You could also clear the Text property so they appear empty. There is a label at the top with instructions, plus a label for each of the text boxes to identify them. All we need in addition to this is a small amount of code to handle the input.

You need to implement a subroutine to handle a **KeyPress** event for the **txtHScanMax** text box, as follows:

```
Private Sub txtHScanMax_KeyPress(KeyAscii As Integer)
   Dim objRefRate As New RefRate
   If (KeyAscii = 13) Then
      txtRRate.Text = objRefRate.RefreshRate(HScan:=Val(txtHScanMax.Text))
      txtHRes.Text = objRefRate.GetHRes
      txtVRes.Text = objRefRate.GetVRes
   End If
End Sub
```

The **Dim** statement declares an object variable, **objRefRate**, that's an instance of the **RefRate** component. We can use this variable to call the interface functions for the component. The **If** statement tests for the *Enter* key being pressed (code 13). If it is, it passes the value entered in the **txtHScanMax** text box as the argument to the interface function **RefreshRate()**. The refresh rate is then displayed in the text box **txtRRate**. In practice, it would be a good idea to verify that the **txtHScanMax** text box is not zero before passing the value to the COM interface function. We call the other two interface functions for the **RefRate** object and display the output in the appropriate text box.

You can paste the calls to the component interface functions into your code from the Object Browser. Press the *F2* function key to display it:

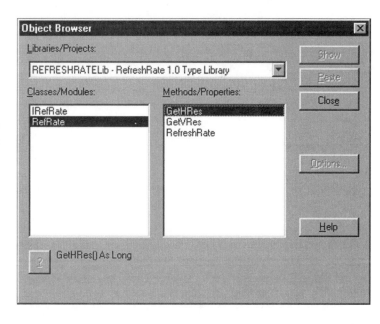

With the cursor positioned in your code where you want to call an interface function, you can highlight the function in the Methods/Properties: list and paste it into your code by clicking the

Paste button. Running the program on my machine and typing in a value of 90 for the horizontal scan rate, I get this output:

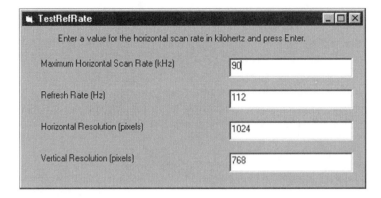

Using ATL-based COM objects in Visual Basic is very straightforward, once Visual Basic is aware of them. All you do is create a variable representing an instance of the component, and use the object variable to access the interface. What could be simpler than that?

Using the COM Component in C++

The simplest way we can explore the mechanics of using a COM component in Visual C++ is to create a project specifically to do this. Use MFC AppWizard (exe) to create a new project for an SDI program. I gave the project the name **UseRefRate**, but you can use whatever you want. You can leave the ActiveX Controls box on Step 3 checked, and on Step 6 change the base class for the view to **CFormView**. This will make it easy to set up some controls to operate the component.

The first thing we need to do is set up the dialog that's used in the view. Go to ResourceView and double-click on the dialog ID—with the name I assigned to the project it's **IDD_USEREFRATE_FORM**. We can set it up to look very similar to the Visual Basic form we had previously:

There are four edit boxes, each with a static text item alongside, and a static text item to indicate how to use the dialog. There's also a button labeled Calculate at the bottom. You can give the button the ID **IDC_CALCULATE**, and the edit boxes the IDs **IDC_HSCAN**, **IDC_REFRESH**, **IDC_HRES** and **IDC_VRES**. All the edit boxes should have the Number option checked on the Styles tab in the Properties dialog, and the bottom three should have the Read-only option checked as well.

Now we can add variables corresponding to the three edit boxes. You will recall that we can do this by double-clicking the edit box while holding down the *Ctrl* key. They should all be of type **long**, since each of the entries is an integer, and you can give them the names **m_lHScan**, **m_lRefresh**, **m_lHRes** and **m_lVRes**. They will be added to the view class definition and initialized in the constructor. You could change the default value set in the view class constructor for **m_lHScan** to 50, since this should always be non-zero. All the code necessary to pass data between the variables and the controls will already have been added to the **DoDataExchange()** function in the view class. We just need to add a handler for the button.

You can add the button handler in the same way as you added the variables for the edit boxes: just double-click the button in the dialog while holding down the *Ctrl* key. The **OnCalculate()** handler will do all of the work to call the COM component interface methods, but first we need to connect our program to an instance of the COM component. We'll need to do two basic things to make this happen: we must create an instance of the component, and we must implement a means of accessing the interface to the component. Since we get a lot of help from ClassWizard for the latter, let's do that first.

Creating the Interface

For the representation of the interface to the COM component, it's natural in C++ to think of a class. ClassWizard can create the class that we need automatically from the type library for the component.

Open the ClassWizard dialog by right clicking in the editor window and selecting from the context menu, and click on the Add Class... button. From the pop-up that appears, select the From a type library... option. You will then see this dialog:

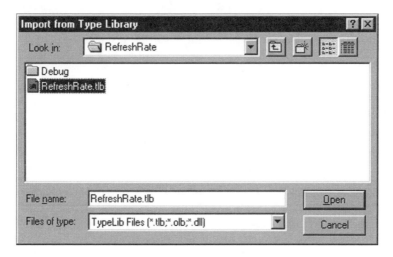

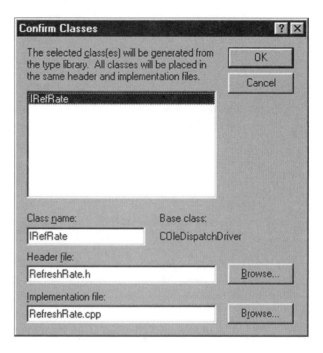

Navigate to the directory containing the type library for **RefreshRate**, select the file and click on <u>O</u>pen. You will then see a dialog showing details of the class that will be created from the type library:

A class **IRefRate** will be derived from **COleDispatchDriver** to implement the interface defined in the type library file **RefreshRate.tlb**. Click on OK in the dialog to accept this, and then click on the OK button to close ClassWizard. If you look in ClassView you will see the class has been added to your project, and is defined as:

```
class IRefRate : public COleDispatchDriver
{
public:
    IRefRate() {}        // Calls COleDispatchDriver default constructor
    IRefRate(LPDISPATCH pDispatch) : COleDispatchDriver(pDispatch) {}
    IRefRate(const IRefRate& dispatchSrc) : COleDispatchDriver(dispatchSrc) {}

// Attributes
public:

// Operations
public:
    long RefreshRate(long HScan);
    long GetVRes();
    long GetHRes();
};
```

The base class **COleDispatchDriver** enables COM interface functions to be called using the **IDispatch** interface. **COleDispatchDriver** has three constructors: one connects to a COM object by using an existing **COleDispatchDriver** object that has already established an interface to the COM object; one accepts a pointer to an **IDispatch** interface; the third is a default constructor that accepts no arguments. If you use the default constructor to create a **COleDispatchDriver**-derived object, you can use **CreateDispatch()** or **AttachDispatch()** to attach the dispatch interface to the object.

If you look in **RefreshRate.cpp**, you'll see how the interface functions have been implemented:

```
long IRefRate::RefreshRate(long HScan)
{
   long result;
   static BYTE parms[] =
      VTS_I4;
   InvokeHelper(0x60020000, DISPATCH_METHOD, VT_I4, (void*)&result, parms,
      HScan);
   return result;
}

long IRefRate::GetVRes()
{
   long result;
   InvokeHelper(0x60020001, DISPATCH_METHOD, VT_I4, (void*)&result, NULL);
   return result;
}

long IRefRate::GetHRes()
{
   long result;
   InvokeHelper(0x60020002, DISPATCH_METHOD, VT_I4, (void*)&result, NULL);
   return result;
}
```

Each of the three functions calls the function **InvokeHelper()** that's inherited from the base class. This function packages the **Invoke()** function in the **IDispatch** interface and can accept five or more arguments, which we can use to find out how it works.

The first argument to **InvokeHelper()** is the DispID for the interface function that's to be called; the DispID was obtained from the type library for the component by ClassWizard. The second argument determines that a method is being called, rather than a property value being set or obtained. The third argument specifies the type of the return value—**VT_I4** corresponds to **long**. The types acceptable in the COM context are encoded so that they can be interpreted appropriately in any programming context, and there is a predefined set of symbols that correspond to these types. The fourth argument is a pointer to a variable that is to receive the return value from the interface function. This is the **retval** value, not the value of type **HRESULT** returned to COM. If the **HRESULT** value returned when the interface function is called indicates a failure, the **InvokeHelper()** function will throw an exception.

The fifth argument is a pointer to a string that indicates the type of each of the following arguments. If there are none, as is the case with **GetVRes()** and **GetHRes()**, this pointer is **NULL**. The types are specified in a language-neutral form similar to that for the return value. **VTS_I4** is used for **HScan**, which corresponds to **long**.

Once we've a created component object, we'll be able to access the interface functions for the **RefRate** component through the driver class, **IRefRate**, so add the following declaration to the **CUseRefRateView** class definition:

```
public:
   IRefRate* m_pRefRateDriver;    // Pointer to dispatch driver for RefRate
```

We'll be using this pointer in the button handler to call the interface functions for the component. You can also add an incomplete declaration for the **IRefRate** class immediately before the view class definition:

```
class IRefRate;                    // The RefRate dispatch driver class
```

Of course, we'll need the definition of the class **IRefRate** when we include the view class definition into the view implementation file, so add the following **#include** directive to the **UseRefRateView.cpp** file, just before the **#include** directive for **UseRefRateView.h**:

```
#include "RefreshRate.h"
```

You need to add the same **#include** directive to the **UseRefRate.cpp** file.

Using the COM Library

Before you can do anything with a COM component, even before constructing it, you need access to the **COM library** in your program. The COM library contains functions that enable you to create COM components, as well as a variety of other functions for working with COM objects. To make the COM library functions available to your program, you call a function **CoInitialize()**.

When you call this function, it requires an argument of **NULL** to be specified because the parameter is reserved for possible future use. Because it's a COM function, it returns a value of type **HRESULT**. The normal return value is **S_OK** if the COM library initialization was successful. **CoInitialize()** returns **S_FALSE** if the library was already initialized. Remember that you should not use an **if** to check for these values directly. Because there are several possible success or failure codes, you should use the macros **SUCCEEDED()** or **FAILED()** to test an **HRESULT** value.

Note that the COM library is part of the OLE library that's a prerequisite for OLE (ActiveX) controls. The OLE library is initialized by a call to **OleInitialize()**, which in turn calls **CoInitialize()**. If you think you'll need the full facilities of the OLE library at some point, you can call **OleInitialize()** instead of **CoInitialize()**. You must then call **OleUninitialize()** (rather than **CoUninitialize()**) when you're done. We only need COM in the present context, so we'll stick with that in our example.

All our usage of COM library facilities will be within the view class for our program. We can add the following statements to the constructor for the **CUseRefRateView** class, following the block of code bounded by the **AFX_DATA_INIT** comments:

```
    if(FAILED(CoInitialize(NULL)))                // Initialize COM library
    {
      AfxMessageBox("COM Library init failed");
      AfxAbort();                                 // End the program
    }
```

This uses the **FAILED()** macro to test whether the **HRESULT** value returned indicates that the COM library was not initialized. If it wasn't, we can't proceed, so we display a message and end the program.

When you've finished with the library in your program, you should call the function **CoUninitialize()**, so add the following statement to the view class destructor:

```
CoUninitialize();    // Uninitialize the COM library
```

With the COM library initialized, we are ready to create our first COM object.

Component Objects

A COM object is not a class object. Although we used a class to implement **RefRate**, doing so was a C++ convenience, nothing more. A COM component can be implemented without using classes at all. To create an instance of a COM component, you can call the COM library function **CoCreateInstance()**. This function will create the COM object by calling the **GetClassObject()** member of the **_Module** object in the component implementation, and supplying a pointer to the COM interface that you request. The function requires five arguments:

1 The CLSID for the component, of type **REFCLSID**.

2 A pointer of type **IUnknown**. If this is **NULL**, it indicates that the component isn't embedded in another component; a component incorporated into another component is said to be **aggregated**. If the component is aggregated, this pointer points to the **IUnknown** interface for the component that contains the component you want.

3 A value indicating the context in which the component is to run—this could be as an in-process server, as an out-of-process server, or as a remote server on a separate machine.

4 A reference to the ID for the interface to be used.

5 A pointer to a pointer to the required interface.

Luckily, **COleDispatchDriver** wraps up this function in a member function called **CreateDispatch()**. All that **CreateDispatch()** needs is a CLSID to be able to create an object and attach its **IDispatch** interface to the **COleDispatchDriver**-derived class. This is precisely what we need it to do, so let's investigate how we can get hold of the CLSID.

Obtaining the CLSID for a Component

There are several ways to get hold of a CLSID. The easy way out in this case would be to copy the definition of **CLSID_RefRate** from the **RefreshRate_i.c** file that was generated by the MIDL compiler when we compiled the code for the component. However, for other components, we can't be sure that this will always be available so we need a more general approach for the COM components you have on your system.

You can view information about **RefRate** and other COM components by using the **OLE/COM Object Viewer** (**Oleview.exe**) that you can access through the Developer Studio <u>T</u>ools menu. It runs as a completely independent program so you could execute it separately from Developer Studio if you wanted to.

To display information about our component using the OLE/COM Object Viewer, make sure Expert Mode is checked in the <u>V</u>iew menu, and extend the All Objects folder in the left hand pane. You will then see a list of all the COM objects on your system in alphabetical order. You should find the **RefRate** entry in the list.

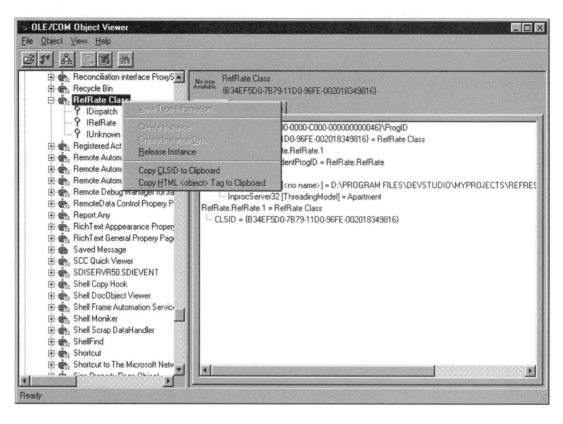

If you click on the entry to highlight it, the registry data will be displayed in the right hand window. Right clicking the entry will bring up a context menu, as shown, where you have an option to copy the CLSID to the clipboard. You will then be able to copy the CLSID from the clipboard into your program. However, there's a problem with that: the CLSID is actually a 128-bit binary number. When we copy the CLSID from the clipboard, we end up with a string of characters:

```
{B34EF5D0-7B79-11D0-96FE-002018349816}
```

You need to convert this to the 16-*byte* numeric value for the CLSID for it to be of any use. Fortunately, the COM library provides a function called **CLSIDFromString()** that will do the conversion for you. You must supply two arguments to the function: a pointer to the string representation of the CLSID, and the address of a variable of type CLSID. You could therefore get the CLSID with the statements:

```
CLSID CLSID_RefRate;                              // Object class ID
::CLSIDFromString(L"{B34EF5D0-7B79-11D0-96FE-002018349816}", &CLSID_RefRate);
```

You'll have noticed the **L** preceding the first quote for the string representation of the CLSID. No, it isn't a typo! The **L** specifies the string constant as being a wide character string—of type **wchar_t**. The **L** is a cast to **long** which is the underlying type of **wchar_t**. With this type of string, each character requires 16 bits (two bytes), rather than the single byte for ASCII. You can just paste the string representation direct from the clipboard (including the braces), put quotes around it and add the initial **L**. In fact, it won't work if you remove the braces, so don't be tempted to delete them.

There's yet another way to get the CLSID. The registry contains a **ProgID** (a program ID) for each COM component. The ProgID is usually in the form **Program_Name.Component_Name.Version**. In our case, the program name is **RefRate**, the component name is **RefRate**, and the version is 1. If you look in the registry under **HKEY_CLASSES_ROOT**, you'll see a key for **RefRate.RefRate.1** which is the ProgID of our component. This key contains a subkey called **CLSID** that contains the CLSID for our component. Given that you've declared **CLSID_RefRate** as above, you can use the ProgID to produce the CLSID using the COM library function **CLSIDFromProgID()**, like this:

```
::CLSIDFromProgID(L"RefRate.RefRate.1",&CLSID_RefRate);
```

This is quite a nice way of getting a CLSID to use for creating an instance of a COM class, but it turns out that **COleDispatchDriver** provides an overloaded version of **CreateDispatch()** that accepts a string for the ProgID of the object to create, so we don't need to call **CLSIDFromProgID()** ourselves.

Creating an Instance of a Component

We can add the code to create an instance of **RefRate** to the view constructor:

```
CUseRefRateView::CUseRefRateView()
 : CFormView(CUseRefRateView::IDD)
{
//{{AFX_DATA_INIT(CUseRefRateView)
m_lHScan = 50;
m_lRefresh = 0;
m_lHRes = 0;
m_lVRes = 0;
//}}AFX_DATA_INIT

    if(FAILED(CoInitialize(NULL)))              // Initialize COM library
    {
        AfxMessageBox("COM Library init failed");
        AfxAbort();                             // End the program
    }

    // Create a new driver object to handle our COM object
    m_pRefRateDriver = new IRefRate;

    // Create an instance of our COM object using the ProgID
    // and attach the dispinterface
    // to our OleDispatchDriver-derived object
    m_pRefRateDriver->CreateDispatch(_T("RefRate.RefRate.1"));
}
```

This is really just putting together what we've discussed. The only thing to notice is the **_T()** macro around the ProgID. If you've compiled your application for Unicode then the **CreateDispatch()** function accepts a wide string, but if you haven't then you must pass a standard string without prefixing it with an **L**. In our (non-Unicode) case we could get away with passing the string directly to the function, but it would be better if we wrapped the string up in a **_T()** macro. This macro is exactly the same as the **L** prefix if Unicode is used, but it means nothing if it isn't, so we're covered in either case. You'll see this macro used a lot in MFC itself.

Note that the pointer, **m_pRefRateDriver**, that we're using here is *not* a pointer to the **IDispatch** interface of the **RefRate** object. **m_pRefRateDriver** is a pointer to a **COleDispatchDriver**-derived class that implements functions corresponding to those in the **RefRate** dispatch interface. If you want to manipulate the dispatch interface directly, you can get a pointer to it from the public **m_lpDispatch** member of **COleDispatchDriver**.

Releasing the Component

The next thing we need to do is add code to the destructor to clean up the driver object that we've allocated with the **new** operator, so add the following statement to the **CUseRefRateView** class destructor:

```
CUseRefRateView::~CUseRefRateView()
{
    delete m_pRefRateDriver;
    CoUninitialize();   // Uninitialize the COM library
}
```

Note that the code must come *before* the call to **CoUninitialize()**. We can't uninitialize the COM library until all the COM objects that we've created have been released. Remember that each time you call **QueryInterface()** or **AddRef()** on an interface, you are increasing the reference count for that interface and that you need to call **Release()** when you've finished using the interface so that the reference count is decreased and the object can remove itself from memory when appropriate.

Although it doesn't look like we're calling **Release()** on the **IDispatch** interface that's wrapped up in the driver class, it is happening. The destructor for **COleDispatchDriver** calls **Release()** on the dispatch interface pointer that it has, as long as a member variable called **m_bAutoRelease** is set to **TRUE**. Since it is **TRUE** by default, the **delete** operation on **m_pRefRateDriver** does call **IDispatch::Release()** in our case.

Now we have an instance of the **RefRate** component and the interface is available to us, so we can implement the handler for the Calculate button.

Using Component Interface Functions

We're back on familiar ground now. We can use the functions in the **IRefRate** class object that connects to the COM object just like any other class member function. The implementation of the handler will be:

```
void CUseRefRateView::OnCalculate()
{
    UpdateData(TRUE);                        // Get m_HScan from the dialog
    m_lRefresh = m_pRefRateDriver->RefreshRate(m_lHScan);
    m_lHRes = m_pRefRateDriver->GetHRes();
    m_lVRes = m_pRefRateDriver->GetVRes();
    UpdateData(FALSE);                       // Set the values in the dialog
}
```

We first call the **UpdateData()** member of our view class (inherited from **CWnd**) with the argument **TRUE**. This causes **DoDataExchange()** to be called to retrieve data from the form dialog controls—on this occasion, just the value entered for the scan rate. After calling the component interface functions to calculate the refresh rate and the screen resolution, we call **UpdateData()** with the argument **FALSE** to store these values back in the controls in the form dialog.

Our client for the component is complete. You can now build it and give it a whirl. You should get a dialog that looks like this one:

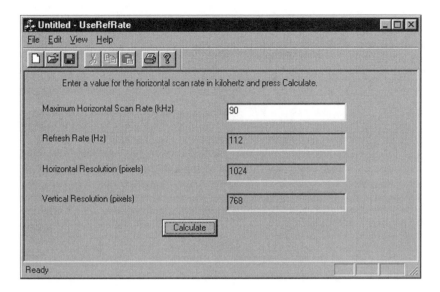

Using ATL to Create an ActiveX Control

Now that we've staggered through creating and using an elementary ATL-based COM object, we're ready for something a bit more challenging. We can see how to put together an ATL-based equivalent of the traffic signal control that we produced using MFC.

The first step is to create a project using the ATL COM AppWizard, exactly as before, but name the project **ATLSignal**. Once that's done you can add a COM object. Click on the button on the ATL toolbar, or select Insert | New ATL Object... from the menu.

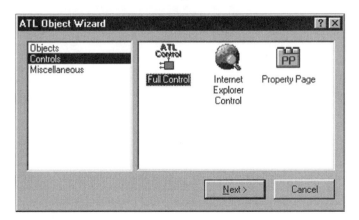

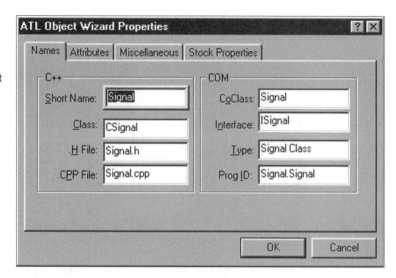

This time we want to insert a full ATL control from the Controls set of COM components, so make sure it's highlighted as shown, and click on Next >. You can enter **Signal** as the short name on the Names tab in the ATL Object Wizard Properties dialog:

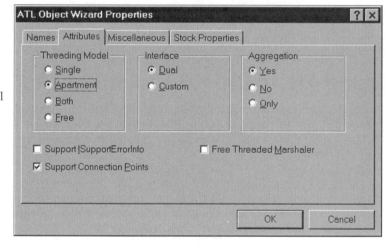

The Stock Properties tab enables you to add support for stock properties to the ATL control object that will be accessible from a client. If you look at the tab, you'll see that there are a greater variety of stock properties available here than through **COleControl** in MFC. However, we don't need to add any of these to our control. Take a look at the attributes tab:

Check the box for Support Connection Points—this will be needed when we add the event to the control which signals the container when our traffic signal changes state. We had the capability in the MFC version to do this, so we should see how to implement it using ATL. That's all we need from the options, so just click on OK to add the files defining the control to our project. Let's take a look at what's been added.

The ATL Control Class

If you look at ClassView, you'll see that we have just one class added to our project, **CSignal**, and an interface, **ISignal**. If you look at the class definition though, there's some real meat here. Let's explore the interesting bits piecemeal:

```
class ATL_NO_VTABLE CSignal :
    public CComObjectRootEx<CComSingleThreadModel>,
```

```
        public CComCoClass<CSignal, &CLSID_Signal>,
        public CComControl<CSignal>,
        public IDispatchImpl<ISignal, &IID_ISignal, &LIBID_ATLSIGNALLib>,
        public IProvideClassInfo2Impl<&CLSID_Signal, NULL, &LIBID_ATLSIGNALLib>,
        public IPersistStreamInitImpl<CSignal>,
        public IPersistStorageImpl<CSignal>,
        public IQuickActivateImpl<CSignal>,
        public IOleControlImpl<CSignal>,
        public IOleObjectImpl<CSignal>,
        public IOleInPlaceActiveObjectImpl<CSignal>,
        public IViewObjectExImpl<CSignal>,
        public IOleInPlaceObjectWindowlessImpl<CSignal>,
        public IDataObjectImpl<CSignal>,
        public IConnectionPointContainerImpl<CSignal>,
        public ISpecifyPropertyPagesImpl<CSignal>
{
    // Details of the class definition...
};
```

Our class **CSignal** has no fewer than *sixteen* base classes, all of which are templates, so they're customized to fit with our class. Our class will inherit the functionality of all these classes, so you'd need to look into the members of all them if you wanted to appreciate the full capabilities of **CSignal**. We won't be doing that here, but we will pick a few that are of interest to us. You can get to the documentation on any of the base classes by placing the cursor on the class name and pressing *F1*.

The first four base classes implement the basic COM capability that we discussed in the context of the previous COM example, so we won't repeat it here. We won't go through the others in detail, but a rough guide to the services that the other base classes provide is as follows:

Class Name	Purpose
IProvideClassInfo2Impl	Provides functions that make the type information for an object available.
IPersistStreamInitImpl	Provides a client interface to initiate saving and loading of the persistent data for an object in a stream.
IPersistStorageImpl	Provides a client interface to initiate saving and loading of the persistent data for an object in a structured form called a **storage** that can improve I/O performance with complex objects.
IQuickActivateImpl	Enables rapid loading of the control.
IOleControlImpl	Provides a default implementation of the **IOleControl** interface that supports signaling ambient property changes, among other things.
IOleObjectImpl	Provides a default implementation of **IOleObject** which provides the primary interface by which a container communicates with a control.
IOleInPlaceActiveObjectImpl	Provides a default implementation of the **IOleInPlaceActiveObject** interface which supports communications between a container and an in-place active control.

Table Continued on Following Page

Class Name	Purpose
`IViewObjectExImpl`	Provides a default implementation of the `IViewObject` interface which enables a control to display itself in the container.
`IOleInPlaceObjectWindowlessImpl`	Provides an implementation of the `IOleInPlaceObjectWindowless` interface which enables a windowless control to receive Windows messages.
`IDataObjectImpl`	Provides an implementation of the `IDataObject` interface that supports the uniform data transfer which applies to transferring data via the clipboard and drag and drop operations.
`IConnectionPointContainerImpl`	Provides a container class for connection points which support events that are signaled from our control to the container.
`ISpecifyPropertyPagesImpl`	Provides an implementation of the `ISpecifyPropertyPages` interface which enables a container to obtain the CLSIDs for the property pages for a control.

The COM AppWizard automatically deals with the registration of the control. The statement:

```
DECLARE_REGISTRY_RESOURCEID(IDR_SIGNAL)
```

is a macro that will generate the definition of a **static** function in the class that will register the control. The symbol **IDR_SIGNAL** is defined by the COM AppWizard and identifies the **.rgs** file containing the registry script.

This block of code in the class definition defines the COM map for the control:

```
BEGIN_COM_MAP(CSignal)
    COM_INTERFACE_ENTRY(ISignal)
    COM_INTERFACE_ENTRY(IDispatch)
    COM_INTERFACE_ENTRY_IMPL(IViewObjectEx)
    COM_INTERFACE_ENTRY_IMPL_IID(IID_IViewObject2, IViewObjectEx)
    COM_INTERFACE_ENTRY_IMPL_IID(IID_IViewObject, IViewObjectEx)
    COM_INTERFACE_ENTRY_IMPL(IOleInPlaceObjectWindowless)
    COM_INTERFACE_ENTRY_IMPL_IID(IID_IOleInPlaceObject,
IOleInPlaceObjectWindowless)
    COM_INTERFACE_ENTRY_IMPL_IID(IID_IOleWindow, IOleInPlaceObjectWindowless)
    COM_INTERFACE_ENTRY_IMPL(IOleInPlaceActiveObject)
    COM_INTERFACE_ENTRY_IMPL(IOleControl)
    COM_INTERFACE_ENTRY_IMPL(IOleObject)
    COM_INTERFACE_ENTRY_IMPL(IQuickActivate)
    COM_INTERFACE_ENTRY_IMPL(IPersistStorage)
    COM_INTERFACE_ENTRY_IMPL(IPersistStreamInit)
    COM_INTERFACE_ENTRY_IMPL(ISpecifyPropertyPages)
    COM_INTERFACE_ENTRY_IMPL(IDataObject)
    COM_INTERFACE_ENTRY(IProvideClassInfo)
    COM_INTERFACE_ENTRY(IProvideClassInfo2)
    COM_INTERFACE_ENTRY_IMPL(IConnectionPointContainer)
END_COM_MAP()
```

Each entry is an interface which can be accessed by a container. All the functions that a container can call in the control will appear in one or other of the interfaces that appear here.

The property map defines the CLSIDs and other information relating to property pages supported by the control:

```
BEGIN_PROPERTY_MAP(CSignal)
    // Example entries
    // PROP_ENTRY("Property Description", dispid, clsid)
    PROP_PAGE(CLSID_StockColorPage)
END_PROPERTY_MAP()
```

Next we have a connection point map:

```
BEGIN_CONNECTION_POINT_MAP(CSignal)
END_CONNECTION_POINT_MAP()
```

This is empty at the moment, but you add an entry here for each event that the control supports. Each event will be represented by a connection point that is specified in this map.

The message map defines the message handlers that the control provides:

```
BEGIN_MSG_MAP(CSignal)
    MESSAGE_HANDLER(WM_PAINT, OnPaint)
    MESSAGE_HANDLER(WM_SETFOCUS, OnSetFocus)
    MESSAGE_HANDLER(WM_KILLFOCUS, OnKillFocus)
END_MSG_MAP()
```

Each entry in the message map relates a function implemented in the control class **CSignal** with a Windows **WM_** message. We'll be adding handlers to the message map a little later in the chapter.

The **GetViewStatus()** function provides information to a container about whether the control has a solid background and is opaque or not. It will be called by a container when the view containing the control needs to be redrawn. This allows the container to make the drawing process more efficient, since items in the view that are covered by an opaque object with a solid background will not need to be redrawn.

At the end of the class definition there's a declaration for the **OnDraw()** function which will draw the control in the container:

```
// ISignal
public:
    HRESULT OnDraw(ATL_DRAWINFO& di);
```

Before we can do much about drawing the control, however, we need to define a traffic signal. That means we need to add a class to the project.

Defining the Signal

We can implement the class to define the signal much as we did with the MFC-based version. However, we'll need to make a few changes because we no longer have MFC available to us.

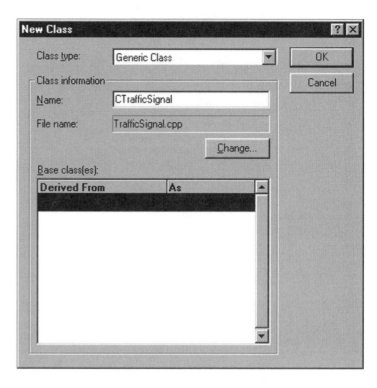

Create a new class by selecting the Insert | New Class... menu item. Set the Class type to Generic in the New Class dialog and give the class the name **CTrafficSignal**, then click OK.

Now go to the class definition and add the following code:

```
#if !defined(AFX_TRAFFICSIGNAL_H__...__INCLUDED_)
#define AFX_TRAFFICSIGNAL_H__...__INCLUDED_

#if _MSC_VER >= 1000
#pragma once
#endif // _MSC_VER >= 1000

class CTrafficSignal
{
public:
    CTrafficSignal();
    virtual ~CTrafficSignal();

// Class interface
    void SetPosition(int x, int y)
    {
        m_ptPosition.x = x;
        m_ptPosition.y = y;
    }

    void SetHeight(int nHeight)
        { m_nHeight =nHeight; }
    void SetSignalState(int nSignalState)
        { m_nSignalState = nSignalState; }
    int NextState();                        // Change to the next state
    void Draw(HDC& hDC);                     // Draw the traffic signal
```

534

```
  private:
    POINT m_ptPosition;     // Bottom center of signal
    int m_nHeight;          // Height of signal
    int m_nSignalState;     // State of signal
};

#endif // !defined(AFX_TRAFFICSIGNAL_H__...__INCLUDED_)
```

This is almost the same as the definition we had in the MFC implementation in Chapter 21, but there are some differences you should note.

The **CPoint** class isn't available because we're not using MFC. To declare the member **m_ptPosition** to store the reference point for the signal we use the **POINT** structure which is defined for the Windows API. This has public members **x** and **y** storing the coordinates. The **SetPosition()** member of the original class accepted a **CPoint** argument; now it accepts two arguments of type **int**. We could use a **POINT** structure for the point here, but it will be easier to use the coordinates as arguments in this case.

The **Draw()** function has a different parameter type specified from the original version too. The **HDC** type is another Windows type defining a handle to a device context. A device context in Windows is a structure that you refer to with a variable of type **HDC**. All our drawing operations will need to use the Windows API, since we have no MFC facilities in our control, but it's not going to be that difficult, as you will see.

Implementing CTrafficSignal

In **TrafficSignal.cpp**, we need to implement three functions: the constructor, the **NextState()** function, and the **Draw()** function. We'll use the same constants that we used in the MFC version, so copy the **OurConstants.h** file to the current project directory. The contents are exactly as before:

```
// Definition of constants

#if !defined(__OURCONSTANTS_H__)
#define __OURCONSTANTS_H__

const int STOP          = 101;
const int GO            = 103;
const int READY_TO_STOP = 104;

const COLORREF RED      = RGB(255, 0, 0);
const COLORREF ORANGE   = RGB(200, 100, 0);
const COLORREF GREEN    = RGB(0, 255, 0);
const COLORREF GRAY     = RGB(100, 100, 100);

#endif // !defined(__OURCONSTANTS_H__)
```

We can implement the constructor for the **CTrafficSignal** class first, since that's the easiest function. The initial additions to **TrafficSignal.cpp** will be:

```
#include "stdafx.h"
#include "OurConstants.h"
#include "ATLSignal.h"
#include "TrafficSignal.h"
```

```
#ifdef _DEBUG
#undef THIS_FILE
static char THIS_FILE[]=__FILE__;
#define new DEBUG_NEW
#endif

//////////////////////////////////////////////////////////////////////
// Construction/Destruction
//////////////////////////////////////////////////////////////////////

CTrafficSignal::CTrafficSignal()
{
   m_ptPosition.x = m_ptPosition.y = 0; // Set arbitrary position
   m_nHeight = 1000;                    // Set arbitrary height
   m_nSignalState = STOP;               // Set initial state to STOP
}
```

This just initializes the data members of the class to arbitrary values. The values for these data members will be set externally by the control.

We can implement the **NextState()** member function almost exactly as in the original version, so add the following code to **TrafficSignal.cpp**:

```
// Change the signal state to the next in sequence
int CTrafficSignal::NextState()
{
   switch (m_nSignalState)
   {
      case STOP:                          // Next after STOP is GO
         m_nSignalState = GO;
         break;
      case GO:                            // Next after GO is READY_TO_STOP
         m_nSignalState = READY_TO_STOP;
         break;
      case READY_TO_STOP:                 // Next after READY_TO_STOP is STOP
         m_nSignalState = STOP;
         break;
      default:                            // We should never get to here
         m_nSignalState = STOP;
         MessageBox(NULL, "Invalid signal state", "ATLSignal Error", MB_OK);
   }
   return m_nSignalState;
}
```

However, note that the original call to **AfxMessageBox()** has to be replaced with a call to the Win32 **MessageBox()** function. The last function we need to implement in the **CTrafficSignal** class is **Draw()**.

Drawing the Signal

The visual representation of the signal is exactly the same as in the previous chapter. The reference point for describing the signal geometry is at the bottom center of the signal.

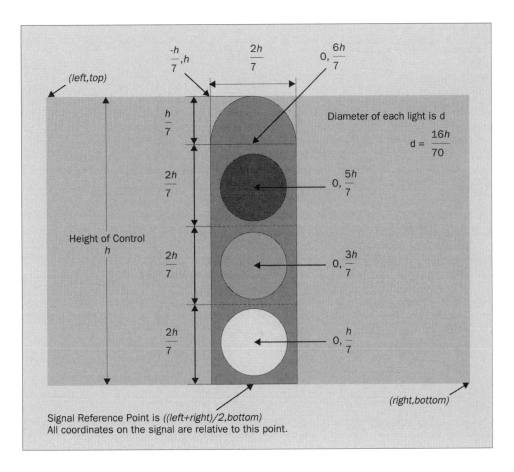

$$\frac{-h}{7}, h \qquad \frac{2h}{7} \qquad 0, \frac{6h}{7}$$

(left,top)

$$\frac{h}{7}$$

Diameter of each light is d

$$d = \frac{16h}{70}$$

$$\frac{2h}{7} \qquad 0, \frac{5h}{7}$$

Height of Control
h

$$\frac{2h}{7} \qquad 0, \frac{3h}{7}$$

$$\frac{2h}{7} \qquad 0, \frac{h}{7}$$

(right,bottom)

Signal Reference Point is *((left+right)/2,bottom)*
All coordinates on the signal are relative to this point.

The dimensions for the signal are determined from the height of the control, and the signal will be drawn relative to the reference point. The reference point will be set by the control as being midway between the left and right boundaries of the control, on the bottom boundary.

Let's go through the code for the **Draw()** function step by step. There's quite a lot of it, although much will be essentially the same as the previous version in Chapter 12. We can start by setting up the brushes and pens we need to draw the traffic signal:

```
void CTrafficSignal::Draw(HDC& hDC)
{
    // Set the pen and brush to draw the signal
    HBRUSH hGrayBrush = (HBRUSH)GetStockObject(GRAY_BRUSH);
    HBRUSH hOldBrush = (HBRUSH)SelectObject(hDC, hGrayBrush);
    HPEN hBlackPen = (HPEN)GetStockObject(BLACK_PEN);
    HPEN hOldPen = (HPEN)SelectObject(hDC, hBlackPen);

    // Plus the rest of the code for the function...
}
```

The Windows API uses **HBRUSH** and **HPEN** types to specify brushes and pens to be used in a device context. These are handles—pointers to the structures representing those entities. Here we need a stock pen and a stock brush, so we can use the API function **GetStockObject()** to obtain them. The type of object that is returned is determined by the argument passed to the function. The object is returned as type **HGDIOBJ**, which is a generic type for all of the stock objects, so we must cast the handle returned to the type we want.

To select a pen or a brush into the device context, we call the API function **SelectObject()**. This works similarly to the **CDC** class member function (which in fact calls the API function eventually). Here we pass the handle to the device context as an argument, as well as the handle to the drawing object we want to select. Of course, we must save the handles to the pen and brush we displace in the device context so that we can restore them when we are done.

Next we can add the code to draw the basic outline of the signal:

```
void CTrafficSignal::Draw(HDC& hDC)
{
    // Set the pen and brush to draw the signal...

    // Define the main body of the signal
    int nLeft = m_ptPosition.x - m_nHeight/7;
    int nTop = m_ptPosition.y - (long)m_nHeight*6L/7L;
    int nRight = m_ptPosition.x + m_nHeight/7;
    int nBottom = m_ptPosition.y;

    Rectangle(hDC, nLeft, nTop, nRight, nBottom);  // Draw the body

    // Draw the semi-circular top of the signal
    Chord(hDC,                                // Device context
          nLeft, nTop - m_nHeight/7,    // Bounding rectangle top-left
          nRight, nTop + m_nHeight/7,   // Bounding rectangle bottom-right
          nRight, nTop,                 // Start point
          nLeft, nTop);                 // End Point

    // Plus the rest of the code for the function...
}
```

The coordinates we need are calculated exactly as before. You should be able to relate them to the diagram. To draw the outline of the signal we call the **Rectangle()** and **Chord()** functions from the Windows API. The MFC functions are just wrappers for these functions, so the argument list is very similar. The only hardship we have to endure is to enter the coordinates for the bounding rectangle explicitly.

Next we can add the code to create the brushes we need to draw the lights:

```
void CTrafficSignal::Draw(HDC& hDC)
{
    // Set the pen and brush to draw the signal...

    // Define the main body of the signal...

    // Create brushes for the lights
    HBRUSH hbrStop;        // A brush to fill the stop light
    HBRUSH hbrReady;       // A brush to fill the ready light
    HBRUSH hbrGo;          // A brush to fill the go light

    switch (m_nSignalState)
    {
```

```
        case STOP:                                  // Red only
           hbrStop = CreateSolidBrush(RED);
           hbrReady = CreateSolidBrush(GRAY);
           hbrGo = CreateSolidBrush(GRAY);
           break;
        case GO:                                    // Green only
           hbrStop = CreateSolidBrush(GRAY);
           hbrReady = CreateSolidBrush(GRAY);
           hbrGo = CreateSolidBrush(GREEN);
           break;
        case READY_TO_STOP:                         // Orange only
           hbrStop = CreateSolidBrush(GRAY);
           hbrReady = CreateSolidBrush(ORANGE);
           hbrGo = CreateSolidBrush(GRAY);
           break;
        default:
           hbrStop = CreateSolidBrush(GRAY);
           hbrReady = CreateSolidBrush(GRAY);
           hbrGo = CreateSolidBrush(GRAY);
     }

     // Plus the rest of the code for the function...
  }
```

To draw the lights, we must set up the appropriately colored brush that we'll use to fill each light, depending on the current signal state stored in the **m_nSignalState** data member. We have a variable of type **HBRUSH** declared for each of the three lights. To create a brush, we can use the API function, **CreateSolidBrush()**. This will return a handle to a brush defined by the argument specified, which is of type **COLORREF**. Here we can use the symbols for the standard colors, but you can use the **RGB()** macro to specify the color if necessary. The overall logic here is exactly the same as before.

The last block of code we need to add will draw the lights using the brushes we have created:

```
void CTrafficSignal::Draw(HDC& hDC)
{
   // Set the pen and brush to draw the signal...

   // Define the main body of the signal...

   // Create brushes for the lights...

   // Define the rectangle bounding the stop light
   int nMargin = (long)m_nHeight * 2L/70L;     // Ten percent of the width
   nLeft += nMargin;                           // Left side of stop light
   nTop += nMargin;                            // Top of stop light
   nRight -= nMargin;                          // Right side of stop light
   int nStep = (long)m_nHeight * 2L/7L;        // Distance between lights
   nBottom = nTop + nStep - 2 * nMargin;       // Bottom of stop light

   // Draw the stop light
   SelectObject(hDC, hbrStop);
   Ellipse(hDC, nLeft, nTop, nRight, nBottom);

   // Set the position of the ready light
   nTop += nStep;
   nBottom += nStep;
```

```
        // Draw the ready light
        SelectObject(hDC, hbrReady);
        Ellipse(hDC, nLeft, nTop, nRight, nBottom);

        // Set the position of the go light
        nTop += nStep;
        nBottom += nStep;

        // Draw the go light
        SelectObject(hDC, hbrGo);
        Ellipse(hDC, nLeft, nTop, nRight, nBottom);

        SelectObject(hDC, hOldBrush);           // Put the old brush back
        SelectObject(hDC, hOldPen);             // Put the old pen back

        // Delete the brushes we have created
        DeleteObject(hbrStop);
        DeleteObject(hbrReady);
        DeleteObject(hbrGo);
    }
```

The main difference from the original code is that we call Windows API functions to select a brush, to do the drawing and to restore the original brush and pen. We also have to delete the brushes we create in the function. Using an MFC class, **CBrush**, in the previous chapter, the brush was deleted automatically when the **CBrush** object was destroyed. This would occur when the **Draw()** function exited. Here, if we don't delete the brushes, we will consume more and more GDI resources till we eventually run out and no programs will execute.

The names of the functions we use are the same as the equivalent **CDC** class members, so the basic logic is exactly the same. Only the arguments are a little different. Piece of cake, wasn't it?

Adding the Signal to the Control

Our control class **CSignal** will need an instance of **CTrafficSignal**, together with the data members that will keep track of the state of the signal. Add the following **private** members to the **CSignal** class definition:

```
private:
    CTrafficSignal m_TrafficSignal;      // The traffic signal
    long m_lStopOrGoTime;                // Stop/Go duration in msecs
    BOOL m_bStartRed;                    // TRUE to start on red
    BOOL m_bSignalGo;                    // True to start the signal
    int m_nTimerID;                      // ID of timer controlling the signal
    int m_nChangeTime;                   // Time for READY_TO_STOP in msecs.
```

Because the class contains a member of type **CTrafficSignal**, we must add a **#include** directive for **TrafficSignal.h** to **Signal.cpp**, immediately preceding the one for **Signal.h**. Later, we'll be using the constants we've defined in **OurConstants.h**, so you can add a **#include** for this too while you're about it. Another place that needs access to the **CTrafficSignal** class that's easy to overlook is the **ATLSignal.cpp** file. This includes **Signal.h**, so you must add a **#include** directive for **TrafficSignal.h** before it does so.

Of course, we need to initialize the new data members in the constructor, which has its definition within the class definition:

```
public:
   CSignal()
   {
      m_bSignalGo = FALSE;          // Not running initially
      m_bStartRed = TRUE;           // Start on red
      m_nTimerID = 100;             // Arbitrary ID for timer
      m_lStopOrGoTime = 5000L;      // Stop or go light on for 5 seconds
      m_nChangeTime = 2000;         // Orange light on for 2 seconds
   }
```

There's nothing new here; we can go straight on to drawing the control.

Drawing the Control

We already have an **OnDraw()** member implemented for us in the **CSignal** class by the ATL Object Wizard:

```
HRESULT CSignal::OnDraw(ATL_DRAWINFO& di)
{
   RECT& rc = *(RECT*)di.prcBounds;
   Rectangle(di.hdcDraw, rc.left, rc.top, rc.right, rc.bottom);
   DrawText(di.hdcDraw, _T("ATL 2.0"), -1, &rc,
                            DT_CENTER | DT_VCENTER | DT_SINGLELINE);

   return S_OK;
}
```

This is a COM function, so it returns a value of type **HRESULT**. The return value here is **S_OK**, but you can return other **HRESULT** values if you have a reason to do so. The parameter, **di**, that gets passed to the function is a reference to a structure of type **ATL_DRAWINFO**. This contains the information we need to implement drawing the control. It contains a member **prcBounds**, which is a pointer to the bounding rectangle for the control, and a member **hdcDraw**, which is a handle to a device context. The code here arbitrarily draws a rectangle around the boundary and displays some text. We'll replace this with our own code to draw the signal:

```
HRESULT CSignal::OnDraw(ATL_DRAWINFO& di)
{
   RECT& rc = *(RECT*)di.prcBounds;         // Get control rectangle
   HDC hDC = di.hdcDraw;                     // Get the device context
   COLORREF clrBackGround;                   // Control background color
   OLE_COLOR clrClientBackColor;             // Client background color

   // Get client backgound color and convert to COLORREF
   GetAmbientBackColor(clrClientBackColor);
   ::OleTranslateColor(clrClientBackColor,NULL,&clrBackGround);

   HBRUSH hbrBackground = CreateSolidBrush(clrBackGround); // Create brush
   FillRect(hDC,&rc,hbrBackground);          // Fill control area

   // Define position and height of the traffic signal
   m_TrafficSignal.SetPosition((rc.right+rc.left)/2,rc.bottom);
   m_TrafficSignal.SetHeight(rc.bottom-rc.top);

   m_TrafficSignal.Draw(hDC);                // Draw the signal
   return S_OK;
}
```

We get a **RECT** structure, **rc**, from the **prcBounds** member of **di** that corresponds to the rectangle bounding the control. The type **RECT** is a **struct** with members **left**, **top**, **right** and **bottom** corresponding to the x and y coordinates of the top-left and bottom-right corners of the rectangle. Since **prcBounds** is a pointer, we first cast it to type **RECT***, then dereference the result to get the rectangle. We also obtain a handle to the device context for the control which we store in **hDC**.

The ambient background color for the container is obtained by calling the **GetAmbientBackColor()** function inherited from the **CComControl** base class. The ambient background color is stored in the variable passed as an argument of type **OLE_COLOR**. Before we can use this value, we must convert it to a **COLORREF** value. This is done by the global function **OleTranslateColor()**, and the result is returned in the variable passed as the third argument, **clrBackground**. The second argument to the function gives you the opportunity of supplying a handle to a color palette to be used in the conversion.

To draw the background in the container background color, we create a brush corresponding to the background color and use the API function **FillRect()** to fill the rectangle **rc** with that color by using the brush we've created. The traffic signal will be drawn on top of this background.

To draw the traffic signal, we set the values for its position and height using the coordinates stored in the rectangle **rc**. We then call the **Draw()** function of the traffic signal object **m_TrafficSignal**.

Starting and Stopping the Signal

To start and stop the signal, we need to intercept mouse messages in our control. The **WM_LBUTTONDOWN** message is the one we want. We must first add our handler, **OnLButtonDown()** to the message map for the **CSignal** class. We need one extra line in the definition of the **CSignal** class:

```
BEGIN_MSG_MAP(CSignal)
    MESSAGE_HANDLER(WM_PAINT, OnPaint)
    MESSAGE_HANDLER(WM_SETFOCUS, OnSetFocus)
    MESSAGE_HANDLER(WM_KILLFOCUS, OnKillFocus)
    MESSAGE_HANDLER(WM_LBUTTONDOWN, OnLButtonDown)
END_MSG_MAP()
```

With an MFC-based program we wouldn't meddle with the message map because ClassWizard would have managed it, but since we're using ATL here we don't have that support and must take care of the message map entries ourselves. Of course, we must also add the function **OnLButtonDown()** as a member of the class. You can add it as a **public** class member, following the declaration of the **OnDraw()** member:

```
public:
    HRESULT OnDraw(ATL_DRAWINFO& di);
    LRESULT OnLButtonDown(UINT uMsg, WPARAM wParam, LPARAM lParam, BOOL& bHandled);
```

In fact, all message handlers that are specified using the **MESSAGE_HANDLER()** macro must have the same prototype:

```
LRESULT MessageHandler(UINT uMsg, WPARAM wParam, LPARAM lParam, BOOL& bHandled);
```

The first parameter identifies the message, and the second and third parameters are standard parameter values passed to the handler by Windows that provide additional information about the message. The contents of both **wParam** and **lParam** depend on the message. For example, in the case of the **WM_LBUTTONDOWN** message, the **lParam** parameter contains the coordinates of the cursor when the button was clicked and the **wParam** parameter will indicate whether any of the mouse buttons, or the *Shift* or *Ctrl* keys were pressed. The *x* coordinate for the cursor position is retrieved from **lParam** by using the **LOWORD()** macro, and the *y* coordinate by using the **HIWORD()** macro. The last argument is set to **TRUE** before a handler is called. If you want the message to be handled elsewhere, you can set it to **FALSE** in your handler. The return value type is a 32-bit value used by Windows message handlers and callback functions.

We can implement the **WM_LBUTTONDOWN** message handler in **Signal.cpp** as:

```
LRESULT CSignal::OnLButtonDown(UINT uMsg, WPARAM wParam,
                               LPARAM lParam, BOOL& bHandled)
{
   // If the signal is stopped, start it
   // If the signal is running, stop it
   m_bSignalGo = !m_bSignalGo;
   if(m_bSignalGo)
      StartSignal();
   else
      StopSignal();
   return 0;
}
```

We're not interested in the cursor position. If the button is clicked we switch the running state of the signal—if it's stopped we start it, and if it's running we stop it. To make this work we need to add the **StartSignal()** and **StopSignal()** functions to the **CSignal** class. The declarations in the class definition will be:

```
public:
   HRESULT OnDraw(ATL_DRAWINFO& di);
   LRESULT OnLButtonDown(UINT uMsg, WPARAM wParam, LPARAM lParam, BOOL& bHandled);
   void StartSignal();            // Start the signal
   void StopSignal();             // Stop the signal
```

We can implement these in **Signal.cpp** as:

```
// Start the signal
void CSignal::StartSignal()
{
   // Setup a timer with the required interval
   m_TrafficSignal.SetSignalState(m_bStartRed ? STOP : GO);
   m_nTimerID = SetTimer(m_nTimerID, (UINT)m_lStopOrGoTime, NULL);

   if (!m_nTimerID)
      exit(1);                    // No timer so exit

   Invalidate();                  // Get the control redrawn
}

// Stop the signal
void CSignal::StopSignal()
```

```
    {
        KillTimer(m_nTimerID);      // Destroy the timer
        Invalidate();               // Redraw the control
    }
```

These work just like the versions we had in the last chapter. In **StartSignal()** we call the function **SetTimer()** to create a timer for the required interval; this function is inherited from the base class **CComControl**. The **SetTimer()** arguments are the timer ID, the time interval in milliseconds, and a pointer to a callback function for the timer. Because we specify this last argument as **NULL**, Windows will generate a **WM_TIMER** message when the timed interval is up.

The **KillTimer()** function used in the **StopSignal()** function is also inherited from **CComControl** and it destroys the timer identified by the ID passed as an argument. To get the control redrawn we call the function **Invalidate()** which invalidates the whole area of the control, which will result in the **OnDraw()** member being called. **Invalidate()** is also inherited from the base class **CComControl**.

Controlling the Signal

To manage the operation of the signal in **CSignal** we use a timer, so we need to add a handler for **WM_TIMER** messages to the class. We do this in the same way as for the **WM_LBUTTONDOWN** message. First, add the message handler to the message map in the class definition:

```
BEGIN_MSG_MAP(CSignal)
    MESSAGE_HANDLER(WM_PAINT, OnPaint)
    MESSAGE_HANDLER(WM_SETFOCUS, OnSetFocus)
    MESSAGE_HANDLER(WM_KILLFOCUS, OnKillFocus)
    MESSAGE_HANDLER(WM_LBUTTONDOWN, OnLButtonDown)
    MESSAGE_HANDLER(WM_TIMER, OnTimer)
END_MSG_MAP()
```

We also need to add a declaration for the handler function to the class definition:

```
public:
    HRESULT OnDraw(ATL_DRAWINFO& di);
    LRESULT OnLButtonDown(UINT uMsg, WPARAM wParam, LPARAM lParam, BOOL& bHandled);
    void StartSignal();                     // Start the signal
    void StopSignal();                      // Stop the signal
    LRESULT OnTimer(UINT nIDEvent, WPARAM wParam, LPARAM lParam, BOOL& bHandled);
```

The declaration has the standard form for a handler specified in a **MESSAGE_HANDLER()** macro that we discussed earlier. In this case, the first parameter will be the ID of the timer. We can implement the handler by adding the following code to **Signal.cpp**:

```
LRESULT CSignal::OnTimer(UINT nIDEvent, WPARAM wParam,
                         LPARAM lParam, BOOL& bHandled)
{
    UINT nInterval = 0;                          // Interval in milliseconds

    // Step to the next signal state and set the time interval
    // based on the new state
    int nNewState = m_TrafficSignal.NextState();  // Go to next state

    switch (nNewState)
```

```
{
   case STOP: case GO:
      nInterval = (UINT)m_lStopOrGoTime;        // Stop or Go interval
      break;

   default:
      nInterval = m_nChangeTime;                // Transient interval
}

Invalidate();                                    // Redraw the signal
KillTimer(m_nTimerID);                // Make sure the old timer is dead

// Set a new timer event
m_nTimerID = SetTimer(m_nTimerID, nInterval, NULL);
if (!m_nTimerID)                                 // No timer...
   exit(1);                                      // ...so end the program

return 0;
}
```

This follows the same logic as in Chapter 12, so we don't need to go through it again.

Exercising the Control

If you build the control, you should be able to run it in the ActiveX Control Test Container that's available through the Tools menu. It will appear in the list of objects in the Insert OLE Control dialog as Signal Class. Here are two copies running:

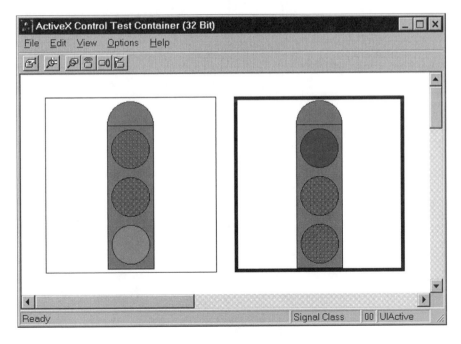

Our control will respond to the background color being set in the container, but we can't set the stop and go interval, or whether it starts on red or green. For that we need to add some properties to the control.

Adding Custom Properties

We add properties through the interface to
the control. If you right-click on ISignal in
ClassView, you'll see the context menu shown
here:

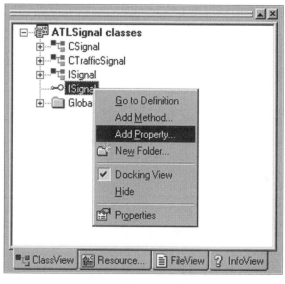

If you select Add Property...
from the context menu, you'll
be able to specify the property
you want to add through the
Add Property to Interface
dialog:

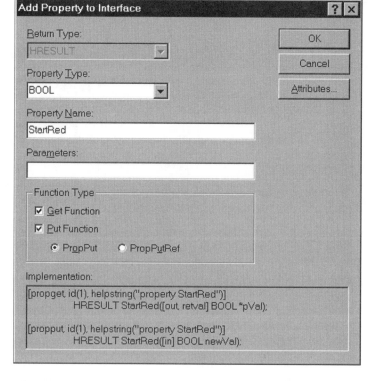

Select the type as BOOL and enter the name as **StartRed**. The information in the lower part of
the dialog shown here appears when you click in, or tab to the Parameters edit box after

entering the Property Type and Property Name data. This shows the **get** and **put** functions that will be added to the interface for retrieving and setting the property value. You should always select the property type from the drop down list, because only these are supported by COM. Click on the OK button to add the property to the interface.

If you look at the definition of **CSignal**, you'll see that the **get_StartRed()** and **put_StartRed()** functions for the property have been added, and there's a skeleton implementation in the file **Signal.cpp**. The implementations are trivial:

```
STDMETHODIMP CSignal::get_StartRed(BOOL * pVal)
{
    *pVal = m_bStartRed;     // Return StartRed status
    return S_OK;
}

STDMETHODIMP CSignal::put_StartRed(BOOL newVal)
{
    m_bStartRed = newVal;    // Set new StartRed status
    return S_OK;
}
```

The **get_StartRed()** function is passed a pointer to the location where the return value is to be stored, so we must dereference the parameter, **pVal**, to store the current value from **m_bStartRed**.

You can use the same procedure to add a property with the name **StopOrGoTime** of type **long** to the **ISignal** interface. The implementations of the **get** and **put** methods require just one extra line of code in each:

```
STDMETHODIMP CSignal::get_StopOrGoTime(long * pVal)
{
    *pVal = m_lStopOrGoTime;    // Return the current interval
    return S_OK;
}

STDMETHODIMP CSignal::put_StopOrGoTime(long newVal)
{
    m_lStopOrGoTime = newVal;  // Store the new interval
    return S_OK;
}
```

That's all we need for the container to be able to control these properties. We should do one more thing to match the functionality of the MFC-based control: add an event to signal the container when the light changes.

Adding Events

An event is a very different animal to the interface functions or properties, which are functions in the control that can be called by the container. An event puts the boot on the other foot: we want the control to be able to call a function in the container.

To add an event to the control, we must first add a new interface to the control that has this capability. We'll add the interface definition to the IDL code for the type library in **ATLSignal.idl**:

```
[
   uuid(862501DB-7DB1-11D0-96FE-002018349816),
   version(1.0),
   helpstring("ATLSignal 1.0 Type Library")
]
library ATLSIGNALLib
{
   importlib("stdole32.tlb");

   // Event Interface
   [
      uuid( /*insert GUID here*/ ),
      helpstring("Event interface for ISignal")
   ]
   dispinterface _SignalEvents
   {
      properties:
      methods:
         [id(1)] void SignalChanged([in]long lSignalState);
   };

   // Plus the code defining the coclass...
};
```

You'll have to obtain a GUID using the **GUID Generator** in the Component Gallery as we did in Chapter 12. Copy the GUID to the clipboard, then paste it between the parentheses after **uuid** and remove the braces from around it. This will identify the interface in the type library entry in the registry.

A **dispinterface** is just a dispatch interface. The interface name, **_SignalEvents**, begins with an underscore. By COM convention, this indicates it's an outgoing interface—in other words, it's an interface that the control's container needs to implement. We'll specify that this is an outgoing interface from the control in the type library entry in the **.idl** file. Add the following line to the **coclass** in the type library definition:

```
library ATLSIGNALLib
{
   importlib("stdole32.tlb");

   // Event Interface as shown above

   [
      uuid(862501E9-7DB1-11D0-96FE-002018349816),
      helpstring("Signal Class")
   ]
   coclass Signal
   {
      [default] interface ISignal;
      [default, source] interface _SignalEvents;
   };
};
```

The attributes in square brackets define the nature of the interface. The **default** attribute indicates it's the default interface, and the **source** attribute specifies that it's outgoing from the control. To fire the event, you just call the function **Fire_SignalChanged()** with an argument specifying the current state of the signal. We need to do this in the **CSignal::OnTimer()**

handler, so add the following statement immediately preceding the call to the **Invalidate()** function:

```
Fire_SignalChanged(nNewState);      // Signal the container
Invalidate();                       // Redraw the signal
KillTimer(m_nTimerID);              // Make sure the old timer is dead
```

Is that it, then? Unfortunately, no. We haven't defined how the container is going to connect to the interface. The **Fire_SignalChanged()** function needs to be implemented and must connect to a container in some way. After all, we're calling a container function here to communicate that the signal has changed. This is done through something called a **connection point**.

Adding a Connection Point

A connection point on a control that represents an event is implemented through an interface called **IConnectionPoint**. It couldn't be anything else really, could it? Since we know nothing about any prospective container, the only way to communicate an event is through an outgoing interface. The connection point interface defines how the event will be communicated to the container. Because a control may have more than one connection point, something called a **connection point container** is used to contain however many connection points we need. A connection point container is implemented through an interface **IConnectionPointContainer**, which the container application will use to find out what connection points are supported. Conveniently, we already have a connection point container implemented in our control, courtesy of the ATL AppWizard.

We can get the code for the connection point generated automatically using the type library for our control. To get an up-to-date version of the type library, including the new event interface, we need to recompile the **.idl** file. We don't want to rebuild the whole project right now, as we'll get compiler errors—it isn't finished yet, after all. You can compile the **.idl** file alone by right-clicking it in FileView, and selecting Compile ATLSignal.idl from the context menu.

With the type library file generated we can add the **IConnectionPoint** interface. To do this, select Add to Project | Components and Controls... from the Project menu.

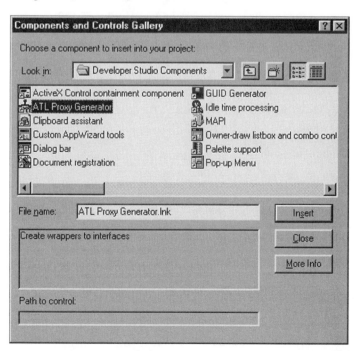

In the dialog that's displayed, select ATL Proxy Generator from the list and click on the Insert button. The ATL Proxy Generator will generate the code for the connection point. This is the code that will implement the **Fire_SignalChanged()** function so that it calls a container function through the connection point interface.

In the ATL Proxy Generator dialog, enter the name or browse for the type library for our control—you're looking for **ATLSignal.tlb**. Highlight the **_SignalEvents** interface in the left hand Not selected pane, and click on the > button to move it to the Selected pane.

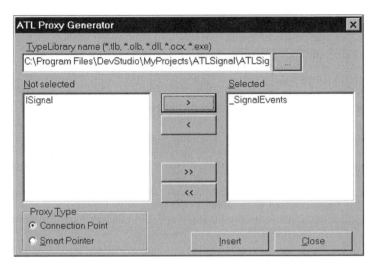

Since the Proxy Type has already been selected as Connection Point, you can click on the Insert button to generate the code. In the Save dialog that follows, you can accept the file name **CPATLSignal.h** to contain the code, and then close the remaining dialogs.

To get the new file displayed in FileView, right-click on the Header files folder and add the file to the folder. If you look in this file you'll see that a class template, **CProxy_SignalEvents**, has been defined. It's derived from **IConnectionPointImpl**, which implements a connection point. We must add the new class as a base class to our control class **CSignal**, and we must change the second argument to the **IProvideClassInfo2Impl** base class template:

```
class ATL_NO_VTABLE CSignal :
    public CComObjectRootEx<CComSingleThreadModel>,
    public CComCoClass<CSignal, &CLSID_Signal>,
    public CComControl<CSignal>,
    public IDispatchImpl<ISignal, &IID_ISignal, &LIBID_ATLSIGNALLib>,
    public IProvideClassInfo2Impl<&CLSID_Signal, &DIID__SignalEvents,
                                              &LIBID_ATLSIGNALLib>,
    public IPersistStreamInitImpl<CSignal>,
    public IPersistStorageImpl<CSignal>,
    public IQuickActivateImpl<CSignal>,
    public IOleControlImpl<CSignal>,
    public IOleObjectImpl<CSignal>,
    public IOleInPlaceActiveObjectImpl<CSignal>,
    public IViewObjectExImpl<CSignal>,
    public IOleInPlaceObjectWindowlessImpl<CSignal>,
    public IDataObjectImpl<CSignal>,
    public IConnectionPointContainerImpl<CSignal>,
    public ISpecifyPropertyPagesImpl<CSignal>,
    public CProxy_SignalEvents<CSignal>        // Added for event proxy
```

```
{
   // Detail of the class definition...
};
```

Don't forget to add the comma to the end of the line preceding the new base class. Note that the addition is a template class that requires **CSignal** as a parameter value. You'll also need to add a **#include** directive for **CPATLSignal.h** to **Signal.h**. As well as adding the new base class, we have changed the second parameter of the **IProvideClassInfo2Impl** class template from **NULL** to **&DIID__SignalEvents**. This identifies the new interface as an outgoing interface for the control.

The **CProxy_SignalEvents** class adds the **Fire_SignalChanged()** function that will communicate with the container. The **IConnectionPointContainerImpl** class that was added by the COM AppWizard implements an interface **IConnectionPointContainer** for the container to access the connection points on the control.

Finally, we must make the connection point itself available to COM by adding an entry in the connection point map in the **CSignal** class definition:

```
BEGIN_CONNECTION_POINT_MAP(CSignal)
   CONNECTION_POINT_ENTRY(DIID__SignalEvents)
END_CONNECTION_POINT_MAP()
```

All connection points for a control must appear in the connection point map. Each entry represents an outgoing interface from the control to the container, so there will be one entry here for each event interface that you define. Connection points are identified by their ID, which is generated by the MIDL compiler. We have just the one defined by the ID **DIID__SignalEvents**. You will find that this has been defined in the file **ATLSignal_i.c** that appears in the External Dependencies folder in FileView.

If you've done everything correctly, the control is ready for another trial.

Running the Control

If you build the control once more, you can exercise it again using the ActiveX Test Container. You'll be able to trace the events being fired and change the properties.

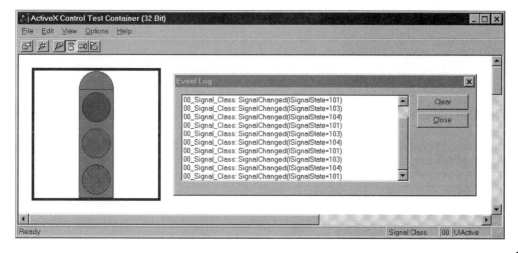

Note that to change the properties you need to use the **put** method. Remember that properties in COM use **get** and **put** methods to operate on property values. You can change the stop and go time interval and the starting condition. An event should fire each time the signal changes.

Summary

If you've made it this far without too much trouble, you should have little difficulty progressing further into using Visual C++ on a wider basis and getting deeper into COM. We only scratched the surface of COM here because, as you will surely appreciate, it's a topic of above average complexity. You shouldn't find it particularly difficult; there's just rather a lot to it. I hope that you've found as much pleasure in getting to here as I have. Enjoy your programming!

Exercises

Ex13-1: 'Mission: Impossible?'
In this chapter, you've seen how to create a client for the **RefRate** ATL component. In fact, you've already created two versions of the client, one in Visual Basic and the other using MFC. Your final mission, should you choose to accept it, is to create yet another client for the **RefRate** component. This time, however, the only tool at your disposal is the Active Template Library. You'll need to prepare well for this expedition. Good luck!

Hints:
Use the documentation to help you learn more about ATL.
Start with an ATL executable project.
Discover how to use the compiler COM support, particularly the **#import** statement.

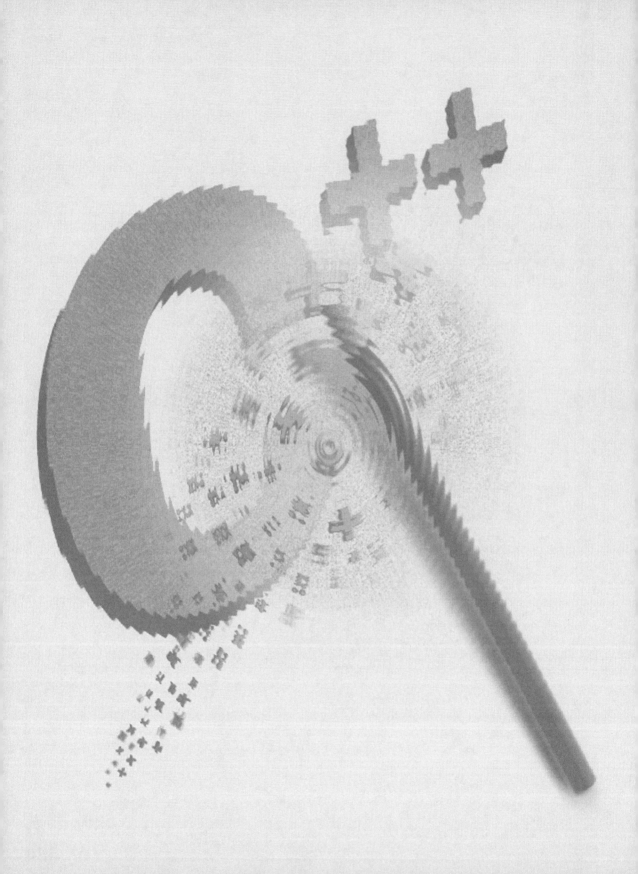

Keywords in Visual C++

Keywords are words used for special purposes. You must not use these words as names of objects in your programs. The following is a list of Visual C++ keywords:

asm	dynamic_cast	namespace	throw
auto	else	new	true
bad_cast	enum	operator	try
bad_typeid	except	private	type_info
bool	explicit	protected	typedef
break	extern	public	typeid
case	false	register	typename
catch	finally	reinterpret_cast	union
char	float	return	unsigned
class	for	short	using
const	friend	signed	uuid
const_cast	goto	sizeof	virtual
continue	if	static	void
default	inline	static_cast	volatile
delete	int	struct	while
dllexport	long	switch	wmain
dllimport	main	template	xalloc
do	mutable	this	
double	naked	thread	

The C++ language is still evolving. There are a number of C++ keywords not at present supported in Visual C++, but they may well be in the future. Other compilers support at least some of them at the moment. You should therefore also avoid using these for your own identifiers. Accidental use of some of them is quite possible, as you can see from the following list:

and	compl	or_eq
and_eq	not	xor
bitand	not_eq	xor_eq
bitor	or	

You should also avoid using identifiers beginning with a double underscore (__), as Visual C++ reserves a considerable number of keywords of this form.

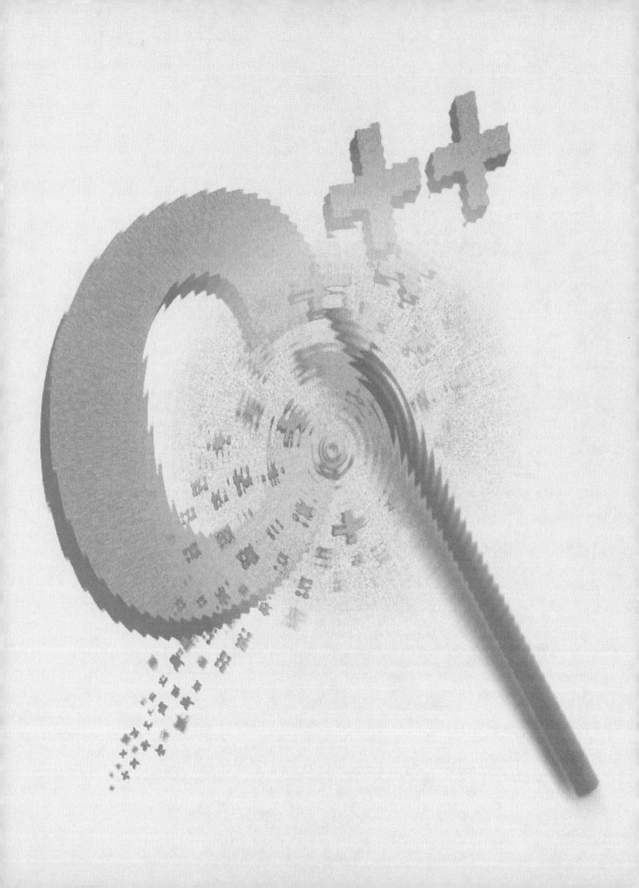

The ASCII Table

The American Standard Code for Information Interchange or ASCII assigns values between 0 and 255 for upper and lower case letters, numeric digits, punctuation marks and other symbols. ASCII characters can be split into the following sections:

0 – 31	Control functions
32 – 127	Standard, implementation-independent characters
128 – 255	Special symbols, international character sets—generally, non-standard characters.

Since the latter 128 characters are implementation-dependent and have no fixed entry in the ASCII table, we shall only cover the first two groups in the following table:

ASCII Characters 0 - 31

Decimal	Hexadecimal	Character	Control
000	00	null	NUL
001	01	☺	SOH
002	02	●	STX
003	03	♥	ETX
004	04	♦	EOT
005	05	♣	ENQ
006	06	♠	ACK
007	07	●	BEL (Audible bell)
008	08		Backspace
009	09		HT
010	0A		LF (Line feed)
011	0B		VT (Vertical feed)
012	0C		FF (Form feed)
013	0D		CR (Carriage return)
014	0E		SO
015	0F	¤	SI
016	10		DLE
017	11		DC1

Decimal	Hexadecimal	Character	Control
018	12		DC2
019	13		DC3
020	14		DC4
021	15		NAK
022	16		SYN
023	17		ETB
024	18		CAN
025	19		EM
026	1A	→	SUB
027	1B	←	ESC (Escape)
028	1C	⌊	FS
029	1D		GS
030	1E		RS
031	1F		US

ASCII Characters 32 - 127

Decimal	Hexadecimal	Character	Decimal	Hexadecimal	Character
032	20	space	060	3C	<
033	21	!	061	3D	=
034	22	"	062	3E	>
035	23	#	063	3F	?
036	24	$	064	40	@
037	25	%	065	41	A
038	26	&	066	42	B
039	27	'	067	43	C
040	28	(	068	44	D
041	29	)	069	45	E
042	2A	*	070	46	F
043	2B	+	071	47	G
044	2C	,	072	48	H
045	2D	-	073	49	I
046	2E	.	074	4A	J
047	2F	/	075	4B	K
048	30	0	076	4C	L
049	31	1	077	4D	M
050	32	2	078	4E	N
051	33	3	079	4F	O
052	34	4	080	50	P
053	35	5	081	51	Q
054	36	6	082	52	R
055	37	7	083	53	S
056	38	8	084	54	T
057	39	9	085	55	U
058	3A	:	086	56	V
059	3B	;	087	57	W

Decimal	Hexadecimal	Character	Decimal	Hexadecimal	Character
088	58	X	108	6C	l
089	59	Y	109	6D	m
090	5A	Z	110	6E	n
091	5B	[	111	6F	o
092	5C	\	112	70	p
093	5D	]	113	71	q
094	5E	^	114	72	r
095	5F	_	115	73	s
096	60	`	116	74	t
097	61	a	117	75	u
098	62	b	118	76	v
099	63	c	119	77	w
100	64	d	120	78	x
101	65	e	121	79	y
102	66	f	122	7A	z
103	67	g	123	7B	{
104	68	h	124	7C		
105	69	i	125	7D	}
106	6A	j	126	7E	~
107	6B	k	127	7F	delete

Solutions to Exercises

Chapter 1

Ex1-1: There are four direct ways to build a project:

▶ Press the Build button on the Build toolbar

▶ Press the *F7* function key

▶ Choose the <u>B</u>uild | <u>B</u>uild menu item

▶ Click the right mouse button on the files item in the tree in the FileView pane, and select Build from the context menu

Ex1-2: The three files used to store information about a project are the **.dsp**, **.ncb** and **.dsw** files. The **.dsp** file stores information about the files which make up the project, the **.ncb** file stores various Visual C++ settings, and the **.dsw** saves the Developer Studio settings.

Ex1-3: File types:

▶ **.obj** files hold the intermediate object code files produced by the compiler

▶ **.pch** files hold precompiled header information (more about this later!)

▶ **.pdb** files hold debugging information

▶ **.exe** files hold the final, executable program produced by the linker

Chapter 2

Ex2-1: The **GetSystemMetrics()** API call can be used to get the width and height of the screen in pixels, so you can use it to calculate the position and size of your window before you create it in **WinMain()**.

```
    int nXCenter = GetSystemMetrics(SM_CXSCREEN)/2;
    int nYCenter = GetSystemMetrics(SM_CYSCREEN)/2;
    int nWidth = 400;
```

```
    int nHeight = 200;

    hWnd = CreateWindow(
        szAppName,                      // The window class name
        "A Basic Window the Hard Way",  // The window title
        WS_OVERLAPPEDWINDOW,            // The window style
        nXCenter - nWidth/2,            // Upper-left x position
        nYCenter - nHeight/2,           // Upper-left y position
        nWidth,                         // The window width
        nHeight,                        // The window height
        0,                              // No parent window
        0,                              // No menu
        hInstance,                      // Program instance handle
        0                               // No window creation data
        );
```

Ex 2-2: The program contained 10 errors. Did you get them all?

```
//EX2_02.CPP
// Debugging example for exercise 2-2
#include <iostream.h>

int len(char * strArray);

int main()
{
    char strInput[256];
```

Can't use a pointer without allocating some memory - making it an array is the easiest thing to do in this case.

```
    cout << "Enter some text to process";
    cin.getline(strInput,255);
```

*Can't use **cin**'s **<<** operator as the user could go past the end of the array.*

```
    int length = len(strInput);
```

*This line needs adding to replace the multiple calls to **len()**. This is required because the lines which swap the characters could cause the character's value to be temporarily zero. This causes **len()** to return the wrong length, making the **for()** loop exit early.*

```
    // Processed entered text swapping around the text
    for(int i = 0; i <= length/2 - 1; i++ )
```

*A couple of errors here. First, **i** needs initializing to 0 not 1, otherwise the first character is missed. Second, the comparison needs to be completely changed: you should always be wary of using single value comparisons with **!=** and **==** as it is possible to jump outside the range you expect the loop to operate in. We also only need to do half the string - otherwise we would swap the string around, and then swap it back again.*

```
    {
        strInput[i] ^= strInput[length - i - 1];
```

*The array subscript needs changing to use **length** and we need to remember to subtract 1 so that we aren't referencing past the end of the array.*

```
        strInput[length - i - 1] ^= strInput[i];
```

*Same as the last error, plus we don't want to increment **i** here.*

```
        strInput[i] ^= strInput[length - i - 1];
```

This line needs adding to loop to complete the swap operation.

```
    }

    cout << strInput << endl;

    return 0;
}


int len(char * strArray)
{
    int length = 0;

    do
    {
        if(strArray[length] == '\0')
```

Opps! An assignment here that needs changing to a comparison. This kind of error can be caught by always placing the constant on the left and the variable on the right. If you then use an assignment, the compiler will throw an error your way.

```
            return length;
    }while(++length);
```

Need the increment before the variable here, not after so that the comparison occurs after the increment. Otherwise the test will fail the first time around.

```
    return -1;
}
```

Chapter 3

Ex3-1: A document is a class which holds data for an application, while a view presents the data to the user in some form. There may be more than one type of view associated with a given document.

Ex3-2: The document template ties together the document, view and window types used by an application.

Ex3-3: You need to be careful when using AppWizard because you can't go back and modify your choices later! If you didn't select (say) database support when you generated the application, it can be hard to go back and manually edit in all the necessary code yourself.

Chapter 4

Ex4-1: Open the menu resource **IDR_SKETCHTYPE** in ResourceView, and add the item &Ellipse to the vacant position at the end of the Element pop-up. Assign the ID **ID_ELEMENT_ELLIPSE**. Add a prompt reading Draw an ellipse. Save the menu.

Ex4-2: Add a definition for **ELLIPSE** to **OurConstants.h**:

```
const WORD ELLIPSE = 105U;
```

Open ClassWizard and add a **COMMAND** handler and an **UPDATE_COMMAND_UI** handler to **CSketcherDoc,** corresponding to the ID **ID_ELEMENT_ELLIPSE**.

Implement the command handler as:

```
void CSketcherDoc::OnElementEllipse()
{
    m_Element = ELLIPSE; // Set element type as a ellipse
}
```

Add a command update handler as:

```
void CSketcherDoc::OnUpdateElementEllipse(CCmdUI* pCmdUI)
{
    // Set Checked if the current element is an ellipse
    pCmdUI->SetCheck(m_Element==ELLIPSE);
}
```

Ex4-3: Open the toolbar **IDR_MAINFRAME** in ResourceView. Draw a new toolbar button to represent an ellipse. Drag it to the group of buttons for elements types. Change its ID to that of the corresponding menu item, **ID_ELEMENT_ELLIPSE**. Save the toolbar.

Open the menu resource with the ID **IDR_SKETCHTYPE**. Open the properties box for the menu item Ellipse. Modify the prompt to include the tooltip.

Ex4-4: Use the **SetText()** member of the class **CCmdUI** to set the menu item text for each color to upper or lower case, depending on the current value of **m_Color**. A typical update handler will be modified as follows:

```
void CSketcherDoc::OnUpdateColorBlack(CCmdUI* pCmdUI)
{
    // Set Checked if the current color is black
    pCmdUI->SetCheck(m_Color==BLACK);
```

```
   // Set upper case for a selected item, lower case otherwise
   if(m_Color == BLACK)
      pCmdUI->SetText("BLACK");
   else
      pCmdUI->SetText("black");
}
```

This modification does not affect the corresponding toolbar button.

Chapter 5

Ex5-1: The class definition should be:

```
// Class defining an ellipse object
class CEllipse: public CElement
{
   public:
      virtual void Draw(CDC* pDC);

      // Constructor for an ellipse
      CEllipse(CPoint Start, CPoint End, COLORREF aColor);

   protected:
      CEllipse(){}            // Default constructor - should not be used
};
```

The implementation of the **CEllipse** class constructor is:

```
// Constructor for an ellipse object
CEllipse:: CEllipse(CPoint Start, CPoint End, COLORREF Color)
{
   m_Color = Color;           // Set ellipse color
   m_Pen = 1;                 // Set pen width

   // Define the enclosing rectangle
   m_EnclosingRect = CRect(Start, End);
   m_EnclosingRect.NormalizeRect();
}
```

The implementation of the **Draw()** function for an ellipse object is:

```
// Draw an ellipse
void CEllipse::Draw(CDC* pDC)
{
   // Create a pen for this object and
   // initialize it to the object color and line width of 1 pixel
   CPen aPen;
   if(!aPen.CreatePen(PS_SOLID, m_Pen, m_Color))
   {                                          // Pen creation failed
      AfxMessageBox("Pen creation failed drawing an ellipse", MB_OK);
      AfxAbort();
   }

   CPen* pOldPen = pDC->SelectObject(&aPen);  // Select the pen
```

```
    // Select a null brush
    CBrush* pOldBrush = (CBrush*)pDC->SelectStockObject(NULL_BRUSH);

    // Now draw the ellipse
    pDC->Ellipse(m_EnclosingRect);

    pDC->SelectObject(pOldPen);             // Restore the old pen
    pDC->SelectObject(pOldBrush);           // Restore the old brush
}
```

Ex5-2: Only the **CreateElement()** element function needs to be modified:

```
CElement* CSketcherView::CreateElement()
{
    // Get a pointer to the document for this view
    CSketcherDoc* pDoc = GetDocument();
    ASSERT_VALID(pDoc);                     // Verify the pointer is good

    // Now select the element using the type stored in the document
    switch(pDoc->GetElementType())
    {
        case RECTANGLE:
            return new CRectangle(m_FirstPoint, m_SecondPoint,
                                        pDoc->GetElementColor());
        case CIRCLE:
            return new CCircle(m_FirstPoint, m_SecondPoint,
                                    pDoc->GetElementColor());
        case CURVE:
            return new CCurve(pDoc->GetElementColor());

        case LINE:
            return new CLine(m_FirstPoint, m_SecondPoint,
                                    pDoc->GetElementColor());
        case ELLIPSE:
            return new CEllipse(m_FirstPoint, m_SecondPoint,
                                        pDoc->GetElementColor());

        default:                    // Something's gone wrong
            AfxMessageBox("Bad Element code", MB_OK);
            AfxAbort();
    }
}
```

Ex5-3: Only the class constructor needs to be modified:

```
CEllipse:: CEllipse(CPoint Start, CPoint End, COLORREF Color)
{
    m_Color = Color;             // Set ellipse color
    m_Pen = 1;                   // Set pen width

    // Define the enclosing rectangle
    m_EnclosingRect = CRect(Start - (End-Start), End);
    m_EnclosingRect.NormalizeRect();
}
```

The modified statement uses two different versions of the overloaded operator—in the **CPoint** class. The expression **(End-Start)** returns the difference between the two points as an object of class **CSize**. This object is then subtracted from the **CPoint** object **Start** to offset it by the **CSize** value.

Ex5-4: Open the menu **IDR_SKETCHTYPE** in ResourceView. Add a new pop-up to the menu bar, labeled P̲en Style. Add menu items to the pop-up for Solid, Dashed, Dotted, Dash-dotted, and Dash-dot-dotted lines. Save the resource.

Ex5-5: The following modifications are necessary:

- Add a protected member of type **int**, **m_PenStyle**, and a function to retrieve its value, to the **CSketcherDoc** class.
- Add initialization of **m_PenStyle** to **PS_SOLID** in the **CSketcherDoc** constructor.
- Add **COMMAND** and **UPDATE_COMMAND_UI** handlers for each of the new menu items.
- Add a protected member of type **int**, **m_PenStyle**, to the **CElement** class.
- Modify the constructors for each of the element classes to accept an argument of type **int** specifying the pen style.
- Modify the **CreateElement()** function member of **CSketcherView** to call the constructors using the additional parameter for pen style.
- Modify the **Draw()** functions in each of the element classes to draw using the pen style specified in the **m_PenStyle** member of each element class.

Ex5-6: The following line must be added to the protected section of the **CSketcherDoc** class definition:

```
    int m_PenStyle;                 // Current pen style
```

Add the following function to retrieve the pen style from the document:

```
    int GetPenStyle()               // Get the pen style
      { return m_PenStyle; }
```

The following line should be added to the constructor, **CSketcherDoc()**:

```
    m_PenStyle = PS_SOLID;          // Set initial style as solid
```

A typical **COMMAND** menu handler is:

```
  void CSketcherDoc::OnPenstyleDashdotted()
  {
    m_PenStyle = PS_DASHDOT;
  }
```

A typical **UPDATE_COMMAND_UI** handler is:

```
  void CSketcherDoc::OnUpdatePenstyleDashdotted(CCmdUI* pCmdUI)
  {
    pCmdUI->SetCheck(m_PenStyle==PS_DASHDOT);
  }
```

The following declaration should be added to the protected section of the **CElement** class:

```
int m_PenStyle;                         // Element pen style
```

The constructor declaration in each derived element class definition should be modified to add the extra parameter. The **CCircle** class is typical:

```
CCircle(CPoint Start, CPoint End, COLORREF aColor, int aPenStyle);
```

The typical change to the constructor to support the pen style is:

```
CCircle::CCircle(CPoint Start, CPoint End, COLORREF aColor,
                                                int aPenStyle)
{
    // First calculate the radius
    // We use floating point because that is required by
    // the library function (in math.h) for calculating a square root.
    long Radius = (long) sqrt((double)((End.x-Start.x)*(End.x-Start.x)+
                                (End.y-Start.y)*(End.y-Start.y)));

    // Now calculate the rectangle enclosing
    // the circle assuming the MM_TEXT mapping mode
    m_EnclosingRect = CRect(Start.x-Radius, Start.y-Radius,
                            Start.x+Radius, Start.y+Radius);

    m_Color = aColor;          // Set the color for the circle
    m_Pen = 1;                 // Set pen width to 1
    m_PenStyle = aPenStyle;    // Set the pen style
}
```

The **CreateElement()** member of **CSketcherView** is modified to:

```
CElement* CSketcherView::CreateElement()
{
    // Get a pointer to the document for this view
    CSketcherDoc* pDoc = GetDocument();
    ASSERT_VALID(pDoc);                     // Verify the pointer is good

    // Now select the element using the type stored in the document
    switch(pDoc->GetElementType())
    {
        case RECTANGLE:
            return new CRectangle(m_FirstPoint, m_SecondPoint,
                        pDoc->GetElementColor(), pDoc->GetPenStyle());
        case CIRCLE:
            return new CCircle(pDoc->GetElementColor(), pDoc->GetPenStyle());
        case CURVE:
            return new CCurve(m_FirstPoint, m_SecondPoint,
                        pDoc->GetElementColor(), pDoc->GetPenStyle());
        case LINE:
            return new CLine(m_FirstPoint, m_SecondPoint,
                        pDoc->GetElementColor(), pDoc->GetPenStyle());
        case ELLIPSE:
            return new CEllipse(m_FirstPoint, m_SecondPoint,
                        pDoc->GetElementColor(), pDoc->GetPenStyle());
```

```
      default:                          // Something's gone wrong
         AfxMessageBox("Bad Element code", MB_OK);
         AfxAbort();
         return NULL;
   }
}
```

The typical change to the implementation of the **Draw()** members of the element classes is:

```
void CCircle::Draw(CDC* pDC, BOOL Select)
{
   // Create a pen for this object and
   // initialize it to the object color and line width of 1 pixel
   CPen aPen;
   COLORREF Color = m_Color;                    // Initialize with element color

   if(Select)
      Color = SELECT_COLOR;                     // Set selected color

   if(!aPen.CreatePen(m_PenStyle, m_Pen, Color))
      {                                         // Pen creation failed
         AfxMessageBox("Pen creation failed drawing a circle", MB_OK);
         AfxAbort();
      }

   CPen* pOldPen = pDC->SelectObject(&aPen);  // Select the pen

   // Select a null brush
   CBrush* pOldBrush = (CBrush*)pDC->SelectStockObject(NULL_BRUSH);

   // Now draw the circle
   pDC->Ellipse(m_EnclosingRect);

   pDC->SelectObject(pOldPen);                  // Restore the old pen
   pDC->SelectObject(pOldBrush);                // Restore the old brush
}
```

Chapter 6

Ex6-1: When the points are added to the head of the list, they will be in reverse order. We must modify the constructor and the **AddSegment()** function to add points to the head of the list, and change the **Draw()** function to process the points from the tail to the head.

The code for the constructor is:

```
CCurve::CCurve(CPoint& FirstPoint,CPoint& SecondPoint, COLORREF aColor, int
aPenStyle)
{
   m_PointList.AddHead(FirstPoint);     // Add the 1st point to the list
   m_PointList.AddHead(SecondPoint);    // Add the 2nd point to the list
   m_Color = aColor;                    // Store the color
   m_Pen = 1;                           // Set the pen width
   m_PenStyle = aPenStyle;              // Set the pen style
```

```
    // Construct the enclosing rectangle assuming MM_TEXT mode
    m_EnclosingRect = CRect(FirstPoint, SecondPoint);
    m_EnclosingRect.NormalizeRect();
}
```

Here we just use the **AddHead()** function instead of **AddTail()**. The code for the **AddSegment()** member is:

```
void CCurve::AddSegment(CPoint& aPoint)
{
    m_PointList.AddHead(aPoint);      // Add the point to the list

    // Modify the enclosing rectangle for the new point
    m_EnclosingRect = CRect( min(aPoint.x, m_EnclosingRect.left),
                             min(aPoint.y, m_EnclosingRect.top),
                             max(aPoint.x, m_EnclosingRect.right),
                             max(aPoint.y, m_EnclosingRect.bottom) );
}
```

Again, the change is just to use **AddHead()** in place of **AddTail()**. The code for the **Draw()** member function is:

```
void CCurve::Draw(CDC* pDC, CElement* pElement)
{
    // Create a pen for this object and
    // initialize it to the object color and line width of 1 pixel
    CPen aPen;
    COLORREF aColor = m_Color;          // Initialize with element color
    if(this == pElement)                // This element selected?
        aColor = SELECT_COLOR;          // Set highlight color
    if(!aPen.CreatePen(PS_SOLID, m_Pen, aColor))
    {
        // Pen creation failed. Close the program
        AfxMessageBox("Pen creation failed drawing a curve", MB_OK);
        AfxAbort();
    }

    CPen* pOldPen = pDC->SelectObject(&aPen);  // Select the pen

    // Now draw the curve
    // Get the position in the list of the first element
    POSITION aPosition = m_PointList.GetTailPosition();

    // As long as it's good, move to that point
    if(aPosition)
        pDC->MoveTo(m_PointList.GetPrev(aPosition));

    // Draw a segment for each of the following points
    while(aPosition)
        pDC->LineTo(m_PointList.GetPrev(aPosition));

    pDC->SelectObject(pOldPen);                 // Restore the old pen
}
```

The **GetTailPosition()** function returns the **POSITION** value for the last member of the list, which will correspond to the first point. We then step backwards through the list by using the **GetPrev()** function.

570

Ex6-2: The declaration in the **CCurve** class for the list should be changed to:

```
// Type safe point pointer list
CTypedPtrList<CPtrList, CPoint*> m_PointPtrList;
```

The constructor will now be implemented as:

```
CCurve::CCurve(CPoint FirstPoint,CPoint SecondPoint, COLORREF aColor)
{
    // Add the points to the list
    m_PointPtrList.AddTail(new CPoint(FirstPoint));
    m_PointPtrList.AddTail(new CPoint(SecondPoint));
    m_Color = aColor;                   // Store the color
    m_Pen = 1;                          // Set the pen width

    // Construct the enclosing rectangle assuming MM_TEXT mode
    m_EnclosingRect = CRect(FirstPoint, SecondPoint);
    m_EnclosingRect.NormalizeRect();
}
```

This now creates new points on the heap that are initialized with the points passed as arguments to the constructor, and passes their addresses to the **AddTail()** function. Since we're using a pointer list, we need to implement the destructor for the **CCurve** class:

```
CCurve::~CCurve()
{
    POSITION aPos = m_PointPtrList.GetHeadPosition();
    while(aPos)
        delete m_PointPtrList.GetNext(aPos);   // Delete CPoint objects
    m_PointPtrList.RemoveAll();                // Delete the pointers
}
```

Don't forget to add a declaration for the destructor in **Elements.h**! The **AddSegment()** member of the **CCurve** class also needs to be modified:

```
void CCurve::AddSegment(CPoint& aPoint)
{
    //Add the point to the end
    m_PointPtrList.AddTail(new CPoint(aPoint));

    // Modify the enclosing rectangle for the new point
    m_EnclosingRect = CRect( min(aPoint.x, m_EnclosingRect.left),
                             min(aPoint.y, m_EnclosingRect.top),
                             max(aPoint.x, m_EnclosingRect.right),
                             max(aPoint.y, m_EnclosingRect.bottom) );
}
```

The **Move()** member function is also affected:

```
void CCurve::Move(CSize& aSize)
{
    m_EnclosingRect+= aSize;                               // Move the rectangle

    // Get the 1st element position
    POSITION aPosition = m_PointPtrList.GetHeadPosition();
```

```
        while(aPosition)
            *m_PointPtrList.GetNext(aPosition)+= aSize;   // Move each point
}
```

Lastly, the **Draw()** function in the **CCurve** class must be changed:

```
void CCurve::Draw(CDC* pDC, CElement* pElement)
{
    // Create a pen for this object and
    // initialize it to the object color and line width of 1 pixel
    CPen aPen;
    COLORREF aColor = m_Color;              // Initialize with element color
    if(this == pElement)                    // This element selected?
        aColor = SELECT_COLOR;              // Set highlight color
    if(!aPen.CreatePen(PS_SOLID, m_Pen, aColor))
    {
        // Pen creation failed. Close the program
        AfxMessageBox("Pen creation failed drawing a curve", MB_OK);
        AfxAbort();
    }

    CPen* pOldPen = pDC->SelectObject(&aPen);   // Select the pen

    // Now draw the curve
    // Get the position in the list of the first element
    POSITION aPosition = m_PointPtrList.GetHeadPosition();

    // As long as it's good, move to that point
    if(aPosition)
        pDC->MoveTo(*m_PointPtrList.GetNext(aPosition));

    // Draw a segment for each of the following points
    while(aPosition)
        pDC->LineTo(*m_PointPtrList.GetNext(aPosition));

    pDC->SelectObject(pOldPen);                 // Restore the old pen
}
```

Ex6-3: The declaration of the **CArray** data member in the **CCurve** class is:

```
    CArray<CPoint, CPoint&> m_PointArray;       // Type safe point array
```

The second argument to the template specifies that arguments will be passed to function members of **m_PointArray** as references.

We can also add a protected data member to keep track of how many points we have in a curve:

```
    int m_nPoints;                              // Number of points
```

The constructor needs to be modified to:

```
CCurve::CCurve(CPoint& FirstPoint,CPoint& SecondPoint, COLORREF aColor)
{
    m_PointArray.SetSize(10);
    m_PointArray[0] = FirstPoint;       // Add the 1st point to the array
```

572

```
    m_PointArray[1] = SecondPoint;    // Add the 2nd point to the array
    m_nPoints = 2;                    // Set the point count
    m_Color = aColor;                 // Store the color
    m_Pen = 1;                        // Set the pen width

    // Construct the enclosing rectangle assuming MM_TEXT mode
    m_EnclosingRect = CRect(FirstPoint, SecondPoint);
    m_EnclosingRect.NormalizeRect();
}
```

By setting the initial size of the array, we avoid unnecessary creation of array elements. The default situation allocates array elements one at a time. You can specify a second argument to the **SetSize()** function to define the number of additional elements to be created when it becomes necessary. If you omit the second argument, the framework will decide how many to create, based on the initial array size.

The **CArray** template provides overloading for **[]** so that you can use indexing to reference members of the array. The **AddSegment()** member of **CCurve** can be implemented as:

```
void CCurve::AddSegment(CPoint& aPoint)
{
    //Add the point to the array and increment the count
    m_PointArray.SetAtGrow(m_nPoints++, aPoint);

    // Modify the enclosing rectangle for the new point
    m_EnclosingRect = CRect( min(aPoint.x, m_EnclosingRect.left),
                             min(aPoint.y, m_EnclosingRect.top),
                             max(aPoint.x, m_EnclosingRect.right),
                             max(aPoint.y, m_EnclosingRect.bottom) );
}
```

The **SetAtGrow()** member of **CArray** sets the array element specified by the first argument to the value passed as the second argument. If the first argument is beyond the extent of the array, the array will be automatically increased in size.

As in the previous exercises, we'll also need to modify the **Draw()** and **Move()** members. Here's the first of those two:

```
void CCurve::Draw(CDC* pDC, CElement* pElement)
{
    // Create a pen for this object and
    // initialize it to the object color and line width of 1 pixel
    CPen aPen;
    COLORREF aColor = m_Color;           // Initialize with element color
    if(this == pElement)                 // This element selected?
        aColor = SELECT_COLOR;           // Set highlight color
    if(!aPen.CreatePen(PS_SOLID, m_Pen, aColor))
    {
        // Pen creation failed. Close the program
        AfxMessageBox("Pen creation failed drawing a curve", MB_OK);
        AfxAbort();
    }

    CPen* pOldPen = pDC->SelectObject(&aPen);  // Select the pen

    // Now draw the curve
```

```
        // Set the position counter to the first element of the array
        int aPosition = 0;

        // Move to the first point in the curve
        pDC->MoveTo(m_PointArray[aPosition++]);

        // Draw a segment for each of the following points
        while(aPosition < m_nPoints)
            pDC->LineTo(m_PointArray[aPosition++]);

        pDC->SelectObject(pOldPen);                    // Restore the old pen
    }
```

And these are the changes you need to make to **Move()**:

```
    void CCurve::Move(CSize& aSize)
    {
        m_EnclosingRect += aSize;              // Move the rectangle

        // Set a counter to the 1st element
        int aPosition = 0;

        while(aPosition < m_nPoints)
            m_PointArray[aPosition++] += aSize; // Move each point in the array
    }
```

Chapter 7

Ex7-1: Modify the scale dialog to appear as shown below:

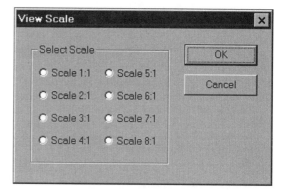

Make sure that each radio button has a unique ID, such as **IDC_SCALE1**, **IDC_SCALE2**, etc., then use ClassWizard to add functions to handle the **BN_CLICKED** message for each radio button. The implementations for these are all very similar. For example, the first two are:

```
    void CScaleDialog::OnScale1()
    {
        m_Scale = 1;
    }
```

```
    void CScaleDialog::OnScale2()
    {
        m_Scale = 2;
    }
```

Modify the **OnInitDialog()** member of **CScaleDialog** to check the appropriate radio button, based on the current scale, as follows:

```
BOOL CScaleDialog::OnInitDialog()
{
   CDialog::OnInitDialog();

   // Check the radio button corresponding to the scale
   switch(m_Scale)
   {
      case 1:
         CheckDlgButton(IDC_SCALE1,1);
         break;
      case 2:
         CheckDlgButton(IDC_SCALE2,1);
         break;
      case 3:
         CheckDlgButton(IDC_SCALE3,1);
         break;
      case 4:
         CheckDlgButton(IDC_SCALE4,1);
         break;
      case 5:
         CheckDlgButton(IDC_SCALE5,1);
         break;
      case 6:
         CheckDlgButton(IDC_SCALE6,1);
         break;
      case 7:
         CheckDlgButton(IDC_SCALE7,1);
         break;
      case 8:
         CheckDlgButton(IDC_SCALE8,1);
         break;
      default:
         CheckDlgButton(IDC_SCALE8,1);
         AfxMessageBox("Invalid scale set.");
   }

   return TRUE;  // return TRUE unless you set the focus to a control
                 // EXCEPTION: OCX Property Pages should return FALSE
}
```

Delete the code from the **DoDataExchange()** member of **CScaleDialog** that handled the previous version of the dialog controls, so it becomes:

```
void CScaleDialog::DoDataExchange(CDataExchange* pDX)
{
   CDialog::DoDataExchange(pDX);
   //{{AFX_DATA_MAP(CScaleDialog)
      // NOTE: the ClassWizard will add DDX and DDV calls here
   //}}AFX_DATA_MAP
}
```

That completes all the necessary modifications. Compile and run Sketcher as normal to see the new dialog in operation.

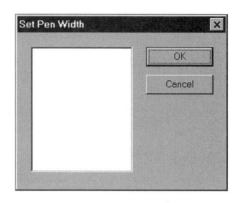

Ex7-2: Modify the pen width dialog box resource to the following:

Assign a suitable ID, such as **IDC_PENWIDTH** to the list box, and make sure the Sort style is unchecked. Now delete the **m_PenWidth** data member of **CPenDialog** and the functions handling the previous **BN_CLICKED** messages for the radio buttons. Don't forget to delete them from the class definition, as well as from the message map in the implementation file. Save the two files so ClassWizard recognizes that the variable has been deleted.

Use ClassWizard to add a new variable for the dialog, **m_PenWidth**, of type **int** and corresponding to the list box ID, **IDC_PENWIDTH**. The variable will store the index to the selected list box item, and will also represent the pen width.

Modify the **OnInitDialog()** member of **CPenDialog** to add the strings to the list box, and highlight the string corresponding to the current pen width:

```
BOOL CPenDialog::OnInitDialog()
{
   CDialog::OnInitDialog();
   CListBox* pLBox = (CListBox*)GetDlgItem(IDC_PENWIDTH);  // Initialize aBox
   pLBox->AddString("Pen Width 0");      // Add the strings to the box
   pLBox->AddString("Pen Width 1");
   pLBox->AddString("Pen Width 2");
   pLBox->AddString("Pen Width 3");
   pLBox->AddString("Pen Width 4");
   pLBox->AddString("Pen Width 5");
   pLBox->SetCurSel(m_PenWidth);         // Highlight the current pen width

   return TRUE;  // return TRUE unless you set the focus to a control
                 // EXCEPTION: OCX Property Pages should return FALSE
}
```

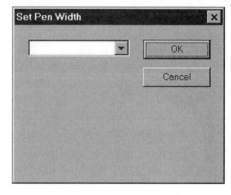

Ex7-3: Change the dialog again by removing the list box and replacing it by a combo box with the same ID. The dialog will look like this:

It's important to allow enough space in the dialog for the combo box to drop down, otherwise you will not see the complete list. Do this by clicking the down arrow and increasing the size of the area displayed.

You could delete the existing **m_PenWidth** member of **CPenDialog** and add it back as the variable to support the combo box, but because the differences are so slight the shortest way to implement the support for the combo box is to modify the existing code. The **DoDataExchange()** member of **CPenDialog** should be modified to:

```
void CPenDialog::DoDataExchange(CDataExchange* pDX)
{
CDialog::DoDataExchange(pDX);
//{{AFX_DATA_MAP(CPenDialog)
    DDX_CBIndex(pDX, IDC_PENWIDTH, m_PenWidth);
//}}AFX_DATA_MAP
}
```

This calls **DDX_CBIndex()** instead of **DDX_LBIndex()**, because we're now using a combo box, not a list box. The only other modification necessary is to the **OnInitDialog()** member of **CPenDialog**:

```
BOOL CPenDialog::OnInitDialog()
{
    CDialog::OnInitDialog();

// Initialize aBox
    CComboBox* pCBox = (CComboBox*)GetDlgItem(IDC_PENWIDTH);
    pCBox->AddString("Pen Width 0");      // Add the strings to the box
    pCBox->AddString("Pen Width 1");
    pCBox->AddString("Pen Width 2");
    pCBox->AddString("Pen Width 3");
    pCBox->AddString("Pen Width 4");
    pCBox->AddString("Pen Width 5");
    pCBox->SetCurSel(m_PenWidth);          // Highlight the current pen width

    return TRUE;  // return TRUE unless you set the focus to a control
                  // EXCEPTION: OCX Property Pages should return FALSE
}
```

The changed lines here are highlighted. The first statement creates a pointer to a **CComboBox** object instead of a pointer to a **CListBox** object, and casts the pointer returned by **GetDlgItem()** accordingly. You should also change the pointer name to **pCBox** for consistency. You also have to change all the succeeding statements which refer to it, of course.

Chapter 8

Ex8-1: Printing page numbers. These are the lines you need to add to **OnPrint()**:

```
// Output the document file name
    pDC->SetTextAlign(TA_CENTER);              // Center the following text
    pDC->TextOut(pInfo->m_rectDraw.right/2, -20,
                    ((CPrintData*)(pInfo->m_lpUserData))->m_DocTitle);
```

```
      CString PageNum;
      PageNum.Format("Page %d", pInfo->m_nCurPage);
      pDC->TextOut(pInfo->m_rectDraw.right/2,-1050, PageNum);

      pDC->SetTextAlign(TA_LEFT);              // Left justify text
```

Using **CString**, it's easy! You create a string object, initialize it using the member function **Format()** with the **m_nCurPage** value we're already using elsewhere in **OnPrint()**, and output it just as we did with the document title (although in a different position, of course).

Ex8-2: Scaling text correctly. This is a matter of working out how and where to specify the font to be used. In fact, you need to do it twice: once in the **CText::Draw()** function, and then again in **CSketcherView::OnLButtonDown()**, to make sure the text rectangle gets set up correctly. Here are the changes to **CText::Draw()**:

```
   void CText::Draw(CDC* pDC, CElement* pElement)
   {
      CFont aFont;
      aFont.CreatePointFont(100, "");
      CFont* pOldFont = pDC->SelectObject(&aFont);

      COLORREF Color(m_Color);              // Initialize with element color

      if(this==pElement)
         Color = SELECT_COLOR;              // Set selected color

      // Set the text color and output the text
      pDC->SetTextColor(Color);
      pDC->TextOut(m_StartPoint.x, m_StartPoint.y, m_String);
      pDC->SelectObject(pOldFont);
   }
```

The new code simply creates a new object of the **CFont** class, calls its member function **CreatePointFont()** to select a default 10 point font, selects it into the device context before the text is output, and selects it out again afterwards. Four very similar lines get added to **CSketcherView::OnLButtonDown()**:

```
      if(pDoc->GetElementType() == TEXT)
      {
         CTextDialog aDlg;
         if(aDlg.DoModal() == IDOK)
         {
            // Exit OK so create a text element
            CFont aFont;
            aFont.CreatePointFont(100, "");
            CFont* pOldFont = aDC.SelectObject(&aFont);

            CSketcherDoc* pDoc = GetDocument();
            CSize TextExtent = aDC.GetTextExtent(aDlg.m_TextString);

            // Get bottom right of text rectangle - MM_LOENGLISH
            CPoint BottomRt(point.x+TextExtent.cx, point.y-TextExtent.cy);
            CText* pTextElement = new CText(point, BottomRt,
                        aDlg.m_TextString, pDoc->GetElementColor()));
```

```
                    // Add the element to the document
                    pDoc->AddElement(pTextElement);

                    // Get all views updated
                    pDoc->UpdateAllViews(0,0,pTextElement);

               aDC.SelectObject(pOldFont);
          }
          return;
     }
```

Chapter 9

Ex9-1: Start off by using AppWizard to generate a new SDI application. You can turn off printer support if you like, and the name really isn't important. The files and classes here assume a project called SkView.

Copy the **DllImports.h** file into the project folder and add it to the project; insert **#include**s for this file into **SkView.cpp**, **SkViewDoc.cpp** and **SkViewView.cpp**. Just like in the chapter, amend the project settings so the **ExtDLLExample.lib** file is linked in, and don't forget to copy **ExtDLLExample.dll** to the **Debug** directory once that's been created. You'll also need to add a **#include** for **afxtempl.h** to **stdafx.h**.

To the document class definition, you need to add five member variables and three member functions, all of which you've used before:

```
// Attributes
protected:
   COLORREF m_Color;
   WORD m_Element;
   CTypedPtrList<CObList, CElement*> m_ElementList;
   int m_PenWidth;
   CSize m_DocSize;

// Operations
public:
   POSITION GetListHeadPosition()
      { return m_ElementList.GetHeadPosition(); }
   CElement* GetNext(POSITION &aPos)
      { return m_ElementList.GetNext(aPos); }
   CSize GetDocSize()
      { return m_DocSize; }
```

As for the implementation, since we're only dealing with documents held in files, we don't need to do any initialization in the constructor. However, we should add the code which deletes the element list cleanly to the destructor:

```
CSkViewDoc::~CSkViewDoc()
{
   POSITION aPosition = m_ElementList.GetHeadPosition();
   while(aPosition)
      delete m_ElementList.GetNext(aPosition);
```

```
      m_ElementList.RemoveAll();
}
```

The only other code to add to the document class is that required to enable serialization from a file. (Remember, we aren't worried about saving files because we never alter them in this application.) The **Serialize()** function looks like this:

```
void CSkViewDoc::Serialize(CArchive& ar)
{
   m_ElementList.Serialize(ar);

   if (ar.IsStoring())
   {
   }
   else
   {
      ar >> m_Color
         >> m_Element
         >> m_PenWidth
         >> m_DocSize;
   }
}
```

The view class requires a little more work, although not much. For a start, it doesn't need any new member variables, although you will need to use ClassWizard to add two new member functions: **OnPrepareDC()** and **OnOpenDocument()**. Once again, nothing needs adding to the constructor, and this time the destructor can be left empty as well. You should add some code **OnDraw()**, but only the same as we had in Sketcher itself:

```
void CSkViewView::OnDraw(CDC* pDC)
{
   CSkViewDoc* pDoc = GetDocument();
   ASSERT_VALID(pDoc);

   POSITION aPos = pDoc->GetListHeadPosition();
   CElement* pElement = 0;
   while(aPos)
   {
      pElement = pDoc->GetNext(aPos);
      if(pDC->RectVisible(pElement->GetBoundRect()))
         pElement->Draw(pDC);
   }
}
```

OnPrepareDC() bears a little more inspection, and looks like this:

```
void CSkViewView::OnPrepareDC(CDC* pDC, CPrintInfo* pInfo)
{
   CView::OnPrepareDC(pDC, pInfo);
   CSkViewDoc* pDoc = GetDocument();
   pDC->SetMapMode(MM_ANISOTROPIC);

   CSize DocSize = pDoc->GetDocSize();
   DocSize.cy = -DocSize.cy;
   pDC->SetWindowExt(DocSize);
```

```
        int xLogPixels = pDC->GetDeviceCaps(LOGPIXELSX);
        int yLogPixels = pDC->GetDeviceCaps(LOGPIXELSY);

        CRect WinRect;
        GetWindowRect(&WinRect);

        double xScale = (double(WinRect.right -
                            WinRect.left))/(DocSize.cx/100*xLogPixels);
        double yScale = -(double(WinRect.bottom -
                            WinRect.top))/(DocSize.cy/100*yLogPixels);

        long xExtent = (long)(DocSize.cx*xScale*xLogPixels/100L);
        long yExtent = (long)(DocSize.cy*yScale*yLogPixels/100L);

        pDC->SetViewportExt((int)xExtent, (int)-yExtent);
    }
```

The new lines here are the ones which handle the scaling. **GetWindowRect()** returns in its argument the coordinates in pixels of the view window. From these values, we contrive to produce two scaling factors (in general, they're different for the x and y directions) which map the document stored in **DocSize** to our view window—the expressions come down to (window width/document width) and (window height/document height), with all measurements in pixels.

You need to implement **OnOpenDocument()** in order that you have somewhere to delete the old document before opening a new one. If you don't do this, any new documents you open will just be superimposed on top of old ones, which is hardly ideal. The code you need to add is exactly the same as the code in the destructor:

```
    BOOL CSkViewDoc::OnOpenDocument(LPCTSTR lpszPathName)
    {
        POSITION aPosition = m_ElementList.GetHeadPosition();
        while(aPosition)
            delete m_ElementList.GetNext(aPosition);

        m_ElementList.RemoveAll();

        if (!CDocument::OnOpenDocument(lpszPathName))
            return FALSE;

        return TRUE;
    }
```

That's everything required for the problem as specified, although you might like to include the text scaling we introduced in the last chapter's exercises, as the text is disproportionately large at these scales otherwise.

Chapter 10

Ex10-1: There are a number of things to do here. Start by adding a new button labeled something like Stock Info to the products dialog, and amend its ID appropriately. Implement a handler for it using ClassWizard and add this code:

```
void CProductView::OnStockinfo()
{
    ((CMainFrame*)GetParentFrame())->SelectView(STOCK_VIEW);
}
```

For this to work, you must also define a new constant in **OurConstants.h**

```
// Arbitrary constants to identify record views
const UINT PRODUCT_VIEW = 1U;
const UINT ORDER_VIEW = 2U;
const UINT CUSTOMER_VIEW = 3U;
const UINT STOCK_VIEW = 4U;
```

and add code to handle it in **CMainFrame::SelectView()**. The new class for the stock control dialog will be called **CStockView**:

```
if (pNewActiveView == NULL)
    {
        switch(ViewID)
        {
            case ORDER_VIEW:        // Create an Order view
                pNewActiveView = (CView*)new COrderView;
                break;
            case CUSTOMER_VIEW:     // Create a customer view
                pNewActiveView = (CView*)new CCustomerView;
                break;
            case STOCK_VIEW:        // Create a stock view
                pNewActiveView = (CView*)new CStockView;
                break;
```

Don't forget that you'll need to add a **#include** for **StockView.h** to **MainFrm.cpp**. Next, call up ClassWizard and use it to create a new class called **CStockSet**, with **CRecordset** as its base. Choose to use the **Products** table from the **Sample Data** database, and once you've done that, add a **public** member variable to the document class:

```
public:
    CStockSet    m_StockSet;
    CCustomerSet m_CustomerSet;
    COrderSet    m_OrderSet;
```

The next step is to add the dialog itself. Go to the ResourceView and insert a new dialog called **IDD_STOCK_FORM**. Make sure its Style and Border are set to Child and None respectively, delete the default controls and add new ones so it looks something like this:

After giving the important controls sensible IDs and ensuring that the tab order of the controls is such that each edit control immediately succeeds its partnering static text control, call up ClassWizard and create a new class called **CStockView**. Base this class on **CRecordView**, select **IDD_STOCK_FORM** as the dialog to be associated with it, and choose **CStockSet** as its recordset.

You can now *Ctrl*-double-click on all the edit controls to tie them to the recordset data members, and on the Products button so that you can implement the handler, which looks like this:

```
void CStockView::OnSkproducts()
{
    ((CMainFrame*)GetParentFrame())->SelectView(PRODUCT_VIEW);
}
```

Just three things remain: make the constructor for **CStockView** public, delete the code from the destructor, and add two **#include**s to **StockView.cpp**:

```
#include "stdafx.h"
#include "DBSample.h"
#include "OurConstants.h"
#include "Mainfrm.h"
#include "StockView.h"
```

Ex10-2: Add the **public** member variable **m_ProductIDparam**, of type **long**, to the definition of **CStockSet**. Initialize it and the parameter count **m_nParams** in the constructor in **StockSet.cpp**:

```
m_ProductIDparam = 0L;
m_nParams = 1;
```

Set up the parameter by adding a couple of lines to the **CStockSet::DoFieldExchange()** function:

```
void CStockSet::DoFieldExchange(CFieldExchange* pFX)
{
    //{{AFX_FIELD_MAP(CStockSet)
    pFX->SetFieldType(CFieldExchange::outputColumn);

    // Various RFX_... commands

    //}}AFX_FIELD_MAP
    pFX->SetFieldType(CFieldExchange::param);
    RFX_Long(pFX, _T("ProductIDparam"), m_ProductIDparam);
}
```

Next, you need to add code to define a filter in the **CStockView::OnInitialUpdate()** function:

```
void CStockView::OnInitialUpdate()
{
    BeginWaitCursor();

    CDBSampleDoc* pDoc = (CDBSampleDoc*)GetDocument();
    m_pSet = &pDoc->m_StockSet;  // Initialize the recordset pointer
```

```
   // Set the database for the recordset
   m_pSet->m_pDatabase = pDoc->m_productSet.m_pDatabase;

   // Set the current Product ID as the parameter
   m_pSet->m_ProductIDparam = pDoc->m_productSet.m_ProductID;

   // Filter on the Product ID field
   m_pSet->m_strFilter = "ProductID = ?";

   GetRecordset();
   CRecordView::OnInitialUpdate();
   if (m_pSet->IsOpen())
   {
      CString strTitle = m_pSet->m_pDatabase->GetDatabaseName();
      CString strTable = m_pSet->GetTableName();
      if (!strTable.IsEmpty())
         strTitle += _T(":") + strTable;
      GetDocument()->SetTitle(strTitle);
   }
   EndWaitCursor();
}
```

Like in the chapter, you need to add an **OnActiveView()** handler to **CStockView**. Here's the code you need to insert:

```
void CStockView::OnActivateView(BOOL bActivate, CView* pActivateView,
                                               CView* pDeactiveView)
{
   if(bActivate)
   {
      CDBSampleDoc* pDoc = (CDBSampleDoc*)GetDocument();

      // Set current Product ID as parameter and requery the database
      m_pSet->m_ProductIDparam = pDoc->m_productSet.m_ProductID;
      m_pSet->Requery();
      CRecordView::OnInitialUpdate();
   }
   CRecordView::OnActivateView(bActivate, pActivateView, pDeactiveView);
}
```

Finally, you should add **#include**s for **ProductSet.h** and **DBSampleDoc.h** to **StockView.cpp**.

Ex10-3: There are all kinds of ways you could approach this; here's a fairly easy method. Add a new edit control to the stock dialog and label it something like Stock Position. *Ctrl*-double-click on the edit box and add a new **CString** variable called **m_StockPosn**. Then you can simply add a few lines to **CStockView::DoDataExchange()**:

```
void CStockView::DoDataExchange(CDataExchange* pDX)
{
   CRecordView::DoDataExchange(pDX);

   m_StockPosn = "Situation normal";
   long StockBalance = m_pSet->m_UnitsInStock - m_pSet->m_ReorderLevel;
```

```
    if (m_pSet->m_ReorderLevel != 0)
    {
       if ((StockBalance > 0) && (StockBalance < 11))
          m_StockPosn = "*Warning: low stock*";
       if (StockBalance < 1)
          m_StockPosn = "**Urgent: reorder now**";
    }
```

```
    //{{AFX_DATA_MAP(CStockView)
    DDX_FieldText(pDX, IDC_SKPRODUCTNAME, m_pSet->m_ProductName, m_pSet);
    DDX_FieldText(pDX, IDC_SKPRODUCTID, m_pSet->m_ProductID, m_pSet);
    DDX_FieldText(pDX, IDC_SKUNITPRICE, m_pSet->m_UnitPrice, m_pSet);
    DDX_FieldText(pDX, IDC_SKUNITSINSTOCK, m_pSet->m_UnitsInStock, m_pSet);
    DDX_FieldText(pDX, IDC_SKREORDERLEVEL, m_pSet->m_ReorderLevel, m_pSet);
    DDX_Text(pDX, IDC_STOCKPOSN, m_StockPosn);
    //}}AFX_DATA_MAP
}
```

If all has gone well, you'll have a dialog which looks something like this:

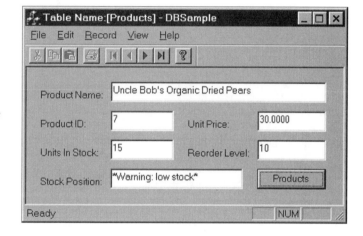

Chapter 11

Ex11-1: First, open the resource for the menu **IDR_WRXCONTYPE** and add a new menu item to the <u>E</u>dit menu with the properties shown below.

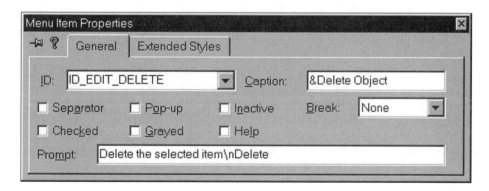

585

Ctrl-double-click on the new menu item to activate ClassWizard, then add **COMMAND** and **UPDATE_COMMAND_UI** handlers to the view class, **CWrxContainerView**. You can accept the default function names of **OnEditDelete()** and **OnUpdateEditDelete()**. Once the new handlers have been added, you can close ClassWizard and start adding some code to the new functions.

We need the new menu item to be enabled only when one of the items in the container is selected. We can determine whether an item is selected by looking at the **m_pSelection** member of the view class. Add the code shown to **OnUpdateEditDelete()**.

```
void CWrxContainerView::OnUpdateEditDelete(CCmdUI* pCmdUI)
{
    if (m_pSelection == NULL)
        pCmdUI->Enable(FALSE);
    else
        pCmdUI->Enable(TRUE);
}
```

This code enables the menu item when there's a valid pointer in **m_pSelection** and disables it when **m_pSelection** is **NULL**. This prevents the user of the container from trying to delete an item without first selecting one.

Deleting an item is simplicity itself—you can just call **COleClientItem::Delete()** to remove a client from a document. The code you should add to **OnEditDelete()** is shown below:

```
void CWrxContainerView::OnEditDelete()
{
    ASSERT(m_pSelection != NULL);
    if (m_pSelection != NULL)
    {
        CWrxContainerDoc* pDoc = GetDocument();
        m_pSelection->Delete();
        m_pSelection = NULL;
        pDoc->SetModifiedFlag();
        Invalidate();
    }
}
```

There's actually a bit more to this code than the single line that deletes the selected item because we need to ensure the integrity of our application. The first line uses the **ASSERT()** macro to alert us if **m_pSelection** is **NULL**. This also serves as documentation to show readers of this code that **m_pSelection** shouldn't be **NULL** when the function is called. We expect **m_pSelection** not to be **NULL** because of the way that we enable and disable the menu item, but this macro helps make doubly sure that **m_pSelection** is in the state we expect.

The **ASSERT()** macro is only active in debug builds so the **if** statement is also necessary to ensure that our code is robust in release builds. If **m_pSelection** does somehow turn out to be **NULL** when this function is called then we don't want to take any action in a release build.

If **m_pSelection** isn't **NULL**, we get a pointer to the document class, then delete the selected item. Next, we set **m_pSelection** to **NULL** because the selected item no longer exists. We need to let the framework know that the document has been modified so that it can save it when necessary, so we call **SetModifiedFlag()** through the document pointer. Finally, we **Invalidate()** the view so that it gets redrawn without the item that has just been deleted.

Chapter 12

Ex12-1: Limitations of the **StartRed** property. There are two main flaws:

1 It limits the starting state of the signal to one of two values: red or not red. This is a problem because there are more than two states that our signal can be in, and it seems unreasonable to exclude valid signal states from the possible start states. We should provide optimum flexibility to the users of our control.

2 Its name unnecessarily relates the state of the signal to a color. The interface of our control is inconsistent because we have one property (**StartRed**) that describes the state of the signal in terms of its color (red or not red) and another property (**StopOrGoTime**) and an event (**SignalChanged**) that describe the state of the signal in terms of the information it conveys (stop, go, or ready to stop). We should rationalize these inconsistencies and always describe the state of the signal in the same way. Since the signal is better defined in terms of the information it conveys than the colors it uses to convey that information, **StartRed** should be replaced or renamed.

To rectify the problems with **StartRed**, we could replace it with a property called **StartState**. This property could use the same enumeration for its possible values as we defined for the **SignalChanged** event. This means that we can provide greater flexibility to our control's users, and provide a consistent interface to our control.

Replacing **StartRed** with **StartState** would also allow us to alter the drawing code for the signal without worrying about whether the property name remained relevant to the control. If we wanted to provide a signal that used icons to represent the different states of the signal, all we would need to change would be the drawing code. The user of our control would be able to use the new version instantly without getting confused by our choice of property name.

Ex12-2: Implementing the **StartState** property. First, use ClassWizard to remove all traces of the **StartRed** property. Go to the Automation tab for the **CTrafficSignalCtrl** class, select **StartRed** and then click Delete. Follow the instructions you're given. Next, use ClassWizard again to add a new Automation property to **CTrafficSignalCtrl** using the settings shown in the screenshot:

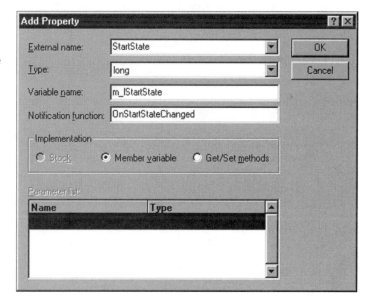

Add the following code to **CTrafficSignalCtrl::OnStartStateChanged()**:

```
void CTrafficSignalCtrl::OnStartStateChanged()
{
    // Stop the signal if necessary
    if (m_bSignalGo)
    {
        m_bSignalGo = FALSE;   // Set signal not running
        StopSignal();          // Stop the signal
    }
    // Set the signal object to the appropriate state
    m_pSignal->SetSignalState(m_lStartState);

    InvalidateControl();   // Get the control redrawn

    SetModifiedFlag();
}
```

Update the code in **CTrafficSignalCtrl::DoPropExchange()** as shown:

```
void CTrafficSignalCtrl::DoPropExchange(CPropExchange* pPX)
{
    ExchangeVersion(pPX, MAKELONG(_wVerMinor, _wVerMajor));
    COleControl::DoPropExchange(pPX);

    // TODO: Call PX_ functions for each persistent custom property.
    PX_Long(pPX, _T("StartState"), m_lStartState, STOP);
    PX_Long(pPX, _T("StopOrGoTime"), m_lStopOrGoTime, 5000);

    // Set the signal object to the appropriate state
    m_pSignal->SetSignalState(m_lStartState);
}
```

Update **CTrafficSignalCtrl::SetStopOrGoTime()** to use the new property notification function:

```
void CTrafficSignalCtrl::SetStopOrGoTime(long nNewValue)
{
    // Only alter the control if the value is different
    if (m_lStopOrGoTime != nNewValue)
    {
        m_lStopOrGoTime = nNewValue;      // Set the new stop or go time

        OnStartStateChanged();            // Set the initial state
        SetModifiedFlag();
    }
}
```

Update the **.odl** file as shown so that the new property uses the enumeration:

```
        [id(2)] long StopOrGoTime;
        [id(1)] SignalState StartState;
```

Ex12-3: Updating a control that has existing users needs to be handled sensitively if you want those users to upgrade to the new version. It can be quite tricky when you're just adding functionality, but that's as nothing compared with when you want to remove properties, methods or events from a control. Removing items from the public interface of a control is *not* something that should be done lightly, and you should try to avoid being in the position of wanting to remove something by carefully designing, implementing and testing your control *before* releasing it to the public.

In our case, we'll plan to remove the **StartRed** property in two stages which in the real world might be separated by months or even years. First, we'll release a control that retains the **StartRed** property and is completely compatible with the first version of the control. All code written to use the first version of the control will work fully with the new version. However, the new version of the control will discourage the use of the **StartRed** property so that in the future we may be able to release a version of the control that drops support for the **StartRed** property completely.

In fact, we may decide never to drop the **StartRed** property from our control because of the large amount of existing code that uses it. It might not be a problem with our simple traffic signal, but it's certainly a possibility for professionally produced ActiveX controls. With that in mind, the first thing that we'd do differently from the implementation of **StartState** in *Ex12-2* is not to delete the **StartRed** property!

> *When updating a control, make sure that you keep a clean backup copy of the source code for the existing control—you never know what might happen!*

We can add the **StartState** property to the control in the same way as before, but after doing so we need to make that it hasn't altered the DispIDs used for the existing methods and properties. It's a good idea to keep DispIDs consistent between versions of a control, even though it's quite unlikely for a client to be using the DispIDs directly. (It could be important if you distribute type libraries for the control separately from the control itself.)

There are two places that you need to check the values of the DispIDs. Towards the end of **TrafficSignalCtl.h** you'll find the following:

```
enum {
//{{AFX_DISP_ID(CTrafficSignalCtrl)
dispidStartRed = 1L,
dispidStopOrGoTime = 3L,
dispidStartState = 2L,
eventidSignalChanged = 1L,
//}}AFX_DISP_ID
};
```

If you compare this with the original control, you may find that the DispID for the **StopOrGoTime** property has changed so change the code like this:

```
enum {
//{{AFX_DISP_ID(CTrafficSignalCtrl)
dispidStartRed = 1L,
dispidStopOrGoTime = 2L,
dispidStartState = 3L,
eventidSignalChanged = 1L,
//}}AFX_DISP_ID
};
```

You'll also need to change the values of the **id**s in the **.odl** file to corresponding values. Always make sure that the IDs for the properties and methods are unique, positive integers.

```
properties:
    // NOTE - ClassWizard will maintain property information here.
    //    Use extreme caution when editing this section.
    //{{AFX_ODL_PROP(CTrafficSignalCtrl)
    [id(DISPID_BACKCOLOR), bindable, requestedit] OLE_COLOR BackColor;
    [id(1)] boolean StartRed;
    [id(2)] long StopOrGoTime;
    [id(3)] SignalState StartState;
    //}}AFX_ODL_PROP
```

Note that we have changed the type of the **StartState** property so that it uses the enumeration, just as we did in *Ex12-2*.

If you change the DispIDs, the last area you'll need to change is the dispatch map itself, which you'll find in **TrafficSignalCtl.cpp**. The order of the entries in the map should match the DispIDs that you've assigned in the header and **.odl** files, so make sure that the code matches this:

```
BEGIN_DISPATCH_MAP(CTrafficSignalCtrl, COleControl)
    //{{AFX_DISPATCH_MAP(CTrafficSignalCtrl)
    DISP_PROPERTY_NOTIFY(CTrafficSignalCtrl, "StartRed",
                    m_bStartRed, OnStartRedChanged, VT_BOOL)
    DISP_PROPERTY_EX(CTrafficSignalCtrl, "StopOrGoTime",
                    GetStopOrGoTime, SetStopOrGoTime, VT_I4)
    DISP_PROPERTY_NOTIFY(CTrafficSignalCtrl, "StartState",
                    m_lStartState, OnStartStateChanged, VT_I4)
    DISP_STOCKPROP_BACKCOLOR()
    //}}AFX_DISPATCH_MAP
    DISP_FUNCTION_ID(CTrafficSignalCtrl, "AboutBox",
                    DISPID_ABOUTBOX, AboutBox, VT_EMPTY, VTS_NONE)
END_DISPATCH_MAP()
```

> *As you've seen, ClassWizard provides DispIDs that match the alphabetical order of the properties you supply. This may be inappropriate if you're modifying a control that needs to maintain the DispIDs for its existing members. However, you can set the DispIDs of the properties manually by using the technique outlined above. Remember to match up the DispIDs in the control's header file, the *.odl* file and dispatch map.*

Now add the code for **OnStartStateChanged()**. The highlighted code shows up the differences between this version and *Ex12-2*, when we didn't have to worry about **StartRed**.

```
void CTrafficSignalCtrl::OnStartStateChanged()
{
    // Stop the signal if necessary
    if (m_bSignalGo)
    {
        m_bSignalGo = FALSE;   // Set signal not running
        StopSignal();          // Stop the signal
    }
    // Set the signal object to the appropriate state
    m_pSignal->SetSignalState(m_lStartState);
```

```
   // The following is only necessary if you are continuing
   // to support the StartRed property
   if (STOP == m_lStartState)
      m_bStartRed = TRUE;
   else
      m_bStartRed = FALSE;

   InvalidateControl();      // Get the control redrawn

   SetModifiedFlag();
}
```

Now change the code for **DoPropExchange()**. This is significantly different to the code we had previously:

```
void CTrafficSignalCtrl::DoPropExchange(CPropExchange* pPX)
{
   ExchangeVersion(pPX, MAKELONG(_wVerMinor, _wVerMajor));
   COleControl::DoPropExchange(pPX);

   // TODO: Call PX_ functions for each persistent custom property.
   if (pPX->GetVersion() < MAKELONG(0, 2))
   {
      // If we are loading information from before version 2.0
      // then we know that StartRed will have been saved
      PX_Bool(pPX, _T("StartRed"), m_bStartRed, TRUE);
      PX_Long(pPX, _T("StopOrGoTime"), m_lStopOrGoTime, 5000);

      // Set the signal object to the appropriate state
      if (m_bStartRed)
      {
         m_pSignal->SetSignalState(STOP);
         m_lStartState = STOP; // Added to support the new StartState property
      }
      else
      {
         m_pSignal->SetSignalState(GO);
         m_lStartState = GO; // Added to support the new StartState property
      }
   }
   else
   {
      // If we are loading/saving info from a version 2.0 or later file,
      // we don't have to worry about StartRed, we use StartState instead
      PX_Long(pPX, _T("StopOrGoTime"), m_lStopOrGoTime, 5000);
      PX_Long(pPX, _T("StartState"), m_lStartState, STOP);

      // Set the signal object to the appropriate state
      m_pSignal->SetSignalState(m_lStartState);

      // This is only necessary if you are continuing to support
      // the StartRed property
      if (STOP == m_lStartState)
         m_bStartRed = TRUE;
      else
         m_bStartRed = FALSE;
   }
}
```

Note the use of **CPropExchange::GetVersion()**. This function returns the version of the control, which is retrieved from the persistent data when loading properties and is taken from the values of the global constants **wVerMajor** and **wVerMinor** when saving properties. The function will save data in version 2.0 format just so long as we make sure that the control knows that it's a version 2.0 control. You can do this by changing the values of **wVerMajor** and **wVerMinor**, which you'll find at the top of **TrafficSignal.cpp**:

```
const WORD _wVerMajor = 2;
const WORD _wVerMinor = 0;
```

This code means that regardless of whether we load our properties from a version 1.0 or version 2.0 property store, they will always be saved in version 2.0 format. This means that we are already making a small step towards eliminating the use of the **StartRed** property.

> If you want a way to save persistent properties using the same version format as they were loaded with, check out the documentation for **ExchangeVersion()**.

The only thing left to do is to discourage the use of the **StartRed** property in new code. The best way to do this is to document the function as being out of date and point the programmer to the new **StartState** property. However, you can also hide the property from Visual Basic users by applying the **hidden** keyword to the property in the **.odl** file:

```
[id(DISPID_BACKCOLOR), bindable, requestedit] OLE_COLOR BackColor;
[id(1), hidden] boolean StartRed;
[id(2)] long StopOrGoTime;
```

This will tell Visual Basic (and other environments that respect this property) not to show the item to the user of your control. Thus **StartRed** will no longer appear in Visual Basic's Properties Window or the Object Browser. However, any code that uses **StartRed** will continue to work just as before.

Chapter 13

Ex13-1: Start by creating a new project with the ATL COM AppWizard. Call it **CtrlClient** and select Executable (EXE) as the Server Type. Now add a dialog to the project by selecting Insert | New ATL Object..., and then Miscellaneous from the list in the ATL Object Wizard. Hit Next > and give the dialog a Short Name of **ClientDlg**. Then click OK.

Once the dialog class has been added to the project, we need to create an instance of the class when the executable starts. Open **CtrlClient.cpp** and add a **#include** statement for **ClientDlg.h** to the top of the file, just below the other **#include**s.

Now move down the file to the **_tWinMain()** function. This serves exactly the same purpose as the **WinMain()** function you saw back in Chapter 2, and acts as the entry point for the executable. (The **_t** prefix indicates that it will receive command line arguments as ASCII characters normally, or Unicode (wide) characters if **_UNICODE** is defined.)

The first half of the code provided by the Wizard for this function deals with parsing the command line arguments and registering or unregistering any components if the command line contains the **RegServer** or **UnregServer** switches. We don't need to worry about this because our client won't be exposing any COM objects. The code we're interested in will go in the second half of the function, after the **if (bRun)** check.

Add or modify the highlighted code shown below:

```
if (bRun)
    {
        hRes = _Module.RegisterClassObjects(CLSCTX_LOCAL_SERVER,
            REGCLS_MULTIPLEUSE);
        _ASSERTE(SUCCEEDED(hRes));

        CClientDlg* pdlgClient = new CClientDlg;
        pdlgClient->Create(NULL);
        pdlgClient->ShowWindow(SW_SHOW);

        MSG msg;
        while (GetMessage(&msg, 0, 0, 0) == TRUE)
        {
            TranslateMessage(&msg);       // Translate the message
            DispatchMessage(&msg);        // Dispatch the message
        }

        if (pdlgClient)
        {
            delete pdlgClient;
            pdlgClient = NULL;
        }

        _Module.RevokeClassObjects();
    }
```

The first section of code before the message loop just creates a new dialog object, then displays it to the user. Once the message loop exits (when it receives a **WM_CLOSE** message and **GetMessage()** returns zero), the dialog object is deleted to free the memory we used.

Now we have to make sure that that the application closes when the user closes the dialog. This means that we need to post a **WM_QUIT** message when the user clicks OK or Cancel on the dialog—for our purposes, both buttons perform the same action. If you look at the dialog class, you'll see that it already has functions (**OnOK()** and **OnCancel()**) to handle the buttons. The Wizard-produced code assumes that the dialog is modal, so it includes calls to **EndDialog()**. We're using a modeless dialog, so we need to replace this code with a call to **DestroyWindow()**.

Add the highlighted code shown below:

```
LRESULT CClientDlg::OnOK(WORD wNotifyCode, WORD wID, HWND hWndCtl, BOOL& bHandled)
{
    PostMessage(WM_QUIT);
    DestroyWindow();
    return 0;
}
```

```
LRESULT CClientDlg::OnCancel(WORD wNotifyCode, WORD wID, HWND hWndCtl, BOOL&
bHandled)
{
    PostMessage(WM_QUIT);
    DestroyWindow();
    return 0;
}
```

Now modify the dialog resource to include the controls necessary for the client. You can copy these controls from the existing dialog resource that you created for the MFC-based client. That done, the next step is to set up the variables that can be used to store the values associated with the controls, so add the following declarations to the **CClientDlg** class definition.

```
private:
    long m_lVRes;
    long m_lHRes;
    long m_lRefresh;
    long m_lHScan;
```

You should also initialize these variables in the class constructor. The top three can be initialized to zero, whereas **m_lHScan** should start at 50, just as it did in the MFC client.

Unfortunately, things get a little harder here. We can no longer use ClassWizard to add these variables, so you'll have to add them by hand. In addition, there's no ATL equivalent of the **UpdateData()** function so you'll need to write your own.

Add the function shown below to **CClientDlg** and give the single **bool** parameter a default value of **true**. This will work just like the **UpdateData()** member function in an MFC dialog.

```
void CClientDlg::UpdateData(bool bSave /* = true */)
{
    Exchange_Text(bSave, IDC_HSCAN, m_lHScan);
    Exchange_Text(bSave, IDC_REFRESH, m_lRefresh);
    Exchange_Text(bSave, IDC_HRES, m_lHRes);
    Exchange_Text(bSave, IDC_VRES, m_lVRes);
}
```

If you pass **true**, the **Exchange_Text()** function will take the strings stored in the control specified by the ID passed as the second parameter and convert their contents to a type compatible with the member variables passed as the third parameter. If you pass **false**, the **Exchange_Text()** function will take the values stored in the third parameter and display them in the control passed in the second parameter.

Your **Exchange_Text()** function should be added to **CClientDlg**, and could look something like this:

```
void CClientDlg::Exchange_Text(bool bSave, int nID, long& lValue)
{
    CComVariant converter = 0;
    if (bSave)
    {
        const int MAX_COUNT = 12;
        TCHAR strText[MAX_COUNT + 1] = {0};
        GetDlgItemText(nID, strText, MAX_COUNT);
```

```
         converter = strText;
         converter.ChangeType(VT_I4);
         lValue = converter.lVal;
      }
      else
      {
         USES_CONVERSION;
         converter = lValue;
         converter.ChangeType(VT_BSTR);
         LPCTSTR strText = OLE2T(converter.bstrVal);
         SetDlgItemText(nID, strText);
      }
   }
```

This function is pretty rough-and-ready, but it does show how you might use a **VARIANT** (or the **CComVariant** wrapper class) to convert between a string and a **long**, and vice versa. It also demonstrates the use of the **OLE2T()** macro to convert from a **BSTR** to a **LPCTSTR**. In your own code, you'd probably want to provide something rather more robust.

Now we need to get hold of the server component so that we can use it to provide information about the refresh rate of our monitor. In contrast to the MFC client, we're going to use the compiler COM support to create a smart pointer class to wrap the **IRefRate** interface.

First, copy the type library for the RefreshRate component (**RefreshRate.tlb**) into the **CtrlClient** project directory. This is just so that we don't have to type a long path name into the **#import** statement for the library. Add **#import "RefreshRate.tlb" no_namespace** to the end of **StdAfx.h**.

Once you compile the project, this statement will produce two files in the output (**Debug** or **Release**) directory for the project, **RefreshRate.tlh** and **RefreshRate.tli**. These files contain class definitions for wrappers for the interfaces and classes contained in the type library. These output files are really for your reference (you don't need to include these files in your project explicitly since this is all handled by the **#import** statement), but it's worth taking a look at them to see what's available to you.

The smart pointer class that wraps the **IRefRate** interface is **typedef**'d to **IRefRatePtr**, so add a new member variable to the dialog class:

```
IRefRatePtr m_IRefRate;
```

Now we can use this member in **OnInitDialog()** and create an instance of the **RefRate** class:

```
LRESULT CClientDlg::OnInitDialog(UINT uMsg, WPARAM wParam, LPARAM lParam, BOOL&
bHandled)
{
   HRESULT hr = m_IRefRate.CreateInstance(__uuidof(RefRate));
   if SUCCEEDED(hr)
   {
      m_lVRes = m_IRefRate->GetVRes();
      m_lHRes = m_IRefRate->GetHRes();
      m_lRefresh = m_IRefRate->RefreshRate(m_lHScan);
      UpdateData(false);
   }

   return 1;  // Let the system set the focus
}
```

595

Similarly, we can add code to respond to the Calculate button. You'll need to add an entry to the message map and a declaration for the **OnCalculate()** function to the **CClientDlg** class:

```
BEGIN_MSG_MAP(CClientDlg)
    MESSAGE_HANDLER(WM_INITDIALOG, OnInitDialog)
    COMMAND_ID_HANDLER(IDOK, OnOK)
    COMMAND_ID_HANDLER(IDCANCEL, OnCancel)
    COMMAND_ID_HANDLER(IDC_CALCULATE, OnCalculate)
END_MSG_MAP()

    LRESULT OnInitDialog(UINT uMsg, WPARAM wParam, LPARAM lParam, BOOL& bHandled);
    LRESULT OnOK(WORD wNotifyCode, WORD wID, HWND hWndCtl, BOOL& bHandled);
    LRESULT OnCancel(WORD wNotifyCode, WORD wID, HWND hWndCtl, BOOL& bHandled);
    LRESULT OnCalculate(WORD wNotifyCode, WORD wID, HWND hWndCtl, BOOL& bHandled);
```

The **OnCalculate()** function looks very similar to the **OnCalculate()** function in the MFC-based client:

```
LRESULT CClientDlg::OnCalculate(WORD wNotifyCode, WORD wID, HWND hWndCtl, BOOL&
bHandled)
{
    UpdateData();
    m_lVRes = m_IRefRate->GetVRes();
    m_lHRes = m_IRefRate->GetHRes();
    m_lRefresh = m_IRefRate->RefreshRate(m_lHScan);
    UpdateData(false);
    return 0;
}
```

That's all there is to it. Now you can compile and run your ATL client just as you did with the MFC and Visual Basic clients. You don't need to worry about releasing the **IRefRate** pointer because it's all handled by the **IRefRatePtr** wrapper class.

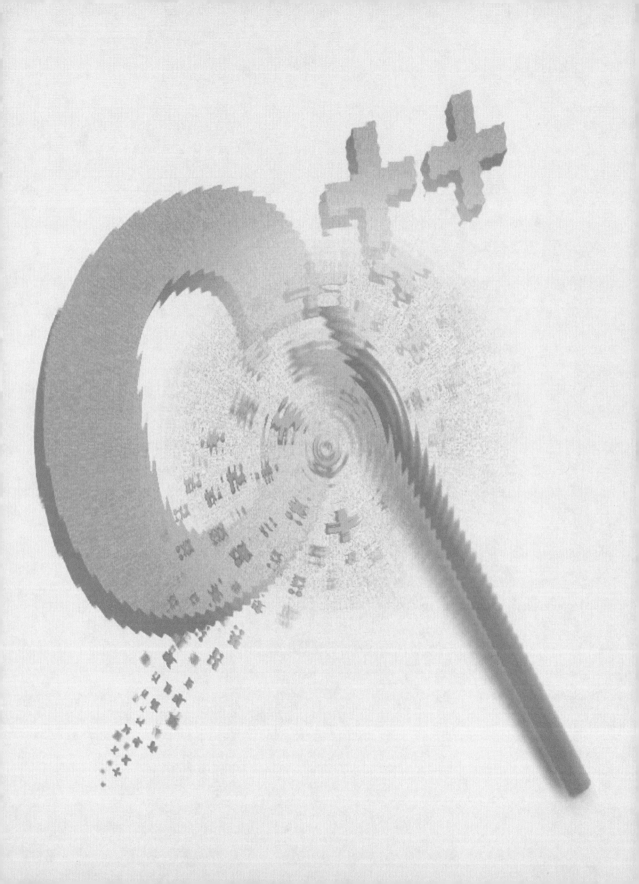

Beginning
MFC
Programming

Symbols

#define, macro definition 92
.bsc 27
.c 20
.cpp 20
.cxx 20
.dll 329
.dsp 14
.dsw 15
.exe 23
.h 30
.ico 30
.ilk 23
.lib, library files 327
.mak 14
.mdb 357
.obj 23
.ocx 329
   DLL file extensions 329
   OLE controls 452
.odl 489
   Object Description Language files
   457
.opt 14
.pch 23
.pch, precompiled header files 97
.pdb 23
.tlb
   type library files 457
.vbx 329

A

Active Template Library (ATL). *see*
ActiveX controls

ActiveX Control Pad, URL 495
ActiveX controls 85
   Active Template Library, using
   Template Library to create ActiveX
   controls 529
     connection point, adding 549
     controls
       developing 505
       drawing 541
     custom properties, adding 546
     events, adding 547
   enumeration, adding 491
   example, traffic signal object 464
     constructor 471
     custom properties, adding 477
     drawing the object 467
     testing 473
   HTML (HyperText Markup
   Language) 495
   introduction 451
   web pages, embedding 495
AddElement() 290, 301
AddRef(), IUnknown interface 407,
502
AddSegment() 206, 208
AddString() 281
AFX_EXT_CLASS keyword 338
afx_msg, message handler 110
AfxAbort() 170
AfxMessageBox() 170
Afxtempl.h 209
afxwin.h 75
aggregation, COM components 511
ambient properties, OLE controls
454
   using 473
AmbientBackColor() 475
AND, SQL 353
AND, bitwise operator 162
animate controls 251

API (Application Programming
Interface), Windows 38, 73
application class, MFC 75
application framework 11
AppWizard 83
   AppWizard-generated code,
   comments 95
   Developer Studio 11
     files created 30
       information 30
     using 27
   MDI application, creating 101
   menus, available functions 85
   message maps 110
   ODBC programs, generating 362
   SDI application, creating 84, 97
     class definitions 92
     executable module, creating 96
     InitInstance() 98
     Run() 100
     viewing classes 91
     viewing project files 90
   toolbars, available functions 85
   WOSA (Windows Open Services
   Architecture) 86
Arc(), drawing circles 149
arrays 192, 194
ASC keyword 356
AssertValid() 183
ATL COM AppWizard
   aggregation 511
   basic code 508
   COM components
     developing 506
     registering 509
   COM server interface 507
   projects, adding COM objects 509
AttachDispatch(), dispatch
interface 522
attributes, Windows GDI 143
Automation, OLE controls 456

B

BEGIN_MESSAGE_MAP, macro 112
BeginPaint() 53
bitwise operators 162
border, windows 36
breakpoints, setting 59
brush, graphics 149
  creating a brush 154
  using a brush 155
buddy control 263
Build options 59
building a project 21
  .dsp 21
  files created 22
button controls 250
  handling messages 259

C

C++ compiler 10
C++ keywords 555
C++ libraries 10
C++ linker 10
C++ programs 38
CArchive 296
  CFile object 296
  IsStoring() 297
  operators 297
CArray 192, 193
CBrush 149, 154
CClientDC 147
CComCoClass 512
CComObjectRootEx 512
CCurve 177, 205
CDC, MFC
  CClientDC 147
  colour 151
  graphics 145, 146
  rectangles, drawing 150
CDialog, dialog class 254
CDocument 81
CDocTemplate 81
CEditView 95, 98
ceil() 318, 327
CFile object 296
CFormView 520

CFrameWnd 76
child window 36
circles, drawing 149
class factory 463
Class ID (CLSID), OLE 407
class interfaces
  COM interfaces, comparison 504
Class Wizard 83
classes
  associaitng menus with 226
  CArchive 296
    CFile object 296
    IsStoring() 297
    operators 297
  class templates 192
  CMenu 227
  CObject
    functionality 298
  collection 191
    arrays 192
    lists 192
    maps 192
    shape 192
    type-safe handling 192
  CPrintInfo 312
    data members 312
    member functions, public 313
  DAO, supporting 358
  supporting ODBC 359
  dialogs, adding 254
  DLLs
    adding 337
    exporting 338
  foreign classes 382
  nested 463
  OLE, implementation of control class 462
  property page class 463
    implementation 464
  registering a class 44
  serialization 293
  templates
    CArray 193
    CList 193, 195, 204
    CMap 193, 200
    CTypedPtrArray 193
    CTypedPtrList 193, 202
    CTypedPtrMap 193
ClassView, Project Workspace window 18
ClassWizard 103
  adding a dialog class 254
  ATL support 505
  custom properties, adding 477

Developer Studio 11
  menu messages 121
  message handlers, definition 112
  message maps 110
client area
  initializing 46
  drawing 53
  window s 36, 142
    current position 147
    redrawing client area 164
client, COM components 502
client coordinates 220, 221, 269
clip rectangle 323
CList 192, 195, 204
CLSID, obtaining for a COM component 525
CMainFrame 89
CMap 192, 200
CMDIChildWnd 101
CMenu 227
CMultiDocTemplate 81
CObject
  functionality 298
  MFC 165
  serialization macros 295
CoCreateInstance(), COM library 525
code comments, AppWizard-generated code 95
COleClientItem 410
COleControl, MFC control base class 455
  stock methods, listed 456
ColeDispatchDriver, base class 522
COleDocument 411
COleLinkingDoc 411
COleServerItem 411
collection classes 191
  arrays 192
  lists 192
    doubly linked 192
  maps 192
  objects 193
  type-safe handling 192
  typed pointer 202
    CTypedPtrList 202, 211
color, graphics 151
COM (Component Object Model)
  components, registering 509
  library, using 524
  objects 502

OLE interface 406
Active Template Library (ATL), using 501
and C++ 520
  COM library 524
  component interface functions, using 528
    component objects 525
      CLSID, obtaining 525
      creating an instance 527
      releasing 528
    interface, creating 521
  class interfaces, comparison 504
  client 502
  CLSID, obtaining for a COM component 525
  COM AppWizard 506
    basic code 508
  COM object (instance) 502
  data types 503
  dispatch interfaces 503
  IDispatch, standard interface 503
  in-process servers 507
  interfaces 502
  IUnknown 406
  objects, adding to projects 509
  OLE/COM Object Viewer 525
  out-of-process servers 507
  proxy 507
  registering
    DLLRegisterServer() 509
    DLLUnRegisterServer() 509
  server 502
  server interface
    marshaling 507
    proxy 507
    stub 507
    unmarshaling 507
combo boxes 251
command messages 111, 113
  processing the messages 114
comments, in AppWizard-generated code 95
common controls 251
comparison operators, SQL 353
compiler, Developer Studio 10
compound documents, OLE 404
  embedded object, activating 405
  in-place activation 405
configuration, projects 15
connection point container, ActiveX controls 549
ConstructElements() 195, 199
containers
  connection point containers, ActiveX

controls 549
OLE 404
  controls 453
  implementing a container 412, 417, 419, 421
    activating an embedded object 426
    initializing a container application 413
    multiple embedded objects, drawing 426
    multiple embedded objects, managing 420
    object insertion, dealing with 427
context menus 225
ContinueRouting() 130
control menu 37
control notification messages 112, 113
control properties, OLE controls 454, 455
  ActiveX Control Wizard, using 455
controls
  see also ActiveX controls
  animate 251
  buddy 263
  button 250
    button handling messages 259
  combo boxes 251
  common 251
  dialog boxes 249
    adding controls to 252
  edit 251
    creating edit box resource 282
  HTML (HyperText Markup Language) 495
  initializing 258
  list boxes 250
    creating 279
  MFC, CDialog 250
  OLE controls
    ActiveX Control Wizard, using 455
    automation 456
    class factory, creating OLE objects 463
    container 453
    creating 458, 460
    enumeration, adding 491
    events 456, 487
    interface 457
    introduction 451
    methods 456
    properties 453
      ambient 454
        using 473
      connecting 485
      control 454, 455

      custom 455
        adding 477
        initialization 479
      extended 454, 455
      standard 453
      stock 455
        using 473
    property pages 456
    type library 489
  scroll bars 250
    scaling 272
    setting up 273
  spin button 263
    displaying 268
  static 250
  tab sequence 265
  tree 251
  web pages, embedding 495
controls, developing with ATL 505
cooperative multi-tasking 48
coordinates
  client 220, 221, 269
  device 269
  logical 220, 269
  page 269
  screen 227, 269
CPen, MFC 151
CPoint 147
CPrintInfo 312
CPropertySheet 456
Create() 255
CreateDispatch(), dispatch interface 522
CreateHatchBrush() 154
CreatePen() 152
CreateSolid Brush() 154, 539
CreateWindow() 44
CRecordset 359, 376
CRecordView 381
CRect 53
CRectTracker 421
CS_HREDRAW 43
CS_VREDRAW 43
CScrollView 218
CSingleDocTemplate 81
CStatusBar 93
CString class 284
  heap, using 285
  operators 284
CToolBar 93
CTypedPtrArray 192

CTypedPtrList 192
  using 211
CTypedPtrMap 192
current position, client area 147
cursor menus
  displaying pop-up at cursor 227
curves, drawing
custom properties, OLE controls 455
  adding 477
  ClassWizard, using 477
  DISP_PROPERTY 477
  DISP_PROPERTY_EX 477
  DISP_PROPERTY_NOTIFY 477
  DISP_PROPERTY_PARAM 477
  initialization 479
customizing Developer Studio 25
CView 80
  VC++ drawing mechanism 145
CWinApp, MFC 75
CWnd 81

D

DAO 356
  classes supporting 358
  vs. ODBC 357
data blocks. *see* complex data types
data members, classes
data types, COM 503
databases
  see also SQL
  .mdb 357
  basics 349
  creating a database application 359
  DAO 356
    classes supporting 358
    ODBC 357
  data transfer, between database and recordset 368
  filters, adding 395
  foreign key 351
  Jet engine 356
  MFC database support 356
  multivalue key 350
  ODBC
    classes supporting 359
    DAO, comparison 357
    registering an ODBC database 360
    using AppWizard to generate an ODBC program 362

orders for product, viewing 392
primary key 350
recordsets
  controls, linking to 373
  creating 366
  sorting 375
relational databases 349
  RDBMS 351
SQL 352
  recordsets and querying the database 367
  retrieving data 352
tables
  joining with SQL 354
  multiple, accessing 387
  table join 351
DDV (Dialog Data Validation) 266
DDX (Dialog Data Exchange) 266
DDX_() 374
DDX_Text() 266
debugging 58
  breakpoints
    removing 60
    setting 59
  Build options 59
  Debug build options 59
  Debug menu
    Go option 61
    QuickWatch 64
    Step into 61
    Step Over 62
    Step-to 61
  Project build options 59
  Release build options 59
  stepping 66
  variables
    changing their value 66
    viewing 63
DECLARE_DYNCREATE, macro 94
DECLARE_MESSAGE_MAP(), macro 92, 94, 110
DECLARE_SERIAL() macro 298
decoding messages 52
decorated names 338
DefWindowProc() 38, 52
DeleteElement() 238, 301
DESC keyword 356
DestructElements() 199
destructors
  implementing document destructor 212
Developer Studio
  AppWizard 11

files created 30
ClassWizard 11
compiler 10
components 10
customizing 25
debug capabilities 58
  Build options 59
  Debug build options 59
  Debug menu 61
  Project Build options 59
  Release build options 59
  setting watches 62
editor window 10, 12
introduction 11
libraries 10
linker 10
options, setting 25
output window 12
  Help, using 22
project configuration 15
project workspace window 12
toolbar functions 12
  options 12
what is Developer Studio? 10
Wizard Bar 11
device context, printing documents 318
device context, Windows GDI 143
  mapping modes 143
device coordinates 269
  transforming logical coordinates into 269
dialog class, creating 280, 284
Dialog Data Exchange 266
Dialog Data Validation 266
dialogs 249
  CDialog 254
  controls 249
  creating View dialog 371
  dialog box
    adding controls 252
    group box 252
  dialog class
    adding 254
    CDialog 254
  dialog data exchange and validation 266
  dialog resource, creating 252
  displaying dialogs 256, 281
  modal and modeless 255
direct exposure, custom properties 477
directed beam displays 179
Dispatch ID 453

dispatch interfaces, COM interface 503

dispatch maps 462

DispatchMessage() 47, 49

DispID (Dispatch ID), dispatch interface 503

DispID. *see* Dispatch ID

display context 53

DLLCanUnloadNow(), COM components 509

dllimport keyword 342

DllMain() 332, 336

DLLRegisterServer(), COM components 509

DLLs
  .dll 329
  .ocx 329
  .vbx 329
  building 339
  classes
    adding 337
    exporting 338
  contents 332
    DllMain() 332
    interface 332
  decorated names 338
    ordinal 338
  DllMain() 336
  dynamic linking
    load time 330
    run time 330
  extension 339
  files required, .h, .lib, .dll 341
  functions, exporting 341
  MFC extension DLL 332
  symbols, exporting into a program 342
  variables, exporting 341
  writing and using an extension DLL 334

DLLUnRegisterServer(), COM components 509

dockable toolbars 13

document interfaces, MFC 79

document size, setting 270

document templates, MFC 81
  document template classes 81

document/view, MFC 79
  linking a document and its views 80
  what is a document? 79
    document interfaces 79

documents, printing 310

printing process 311

documents, serializing 294
  how serialization works 299

DoDataExchange() 266, 464

DoModal() 255

DoPropExchange() 461

DoVerb(), OLE 426

DPtoLP() 221

Draw() 170, 209, 213, 467

drawing modes 178
  list 179

DrawText() 54, 276

driver, ODBC 357

dynamic linking
  load time 330
  run time 330

dynamic-link libraries. *see* DLLs

dynaset, vs. snapshot 364

E

early binding 330

edit controls 251
  creating edit box resource 282

editor window, Developer Studio 10, 12

element menu 117
  adding items to 117

elements
  adding to a list 195
  arrays 194
  classes
    serialization 303
  creating in the view 261
  deleting 238
  highlighting 233
  masked 244
  menus
    creating a text element 288
  moving 238
    getting them to move themselves 241
    modifying WM_MOUSEMOVE 240
    text 308

Ellipse(), drawing circles 149

Enable() 130

EndPage() 312

EndPaint() function 54

enumeration, adding with odl file 491

EqualRect() 53

errors, dealing with 22

event maps 462

event-driven programs 8, 38

events 38
  OLE controls 456
    events, adding 487
    listed common 456

executing a program 24
  executing a Windows program 27, 30

ExitInstance() 460

extended properties, OLE controls 454, 455

F

fields, databases 349

files
  .idl 504
  .rgs, registry 511
  resource 37
    defining menus 115
  type library 457

FileView, Project Workspace window 18

FillRect(), ATL ActiveX 542

filters, recordsets 383
  adding a filter to recordset 383
  filter parameters
    defining 384
    implementing 397

FindIndex() 198

Fire_SignalChanged(), ATL ActiveX 548

flags 161

floating toolbars 13

foreign class, databases 382

foreign key, databases 351

frame window, MFC 76

frame window, view 80

FreeLibrary() 331

FROM keyword 352

full server, OLE 404

functions
  general
    AddSegment() 206, 208
    AmbientBackColor() 475
    ceil() 318, 327
    Create() 255
    CreateElement() 206, 261
    CreateWindow() 44

DDV_MinMaxInt() 266
DDX_() 374
DDX_Text() 266
DefWindowProc() 38, 52
DeleteElement() 238
DispatchMessage() 47, 49
DLLs, exporting 341
DllMain() 332, 336
DoDataExchange() 266, 464
DoModal() 255
DoPropExchange() 461
DPtoLP() 221
Draw() 213, 467
DrawText() 54
EndPage() 312
EqualRect() 53
ExitInstance() 460
FindIndex() 198
GetAt() 194
GetBackColor() 475
GetBoundRect() 214, 260
GetClientRect() 54
GetDefaultConnect() 367
GetDefaultSQL() 368
GetDlgItem() 267
GetForeColor() 475
GetMessage() 47
GetNext() 197, 209, 212
GetScaleUnits() 475
GetStockObject() 44
GetSubMenu() 227
Helper
  ConstructElements() 195, 199
  DestructElements() 199
  HashKey() 201
InflateRect() 53
InitInstance() 460
InsertBefore() 197
InvalidateRect() 215
IsEmpty() 199
IsStoring() 297
LoadMenu() 227
LookUp() 201
Move() 241
NextState() 466
notify() 483
OnAppAbout() 112
OnBeginPrinting() 316
OnCreate() 276
OnDraw() 213, 461, 475
OnEndPrinting() 316
OnFileNew() 112
OnInitDialog() 258
OnInitialUpdate() 218, 223
OnLButtonDown() 221, 282, 302
OnLButtonUp() 215, 216
OnMouseMove() 206, 235, 238

OnPenWidth() 259
OnPreparePrinting() 315
OnPrint() 319
OnResetState() 462
OnUpdate() 217
OnUpdateColorBlack() 129
OnViewScale() 273
PeekMessage() 48
RectVisible() 214
RegisterClass() 44
ResetScrollSizes() 272
RFX_() 369
SelectObject() 276
Serialize() 296
SetAt() 194
SetBkMode() 54
SetFieldType() 369
SetMapMode() 223
SetMaxPage() 313
SetMinPage() 313
SetScrollSizes() 218, 223
SetViewportExt() 270
SetViewportOrg() 270
SetWindowExt() 270
SetWindowOrg() 270
ShowWindow() 45
TrackPopupMenu() 227
TranslateColor() 475
TranslateMessage() 47, 49
UpdateAllViews() 216
UpdateWindow() 46
Serialize() 295
WindowProc() 38, 51
WinMain() 40, 41, 49, 72
WndProc() 38
member functions
  AddElement() 290, 301
  AddHead() 195
  AddString() 281
  AddTail() 195, 208
  ContinueRouting() 130
  DeleteElement() 301
  Draw() 234
  DrawText() 276
  Enable() 130
  GetDeviceCaps() 271, 319
  GetDocExtent() 317
  GetElementColor() 289
  GetFromPage() 313
  GetHeadPosition() 197, 209, 212
  GetParentFrame() 278
  GetPenWidth() 289
  GetTailPosition() 197
  GetTextExtent() 289
  GetToPage() 313
  IsKindOf() 309
  IsPrinting() 319

LPtoDP() 272
MoveElement() 302
OnPrepareDC() 221, 270
OnPreparePrinting() 313
RemoveHead() 199
RemoveTail() 199
SetAt() 201
SetCheck() 130
SetModifiedFlag() 301
SetParts() 276
SetRadio() 130
SetRange() 267
SetSize() 194
SetText() 130
SetTextAlign() 322
SetTextColor() 288
SetTimer() 481
StartSignal() 481
StopSignal() 482
TextOut() 288
UnionRect() 315

G

GDI (Graphical Device Interface),
Windows 143
Get/Set functions,
DISP_PROPERTY 477
GetAmbientBackColor(), ATL
ActiveX 542
GetAt() 194
GetBackColor() 475
GetBoundRect() 168, 214, 260
GetClassObject(), COM library
525
GetClientRect() 54
GetDefaultConnect() 367
GetDefaultSQL() 368
GetDeviceCaps() 271, 319
GetDlgItem() 267
GetDocExtent() 317
GetDocument() 95, 96
GetElementColor() 289
GetElementType() 183
GetForeColor() 475
GetFromPage() 313
GetHeadPosition() 197, 209, 212
GetIDsOfNames(), dispatch
interface 504
GetMessage() 47
GetNext() 197, 209, 212

GetParentFrame() 278
GetPenWidth() 289
GetProcessAddress() 331
GetScaleUnits() 475
GetStockObject() 44
GetStockObject(), ATL ActiveX 538
GetSubMenu() 227
GetSystemMetrics(), Windows API function 516
GetTailPosition() 197
GetTextExtent() 289
GetToPage() 313
GetViewStatus(), ATL control class 533
Globally Unique ID generator 492
   globally unique IDs (GUIDs), OLE 407
Go 61
graphics
   brush
      creating a brush 154
      using a brush 155
   CDC, MFC 146
   circles, drawing 149
      CCircle 175
   client area, window 142
      redrawing client area 164
   colour, drawing in 151
   context menu, implementing 225
   coordinates 220
   curves, drawing 205
   drawing, in practice 156
      mouse, programming 157
      rubber-banding 156
   drawing modes 178, 179
   GDI (Graphical Device Interface), Windows 143
   lines, drawing 148
      drawing with a mouse 170
   output display 141
      GDI (Graphical Device Interface), Windows 143
   pen object 151
      creating a pen 151
      using a pen 153
   raster displays 179
   rectangles, drawing 150
      normalizing rectangles 173
   SetROP2(), drawing modes 178, 179
   shapes, deleting and moving 224
   update region 164
   views
      scrolling 218

updating multiple 216
group box 252
GUID (Globally Unique ID) generator 492
   Guidgen.exe 492
Guidgen.exe 492

H

handlers. *see* message handlers
handles
hashing 200
HashKey() 201
hbrBackground, WNDCLASS 44
HBRUSH, ATL ActiveX 537
HDC 53
header files
   Afxtempl.h 209
   afxwin.h 75
   ChildFrm.h 278
   CScaleDialog.h 279
   DllImports.h 344
   Elements.h 165, 286, 337
   OurConstants.h 286, 337
   PrintData.h 318
   ScaleDialog.h 268
   Sketcher.h 127
   Stdafx.h 209
   TextDialog.h 290
   Windows.h 126
   windows.h 41, 53
   Wingdi.h 126
   Winuser.h 112
Help, dealing with errors 22
helper functions 195, 201
   lists 199
highlighting, syntax 20
HINSTANCE, type 41
HIWORD(), macro 543
HPEN, ATL ActiveX 537
HTML (HyperText Markup Language) 495
Hungarian notation 39, 74
HyperText Markup Language (HTML) 495

I

IDE (Integrated Development Environment). *see* Developer Studio
IDispatch, standard interface 503
   Invoke() 503
IDispatchImpl 512
IDL. *see* Interface Definition Language
IMPLEMENT_SERIAL(), macro 299, 337
in-place activation, OLE 405
   embedded object, activating 405
in-process server, COM components 507
index arrays 194
indirect exposure, custom properties 477
InfoView, Project Workspace window 18
initialization
   client area 46
   controls 258
   custom properties 479
   program window 44
InitInstance() 76, 98, 460
InsertBefore() 197
instance, COM object 502
Integrated Development Environment (IDE). *see* Developer Studio
Interface Definition Language (IDL) 457
   Microsoft IDL processor (MIDL) 457
interface, DLLs 332
interface ID (IID), OLE 407
interfaces
   COM 502
      dispatch interfaces 503
      IDispatch, standard interface 503
      IUnknown 502
      Iunknown, functions 502
   dispatch 503
   IDispatch, standard interface 503
   IUnknown 502
   virtual function table (vtable) 503
   OLE controls 457
Internet Explorer, URL 495
IntersectClipRect(), printing regions 323

Invalidate(), ATL ActiveX 549
InvalidateRect() 215
   redrawing client area 164
invisible controls, developing with
ATL 505
Invoke(), IDispatch interface 503
IsEmpty() 199
IsKindOf() 309
IsPrinting() 319
IsStoring() 297
IUnknown, COM interface 452,
502
   functions 502

J

Jet database engine 356
   .mdb 357
   ODBC 357
joins, database tables 351
   SQL, using 354

K

keys, databases 350
   foreign 351
   multivalue 350
   primary 350
keywords 555
KillTimer(), 544

L

late binding 330
libraries
   MFC (Microsoft Foundation Class)
   11
   standard library 10
   type library 489
lines, drawing 148
   drawing with a mouse 170
LineTo(), drawing lines 148
linker, Developer Studio 10
list boxes 250, 251
   creating control 279
   using 278
lists 192

adding elements to 195
helper functions 199
iterating through 197
removing objects 199
searching 198
load time dynamic linking. *see*
early binding
LoadLibrary() 331
LoadMenu() 227
LoadStdProfileSettings() 100
logical coordinates 220, 269
   transforming into device coordinates
   269
LookUp() 201
LOWORD(), macro 543
LPARAM 47
LPSTR, type 42
LPtoDP() 272

M

macros
   #define 92
   adding serialization to a class 298
   ASSERT_VALID() 183
   BEGIN_MESSAGE_MAP 112
   BEGIN_MESSAGE_MAP() 110
   DECLARE_DYNCREATE 94
   DECLARE_MESSAGE_MAP() 92,
   94, 110
   END_MESSAGE_MAP() 110
   IMPLEMENT_SERIAL() 337
   ON_COMMAND 112, 124
   ON_UPDATE_COMMAND_UI()
   129
   RUNTIME_CLASS() 100
Makefile 14
MAPI (messaging API), WOSA 86
mapping modes
   device context 143, 442
   logical and client coordinates 220
   MM_LOENGLISH 222
   scaleable 269
   setting 270
maps 192
marshaling, COM server interface
507
masked elements 244
mdb, Jet database engine 357
MDI (Multiple Document

Interface), MFC 79
   AppWizard MDI application,
   creating 101
   command messages, how they are
   processed 114
member functions. *see* functions
menu bar, windows 37
menus 115
   AppWizard, available functions 85
   associating with a class 226
   context 225
   control 37
   element menu, adding items to 117
   menu items
      adding 285
         to the menu bar 117
      defining properties 118
      modifying existing items 119
      text elements, defining 286
   menu messages
      choosing a class to handle menu messages
      121
      coding menu message functions 125
      creating menu message functions 121
      servicing 237
   pop-up, displaying at cursor 227
   resource file 115
   scale, adding to scale dialog 263
   system 37
message handlers 109
   adding to user interface 129
   definitions 111
message loop, Windows messages
46, 47
message maps 109, 462
   BEGIN_MESSAGE_MAP() macro
   110
   DECLARE_MESSAGE_MAP()
   macro 110
   END_MESSAGE_MAP() macro 110
   understanding 110
MESSAGE_HANDLER(), macro
542
messages 46, 109
   button controls 259
   decoding 52
   default message processing 38
   menu messages
      choosing a class to handle menu messages
      121
      coding menu message functions 125
      creating menu message functions 121
      servicing 237
   message handlers, adding to user

interface 129
mouse and graphics 158
processing functions, messages 51
queued and non-queued 46
windows 38
metafile, OLE 427
methods. *see* member functions
MFC 73
AppWizard 83
Classes, serialization 300
ClassWizard 103
CMenu 227
collection classes 191
common controls 251
database support 356
DAO vs. ODBC 357
Database Access Objects (DAO) 356, 358
Jet engine 356
ODBC (Open Database Connectivity) 357, 359
DLL, MFC extension 332
document templates 81
document/view 79
document templates 81
linking a document and its views 80
fundamental SDI classes 82
messages 109
categories 113
message handlers 109, 111
message map 109
MFC application 74
notation 74
OLE support 408
OLE document classes 411
OLE object classes 409
embedded object in a container 410
embedded object in a server 411
program structure 74
view 80
MFC extension DLL 332
Microsoft ActiveX Control Pad 496
Microsoft Guidgen.exe 492
Microsoft Foundation Classes. *see* MFC
Microsoft IDL processor (MIDL) 457
Microsoft Internet Explorer (IE), URL 495
MIDL. *see* Microsoft IDL processor
mini-server, OLE 404
MM_ANISOTROPIC, mapping mode 268

MM_ISOTROPIC, mapping mode 268
MM_LOENGLISH 222, 269
modal dialogs 255
modeless dialogs 255
mouse, graphics 157
ClassWizard generated code 161
drawing using the mouse 162, 166
classes for elements, defining 165
client area, redrawing 164
mouse message handlers 178
messages from the mouse 158
catpuring messages 186
mouse message handlers 160, 180
Move() 241
MoveElement() 302
MoveTo(), current position 147
MSG, type 47
multipage printing
implementing 314
overall document size 315
multitasking, Windows 48
multivalue key, databases 350

N

nested classes, example 463
non-queued messages, Windows 46
notation, MFC 74
Hungarian notation 74
notify() 483

O

object code 10
Object Description Language (ODL) 457
object files 10
Object Linking and Embedding. *see* OLE
Objects, collections 193
OCX, OLE controls 452
ODBC 357
ODBC (Open Database Connectivity)
classes supporting 359
DAO, comparison 357

database example 359
ODBC programs, generating with AppWizard 362
registering an ODBC database 360
odl, Object Description Language files 457, 489
enumeration, adding 491
UUID (Universally Unique Identifier) tag 491
see also GUID
OLE
see also ActiveX
Automation, DLLs 335
COM (Component Object Model), OLE interface
interface ID (IID) 407
IUnknown 406
compound document 404
embedded object, activating 405
in-place activation 405
containers 404, 413, 420, 426, 427
implementing 412
controls, OLE
automation 456
class factory, creating OLE objects 463
container 453
creating 458
application class 460
control class 460
structure 460
enumeration, adding 491
events 456
adding 487
listed common 456
how they work 453
interface 457
introduction 451
methods 456
OLE servers, comparison 452, 453
properties 453
ambient properties 454
using 473
connecting 485
control properties 454, 455
ActiveX Control Wizard, using 455
custom properties 455
adding 477
initialization 479
extended 454, 455
standard 453
stock properties 455, 473
property pages 456
property sheets 456
OLE servers, comparison 452, 453
type library 489

what are OLE controls? 452

full server 404

how does OLE work? 406

in-place activation 405

  embedded object, activating 405

metafile 427

MFC support 408

  OLE document classes 411

  OLE object classes 409

   embedded objects

    in a container 410

    in a server 411

mini-server 404

registry, OLE 407

  Class ID (CLSID) 407

servers

  applications, generating 431

  embedded object, implementing 442

  executing 447

  functionality, adding 441

  implementing 430, 431

  OLE controls, comparison 452, 453

  view, updating 443

tracker, multiple embedded objects 421

verb 426

OLE/COM Object Viewer 525

ON_COMMAND, macro 112, 124

ON_UPDATE_COMMAND_UI(), macro 129

OnAppAbout() 92, 112

OnBeginPrinting() 316

OnCreate() 276

OnDraw() 185, 213, 461, 475

OnDraw(), graphics 145

OnEndPrinting() 316

OnFileNew() 112

OnInitDialog() 258

OnInitialUpdate() 218, 223

OnLButtonDown() 160, 221, 282, 302

OnLButtonUp() 160, 215, 216

OnMouseMove() 160, 206, 235, 238

  handler, coding 180

OnPenWidth() 259

OnPrepareDC() 221, 270

OnPreparePrinting() 313, 315

OnPrint() 319

OnResetState() 462

OnUpdate() 217

OnUpdateColorBlack() 129

OnViewScale() 273

Open Database Connectivity. *see* **ODBC**

Open Software Foundation

  UUID (Universally Unique Identifier 492

options

  Developer Studio 25

  projects 26

  setting 24

OR, SQL 353

OR operator 43

ORDER BY 356

ordinal, decorated names 338

out-of-process server, COM components 507

output window, Developer Studio 12

P

page coordinates 269

PAINTSTRUCT 53

panes 274

parameters

parent window 36

PeekMessage() 48

pen object, graphics 151

  creating a pen 151

  using a pen 153

points, font 144

pre-compiled headers 23

pre-emptive multi-tasking 48

precompiled headers 97

primary key, databases 350

printing

  cleaning up afterwards 318

  clip rectangle 323

  CPrintInfo class 312

  device context 318

  documents 310

   clip rectangle 323

   multiple pages 314

   overall document size 315

   printing process 311

   recording changes in 301

   regions 323

  preparing to print 316

  print data, storing 315

  regions 323

   IntersectClipRect() 323

   SetClipRgn() 323

printing process 311

program window

  creating and initializing 44

  specifying 42

programs

  event driven 8, 38

  executing 24

Project build options 59

Project name 16

Project type 16

project workspace window, Developer Studio 12

projects 14

  building 21

  ClassView 18

  COM objects, adding 509

  configuration 15

  creating 16

  customizing 26

  defining 14

  options, setting 26

  project workspace 14

  Project Workspace window 14

   FileView 18

   InfoView 18

   project name 16

   project type 16

   ResourceView 18

  source files, adding 21

  subprojects 14

  type 16

properties

  direct exposure 477

  indirect exposure 477

properties, OLE controls 453

  ambient properties 454

   list, partial 454

   using 473

  control properties 454, 455

   ActiveX Control Wizard, using 455

  custom properties 455

   adding 477

   ClassWizard, using 477

   DISP_PROPERTY 477

   DISP_PROPERTY_EX 477

   DISP_PROPERTY_NOTIFY 477

   DISP_PROPERTY_PARAM 477

   initialization 479

  extended properties 454, 455

  properties, connecting 485

  property pages 456

  standard properties 453

stock properties 455
  listed 455
  using 473
property pages 456
  property page class 463
  using 484
proxy, COM server interface 507

Q

QBE (Query By Example). *see*
Graphical Query Generator
QueryInterface(), IUnknown
interface 407, 502
queued messages, Windows 46
QuickWatch 64

R

rand() 327
raster displays 179
RDBMS (relational database
management systems) 350
record view 369
  creating View dialog 371
records. *see* complex data types
  databases 349
  SQL, sorting 356
recordsets
  controls, linking to 373
  creating 366
  data transfer between database and
  recordset 368
  dynaset vs. snapshot 364
  filters 383
    adding a filter to recordset 383
    filter parameters, defining 384
  querying the database 367
  record view 369
  SELECT 352
  snapshot vs. dynaset 364
  sorting 375
RECT 53
rectangles, drawing 150, 173
RectVisible() 214
Regedit.exe, registry 407
regions, printing 323
RegisterClass() 44
registry

globally unique IDs (GUIDs) 407
OLE 407
registering COM components 509
  .rgs files 511
window class 44
Relational Database Management
Systems. *see* RDBMS
relational databases 349
Release build option 59
Release(), IUnknown interface 407,
502
ReleaseCapture() 186
RemoveHead() 199
RemoveTail() 199
ResetScrollSizes() 272
Resource Editor 83
resource files 37
resources 115
ResourceView, Project Workspace
window 18
RFX_() 369
RGB() 126
rubber-banding, graphics 156
Run() 98, 100
run-time dynamic linking 330
running a program 24
RUNTIME_CLASS(), macro 100,
309

S

scale dialogs 265
  adding scale menu and toolbar 263
  removing 279
scale factor, Windows 268
  mapping modes 269
schema numbers, programs 299
screen coordinates 227, 269
scroll bars 250, 251
  scrolling, implementing with scaling
  272
  setting up 273
SDI (Single Document Interface),
MFC 79
  AppWizard
    SDI application
    creating 84
    executable module 96
  command messages
    how they are processed 114

fundamental SDI classes 82
  serialization 94
SELECT 352
SelectObject() 153, 155, 276
SelectObject(), ATL ActiveX 538
SelectStockObject() 155, 468
serialization 94, 293
  CArchive 296
    CFile object 296
    IsStoring() 297
    operators 297
  classes
    serialization, implementing 300
    serialization with macros, adding 298
  CObject 298
  element classes 303
  how serialization works 299
  macros, adding serialization to a
  class 298
  serializing documents 294, 300
    document class definition 294
    document class implementation 295
    recording changes in 301
  shape classes 305
Serialize() 295, 296
server, COM component 502
servers, OLE
  adding server functionality 441
  full server 404
  implementing an OLE server 430,
  431
    server application, generating 431
  mini-server 404
  server, executing 447
  server functionality, adding
    embedded object, implementing 442
    view, updating 443
Set/Get functions,
DISP_PROPERTY 477
SetAt() 194, 201
SetBkMode() 54
SetCapture() 186
SetCheck() 130
SetClipRgn(), printing regions 323
SetFieldType() 369
SetMapMode() 223
SetMaxPage() 313
SetMinPage() 313
SetModifiedFlag() 301
SetParts() 276
SetRadio() 130
SetRange() 267

SetRegistryKey() 99
SetROP2() 178
SetScrollSizes() 218, 223
SetSize() 194
SetText() 130
SetTextAlign() 322
SetTextColor() 288
SetTimer() 481
setting a watch, debugging 62
SetViewportExt() 270
SetViewportOrg() 145, 270
SetWindowOrg() 270
SetWindowsExt() 270
shape classes, serializing 305
ShowWindow() 45
Sketcher example 185
slow watch. see watch
snapshot vs. dynaset 364
source files, adding to a project 21
spin button 251, 263
   displaying 268
SQL (Structured Query Language) 352
   ASC keyword 356
   comparison operators 353
   DESC keyword 356
   FROM keyword 352
   joining tables 354
   ORDER BY 356
   recordsets
     controls, linking to 373
     creating 366
     data transfer between database and recordset 368
     dynaset 364
     record view 369
     recordsets and querying the database 367
     second recordset object, using 376
     snapshot 364
     sorting 375
   retrieving data 352
   SELECT 352
   sorting records 356
   WHERE keyword 353
sqrt() 327
standard interface, OLE 406
standard library 10
StartSignal(), ATL ActiveX 481, 543
static controls 250
static linking 327
status bar

adding to a frame 275
creating 274
flicker problems 275
panes 274
parts, defining 276
Stdafx.h 209
Step into 61
Step Over 62
Step-to 61
stepping, debugging 66
stock properties, OLE controls 455
   listed 455
   using 473
strings
   CString class 284
     heap, using 285
     operators 284
struct keyword 53
Structured Query Language. *see* SQL
stub, COM server interface 507
Sushi, use in programming 32
SW_HIDE 42
SW_SHOWMAXIMIZED 42
SW_SHOWMINNOACTIVE 42
SW_SHOWNORMAL 42
switch statement 52
symbols
   DLL, exporting into a program 342
syntax color highlighting 20
system menu 37

T

tab sequence 265
table join, databases 351
tables, databases 349
   joining, using SQL 354
   multiple tables, accessing 387
     switching views 387
     switching views, enabling the switching operation 390
     view activation , handling 391
templates
   class templates
     CArray 192
     CList 192, 195, 204
     CMap 192, 200
     CTypedPtrArray 192
     CTypedPtrList 192, 202

     CTypedPtrMap 192
     type-safe handling 192
   document templates, MFC 81
text, moving 308
TextDialog.h 290
TextOut() 288
title bar, windows 36
tlb, type library files 457
toolbars
   AppWizard, available functions 85
   Developer Studio 12
     options 12
   dockable 13
   floating 13
   toolbar buttons
     adding 132
     editing properties 134
     tooltips 136
   windows 37
tooltips 136
tracker, OLE
   multiple embedded objects 421
     cursor, setting 425
     tracker style, setting 424
TrackPopupmenu() 227
traffic signal object, example 464
   constructor 471
   custom properties, adding 477
   definition 465
   drawing the object 467
   testing 473
   using 471
TranslateColor() 475
TranslateMessage() 47, 49
tree controls 251
TrialRun, example project 16
type libraries 489
type library files 457
   Object Description Language (ODL) 457
typed pointer collections
   CTypedPtrArray 193
   CTypedPtrList 193, 202
     operations 203
     using 211
   CTypedPtrMap 193

U

UnionRect() 315
Universally Unique Identifier
(UUID) tag 491
  see also GUID
unmarshaling, COM server
interface 507
update region, graphics 164
UPDATE_COMMAND_UI, menu
items 286
UpdateAllViews() 216
UpdateWindow() 46
user interfaces
  adding message handlers to 129
  controls
    animate 251
    button 250
    combo boxes 251
    common 251
    edit 251
    edit, using 282
    list boxes 250
    scroll bars 250
    static 250
    tree 251
  dialogs 249
  highlighting elements 233
  list boxes 278
  menus 115
    creating and editing resources 115
    displaying pop-up at cursor 227
    menu item 285
    servicing messages 237
  message handlers, adding to update
  interface 129
  scale dialogs 265
  scroll bars 272
  spin button
    creating 263
    displaying 268
  status bar
    adding to a frame 275
    creating 274
    flicker problems 275
    parts, defining 276
  toolbars
    adding toolbar buttons 132
    editing toolbar button properties 134
    tooltips 136
UUID (Universally Unique
Identifier) tag 491
  see also GUID

V

Variables
  debugging 66
  DLL, exporting 341
  viewing in Edit Window 63
  watches 62
vector displays 179
verb, OLE 426
view, MFC 80
  see also document/view
virtual function table (vtable) 503
virtual functions, Serialize() 295
Visual C++, Windows API 73

W

watches, debugging 64
  setting for a variable 62
web pages
  embedding ActiveX controls 495
WHERE keyword 353
WINAPI 41
  see also functions, API
window class, MFC 75, 76
window, client area 142
window sockets 335
WindowProc() 38, 51
  example function 55
  switch statement 52
WindowProc() function prototype
51
Windows
  API 38
    see also functions, API
  client area, drawing 53
  creating with C++ 38
  defined types 41
  display context 53
  DOS, comparison 37
  GDI (Graphical Device Interface)
  143
    attributes 143
    device context 143
    device context, mapping modes 143
  graphics
    client coordinates 220
    context menu, implementing 225
    curves, drawing 205
    logical coordinates 220
    output display 141

    shapes, deleting and moving 224
    views, scrolling 218
      updating multiple 216
  Hungarian notation 39
  message handlers 109
    adding to user interface 129
    definitions 111
    message map 109
  message loops 46, 47
  messages 38, 109
    categories 113
    decoding 52
    default message processing 38
    message processing functions 51
    queued and non-queued 46
  multitasking 48
    cooperative 48
    pre-emptive multi-tasking 48
  OR operator 43
  program essentials 71
  program structure 8, 40
  program window
    creating and initializing 44
    specifying 42
  programming basics 8, 35, 71
    creating 27
    elements of a window 36
    errors, dealing with 22
    event-driven programs 8
    executing 27, 30
    first program 18
    Help, using 22
    libraries 10
    linking 10
    object code 10
    projects 14
    simple program example 56
    structure 8, 40
    executing programs 24
    first program 18
    running programs 24
  VC++ programming 83
windows
  border 36
  child 36
  client area 36
  elements 36
  menu bar 37
  parent 36
  styles 45
  title bar 36
  toolbar 37
Windows API (Application
Programming Interface) 38, 73
  see also functions, API

C++ programming 73

Windows Sockets 86

windows.h 41, 53, 126

WinMain() 40, 41, 49, 72

    arguments to 41

Winuser.h 112

Wizard Bar, Developer Studio 11

wizards

    AppWizard

        ODBC program, generating 362

    ClassWizard 123

        adding a dialog class 254

        custom properties, adding 477

WM_DESTROY 55

WM_LBUTTONDOWN 159

WM_LBUTTONUP 159, 184

WM_MOUSEFIRST 48

WM_MOUSELAST 48

WM_MOUSEMOVE 159

WM_PAINT 47, 53

    OnDraw() 145

WM_QUIT 47

WM_TIMER

    adding a handler with ClassWizard 482

WNDCLASS 42

WndProc() 38, 72

World Wide Web

    ActiveX controls, embedding 495

WOSA (Windows Open Services Architecture) 86

WPARAM, type 47

WS_CAPTION, window style 45

WS_MAXIMIZEBOX, window style 45

WS_MINIMIZEBOX, window style 45

WS_OVERLAPPED, window style 45

WS_OVERLAPPEDWINDOW 45

WS_SYSMENU, window style 45

WS_THICKFRAME, window style 45

Z

zoom factor, OLE 443

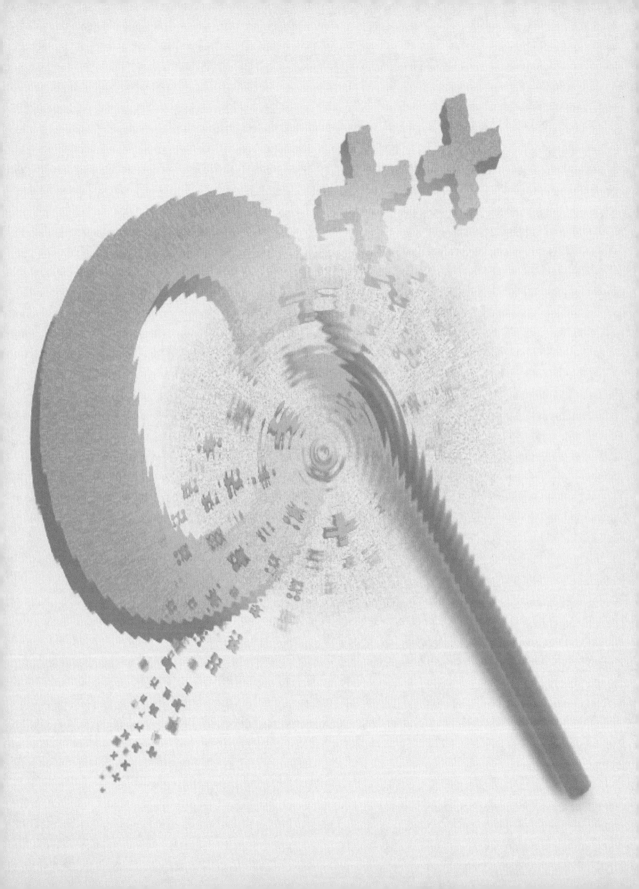

Professional DCOM Programming

Author: Dr. Richard Grimes
ISBN: 186100060X
Price: $49.95 C$69.95 £46.99

The book starts by examining why we need to be able to implement and distribute code objects, and looks at the various systems of distribution that currently exist. It then narrows the focus down to sharing data and functionality on Windows. This leads into an examination of COM, and from there, logically, to DCOM. We show how DCOM builds on the foundations of COM and RPC.

You'll quickly get to grips with the essentials of DCOM programming and we build on this base with thorough coverage of MIDL, Microsoft's Interface Definition Language. MIDL allows you to define your interfaces, create Type Libraries and provide marshaling support. All of these topics are covered in depth and backed up with strong code examples written using the latest tools.

The latter half of the book looks at the design and implementation of distributed applications. Each chapter covers a topic of prime importance to DCOM programmers. Security is fully explained, starting with the NT security model and exploring how it relates to DCOM. You'll then see how to write your DCOM servers as NT services, before being drawn into the murky world of multithreaded applications. The book shows how to use threads in Win32 and in DCOM servers, covers the different threading models and also looks at the issues of passing interface pointers between threads. Finally, you'll see how Microsoft Transaction Server can ease the life of a DCOM developer as well as the new issues introduced by this product

Instant VB5 ActiveX Control Creation

Authors: Alex Homer, Stephen Jakab
and Darren Gill
ISBN: 1861000235
Price: $29.95 C$41.95 £27.99

Aimed at experienced Visual Basic programmers who want to be able to create their own controls using the freely downloadable Visual Basic 5 CCE, this book takes you from an overview of VB5 CCE, right up to how to create your own, highly customized controls. It explains in detail how to create different types of control, including sub-classed, aggregate and owner-draw controls, and also includes coverage of the issues you need to be aware of when distributing your controls.

Wrox Press
http://www.wrox.com/

If you've enjoyed this book, you'll get a lot from Ivor's new book, Beginning Java.

Beginning Java teaches Java 1.1 from scratch, taking in all the fundamental features of the Java language, along with practical applications of Java's extensive class libraries. While it assumes some little familiarity with general programming concepts, Ivor takes time to cover the basics of the language in depth. He assumes no knowledge of object-oriented programming.

Ivor first introduces the essential bits of Java without which no program will run. Then he covers how Java handles data, and the syntax it uses to make decisions and control program flow. The essentials of object-oriented programming with Java are covered, and these concepts are reinforced throughout the book. Chapters on exceptions, threads and I/O follow, before Ivor turns to Java's graphics support and applet ability. Finally the book looks at JDBC and RMI, two additions to the Java 1.1 language which allow Java programs to communicate with databases and other Java programs.

Visual Basic is a great tool for generating applications quickly and easily, but if you really want to create fast, tight programs using the latest technologies, Visual C++ is the only way to go.

Ivor Horton's Beginning Visual C++ 5 is for anyone who wants to learn C++ and Windows programming with Visual C++ 5 and MFC, and the combination of the programming discipline you've learned from this book and Ivor's relaxed and informal teaching style will make it even easier for you to succeed in taming structured programming and writing real Windows applications.

The book begins with a fast-paced but comprehensive tutorial to the C++ language. You'll then go on to learn about object orientation with C++ and how this relates to Windows programming, culminating with the design and implementation of a sizable class-based C++ application. The next part of the book walks you through creating Windows applications using MFC, including sections on output to the screen and printer, how to program menus, toolbars and dialogs, and how to respond to a user's actions. The final few chapters comprise an introduction COM and examples of how to create ActiveX controls using both MFC and the Active Template Library (ATL).